American Prisons and Jails

American Prisons and Jails

An Encyclopedia of Controversies and Trends

VOLUME I: A–M

Vidisha Barua Worley and
Robert M. Worley, Editors

An Imprint of ABC-CLIO, LLC
Santa Barbara, California • Denver, Colorado

Copyright © 2019 by ABC-CLIO, LLC

All rights reserved. No part of this publication may be reproduced, stored in a retrieval system, or transmitted, in any form or by any means, electronic, mechanical, photocopying, recording, or otherwise, except for the inclusion of brief quotations in a review, without prior permission in writing from the publisher.

Library of Congress Cataloging-in-Publication Data

Names: Worley, Vidisha Barua, editor. | Worley, Robert M., editor.
Title: American prisons and jails : an encyclopedia of controversies and
   trends / Vidisha Barua Worley and Robert M. Worley, editors.
Description: Santa Barbara, California : ABC-CLIO, [2019] | Includes
   bibliographical references and index.
Identifiers: LCCN 2018016381 (print) | LCCN 2018016538 (ebook) |
   ISBN 9781610695015 (ebook) | ISBN 9781440847486 (hardcopy : alk. paper) (vol. 1) |
   ISBN 9781440847493 (hardcopy : alk. paper) (vol. 2) | ISBN 9781610695008
   (set : alk. paper)
Subjects: LCSH: Prisons—Law and legislation—United States—Encyclopedias. |
   Correctional law—United States—Encyclopedias. | Prisons—Law and
   legislation—United States—History.
Classification: LCC KF9730.A68 (ebook) | LCC KF9730.A68 A44 2019 (print) |
   DDC 365/.97303—dc23
LC record available at https://lccn.loc.gov/2018016381

ISBN: 978-1-61069-500-8 (set)
      978-1-4408-4748-6 (vol. 1)
      978-1-4408-4749-3 (vol. 2)
      978-1-61069-501-5 (ebook)

23 22 21 20 19   1 2 3 4 5

This book is also available as an eBook.

ABC-CLIO
An Imprint of ABC-CLIO, LLC

ABC-CLIO, LLC
130 Cremona Drive, P.O. Box 1911
Santa Barbara, California 93116-1911
www.abc-clio.com

This book is printed on acid-free paper ∞

Manufactured in the United States of America

Contents

Acknowledgments   xiii

Introduction   xv

Volume 1

Access to the Courts   1

Activism   5

Administration   9

AIDS/HIV among Inmates   12

Alcatraz   15

American Prison Designs   18

Angola   21

Antiterrorism and Effective Death Penalty Act of 1996   23

Arts Programs   25

Attica   26

Auburn System of Penology   29

Australia, Prisons in   31

Baltimore City Detention Center   35

Beccaria, Cesare (1738–1794)   39

Bell v. Wolfish (1979)   41

Benefit of Clergy   42

Biosocial Findings to Increase the Effectiveness of Treatment Programs   44

Boot Camps   48

Building Tenders   50

Canada, Prisons in   53

Capital Punishment, Collateral Consequences of   58

Castration as a Deterrent to Sexual Offending   61

Cell Phones in Prison   63

China, Prisons in   65

Civil Commitment and Postcriminal Sanctions for Sex Offenders   69

Civil Disabilities   73

Cleanliness in Prison   76

Cognitive-Behavioral Therapies in Prison   78

Commissary   81

Compassionate Release   82

Conjugal Visits   85

Consensual Sex between Inmates   88

Constitution as a Source for Prisoners' Rights, The   94

Continuum of Sanctions   98

Convict Criminology   101

Convict Lease System   106

Cooking in Prison   108

Correctional Case Management   111

Correctional Counseling   114

Correctional Employees and Administrators, Job Satisfaction of   117

Correctional Officer Subculture   121

Correctional Officer Training   124

Correctional Officer Unions   128

Correctional Officers, Job Stress among   132

Correctional Officers, Typology of   136

Correctional Officers and Discretion   138

Correctional Officers with Military Experience   141

Cost of Prisons   143

Custody Levels   146

Death Penalty in the Middle East   151

Death Penalty Legal Issues   154

Death Row Correctional Officers   159

Death Row Inmates   161

Deliberate Indifference   164

Deprivation Model   167

Determinate versus Indeterminate Sentencing   169

Disciplinary Hearings   171

DNA Exonerees   174

Drug Use in Prison   178

Economics of Crossing Over, The   181

Education in Prison   183

Elderly Offenders in Prison   186

England, Prisons in   193

Enlightenment and Punishment   196

Environmentally Friendly ("Green") Prisons   199

Equine-Facilitated Prison-Based Programs   202

Escapes   206

Ethical Issues in Prison Counseling   208

Evidence-Based Practice in Corrections   211

Evolving Standards of Decency   214

Execution Methods   218

Fathers behind Bars   223

Federal Sentencing Guidelines   226

Florence ADX   228

Folsom State Prison   230

France, Prisons in   233

Furloughs   236

General Strain Theory and Incarceration   241

Genetics in Sentencing, Role of   244

Good Time   247

Gossip and Rumors   250

Contents

Guantanamo Bay   252

Habeas Corpus Writs   257

Halfway Houses   258

Health Care in Prison Populations   260

Health Promotion in Prison Settings   263

Hunger Strikes   266

Importation Model   269

Inappropriate Correctional Employee–Inmate Relationships   271

Incarcerated Veterans   274

Incarceration, Factors Contributing to the Growth in   278

Incarceration, Impact of Social Progressives on (1900s–1920s)   282

Incarceration, Social Costs of High Rates of   285

Incarceration of Undocumented Immigrants   289

Incarceration Rates   293

Incarceration Rates, Trends in the United States   297

Incarceration Rates and Race   301

Incarceration Rates in the United States Compared to Other Countries   304

Informal Methods of Control Utilized by Correctional Officers   307

Inmate Classification   310

Inmate Dental Care   312

Inmate Subculture   315

Inmate-on-Inmate Sexual Abuse   318

Inmates, Transportation of   324

Inmates and Freedom of Religion   326

Inmates with Co-Occurring Disorders   330

Inmates with Intellectual Disabilities   332

Inmates' Perceptions of Prison versus Alternative Sanctions   335

Innocence Project   339

Inside-Out Prison Exchange Program   341

Inside-Outside Relationships   345

Jailhouse Lawyers   349

Contents ix

Jails Compared to Prisons 351

Judicial Involvement in Prison Administration 354

Juvenile Detention Centers 357

Juveniles in Corrections, Landmark Cases Involving 361

Leavenworth 365

Leaving Prison 368

Legitimate Penological Interests 370

Lockups 373

Maconochie, Alexander (1787–1860) 377

Male Prisoners' Perceptions of Female Officers 379

Masturbation in Prison 381

Maximum Security 383

Medical Experiments on Inmates 386

Mental Health Issues and Jails 388

Mentally Ill Prisoners 392

Methadone Maintenance for Prisoners 395

Misconduct by Correctional Employees 398

Misconduct by Prisoners 401

Mitchell, Joyce (1965–) 406

Muslim Inmates 410

Volume 2

Net Widening 415

Norway, Prisons in 417

Notorious or Infamous Inmates 420

Overcrowding 425

Oz (1997–2003) 428

Pains of Imprisonment 431

Panopticon 432

Parole, History of 434

Parole, Violation of 437

Contents

Parole Board   440

Penn, William (1644–1718)   442

Pennsylvania System of Penology   446

Personnel   448

Peru, Prisons in   450

Political Prisoners   452

Pregnancy and Motherhood in Prisons   455

Presentence Investigation Reports   458

Prison Argot   459

Prison-Based Animal Training Programs   462

Prison-Brewed Alcohol   465

Prison Ethnography   466

Prison Gangs   468

Prison Industries   473

Prison Law Libraries   477

Prison Litigation Reform Act   479

Prison Ministry   482

Prison Museums   484

Prison Populations, Downsizing of   487

Prison Populations, Trends in   491

Prison Rape Elimination Act   494

Prison Reform, Intended and Unintended Consequences of   502

Prison TV Shows, Scripted   504

Prison TV Shows, Unscripted Reality   507

Prison Work Programs   510

Prisoner Handbooks   514

Prisoner Reentry/Family Integration   515

Prisonization   518

Prisons, History of   521

Prisons as Schools for Crime   527

Privatization   529

Contents

xi

Protective Pairing in Men's Prisons   533

Pseudofamilies in Women's Prisons   535

Punishment Philosophies   538

Racial Integration of Inmates   543

Radicalization of Inmates   545

Rapelore in Prisons   547

Recidivism   549

Recidivism of Sex Offenders   551

Religious Programs Outreach   553

Respect   555

Restoration of Rights after Conviction   558

Restorative Justice   559

Rights Are Lost versus Rights Are Retained   562

Riots   565

Ruffin v. Commonwealth (1871)   569

San Quentin   571

Second Chance Act   573

Section 1983 Lawsuits   575

Self-Injury in Prison   577

Sentencing Disparities and Discrimination in Sentencing   579

Sentencing of Mothers and Parental Rights   582

Sex Offenders in Prison   585

Sex Reassignment Surgery among Inmates   590

Sexual Abuse of Inmates by Correctional Staff   592

Sexual Violence against Juveniles in Prison   597

Sexuality in Women's Prisons   602

Sexually Explicit Materials in Prisons   605

Sight and Sound of Juvenile Offenders   607

Snitches   608

Social Contract Theory   610

Solitary Confinement   612

South Africa, Prisons in   615

Sports   619

Stanford Prison Experiment   622

State-Raised Youths   624

Stigmatization versus Reintegrative Shaming   626

Suicide in Custody   629

Sykes, Gresham (1922–2010)   632

Synthetic Sanity   634

Tasers in Prisons and Jails   639

Tattooing in Prison   642

Tests of Adult Basic Education   644

Texas Prison Rodeo, The   646

Three-Strikes Laws   648

Total Institutions   651

Transgender Inmates   654

Treatment in Prisons   660

Treatment Professionals in Prisons   663

Truth in Sentencing   664

Underground Prison Economy   667

UNICOR   670

Use of Force in Prisons   672

Victim Impact Statements   677

Violence in Prison   679

Visitation   682

Vocational Training and Education   686

White-Collar Offenders and the Incarceration Experience   691

Women in Prison   694

Selected Bibliography   699

About the Editors and Contributors   709

Index   731

Acknowledgments

As we complete this two-year-long undertaking, we would like to thank Professor James E. Robertson for recommending us to ABC-CLIO to edit this encyclopedia. We are also very grateful to all the 139 contributors for writing all the wonderful entries, and most importantly, for submitting them on time. Without this team effort, this major project would not be possible. We take this opportunity to thank each one of our esteemed contributors.

Introduction

The United States presently has the dubious distinction of being the world's incarceration leader. Even though Americans comprise less than 5 percent of the global population, this country houses roughly one-quarter of the world's inmates. There are more than 2.3 million incarcerated offenders residing within prisons and jails in the United States. This enormous prison population is something that is unprecedented, not only in the United States but throughout the world. Punishing such a large number of people comes with a price tag of approximately $80 billion per year. Furthermore, it is of particular concern that members of racial minorities are significantly more likely than whites to find themselves behind bars. For example, one in three African American men will be imprisoned at some point during their lifetime. To make matters worse, if a black male does not graduate from high school, there is a 60 percent chance he will spend at least some part of his adulthood in a correctional facility.

As readers peruse through the pages of this two-volume encyclopedia of correctional systems and practices, they will see that incarceration was once considered a benevolent alternative to draconian sanctions, such as mutilations, banishment, branding, and executions. The evidence reveals that early Americans were inspired to use humane punishments by scholars such as Cesare Beccaria, the Italian law professor who argued from across the globe that punishment should be intended to enhance public safety rather than to avenge crime. Around this same time, William Penn, a philosopher, real estate tycoon, and founder of Pennsylvania, proposed the Great Law, a penal code based on tenants of the Quaker religion, which replaced harsher punishments with fines and jail time. In fact, the Walnut Street Jail in Philadelphia, which is often cited by historians as one of the first prisons in the United States, was intended to be a place of refuge where inmates could privately reflect on their misdeeds in individual cells and seek penitence. It would not be long before prisons and jails were referred to as "penitentiaries" all throughout the nation, a term still used today.

By the antebellum era, correctional facilities had become an established part of our culture and virtually as "American as apple pie." However, criminal justice pioneers were not afraid to experiment with new forms of incarceration. For example, Captain Elam Lynds established the Auburn system of penology in 1821. Under the Auburn system, inmates worked together in congregate shops but were expected to work silently to prevent the prison from becoming a "school for criminals." It was not long before industrialists criticized the Auburn system because they were unable to compete with the free labor of the prison regime. Meanwhile, and halfway around the world, Captain Alexander Maconochie devised a system of parole in the penal colony of Norfolk Island near Australia. Beginning around the 1850s, certain states within the United States adopted Maconochie's innovation of early release. This is one of many examples throughout the history of prisons and jails, which illustrates that Americans have long sought to achieve a sense of fairness and balance in administering punishment. Of course, as one reads the various entries throughout this encyclopedia, it will soon become apparent that it is highly debatable as to whether or not contemporary correctional facilities reflect the ideals of fairness, equity, and justice for all.

Prisons and jails in the United States have long targeted individuals of color, as they continue to do so today. In the 19th century, in the aftermath of the Civil War, southern states did not have the infrastructure to feed, clothe, and take care of convicted offenders. Instead, inmates were rented out to private businesses at a rate of around $3 a head per month. Historians have written extensively of the "black codes" that were implemented where African Americans could be imprisoned for the most petty and mundane type of offenses imaginable. It is a sad but well-established fact that the rate of incarceration for African Americans rose by roughly 500 percent following the Civil War. Virginia, South Carolina, Georgia, and Texas were notorious for using variations of the convict leasing system where field hands were literally worked to death. Eventually, when prison officials realized they could make more money by forcing prisoners to work in public facilities, convict leasing was phased out.

Although the layperson may regard prisons and jails as crude facilities that are designed merely to warehouse inmates, in actuality the field of corrections can often be quite progressive. In 1913, Thomas Mott Osborne, a Harvard-educated idealistic prison reformer, spent a week undercover as a convict in the Auburn Prison in order to expose the cruelties of institutional life. Osborne later became a warden of Sing Sing Prison in New York and eventually established the Welfare League Association, an organization designed to assist former prisoners. In the South, during the 1930s, when racial segregation was a way of life in virtually every aspect of society, black inmates competed side by side with their white compatriots for cash prizes at prison rodeos. From a historical perspective, the significance of this feat cannot be overlooked or ignored. By way of comparison, the U.S. military did not become racially integrated until 1948, and even then, it did not completely desegregate until several years later.

As the above paragraph suggests, correctional institutions are capable of providing glimpses of civility, perhaps even hope—not just for the inmates residing within these facilities but also for those living outside the prison walls. The mid-1940s, up until the late 1960s, marked the era of rehabilitation where prisons and jails would become the beneficiaries of scientific advances in treatment and rehabilitation. Correctional psychologists, teachers, and social workers used their expertise to treat offenders in an attempt to "cure" offenders of their criminality. Prisoner classification schemes were also implemented throughout the country in order to meet the educational, psychiatric, and religious needs of the inmate

Introduction xvii

population. During World War II, prisoners donated blood to the Red Cross and also worked on assembly lines to support the war effort. Some inmates were even permitted to enlist and, in fact, served their country with honor.

Shortly after World War II, Gresham M. Sykes, a veteran, used his G.I. Bill to pursue a doctoral degree at Northwestern University in Chicago. In 1958, Sykes published his groundbreaking book, *The Society of Captives*, which today, more than 60 years later, is still regarded as perhaps the most seminal prison ethnography. In this detailed examination of a New Jersey maximum security prison facility, Sykes illustrates how the operational realities of prison life encourage a norm of reciprocity where correctional officers ignore minor rule infractions in exchange for compliance in major areas. This illustrated, perhaps for the first time ever, that contrary to popular opinion, inmates may actually hold some degree of power over their captors. Gresham Sykes also describes how overfamiliarization between the keeper and the kept can lead to the outright corruption of authority. He notes that this is a slow, often subtle process where inmates take advantage of naïve correctional officers who want to be nice, or what he refers to as a "good Joe." Although Sykes later published in other areas of criminology, and is best known for the pivotal, "techniques of neutralization" theory, his early contribution to prison research is still nothing short of revolutionary. He is, without question, someone who has had a profound influence on prison research.

U.S. Supreme Court decisions under the leadership of Chief Justice Earl Warren have had a major impact on prisons and jails well into the 21st century. Most notably, *Cooper v. Pate*, 378 U.S. 546 (1964), forever changed the dynamics of institutional life, as this landmark decision gave inmates the right to sue prison officials in federal court. As a result of this ruling, the "hands-off" policy of judicial noninterference quickly dissipated. Wardens and correctional officers realized they were subject to significant oversight by the courts. The Warren Court forever changed the landscape of prisons and jails.

In spite of the fact that incarceration has become more humane, it is also being used much more frequently than ever before in the history of prisons and jails. In the early 1970s, in the wake of the civil rights movement and President Lyndon B. Johnson's war on poverty, there were fewer than 96 prisoners per every 100,000 American citizens. As Professor Loïc Wacquant notes, some penologists, such as Norval Morris and David Rothman, even began to opine that correctional facilities were in an inevitable state of decline. Unfortunately, however, this trend did not persist. In 1974, criminologist Robert Martinson published what became known as the "nothing works" doctrine in corrections. Even though Martinson's study was replete with methodological errors, it was nevertheless embraced by policy makers. Today, the United States has an incarceration rate of 698 prisoners per every 100,000 people—higher than any other country in the world by far.

President Richard Nixon is one of the first major players in modern history who politicized crime and essentially dismantled the rehabilitation movement in corrections. President Ronald Reagan later borrowed a page from the Nixon playbook in the 1980s when he approved the Sentencing Reform Act, which called for mandatory minimum drug sentences. Under this draconian law, crack cocaine, an illicit substance often used by poor African Americans, was punished 100 times as harshly as powdered cocaine, which was the drug of choice among affluent whites during the 1980s. During the 1990s, President Bill Clinton, a Democrat, gave states $10 billion dollars to expand prisons. It seems as though policy makers of both political parties have learned that it is popular to advocate for stronger punishments, whatever the consequences may be.

In 2010, President Barack Obama signed into law the Fair Sentencing Act, which reduced the disparity between crack and powdered cocaine by 18:1. More recently, voters in California approved Proposition 36, a measure that significantly restricts the usage of three-strikes legislation and even authorizes the resentencing of some offenders who are serving life behind the prison walls. If there is a possible silver lining to the 2008 financial crisis, it is that taxpayers are now more than ever sensitive to the fact that it costs an average of $35,000 a year to imprison an individual. The price tag more than doubles when society incarcerates elderly offenders, which happens to be one of the fastest-growing correctional populations in the United States.

Given the tremendous amount of taxpayer dollars, public resources, and human lives that are devoted to maintaining the criminal justice juggernaut, a number of issues and controversies continue to arise associated with incarceration.

Robert M. Worley, Ph.D., Lamar University and
Vidisha Barua Worley, Ph.D., Esq., Lamar University

Access to the Courts

For much of the 19th and 20th centuries, prisoners were viewed as "slaves of the state" (as decided by the U.S. Supreme Court in 1871, *Ruffin v. Commonwealth*), and due to the crime(s) they committed and the sentences imposed, they were not considered "persons" in the eyes of the law. Prisoners had no civil rights or any type of legal protection. They had no legal standing in court. Therefore, there was no need for them to have access to the courts. This judicial view of prisoners, which was followed by the courts from the *Ruffin* decision up until the 1960s, was known as the "hands-off doctrine." It rendered prisoners essentially "civilly dead" without the ability to obtain any legal remedy even if the prisoner's claim had underlying legal merit. The development of the hands-off doctrine can be traced to one or more of the following rationales: separation of powers doctrine, low level of judicial expertise in penology, fear that judicial intervention would undermine prison discipline, and fear that giving inmates access to the courts would result in a surge in prisoner civil litigation.

The courts were particularly concerned that by reviewing prisoner civil actions, the courts would interfere with, and undercut the ability of, prison administrators to maintain security and control over their facilities and their ability to promulgate necessary correctional policies to do so. Judges did not want to hinder, or second-guess, the ability of prison officials to carry out the objectives of the correctional institutions. This view was consistent with *Coffin v. Reichard* (1944), which stated that a convicted offender retains all the rights that citizens in general have, but when those rights interfere with the administration or correctional institutions' policies, then the prisoner has no legal recourse. Another key reason for the lack of judicial action was the conservative and philosophical nature of the Supreme Court justices that guided their decisions in the late 1800s up until the Warren Court in the 1960s.

Despite the hands-off rationale and conservative nature of the courts, which denied inmates civil access to the courts, there were a handful of prisoner lawsuits prior to the 1960s that slowly opened the doors for inmates to seek judicial redress. One of the first U.S. Supreme Court cases pertaining to prisoners' access to the courts was in 1941: *Ex parte Hull*.

In *Hull,* the court considered whether an inmate had the constitutional right to judicial intervention to prevent their habeas corpus petitions from being screened by prison officials. Despite often being criminal in nature, habeas corpus petitions are considered and treated by the courts as civil actions. The court stated that access to the courts is a basic requirement of due process and is protected—even for convicted prisoners—under the due process clause of the Fourteenth Amendment.

Despite the precedent of *Hull*'s judicial intervention, the courts however still maintained a hands-off approach when dealing with prisoner lawsuits. By the late 1950s under the Warren Court, the U.S. Supreme Court heard two more key cases that addressed prisoners seeking redress and their access to the courts: *Griffin v. Illinois* (1956) and *Burns v. Ohio* (1959). Both cases dealt with indigent prisoners. In the *Griffin* case, the court established that indigent prisoners have the same rights to an appellate review as any other person. In the *Burns* case, the U.S. Supreme Court made it clear that a state cannot require a filing fee when an inmate is seeking an appeal.

Despite the few prisoner lawsuits that did reach the attention of the state and federal courts, the judiciary continued to stay away from prisoner grievances until *Cooper v. Pate* (1964). In the *Cooper* case, the U.S. Supreme Court ruled that inmates could bring a suit against prison administrators under Title 42, Section 1983, of the Civil Rights Act. The U.S. Supreme Court made it clear that prisoners must have an effective remedy for prison abuse. This case is considered by legal scholars to have effectively ended the hands-off doctrine that had dominated the judiciary for over a century.

In 1969, the U.S. Supreme Court heard *Johnson v. Avery*, a case involving a Tennessee prisoner who violated prison regulations by helping another inmate prepare writs. The court stated that prisoners must have access to the courts, and if inmates are able to assist other inmates in their legal claims, the prison administrators, staff, and policies should not interfere.

In the 1974 case, *Wolff v. McDonnell*, the U.S. Supreme Court heard a class action lawsuit from a Nebraska inmate that alleged that the prison disciplinary proceedings violated the due process clause of the Fourteenth Amendment. In the majority opinion, the court famously stated that "(t)here is no Iron Curtain between the Constitution and the prisons of this country." The court found that due process was violated when the prison failed to provide written notice of the charges against the inmate, a written statement of the evidence that would be used against him, and the opportunity for the inmate to call witnesses and present evidence in his own defense. The suit also objected to the prison officials inspecting privileged mail between inmates and their attorneys, which the inmates asserted unconstitutionally "chilled" their ability to freely access the courts without fear of retaliation by the prison officials and employees.

Finally, in *Bounds v. Smith* (1977), accessing the courts was further articulated as a constitutional right for prisoners. The courts stated in *Bounds* that inmates must have *meaningful* access to the courts by providing inmates access to a reasonable law library or the option to hire jailhouse lawyers to assist with filing a petition. These key rulings effectively changed the legal status of prisoners and gave them unprecedented access to the courts.

The right of access to the courts by prisoners, however, is not absolute or automatic; there are limitations. In *Lewis v. Casey* (1996), inmates in Arizona claimed that their access to the courts was denied because the prison administration did not provide inmates with an adequate law library and other legal assistance. Though the lower court decision agreed with the inmates, the U.S. Supreme Court reversed more than 20 years of prisoner access to the court's case law originally established by the *Bounds* decision. The court stated that a prisoner must prove to the courts that prison officials or a prison policy prevented the inmate from asserting a "non-frivolous claim" and suffered an "actual injury." In other words, a prisoner must have a legitimate underlying claim and demonstrate to the court that an "injury" occurred because the prison official or institutional policy prevented that inmate from filing and/or proceeding with their claim. The *Lewis* decision effectively redefined prisoners' rights and further limited inmates' access to the courts.

Today, while prisoners still are not given unfettered access to the courts, prisoners are able to file lawsuits in a number of different ways. There are three basic types of lawsuits an inmate can file to access the courts: (1) a habeas corpus suit, (2) a civil rights suit, and (3) what is typically categorized as "other suits" or "mandamus suits" or civil actions.

Habeas corpus suits are federal civil petitions filed by inmates who challenge the constitutionality of their criminal convictions and sentences. The habeas court is charged with the responsibility of determining if the state court verdict and rulings on appeal violated any federal constitutional right that the defendant retains. The writ of habeas corpus is a crucial tool for prisoners to use when questioning the legality of their imprisonment.

Regardless of whether or not the inmate is confined as a state or federal inmate, if the claim is based on a violation of a provision of the federal constitution, it may be asserted in federal court as a civil rights suit pursuant to 42 U.S.C. §1983. If the civil rights suit is brought in state court, it can be removed by the defendants to be heard by the U.S. District Court located in the jurisdiction in which the prison where the violation occurred is located. So long as the defendant has personal involvement in the underlying constitutional violation or the imposition of the unconstitutional policy, practice, or custom, inmate plaintiffs may initiate lawsuits against jailers, sheriffs, correctional officers, administrators, and even other inmates. Examples of this type of case include claims of denial of the right to access the courts in violation of the Fourteenth Amendment (*Johnson v. Avery*, 1969), denial of freedom of expression and religion in violation of the First Amendment (*Cooper v. Pate*, 1964), denial of freedom of association in violation of the First Amendment (*Jones v. North Carolina Prisoners' Labor Union, Inc.*, 1977), freedom from (excessive force) cruel and unusual punishment in violation of the Eighth Amendment (*Holt v. Sarver*, 1969), freedom from unreasonable searches and seizures in violation of the Fourth Amendment (*Bell v. Wolfish*, 1979), the right to reasonable medical treatment pursuant to the Eighth Amendment (*Newman v. State of Alabama*, 1974), and the limited due process rights related to grievance procedures (*Procunier v. Martinez*, 1974).

In a civil rights suit, it is not sufficient for an inmate to allege that the defendant(s) acted merely negligently. It is the inmate's burden to prove, by a preponderance of the evidence that the defendants acted either with "deliberate indifference" to the inmate's constitutional rights or with "willful disregard" to those rights. These are considerably higher legal standards than negligence and require proof of a higher level of intent on the part of the defendant than in negligence claims.

Some civil rights actions that are filed warrant the attention of the courts, but there are also a significant number of frivolous lawsuits that ultimately hinder the courts' ability to function. According to the Administrative Office of the U.S. Courts, the number of civil rights suits filed in U.S. District Courts pursuant to Title 42 USC § 1983 increased from fewer than 5,000 in 1970 to approximately 40,000 in 1996. However, with the passing of the Prisoner Litigation Reform Act in 1996 and the courts' standard of proof more difficult for prisoners, the number of civil rights petitions filed by prisoners was fewer than 23,000 in 2012.

In addition to habeas petitions and civil rights suits, prisoners can also file civil actions in state court based on violations of state statutory law or case/common law. Examples include "tort" claims of inmates who sustain personal injury due to the negligently maintained real property/real estate (i.e., a stair that the prison knew was uneven caused the inmate to fall and injure his knee) or negligent medical care provided by a privately contracted prison medical provider (i.e., a negligent medical decision made by the prison doctor, not the prison officials, which violated the professional medical standard of care one would reasonably receive outside of prison).

Another type of suit an inmate can file is a mandamus petition, which is filed under the Mandamus Act (28 U.S.C. § 1361). A mandamus lawsuit is filed when an administrative, executive, or judicial officer fails to perform his or her legal duty in providing rights and privileges to prisoners. However, these types of suits at the federal level are less frequent and seldom used.

Gaining access to the courts has given inmates the opportunity to challenge their convictions, improve living conditions, obtain better medical care, expand on legal services and materials, and exercise freedom of religion and expression, freedom of press, freedom from cruel and unusual punishment, the right to rehabilitation and treatment, and other due process rights.

While the U.S. Supreme Court in the 1990s limited some prisoners' rights, Congress also passed two critical statutes in 1996 that had a significant impact on prisoners accessing the courts. In 1996, Congress passed the Prison Litigation Reform Act (PLRA), which placed restrictions on prisoners' ability to access the federal courts. It was specifically aimed at reducing frivolous civil rights lawsuits brought by prisoners. The second act was the Antiterrorism and Effective Death Penalty Act (AEDPA) of 1996. This act limited the federal court's scope of review of state court findings and made it more difficult for prisoners to file multiple/serial habeas corpus petitions. Prisoners now have a one-year statute of limitation to file a habeas petition. That one-year time period is "tolled" or halted temporarily while the inmates exhaust their timely and properly filed appeals in state court. If the inmates wish to file a second/successive habeas petition, they must first seek permission to do so from the Court of Appeals but are still limited. The basis for appealing further to the U.S. Supreme Court are even more limited. Though prisoners have gained significant access to the courts over the last 50 years, judicial decisions and congressional oversight have significantly affected changes to prisoners' ability to access the courts.

Christopher J. Przemieniecki

See also: Antiterrorism and Effective Death Penalty Act of 1996; Constitution as a Source for Prisoners' Rights, The; Habeas Corpus Writs

Further Reading

Branham, L. S. (2002). *The law of sentencing, corrections, and prisoners' rights* (6th ed.). St. Paul, MN: West.

Champion, D. J. (1991). Jail inmate litigation in the 1990's. In J. A. Thompson & G. L. Mays (Eds.), *American jails: Public policy issues* (pp. 197–215). Chicago: Nelson-Hall.

Haas, K. C. (1977). Judicial politics and correctional reform: An analysis of the decline of the "hands-off" doctrine. *Detroit College Law Review, 4,* 796–831.

Haas, K. C., & Alpert, G. P. (Eds.). (1991). American prisoners and the right of access to the court: A vanishing concept of protection. In K. C. Haas & G. P. Albert (Eds.), *The dilemmas of corrections* (pp. 203–226). Prospect Heights, IL: Waveland Press.

Hemmons, C., Belbot, B., & Bennett, K. (2004). *Significant cases in corrections.* Los Angeles: Roxbury.

Jacobs, J. B. (1997). The prisoners' rights movement and its impacts. In J. W. Marquart & J. R. Sorensen (Eds.), *Correctional contexts: Contemporary and classical readings* (pp. 231–247). Los Angeles: Roxbury.

Meeropol, R., & Head, I. (Eds.). (2010). *The jailhouse lawyer's handbook* (5th ed.). New York: Center for Constitutional Rights. Retrieved from http://jailhouselaw.org/category/chapter-3

Palmer, J. D., & Palmer, J. W. (2015). *Constitutional rights of prisoners* (9th ed.). New York: Routledge.

Schlanger, M. (2015). Trends in prisoner litigation, as the PLRA enters adulthood. *UC Irvine Law Review, 5*(1), 153–179.

Smith, C. E. (2007). Prisoners' rights and the Rehnquist era. *The Prison Journal, 87*(4), 457–476.

Thomas, J. (1988). *Prisoner litigation: The paradox of the jailhouse lawyer.* Totowa, NJ: Rowman & Littlefield.

Trammell, R. (1997, September). Out of bounds: *Lewis v. Casey* redefines rights previously found in *Bounds v. Smith*—seriously undermining prison law libraries and the ability of inmates to seek justice. *AALL Spectrum,* 10–11.

University of Pennsylvania. (1962). Constitutional rights of prisoners: The developing law. *University of Pennsylvania Law Review, 110,* 985–1008.

Wallace, D. H. (1997). Prisoners' rights: Historical views. In J. W. Marquart & J. R. Sorensen (Eds.), *Correctional contexts: Contemporary and classical readings* (pp. 248–257). Los Angeles: Roxbury.

Activism

Since the invention of the prison in Europe and later in the United States, a number of individuals and groups have tried to either change correctional policies and practices and/or attempted to cast doubt on the legitimacy of incarceration and have worked to close jails, prisons, and juvenile detention facilities. In general, these efforts are part of a larger discussion of prison abolition, activism, reform, unions, and sentencing reform. Prison activism refers to "a broad-based social movement that addresses injustices in the criminal justice system" (Piper, 2005, p. 7). Although some constituencies want to reform the prison system, others want to abolish it.

Also, it is difficult to date the origins of prison activism and to know exactly how many people and organizations are involved with activities that may fall under this rubric.

A variety of people from different walks of life and professional backgrounds participate in prison activism and abolition. Front and center have been convicts, inmates, and prisoners (Ross, 2010), as their lives are most impacted by the conditions of confinement and have spent considerable effort to change their immediate living environment. Also important are the numerous lawyers or people with legal backgrounds who have participated in calling attention to substandard prison conditions, policies, and practices. In the United States these efforts can be traced back to lawyers like Clarence Darrow (1857–1938) and extend to well-known "radical" celebrity lawyers like William Kuntsler (1919–1995) and Ron Kuby (1956–). Otherwise, a handful of prisoners have managed to garner public recognition for their work behind bars to change prison policies and practices. For example, Caryl Chessman (1920–1961), while on death row at San Quentin Prison (California), managed to change prison policy in that state (Piper, 2005, p. 8).

Likewise, numerous organizations in the United States participate in prison activism (Sudbury, 2004). They vary in terms of their central focus, and each has a slightly different mission and life span. Many of these groups have narrowly focused objectives. Some have religious leanings (e.g., assisting prisoners with their spiritual needs), while others are focused on political issues (e.g., expanding inmates' ability to vote). Others, like Mothers Against Mandatory Minimums, have worked disproportionately on sentencing reform, often forming alliances with like-minded organizations such as The Sentencing Project. Some groups specialize in the plight of juveniles who are behind bars, while others focus on women who are incarcerated (Katzenstein, 2005). Others have a broader set of objectives with respect to corrections in the United States. They want to start or improve rehabilitation programs in correctional facilities, provide better medical, dental, and counseling care, and/or fight against censorship of materials coming into the prison. On the other hand, there are many organizations whose primary focus is correctional system reform, including the Prison Moratorium Project, the Prison Activist Resource Center, and Citizens United for Rehabilitation of Errants (CURE). Some of them focus on one particular correctional facility or those correctional facilities in one particular state. For example, "Schools Not Jails" (Acey, 2000) channeled their energies into reforming correctional facilities in California only.

Meanwhile, there are a number of organizations that have as part of their larger mission a focus on prisoners and on conditions in correctional facilities. This includes international organizations like Amnesty International and Human Rights Watch. The former has a focus on the use of the death penalty, while the latter is concerned with all manner of behaviors that encroach on the rights of individuals who are unnecessarily detained or subjected to substandard conditions of confinement. United States organizations that serve a broad mission include the American Civil Liberties Union (ACLU) and the National Lawyers Guild (NLG). The ACLU, through their National Prison Project, monitors persistent legal violations perpetrated by jails and prisons, and the NLG has two committees focused on assisting incarcerated individuals. Meanwhile, the Sentencing Project works on numerous issues affecting the rights of people who are incarcerated and negatively affected by the criminal justice system.

In this context they have campaigns that bring awareness to certain prisoners or classes of prisoners. Some organizations, like the Soros Foundation, have been involved in prison activism by supporting individuals (e.g., scholars and journalists) who will work on behalf of prison reform. Almost every large city in the United States has a prison activist community who participate in demonstrations, letter-writing campaigns, etc. Many of the people who belong in these groups do not limit their activities to one prison only.

No sooner than the first prisons were constructed that efforts to change and reform them started. British social reformer Jeremy Bentham (1748–1832) and his Panopticon was an attempt to reform. So were the Quakers who formed the Walnut Street jail. Some might even say that the history of corrections is the history of reform. This discussion also includes an expansion of prisoner rights. There has been a constituency of individuals in the United States, like the prison abolitionists who have been prison activists.

During the 1960s, numerous activist groups like the Black Panther Party had prison outreach programs. We also saw the antiwar and civil rights movements take an interest in prisoner rights and join forces with prison activists. It was not until the 1970s, however, that there was an increase in the amount of prison activism in the United States. In many respects, this development began with what is referred to as prisoner movements, in particular prisoner unions, which originally formed inside correctional facilities. In general, "The term 'prisoners unions' [was] used for a variety of movements which have developed in various states since 1970" (Huff, 1974, p. 10). The origins of prisoner unions can be traced back to the early 1970s at Folsom Prison in California. Many of them found considerable opposition from correctional officers, workers, and administrators, despite the alliances they made with activists on the outside (e.g., Black Panther Party and various anarchist groups).

It is understandable that the prisoner movements and unions started during this time, as this was on the heels of the burgeoning civil rights movement and calls for greater racial and ethnic equality in the United States. In the post–Watergate era (1972), a considerable amount of attention was devoted to groups that assisted with religious services in prisons, such as the work by Charles "Chuck" Colson who was convicted of crimes during the Reagan administration, and shortly after his release founded the Prison Fellowship, an evangelical organization that worked with prisoners.

During the 1970s, almost all of the activity by activists was directed toward men. This shortcoming was noticed during the 1980s and soon thereafter.

Groups like Critical Resistance and Women's Advocacy Ministry as well as individuals like Angela Davis and Kathy Boudin have done a great deal to illuminate the conditions in women's prisons and to set out an agenda to reform or abolish women's facilities. (Piper, 2005, p. 9)

Some of the issues that were explored dealt with incarcerated mothers. This has involved women who were pregnant behind bars and also formerly incarcerated women and their struggles with reentry.

Over the past four decades one of the most radical positions has been the prison abolition movement. In the forefront of this movement are activists, ex-convicts, academics, religious actors, politicians, and inmates and their families. The modern origins of prison abolition started during the 1960s in Scandinavia and soon spread to other Western countries. In the United States, the prison abolition movement began in 1976 with the help of Quaker and prison minister Fay Honey Knopp, who established an organization called the Prison Research Education Project and later authored the well-known book, *Instead of Prison: A Handbook for Abolitionists* (1976). In 1981, the Canadian Quaker Committee for Jails and Justice started advocating prison abolition, and in 1983, the very first International Conference on Prison Abolition (ICOPA) was held in Toronto (Ross, 1983). Since then, the organization has evolved, including a name change, substituting the words "circle" for "conference" and "prison" for "penal," so that the organization is now called the International Circle on Penal Abolition. Accompanying this movement is a considerable amount of scholarship exploring the different facets of abolition.

In general, prison reformers have tried to force governments and departments of corrections to change prison conditions and policies, including minimizing crowding/overcrowding, providing educational opportunities, reinstating the loss of pell grants, etc. Some of this work has been in the area of sentencing in an effort to prevent people from going to jail in the first place. Advocates of prison abolition believe that these changes do not go far enough and seek solutions outside the prison system by changes in laws such as decriminalization of drugs and seeing drug addiction as a medical problem rather than a criminal justice problem, as suggested by Piper (2005).

Although numerous constituencies have been involved in prison activism and abolition, some have disproportionately focused their resources on changing particular types of prison sentences that they argue do extreme harm to inmates. This includes efforts organized around abolishing mandatory minimums and the death penalty. With respect to the first effort, starting in 1990 many prison activists have tried to call attention to and lobbied members of Congress on the disproportionate sentencing of young African American males for crack versus the less severe sentences attributed to possession of powder cocaine.

Other constituencies have tried to either curtail or abolish the death penalty. Although not strictly prison reform, it is related to prisons as the death penalty currently exists in 31 states (Ross, 2016, Chap. 11). As early as 1845, an organization called the American Society for the Abolition of Capital Punishment formed. "Since then, . . . These groups fight both for the abolition of the death penalty and for individuals facing execution" (Piper, 2005, p. 10).

Jeffrey Ian Ross

See also: Panopticon; Prison Reform, Intended and Unintended Consequences of; Religious Programs Outreach

Further Reading

Acey, C. E. S. A. (2000). This is an illogical statement: Dangerous trends in anti-prison activism. *Social Justice, 27*(3), 206–211.

Barry, E. M. (2000). Women prisoners on the cutting edge: Development of the activist women's prisoners' rights movement. *Social Justice, 27*(3), 168–175.

Brown, M., & Schept, J. (2016). New abolition, criminology and a critical carceral studies. *Punishment & Society, 19*(4), 440–462.

Greene, D. (2005). Abolition. In M. Bosworth (Ed.), *Encyclopedia of prisons & correctional facilities* (pp. 2–5). Thousand Oaks, CA: Sage.

Haines, H. H. (1996). *Against capital punishment: The anti-death penalty movement in America, 1972–1994*. New York: Oxford University Press.

Huff, C. R. (1974). Unionization behind the walls. *Criminology, 12*(2), 175–194.

Huff, C. R. (1975). The development and diffusion of prisoners' movements. *The Prison Journal, 55*(2), 4–20.

Katzenstein, M. F. (2005). Rights without citizenship: Activist politics and prison reform in the United States. In D. S. Meyer, V. Jenness, & H. M. Ingram (Eds.), *Routing the opposition: Social movements, public policy, and democracy* (pp. 236–258). Minneapolis: University of Minnesota Press.

Knopp, F. H. (1976). *Instead of prisons: A handbook for abolitionists*. Syracuse, NY: Prison Education Action Research Project.

Piper, K. (2005). Activism. In M. Bosworth (Ed.). *Encyclopedia of prisons & correctional facilities* (pp. 7–11). Thousand Oaks, CA: Sage.

Ross, J. I. (1983, June 2–8). Jail dehumanizing say abolitionists. *Now*, p. 5.

Ross, J. I. (2010). Resisting the carceral state: Prisoner resistance from the bottom up. *Social Justice, 36*(3), 28–45.

Ross, J. I. (2016). *Key issues in corrections*. Bristol, U.K.: Policy Press.

Sudbury, J. (2004). A world without prisons: Resisting militarism, globalized punishment, and empire. *Social Justice, 31*(1–2), 9–30.

Zonn, S. (1977). Inmate unions: An appraisal of prisoner rights and labor implications. *University of Miami Law Review, 32*(3), 613–635.

Administration

The administration of corrections facilities is a very complex and stressful process. The days of the warden making all decisions and acting as the final authority of the prison environments are long gone. The reality is that the prison warden is just one "cog" in a very hierarchical ladder of decision makers. The distance between the warden and the governor (or other final authority) now may be through several layers of supervision and control. The bureaucracy of control and supervision for correctional facilities has grown in direct relationship to the increased number of people sentenced to prison in the past 30 years.

Three specific components have been particularly challenging in this time period: (1) changing nature of prison inmates, (2) matrix management, and (3) management by litigation. These three components have added to the complexity of a system that has been directed by competing and changing goals—incapacitation, retribution, rehabilitation, and deterrence—and these conflicting goals require different approaches in prison management. Members of the general public cannot agree on what they want from a prison system, and to further complicate this issue, public opinion is subject to change. The image of the pendulum is often depicted as something that moves between the extremes of rehabilitation on the one end and punishment on the other. This pendulum seems to move continuously throughout history as extremes in punishment are seen as too severe and then the extremes in rehabilitation are seen as too lenient.

The complexity of prison administration has increased as the number of special populations of inmates has increased. The current prison populations include special needs inmates with a variety of management issues, such as mentally ill inmates, sex offenders, transgender inmates, gang-involved inmates, female inmates, young inmates, elderly inmates, religiously diverse groups, and inmates with serious medical conditions. As the number of inmates sentenced to prison has increased, the number of inmates within each of the special populations has also soared. Prison systems must provide specific security and services to each of these individual groups of inmates in order to provide a constitutionally adequate environment. As specific needs are identified, the system must adapt with policy and practice to address the needs. A failure to adapt has often resulted in litigation that forces such change.

One adaptation that has been made by large systems includes an increase in specialization of services and management. Matrix management is a common approach to deal with this type of specialization. Under matrix management, there may be several areas of the prison that are not within the power of the warden at all. One of the most frequently separated areas is that of health care. Often health care is an entirely different chain of command that has its own top administrator. This particular type of matrix management is intended to provide expert supervision to a vital piece of the care and custody of inmates. The result can be a highly effective form of health care service, if the matrix is managed well. In cases where the matrix organizational approach is not managed well, the result can be a fragmented service system that is not accountable to the inmates or the taxpayers or the warden.

Although the warden may not be "really" in charge, the warden is often named as the primary target on litigation from or about inmates. The liability of supervising this type of locked community cannot be understated. A warden must be able to depend on the people who work within the facility, no matter who they actually report to. When an inmate dies from a lack of medical treatment, the warden is the primary person named in litigation. As a result, a warden must have a full understanding of the environment and have the ability to work with a complex and often politically motivated group of providers of services.

The role of litigation and court involvement in prison systems is important to understand. Just as the pendulum has moved from one extreme to the other, the involvement from the judiciary has also changed over time. Prior to 1964, the court systems took a hands-off approach to prison issues. The 1964 decision of *Cooper v. Pate* launched the court system into an era where they exercised a great deal of power on the entire criminal justice system. In this case, the U.S. Supreme Court held that prison inmates could bring lawsuits against prison authorities under Section 1983 of the federal Civil Rights Act *(Cooper v. Pate*, 378 U.S. 546). This decision unleashed a torrent of civil rights litigation against our country's corrections systems.

As a direct result of this decision, many corrections systems were involved in litigation and were ultimately judged as unconstitutional under the Eighth

Amendment of the U.S. Constitution. By 1985, over one-third of the country's corrections systems were under court orders or consent decrees aimed at the conditions of confinement. The cost to the taxpayer and the types of court interventions ordered created a movement in the country to make access to the courts for inmates much more difficult.

The Prison Litigation Reform Act (PLRA) was signed into law in 1996. This act changed the face of prison litigation by requiring a variety of actions by inmates prior to a case proceeding in federal court. These actions were seen by some as barriers to constitutional protections and by others as necessary steps to reduce the number of frivolous lawsuits that were clogging the courts. Although the PLRA makes filing a civil action against a prison system more difficult, it did not totally eliminate court intervention in prison administration. The impact of the courts' involvement in administrative decisions is still an important policy consideration for correctional leaders.

The administration of a prison is impacted by outside entities, such as the court system, and by the increasing need for specialized services due to the changing nature of the types and numbers of inmates sentenced to prison. The complexity of this type of management continues to increase as the pendulum swings from one extreme to the other.

Susan Jones

See also: Legitimate Penological Interests; Personnel; Prison Populations, Trends in; Prison Reform, Intended and Unintended Consequences of; Recidivism

Further Reading

Connor, D. P., & Tewksbury, R. (2013, July/August). Examining prison wardens' perceptions of inmates incarcerated for sex offenses. *Corrections Today, 75*(3), 60, 61, 68.

Cooper v. Pate, 378 U.S. 546 (U.S. Supreme Court 1964).

Cullen, F. T., Latessa, E. J., Burton, V. S., & Lombardo, L. (1993). The correctional orientation of prison wardens: Is the rehabilitative ideal supported? *Criminology, 31*(1), 69–92.

Cullen, F. T., Latessa, E. J., Kopache, R., Lombardo, L. X., & Burton, V. S. (1993). Prison warden's job satisfaction. *The Prison Journal, 73*(2), 141–161.

Dennehy, K. M., & Nantel, K. A. (2006). Improving prison safety: Breaking the code of silence. *Washington University Journal of Law & Policy, 22*(1), 175–185.

Flanagan, T. J., Johnson, W. W., & Bennett, K. (1996). Job satisfaction among correctional executives: A contemporary portrait of wardens of state prisons for adults. *The Prison Journal, 76*(4), 385–397.

Hensley, C., Dumond, R., Tewksbury, R., & Dumond, D. (2002). Possible solutions for preventing inmate sexual assault: Examining wardens' beliefs. *American Journal of Criminal Justice, 27*(1), 19–33.

Jacobs, J. B., & Magdovitz, S. B. (1977). At LEEP'S end? A review of the law enforcement education program. *Journal of Police Science and Administration, 5*(1), 1–18.

Johnson, W. W., Bennett, K., & Flanagan, T. J. (1997). Getting tough on prisoners: Results from the national corrections executive survey, 1995. *Crime & Delinquency, 43*(1), 24–41.

Lipsky, M. (1980). *Street-level bureaucracy: Dilemmas of the individual in public service.* New York: Russell Sage.

Moster, A. N., & Jeglic, E. L. (2009). Prison warden attitudes toward prison rape and sexual assault: Findings since the Prison Rape Elimination Act (PREA). *The Prison Journal, 89*(1), 65–78.

Withrow, P. (Ed.). (2007). *A view from the trenches: A manual for wardens by wardens* (2nd ed.). Ghent, NY: NAAWS.

Zaitzow, B. H. (1998). Doing time: Everybody's doing it. *Criminal Justice Policy Review, 9*(1), 13–42.

Zupan, L. L. (1992). Men guarding women: An analysis of the employment of male correction officers in prisons for women. *Journal of Criminal Justice, 20*(4), 297–309.

AIDS/HIV among Inmates

With more than 2 million people incarcerated in correctional facilities throughout the United States, and the incidence of human immunodeficiency virus, or HIV, five times greater in incarcerated facilities than the general population, HIV presents a significant health concern to prisons and jails. Incidence rates are due in large part to a constellation of factors attributable to the population on the outside prior to detention, including drug use, mental illness, prostitution, poverty, and homelessness. The incidence rates and transmission patterns of HIV in jails and prisons have often been overlooked, underexamined, and neglected.

The potential harms of HIV in correctional settings are borne of two sources of concern. First, HIV presents unique health implications and medical needs including more frequent doctor visits, confidentiality concerns, and complex medication regimens and monitoring for the inmate testing positive for this highly communicable and potentially deadly disease. Second, inmates testing positive for HIV in prisons and jails increases the risk of transmission to other inmates in the correctional facility and then to the broader community outside the institution upon their release and return.

HIV typically enters prison and jail populations in one of two ways. Frequently, inmates have contracted the disease prior to being incarcerated through high-risk lifestyle choices such as intravenous drug use, sex work and prostitution, or other sources of transmission, and entered the facility with the disease either diagnosed or undiagnosed. Another source of infection involves transmission while in the correctional institution where an infected inmate in the facility may spread the disease to other inmates while incarcerated through participation in risk-taking behaviors including needle sharing for tattooing, syringe sharing when using drugs, or engaging in unprotected sexual behavior. Jails and prisons too may inadvertently facilitate transmission within the facility due to lack of oversight and prioritizing of prevention on the part of correctional and state/federal officials.

The large amounts of both financial and human resources invested in prisons are not typically allocated toward prison programming, safe sex or abstinence programs, personal health or services aimed at improving the overall well-being and quality of life of prisoners. These issues are not often viewed as the top priorities; instead, as a way to appeal to the general public's fervor regarding how to treat and secure inmates, most of the financial and human resource capital is deployed for the priority and purpose of making the correctional institutions more secure.

AIDS/HIV among Inmates

Despite rising medical costs, an ever-increasing prison population, and aging inmates, many jails and prisons are underfunded in the area of providing adequate medical care to prison and jail inmates, including in many facilities the funding to test for and treat incidents of HIV. This has had significant negative impact on inmates infected with HIV, and even though the percentage of inmates infected is fairly low, rates continue to exceed those of the general population, and HIV remains a major correctional institution health concern. A lack of adequate resources for testing and treatment undermines early intervention and prevention, increasing transmission risk both inside the correctional facility and to the community where the inmate returns.

It is easy to overlook the kind of impact HIV has had on jails and prisons in the United States as the number of inmates infected with HIV has consistently declined since 2001. The U.S. Department of Justice found that there was a 16 percent drop in HIV-infected inmates from 2001 to 2010 (Maruschak, 2012). Currently, 1.5 percent of inmates are infected with HIV with men comprising approximately 91 percent of HIV-positive inmates (Westergaard, Spaulding, & Flanigan, 2013). Jail-incarcerated African American males test positive for HIV at rates five times greater than white males and two times greater than Hispanic/Latino males. African American females in jails are two times more likely to test positive for HIV than white or Hispanic/Latina females (Centers for Disease Control and Prevention, 2015).

In the earliest era of the HIV epidemic, the controversial issue of segregation emerged as a means of managing the HIV-positive population in correctional facilities to protect the general population of the facility from infection. The American Civil Liberties Union (ACLU) released a report in 2010 condemning the practice of segregating HIV-infected inmates from the rest of the prison population, calling it "cruel, inhumane, and degrading treatment" (ACLU, 2010). Just three years later, South Carolina became the last state to end its policy of segregating HIV-infected prisoners. Today many consider integration to be part of best practice, and though there are no states that continue the practice of segregation, the debate continues.

The ACLU relied on three key points regarding segregation of HIV-status inmates: (1) It dehumanized inmates, (2) it created a climate of discriminatory and cruel behavior, and (3) it attached a negative stigma to the inmates. HIV-positive inmates were more likely to be viewed as inferior, which produced discriminatory behavior by prison staff and other prisoners. Inmates' HIV status disqualified them from many prison jobs, they frequently received poorer housing assignments, and they were denied access to meaningful rehabilitative programs while in prison (2010). On the contrary, many people believe that segregating HIV-infected inmates is necessary to the health and welfare of the larger inmate population. They assert that not only is it necessary to protect other prison inmates from being infected, but it is also important as it limits transmission opportunities and serves to protect the communities that inmates will be released to upon completion of their sentence.

In 2012, the United Nations Office on Drugs and Crime published a brief outlining 15 recommended HIV intervention strategies to be implemented in prisons and other closed settings. The list of recommendations included HIV testing, treatment, care and support, and condom programs. Research reveals that testing is inconsistent in prisons and jails throughout the United States, and while some states implemented mandatory testing, opponents say it violates human rights, takes away personal choice, is costly, and serves to stigmatize the inmate. Those who support mandatory testing and treatment argue that inmates should not have the right to refuse treatment if refusal puts other people's health at risk. Transmission rates are highest among untested and undiagnosed inmates. Studies have found that risk-taking behavior decreases after diagnosis suggesting both individual offender and broader public health benefits (Wakeman & Rich, 2010).

The United Nations (UN) recommendations also encourage condom provision programs, making condoms available to both men and women free of charge and easily accessible without requiring a formal request. Historically, correctional rules and regulations have required abstinence leaving many inmates in a dangerous muddle of criminalized sexual expression, covert efforts at ineffective safe-sex practices, and a high risk of sexual disease contraction and transmission (Krienert, Walsh, & Lesch, 2014). Proponents believe programs allowing prisoners access to condoms and even sterile needles could greatly reduce transmission pathways by introducing barriers to the disease (Stover & Hariga, 2016).

The UN recommendation regarding treatment, care, and support states that anti-retroviral medications, as well as medical care and support, should be at least equivalent to what people living in the community receive. The UN also states that authorities must address concern for treatment protocol desistance by inmates upon release and appropriate links made between the returning inmates and community-based care and support services. In addition, the UN recommends that correctional facilities provide adequate health care to meet the medical needs of inmates, a concern proponents say many facilities throughout the United States are not addressing.

The incarcerated population is a marginalized population at significantly higher risk of contracting and transmitting HIV either prior to incarceration or after incarceration. Considering the disproportionate number of people with HIV coming through the criminal justice system, prisons and jails offer a unique opportunity for diagnosis, treatment, and prevention of HIV. In addition to recommendations for changes in policies and practices, many experts point to information and education as a primary pathway to prevention. By educating inmates on the perils of HIV, as well as dispelling myths and misinformation about transmission, safe-sex practices and appropriate precautions can be implemented. Additionally, addressing and improving on some of the external precursors to disease transmission such as drug abuse, mental illness, poverty, and homelessness will contribute to reductions in correctional facility HIV transmission. Lastly, reducing overcrowding and substandard living conditions in prisons and jails is another way to help control the spread of HIV. Reducing overcrowding would decrease the number of inmates in direct contact with one another and reduce strains on correctional staff responsible for providing supervision. Further, HIV diagnoses tend to be comorbid with HIV-infected inmates, with their weakened immune system, more vulnerable to other infections, diseases, and illnesses including sexually transmitted infections, hepatitis, and AIDS.

Timothy Worman, Jessie L. Krienert, and Jeffrey A. Walsh

See also: Consensual Sex between Inmates; Cost of Prisons; Health Promotion in Prison Settings; Treatment in Prisons

Further Reading

American Civil Liberties Union (ACLU). (2010). *Sentenced to stigma: Segregation of HIV-positive prisoners in Alabama and South Carolina.* New York: Human Rights Watch.

Centers for Disease Control and Prevention. (2015). *HIV among incarcerated populations.* Retrieved August 22, 2016, from http://www.cdc.gov/hiv/group/correctional.html

Krienert, J., Walsh, J., & Lesch, L. (2014). Alternative to abstinence: The practice of (un) safe sex in prison. *Criminal Justice Studies, 27*(4), 387–401.

Maruschak, L. M. (2012). HIV in prisons, 2001–2010. *AIDS, 20,* 25.

Stover, H., & Hariga, F. (2016). Prison-based needle and syringe program (PSNP)—Still highly controversial after all these years. *Drug: Education, Prevention & Policy, 23*(2), 103–112.

Sylla, M. (2008). HIV treatment in US jails and prisons. *San Francisco AIDS Foundation* [Online newsletter]. Retrieved from www.sfaf. org/beta/2008_win/jails _Prisons

Taxman, F. S., Perdoni, M. L., & Harrison, L. D. (2007). Drug treatment services for adult offenders: The state of the state. *Journal of Substance Abuse and Treatment, 32,* 239–254.

UNODC, UNDP, & UNAIDS. (2013). *Prevention, treatment and care in prisons and other closed settings: A comprehensive package of interventions.* Vienna: United Nations Office of Drugs and Crime.

Wakeman, S. E., & Rich, J. D. (2010). HIV treatment in US prisons. *HIV Therapy, 4*(4), 505–510.

Westergaard, R., Spaulding, A., & Flanigan, T. (2013). HIV among persons incarcerated in the USA: A review of evolving concepts in testing, treatment, and linkage to community care. *Current Opinion in Infectious Disease, 26*(1), 10–16.

Alcatraz

Alcatraz Island, or "the Isla de Alcatraces" (Spanish, island of the pelicans), was the site for Alcatraz Federal Prison, a maximum security prison that housed high-profile inmates from 1933 until its closure in 1963. Discovered by the Spanish, the island had little vegetation and was made up primarily of fine-grained sandstone. It was a forbidding place in the middle of San Francisco Bay. The nickname "The Rock" was a fitting description of the island.

In 1850, by presidential order, the island was set aside for possible use as a U.S. military reservation. It was put into use in the early 1850s when the U.S. army built the Citadel (a fortress) on top of the island. The purpose of the Citadel was to protect the bay during the time of the California gold rush. The island also was the site of the first operational lighthouse on the West Coast of the United States. The first prisoners, military prisoners, were housed at the Citadel in the late 1850s.

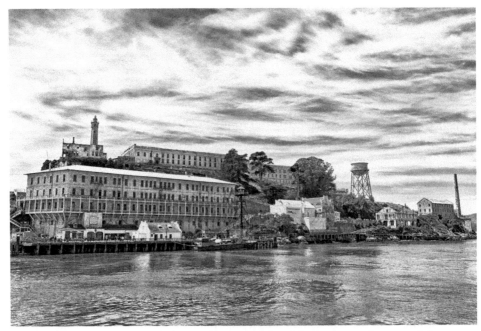

Before closing its doors in 1963, the Alcatraz Federal Prison housed some of the country's most dangerous and troublesome offenders. (Ian Whitmorth/Dreamstime.com)

There was virtually no need for the military presence to protect the San Francisco Bay, but Alcatraz did serve as a military prison until 1933 when it was transferred to the U.S. Department of Justice for use by the Federal Bureau of Prisons. In the United States, in the 1920s and 1930s, there had been an increase in high-publicity crime. The Prohibition period had led to increasing criminal activity as many were involved in bootlegging and operating illegal drinking establishments. Although Prohibition was ended, the gangs and mobsters who had gained money and power during Prohibition were now high-publicity criminals. Al Capone, Machine Gun Kelly, Bonnie and Clyde, and other criminals had caught the public's attention and were an embarrassment to law enforcement agencies. Prisons were crowded, escapes were common, and the federal government needed to show the public that they had a plan.

The Alcatraz prison would be a new type of prison designed to isolate high-profile inmates and problem inmates who could not be controlled in other institutions. Under the leadership of Sanford Bates, the head of the Federal Bureau of Prisons, Alcatraz would be used as a maximum security, minimum privilege institution to show the country that they were tough on crime. Inmates would only come to Alcatraz from other institutions. This prison would be the toughest one in existence in the United States and would be known for the ability to control the worst of the worst.

The military prison was renovated to meet the needs of a maximum security prison. Tool-proof steel was installed on the cell doors and to cover windows in the two cell blocks that would be used. Later, another cell block would be used for the isolation of problem inmates. Gun galleries were built and enclosed with steel bars. Metal detectors were installed in the administrative area, and new towers were equipped with high-intensity lights. There were a total of 348 cells, all single-man units.

The first warden selected to operate the new federal prison was James Johnston. Johnston had been warden of San Quentin and Folsom prisons and served as the warden of Alcatraz from 1934 to 1948. The most highly qualified correctional officers from the federal prison system were also brought to Alcatraz to staff the prison. Inmates who were housed at Alcatraz were controlled completely, and the very limited privileges available had to be earned. Each inmate was housed in a bare cell which measured $5' \times 9' \times 7'$. The cells were equipped with a steel bed with a mattress, two shelves, a foldout table and chair, a toilet, and a sink. Visitation had to be earned and was limited to one family member once a month. No original letters could be received (all were copied after being screened), and no newspapers, magazines, or radios were allowed. There were 13 mandatory head counts each day, 6 verification counts, and random counts as well. The inmates did have access to a library and were allowed to bathe and change clothes twice a week. An early rule also prohibited talking in the cell house, but that was changed in 1940, as it was found to be inhumane.

There were 14 escape attempts from Alcatraz during the time it was a federal prison. Thirty-six men attempted escape: 23 were caught, 6 were shot and killed, 2 drowned, and 5 were classified as missing and drowned. There is some speculation that the missing men could have successfully escaped to the mainland. Due to the strong currents and cold temperature in the San Francisco Bay, this is an unlikely possibility. One failed escape attempt became known as the "Battle of Alcatraz." In May 1946, six inmates attempted to escape from the cell house. Their attempt was not effective as the key they needed to exit the building was missing. The battle went on for three days and ended with the death of three inmates and two guards. Other hostages were also held and shot by the inmates in an effort to leave no witnesses.

As the prison was designed to hold the most dangerous and problematic inmates, there were many famous mobsters and extremely violent inmates housed in Alcatraz. Al Capone and Robert Stroud (the Birdman of Alcatraz) are probably the best known of the prison's famous residents. Al Capone had served time in other federal prisons and was used to being treated with respect and given special privileges. It was said that he had been allowed extensive visits from numerous family members and colleagues, and special meals. Capone would even make suggestions to other wardens regarding how the prisons should be run. When the notorious mobster arrived at Alcatraz, things were completely different.

In Alcatraz, Capone was treated the same as all the other inmates. He received no special privileges due to his infamy and had to work prison jobs as well. Capone actually did not cause any problems while in Alcatraz. Capone was diagnosed with syphilis and initially refused treatment. By the time he agreed to be treated for that ailment, he had suffered irreversible brain damage and was kept in the medical unit of the prison for the remainder of his sentence.

Robert Stroud had a long prison history and was known for violence. Stroud had originally been sentenced to prison for a murder he committed in Alaska. He was first housed at McNeil Island but was transferred to Leavenworth after assaulting an orderly. While at Leavenworth, Stroud attacked and killed an officer. He was sentenced to death, but due to his mother's lobbying and her appeals to Edith Wilson, wife of then-president Woodrow Wilson, Stroud's sentence was changed to life in isolation. While in Leavenworth, Stroud accumulated almost 300 birds and wrote two books on bird care. Stroud was transferred to Alcatraz in 1942 after already serving 33 years in prison. Contrary to popular opinion, he was not allowed birds while in Alcatraz.

In addition to the inmates and officers, more than 300 civilians also lived on the island. The population was composed of the families of the officers and included between 60 and 80 children who grew up there. Ferries traveled frequently to the mainland where the children attended school and then returned to the island. Former residents recall their experiences living on the island as peaceful and with a strong community. Happy memories are reported by those who lived in a unique island environment.

Although Alcatraz was an effective prison, it was extremely costly to operate. By the early 1960s the salt water was causing significant deterioration of the structures that needed expensive renovations. Public opinion had changed since the building of the prison, and there was a national campaign to emphasize rehabilitation of prisoners. In 1963, Attorney General Robert Kennedy announced the closing of Alcatraz Federal Prison. At this time, the prison is a very popular tourist attraction. People can roam the island and tour the cell blocks.

Paige Heather Gordier

See also: Attica; Leavenworth; Notorious or Infamous Inmates

Further Reading

Albright, J. (2008). *Last guard out.* Bloomington, IN: AuthorHouse.

Esslinger, M. (2012). *Alcatraz: A definitive history of the penitentiary.* San Francisco: Ocean View.

Fuller, J. (1982) *Alcatraz: Federal penitentiary, 1934–1963* (15th ed.). San Francisco: Asteron Production.

Hurley, D. J. (1989). *Alcatraz Island maximum security.* Petaluma, CA: Barlow.

Lageson, E. (2012). *Battle at Alcatraz: A desperate attempt.* Omaha, NE: Addicus Books.

Quillen, J. (2015). *Inside Alcatraz: My time on the Rock.* New York: Random House.

Ward, D. (2009). *Alcatraz: The gangster years.* Berkeley: University of California Press.

American Prison Designs

The architectural structure of American penitentiaries has always been aligned with an ideological view about correctional facilities. In America, during the Enlightenment in the 18th century, there was a European-influenced shift from the deontological retributive ideology toward a more utilitarian view in the purpose of prisons. This new perspective included the notion that incarceration can be used as a means of deterrence, incapacitation, and rehabilitation. The use of prisons was not solely viewed as a means of punishment but more so as a way to keep the general public safe. The birth of New York's Auburn Prison and the later development of Pennsylvania's Eastern State Penitentiary are exemplary of this shift, and their architectural designs correspond with the utilitarian motive. By no surprise, the radial layouts of these two prisons were influenced by a utilitarian European scholar named Jeremy Bentham and his panopticon prison design.

Bentham introduced the idea of the correctional institution as a source of power and control over the individual through his panopticon prison design. At the center of his proposed construction was a guard post that had a view of all inmate cells. In addition, the center post was constructed in a fashion where inmates are unaware of when someone is supervising them from this fixture. Bentham's omniscient post enabled the prison guard to supervise all without being seen. The design's purpose was to create a panoptic effect where inmates abide by the institutional rules in fear of being caught breaking them. Arguably, the panoptic design contains the ideological belief of that time, that humans are rational actors. Thus, through the manipulation of facility design, an inmate's behavior could be manipulated.

The layouts of prisons in the United States can be categorized by five main designs: (1) the telephone pole design, (2) the radial design, (3) the courtyard design, (4) the campus-style design, and (5) the high-rise design.

The first is the telephone pole design. This layout is composed of one major corridor that is used for inmate and staff movement throughout the facility. From this central corridor are pathways or wings that protrude parallel to one another and that extend from both sides of the singular corridor. These wings lead to cell blocks and other locations in the correctional facility. The blueprint resembles the manner in which a human's ribs (cell blocks and facility wings) protrude from the sternum (the main corridor).

The second layout is the radial design. In this facility cells are arranged in a linear manner, and all cell blocks and facility wings meet at a central point in the prison. The design resembles the shape of a star or a wheel. At the central point of the facility are controls that open and close the gates to every wing—permitting or denying the access of inmates and personnel to other areas of the facility.

Another layout utilized is the campus-style design, which consists of several independent correctional buildings that are enclosed in a secure perimeter. The standalone buildings are placed at a distance from one another and include various facilities such as housing units, medical services, and more.

The courtyard design encompasses a mixture of both the telephone and campus-style design. Buildings are placed in a manner in which they form a square or rectangular shape. Inmate sleeping quarters and other correctional facility amenities are located inside these structures. Located outside the facility buildings in the center of the square is a shared courtyard.

In the high-rise prison design the layout builds upward in a style resembling inner-city apartment buildings or skyscrapers. The multilayered facility utilizes the individual floors of a facility to separate offenders and dedicate specific landings for certain purposes such as vocational training or administrative offices.

Prison designs allow for the separation or the classification of specific groups of inmates. Separation of individuals are commonly done on the basis of age, gender, and offense. These classifications have observable impacts on the design of a correctional facility. The security levels in federal prisons can be identified by the construction of minimum, low, medium, high, and administrative facilities. For state-controlled prisons, the security levels vary in terms, but definitions follow a similar pattern of low to high level. The placement in one security level over another is based on administrative discretion, the capacity that a facility has, the type of offense convicted of, prior criminal convictions, gang affiliations, other individual level characteristics that may foster security risks, and facility level characteristics that can control those risks.

Federal minimum security facilities have limited or no fencing, lower number of staff per inmate, dormitory housing, and some work and programs for the inmates. Low security level facilities have an increase in staff-to-inmate ratio, doubled fenced perimeters, more work and programs for inmates, and dormitory-style housing. The medium security facility includes stronger enforced perimeters, such as electronic gates, cell-type housing, and an increase in work and treatment programs for inmates. High security level penitentiaries, sometimes referred to as maximum on the state level, are characterized by multiple- and single-cell housing, increased levels in staff-to-inmate ratio, further strengthened perimeters, and a high level of control over inmate movement. In some maximum security facilities, inmates are kept confined in their cells for 23 hours a day, limiting any time spent outside the cell. Administrative facilities are a mixture of institutions designed for different types of offenders, such as inmates with chronic medical issues. Included in administrative facilities are super maximum (supermax) prisons that are built for highly violent and escape-prone inmates.

The structure of the prison begins with the entrance. These facilities are usually encased in exterior barriers such as barbed fencing, natural barriers (e.g., water), or walls in order to maintain security. In addition, one may find correctional officer posts surrounding the perimeter and at various checkpoints throughout the facility. These checkpoints serve the function of identifying and searching all individuals seeking to enter a given facility. Once cleared, individuals may be directed to enter the prison through a sally port, which is a fortified entry. Individuals are likely to encounter more identification and search posts further along entering a prison.

The housing unit is a structure in the prison where the cell blocks and cells can be found. Housing units are strategically classified by offender risk level. This includes classification by inmates on mental health surveillance, inmates who are in protective custody units, inmates with proven histories of good behavior, or any other classification created. The cell block within a housing unit refers to a row of cells, and the cell refers to the sleeping quarters of an inmate. Moreover, the cell may be sealed off by a steel door and include a toilet and a sink inside. Sleeping quarters are found in three main forms: single cells, double cells (e.g., two-person rooms), and dormitories (e.g., multiple beds in an open room). For some facilities one may find a dayroom within the housing unit as well. The dayroom refers to a structure that allows inmates from that specific unit to congregate outside of their cells. The dayroom will include seats and may have a television present as well.

Another structure present in the prison is the control room, which allows officers to log information and monitor inmates from a separate room. This is usually located near the entrance of the housing unit with a physical view and electronic view (e.g., CCTV) of the cell blocks. In addition, the control room allows for not only the surveillance of offenders, but for the opening and closing of cells and the entrance to the housing unit.

There is one last structure used to house inmates: punitive segregation. In some prisons this is also known as the "shoe," "the box," "the bing," or solitary confinement. In these structures, individuals are housed separately with no interaction with other inmates, and depending on the security level, no face-to-face interaction with correctional officers. Inmates may be sent there for various reasons with the most common being violent behavior.

Visitation rooms are utilized in prisons as the location for inmates to meet and spend time with outside visitors. Visitors may include family, friends, lawyers, journalists, researchers, and other approved guests. The visitation room may be set up with seating in an open space that includes many inmates and their families, or it may take place in a private room. A private room may be necessary for inmates who may be restricted from any interaction with other inmates.

Other structures usually found in prisons include gymnasiums for recreational use, chapels for religious services, educational or vocational classrooms, libraries, laundry rooms, cafeterias, kitchens, and administrative offices.

Victor St. John

See also: Alcatraz; Angola; Attica; Custody Levels; Environmentally Friendly ("Green") Prisons; Florence ADX; Inmate Classification; Jails Compared to Prisons; Juvenile Detention Centers; Leavenworth; Maximum Security; Panopticon; Prisons, History of; San Quentin; Solitary Confinement; Visitation

Further Reading

Bentham, J. (1843). *The works of Jeremy Bentham, Vol. 4 (Panopticon, Constitution, Colonies, Codification).*

Bonta, J., & Motiuk, L. L. (1992). Inmate classification. *Journal of Criminal Justice, 20*(4), 343–353.

Emerson, C. S. (2002). *U.S. Patent No. 6,360,494.* Washington, DC: U.S. Patent and Trademark Office.

Fairweather, L., & McConville, S. (2000). *Prison architecture: Policy, design, and experience.* New York: Routledge.

Polson, S. R. (1990). *U.S. Patent No. 4,970,834.* Washington, DC: U.S. Patent and Trademark Office.

Angola

The term "Angola" is a nickname under which the Louisiana State Penitentiary is known because countless slaves in the United States of America came from Angola in Africa. Angola, also known as "The Farm," is the largest maximum security prison in the United States. Given that the prison is the only maximum security facility in Louisiana, it houses inmates convicted of the most serious and violent crimes. Hence, the majority of inmates in Angola have a life sentence, and the facility is also the location of the execution chamber for death row inmates. Although only the condemned men are housed in Angola, the prison carries out executions for both male and female inmates who have been sentenced to death. Due to the high number of aging inmates who will never be released, a hospice program was introduced in the prison in 1998. Two years after the launch of the program, Angola Hospice Chapel was established, which allowed for the inmates to have formal funerals on the prison grounds. In relation to general medical care, a medical center for various inpatient services is available; nonetheless, the inmates with serious medical issues or those who are in need of surgery must be transferred elsewhere. Apart from medical services, a variety of educational and rehabilitative programs are offered at Angola. For example, inmates may learn a trade such as eyeglass repair or participate in a prerelease exit program.

Angola is best known because of its presence in the media mainly due to its penal tourism activities and activism. Since 2001, Louisiana State Penitentiary hosts an Arts and Crafts Festival where inmates with a good record can present and sell the goods that they have created through obtaining craft materials sold by prison-approved vendors. The customers cannot pay the inmates directly, and only a few trustee inmates are allowed to participate in the event without being restricted by bars. Inmate bands also perform at the festival. The event happens during one weekend in spring and every Sunday in October each year. Another significant event takes place during the Arts and Crafts Festival, which is the Angola Prison Rodeo. This is one of the most controversial and famous prison events happening in the United States; however, its purpose is to serve as a positive influence on rehabilitation and reform of the inmates, as specified in the Angola Prison Rodeo Charter. Inmates who choose to participate in the rodeo are financially rewarded whenever they win. Using proper judges has professionalized the rodeo. Nevertheless, the rodeo has gained unwanted attention because participating inmates are not provided with any training; hence, the event is potentially dangerous to them. Additionally, some researchers argue that the rodeo is humiliating and reinforces the inmates' "outsider" status within American society. The prison rodeo has a longer history than the festival, as it was first held in 1965, but it was not open to the public until 1967. The capacity of the rodeo venue is 11,000 visitors, and each ticket costs $20 as of 2016. The proceeds from all of the above-mentioned events go toward the Inmate Welfare Fund, which is meant to cover activities that improve the prison conditions. Louisiana State Penitentiary also partakes in another penal tourism activity where, for $10, members of the public may choose to play golf in the penitentiary's Prison View Golf Course that overlooks parts of the facility. Nonetheless, guests must go through a background check before they are able to play. A museum of Louisiana's prisons within Angola was established in 1998. Admission to the museum is free, and the gift shop offers items such as clothing with the phrase "Angola—A Gated Community" printed on them.

A significant example of activism is inmates' editing and publishing *The Angolite*, which is a nationally recognized prison news magazine. The annual subscription cost is $20 for the public. The magazine used to be coedited by two of Angola's most notable inmates, Billy Wayne Sinclair and Wilbert Rideau, who were both initially sentenced to death. Sinclair coauthored a memoir, *A Life in the Balance: The Billy Wayne Sinclair Story, A Journey from Murder to Redemption Inside America's Worst Prison System*, with his wife in 2012, six years after his release. Rideau continued working in the media upon his release in 2005 and was presented with the George Polk Award in Journalism in 2011. A well-received documentary movie about the prison from 1998, *The Farm: Angola, USA,* was codirected by Rideau.

Angola has also been featured in the media because of Sister Helen Prejean, who wrote the book *Dead Man Walking: The Eyewitness Account of the Death Penalty That Sparked a National Debate,* which portrayed her spiritual advisory of two men on death row in Angola—Elmo Patrick Sonnier and Robert Lee Willie. Both of these inmates were electrocuted in Angola in the 1980s. The book was later made into a movie directed by Tim Robbins and starring Sean Penn and Susan Sarandon, who won an Oscar for her portrayal of Sister Helen Prejean. *Dead Man Walking* was adapted into an opera in 2000 and has recently been introduced as a possible literary curriculum for high school students to promote awareness of the death penalty. Sister Prejean is still involved with Angola and continues to provide spiritual services to death row inmates.

Tereza Trejbalova

See also: Death Row Inmates; Maximum Security; Prison Industries; Prison Museums

Further Reading

Churcher, K. M. A. (2011). Journalism behind bars: The Louisiana State Penitentiary's Angolite magazine. *Communications, Culture & Critique, 4*(4), 382–400.

Evans, C., Herzog, R., & Tillman, T. (2002). The Louisiana State Penitentiary: Angola prison hospice. *Journal of Palliative Medicine, 5*(4), 553–558.

Prejean, H. (1994). *Dead man walking: The eyewitness account of the death penalty that sparked a national debate.* New York: Random House.

Schrift, M. (2004). The Angola Prison Rodeo: Inmate cowboys and institutional tourism. *Ethnology, 43*(4), 331–344.

Schrift, M. (2006). Angola prison art: Captivity, creativity, and consumerism. *Journal of American Folklore, 119*(473), 257–274.

Antiterrorism and Effective Death Penalty Act of 1996

The Antiterrorism and Effective Death Penalty Act (AEDPA) of 1996 was introduced by the Senate majority leader at the time, Senator Bob Dole, in the aftermath of the 1993 World Trade Center bombing and the 1995 Oklahoma City federal building bombing. President Bill Clinton signed it into law on April 24, 1996. The purpose of the act, as stated in the bill summary, was to "deter terrorism, provide justice for victims, [and to] provide for an effective death penalty."

The act had many provisions to fulfill its stated purpose. Title I concerns habeas corpus reform. Title II concerns providing restitution or assistance to victims of terrorism, while Title III refers to the designation of foreign terrorist organizations and prohibitions on providing funding to them. Title IV discusses the removal or exclusion of alien terrorists and modifies asylum procedures.

Title V places restrictions on nuclear, biological, and chemical weapons, and Title VI implements the plastic explosives convention. Title VII made changes to criminal law involving terrorist or explosive offenses, which included increasing penalties and changes to criminal procedure. Title VII-A, Section 709 commissioned a study to determine the constitutionality of putting restrictions on bomb-making materials. Finally, Title VIII changed funding to and clarified jurisdiction of law enforcement related to terroristic threats.

IMPACT ON HABEAS CORPUS

The writ of habeas corpus translates from Latin to "that you have the body." It is a piece of legislation intended to prevent unlawful detention by providing a legal recourse in which the legality of detention can be determined in court. Habeas corpus was originally a piece of English common law, but it has been adopted by many constitutions around the world. The United States took it as part of the U.S. Constitution. In the modern day, it is used frequently in deportation proceedings to challenge the custody of individuals detained by the U.S. Immigration and Customs Enforcement.

AEDPA had a tremendous effect on habeas corpus in the U.S. justice system. The grounds on which a successful habeas corpus claim rests were narrowed considerably in a number of ways. First, it limits the power of federal judges to grant habeas corpus relief unless the decision made by the state court is proven to be contrary to existing federal law as established by the federal court. Second, it imposes time limits on habeas corpus proceedings in death penalty cases. Third, it takes away the U.S. Supreme Court's power to review a court of appeals denial of filing a federal habeas corpus petition.

CRITICISMS

There are two main criticisms of AEDPA. First, it severely limits the rights of a defendant to appeal a ruling. A defendant can only do so if the court ruled in contradiction to already established federal law. Second, it carries the potential to execute innocent people. Previous to its passage, a study was done by Columbia University which found that nearly 70 percent of capital cases in the decade prior had an error, and in 47 percent of cases, this error caused the case to be dismissed. Since the passage of AEDPA, the reversal rate in state level death penalty cases has dropped by 40 percent, but this is not due to the courts doing a better job, but rather to the defendants not being able to appeal the ruling due to AEDPA.

Although the intent of AEDPA was to deter terrorism, the actual effect it had was to prevent appeal in death penalty cases, which might allow the execution of innocent people.

Vrishali Kanvinde

See also: Habeas Corpus Writs

Further Reading

Antiterrorism and Effective Death Penalty Act of 1996. U.S. Government Publishing Office. Retrieved from www.gpo.gov/fdsys/pkg/PLAW-104publ132/html/PLAW -104publ132.htm

Caplan, L. (2015, June 21). The destruction of defendants' rights. *The New Yorker.* Retrieved June 19, 2017, from www.newyorker.com/news/news-desk/the-destruction-of-de fendants-rights

The Constitution of the United States: A transcription. National Archives and Records Administration. Retrieved from www.archives.gov/founding-docs/constitution-transcript

Legal Information Institute, Cornell University. (2009, September 30). Retrieved from www.law.cornell.edu/wex/antiterrorism_and_effective_death_penalty_act_of_1996_aedpa

Arts Programs

Prison arts programs include both individual participation and peer-organized arts experiences. The art forms represented in these programs include music, dance, visual arts, theater, and creative writing. Empirical evaluations of these programs suggest that they may be effective in a number of ways: (1) they help inmates develop prosocial skills and cope with their institutionalization, (2) provide them with a healthy outlet for physical and mental aggression, and (3) simultaneously offer a cost-effective alternative to traditional prison life.

Adult male inmates from a minimum security state prison in the midwestern United States who participated in a prison choir perceived improvement in their interpersonal skills, a short-term reduction in stress, and a sense of accomplishment. Additionally, participation in these programs provides an incentive for model behavior, so prisons become safer as racial tensions and disciplinary infractions decrease. Additionally, advocates of prison-based arts programs assert that they are proven to have long-term rehabilitative potential because, when afforded the opportunity to express themselves and direct their energies in a positive way, inmates are able to develop the communication, collaboration, and conflict resolution skills needed for postrelease success.

The earliest recorded prison arts programs were developed and organized by inmates themselves. During his incarceration in the Ohio Federal Penitentiary from 1898 to 1901, William Sydney Porter, also known as O. Henry, began a Sunday recluse club that was essentially a forum for a group of male inmates to share creative writing and stories. In prison farms such as Parchment in Mississippi and Angola in Louisiana, prisoners used songs to make work pass by more tolerably and, eventually, music became an intrinsic part of the prison culture. A community arts movement began sweeping through the country at the turn of the 20th century with the introduction of settlement houses, which provided inspiration for youth offender education and cultural development. The 1950s and 1960s saw the proliferation of both community- and institution-based programs as the rehabilitation of inmates became a priority. Although rehabilitation was primarily attempted through the use of religious activities, vocational or academic educational programs, library services, recreation, and social education, some prisons began experimenting with the use of programs that emphasized the arts.

One key indicator of the success of prison arts programs is diminished recidivism. A study conducted by the California Department of Corrections found that, after two years on parole, inmates who had participated in prison-based arts programs had lower recidivism rates than nonparticipants. Likewise, inmates at the Queens House of Detention in New York who participated in a drama and theater program enjoyed similar success.

A further measure of the value of a prison arts program is its cost effectiveness. A study from Arizona State University reported savings for the New Mexico Corrections Department of up to $40,000 in costs per semester due to the Prison English Program. California's Arts-in-Corrections (AIC) program saw such a significant decrease in disciplinary actions that administration time spent on managing disciplinary infractions dropped by 4,553 hours, translating into a cost savings of over $75,000. This was in addition to more than $225,000 in measurable social benefits to the California Department of Corrections, which included over $105,000 in taxpayer benefits and more than $123,000 in individual benefits.

Funding for prison-based arts programs is scarce and often short-lived. The Federal Bureau of Prisons published a summary in May 2015 of national programs in federal prisons, and none focus predominantly on art. At the state level, the AIC is an example of a program that was cut due to budgetary constraints and recently reintroduced. Occasionally, programs are kept alive by donations of time and money.

Leanne Havis

See also: Evidence-Based Practice in Corrections; Recidivism

Further Reading
Arizona State University College of Liberal Arts & Sciences. (2013). Calculating impact: Doing the numbers. *Prison English News, 1*(1), 2.
Brewster, L. (2010). The California Arts-in-Corrections music programme: A qualitative study. *International Journal of Community Music, 3*(1), 33–46.
Cleveland, W. (1992). Geese theater: America's national prison theater company. In W. Cleveland (Ed.), *Art in other places: Artists at work in America's community and social institutions* (pp. 51–73). Westport, CT: Praeger.
Cohen, M. L. (2007). Explorations of inmate and volunteer choral experiences among a prison-based choir. *Australian Journal of Music Education, 1,* 61–72.
Gardner, A., Hager, L. L., & Hillman, G. (2014). *Prison Arts Resource Project: An annotated bibliography.* Washington, DC: National Endowment for the Arts.
Melnick, M. (1984). Skills through drama: The use of professional techniques in the treatment and education of prison and ex-offender populations. *Journal of Group Psychotherapy, Psychodrama and Sociometry, 37,* 104–117.

Attica

Attica Prison is a maximum security/supermax facility that opened in 1931. It is currently operated by the state of New York and has a capacity of 2,253 inmates. The prison is based on the Auburn style of prison with immense walls, highly visible guard towers, and stacked tiers of cells. The cells were built to house one or two men.

Attica is most well known for the riot that occurred in 1971. This prison and the riot have been regarded as a symbol of change as the events that occurred there helped move the country toward a dedicated effort of prison reform.

Prior to the riot, the conditions in the prison were very poor, and tensions were high. The prison was built to house 1,200 inmates and in 1971 had 2,225 inmates. Due to the severe level of overcrowding, there was reduced living space for the residents. Access to programs and recreation was limited, and many inmates were idle and restless. Additionally, inmate classification was not being properly done, as there were so many men coming into the prison and little room to put them in the proper security levels within the prison. Many inmates were young, prone to violence, and housed throughout the prison due to improper classification. There were a number of security threat groups active in Attica including the Black Muslims, the Puerto Rican Young Lords, and the Black Panthers.

Prior to the Attica riot, racial tensions were also high between officers and inmates. The inmates were predominantly Puerto Rican and black. Of the 397 officers employed in 1971, one was Puerto Rican, and the rest were white. The inmates were becoming more politically aware due to the civil rights movement and became a united group seeking social justice and improved conditions. The solidarity of the inmates frightened the prison officials.

Earlier in the summer of 1971, there were several peaceful protests, and also a work strike, at the prison. These protests brought attention to the poor conditions in the prison and allowed the inmates to express their frustrations to the administration. Unfortunately, the inmates felt that their complaints were not being addressed, and rumors of a riot began to emerge. The prison administration did not take the rumors seriously.

The riot took place on September 8, 1971. A fight between two inmates occurred the night before. The officers were able to break up the fight without incident and waited until that evening to remove the two inmates from their cells. The other inmates were loud and protested this action. In the morning, the protest continued at breakfast, and the riot began in the dining hall. The inmates quickly took control of the four main cell blocks and took 40 officers hostage. The officers were beaten, and one later died of his wounds. The officers had not been trained to respond to this type of inmate behavior, and there was no plan in place for them to follow.

At the time of the riot, Russell G. Oswald was the new commissioner of the Department of Correctional Services. He had met with the inmates earlier in the year but had to leave that meeting early due to a personal emergency. When he returned to

The prison riot at the Attica Correctional Facility in 1971 involved complex negotiations between inmate leaders and correctional administrators. Ultimately, law enforcement officials would reclaim the prison through excessive force and violence. (Bettmann/Getty Images)

the prison, he found that the inmates had formed a committee, and even though negotiating with inmates was against prison policy, Oswald decided to carry on the talks. The inmates were not well organized, and their demands ranged from those focused on the conditions in the prison to the extreme demands of amnesty for the inmates involved in the riot who also wanted transportation to other countries. Outside observers were invited to view the negotiations, and reporters, lawyers, and politicians became involved. Governor Nelson Rockefeller was also asked by the inmates to come and meet with them, but he refused.

Commissioner Oswald met with the inmate team and was able to agree to most of the inmates' demands regarding improved prison conditions. He was not able to discuss amnesty as an officer had been killed by the inmates. Oswald's response to the inmates was perceived as insincere. He emphasized that amnesty was non-negotiable and that the riot had to be ended immediately. These decisions made the inmates question his sincerity and caused increased tension among the participants.

On September 13, 1971, four days after the riot began, the governor ordered that the prison be retaken. A poorly planned attack was launched by the state police and correctional officers. All were heavily armed, and there was no apparent concern for the safety of the hostages. In a nine-minute time span, the officers retook the prison. Ten hostages and 29 inmates were killed; three hostages and 85 inmates were injured. Including three inmates killed early in the riot by other inmates, the total number of deaths from the riot was 43. This was the largest number of people killed in any prison riot in U.S. history.

Following the riot, allegedly, the officers brutally beat the inmates, tortured them, and used unlimited force to reestablish their control. Injured inmates were left in the yard for long periods of time prior to being treated. Inmates were kicked, stepped on, and further beaten while lying injured. Others were forced to "run the gauntlet" between rows of officers who continued to beat the inmates inside the prison.

Initially, reporters were not allowed in the prison following the riot. Information was withheld, and the officials blamed the deaths of the hostages on the inmates. Investigations later showed that state officials actively covered up evidence, and the information reported to the press had effectively turned the public against the inmates. The public eventually discovered the truth about what happened during the riot and demanded improvements be made to prison conditions across the nation.

The state of New York was sued by the inmates who survived the riot and the families of those who died. In August 2000, the state agreed to pay more than 500 inmates and relatives a sum of $12 million for the abuse the inmates suffered during and following the riot. Attica is still in operation today, and many people still believe that the conditions in that facility have not improved. In September 2016, the 45th anniversary of the riot was recognized throughout the country with peaceful protests in a number of prisons.

Paige Heather Gordier

See also: Alcatraz; Leavenworth; Prison Reform, Intended and Unintended Consequences of; Riots; Violence in Prison

Further Reading

New York Special Commission on Attica. (1972). *Attica*. New York: Praeger.

New York Times (1992, February 5). Unanswered questions in Attica case: High level accountability, B5:1.

Oppenheimer, M. (2016). *Attica, Attica: The story of the legendary prison uprising*. New York: Pantheon Books.

Thompson, H. (2016). *Blood in the water: The Attica prison uprising of 1971 and its legacy*. New York: Knopf Doubleday.

Auburn System of Penology

The Auburn system, which opened with the creation of Auburn Penitentiary in New York in 1819, was quickly adopted as the ideal model for future prisons. The system combined labor with incarceration to form a silent yet productive version of punishment. The Auburn system emphasized isolation, obedience, and labor. Correctional facilities used silence to maintain compliance, coupled with a forced inmate labor system meant to aid in rehabilitation through hard work. Dignitaries from around the world came to see this new, innovative approach to penal care, and, in fact, tourists also viewed prisoners by paying an admission fee to watch inmates working in the factory.

Often referred to as the congregate system, Auburn enacted the philosophy that offenders should work in silence as penance for their crimes (Gill, 1962). In order for reform to be successful, correctional philosophers believed that breaking the spirit of the criminal was necessary. Strict routines involving work, silence, and obedience were implemented to reform offenders into productive societal members. During the day, inmates were required to work in the institution's factories, and although they shared meals with other inmates, workers ate back-to-back and silence was enforced at all times. At night, prisoners returned to small, isolated cells where they were encouraged to read the Bible and pray. Not only were prisoners isolated from each other, but they were also isolated from the outside world. No written or verbal communication with families was allowed. A regimen of hard work and religious instruction were considered humane penal advancements used in an attempt to restore inmates to the role of productive citizen.

Auburn Prison had many innovations that set it apart from its rival, the Pennsylvania system. The use of prison labor was an attractive and lucrative design for future prisons. In early years, inmate labor produced a financial profit through contracts within the community. Auburn and subsequent prisons using this model were designed as industry facilities with a factory for material output. This was the defining feature of the Auburn system. The state contracted with private manufacturers to provide the materials necessary for the inmate laborers. Products produced during this time included furniture, clothing, footwear, carpets, and even weapons. The use of prison labor attributed to the Auburn system's economic success, which offset the cost of housing inmates and led to widespread replication.

The physical design of the prison was innovative as well. As inmates were only to remain in their cells to sleep, the cells were very small, roughly three and a half feet wide by seven feet long, and designed for a single inmate. The system utilized two back-to-back rows of cells that were five tiers high. This cost less to build and maintain than other fortress-style systems and increased the capacity of inmates that could be housed within the prison (Morris & Rothman, 1995). Although cells were only meant for sleep, no work was allowed on Sunday, leaving inmates to experience lengthy periods of complete isolation in very small cells.

Mental health issues were rampant within the institution. In 1857 an asylum, the Lunatic Asylum for Insane Convicts, was built on grounds to care for the mentally ill. Women were also incarcerated in Auburn. In the beginning, they were housed together in a dark attic space, receiving food and supplies once a day. After a series of events, including inmate pregnancy, Auburn became the first prison in the nation to hire a female matron. Later, following the closure of the asylum in 1892, a women's wing was built (McHugh, 2010).

Discipline in the Auburn Prison was punitive and harsh. Inmates were forced to follow strict regimentation. The prison was designed using a quasi-military model, and inmates were given only the most basic of necessities. Silence was strictly enforced, with guards holding the responsibility for punishing a prisoner who broke the silence. Keepers were vigilant in detecting whispers, and punishment was swift and painful. Inmates were commonly flogged for communicating (Morris & Rothman, 1995).

The Auburn system was one of the first prison systems to require inmates to wear uniforms, the now iconic black-and-white stripes. Another defining feature of the prison was the use of the lockstep. The lockstep required prisoners to be chained together when moving about the institution. They shuffled in a single file line, feet not leaving the ground, and faces turned in unison in a single direction. This was used to ensure that no communication occurred during prison movement. Inmates developed complex nonverbal communication techniques including song, whistles, tapping, and rudimentary sign language. Keepers watched for any form of communication and swiftly punished verbal and nonverbal violators. In 1890, Auburn experienced another first—the use of the electric chair as a new form of execution.

The Auburn system became widely adopted by the other states. Many adopted the administrative pattern and architectural design for their own prisons (Barnes, 1921). The use of prison labor to offset the cost of housing inmates made this system appealing to other states. The design of the prison was also cost efficient, making it easier for states to fund. This design of prison became one of historical significance, replicated around the world.

Many prisons today still hold remnants of the Auburn system (Gill, 1962). Eventually, the prison system of labor, silence, and obedience ceased to exist. Flogging was outlawed in 1847, and by the early 1900s, the contract labor system, the striped uniforms, and the lockstep were removed from use (McHugh, 2010). Overcrowding plagued the institution, making enforcing silence and solitary cells nearly impossible.

Genoa V. Cole, Jessie L. Krienert, and Jeffrey A. Walsh

See also: Pennsylvania System of Penology; Prisons, History of

Further Reading

Barnes, H. E. (1921). The historical origin of the prison system in America. *Journal of the American Institute of Criminal Law and Criminology, 12*(1), 35–60.

Gill, H. B. (1962). Correctional philosophy and architecture. *The Journal of Criminal Law, Criminology, and Police Science, 53*(3), 312–322.

McHugh, E. (2010). *Auburn Correctional Facility.* New York: Arcadia.

Morris, N., & Rothman, D. J. (Eds.). (1995). *The Oxford history of the prison: The practice of punishment in Western society.* New York: Oxford University Press.

Australia, Prisons in

Australia's criminal justice system has established both private and government-owned prisons. The prisons are governed by the laws of the territories where they have been placed. The Department of Corrections of various states operates the public prisons. Private corporations manage the private prisons (Australian correctional agencies and facilities, 2013).

The first private prison was operated by the Correctional Corporation of Australia, an international venture of Corrections Corporation of America. In 1990 the Queensland facility began operations, which has led to other states doing the same. Privatization of prisons is being expanded by for-profit corporations. In 2011, there were 5,520 prisoners being held privately representing 19 percent of Australia's 28,711 total prisoners. It was an increase of 95 percent compared to 1998 (Australian Bureau of Statistics, 2015; Australian correctional agencies and facilities, 2013; Prison—Australia/World Prison Brief, 2014).

The private Australian prisons are Fulham Correctional Centre (Melbourne, Victoria), Mount Gambier Prison (Mount Gambier, South Australia), Port Phillip Correctional Centre (Trucanina, Victoria), Arthur Gorrie Correctional Centre (Wacol, Queensland), Parklea Correctional Centre (Parklea, New South Wales), Junee Correctional Centre (Junee, New South Wales), and Acacia Prison (Wooroloo, Western Australia) (Australian Institute of Criminology, 2013).

Australia is using the Papua New Guinea's Nauru and Manus islands to process immigration applications of refugees and asylum seekers. The applicants are housed on those islands in detention centers that are like prisons, heavily guarded. These detention centers are part of Australia criminal justice system and are being outsourced by the Department of Immigration and Border Protection. They are owned privately by Broadspectrum, formerly Transfield Services Ltd. It takes a long time, sometimes years for the immigration applications to be processed. These detainees are kept in these prisons and are not sent back to their country of origin. Not everyone is admitted into Australia under their immigration laws (Australian correctional agencies and facilities, 2013; Manus Island takes Australia to the edge of outsourcing, 2014).

Prisoners' lives are heavily structured in an effort to rehabilitate them. Prisoners are encouraged to work or learn. Work may be in metal or wood shops, in kitchens, in landscaping, and in cleaning. Clerical positions in the administration or library and wherever else required can also be filled by prisoners. Work or study or both is mandatory. There are libraries with books and computers. However,

Internet is not allowed. Some low security prisoners are allowed to work in the community doing cleaning, landscaping, building picnic tables, or other community-building projects. A sentence management team designates what each prisoner does. Technical instructors escort prisoners to their places of activity (A day in the life of an Australian residential inmate, 2004).

Food is served three times daily for breakfast, lunch, and dinner in an effort to provide nutrition to prisoners. Each territory has its own system of managing the kitchen. In most prisons the inmates work in the kitchen under the direction of chefs. They grow vegetables and grains used in the prison. Meals consist of bread, multigrain cereals, meats, salads, and fruits. They are allowed milk and juice per day. Twice a week hot lunch such as meat pies and stews are allowed. Dinner is based on a weekly menu based on dietary recommendations (A day in the life of an Australian residential inmate, 2004).

In most prisons, a prisoner's day begins with a wake-up call at 6:30 in the morning, and by 7:30 they are expected to have cleaned their rooms, showered, and breakfasted. They must present themselves for muster in front of their cells, when they are head counted, and then escorted for work or education. About 95 percent of prisoners work full-time. However, some work part-time and join classes that could be work related or hobby classes. New prisoners must complete work applications and until approved for some work are allowed to clean or wash the premises. In the afternoon, around 12:15 and again at 4:45 p.m., inmates are head counted. At 5 p.m. is dinner time after which the prisoners can stay in the compound within boundaries. They can use the phone to call people who have been preapproved from the list of people provided by the prisoner. At most prisons, after 6:30 p.m. is lockdown time after which a prisoner cannot leave his cell. Inmates are free to play games, watch TV, or write letters after that. Every 2 hours guards make a round to check that all prisoners are within the unit (A day in the life of an Australian residential inmate, 2004).

Prisoners go through three processes when they go to jail, namely admission, induction, and classification. When prisoners are admitted into jail, their clothing is removed for a search. They are allowed to shower and wear prison clothes. Their personal items including watches and jewelry except plain wedding bands are taken away. They receive a medical examination, are photographed, are interviewed by a counselor, and are given an identity card and allocated a cell. All their personal details are recorded. During induction, prisoners are explained the rules and regulations and what they are expected to do in jail. For classification purposes, which takes three weeks, prisoners are assessed for their health, employment, education, training, or any interventional need. Once classification is complete, a different cell, suited to the needs of the prisoner, is allotted (A day in the life of an Australian residential inmate, 2004).

Different prisons have different types of cells. Usually a cell has a bed, cubby holes for storage of clothes, a desk, and a swivel for television that an inmate can purchase from the jail. Six inmate cells form a unit. Each unit has three showers and three toilets, a washer and a dryer, a fridge, a microwave, a toaster, and a storage place for plastic plates, bowls, and eating utensils. Each cell has a 21-inch television set and two steel benches to sit. Space is provided to store games and newspapers. Four units make a block, and three blocks form a cluster. Each cluster has its own office and guards. The entire compound could be made of three or more clusters. The compound is covered by video cameras (A day in the life of an Australian residential inmate, 2004).

The prisoners have basic rights. They are entitled to a lawyer from legal aid if they cannot afford to hire one. They can complain about any discrimination by the prison authority and can sue for damages. The prisoners can expect to get medical assistance when requested. They may request treatment from private doctors if they are able to pay. Voting in federal elections is allowed if the prisoner's sentence is for less than three years. Transfer to other jails is allowed provided there is no history of bad behavior and the victim is not distressed by it. Transfer may be requested to be near families, for health care, or for safety (Standards for health services in Australian prisoners, 2011).

The prisoners are not allowed to keep mobile phones. They can make calls but usually cannot receive them. If they anticipate an emergency at home, they may request that they be allowed to receive calls. They can receive and write unlimited letters. Some letters that are privileged can be read by the prison staff. The prisoners are allowed to have visitors once a week (A day in the life of an Australian residential inmate, 2004; Woodward, 2003).

Prisoners are allowed to keep money in their prison trust account from which they can transfer money toward making phone calls as they are not free. They can buy food from the cafeteria from that money or buy games, clothes, necessary items, and TV. They have no access to anything intoxicating or dangerous such as articles that can be used as weapons (A day in the life of an Australian residential inmate, 2004).

The prisoners such as those convicted for rapes, armed robbery, or murders in need of maximum security are housed in Goulburn Supermax in New South Wales (Phelps, 2015). Prisoners there are X-rayed for security checks regularly, and they are transferred to a different cell every two weeks for security reasons. Even visitors are required to go through tough security checks prior to being admitted. There are security checks 24 hours every day. Not all prisoners are allowed to work there. They are housed in cold cells with just a bunk bed, shelves, toilet, and a sink (Phelps, 2016).

Australian prisons have been criticized for having disproportionately high numbers of Aboriginals and Torres Strait Islanders in the prisons. These natives are reported to be repeatedly incarcerated for incredibly trivial offences. There is overcrowding in the prisons with inadequate medical and mental health services. The Department of Correction's state prisons are therefore endeavoring to provide rehabilitative services conducive to the native people. They are hiring some staff from the native population. Private companies who run the prisons are more focused on their profit than the rehabilitation and reform of prisoners, which should be the proper goal (Baidawi et al., 2011; Weatherburn, 2014).

Rupendra Simlot and Alka Simlot

See also: Health Care in Prison Populations; Prison Populations, Trends in; Privatization; Treatment in Prisons

Further Reading

Australian Bureau of Statistics. (2015). *Prisoners in Australia.* Retrieved from http://www.abs.gov.au/ausstats/abs@.nsf/Lookup/by%20Subject/4517.0~2015~Main%20Features~Aboriginal%20and%20Torres%20Strait%20Islander%20prisoner%20characteristics~7

Australian correctional agencies and facilities. (2013). Canberra, Australia: Australian Institute of Criminology.

Baidawi, S., Turner, S., Trotter, C., Browning Collier, C., O'Connor, D., & Sheehan, R. (2011, August). Older prisoners: A challenge for Australian corrections. *Trends and Issues in Crime and Criminal Justice.* Canberra, Australia: Australian Institute of Criminology.

A day in the life of an Australian residential inmate. (2004). Retrieved from www.prisontalk.com/forums/archive/index.php/t-4913.html

Manus Island takes Australia to the edge of outsourcing. (2014, March 5). Retrieved from https://theconversation.com/manus-island-takes-australia-to-the-edge-of-outsourcing-23647

Phelps, J. (2015). *Australia's most murderous prison, behind the walls of Goulburn Jail.* North Sydney, NSW: Random House Australia.

Phelps, J. (2016). *Australia's hardest prison, inside the walls of Long Bay Jail.* North Sydney, NSW: Random House Australia.

Prison—Australia/World Prison Brief. (2014). Institute of Criminal Policy Research, Birkbeck, University of London, London, U.K.

Standards for health services in Australian prisoners. (2011). The Royal Australian College of General Practitioners, North Sydney, NSW, Australia.

Weatherburn, D. (2014). *Arresting incarceration: Pathways out of indigenous imprisonment.* Canberra, Australia: Aboriginal Studies Press.

Woodward, R. (2003). *Families of prisoners: Literature review on issues and difficulties.* Australian Government Department of Family and Community Services.

B

Baltimore City Detention Center

In July 2015, Maryland governor Larry Hogan ordered the immediate closing of the Baltimore City Detention Center (BCDC). The state's oldest correctional institution, BCDC was widely considered to be dangerous and unsafe for the inmates and the staff that operated the facility. The decision to close the facility came on the heels of a scandal that exposed complete chaos and anarchy inside the walls of the facility. The scandal implicated corrections staff in a prison gang enterprise operated by the Black Guerilla Family (BGF) prison gang. Corrupt correctional officers allowed BGF members to virtually seize control of the facility.

The Baltimore City Jail predates the Civil War (1861–1865) and was first opened in 1859. At the time of its construction, the gothic-style building was deemed an architectural marvel. However, the design of the facility, which predated modern design standards for penal facilities, made its blind corners, dark corridors, and other hazardous conditions extremely dangerous.

By 1885, fewer than 30 years after the facility was constructed, there were complaints regarding lack of reasonable accommodation and concerns regarding the safety of the inmates and staff. In 1938, there was a significant push for the facility to be closed down due to reports of poor sanitation and corruption. C. Delano Ames, president of the city's Criminal Justice Commission, called the facility a disgrace to the city of Baltimore. Plans to renovate the facility were considered a waste of taxpayer money. As such, the facility remained open and continued to operate under negligent conditions.

In 1940, as a result of the negative publicity surrounding the facility, a grand jury subcommittee voted for a new facility to be constructed. Despite this recommendation, members of the grand jury were not optimistic that the city would move forward with their recommendation. However, in 1952, a plan was voted on to construct a new $6 million jail near City Hospital in East Baltimore (what is now John Hopkins Bayview Medical Center). The plan to construct a new facility was ultimately voted down. Residents in the city's east side protested the construction of a new jail in fear that the community would become a loitering ground for inmates.

Instead of building a new jail, the city voted to renovate the facility. The renovation plans called for improvements to the interior and exterior of the building. The three-stage renovation included a gym and office spaces. The newly renovated facility, completed in 1967, housed 1,500 men and included new space for 200 female inmates.

In 1972, five years after the renovations were completed, the Federal Bureau of Prisons conducted a review of the facility due to numerous incidents citing

The Baltimore City Detention Center, where correctional officers colluded with inmates and committed crimes such as racketeering, conspiracy, money laundering, and the distribution of illicit substances. Some of the female officers also engaged in sexual relationships with inmate gang members. (Library of Congress)

corruption and inmate safety. The review concluded that correctional officers were poorly trained, security measures were poor and inadequate, and the programs offered to inmates were substandard. As a result, in 1991, the state of Maryland assumed control of the Baltimore City Jail and renamed it the Baltimore City Detention Center.

The facility, unfortunately, did not fare any better under state control. In 2002, the U.S. Department of Justice (DOJ) stepped in and found that the conditions inside the facility violated the constitutional rights of the inmates. Several inmate deaths were attributed to the conditions at the facility. The DOJ concluded that officials in the facility failed to provide adequate medical services for chronic health problems.

SCANDAL

In 2013, the BCDC became the center of national headlines after a federal grand jury indicted 44 people, including 13 female corrections officers, on charges of racketeering and drug violations. At the center of the indictment was Tavon White, top lieutenant for the Black Guerilla Family prison gang. White, also known as "Bulldog," assumed leadership of the Black Guerilla Family prison gang in 2009 shortly after he was incarcerated on an attempted murder charge. In a conversation captured on a Federal Bureau of Investigation (FBI) wiretap, White was overheard claiming that he had complete control of the inmates and correctional officers in the BCDC. During the taped conversation, White exclaimed, "I got elevated to the seat where as though nobody in the jail could outrank me . . . Like, I am the law . . . So if I told any fucking body they had to do this, hit a police, do this, kill a motherfucker, anything, it got to be done. Period" (Toobin, 2014).

The BGF, which has roots in California, has seen a tremendous rise in Baltimore. It is currently the largest prison gang in the state. Over one-third, more than 3,000 identified gang members, are affiliated with the BGF. The gang is known for being extremely violent. Inmates who refused to comply with BGF demands are brutally attacked and beaten.

White along with other BGF members, manipulated correctional officers who helped them to grow a profitable prison enterprise by smuggling in drugs, cell phones, and other contraband into the facility. According to court documents, corrections officers agreed to turn a blind eye to BGF activities in exchange for them maintaining order in the facility. In a recorded conversation, White claimed that he made more than $15,000 in one month selling drugs and other contraband in the jail. The BGF developed an elaborate payment system utilizing Green Dot Money Pak. Cards belonging to BGF members were used to exchange money inside and outside of the facility. Customers (inmates) were required to text payments to the Green Dot cards using 14-digit account numbers.

A key factor in White's control of BCDC was his relationship with female correctional officers. White was very adept at preying on women who he deemed to be weak and vulnerable. Court documents detailed how BGF recruits were taught to prey on specific correctional officers. These officers were described as having low self-esteem, insecurities, and certain physical attributes. The BGF members would befriend these officers with compliments and gifts and then manipulate them into smuggling contraband and serving as informants. In addition to smuggling contraband and having sex with BGF members, female correctional officers also served as lookouts. They would warn BGF inmates about upcoming law enforcement operations. For instance, they would notify BGF members about upcoming canine scans and cell searches.

Investigations also revealed that BGF members had engaged in sexual activity with multiple female correctional officers. More specifically, White fathered five children with four different women. Two of the women had White's name tattooed on their bodies.

White was also able to exert control and influence over these female correctional officers by purchasing expensive gifts for them. Court records revealed that he also helped to pay their rent. White also used the proceeds from his illegal sale of contraband to purchase luxury vehicles for them.

On February 9, 2015, White pleaded guilty to federal racketeering conspiracy charges. He was sentenced to 12 years in prison for his role in the operation. In addition to the federal charges, White pleaded guilty to a state charge for attempted murder. White became a key witness for prosecutors during trial. In exchange for a reduced sentence, he testified against numerous correctional officers and jail staff who helped him run his operation in the prison. White's testimony helped prosecutors to secure numerous convictions.

CURRENT STATUS

The Baltimore City Detention Center officially closed on August 26, 2015. Governor Larry Hogan ordered that all 1,100-plus inmates in the facility be transported to other local facilities. All detainees would remain local and in proximity to the courthouse. The 700-plus employees impacted by the closing of the facility were transferred to other institutions across the state.

Recent declines in the city's jail population make it feasible to house inmates in other existing facilities. The closing of the facility will save approximately

$10–$15 million dollars annually. According to Governor Hogan, "The final closure of this detention center removes a stain on the reputation of our state and Maryland's correctional system. For years, corruption, criminal activity has plagued this facility, but that ends today" (Broadwater, 2015).

Kevin D. Stewart

See also: Economics of Crossing Over, The; Inappropriate Correctional Employee–Inmate Relationships; Prison Gangs

Further Reading

Beck, A., Rantala, R., & Rexroat, J. (2014). *Sexual victimization reported by adult correctional authorities, 2009–11* (NCJ 243904). Washington, DC: U.S. Department of Justice.

Blackburn, A., Fowler, S., Mullings, J., & Marquart, J. (2011). When boundaries are broken: Inmate perceptions of correctional staff boundary violations. *Deviant Behavior, 32,* 351–378.

Broadwater, L. (2015). Hogan administration moves last detainees out of closed Baltimore jail. *The Baltimore Sun.* Retrieved from http://www.baltimoresun.com/news/mary land/baltimore-city/bs-md-ci-bcdc-20150825-story.html

Cheeseman Dial, K., & Worley, R. (2008). Crossing the line: A quantitative analysis of inmate boundary violators in a southern prison system. *American Journal of Criminal Justice, 33,* 69–84.

Fenton, J. (2016, March 9). Tavon White, center of Baltimore jail corruption scandal, returns as murder trail witness. *The Baltimore Sun.* Retrieved from http://www.baltimoresun .com

Jones, S. (2015). Recommendations for correctional leaders to reduce boundary violations: Female correctional employees and male inmates. *Women & Criminal Justice, 25,* 360–378.

Marquart, J., Barnhill, M., & Balshaw-Biddle, K. (2001). Fatal attraction: An analysis of employee boundary violations in a southern prison system, 1995–1998. *Justice Quarterly, 18,* 877–910.

Ross, J., Tewksbury, R., & Rolfe, S. (2016). Inmate responses to correctional officer deviance. *Corrections: Policy, Practice, and Research, 1,* 139–153.

Toobin, J. (2014). This is my jail. *The New Yorker.* Retrieved from https://www.newyorker .com/magazine/2014/04/14/this-is-my-jail

Trammell, R., Raby, J., Anderson, A., Hampton, S., & Stickney, T. (2014). Maintaining order and following the rules: Gender differences in punishing inmate misconduct. *Deviant Behavior, 34,* 805–821.

U.S. Attorney's Office, District of Maryland. (2015, September 15). Former correctional officer sentenced to over six years in prison in Baltimore jail racketeering conspiracy. *The Federal Bureau of Investigation.* Retrieved from http://www.fbi.gov

Worley, R. (2016). Memoirs of a guard-researcher: Deconstructing the games inmates play behind the prison walls. *Deviant Behavior, 37,* 1215–1226.

Worley, R., Marquart, J., & Mullings, J. (2003). Prison guard predators: An analysis of inmates who establish inappropriate relationships with prison staff, 1995–1998. *Deviant Behavior, 24,* 175–198.

Worley, R., & Worley, V. (2011). Guards gone wild: A self-report study of correctional officer misconduct and the effect of institutional deviance on "care" within the Texas prison system. *Deviant Behavior, 32,* 293–319.

Worley, R., & Worley, V. (2016). The economics of "crossing over": Examining the link between correctional officer pay and guard-inmate boundary violations. *Deviant Behavior, 37,* 16–29.

Zoukis, C. (2015, April 9). Forty defendants, including 24 guards, convicted in widespread corruption scandal at Baltimore City Jail. *Prison Legal News.* Retrieved from http://www.prisonlegalnews.com

Beccaria, Cesare (1738–1794)

Cesare Beccaria is an intellectual from the 18th century who is recognized as an integral part of European penology post-Middle Ages. The Middle Ages, or Dark Ages, was a period where spiritual explanations and approaches to crime were the ideological norm. This encompassed the notion that criminal acts were driven by demonic forces and resulted in the use of severe punishments (e.g., quartering, decapitation, or the use of stocks) and excessive torture (e.g., prolonged imprisonment, use of the Judas cradle, or use of the cat's paw). The shift away from this era into the period of the Enlightenment (also known as the Age of Reason) marked the birth of classical criminology and penal reform. Most notably in the field of criminal justice, Beccaria is known for his perspective on human nature and crime, his rationale for punishment and guidelines on how punishments should be implemented, and his views on the role of legislation and the judiciary.

Beccaria published *On Crimes and Punishments* in 1764. In it he argued that people commit criminal acts out of their own free will or rational choice. In doing so, Beccaria placed criminal culpability back on the individual offender and away from external influences or explanations for criminal acts such as demonic possession. Additionally, Beccaria theorized that hedonism (doctrine that pleasure or happiness is the sole or chief good in life) is a natural characteristic among humans. Thus, when individuals make decisions freely, they calculate the costs and the benefits of their actions with reference to pleasure. The benefits reaped from a decision equate to any act that produces self-gratification or pleasure, while the costs of a decision equate to the pain or unpleasant outcomes. Ultimately, Beccaria attributes crime to the pleasurable benefits of a criminal act outweighing the costs and the government's inability to regulate these costs and benefits.

Beccaria posited that the purpose of punishment is to deter crime. Deterrence is the ability to reduce the repetition of a criminal act by a previous offender and other members of society through fear. The hedonistic ideology of human nature further supports his belief that humans will avoid or be deterred from committing a crime due to the fear of an unpleasant punishment. For Beccaria, penal legislation should follow the same hedonistic reasoning; that is, the consequences or costs of crime should outweigh the benefits from committing the act.

Alongside the ability to deter crime, the purpose of punishment is also a means to legitimize the presence of a fair government through what is known as the social contract. The social contract was the mainstream ideology during the Enlightenment, which stated that citizens of a given society agree to give up particular freedoms and in exchange the governing body will protect all other rights.

Beccaria delineated a detailed guide on how punishment should be implemented. He emphasized that criminal consequences should be swift, certain, and severe. Beccaria's requirement of swiftness refers to the quickness or immediacy of a punishment. The rationale behind a prompt sanction is that it will allow criminals to associate a specific punishment with the crime that was committed.

In *On Crimes and Punishments,* certainty is regarded as the most salient prong when administering punishment. Beccaria went further in his ranking of these three prongs when he writes that the certainty behind a moderate sanction will produce greater deterrence than an uncertain yet severe sanction. Beccaria's logic tied into his belief that if an individual commits a crime and is not punished, it weakens the legitimacy of the government by failing to uphold the social contract.

The concept of severity is mentioned in regard to proportionality between crime and punishment. The costs should be more severe in comparison to the rewards of crime; the more serious the crime the more severe the punishment. However, Beccaria cautioned that the proportionality or level of severity administered must not excessively outweigh the crime because then the government becomes unjust and tyrannical. Beccaria also stated that excessive punishments beget more offenses. For instance, if a sentence for drug possession is life in prison and a sentence for murder is life in prison, one might choose to murder all witnesses in a drug possession case because either way life in prison would be the end result for both murder and drug possession.

In his discussion of severity, Beccaria denounced the use of torturous confessions and capital punishment. He argued that the use of torture is not only cruel but may yield inaccurate confessions. As for capital punishment, Beccaria deemed it excessive and ineffective. He viewed the killing of an offender as a hypocritical means to deter the public from committing murder. As an alternative, Beccaria promoted the use of longer imprisonment sentences as a more effective deterrent for severe crimes such as murder.

Beccaria argued that laws must be clear and that the general population must be cognizant of their meanings. His belief was that when offenders understand the consequences of a crime that they will effectively conduct a cost-benefit analysis before breaking the law. In this calculation, an offender might then become deterred from completing a criminal act. Beccaria also proposed that penal legislation must be specific for every crime and nondiscretionary in the consequences administered for breaking the law. This meant that punitive law should predetermine the imprisonment length or fine for crimes and attempts at certain crimes. Furthermore, the law should incorporate punishments for lone offenders and coconspirators. The predetermination of such rules would allow for equality among sentencing.

Additionally, Beccaria advanced that the role of the judiciary is solely to conclude whether or not the crime was committed by the accused. The focus here is on the criminal act or *actus reus* and less on the offender or *mens rea.* Beccaria wrote that defendants should be judged by a jury of peers and that judges should not have any personal ties to the defendant or victim, nor any opportunity for personal gains from a given verdict. Beccaria also outlined that judicial hearings should be public and criticized the use of secret hearings as an abuse of governmental power.

Victor St. John

See also: Determinate versus Indeterminate Sentencing; Enlightenment and Punishment; Federal Sentencing Guidelines; Legitimate Penological Interests; Punishment Philosophies; Sentencing Disparities and Discrimination in Sentencing; Social Contract Theory

Further Reading

Hostettler, J. (2011). *Cesare Beccaria: The genius of 'On Crimes and Punishments.'* London: Waterside Press.

Thomas, A. (Ed.). (2008). *Cesare Beccaria: On crimes and punishments and other writings*. Toronto: University of Toronto Press.

Bell v. Wolfish (1979)

As Americans, citizens have the right to be presumed innocent until proven guilty. However, if an individual is suspected of a crime, it is common for them to be arrested and placed behind bars before any sort of proceeding in a courtroom takes place. *Bell v. Wolfish*, 441 U.S. 520 (1979), was a class action lawsuit that challenged the legality of conditions facing pretrial detainees in a New York City correctional facility.

The case involved the Metropolitan Correctional Center (MCC) in New York, which was built in 1975. Initially, it was intended to house 449 inmates, but it was not built like a traditional jail facility. It did not have jail cells like a traditional facility and instead had dormitories that were somewhat open and private rooms as well. There were also common rooms that the inmates had access to for a specific number of hours per day.

Unfortunately, it soon became obvious that the facility was not large enough. Overcrowding quickly became a problem, and rooms that were meant for just one inmate soon held two, while other inmates waiting for a room slept on cots in common areas. The overcrowding was an issue, and the practice of placing two inmates in a room meant for one became known as double-bunking. Inmates were also prohibited from receiving particular reading material while incarcerated at MCC. Finally, the practice of requiring inmates to stand outside of their rooms while they were being searched as well as being subjected to body cavity searches after visitation were called into question.

A class action lawsuit was filed in Federal District Court with the plaintiffs claiming that their constitutional rights were violated due to the practices at the prison. They claimed that these practices violated their First, Fourth, Fifth, and Fourteenth Amendment rights. Initially, the outcome was a victory for the plaintiffs as the Federal District Court found in their favor and forbade MCC from engaging in the practices communicated in the case. The case was appealed to the Court of Appeals, who affirmed the findings. In addition, the Court of Appeals found that MCC did not make a showing of compelling necessity in regard to the practice of double-bunking.

The case was then appealed to the U.S. Supreme Court, which made a decision on the case in May 1979. The lower courts found the MCC lacking in several areas, but the U.S. Supreme Court found (5–4) that:

1. Double-bunking of inmates was not "punishment."
2. The publishers only rule was constitutional.

3. The package receipt restriction was not a violation of due process.
4. Room/cell searches of pretrial detainees were not a violation of the right to privacy.
5. Visual body cavity searches were not unreasonable.

The underlying question in this case was: at what point do suspects lose some of their right to liberty when incarcerated as pretrial detainees? Specifically, the case asked if certain conditions of confinement violate the individual liberty, due process, and privacy of pretrial detainees as protected by the First, Fourth, and Fifth Amendments through the Fourteenth Amendment. To answer the question, the personal liberties of the pretrial detainee had to be balanced against the necessity of keeping the facility itself and the public outside safe.

The Court found that the conditions of confinement did not infringe on a pretrial detainee's rights. The opinion argued that the issue of prison management is ripe with "judgment calls" that rest outside the jurisdiction of the judiciary. As long as administrative practices are implemented in the genuine interest of "safeguarding institutional security," they do not warrant judicial scrutiny and are consistent with the Constitution.

This case arose as a challenge to the conditions under which pretrial defendants are confined. The petitioners claimed that in the absence of a conviction, subjecting incarcerated defendants automatically to the same conditions as convicted felons was unconstitutional punishment. The Federal District Court agreed with this view, holding that defendants could only be deprived of liberty as a matter of "compelling necessity." It was also determined that the Supreme Court felt that the possible innocence of pretrial detainees should not prevent corrections officials from taking necessary steps to maintain their facility.

Katrina Cathcart

See also: Constitution as a Source for Prisoners' Rights, The; Jails Compared to Prisons; Judicial Involvement in Prison Administration; Treatment in Prisons

Further Reading

Hartman, G. R., Mersky, R. M., & Tate, C. L. (2012). *Landmark Supreme Court cases: The most influential decisions of the Supreme Court of the United States.* New York: Checkmark Books.

Robertson, J. E. (2010). Recent legal developments: Correctional case law: 2009. *Criminal Justice Review, 35*(2), 260–272.

Rudovsky, D. (1988). *The rights of prisoners: The basic ACLU guide to prisoners' rights.* Carbondale: Southern Illinois University Press.

Benefit of Clergy

The term "benefit of clergy" refers to the historical existence of an ecclesiastical alternative to secular courts and the harsh physical punishments that were often associated with these secular courts. Although the concept of the benefit of clergy is commonly associated with English courts, it was not solely limited to these courts. Other countries, such as the United States, also recognized the benefit of clergy

Benefit of Clergy

either explicitly through legal provisions or implicitly through commonly accepted legal practice. In England, the practice of the benefit of clergy originated during the 12th century when secular authorities attempted to circumvent traditional legal practice, which had given ecclesiastical authorities a voice in legal processes and outcomes. As English authorities sought to limit religious influence, the church responded with the establishment of an ecclesiastical court developed for clergy members who would have otherwise been prosecuted in secular courts. The benefit of such a system for clergy members was that they would often be found not guilty or would receive sanctions that were substantively less severe than those that would have been issued in secular courts.

With the establishment of the benefit of clergy, a reliable manner for determining who could avail themselves to its benefits was needed. In 12th- and 13th-century England, clergy members were among the few in society with basic literacy and elevated levels of formal education. As a result, literacy tests in the form of the verbal recitation of Bible passages became a standard test for differentiating those who could and could not avail themselves of the benefit of clergy. Over time, the right to the benefit of clergy expanded as individuals who could read or were capable of rote memorization of specific Bible verses were able to seek shelter from secular persecution in ecclesiastical courts. In some instances, the benefit of clergy was extended to individuals who had no direct attachment to the church. Over time, the benefit of clergy was employed so commonly that many first-time offenders sought lessened punishments through its invocation. As public reliance on the benefit of clergy increased, secular authorities became progressively more concerned with both the frequency of its use, especially among the secular population, and the severity of the offenses for which it was being invoked.

As a result of these concerns, secular authorities sought to limit ecclesiastical authority over legal processes and the criminal sanctions that stemmed from them. Although an outright revocation of the benefit of clergy was not initially feasible, secular authorities sought to slowly undermine the concept's foundation. Restrictions were placed on the types of crimes for which the benefit of clergy could be claimed, thereby creating a list of exempted offenses. This was especially significant for those offenses punishable by death, as avoiding this punishment had previously been a major motivator for the reliance on the benefit of clergy. As the list of exempted offenses lengthened, the practical outcome was that fewer and fewer individuals could ultimately avail themselves of the protections that were associated with the benefit of clergy. Various legislative and political developments in the 19th century contributed to the ongoing decline in the use of the benefit of clergy in England and the United States. Today, the practice has either been formally eliminated through legislation or has fallen out of practice through a lack of use.

Jason R. Jolicoeur

See also: England, Prisons in; Inmates and Freedom of Religion; Prisons, History of; Religious Programs Outreach

Further Reading

Baker, N. F. (1927). Benefit of clergy: A legal anomaly. *Kentucky Law Journal, 15*(2), 85–115.

Beattie, J. M. (1986). *Crime and the courts in England, 1660–1800*. Princeton, NJ: Princeton University Press.

Berman, H. J. (1983). *Law and revolution: The formation of the western legal tradition*. Cambridge, MA: Harvard University Press.

Cross, A. L. (1917). The English criminal law and benefit of clergy during the eighteenth and early nineteenth century. *The American Historical Review, 3*(22), 544–565.

Dalzell, G. W. (1955). *Benefit of clergy in America and related matters*. Winston-Salem, NC: John F. Blair.

Firth, C. B. (1917). Benefit of clergy in the time of Edward IV. *The English Historical Review, 126*(32), 175–191.

Lea, H. C. (1869). *Studies in church history: The rise of the temporal power-benefit of clergy-excommunication*. London: Sampson, Low, Son, and Marston.

McLynn, F. (2013). *Crime and punishment in eighteenth-century England*. New York: Routledge.

Plucknett, T. (2001). *A concise history of the common law* (5th ed.). Union, NJ: Lawbook Exchange.

Sawyer, J. K. (1990). Benefit of clergy in Maryland and Virginia. *The American Journal of Legal History, 34*(1), 49–68.

Biosocial Findings to Increase the Effectiveness of Treatment Programs

During the past two decades, there has been a considerable amount of criminological research underscoring the role that genetic and biological influences have on the development of criminal behavior. These results have largely been referred to as "biosocial findings" because they showcase the importance of genetic, biological, and environmental influences when it comes to criminal offending behaviors. Despite the consistent findings of a strong genetic effect on criminal behavior, there is an almost knee-jerk reaction among critics that these findings can only lead to oppressive and inhumane crime-control policies. Forced sterilization, lifelong prison sentences, and an eradication of all rehabilitation programs are often viewed as the only policies that a biosocial perspective could support.

In reality, however, the findings of biosocial research can be used to help guide and inform programs that are designed to provide treatment and rehabilitation to offenders. In addition, integrating biosocial findings into existing treatment programs can actually lead to an increase in the effectiveness of such programs. To understand how this can be the case, it is first important to understand that environmental effects are typically not ubiquitous across all people; rather, there is a great deal of variability in how people respond to the same environments, which is why two people who are exposed to the same salient environments often turn out quite differently from each other.

This same general finding holds true for treatment and rehabilitation programs, wherein participants who complete the programs often are affected by it in different ways. Some participants, for instance, are changed by the program and thus refrain from criminal offending for the rest of their lives. Other participants who might complete the same program are unaffected by it and return to a life of crime

Biosocial Findings and Treatment Programs

as soon as they are released from the criminal justice system. And still other participants might be partially affected by the program and reduce their criminal involvement but continue to engage in less serious forms of antisocial behaviors.

This variability in response to treatment services is likely to occur across all programs, even those that are consistently revealed to be the most effective at reducing recidivism. If there was a more complete understanding of who is likely to be affected by the program and who is likely to remain immune to it, and what separates the two groups, then it might be possible to increase the effectiveness of such programs to even higher levels. To date, however, outside of a few notable findings there has not been a tremendous amount of success in this endeavor.

Although countless explanations have been advanced for why people respond to the same environments—including the same treatment and rehabilitation programs—differently, for this phenomenon, one of the more promising is derived from the logic of gene-environment interactions. Gene-environment interactions focus on the ways in which genes moderate environmental effects and how environments moderate genetic effects. As it applies to treatment success, however, the former is the only one that is applicable.

Gene-environment interactions occur when the intersection of genetics and environments produces an outcome that is above and beyond the additive effects of genes and the environment. Thought of in a different way, gene-environment interactions produce particular outcomes when there is a certain balance of genetic and environmental influences. Consider, for instance, why childhood maltreatment represents a risk factor for a wide range of maladaptive outcomes, including crime, delinquency, and depression. Somewhat paradoxically, however, is that most children who are maltreated do not develop any type of serious behavioral, emotional, or cognitive deficit. Even in the face of severe disadvantaged environments, most children will mature into adolescents and adults who lack any type of serious negative outcome associated with the maltreatment—that is, they are resilient to maltreatment. Only a relatively small percentage of youth will develop deleterious outcomes—that is, they are susceptible to maltreatment.

Gene-environment interactions explain resiliency and susceptibility to any environmental stimuli (whether it is maltreatment, neighborhood influences, or rehabilitation programs) by underscoring the role of genetic influences. Each person possesses his or her own unique suite of genes, known as a genotype. Genotypes, in turn, are able to moderate how people respond to environments. For instance, consider a person who has a genotype that confers a genetic risk for heart disease. Contrast this person with someone else whose genotype does not confer a genetic risk for heart disease. Now consider that both of these people experience an environment that consists of a sedentary lifestyle and where their diets are high in sodium, cholesterol, and fat. These environments are clearly not healthy, but these unhealthy lifestyles are likely to lead to heart disease much quicker and at a much higher rate for the person with the risky genotype when compared to the person without the risky genotype. In this case, genotype is moderating the effect of an unhealthy lifestyle on the development of heart disease.

The logic of gene-environment interactions can easily be applied to the study of treatment effectiveness for criminal offenders. Offenders who are processed through different treatment programs may be more or less susceptible to them depending on their own unique genotype. Persons who possess certain genotypes, for instance, may be more apt to benefit from a program (i.e., to not engage in future criminal behaviors) when compared to persons who possess different genotypes. The end result is that treatment effectiveness is determined, in part, by the genotypes possessed by program participants.

If research shows that program effectiveness is moderated by genotype, then genotype could be used to help match offenders to particular treatment programs. For instance, persons who possess certain genotypes might be funneled into Program A, whereas persons who possess different genotypes might be ushered into Program B. When used in this way, genotypic information is used to sort offenders into programs that provide the highest chances of success.

The medical field has already embraced such an approach. For certain medications, patients are genotyped, and depending on the results of the genetic testing, they may or may not be prescribed a particular type of medication. Studies have shown that genotype moderates the medicine's effectiveness, and without that genotype the effects of the medication are either null or harmful. Whether this same finding would apply to criminal offenders is generally unknown because it has not been fully explored at this time. There is, however, circumstantial evidence from studies of interventions on children and youth suggesting it would be effective. In one study, for example, researchers examined whether family-based interventions would reduce risky behavior. The results of their study revealed that the family-based intervention was effective but only for respondents who possessed a particular genotype; the program was ineffective for respondents without that particular genotype. Whether this finding would apply to adult offenders remains to be determined by future research.

Gene-environment interactions are not the only way in which genetic research findings can be used to potentially determine the effectiveness of rehabilitation programs. The second way in which genetic influences could be folded into treatment programs is by focusing on genetic risk. To understand how genetic risk might be applicable, it is first necessary to understand the role of offender risk when it comes to program effectiveness. Offender risk levels are typically assessed prior to them being assigned to a particular program. Risk level is most reliably measured via some type of actuarial tool, such as the Level of Service Inventory–Revised (LSI–R). The results of these tools will then allow criminal justice practitioners to assign a risk level to each offender (e.g., low-, medium-, or high-risk levels). These risk levels can then be used to help match each offender to the most appropriate program for him or her to achieve optimum success.

What is interesting to consider is the risk level of offenders who are most amenable to treatment. Although it seems commonsensical to believe that low-risk offenders would be the offenders who would be most likely to remain crime-free, research has shown a very different finding—that is, high-risk offenders are the offenders who are the most likely to benefit from treatment programs. Low-risk offenders, in fact, have actually been shown to become more criminal after they complete a treatment or rehabilitation program.

Biosocial Findings and Treatment Programs

For the most part, the overarching belief is that if individuals are found to possess a high genetic propensity for violence, aggression, and crime, then the only way to deal with them is by incarcerating them for long periods of time. Given the finding that high-risk offenders are the most amenable to behavioral change, then it seems logical to conclude that offenders who possess an elevated genetic risk for crime would also be the very offenders who would benefit the most from a treatment or rehabilitation program. There is no research bearing directly on this possibility, meaning that at this point no hard-and-fast conclusions can be drawn regarding the link between high genetic risk for crime and the success of treatment programs.

Although social scientists tend to be quite wary of the way in which genetic research can be used to process offenders through the criminal justice system, there is a good reason to believe that the findings from biosocial criminological research can be used to increase the effectiveness of rehabilitation and treatment programs. Findings from studies testing for gene-environment interactions could be used to help sort offenders into treatment programs that are individually tailored to the genotypes of criminals. If successful, then the success rates of such programs should increase. In addition, assessing offenders for their genetic risk could also lead to a better understanding of which offenders should be processed through treatment programs (e.g., offenders high in genetic risk) and which offenders should be diverted away from such programs (e.g., offenders low in genetic risk). Depending on the results of studies, and whether these potential ideas are successful, it is quite possible that biosocial research could result in a much more successful and effective criminal justice system when it comes to the ability to reduce recidivism and make society a safer place.

Kevin M. Beaver

See also: Recidivism; Treatment in Prisons

Further Reading

Beaver, K. M. (2008). The interaction between genetic risk and childhood sexual abuse in the prediction of adolescent violent behavior. *Sexual Abuse: A Journal of Research and Treatment, 20*, 426–443.

Beaver, K. M. (2016). *Biosocial criminology: A primer* (3rd ed.). Dubuque, IA: Kendall/ Hunt.

Brody, G. H., Beach, S. R. H., Philibert, R. A., Chen, Y. F., & Murry, V. M. (2009). Prevention effects moderate the association of 5-HTTLPR and youth risk behavior initiation: Gene x environment hypotheses tested via a randomized prevention design. *Child Development, 80*, 645–661.

Brody, G. H., Chen, Y. F., Beach, R. J., Kogan, S. M., Yu, T., DiClemente, R. J., Wingood, G. M., Windle, M., & Philibert, R. A. (2014). Differential sensitivity to prevention programming: A dopaminergic polymorphism-enhanced prevention effect on protective parenting and adolescent substance use. *Health Psychology, 33*, 182–191.

Ferguson, C. J. (2010). Genetic contributions to antisocial personality and behavior: A meta-analytic review from an evolutionary perspective. *Journal of Social Psychology, 150*, 160–180.

Gajos, J. M., Fagan, A. A., & Beaver, K. M. (2016). Use of genetically informed evidence-based prevention science to understand and prevent crime and related behavioral disorders. *Criminology and Public Policy, 15*, 683–701.

Lipsey, M. W., & Cullen, F. T. (2007). The effectiveness of correctional rehabilitation: A review of systematic reviews. *Annual Review of Law and Social Science, 3*, 297–320.

Lowenkamp, C. T., Latessa, E. J., & Holsinger, A. M. (2006). The risk principle in action: What have we learned from 13,676 offenders and 97 correctional programs? *Crime and Delinquency, 52*, 77–93.

Boot Camps

Intermediate sanctions are a vital component of the criminal and juvenile justice systems, in which offenders have alternative options of rehabilitation. Rather than being incarcerated or placed on probation, the justice system has the ability to use an intermediate sanction to rehabilitate an offender. Boot camps represent a type of intermediate sanction. Boot camps, also referred to as shock or intensive incarceration programs, are short-term, in-prison programs that largely resemble military basic training. These programs are heavily structured and emphasize rigorous physical activity and manual labor. They were originally designed to reduce prison populations and associated operating costs as well as reduce recidivism rates through modifying offenders' negative behaviors.

Although some speculate that correctional boot camps have been around in the United States since the early 1970s, the first recognized programs were not established until 1983 in Georgia and Oklahoma. Following their initial implementation, boot camps proliferated across the country throughout the late 1980s and early 1990s. By 1995, there were 75 state-facilitated boot camps for adults. The use of boot camps was not isolated to adult offenders, however. In 1985, the first juvenile boot camp was established in Louisiana. During the 1990s, partially in response to the tough-on-crime ideology, juvenile boot camps became a popular sentencing option. In 1996, there were 48 established juvenile boot camps in 27 different states. The fascination with boot camps began to wane during the latter part of the 1990s, with nearly one-third of state-run prison boot camps being shut down by 2000. As of 2009, only 11 states operated boot camps for juvenile offenders. Though the number of camps have dwindled in recent decades, boot camps continue to be an alternative to long-term incarceration for both juvenile and adult offenders in some states.

Boot camps are not utilized or well suited for all types of offenders. The majority of adult boot camps reserve participation for young, first-time, nonviolent offenders. For juvenile boot camps, eligible offenders are typically in their mid-to-late teens who have prior experience with the juvenile justice system and have failed to be successful with less severe sanctions, but who are not serious enough offenders to be eligible for placement in a state facility. For both juvenile and adult boot camps, participation is largely restricted to male offenders, though there are some female boot camps in existence.

Boot camps are designed to resemble military basic training. Therefore, there is a large emphasis on structure, physical training, manual labor, drill and ceremony, and summary punishment (i.e., immediate sanction for an infraction such as extra chores, pushups, etc.). Many programs also have rehabilitative and treatment components, though the types of activities included as part of these components vary greatly from program to program. Many boot camps with treatment components include academic and vocational education, drug and alcohol treatment, different types of therapy, and life skills training. In juvenile boot camps, this emphasis on rehabilitation is particularly salient. According to a study conducted jointly by the Institute for Criminological Research and the National Institute of Justice, juvenile boot camps spend more than half of each day on education and counseling activities. Additionally, most juvenile boot camp programs include substance abuse treatment, rehabilitative counseling, and intensive community supervision upon release.

Boot camps were designed to achieve three main goals. The main goal is to reduce recidivism among offenders by modifying their behavior through positive reinforcement of appropriate behavior and immediate punishment of negative behavior. Another goal is to reduce the number of incarcerated offenders by diverting them from traditional incarceration facilities to boot camps. A final goal, which is partially dependent on the first two goals, is the reduction of correctional operating costs. If boot camps are able to reduce the number of incarcerated offenders as well as rehabilitate boot camp participants, then theoretically, correctional operating costs should be reduced.

Evaluations have been conducted to assess whether adult and juvenile boot camps are successful in achieving these goals. Studies have consistently found that boot camps do not significantly reduce recidivism rates. This finding holds true for both juvenile and adult boot camps. Additionally, it has been found that the emphasis of the program, whether heavily militarized or more focused on treatment, does not have an impact on recidivism. Both types of programs fail to significantly reduce recidivism rates. Researchers have identified a number of limitations to explain the failure to reduce recidivism including low "dosage" effects and insufficient preparation of participants for reentry. Some researchers argue that recidivism is not impacted because the length of stay is too short to have any realistic effect. Essentially, they argue that real and long-lasting changes in behavior cannot be achieved in the 90 to 120 days that is typical of most boot camp programs. Other researchers argue that recidivism is not impacted because boot camps do not prepare graduates for life after release. Many programs provide little to no postrelease programming to prepare graduates to be successful once released. However, many programs require intensive supervision upon release. The lack of adequate preparation coupled with intensive surveillance increases the likelihood that graduates will violate probation or reoffend.

Mixed results have been found regarding whether boot camps reduce prison populations. An NIJ multisite study on adult boot camps in Louisiana and New York found that the programs did reduce the need for prison beds in these states. A study exploring juvenile boot camps in South Dakota and Oregon found similar findings.

However, the restrictive criteria for boot camp participants, particularly for adult boot camps, impact the ability to significantly reduce prison populations. Due to the failure of boot camps to either reduce recidivism or have a significant impact on prison populations, the goal of reducing operating costs is also usually not achieved. Despite the shortcomings of most boot camp programs, they continue to be used in many states across the country. Many of the boot camps that remain in existence today have reviewed the findings from previous evaluations and are making changes to their programs in order to attempt to increase their effectiveness.

Riane M. Bolin and Christina Poole

See also: Continuum of Sanctions; Correctional Officers with Military Experience; Cost of Prisons; Evidence-Based Practice in Corrections; Inmates' Perceptions of Prison versus Alternative Sanctions; Prison Populations, Downsizing of; Recidivism

Further Reading

Bottcher, J., & Ezell, M. E. (2005). Examining the effectiveness of boot camps: A randomized experiment with a long-term follow up. *Journal of Research in Crime and Delinquency, 42*(30), 309–332.

MacKenzie, D. L., & Armstrong, G. S. (2004). *Correctional boot camps: Military basic training or a model for corrections?* Thousand Oaks, CA: Sage.

MacKenzie, D. L., Gover, A. R., Armstrong, G. S., & Mitchell, O. (2001). *A national study comparing the environments of boot camps with traditional facilities for juvenile offenders.* Washington, DC: U.S. Department of Justice.

MacKenzie, D. L., & Hebert, E. E. (1996). *Correctional boot camps: A tough intermediate sanction.* Washington, DC: U.S. Department of Justice.

Meade, B., & Steiner, B. (2010). Total effects of boot camps that house juveniles: A systematic review of the evidence. *Journal of Criminal Justice, 38*(5), 841–853.

Peters, M., Thomas, D., & Zamberlan, C. (1997). *Boot camps for juvenile offenders.* Washington, DC: Office of Juvenile Justice and Delinquency Prevention.

Building Tenders

The term "building tenders" refers to the historical use of inmates as a correctional management tool. Although building tenders is often used interchangeably with the related term "inmate trusty," the two terms have come to have different connotations over time. In a contemporary sense, prison or jail trusties are commonly characterized as lower risk inmates who are allotted additional privileges in exchange for the labor that they provide to correctional institutions. Building tenders, on the other hand, refers to a group of inmates who were historically granted substantive power and authority over other inmates by prison administrators in exchange for their ability to maintain order within correctional institutions and ensure inmate compliance with institutional directives. The use of building tenders in the American prison system was most prominent during the 1960s and 1970s and was at least partially driven by increasing prison populations, which challenged the ability of prison officials to maintain institutional order. Although the use of building tenders in the United States is most strongly linked to the Texas prison system, building tenders were also commonly employed by prison systems in Arkansas, Louisiana, Alabama, and Mississippi.

Building tenders were frequently selected precisely because they were intimidating inmates who were willing and able to use violence to accomplish their assigned duties within the institutions that incarcerated them. This willingness to use force in the form of extortion, threats, and beatings ultimately contributed to tenders having fearsome institutional reputations. Due to their willingness to harm other inmates, the special privileges that they enjoyed as a result of this propensity, and the symbiotic relationships that they cultivated with institutional staff, building tenders were both feared and despised by the rest of the inmate population. In order to accomplish their duties, building tenders were allowed to enlist the help of other inmates, were given access to otherwise off limits areas of the institutions that housed them, and often had access to crude weapons. The continuation of the building tender system was possible largely because of the tacit support of prison officials. Prison administrators supported the building tender system largely because of the dramatic increase in prison populations, changing types of inmates who became increasingly more difficult to manage, and stagnant levels of fiscal support that resulted in insufficient correctional staffing levels. Collectively, these factors made inmate management more challenging and dangerous, causing prison officials to seek out alternative means of more effectively managing inmate populations.

Building tenders were typically effective at maintaining order in the prisons that they supervised. Perhaps more importantly, building tenders were able to maintain order without the increased costs that would have been associated with hiring additional correctional officers. This was a critical benefit in an era of stagnating or declining correctional budgets. However, the benefits associated with the reliance on building tenders came at a cost. Instances of predatory behavior, including physical assaults on other inmates, became commonplace in institutions using building tenders. Additionally, the tactics employed by building tenders contributed to growing resentment among the inmate population. This had a deleterious influence on inmate morale and contributed to violent attacks on both building tenders and other prison staff. Finally, the abusive practices associated with building tenders undermined the ongoing legitimacy of the correctional function in the minds of many.

As the prisoner rights movement developed during the latter half of the 20th century, courts increasingly abandoned the hands-off doctrine, which had limited their prior willingness to arbitrate inmate challenges concerning the perceived unconstitutional nature of their conditions of confinement. As the courts pursued a more engaged orientation toward the conditions of imprisonment within the American penal system, inmates increasingly pressed their rights. The abusive nature of the building tender system, along with other correctional practices and policies, fueled civil litigation involving penal institutions. One of the most significant cases regarding the reliance on building tenders was *Ruiz v. Estelle* (1980). This case challenged a variety of conditions of confinement then existing within the Texas correctional system, including a lack of inmate safety brought about by insufficient staffing and a reliance on building tenders. The courts ruled in favor of the inmates in this case finding that these conditions amounted to a violation of their constitutional rights. With this ruling, the building tender system was eliminated within the Texas Department of Corrections.

As the use of building tenders was abandoned, violence increased when prison gangs attempted to fill the resulting power void in Texas prisons. In spite of the unintended consequences associated with the elimination of the Texas building tender system, its demise served as a portent of the future facing other states still employing building tenders. Additional court cases with similar findings and changing public opinion contributed to the eventual elimination of building tenders as a prison management tool in American prisons.

Jason R. Jolicoeur

See also: Constitution as a Source for Prisoners' Rights, The; Prison Gangs; Prisons, History of; Violence in Prison; Vocational Training and Education

Further Reading

DiIulio, J. J. (1987). *Governing prisons: A comparative study of correctional management.* New York: Free Press.

DiIulio, J. J. (1987). Prison discipline and prison reform. *The Public Interest, 89*(4), 71–90.

DiIulio, J. J. (Ed.). (1990). *Courts, corrections, and the Constitution: The impact of judicial intervention on prisons and jails.* New York: Oxford University Press.

Channels, S. (Ed.). (1985). *Prisons and prisoners: Historical documents.* Philadelphia: Haworth Press.

Chase, R. T. (2015). We are not slaves: Rethinking the rise of carceral states through the lens of the prisoners' rights movement. *The Journal of American History, 102*(1), 73–86.

Crouch, B. M., & Marquart, J. W. (1989). *An appeal to justice: Litigated reform of Texas prisons.* Austin: University of Texas Press.

Parkinson, R. (2010). *Texas tough: The rise of America's prison empire.* New York: Henry Holt.

Pollock, J. (Ed). (1997). *Prisons: Today and tomorrow.* Gaithersburg, MD: Aspen.

Price, J. K., & Coleman, S. (2011). Narrative of neglect: Texas prisons for men. *East Texas Historical Journal, 49*(2), 44–68.

Taylor, W. B. (1999). *Down on Parchman Farm.* Columbus: Ohio State University Press.

Canada, Prisons in

Canadian law and legal institutions offer a unique blend of principles and practices drawn from both the United Kingdom and the United States. This "blend" may be best understood in terms of the colonial and Commonwealth relationships that Canada has had with the United Kingdom coupled with the nation's proximity to the United States, its closest neighbor and trading partner. The same is true when discussing correctional institutions and practices.

CORRECTIONAL JURISDICTIONS

Canada operates 15 correctional jurisdictions: one federal, ten provincial, and three territorial services as well as one military correctional "service" within the Security Branch. This diversity reflects Canada's constitutional and legal history. *The Constitution Act*, 1867, 30 & 31 Victoria, c. 3 (U.K.) (formally known as the British North America Act [1867]) established that while the federal government had sole responsibility for the creation of the criminal law, the provinces (state-level governments) would be responsible for the administration of those laws; thus, the same criminal law would apply across the nation while its administration would reflect the cultural values and norms of each province and territory.

The Constitution Act (1867) also split the responsibility for correctional operations between the federal and provinces/territories but in a manner quite different from its American neighbors. While U.S. correctional services operate on the basis of the laws of the specific jurisdiction that were transgressed, that is, state and federal prisons for those sentenced under state and federal laws, respectively, Canadian correctional jurisdiction is determined by the length of sentence imposed. Those offenders convicted and sentenced to incarceration of up to two years less one day serve their sentence in a provincial/territorial institution, while those offenders incarcerated for single terms of two years or more or multiple shorter sentences totaling more than two years serve their sentences in a federal institution. Thus, the Canadian constitutional arrangements have resulted in locally operated lockups (police detention while booking), provincially operated prisons (short-term, unified jail-prison function), and federally operated penitentiaries (long-term prison function).

The *National Defence Act* (R.S.C., 1985, c. N-5) provides for members of the Canadian Armed Forces to be incarcerated for offenses under military law. Those offenders sentenced to less than two years of incarceration serve their sentences in garrison guard rooms if less than 30 days or one of the strict-regime, military detention barracks for longer sentences; military offenders sentenced to longer sentences serve the first two years of their sentences within the strict-regime, military detention barracks and are transferred to a federal correctional institution to serve the remainder of their sentence.

OFFENDER POPULATION ISSUES

Although the size of the overall Canadian population is similar to that of the state of California, Canada's incarceration rate is far lower than that state since Canadian judges tend to rely more on fines and community sanctions than imprisonment at a ratio of 4:1 over custodial sentences. The on-register count of inmates in Canada was 39,623 during 2014–2015. Having said this, however, political changes toward a conservative penal populism during the past decade have been only slightly mirrored by increases in the prison population. The overall Canadian rate of imprisonment increased by 23 percent, from 129 to 138 inmates per 100,000 adult population members, between 2005 and 2015. The proportion of provincial/territorial to federal inmates has remained relatively constant at approximately 61 percent to 39 percent, respectively, during the same 10-year period. The number of remanded inmates (pretrial and presentence detainees) also increased steadily by nearly 39 percent during that same decade. During the same period, the proportion of remanded inmates only increased from 49.5 percent to 56.8 percent of the national prison population (Statistics Canada, 2017a).

SIMILAR CHALLENGES, DIFFERENT APPROACHES

Among the many challenges facing correctional agencies across North America are the aging, minority, female, mentally ill, and remand (pretrial) inmate populations; what makes the Canadian situation different is that the former is primarily a federal issue while the latter is exclusively a provincial (state-level) issue. The "graying," or aging, of the federal inmate population (calculated as 50 years of age and older) may be attributed to (1) changes in the criminal law over the past decade that added to the number of mandatory prison sentences; (2) increased sentence lengths imposed for violent, sexual, and drug offences; (3) older age of inmates upon committal (averaging 33 years and increasing); and (4) increasingly restrictive release policies (especially for violent and sexual offenders) of risk-averse agencies. Inmates in this age category comprise 24 percent of the federal inmate population, and significant increases are expected during upcoming years as the Canadian population ages; the current lack of geriatric and hospice care will need to be addressed especially since 20 percent of federal inmates are serving life sentences (Public Safety Canada, 2017).

Whereas jurisdictions in the United States are used to dealing with high percentages of Hispanic and African Americans incarcerated, the Canadian situation deals with the disproportionate confinement of Aboriginal offenders: First Nations (Amerindian), Métis (mixed Amerindian-European), and Inuit (Eskimoan) offenders. Although the proportion of Aboriginal persons within the overall Canadian

Inuit prisoners carve soapstone sculptures to raise money for a charity auction at the Beaver Creek Institution, a minimum security federal prison in Gravenhurst, Ontario. (Ron Bull/Toronto Star via Getty Images)

population is approximately 4.3 percent, both federal and provincial/territorial incarcerated populations average 24–25 percent; the percentage of Aboriginal offenders in provincial/territorial custody may range as high as 65–85 percent in individual provinces and territories as one moves across the country from east to west and into the northern territories (Public Safety Canada, 2017; Statistics Canada, 2017a). Aboriginal offenders are remanded into custody more frequently than other groups and tend to serve more of their sentence prior to release; the latter is especially the case for Aboriginal women.

Services for female inmates continue to be a challenge for Canadian correctional jurisdictions due to the economy of scale and physical distances involved. Although federally sentenced women are housed in the nearest of five multilevel regional women's facilities across the country and/or the one Aboriginal Healing Lodge, each province/territory has at least one female institution; the problems with this arrangement are that female offenders are routinely kept in a facility that is located hundreds of miles from family members, which impedes the maintenance of family bonds and the rehabilitation process. As in the United States, their smaller number often results in the provision of limited programming and services with limited value for released women in relation to her male counterparts. Many programs reflect patriarchal views of what a woman "needs" for her gender roles in society, while classification and other diagnostic services are often adapted from the existing male instruments; the latter often results in female offenders being classified at higher levels than their male counterparts.

The number of inmates who enter with or develop mental illnesses while in custody continue to be a problem for both provincial/territorial and federal corrections. The correctional investigator for Canada (an investigative ombudsman for federal inmates) identified that the proportion of federal inmates with mental illnesses is high with 40 percent of incoming federal inmates having at least one mental disorder (Correctional Investigator for Canada, 2015). The limited number of programs for this population coupled with limited training for staff exacerbates this problem. For example, although it is estimated that 9.8 percent to 23.3 percent of federal inmates have fetal alcohol spectrum disorder (FASD), many correctional staff and their agencies continue to deal with behaviors by members of this cognitively impaired group using cognitively oriented interventions and/or sanctions. The incidence of self-harm among female inmates far exceeds that among males with Aboriginal female offenders accounting for the highest numbers of cuttings and attempted suicides. The nexus between mental health and suicide was recently brought to national attention through the case of 19-year-old Ashley Smith, a young, mentally ill inmate who hanged herself in 2007 while in federal custody after being primarily treated as a behavioral problem. Subsequent inquiries revealed how this woman's mental health rapidly deteriorated, and the psychiatric interventions that she received were minimal at best.

Remand (pretrial detention) is exclusively a provincial responsibility in Canada. The provinces hold remand inmates in purpose-designed remand centers (usually in or near large urban centers) and in the remand sections of most jails. The remand population has increased by 39 percent over the past decade and consistently outpaces the sentenced population. Recent statistics indicate the extent of the "remand crisis" that exists in Canada whereby the average percentage of remand is 57 percent compared to 43 percent for sentenced inmates. Probable contributors to this "crisis" may be familiar to many Americans: (1) increased complexity of cases brought before the courts, (2) increased numbers of not-guilty pleas for offenses that carry mandatory sentences, (3) increasing number of offenders who fail to meet primary and secondary bail eligibility conditions (likelihood of flight and/or reoffending while on bail), and (4) financial inability to secure bail. Although Canada does not have the strict "speedy trial" legislation that operates in American jurisdictions, the typical time spent on remand in Canada is between 36–45 days (Statistics Canada, 2017b).

Related to the "graying" of the inmate population are the ages of the correctional staff and the prisons themselves. Although provincial/territorial data are not available, the federal correctional service identified that over half of its staff are more than 50 years of age with 20.8 percent of its staff having retired between 1998 and 2007; this includes 6.9 percent of its executive management personnel (Correctional Service of Canada, 2008). During the 1950s and 1960s, both provincial and federal services replaced most of the facilities built prior to the 20th century. Many of these "new" facilities are now reaching their maximum effective age without major renovation, and most will need to be replaced in the coming years to comply with contemporary codes and standards.

Institutional size and crowding is not an issue to the same extent found in American corrections; however, crowding/overcrowding still exists in Canadian facilities. Unlike many American jurisdictions, however, Canadian prisons tend to be smaller and house between 100 and 500 inmates which, in turn, mediates but does not eliminate many of the problems associated with crowding/overcrowding several thousand inmates in facilities designed for only one or two thousand beds. In Canada, crowding occurs at the institutional level, while the correctional service as a whole may not have reached its overall design capacity; hypothetically, therefore, the population of the Edmonton Remand Centre may be over its design capacity, while the overall provincial inmate population in Alberta (of which the Centre is part) remains under its overall design capacity. The northern territories are the exception as they are chronically overcrowded due to the lack of facilities in those jurisdictions.

The riots and hostage takings that plagued many American jurisdictions during the 1960s and 1970s were mirrored in Canada, yet the loss of life and destruction of public property were far less. This was due, in part, to smaller size and relatively new construction of its institutions as most disturbances occurred in older, higher security institutions built around the turn of the century. The federal approach was to institute a Royal Commission (similar to a presidential or blue-ribbon committee), which resulted in wide-ranging changes to that system, including the amalgamation of the penitentiary and parole services as the Correctional Service of Canada.

CONCLUSION

The operation of institutional corrections in Canada has both subtle and gross differences to those operated at the county, state, and federal levels in the United States. Although the provinces and territories provide combined jail-prison services, they may be best compared to the county facilities in most states, accounting for the majority of custodial admissions and having the least resources available per inmate. The federal Correctional Service of Canada operates a long-term penitentiary system akin to those operated by states and the federal Bureau of Prisons. Disproportionate minority confinement in Canada deals with persons of Aboriginal descent rather than black and/or Hispanic inmates. As with the American prison population, a large percentage of inmates either enter with or develop one or more forms of mental illness while incarcerated with the incidence of self-harm events being far greater than that among the nonincarcerated population. Like their American counterparts, Canadian correctional services are experiencing a "graying" of its long-term inmate population coupled with a dramatic increase in staff retirements.

Allan L. Patenaude

See also: Incarceration Rates in the United States Compared to Other Countries; Mentally Ill Prisoners; Overcrowding

Further Reading

Beaudette, J. N., Power, J., & Stewart, L. A. (2015). *National prevalence of mental disorders among incoming federally-sentenced men offenders*. Ottawa, ON: Correctional Service of Canada.

Correctional Investigator for Canada. (2015). *Annual report of the correctional investigator of Canada, 2014–2015*. Ottawa, ON: Office of the Correctional Investigator for Canada.

Correctional Service of Canada. (2008). *Correctional Service of Canada retirement overview*. Ottawa, ON: Human Resource Planning, Reporting and Information Management, Correctional Service of Canada.

Jones, N. A., & Patenaude, A. L. (2011). The criminal justice system. In M. A. Hurlbert (Ed.), *Pursuing justice: An introduction to justice studies* (pp. 244–267). Black Point, NS: Fernwood.

MacGuigan, M. (1977). *Report to Parliament by the Sub-Committee on the Penitentiary System in Canada*. Ottawa, ON: Supply and Services Canada.

Public Safety Canada. (2017). *2016 Annual report corrections and conditional release statistical overview*. Ottawa, ON: Public Safety Canada Portfolio Corrections Statistics Committee.

Reitano, J. (2016). *Adult correctional statistics in Canada, 2014/2015*. Ottawa, ON: Statistics Canada.

Service, J. (2010). *Under warrant: A review of the implementation of the Correctional Service of Canada's 'mental health strategy.'* Ottawa, ON: Office of the Correctional Investigator of Canada.

Statistics Canada. (2017a). *Adult correctional statistics in Canada, 2015/2016*. Ottawa, ON: Author.

Statistics Canada. (2017b). *Trends in the use of remand in Canada, 2004/2005 to 2014/2015*. Ottawa, ON: Author.

Winterdyck, J. A., & Weinrath, M. (Eds.). (2013). *Adult corrections in Canada: A comprehensive overview* (pp. 225–248). Whitby, ON: de Sitter.

Capital Punishment, Collateral Consequences of

Capital punishment, as the ultimate sanction for crime, is designed to have a potent impact on society. Some of the intended impacts or consequences are general deterrence, retribution and justice (righting wrongs through proportional punitive response), and closure for covictims. Less often considered are the collateral consequences of this ultimate punishment, what might be considered the ripple effects of the death penalty. These ripples represent sharp contrast to the stated purposes of the death penalty, often revealing consequences in direct opposition to the intended effects. These collateral consequences manifest at both the individual and societal level. There are obvious individual-level consequences for family and friends of both the condemned and their victims and less obvious consequences for those who work in the criminal justice system and those who work with or experience the death penalty and execution processes. The latter includes the impact on lawyers, capital jurors, prison staff, and media witnesses, among others. There are also collateral consequences that reverberate more broadly throughout society and potentially rupture the very foundations the death penalty is supposed to strengthen, including the sanctity of life and rule of law. The flaws and failings of capital punishment exposed over the years of its use further threaten to undermine these foundations with the collateral consequence of diminishing the legitimacy of the criminal justice system.

Capital Punishment, Collateral Consequences of

At the individual level, the family and loved ones of offenders and victims suffer the most direct, and acute, collateral consequences of capital punishment. Though the offender may be guilty of a crime for which the death penalty is deemed warranted, his or her family members are not. Nevertheless, they must withstand the excruciating process of watching a loved one be condemned to death and eventually killed. At minimum, this is a loss of a family member; but it is often more than that as family members experience social stigmatization typically accompanied by invasive media contact. Victims' family and friends (covictims) are often evoked as a key rationale for capital punishment. It is proclaimed that, in cases of particularly brutal murders, execution is the only way to provide justice and closure. However, research shows that these outcomes are elusive for covictims and that execution does not necessarily provide the promised catharsis. In fact, many accounts of covictim experiences suggest that the lengthy process associated with the death penalty contributes to a form of suspended grief, prolonging the agony of the loss of a loved one to murder. To be sure, the experiences of murder covictims vary greatly, but there is no question that many become collateral casualties of the capital punishment process.

The individual collateral consequences extend beyond those directly connected to the offenders or victims in capital cases. Beginning with the murder itself and ending with execution, numerous criminal justice functionaries are directly impacted by the death penalty and the surrounding legal apparatuses. Unlike offenders' and victims' family members, these individuals are involved with the death penalty, typically by choice. This choice does not mitigate the harmful consequences many of them experience. Police officers, investigators, and other law enforcement officials not only experience the murder and its aftermath but are also often drawn into the lengthy and demanding capital trial and subsequent hearings. At this stage, attorneys, judges, and witnesses begin to play a direct role in the capital punishment process.

What makes this experience different for many of these individuals is that a life is on the line, and they play a role in whether that individual lives or dies. The consequences include often profound emotional stress as they attempt to manage the dissonance that comes with making decisions that may contribute to the death of another person. This may be most acute for jurors who have less choice in their level of involvement but carry the greatest burden of the final judgment of both guilt and sentence—explicitly deciding whether the defendant lives or dies.

Once sentenced to death, offenders are placed on death row, typically characterized by supermax-style lockdown during which the inmate will spend the vast majority of his or her time alone in a cell. This is not to say there is no interaction with others during this time. Indeed, there is a "death row community" that includes those who work with death row inmates such as correctional officers, religious advisers, counselors, and medical staff, as well as the other death row inmates. Emotions run high in this unique community, especially when an inmate is executed and those who knew and/or worked with him or her must reconcile this reality of the relationships they have and continue to establish.

Some of those who work or interact with death row inmates also are present at their execution. The actual execution typically includes a team of correctional officers, medical personnel, the prison chaplain, and the warden, each playing an integral role in the execution routine. Also present at executions are a variety of witnesses including covictims, those there on behalf of the condemned, and media witnesses. We know from research and personal accounts that the execution profoundly impacts those who participate in or witness it. Members of the execution team often must see counselors after executions, and some have reported PTSD symptoms similar to those experienced by survivors of natural disasters and military combat. Witnesses, likewise, have characterized the experience as traumatic. Executions take a significant short- and long-term toll on those involved.

There are also collateral consequences at the societal level. Contrary to the deterrence hypothesis, for example, some studies have shown the death penalty to be associated with an actual increase in levels of violence and homicide in society. This has been termed the "brutalization" effect of the death penalty. The cost of capital punishment and the associated tax burden on society has been found to exceed the cost of life in prison in most states, typically by many millions of dollars. In terms of both public safety and expense, there is ample evidence that detrimental consequences associated with capital punishment rival the purported benefits.

There is no greater detriment than when errors are made in capital cases. Wrongful convictions and wrongful executions are arguably the most far-reaching and profound ripple effects of the death penalty. Over the last 40 years, there have been 156 exonerations of innocent death row inmates—approximately 1 exoneration for every 9 executions. Moreover, research has shown that the probability of wrongful convictions is elevated in capital cases, with the added pressures on police and prosecutors and unique jury selection processes found to bias a jury toward guilt. This associated increase in risk of error coupled with the particular gravity of such mistakes amplifies the death penalty's collateral consequences, impacting the criminal justice system, the people who come in contact with it, and society at large.

The most immediate collateral consequence of these errors is the wrongful incarceration of an innocent person. The most egregious is the execution of that person, a tragedy that, though rare, has happened throughout history. These tragic circumstances create victims out of not only the wrongfully condemned but their families and loved ones. But the impact of wrongful convictions in capital cases is not limited to these most proximate outcomes. There is no justice or closure for covictims; in fact, the real offender remains unapprehended. Juries and others in the criminal justice system must face the reality of having played a role in wrongfully condemning a person to death. This is a significant burden and, unfortunately, one that is being experienced regularly.

In the end, the greatest casualty may be the legitimacy of our criminal justice system and the rule of law. The failings of the system surrounding capital punishment serve to produce deeply demoralizing and delegitimizing forces throughout the criminal justice system and threaten the very foundations of justice, retribution, and sanctity of life central to the rationale for the death penalty. These are collateral consequences that extend far beyond this singular penal policy and that produce ripple effects throughout society. The death penalty is a punishment intended to have a great impact on society and the people within it. With this come just as potent unintended, collateral consequences.

Scott Vollum

See also: Antiterrorism and Effective Death Penalty Act of 1996; Death Penalty Legal Issues; Death Row Inmates; Innocence Project; Restorative Justice

Further Reading

Arrigo, B. A., & Fowler, C. R. (2001). The "death row community": A community psychology perspective. *Deviant Behavior, 22*, 43–71.

Bohm, R. M. (2013). *Capital punishment's collateral damage.* Durham, NC: Carolina Academic Press.

Cochran, J. K., & Chamlin, M. B. (2000). Deterrence or brutalization: The dual effects of executions. *Justice Quarterly, 17*(4), 685–706.

Dicks, S. (1991). *Victims of crime and punishment: Interviews with victims, convicts, their families, and support groups.* Jefferson, NC: McFarland.

Gross, S. R. (1996). The risks of death: Why erroneous convictions are common in capital cases. *Buffalo Law Review, 44*, 469–500.

Gross, S. R., O'Brien, B., Hu, C., & Kennedy, E. H. (2014). Rate of false conviction of criminal defendants who are sentenced to death. *Proceedings of the National Academy of Sciences, 111*(20), 7230–7235.

Haney, C. (1997). Violence and the capital jury: Mechanisms of moral disengagement and the impulse to condemn to death. *Stanford Law Review, 49*, 1447–1486.

Johnson, R. (1997). *Death work: A study of the modern execution process.* Belmont, CA: Wadsworth.

Liebman, J. S. (2014). *The wrong Carlos: Anatomy of a wrongful execution.* New York: Columbia University Press.

Lifton, R. J., & Mitchell, G. (2000). *Who owns death? Capital punishment, the American conscience, and the end of executions.* New York: William Morrow.

Radelet, M. L. (Ed.). (1989). *Facing the death penalty: Essays on a cruel and unusual punishment.* Philadelphia: Temple University Press.

Sarat, A. (2014). *Gruesome spectacles: Botched executions and America's death penalty.* Redwood City, CA: Stanford University Press.

Smykla, J. O. (1987). The human impact of capital punishment: Interviews with families of persons on death row. *Journal of Criminal Justice, 15*, 331–347.

Vollum, S. (2008). *Last words and the death penalty: Voices of the condemned and their co-victims.* New York: LFB Scholarly.

Westervelt, S. D., & Cook, K. J. (2012). *Life after death row: Exonerees' search for community and identity.* New Brunswick, NJ: Rutgers University Press.

Castration as a Deterrent to Sexual Offending

Castration as a deterrent to sexual offending involves several medical, legal, and ethical issues. Castration is a great example of a lockdown nation because the state is exercising control over the physical body after release from prison. Through castration the state is able to control hormones of convicted sex offenders, which is believed to be related to an offender's sexual desire. Castration is more commonly used as a method of control to prevent repeat sexual offenses of minors.

The two main types of castration are chemical and surgical. Chemical castration involves using antiandrogen medication, which reduces testosterone to prepuberty levels. The most common forms of chemical castration include medroxyprogesterone acetate (commonly known as depo-Provera) and depo-leuprolide (Lupron). Due to its less invasive nature chemical castration is more likely to be used in comparison to surgical castration, which involves an orchiectomy or removal of the testicles. Chemical castration might permit sexual offenders to engage in normal sexual activity, and the side effects may be reversible after discontinuation.

The main argument in support of castration is male focused and centers on the role testosterone plays in aggression and sexual desire. Based off human and animal studies it is argued that reducing testosterone will leave sexual offenders with little to no sexual desire, which in turn would prevent future offenses. Although there are conflicting results concerning if sexual offenders have higher (or lower) levels of testosterone than the general public, understanding the causes of sexual aggression is important in order to better inform social policy on treatment options. For example, through studying saliva and blood samples of testosterone levels comparing convicted sexual offenders worldwide, rapists had significantly higher levels of testosterone whereas child molesters had lower levels. It is unknown if castration among offenders with lower levels of testosterone would be as effective in comparison to those with higher levels of testosterone. These results show that due to the variety of sexual offenses and the variation in offenders there cannot be a one-size-fits-all approach to treatment.

There are also mixed findings on whether castration works as a deterrent. Unlike other deterrents that may focus on preventing crime among the general public, castration typically focuses on repeat offenders. This means the aim of using castration as a deterrent is centered on offender recidivism. Of the relatively small group of repeat sexual offenders, recidivism research typically focuses on the benefits of psychosocial programs and does not address the effectiveness of castration. There is some research on the effect of surgical castration on sexual offender recidivism, and there appear to be significant positive outcomes for surgical castration in comparison to chemical castration or psychosocial programs. Still, there are extremely few sexual offenders worldwide who have undergone surgical castration in comparison to other forms of treatment such as chemical castration. Additionally, research on recidivism using any form of castration is flawed. Due to the limited availability of sexual offender programs in prison, recidivism research rarely includes a control group for comparison. There is also a lack of information about convicted sexual offenders who may be offered chemical castration as part of a parole option who decline.

Beyond the questionable effectiveness of castration on recidivism, the medical community and others have expressed concern over the lifelong effects of chemical castration in particular. Depression, reduced brain function, infertility, osteoporosis, and cardiovascular disease are some of the many side effects an offender may be at risk for developing especially with long-term use of antiandrogen medication.

Worldwide few countries use castration to deter sex offenses and included among others are Argentina, Australia, Israel, New Zealand, Russia, the United Kingdom, and the United States. Since 2012, several more countries are engaged in an ongoing debate on the implementation of chemical castration including India, Indonesia, and South Korea. Two of these countries, Indonesia and South Korea, passed laws and chemically castrated convicted rapists of minors. In 2012, a congressional antirape law in India was proposed that included chemical castration for convicted rapists. The following year a committee rejected chemical castration as a human rights violation because of the unknown and potentially dangerous side effects. The committee also expressed concern that passing such a law allowing chemical castration would not address the social foundations of rape.

Focusing on the United States, nine states permit castration for convicted sexual offenders. Two states, California and Florida, require mandatory chemical castration for repeat offenders. If ordered to undergo chemical castration, offenders may choose surgical castration as an alternative. A majority of these nine states do not allow elective castration to be taken into consideration when an offender is eligible for probation or parole. Typically, castration as a deterrent to sexual offending is initiated while an offender is incarcerated and scheduled to be paroled or released within a few weeks. Occasionally, castration is used as an alternative to imprisonment while an offender is on probation. When chemical castration is part of probation or parole, the length of treatment imposed may be temporary or for life.

Chastity Blankenship

See also: Recidivism of Sex Offenders; Sex Offenders in Prison

Further Reading

Cochrane, J. (2016, May 25). Indonesia approves castration for sex offenders who prey on children. *New York Times*. Retrieved from http://www.nytimes.com/2016/05/26/world/asia/indonesia-chemical-castration.html

Lee, J. Y., & Cho, K. S. (2013). Chemical castration for sexual offenders: physicians' views. *Journal of Korean Medical Science, 28*(2), 171–172.

Lösel, F., & Schmucker, M. (2005). The effectiveness of treatment for sexual offenders: A comprehensive meta-analysis. *Journal of Experimental Criminology, 1*(1), 117–146.

Maletzky, B. M., Tolan, A., & McFarland, B. (2006). The Oregon depo-provera program: A five-year follow-up. *Sexual Abuse: A Journal of Research and Treatment, 18*(3), 303–316.

Norman-Eady, S. (2006). *Castration of sex offenders.* Connecticut General Assembly, Office of Legislative Research. Retrieved from https://www.cga.ct.gov/2006/rpt/2006-R-0183.htm

Verma panel rejects chemical castration, death for rapists. (2013, January 23). *The Times of India.* Retrieved from http://timesofindia.indiatimes.com/india/Verma-panel-rejects-chemical-castration-death-for-rapists/articleshow/18154252.cms

Wong, J. S., & Gravel, J. (2016). Do sex offenders have higher levels of testosterone? Results from a meta-analysis. *Sexual Abuse: A Journal of Research and Treatment*, Online-First, 1–22.

Cell Phones in Prison

In most prisons, cell phones are forbidden items for incarcerated individuals. For prisoners, cell phones are banned, due to the ability of prisoners to communicate with persons outside the prison walls for nefarious reasons such as the intimidation of witnesses, management of their criminal enterprises, and to plot the murder of witnesses and state officials. Cell phones also allow inmates to use social media, plan and coordinate prison breaks, plan attacks on correctional officers within prisons, and to send and receive e-mail and text messages. In light of this, cell phones in prisons have been deemed a security threat by courts in the United States and their usage among federal and state prisoners is of grave concern to correctional administrators. Not surprisingly, corrections officials have identified the problem of cell phones in prisons as one of the toughest issues they face.

It has been argued that contraband cell phones usually find their way into prisons as a result of the outrageously high costs associated with making or receiving telephone calls from prescribed prison landline telephones. These cell phones are then used for numerous nefarious acts that jeopardize the safety and security of a host of individuals. Not all prisoners however, use cell phones for criminal acts, as some may use these illegally obtained cell phones to surf the Internet, communicate with family and friends, and to facilitate their continued presence on social media. For instance, in September 2012, an inmate in South Carolina used a contraband cell phone to alert prison officials about a correctional officer who was being held hostage by prisoners.

Prisoners' use of contraband cell phones is often intended to evade prison officials from listening in on their (prisoners') conversations. Prisoners secure these cell phones through a variety of methods. Some cell phones are smuggled into correctional facilities by corrupt prison staff who generally do not face stringent security checks as visitors do, as well as by corrupt visitors. Other means include the smuggling of cell phones into prisons via body orifices, throwing them over prison fences, launching them from a device called a potato cannon or spud gun, by hiding them in footballs and/or by inmates convicted of misdemeanors with lower security restrictions. In some instances, family members and friends are complicit in this act as they pay the monthly costs and maintenance fees for the contraband cell phones.

Contraband cell phones in prisons can cost a prisoner from $300 to $1,200 depending on the make, model, and capability of the phone. However, in an attempt to combat contraband cell phones in prisons, several jurisdictions have attached stiff penalties for prisoners found in possession of cell phones or for visitors and/or prison staff who are found guilty of smuggling or attempting to smuggle cell phones into prisons. Staff penalties range from disciplinary action to job loss and criminal charges; prisoners may face new criminal charges and lose sentence credit and/or the withdrawal of privileges, while visitors face stiff fines and/or imprisonment.

Wendell C. Wallace

See also: Inappropriate Correctional Employee–Inmate Relationships

Further Reading

Burke, T. W., & Owen, S. S. (2010). Cell phones as prison contraband. *FBI Law Enforcement Bulletin, 79*(7), 10–15.

Estevez., D. J., & Gutierrez, I. M. (2011). *Contraband cell phones in prisons: Technology solutions and perspectives.* New York: Nova Science.

Farber, B. J. (2008). Legal issues pertaining to inmate telephone use. (2) *AELE Monthly Law Journal* 301, Jail & Prisoner Law Section. Retrieved from http://www.aele.org /law/2008JBFEB/2008-2MLJ301.pdf

Goldman, R. (September 14, 2012). *Hostage prison guard saved by inmates' contraband cell phones.* ABC News. Retrieved from http://abcnews.go.com/US/sc-hostage -prison-guard-saved-inmates-contraband-cell/story?id=17238164

Locke, G., & Strickling, L. E. (2010). *Contraband cell phones in prisons: Possible wireless technology solutions.* U.S. Department of Commerce.

Rhoden-Trader, J., & Brunson, T. (2014). Fighting back against contraband cell phones: A corrections dilemma in an ever changing technology driven society. *International Journal of Humanities and Social Science, 4*(11–1), 1–8.

van Doorn, E., Bhat, A., Lonske, B., Guo, Z., Hovareshti, P., & Gaddam, S. (2015). *Time difference of arrival system for cell phone localization in correctional facilities.* U.S. Department of Justice.

China, Prisons in

The People's Republic of China (PRC) has one of the most controversial prison systems in the entire international community. There are several reasons for this, and among them are the fact that the Chinese tend to lack transparency on most issues related to crime, punishment, and human rights abuses. This is in spite of the fact that these are continual areas of concern among Western governments, including the State Department of the United States, Human Rights Watch researchers, and activists around the world.

The term used to refer to the Chinese prison system has traditionally been *laogai*, which simply means "reform through labor" (Seymour & Anderson, 1999; Wu, 2005). Although this was true for generations and although the concept of reform through labor continues to be the primary mode of facility operation in China, the government has attempted to distance itself from the specific term of *laogai* due to the negative publicity that it has received throughout the international community. Rather, the Chinese government now officially uses the term *prison,* hoping that this will be perceived as positive change by other countries and to give the impression that the Chinese system is similar to penal systems found in the West.

Although the historical circumstances have changed for China since the days of Chairman Mao Zedong's rule (1945–1976), including the changes since the end of the Cold War, the means of operation within Chinese prisons have remained constant. The only major difference has been that, unlike past historical circumstances where the majority of inmates were incarcerated for political reasons, most inmates in more recent years are incarcerated due to the commission of common crimes. Regardless, the use of the laogai method, through brutal suppression and exhausting labor requirements, remains intact.

Within the Chinese prison system, the primary slogan known to both staff and inmates alike is "reform first, production second." This means that political propaganda, brainwashing techniques, as well as conditions designed to break down one's resistance are pervasive within Chinese prisons and take priority over the amount of work that is completed by an inmate in a Chinese prison. In regard to production, the Chinese Ministry of Justice emphasizes the need to organize the inmate system of labor and production so that it is maximally efficient, thereby creating wealth for the People's Republic of China. In fact, there is widespread concern that

66 China, Prisons in

most of the amazingly low prices on goods produced in China that are exported throughout the world are, in fact, produced through prison labor. This is, of course, illegal by international trade standards but allows China to generate enormous amounts of revenue and, quite naturally, this then fuels the desire to build more prisons and keep those that exist full of productive inmates as a form of slave labor.

STRUCTURE AND POPULATION

In 1994, the People's Republic of China drafted and adopted what is referred to as the Prison Law, which largely is still in force today, with only a few notable revisions. This law held that the State Council judicial administration (known more commonly as the Ministry of Justice) would be responsible for the operation and supervision of prisons throughout the nation. However, this is parceled out among the various provinces of China (some are operated at the regional or city level of government), where offices of justice are tasked with managing prisons in their jurisdiction through their prison administrative sections of that localized government (Jiancang, 2014). Thus, each province (or occasionally a region or a city) with a prison located therein will have a Prison Administration Bureau, which then answers to the Ministry of Justice for the People's Republic of China.

According to data available through the Ministry of Justice, there are approximately 700 prisons throughout the nation of China, along with an additional 30 juvenile centers throughout the eastern part of the nation. In 2009, the ministry reported that there were approximately 320 reeducation camps but, in 2015, it was reported that these facilities had been closed. There was no explanation as to where individuals in reeducation facilities were sent or how this transition took place (Institute for Criminal Policy Research, 2015). Lastly, it is unknown how many persons are in pretrial detention and/or special detention facilities for drug and/or prostitution crimes.

Information from the Ministry of Justice indicates that, within the actual prison population alone, there are approximately 2,300,000 incarcerated individuals. When compared to the overall population of China (approximately 1.4 billion people in 2015), this would make the rate of incarceration in the PRC somewhere around 164 per 100,000 people. It is estimated that another 250,000 or so pretrial detainees also are incarcerated for a period of approximately three months or so at any given time throughout the year based on numbers provided by the Supreme People's Procuratorate (Institute for Criminal Policy Research, 2015).

ADMINISTRATION AND ORDER

According to the Ministry of Justice (2009), offenders are classified by the nature of their crime, the type of penalty they have received, the length of their sentence, their age, gender, and other characteristics. The overarching idea is that inmates are not housed in a manner that contributes to their potential victimization. In no case are women housed with men, nor are juvenile offenders kept with adult offenders.

Officers within the facility are referred to as prison police; they are tasked with maintaining order and security inside the prison. As the Ministry of Justice (MOJ) indicates, the use of restrictive or preventative devices on inmates should be reserved for those offenders who commit dangerous acts. The MOJ notes that such devices should not be used on inmates who have an advanced illness or are advanced in age. Likewise, the MOJ (2009) notes that such devices are to only be used on female inmates in the rarest of circumstances. In all cases, such devices should not be used on inmates who are involved in labor activities supervised by prison authorities. Lastly, armed police and prison police may use firearms only in emergencies when there are serious emergency situations in maintaining inmate compliance.

In regard to living conditions, the MOJ (2009) notes that adult inmates are normally expected to work 8 hours a day, with any extended work hours being approved by prison authorities to fulfill production plans. In addition, the MOJ has indicated that inmates are to be given 2 hours of daily study time as well as a full 8 hours of sleep, every day. Further, juvenile offenders are only expected to work half a day and study half a day, with sleep granted being no less than 8 hours, daily. Youth are not expected to work in a manner that is beyond their physical abilities.

Lastly, the MOJ requires that inmates should be given time, every day, for cultural or sport activities and that they should have all statutory holidays and weekends off. This is in addition to the expectation that food and beverages provided be equivalent to those provided to laborers at other local- and state-owned enterprises of similar conditions. The MOJ goes further to note that prison kitchens should be managed by staff who make efforts to improve dietary offerings as much as is possible within the facility (2009).

From the information provided by the MOJ, it would seem that China provides for a very reasonable set of standards for prison operations. The likely truth to these posted statements is questionable, of course. The fact that the People's Republic of China is so restrictive in allowing access to prison facilities further diminishes the credibility of the public stance provided by the MOJ.

FEMALE OFFENDERS

In China, there has been a rise in the rate of women who are incarcerated. Indeed, the current rate of women who are incarcerated is thought to have increased by nearly 50 percent, during the past decade, as opposed to the much slower rate of growth—10 percent—for the male prison population (Dui Hua, 2016; Hatton, 2015). In 2015, it was estimated that more than 107,000 women were officially incarcerated in China (Dui Hua, 2016). Currently, female offenders are only 6 percent of the prison population in China. However, if incarceration trends continue, it is estimated that within five years, China will have more women in prison than the United States, which has the world's largest prison population (Dui Hua, 2016; Hatton, 2015). While it is known that female prisons tend to be overcrowded, little is known about their specific conditions. Problems associated with accommodating female inmates are similar to those encountered in other countries, including issues of being the primary caretaker for children. Also, most Chinese female offenders have characteristics of offenders in other countries, being convicted of nonviolent crimes, poorly educated, and unmarried, with histories of abuse and substance misuse. To further exacerbate these conditions, it is known that Chinese prisons do not have family visits on a routine basis, meaning that most female offenders cannot see their family (including children) consistently. Further still, official programming is not provided to female offenders. Rather, any assistance gained is through prison correctional officers or, when allowed, volunteers. Thus, it would appear that China is ill-equipped to address its growing rate of female offenders who are incarcerated. This is not unlike experiences of many other nations that saw growth among their female offender population. However, in most other circumstances, other nations are much more transparent than are the Chinese, making it even more likely that this group of offenders will be denied adequate and gender-responsive health care and support systems (Dui Hua, 2016; Hatton, 2015).

REFORM

In 2004, China's Second Session of the Tenth National People's Congress passed an amendment to its basic law, the Constitution of the People's Republic of China, where it was intended to showcase China's willingness to protect human rights (Jiancang, 2014). Since this time, a series of white papers have shown improvements in addressing human rights, newspaper releases that showcase positive developments in Chinese penology, and press releases to highlight advances have been seen.

However, human rights abuses by the Chinese government have been widely publicized and, for the most part, are not debated by most anyone but the Chinese government itself. Hundreds of personal accounts of torture, inhumane deprivations, and cruel forms of exploitative working conditions have been recounted during the past 10 to 20 years to external governments, advocacy groups, and new agencies (Human Rights Watch, 2009). The U.S. Department of State remains skeptical and critical of improvements in human rights issues related to China, both in regard to prison operations, as well as the fundamental fairness of processes that lead to incarceration.

It would appear that the prison system of the People's Republic of China maintains standards of care and treatment that would be viewed as abusive by most other developed countries throughout the world. The fact that the PRC maintains such strict secrecy by restricting access to these facilities heightens suspicion in regard to inmate treatment. It is clear that, though reforms have been made, at least as claimed by Chinese news sources, the prison population is viewed as an economic tool. When such economic exploitation is allowed to persist behind a shroud of secrecy, it becomes questionable whether the PRC will ever have sufficient incentive to truly improve human rights conditions to a standard that is considered appropriate by the modern world of correctional practice.

Robert D. Hanser

See also: Incarceration Rates in the United States Compared to Other Countries; Punishment Philosophies; Treatment in Prisons

Further Reading

Dikotter, F. (2002). The promise of repentance: Prison reform in modern China. *British Journal of Criminology, 42*(2), 240–249.

Dui Hua. (2016). *2015 Annual report.* San Francisco: Author.

Hatton, C. (2015, June 25). *Why is China's female prison population growing?* British Broadcast News. Retrieved from http://www.bbc.com/news/blogs-china-blog-332 68611

Human Rights Watch. (2009). *China: Secret "black jails" hide severe rights abuses: Unlawful detention facilities breed violence, threats, extortion.* Retrieved from https://www.hrw.org/news/2009/11/11/china-secret-black-jails-hide-severe-rights-abuses

Institute for Criminal Policy Research. (2015). *World prison brief: China.* London: Institute for Criminal Policy Research.

Jiancang, F. (2014). *Inmates' rights protection in China's prisons.* Beijing: China Society for Human Rights Studies.

Ministry of Justice. (2009). *Prison administration.* Beijing: Ministry of Justice, People's Republic of China.

Seymour, J. D., & Anderson, R. (1999). *New ghosts, old ghosts: Prison and labor reform camps in China.* New York: Routledge.

Wu, H. (2005). *Congressional-Executive Commission on China Roundtable on forced labor in China.* Washington, DC: State Department of the United States.

Civil Commitment and Postcriminal Sanctions for Sex Offenders

Mental health conditions are common for many Americans, and researchers suggest that approximately one in five adults annually experience some sort of mental illness. Estimates expand to 20 percent of state prison inmates who currently suffer from a mental health condition. Yet despite the high frequency of mental illness in civilian and incarcerated populations in the United States, many individuals do not receive medical or psychiatric help for their symptoms. Jail and prison inmates are even less likely than civilians to receive help, mainly due to budget deficits.

Mental illness can be a contributing factor as to why individuals commit offenses—in this case, sex offenses. During manic episodes, individuals can engage in sexual deviance that leads to arrest and subsequent conviction of a sex crime. Although researchers have mixed opinions on the connections between sexual offenses and mental health conditions, a significant amount of research suggests that sex offenders have higher rates of mental illness compared to individuals who do not sexually offend. Recent research suggests that male sex offenders are six times more likely to display mental health symptoms, and even be hospitalized, compared to men in the general population.

Sex offenders are commonly divided into two groups—those who are opportunistic and those who are paraphilic. Those who are opportunistic typically do not have strong victim preferences or offending scripts. Those who are paraphilic often meet the criteria for a specific paraphilia listed in the *Diagnostic and Statistical Manual of Mental Disorders* (DSM-5). In order to be diagnosed with a specific paraphilia, an individual must meet two qualifications. First, the individual must experience distress in relation to the specific sexual desire. This can be self-induced distress related to personal shame, or it can result from societal pressures. Second, the individual must experience "a sexual desire or behavior that involves another person's psychological distress, injury, or death, or a desire for sexual behaviors involving unwilling persons or persons unable to give legal consent" (American Psychiatric Association, 2013). Common paraphilias extend to child victims (pedophilia), personal harm or humiliation (sexual masochism), or the harm or humiliation of a willing or unwilling partner (sexual masochism).

Traditionally, civil commitment programs have been used for the involuntary hospitalization of any individual who needs psychiatric intervention. States have the legal ability to protect citizens from harming themselves or others, if they pose a threat or are considered dangerous, during a mental health incident. Often the hospitalization is of a short duration, and treatment can be maintained by an outpatient treatment provider. For sexual offenders who are deemed "sexually violent predators," involuntary hospitalization can last for years at a time.

CIVIL COMMITMENT IN THE UNITED STATES

Currently, sex offender civil commitment is used in 20 states throughout the country and the federal government, which created civil commitment provisions within the passage of the Adam Walsh Act of 2006. Of these states, 13 allow for juvenile sex offenders to be civilly committed in addition to their adult counterparts. Sex offender civil commitment programs were established due, in part, to the rising concerns surrounding high rates of sexual offense recidivism. Civil commitment is built around the incapacitation model of institutionalization, which suggests that if offenders are removed from an environment in which they can reoffend then they will be unable to reoffend. While they are removed from the community, sexually violent predators (SVPs) would have access to rehabilitation programs, thus lowering recidivism rates even further. However, research suggests that in general, sexual offense recidivism levels are 5.3 percent over a three-year period and are between 13 and 15 percent after five years. However, when examining offense specific groups, the recidivism rates differ quite significantly.

As of 2016, nearly 5,400 individuals are currently supervised by state or federal sexually violent predator programs. This equates to 0.6 percent of the total population of registered sex offenders who are civilly committed in the United States. SVP programs require the individual to be convicted of a sexually violent crime and to be diagnosed with a mental health condition that causes them to be a safety risk. Individuals deemed SVPs can be institutionalized indefinitely until the state determines that they no longer are at a high risk for sexual recidivism. Typically, civil commitment occurs after the SVP is released from prison. Commitment centers often report low release rates of SVPs—some having never released a client. Recent research discussing the frequency of SVP release rates has caused many treatment programs to become the recipients of harsh criticism for not discharging patients and has caused some to question the rigor of the treatment programs themselves.

Before an SVP can be involuntarily hospitalized, the state must complete risk assessments for the individual in question. Most jurisdictions use the Static-99R (developed by R. Karl Hanson and David Thornton), which comprises 10 items that can be used to evaluate adult male sex offenders. The Static-99R evaluates offenders based on a number of criteria including the age of the offender, prior history of nonsexual violence, prior history of sex offenses, having been previously sentenced to a criminal sentence, prior history of noncontact sexual offenses, and the type of individual victimized during the offense.

Research suggests that those offenders who are younger than 25 years of age, who never had an intimate adult relationship lasting more than two years, who have an official history of nonsexual violence, who have an official history of sexual offenses, and who have unrelated, stranger, or male victims all have higher rates of recidivism than their item counterparts. The Static-99R coding form allows for a tallied score from 0 to 12 points. Most of the 10 items are scored using a 0 or 1 dichotomous score sheet, with the exception of the prior history of sexual offense items, which are scored from 0 to 3 based on the number of prior convictions an offender has. Any individual who scores a 6 or higher is then considered high risk and likely to recidivate. This offender is then compared to others in the same jurisdiction who have been evaluated for similar risk factors and outcomes.

Once committed, SVPs are required to attend treatment programs that vary in intensity and weekly duration. Some offenders only receive a few hours of treatment per week, whereas others attend 30-plus hours of counseling and treatment. Most programs are similar in design, relying heavily on cognitive-behavioral treatment structures and the use of group therapy techniques.

CONSTITUTIONAL CHALLENGES

Although 20 states plus the federal government have civil commitment programs, they have not gone without criticism and review. Many have objected based on legal and ethical considerations as to whether the indefinite institutionalization of sexually violent predators is in violation of the offenders' constitutional protections. The U.S. Supreme Court has heard three cases reviewing the constitutionality of state and federal sex offender civil commitment programs. All three cases have resulted in rulings suggesting that the programs are not in conflict with the safeguards protecting the offenders' constitutional rights.

In 1997, the U.S. Supreme Court reviewed the case *Kansas v. Hendricks*, which called into question the Kansas Sexually Violent Predator Act. The act established Kansas's first civil commitment program in which the state was authorized to indefinitely detain any offenders who were evaluated as high risk. The offenders could be detained after the completion of an incarceration sentence. The petitioner, Leroy Hendricks, had an extensive history of child molestation convictions and was involuntarily committed under the new law. Hendricks argued that the new law violated his double jeopardy and due process protections, and that it was in violation of the ex-post facto clause embedded in Article 1 of the Constitution.

The U.S. Supreme Court disagreed with Hendricks and upheld the Kansas Sexually Violent Predator Act in a 5–4 vote. In the ruling the state's threshold for commitment—establishing a debilitating "mental abnormality or personality disorder" that caused the offender to lose all self-control—was acceptable. But the court did not make a recommendation as to where the threshold should be in determining what loss of self-control actually meant. Additionally, the court stated that the law established a civil protection and did not establish criminal proceedings, and therefore it was constitutional since it was not punitive in nature.

Five years after the *Hendricks* ruling, the Kansas Sexually Violent Predator Act was once again challenged when the court reviewed the act in *Kansas v. Crane* (2002). In this case the petitioner, Michael Crane, challenged the *Hendricks* ruling and the court's failure to establish the threshold surrounding a total loss of self-control. In a 7–2 decision, the U.S. Supreme Court ruled that the state must evaluate all offenders' control levels prior to detainment, but that a total lack of control was not necessary to establish. With this ruling, the state only had to determine that the offender had a mental health condition and that he was unable to control his behavior.

In the third and final challenge, the federal civil commitment policies established in the Adam Walsh Act (2006) were reviewed in *United States v. Comstock* (2010). In this case, several convicted sex offenders in federal prison custody were about to be released upon completion of their sentences. However, the attorney general had already classified them as sexually violent predators, which required them to be indefinitely detained under the civil commitment provisions of the Adam Walsh Act. In challenging the law, lower federal appeals courts determined that the law was unconstitutional and overstepped congressional power. The U.S. Supreme Court disagreed and in a 7–2 ruling reversed the lower court's decision.

The court ruled that the federal civil commitment was constitutional, based on the necessary and proper clause that allows for further detainment of individuals already in federal custody. No further challenges have been made in objection to civil commitment laws. Civil commitment laws have been upheld by the U.S. Supreme Court and continue to be used by 20 states and the federal system, despite objections to their legal and ethical value.

Jennifer L. Klein

See also: Sex Offenders in Prison

Further Reading

American Psychiatric Association. (2013). *Diagnostic and statistical manual of mental disorders* (5th ed.). Washington, DC: Author.

Duwe, G. (2014). To what extent does civil commitment reduce sexual recidivism? Estimating the selective incapacitation effects in Minnesota. *Journal of Criminal Justice, 42,* 193–202.

Kansas v. Crane, 534 U.S. 407 (2002).

Kansas v. Hendricks, 521 U.S. 346 (1997).

Knighton, J. C., Murrie, D. C., Boccaccini, M. T., & Turner, D. B. (2014). How likely is "likely to reoffend" in sex offender civil commitment trials? *Law and Human Behavior, 38*(3), 293–304.

Levenson, J. (2004). Sexual predator civil commitment: A comparison of selected and released offenders. *International Journal of Offender Therapy and Comparative Criminology, 48*(6), 638–648.

Levenson, J., Prescott, D. S., & Jumper, S. (2014). A consumer satisfaction survey of civilly committed sex offenders in Illinois. *International Journal of Offender Therapy and Comparative Criminology, 58*(4), 474–495.

Lu, Y., Freeman, N. J., & Sandler, J. C. (2015). Predictors of the sex offender civil commitment trial outcomes in New York State. *Law and Human Behavior, 39*(5), 514–524.

Testa, M., & West, S. G. (2010). Civil commitment in the United States. *Psychiatry, 7*(10), 30–40.

United States v. Comstock, 560 U.S. 126 (2010).

Wilson, R. J., Looman, J., Abracen, J., & Pake, D. R., Jr. (2013). Comparing sexual offenders at the Regional Treatment Center (Ontario) and the Florida Civil Commitment Center. *International Journal of Offender Therapy and Comparative Criminology, 57*(3), 377–395.

Civil Disabilities

Nearly 20 million adults living in the United States are estimated to have a felony conviction (Shannon et al., 2011). Of that number, about one-fifth are currently under correctional supervision. Unlike misdemeanor convictions, having a felony conviction has historically been associated with losing certain civil and political rights based on the fact that one's reputation or trust becomes tarnished in the eyes of the community. As a result, people with felony convictions not only have their criminal sentence to serve, but they also face long-lasting barriers that may remain for the rest of their lives. These limitations are known as "civil disabilities" or "collateral consequences," and they vary widely in number and duration within each state.

Many theories abound as to why civil disabilities became possible in the first place. Historically, some believe that it was to preserve confidence in government and other positions of trust. Others believe that disabilities were expanded to keep certain classes of persons outside of regular society—similar to a form of permanent banishment or civil death. As social welfare and pension programs were reduced, qualifying for these programs became more difficult. Law-abiding persons argued that they should not have to compete with a person who has broken the law.

Although some civil disabilities apply to persons convicted of a federal felony offense, most disabilities are left up to each individual state to decide for state-level felony offenders. Thus, what may be restricted in one state is possible in another state. Also, some civil disabilities are temporarily lost only during incarceration, and/or community correctional supervision, while others are permanently lost for the rest of one's life, unless measures have been taken to restore one's civil rights. Some restrictions are specifically limited to only certain types of felony offenses, such as drug-related or sex-related crimes (Alarid, 2017). There are 10 types of civil disabilities that are most common:

Becoming Occupational Licensed or Certified. Each state occupational licensing board regulates laws that define job qualifications that apply in their state. For example, some licensing boards will disqualify all felony convictions. Nearly half of all states now require that the licensing board show how the conviction was related to the knowledge, skills, and abilities for that particular job. For example, a locksmith licensing board would have no trouble convincing the state that a person who was convicted of breaking and entering or burglary should not become licensed as a locksmith.

Getting Hired for a Job. Some states have also passed legislation that regulates what kinds of information employers can ask on initial job applications, unless the employer can show that the question is necessary to a particular job. This legislation is known as "ban-the-box" because it allows convicted felons to not have to disclose their criminal background until later in the hiring process (Uggen et al., 2014).

Public Housing Eligibility. The U.S. Department of Housing and Urban Development (HUD) supports public housing agencies that ban felony convictions when they are not suitable for tenancy, such as registered sex offenders and individuals who were convicted for manufacturing methamphetamine on public housing property. Eligibility for public housing narrowed significantly when public housing agencies routinely used arrest records, rather than conviction records, to deny housing and/or evict existing tenants. Although landlords can still exercise discretion, HUD no longer allows the presence of an arrest record by itself as evidence to deny housing.

Jury Duty. Felons may not serve on a jury (half of all states), and a felony conviction can be brought up to a judge or jury in order to purposefully discredit their testimony.

Voting Rights. Felons are generally prohibited from voting during correctional supervision or while in confinement. Once the sentence has been completed, voting rights can be restored in all but 12 states. However, nearly 6 million citizens in 12 states will not be allowed to vote because of a felony conviction. When the right to vote, considered a fundamental right in democratic societies, is lost, this is also known as "felony disenfranchisement." An increasing number of states have loosened eligibility and have now restored this right after the sentence is complete.

Possession of Firearms. The limits on firearm possession for convicted felons depend mainly on whether the felony conviction is a federal or state conviction. For any federal felony conviction, federal law prohibits possession or any related activity to firearms or ammunition, even if state law allows it in the state that the federal offender happens to reside (*Beecham v. United States,* 1994). For state felony convictions, states can choose to adopt federal law or to make exceptions. Some states will allow firearm restrictions to be eventually restored with the passage of time and no new felony convictions.

Parental Rights and Custody. For long-term prison confinement or life sentences, about one in five states allow the other nonincarcerated parent to sever parental rights. Since most terms of confinement will result in release, most states will award other suitable family members temporary custody until the parent with the conviction is finished with the sentence and is in a stable environment to apply for permanent custody. For crimes committed by a parent against one or more children where the continuation of the convicted parent's relationship with that child threatens their safety, parental rights are terminated.

Financial Aid Eligibility. College students who are convicted of any misdemeanor or felony drug offense during the time they receive federal financial aid for school are ineligible to receive future financial aid for a minimum of one year and indefinitely for repeat convictions. Half of all states also disqualify students from state financial aid programs.

Eligibility for Food Stamps and Welfare Benefits. The Temporary Assistance for Needy Families Act denies food stamps and welfare benefits to anyone convicted of possession/sale of drugs. However, like most of the federal bans, states are allowed to opt out or to make exceptions because of the negative impact this ban has on dependent children. Only 11 states have chosen to deny welfare benefits to convicted drug offenders (Ewald, 2012).

Eligibility for Social Security, Disability, and Medicaid. An incarcerated offender becomes ineligible for Social Security, Social Security Disability Insurance, Supplemental Security Income, and Medicaid. This is because an offender's food, clothing, and shelter needs are already met by the institution. Once released, federal benefits can begin again, but reapplication takes between two to three months—one month to become eligible to get the benefits reinstated, and then the payment comes one month later in arrears. If offenders need to reapply for benefits because they were confined longer than one year, they need to provide proof of the date they were released from jail or prison. Some prison reentry programs have begun to help offenders start the application process once they have a parole or release date scheduled in writing.

More recently, concerns about the high number of collateral consequences and the subjective interpretation of existing limitations have caused convicted felons to be quickly excluded from too many programs and opportunities that might help them become law-abiding citizens. Due to the potential for discrimination in the areas of housing and employment, the political tide seems to have turned away from blanket and permanent exclusion policies to requiring landlords, employers, and other gatekeepers to more specifically list types of criminal activities that it makes sense to exclude.

Leanne Fiftal Alarid

See also: Capital Punishment, Collateral Consequences of; Prisoner Reentry/Family Integration; Restoration of Rights after Conviction

Further Reading
Alarid, L. F. (2017). *Community-based corrections* (11th ed.). Boston: Cengage.

Beecham v. United States, 511 U.S. 368 (1994).

Ewald, A. C. (2012). Collateral consequences in the American states. *Social Science Quarterly, 93*(1), 211–247.

National Inventory of the Collateral Consequences of Conviction. Retrieved from http://www.abacollateralconsequences.org

Shannon, S., Uggen, C., Thompson, M., Schnittker, J., & Massoglia, M. (2011). *Growth in the U.S. ex-felon and ex-prisoner population, 1948 to 2010.* An unpublished paper available online at http://paa2011.princeton.edu/papers/111687

Uggen, C., Vuolo, M., Lageson, S., Ruhland, E., & Whitham, H. K. (2014). The edge of stigma: An experimental audit of the effects of low-level criminal records on employment. *Criminology, 52*(4), 627–654.

Cleanliness in Prison

Correctional facilities were initially built to house prisoners, reduce crime in society, and to increase the public's well-being. However, in recent times, the health, welfare, and personal hygiene of inmates in the United States and abroad have come into light in privately run and public prisons. Presidential candidate Hilary Rodham Clinton stated during the first publicly televised presidential debate on September 26, 2016, that it may be time to end privatized prisons in the United States. In her statements she reiterated that prisons today are more focused on profit than on the prisoners themselves. She claimed the profits were not being used equitably to properly maintain private facilities to include cleanliness. As of today, many lawmakers would like to see private correctional facilities be completely phased out at the state and federal levels. If funds are not spent correctly, and correctional facilities are not maintained, inmates will face illness, exposure to contagious infectious diseases, and many other ailments and threats.

Internationally, the United States' allies work diligently to communicate the same cleanliness standards among populations. The Geneva Conventions act as a guiding light for domestic and international prison regulations and cleanliness. The Geneva Conventions demand clean facilities and fair treatment for all prisoners. The United Nations has published an international policy titled *Standard Minimum Rules for Treatment of Prisoners,* which outlines that correctional facilities must keep all areas of the correctional facility meticulously clean and orderly. In certain facilities in the United States, only common areas, cafeterias, restrooms, and living quarters are kept moderately clean. However, more and more public and private facilities in the United States are adopting new polices to ensure that all areas of a facility are addressed. For example, the Wisconsin Secure Program Facility in Boscobel, Wisconsin, has adopted the *No-Touch Cleaning Method.* This method removes two-thirds more contaminants from surfaces than traditional cleaning, thus reducing the risk of spreading communicable diseases and other germs throughout a facility.

In theory, if correctional facilities adopt strict physical cleanliness protocols, then it communicates a message to inmates that personal hygiene is just as important as maintaining a clean facility. It is imperative to understand that when inmates are incarcerated and are in contact with one another, they are at greater risk for infection, sickness, blood-borne pathogens, and contamination. In today's era, prisoners can easily get STDs, staph infections, influenza, and many other viruses and bacterial infections. If all areas of the facility are actively cleaned and maintained, it can reduce the above-stated risks.

Cleanliness in Prison

However, there are many challenges to implementing such policies and procedures, including allocated funding and overcrowding in local, state, and federal facilities. Housing in each of these facilities typically has four inmates to a three-person room. Open dormitories often exceed the allotted number of individuals permitted in a room. In overcrowding scenarios, housing areas and in open dormitories, it is more difficult to control the spread of contagious illnesses such as colds, the norovirus, and other common ailments. Further, access to personal hygiene products can be difficult due to the cost and demand of products while incarcerated. As a result of overcrowding, access to showers, toilets, sinks, and other required facilities is drastically reduced.

In addition to overcrowding and funding, many correctional facilities do not have the resources to staff a custodial team to maintain the facilities. Many facilities rely on the inmate population to fill these vacancies. One of the biggest challenges with using inmates as custodial staff members is their lack of training, education, and access to cleaning equipment and supplies. In order to effectively and efficiently clean a correctional facility, cleaning equipment, chemicals, and supplies are needed to prevent the spread of bacteria, germs, and communicable diseases. However, due to the danger and hazards that each of these resources have, inmate custodial staff are limited to basic tools such as brooms, mops, and dish soap.

Another component to maintaining cleanliness in correctional facilities is to have a well-organized laundry program established. Inmates are typically issued a specific set of garments to wear from the facility including socks, underwear, jumpsuit, coveralls, long sleeve shirts, T-shirts, shower shoes, etc. If additional garments are needed, prisoners often have to purchase these items with independent funds. Dependent on the facility, some have inmates serve on a laundry detail that washes all of the prison garments on a specific cycle and day of the week. Further, the garments are washed with vetted cleaning materials in commercial washers and dryers. Inmates are then reissued garments on a rotational cycle. One of the challenges is that bleach and other strong detergents are banned within correctional facilities due to their ingredients and dangers to the prison population. This can make it difficult to address blood and other bodily fluids that may appear on clothing and prisoner garments.

In sum, cleanliness and personal hygiene in correctional facilities today are the key to maintaining a healthy prison population and workforce. These strategies and suggestions can be implemented with the proper leadership, funding, and dedication from both internal and external stakeholders.

Thomas James Rzemyk

See also: Health Care in Prison Populations; Prison Work Programs

Further Reading

Abgoola, C. (2016). Memories of the 'inside': Prison conditions in South African female correctional facilities. *South African Crime Quarterly, 56*, 19–26.

Bick, J. A. (2007). Infection control in jails and prisons. *Clinical Infectious Diseases, 45*(8), 1047–1055.

Cleaning Industry Research Institute—CIRI. (2016). *Cleaning machine: Wisconsin prison adopts No-Touch Cleaning*. Albany, NY: Author.

Clinton, H. (2016, September 26). *United States Presidential Debate.*

A guide to health needs assessment in Scottish prisons. (2006). Edinburgh: Scottish Prison Service/NHS Scotland.

Primary health care. Report of the International Conference on Primary Health Care, Alma-Ata, USSR, September 6–12, 1978. Geneva: World Health Organization (Health for All Series, No. 1).

Sloan, J. (2012). 'You can see your face in my floor': Examining the function of cleanliness in an adult male prison. *The Howard Journal of Criminal Justice, 51*(4), 400–410.

United Nations Office on Drugs and Crime. (2016). *Standard minimum rules for treatment of prisoners.* Vienna, Austria: Author.

Cognitive-Behavioral Therapies in Prison

Cognitive-behavioral therapy (CBT) is a treatment approach that attempts to address and turn around dysfunctional thoughts (or cognitions) and behaviors in a relatively short period of time. Although the term captures a broad range of prison programming, CBT begins with the assumption that behaviors are the result of problematic or dysfunctional thinking patterns. In the correctional setting, CBT programs typically try to target thinking patterns associated with criminal offending, substance use, or criminal associations. Even though the term is used to refer to a wide variety of correctional processes and programs, the shared foundational argument is that offenders can change core aspects of their thinking patterns and that this will impact subsequent behavioral outcomes including the decision to commit crime. If successful, CBT will help offenders make constructive and prosocial choices in the future. Programs based on CBT principles have become very prominent in American corrections because they can be used in almost any setting (prisons, jails, community-based), can be facilitated by almost any staff member with minimal training, are relatively cheap to administer, and can help reduce recidivism with proper implementation.

As the name implies, CBT combines core features from two prominent theoretical paradigms: cognitive therapy and behavioral therapy. The two approaches are united under the assumption that thinking affects behavior. Those individuals who display antisocial, distorted, and irrational thinking are more likely to act out, have spotty employment histories, have poor and dysfunctional relationships, and use and abuse drugs. Thus, if the goal is to change behavior (i.e., make it less likely that individuals will offend again after prison), then practitioners need to change how prisoners think. The cognitive component of CBT focuses on individual assumptions, beliefs, and thinking patterns. How people act, according to this perspective, is partially determined by how they interpret circumstances and situations. Change is achieved by encouraging clients to be more aware of the connections between thoughts and actions, and especially the way clients think about their life circumstances. Cognitive theory emphasizes that, while individuals may be able to do little about the circumstances they encounter, they can do a lot about how they perceive and interpret these circumstances. The behavioral therapy component of CBT builds on the cognitive component by drawing on psychological

Cognitive-Behavioral Therapies in Prison 79

concepts of social learning as well as the use of rewards and punishments to shape behavior. Behavioral therapy stresses that simply recognizing maladaptive thought patterns is insufficient. Rather, the therapy must provide the client with the right tools to change behavior. This can occur through modeling and practice, or it can occur by adopting principles of operating conditioning, where behavior is met and either reinforced or eliminated with appropriate rewards and punishments.

Combined, then, the cognitive component of CBT helps practitioners determine what to change, and the behavioral component helps practitioners determine how to change it. The "what" in this case are maladaptive thinking patterns, and the "how" are approaches that include rewards, punishments, modeling, and practice. In the correctional setting, criminal justice researchers and practitioners have developed a range of measurement techniques to quantify and categorize antisocial and criminal-thinking patterns. This information is often a component of risk and needs assessments that help prison staff create individualized treatment plans. In addition, a host of surveys have been developed to specifically measure criminal thinking in the correctional population. For example, the Psychological Inventory of Criminal Thinking Styles (PICTS) is an 80-item self-report survey instrument designed to measure how criminals think. Similarly, the Criminal Thinking Scale (CTS), developed by Texas Christian University (TCU), is a 37-item self-report survey instrument meant to capture current or recent criminal thinking patterns. Offenders who score high on these scales are more likely to have thinking patterns associated with serious criminal behavior.

These scales, and others, have been useful in helping researchers and practitioners determine those thought processes that distinguish offenders from nonoffenders. For example, research shows that crime-involved citizens tend to perceive the world in a more fatalistic fashion than nonoffenders. That is, they tend to believe that there is little they can do to change the circumstances in their lives. This is combined with high levels of mollification, meaning that offenders tend to minimize the seriousness of their actions by looking to external circumstances for justification. Offenders also display high levels of entitlement, meaning they feel a strong sense of ownership and privilege leading to a misidentification of wants as needs. Finally, offenders tend to have overall negative views of law enforcement and the criminal justice system. Those who do not see the legitimacy of the criminal justice system are less likely to abide by its rules.

Cognitive-behavioral therapies offered in the correctional setting focus on changing these procriminal thinking patterns. Although there are a wide range of programs and curriculum that have been developed for correctional use, there are a number of features common to CBT programs. Broadly stated, most CBT approaches go about achieving change by first helping offenders define the problems and thought patterns that led them into contact with the criminal justice system. Clients are then encouraged to select current and future goals and generate new prosocial solutions to achieving these goals. Finally, CBT programs work on implementing these solutions through modeling, reinforcement, and practice. Programs are typically offered in highly structured classroom-like settings to groups of 8 to 12 participants. Groups meet once or twice a week and work through lessons individually, in small groups, and as a class as a whole. Manuals and workbooks are common features of CBT programs, which involve skills and activities including written exercises, role play, rehearsal, and homework assignments.

Of vital importance to the success of CBT programs is the counselor or course facilitator. The facilitators do not simply take attendance and make sure that participants make their way through the course materials. Rather, they take an active role in helping clients set new goals and solutions. Successful counselors interact with participants in open and enthusiastic ways, act as prosocial role models, and are the front line in approving (reinforcing) or disapproving (punishing) participant behavior. Ideal facilitators will have background training in areas such as mental health or chemical dependency, but this is typically not a required component for facilitator eligibility.

There is no shortage of programs and curriculum that adopt principles of CBT, but only a handful of these have met the rigorous standards of evidence-based practices. That is, not all programs have been evaluated using statistical designs including random assignment (where some offenders receive the program and others, a control group, do not). Perhaps the best known, and most widely used program is Thinking for a Change (T4C), a 25-lesson curriculum designed in collaboration with the National Institute of Corrections. Participating offenders meet in groups of 8 to 12 ideally two times per week to complete the program. Like many CBT programs, T4C starts by having participants examine thoughts and attitudes. It is then coupled with social-skills training with an emphasis on alternative behaviors. Participants are encouraged to implement these new skills through various problem-solving exercises. Other common CBT curricula include Aggression Replacement Training (ART), Strategies for Self-Improvement and Change, Moving On, Reasoning and Rehabilitation (R&R), and Controlling Anger and Learning to Manage It (CALM).

The most common metric of program success is recidivism, or a return to prison within some specified time period. By this metric, the evidence is fairly positive that CBT programs delivered with fidelity can shift thinking patterns and ultimately decrease recidivism rates. However, it is important to note that only focusing on recidivism is a limited view of the potential effectiveness of CBT programs. Beyond criminal offending, prisoners tend to display a range of deficits including poor employment histories, dysfunctional relationships, and high rates of substance abuse. As a broad theory of change, CBT can lead to better outcomes across these domains by focusing on the present (rather than the past) and basing the approaches in active learning. By focusing on setting goals and implementing prosocial approaches to meeting these goals, involvement in criminal behavior should decrease while involvement in prosocial behavior should increase. Thus, the benefit of CBT programs extends well beyond criminal justice outcomes.

Cody Warner and Jacob Doneux

See also: Evidence-Based Practice in Corrections; Treatment in Prisons; Treatment Professionals in Prisons

Further Reading

Landenberger, N. A., & Lipsey, M. W. (2005). The positive effects of cognitive-behavioral programs for offenders: A meta-analysis of factors associated with effective treatment. *Journal of Experimental Criminology, 1*(4), 451–476.

Lowenkamp, C. T., Hubbard, D., Markarios, M. D., & Latessa, E. J. (2009). A quasi-experimental evaluation of thinking for a change: A 'real world' application. *Criminal Justice and Behavior, 36*(2), 137–146.

Milkman, H., & Wanberg, K. (2007). *Cognitive-behavioral treatment: A review and discussion for corrections professionals.* Washington, DC: U.S. Department of Justice.

Taxman, F. S., Rhodes, A. G., & Dumenci, L. (2011). Construct and predictive validity of criminal thinking scales. *Criminal Justice and Behavior, 38*(2), 174–187.

Walters, G. D. (2016). Proactive and reactive criminal thinking, psychological inertia, and the crime continuity conundrum. *Journal of Criminal Justice, 46*, 45–51.

Wilson, D. B., Bouffard, L. A., & Mackenzie, D. L. (2005). A quantitative review of structured, group-oriented, cognitive-behavioral programs for offenders. *Criminal Justice and Behavior, 32*(2), 172–204.

Commissary

The prison commissary, also referred to as the canteen, operates as a store in the prison and sells various products to inmates. Generally, corporations contract with prison facilities to allow them to sell their goods and services to prisoners and their families. It is not uncommon for commissary items to be similar in prices to stores outside of prison, or in some instances, cost more. As a result, prison commissaries act as a mechanism of prison profitability. For example, commissary sales have been linked to funding prison amenities such as cable television.

Generally, upon first arrival at the facility, a commissary account is established for a prisoner. Money earned from prison jobs or deposited funds from family and friends in an inmate's commissary account are used to shop at the store. The federal prison system regulates how much inmates can spend at the commissary every month. The permitted amount per month varies among prisons and can range between $105 and $300 dollars. The operations and commissary list of items for sale can also differ among prison institutions. Examples of purchasable items in a prison commissary include ramen noodles, soda, chips, packaged meat, pastries, cheeses, cookies, candy, toiletries, stationary items, clothing, and other goods. Inmates may also have access to various brands of cigarettes or loose tobacco at the commissary. Some commissaries allow for inmates to preorder and then pick up goods.

The prison commissary may only be open certain days of the week. Limited funds or opportunity to purchase items has resulted in bartering situations between inmates with their own commissary inventory. Although administration attempts to minimize the stockpiling of purchased goods by prisoners, commissary items are commonly used as currency by inmates to obtain desired goods, services, or settle debts. Forfeiture of commissary privileges, a transfer to solitary confinement, or loss of good behavior credit are punishments that can be implemented if an inmate is discovered by officials to be bartering with commissary items.

The prison commissary amenity serves the purpose of operating as a system of rewards and punishments. The prison commissary provides an incentive to motivate inmates to comply with various day-to-day regulations and work in the prison.

By complying, prisoners avoid any infringement that may disqualify them from visiting the commissary. Additionally, without compensation to utilize at the commissary, inmates may feel less compelled to engage in prison labor. Interestingly, selected inmates are trusted to work in the commissary, and these jobs are considered highly desirable because the positions are well paid and entail minimal physical labor. The commissary workplace is heavily monitored. However, inmates working in the store can receive perks such as getting extra food or novelty items during their shifts.

The prison commissary also provides inmates with access to needed or desired items. Access to these goods can assist in minimizing an inmate's discontentment with imprisonment and resentment toward officials. Further, through the commissary, prisoners are able to maintain relationships with loved ones outside of prison by purchasing gift items, greeting cards, and stamps. Therefore, the prison commissary assists the penitentiary's administration in overall prison management and control.

Kristina M. Lopez

See also: Prison Industries; UNICOR

Further Reading

Chandler, C. (2013). Death and dying in America: The prison industrial complex's impact on women's health. *Berkeley Women's LJ, 18*(1), 40–60.

Finn, P. (1996). No-frills prisons and jails: A movement in flux. *Federal Probation, 60*(3), 35–44.

Fleisher, M. S. (2006). *Societal and correctional context of prison gangs.* Retrieved from http://archive.vera.org/files/fleisher-mark-s.pdf

Harner, H. M., & Riley, S. (2013). Factors contributing to poor physical health in incarcerated women. *Journal of Health Care for the Poor and Underserved, 24*(2), 788–801.

Lenz, N. (2002). "Luxuries" in prison: The relationship between amenity funding and public support. *Crime & Delinquency, 48*(4), 499–525.

Smoyer, A. B. (2013). *Cafeteria, commissary and cooking: Foodways and negotiations of power and identity in a women's prison.* New York: City University of New York.

Sykes, G. M. (1958). *The society of captives: A study of a maximum security prison.* Princeton, NJ: Princeton University Press.

Compassionate Release

Compassionate release is a process of sentence reduction or early release for inmates who face unexpected and compelling circumstances that potentially alter the reason for their incarceration. The purposes of incarceration include retribution, rehabilitation, deterrence, and incapacitation. Given the extraordinary conditions and circumstances in which inmates may find themselves, their current sentence may be deemed as inhumane and excessive under the Eighth Amendment, and therefore, unjust. The Sentencing Reform Act of 1984 provides for the use of compassionate release, and along with the federal government, most states allow for its use. Eligibility for compassionate release is based on "extraordinary and compelling" circumstances, including terminal illness with a life expectancy of 18 months or less, physical or mental incapacitation that prevents self-care, and the death or incapacitation of a caregiver solely responsible for an inmate's minor child. In addition to these release causes, the Bureau of Prison (BOP) recently revised its regulations to include an early release option to inmates 65 years and older who have serious or chronic medical conditions related to aging and whose physical or mental health (e.g., dementia) has deteriorated so as to diminish their ability to function in a correctional facility.

For consideration of compassionate release, there is a need for a prisoner to meet medical and legal eligibility requirements. The process for compassionate release requires a written appeal by the inmate or his or her advocate describing the "extraordinary and compelling" reason(s) for release. The inmate must undergo a medical evaluation and a confirmed medical diagnosis provided by a physician. Once completed, approval is still needed through the legal and correctional system, which requires that a number of additional levels of review take place. Release eligibility does take into account whether or not the individual poses a threat to society.

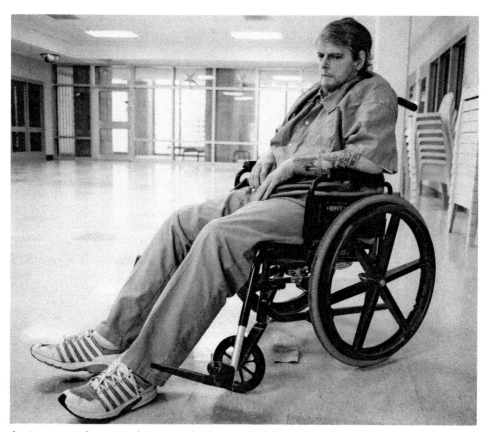

An inmate with terminal cancer who has applied four times for compassionate release sits in his wheelchair during an interview at the Federal Correctional Complex in Butner, North Carolina. (Nikki Kahn/The Washington Post via Getty Images)

Although the process does not seem complex, of concern are the potential barriers regarding the compassionate release mechanism and evidentiary inconsistency among states that limit access and use of this early release mechanism. Among the obstacles is inmate knowledge of this program, which may be lacking and, as such, must be communicated to them. This is followed by an inmate's ability to complete the application, especially if cognitively impaired or facing a lack of social support from family and friends. Jurisdictional differences lead to a lack of consistency in determining details, such as life expectancy, and the reliance on medical doctors, whose opinions can vary, to predict life expectancy and functional decline. In addition, the chances of recovery are also weighed in decision making. Because of this, the process may take months or years to undergo a review, which may result in the inmate's death in prison prior to approval.

Pragmatic uses for compassionate release are the reduction in overcrowding and the cost savings associated with moving prisoners out of the correctional system. Currently, the U.S. prison system houses more than 2 million prisoners and faces an increase in its aging population over the next few decades. Aging inmates are more expensive to incarcerate than their younger counterparts due to increased medical needs. For terminally ill inmates and those with age-related chronic illnesses or psychological/mental health issues, treatment costs are financially unsustainable for the correctional system. For many elderly inmates, they average three chronic illnesses requiring medical treatment and have unique needs their younger counterparts do not have. Included among the costs beyond medical treatment itself are hospital security, medical transport to and from a medical facility for treatment, and disability-accessible, protective housing for elderly inmates. For those who are terminally ill, other options include hospice care provided in prison; however, resources are woefully inadequate. Physicians are limited in prescription formularies and access to urgent care facilities, restrictions on inmate and staff movement, and finding, training, and retaining hospice volunteers, along with a host of other corrections-related barriers.

Although applications for compassionate release have been increasing, the approval of such releases is very low. For example, Texas's use of medically recommended intensive supervision (MRIS) was created to ameliorate issues of cost and overcrowding by expediting the release of inmates and results in a more efficient and cost-effective correctional system. A review found the restrictive nature of its requirements for eligibility limited who could apply, and for those who met age and medical requirements, the convened panel denied most applications based on their decision that the offender constituted a threat to public safety. The BOP's own statistics reflect a very low recidivism rate of 3.5 percent among those approved for compassionate release. This is significantly lower than inmates released from prison via more traditional means (e.g., parole and mandatory release). Limiting release of those who meet medical and legal requirements is most likely due to politically and socially charged reasons, including the public's negative opinion toward compassionate release of inmates, the public's preference for completion of criminal sentence, and apathy of terminally ill inmates by the public and correctional institutions and staff. Although the public takes a hard stance against early release and considers providing high-quality health care to inmates a low priority, and there is a potential of an ethical dilemma based on custody versus care for the correctional system, the judiciary has consistently affirmed inmates' constitutional right to health care via evolving standards of decency.

To date, the compassionate release rate is reported at 0.01 percent for the entire prison population. There are many reasons for such a low rate of release that range from legislative restrictions and variability in requirements by state to public opinion and access to information and support provided to eligible inmates. The implications and issues to be considered with regard to compassionate release include costs associated with medical treatments over time given the increase in age of the prison population, the human right to health, and the right to freedom from cruel and unusual punishment (i.e., Eighth Amendment).

Deborah T. Vegh

See also: Constitution as a Source for Prisoners' Rights, The; Elderly Offenders in Prison; Evolving Standards of Decency; Health Care in Prison Populations; Incarceration Rates, Trends in the United States; Overcrowding; Punishment Philosophies; Recidivism

Further Reading

Berry, W. W. (2009). Extraordinary and compelling: A re-examination of the justifications for compassionate release. *Maryland Law Review, 68*(4), 850–888.

Boothby, J., & Overduin, L. (2007). Attitudes regarding the compassionate release of terminally ill offenders. *The Prison Journal, 87*(4), 408–415.

Ethridge, P. A., & White, T. G. (2015). The use of medically recommended intensive supervision (medical parole) in Texas. *Journal of Correctional Health Care, 21*(4), 375–389.

Ferri, C. N. (2013). Stuck safety valve: The inadequacy of compassionate release for elderly inmates. *Stetson Law Review, 43*, 197–243.

Jefferson-Bullock, J. (2014). Are you (still) my great and worthy opponent? Compassionate release of terminally ill offenders. *University of Missouri–Kansas City Law Review, 83*, 521–564.

Linder, J. F., & Meyers, F. J. (2007). Palliative care for prison inmates: "Don't let me die in prison." *Journal of the American Medical Association, 298*(8), 894–901.

Maschi, T., Marmo, S., & Han, J. (2014). Palliative and end-of-life care in prisons: A content analysis of the literature. *International Journal of Prisoner Health, 10*(3), 172–197.

Stensland, M., & Sanders, S. (2016). Detained and dying: Ethical issues surrounding end-of-life care in prison. *Journal of Social Work in End-of-Life & Palliative Care, 12*(3), 259–276.

Williams, B. A., Sudore, R. L., Greifinger, R., & Morrison, R. S. (2011). Balancing punishment and compassion for seriously ill prisoners. *Annals of Internal Medicine, 155*(2), 122–126.

Conjugal Visits

Conjugal visits refer to the extended visitation time incarcerated inmates may spend privately with a visitor, usually their spouse. The concept has become synonymous with intimate sexual relations while incarcerated, though this is a mischaracterization and oversimplification of its contemporary purpose. Although typically reserved for the inmate's legal spouse and domestic partners, visits can also extend to close family members, including children. Conjugal visits originated at Parchman Prison Farm, today known as the Mississippi State Penitentiary, Mississippi's oldest and only maximum security male institution.

Parchman Prison Farm, built to resemble a plantation-era working farm, opened in 1904 and was run by Warden James Parchman as a business with an interest in maximizing profits for the state. Inmates at Parchman, in an effort to incentivize hard work, productivity, and rule following, were granted several unique privileges uncommon to inmates including sexual relations. Initially prostitutes were shuttled to and from the prison on Sundays each week, the inmates' only day off work at the farm. As interest in the productive workforce at Parchman Prison Farm grew, the conjugal visit policy was amended to reflect family visitations rather than sexual relations. The new policy permitted only inmates with wives to receive conjugal visits, and prostitutes were no longer transported to the prison for these purposes. Parchman with its ever-productive workforce became a model for the merits of conjugal visit programs, and state prisons throughout the United States took notice (see McElreath et al., 2016). Conjugal visitation policies were not extended to include female inmates until sometime during the 1970s. At its peak in 1993, conjugal visit programs were in practice in 17 states. At present, there remain only four states that continue to operate conjugal visitation programs—California, Connecticut, New York, and Washington.

Currently, the primary purpose of conjugal visitation programs is to preserve partner intimacy and promote family unity and bonding. Most states have stepped away from the term "conjugal visits" as it harkens back to earlier days denoting a false connotation that the visits are for the sole purpose of sexual relations. Instead, Extended Family Visits (EFV) or Family Reunification Programs (FRP) reorient the intent of the visits to capture the more holistic family-based focus (Boudin, Stutz, & Littman, 2013). Research has generally found that conjugal visits have had a significant positive effect on sustaining and maintaining an inmate's relationship with his or her family by reducing marital stress, promoting communication, and by allowing the inmate to physically engage with his or her family, strengthening the familial bond as well as the inmate's connection to prosocial priorities outside of the institution.

Though the rules and procedures vary from state to state, conjugal visits, Extended Family Visits, or Family Reunification Programs operate in a generally similar manner. Visits only take place at minimum or medium security prisons or jails, and they only occur at select facilities that operate the programs. The federal prison system does not offer conjugal visitation to inmates, and states with conjugal visitation programs adhere to strict rules, requiring stringent inmate eligibility criteria for program participation. For example, inmates must maintain a good prison disciplinary record, have a clean health record to prevent the spread of HIV/STDs, have no sexual or domestic violence convictions, and cannot be serving a life sentence. Visits are considered a privilege not a right and may be taken away for a variety of institutional infractions including threatening prison staff, attempted escape, or failing a drug or alcohol test.

Conjugal Visits 87

Institutional policies related to the duration of the visit range in time from a few hours to several days, with the majority of programs offering overnight visitations in family living quarters. The visits typically occur in isolated rooms, trailers, or small apartments located within the confines of the prison complex. Some facilities provide basic amenities including condoms, toiletries, TVs, and games during the visit. Similar to other more traditional visitations, visitors must pass a background check and submit to a body search. They are often allowed to bring several approved items with them for their visit. Approved items frequently include food items, toiletries, board or card games, and changes of clothes. If the inmate or his or her visitor is caught with contraband items, the inmate's conjugal visitation rights will be terminated, and the visitor may face criminal charges for the offense committed.

Proponents of conjugal visits assert visits are valuable assets to the inmate's well-being and serve as motivation for success and rule following in the prison. Allowing inmates to see their families while they are incarcerated promotes good behavior and may help to reduce both physical and sexual violence in the prison. Requirements for participation incentivize good behavior and minimize rule infractions. Additionally, maintenance of familial ties may increase the likelihood of positive behavioral change by decreasing the effects of prisonization, providing a necessary conduit to life outside the institution. Research has also found that states with conjugal visit programs report less sexual violence in the prison, theorizing that visits may help to release pent-up sexual frustration thereby reducing the sexual victimization of other inmates (D'Alessio, Flexon, & Stolzenberg, 2013).

One of the more prominent arguments in support of conjugal visits is that they help keep marriages, and families, intact. With conjugal visits extending more broadly to include additional family members such as children, inmates are afforded the opportunity to establish strong ties with family members. One of the hallmarks of successful offender reentry is a strong support network, and the family often serves as the first level of that network, enriching their postprison life. By strengthening their bond with their family, inmates also retain a bond with the community, which may help with future reentry needs related to housing and employment upon release.

Budgetary concerns top the list of problems surrounding conjugal visitation programs. With tighter state budgets, critics of the programs argue that prison is supposed to be a punishment, and taxpayers question the use of limited funds to pay for programs providing for inmates to engage in sexual relations. As a result, many programs have been dramatically reduced or abandoned altogether. Mississippi, the first state to implement a conjugal visitation program, terminated its program in 2014 amid mounting budget costs. The expenses of these family visitation programs can be quite costly with the need for increased security for the visitation area, costs of inmate transportation around the grounds, supplies and maintenance of the living quarters, and preservation of the visitation facility seen as expensive and unnecessary amenities in already tight budgetary times.

Another important area of concern that has been raised relates to public health and community stability. Opponents of conjugal visitation programs raise the concern that such programs may contribute to infectious disease transmission, including

HIV and other sexually transmitted diseases from visitors to the inmate populations and from inmates to their visitors. Similarly, pregnancy is a potential consequence with both the potential for female visitors becoming pregnant resulting in increases in single-parent households in communities throughout the United States or female inmates becoming pregnant and giving birth behind bars with all of the associated increased security and medical costs incurred by the institution. These concerns provided the rationale at the time conjugal visitations ended in the state of Mississippi.

Another concern of this program is that many people believe that inmates are not deserving of the privilege of conjugal visits since prison is meant to be a punishment. Our society's "get tough" stance on criminals has some people questioning the wisdom and hindsight of spending money and deploying resources on programs that are perceived to benefit convicted felons. Conjugal visitation is viewed by many as an unnecessary privilege rather than a necessary bridge toward family stability, unity, and successful offender reentry.

Timothy Worman, Jessie L. Krienert, and Jeffrey A. Walsh

See also: Consensual Sex between Inmates; Prisoner Reentry/Family Integration; Visitation

Further Reading

Boudin, C., Stutz, T., & Littman, A. (2013). Prison visitation policies: A fifty-state survey. *Yale Law & Policy Review, 32*(1), 149–189. Available at SSRN 2171412.

D'Alessio, S. J., Flexon, J., & Stolzenberg, L. (2013). The effect of conjugal visitation on sexual violence in prison. *American Journal of Criminal Justice, 38*(1), 13–26.

Hensley, C., Rutland, S., & Gray-Ray, P. (2002). Conjugal visitation programs: The logical conclusion. In C. Hensley (Ed.), *Prison sex: Practice and policy* (pp. 143–156). Boulder, CO: Lynne Rienner.

McElreath, D. H., Doss, D. A., Jensen, C. J., Wigginton, M. P., Mallory, S., Lyons, T., Williamson, L., & Jones, D. W. (2016). The end of the Mississippi experiment with conjugal visitation. *The Prison Journal, 96*(5), 752–764.

Consensual Sex between Inmates

Some commentators have argued that the Fourteenth Amendment protects some aspects of voluntary sexual expression in prison. Other commentators have questioned the extent to which sexual behavior in prison can be truly consensual. Nonetheless, the U.S. Department of Justice's (2012) Standards to Prevent, Detect, and Respond to Prison Rape advises prison staff not to label every participant in a sexual act as an abuser.

CONSENSUAL SEX AND PRISON RULES

Jails and prisons prohibit all sexual relationships in prison. Given that prisons are single-sex institutions, the assumption of these blanket prohibitions is that any deviation from heterosexuality, coerced or otherwise, is viewed as morally wrong and/or a threat to prison order (Robertson, 2016). Indeed, as Robinson (2011) observed, "Such policies . . . often fail to draw sharp distinctions between consensual and coerced sex, implying that they are equally . . . Such bans may deter inmates from reporting sexual assault because prison officials can characterize a claim of rape as consensual activity, which is forbidden" (p. 1316). Little is known about enforcement of prison rules banning consensual sex and the disciplinary sanctions imposed on participants.

The U.S. Department of Justice's (2012) Standards to Prevent, Detect, and Respond to Prison Rape take a nuanced approach toward consensual sex between inmates. As its executive summary explains:

[t]he Department did not intend to limit agencies' ability to prohibit or otherwise restrict inmate sexual activity. Rather, the Department meant to ensure that such activity is not automatically classified as "sexual abuse." The Department recognizes that it may be difficult to discern whether sexual activity between inmates is truly consensual; activity that may seem to be voluntary may actually be coerced. Yet it is essential that staff make individualized assessments regarding each inmate's behavior, and not simply label as an abuser every inmate caught having sex with another inmate. . . . (U.S. Department of Justice, 2012, p. 11)

Hence, the standards expressly distinguish "consensual sexual contact between inmates" from "sexual abuse," with the latter present when an inmate "is coerced into such act by overt or implied threats of violence, or is unable to consent or refuse. . . ." (U.S. Department of Justice, 2012, at § 115.6). However, the standards permit "discipline for violating any agency policy against [consensual] sexual contact" (U.S. Department of Justice, 2012, p. 8).

Bans on consensual sex are difficult to enforce absent constant surveillance of the inmate population. Also, Eigenberg (2000a) found that 96 percent of surveyed correctional officers reported great difficulty in distinguishing between consensual and coerced sexual activity. Nonetheless, correctional officers sometimes distinguish a "real rape" as one in which force or the threat thereof occurred, from a voluntary-but-coerced category (Buchanan, 2010; Eigenberg, 1994, 2000a, 2000b).

CONSENSUAL SEX AS A LIBERTY INTEREST

Smith (2006) argued that sexual expression is "a core feature of any social environment" (p. 225), including the prison, and thus argues for official recognition of consensual sexual relationships among inmates. "There is a range of legitimate prisoner interests in allowing sexual expression," she posited, "that do not threaten this core correctional mission of safety and security" (p. 201). These prisoner interests are delineated below.

- **Sex as Pleasure.** "[T]he state has little interest in regulating inmates' sexual expression for pleasure, except to the extent that it compromises safety and security or other legitimate penological goals."

- **Sex as Trade.** "In some institutions, there is a menu of sexual practices that are bartered for common items like cigarettes, candy, chips, or a phone call."

- **Sex as Freedom.** "For many prisoners sexual expression is a corollary of freedom."

- **Sex as Transgression.** Sex "as freedom of expression . . . is closely associated with transgression—breaking the rules and going against the normative structures imposed by society, the state, and other institutions."
- **Sex as Procreation.** "[B]oth male and female prisoners desperately want to become parents. . . ."
- **Sex as Love.** "Even in the prison setting, where individuals are legally stripped of their autonomy and dignity and face violence from other prisoners and staff, prisoners manage to establish meaningful and sometimes loving relationships." (Smith, 2006, pp. 204–226)

The Supreme Court in *Lawrence v. Texas* (2003) held that consensual sexual relationships between persons of the same sex are one of the liberty interests protected by the due process clause of the Fourteenth Amendment. In turn, Smith (2006) argues that some degree of sexual expression is not "part of the penalty" and should be recognized as a right enjoyed by inmates. Robinson (2011) is in accord, explaining that "*Lawrence*, properly understood, nonetheless raises serious questions as to whether broad bans on consensual sexual expression between inmates can continue to stand. . . ." (p. 1408).

However, no court in the United States has ruled that inmates have a right to engage in consensual sexual relationships. And while inmates have a right to marry while incarcerated, this constitutional protection does not extend to procreation (*Goodwin v. Turner*, 908 F.2d 1395 (8th Cir. 1990).

CONSENSUAL SEX AS AN IMPAIRED CHOICE

Duress is constantly present in the prisons and jails of the United States: "[A]ll relationships," wrote Gilligan (1997), "are so constrained and limited in the unfree world of the prison that what is normally meant by such terms as 'free' or 'voluntary' does not apply" (p. 165). Consequently, the concept of consensual sex among inmates must be understood as part of a continuum with unqualified coercion at one end and impaired choices at the other end.

Illustrative is a bartered sexual relationship in which an inmate "exchanges" sexual acts for protection from other inmates ("protective pairing"). For one victim of prison rape, Donaldson, protective pairing was about survival. Writing under the pen name of Donald Tucker (1982), Donaldson described his arrangement with his cellmates:

> [F]our white marines came up to me and said, "You're moving in with us!" and so I became the fifth occupant of the four-bunk cell . . . I had become the Punk of these four lads. . . . They provided me with protection and such things as stamps and snacks, in return wanting blowjobs (from three) and ass (in jail called "pussy") from one. (pp. 63–64)

By contrast, Trammell's (2011) interviews with 40 male parolees regarding their perceptions of such relationships, suggest that inmates as a whole view sex-for-protection as a business arrangement—albeit one in which the victim is blamed for being unmanly. Trammell herself characterizes protective pairing as "symbolic violence" (p. 3).

Consensual Sex between Inmates

The impaired sexual choices faced by inmates like Tucker-Donaldson are attributed to several factors. First, the greatest impairment of a prisoner's sexual autonomy arises from a host of intended and unintended deprivations caused by incarceration, what Sykes (1958) labeled and documented as "the pains of imprisonment" (Sykes, 1958, p. 63). These include loss of familial affection, which is widely associated with female inmates forming pseudofamilies, with sexually active pseudofathers and pseudomothers (Giallombardo, 1966; Owen, 1998). In turn, the single-sex prison population deprives inmates of opposite-sex sexual relationships with other inmates and is associated with increased levels of same-sex sexual behavior among male inmates in which the sexual dominant partner is regarded as masculine with a heterosexual orientation, whereas the submissive party is viewed as feminine (Hensley, 2001; Sykes, 1958).

Second, an inmate hierarchy in both men's and women's prisons recreates stark power differentials among inmates and thus render problematic behaviors otherwise suggesting consent (Ristroph, 2006; Robertson, 2012, 2016; Saul, 2009). As Human Rights Watch (2001) concluded, "[T]he relevant inquiry in evaluating sexual activity in prison is not simply 'did the inmate consent to sex?' but also 'did the inmate have the power to refuse unwanted sex?'" (p. 84).

Third, inmates with serious psychological distress, who account for 14.7 percent of prison inmates and 26.3 percent of jail inmates (Beck et al., 2013), can lack the capacity to consent in a meaningful manner (Perlin & Lynch, 2014; Saul, 2009).

PREVALENCE STUDIES

One study, published in 2010, observed that "[r]esearch on male sexual activity in prisons has primarily focused on sexual coercion whereas the research on female sexual activity in prisons has primarily focused on consensual sex. . . ." (Warren et al., 2010, p. 19). Also, many prevalence studies implicitly embraced dichotomous characterizations of same-sex sexual activity, whereby sex behavior was either consensual or coerced. In addition, exposure periods, sample sizes and demographics, and types of same-sex sexual behavior have differed.

Males

Research on consensual sex among male prisoners has been sparse, yielding disparate findings. At the high end, Wooden and Parker (1982) found that 65 percent of their sample of 200 California state inmates reported sexual behavior with fellow inmates during their imprisonment, which included the 14 percent who also reported sexual victimization. By comparison, Nacci and Kane (1984), after querying 330 male federal inmates, found that 12 percent in low security facilities and 30 percent in high security facilities reported sexual behavior with other inmates, including 0.6 percent claiming to be sexual victims. Later, Tewksbury (1989) administered a questionnaire to 150 Ohio state prisoners, of whom 19.4 percent reported same-sex sexual activities the previous year of imprisonment. When Hensley (2001) conducted his face-to-face interviews with 174 men, they provided a laundry list of their consensual sex acts since their imprisonment: 8 percent kissed or had been kissed by another inmate; 23 percent rubbed or had been rubbed in a sexual manner; 24 percent had touched another person's penis or vice versa; 23 percent performed or received oral sex; and 20 percent engaged in anal sex.

In contrast to prior studies, Warren et al.'s (2010) prevalence study of 288 male inmates in state prisons in Ohio and Texas sought to place consensual sex within what they regarded as the "full continuum of sexual behavior in prison," that is, consensual, bartered, and coerced (p. 18). Their findings included the following:

- 12.5 percent reported noncontact sexual victimization, and 5.9 percent reported contact sexual victimization by other inmates;

- 2.4 percent reported bartered noncontact sex acts, and 2.4 percent bartered contact sex acts with other inmates;

- 14.2 percent reported consensual noncontact sex acts, and 5.9 percent reported consensual contact sex acts; and

- .49 correlation between involvement in consensual sex and bartered sex.

Females

In her history of prison sexuality, Kunzel (2008) wrote, "While investigators were struck by the predominance of lesbianism in women's prisons, they struggled with challenges in assessing it empirically" (p. 115). Indeed, the leading studies reported rates of same-sex sexual behavior among female inmates at much higher rates than the prevalence studies of male prisoners. For example. Giallombardo (1966), in her groundbreaking study of the Federal Reformatory for women at Alderson, West Virginia, estimated that 90–95 percent of its residents participated in same-sex sexual behavior. The percentage dropped to 30–60 percent among the inmates interviewed by Owen (1998) at a women's prison in California. By contrast, Greer (2000) pegged the percentage at 42.9 percent in her interviews with 35 women at a midwestern state prison. A similar percentage (46 percent) was reported by Hensley, Tewksbury, and Koscheski (2002) in their study of female inmates in a southern prison.

Warren et al.'s (2010) interviews with 183 female inmates in state prisons located in Ohio and Texas broke with earlier prevalence studies of consensual sex by addressing a continuum of sexual behavior. Their findings included the following:

- 22.4 percent reported noncontact sex victimization (e.g., sexual comments; sexual letters) and 2.7 percent reported contact sexual victimization (e.g., sexual kissing; oral, vaginal, and anal sex) by other inmates;

- 6 percent reported bartered noncontact sex acts, and 3.8 percent reported bartered contact sex acts with other inmates;

- 39.3 percent reported consensual noncontact sex acts, and 26.2 percent reported consensual contact sex acts with other inmates; and

- .40 correlation between involvement in consensual sex and bartered sex.

Consensual Sex between Inmates

Defining consent is complicated by the very nature of the American prison: it confines men and women under abnormal coercive conditions. An acceptable operational definition of consensual sex may not be feasible unless imprisonment is restructured to resemble the broader, normal society, with as few deviations as security and safety permit. And even under those conditions, sexual autonomy will be problematic and so will practices that some inmates deem consensual.

James E. Robertson

See also: Inmate-on-Inmate Sexual Abuse; Prison Rape Elimination Act; Sexual Abuse of Inmates by Correctional Staff

Further Reading

Beck, A. J., Harrison, P. M., Berzofsky, M., & Caspar, R. (2013). *Sexual victimization in prisons and jails reported by inmates, 2011–12.* Washington, DC: Bureau of Justice Statistics.

Beck, A. J., & Johnson, C. (2012). *Sexual victimization by former state prisoners, 2008.* Washington, DC: Bureau of Justice Statistics.

Buchanan, K. S. (2010). Our prisons, ourselves: Race, gender and the rule of law. *Yale Law and Policy Review, 29,* 1–82.

Dolovich, S. (2012). Two models of the prison: Accidental humanity and hypermasculinity in the L.A. County Jail. *Journal of Criminal Law and Criminology, 102,* 965–1117.

Donaldson, S. (2001). A million jockers, punks, and queens. In D. Sabo, T. A. Kupers, & W. London (Eds.), *Prison masculinities* (pp. 118–126). Philadelphia: Temple University Press.

Eigenberg, H. (1994). Rape in male prisons: Examining the relationship between correctional officers' attitudes toward male rape and their willingness to respond to acts of rape. In M. Braswell, R. Montgomery, & L. Lombardo (Eds.), *Prison violence in America* (2nd ed., pp. 145–166). Cincinnati: Anderson.

Eigenberg, H. M. (2000a). Correctional officers' definitions of rape in male prisons. *Journal of Criminal Justice, 28,* 435–449.

Eigenberg, H. M. (2000b). Correctional officers and their perceptions of homosexuality, rape, and prostitution in male prisons. *The Prison Journal, 80,* 415–433.

Einat, T. (2012). Rape and consensual sex in male Israeli prisons: Are there differences with western prisons? *The Prison Journal, 93,* 80–101.

Farmer v. Brennan, 511 U.S. 825 (1994).

Fleisher, M. S., & Krienert, J. L. (2009). *The myth of prison rape: Sexual culture in American prisons.* Lanham, MD: Rowman & Littlefield.

Giallombardo, R. (1966). *Society of women: A study of a women's prison.* New York: Wiley.

Gilligan, J. (1997). *Violence: Reflections on a national epidemic.* New York: Vintage Books.

Greer, K. (2000). The changing nature of interpersonal relationships in a women's prison. *The Prison Journal, 80,* 442–468.

Hensley, C. (2001). Consensual homosexual activity in male prisons. *Corrections Compendium, 26*(1), 1–4.

Hensley, C., Tewksbury, R., & Koscheski, M. (2002). The characteristics and motivations behind female prison sex. *Women & Criminal Justice, 13,* 125–139.

Human Rights Watch. (2001). *No escape: Male rape in U.S. prisons.* New York: Author.

Koscheski, M., Hensley, C., Wright, J., & Tewksbury, R. (2002). Consensual sexual behavior. In C. Hensley (Ed.), *Prison sex: Practice and policy* (pp. 111–132). Boulder, CO: Lynne Rienner.

Kunzel, R. (2008). *Criminal intimacy: Prison and the uneven history of modern American sexuality*. Chicago: University of Chicago Press.

Lawrence v. Texas, 539 U.S. 558 (2003).

Nacci, P., & Kane, T. (1984). The incidence of sex and sexual aggression in federal prisons: Inmate involvement and employee impact. *Federal Probation, 8*, 46–53.

Owen, B. (1998). *In the mix: Struggle and survival in a women's prison*. Albany, NY: State University of New York Press.

Perlin, M. L., & Lynch, A. J. (2014). "All his sexless patients": Persons with mental disabilities and the competence to have sex. *Washington Law Review, 89*, 257–300.

Ristroph, A. (2006). Sexual punishments. *Columbia Journal of Gender and Law, 15*, 139–184.

Robertson, J. E. (2012). Exchanging sex for protection: Do the PREA Standards legitimate "shielding" arrangements between inmates? *Correctional Law Reporter, 24*, 43–44.

Robertson, J. E. (2016). Sex in jails and prisons. In H. Fradella & J. Sumner (Eds.), *Sex, sexuality, law, and (in)justice* (pp. 367–401). New York: Taylor & Francis/Routledge.

Robinson, R. K. (2011). Masculinity as prison: Sexual identity, race, and incarceration. *California Law Review, 90*, 1309–1408.

Saul, J. E. (2009). Of sexual bondage: The "legitimate penological interest" in restricting sexual expression in women's prisons. *Michigan Journal of Gender & Law, 15*, 349–387.

Saum, C., Surratt, H., Inciardi, J., & Bennett, R. (1995). Sex in prison: Exploring the myths and realities. *The Prison Journal, 75*, 413–430.

Smith, B. V. (2006). Rethinking prison sex: Self-expression and safety. *Columbia Journal of Gender and Law, 15*, 185–236.

Sykes, G. M. (1958). *The society of captives: A study of a maximum security prison*. Princeton, NJ: Princeton University Press.

Tewksbury, R. (1989). Measures of sexual behavior in an Ohio prison. *Sociology and Social Research, 74*, 34–39.

Trammell, R. (2011). Symbolic violence and prison wives: Protective pairing in men's prisons. *The Prison Journal, 91*, 305–324.

Tucker, D. (Stephen Donaldson). (1982). A punk's song. In A. M. Scacco Jr., *Male rape: A casebook of sexual aggressions* (pp. 58–79). AMS Studies in Modern Society; Political and Social Issues, *15*. New York: AMS Press.

U.S. Department of Justice. (2012). *Standards to prevent, detect, and respond to prison rape*, 28 CFR Part 115, Docket No. OAG131; AG Order No. RIN 1105.

Warren, J., Jackson, S., Booker, A., Loper, M., & Burnette, M. (2010). *Risk markers for sexual predation and victimization in prison*. Washington, DC: U.S. Department of Justice.

Wooden, W. S., & Parker, J. (1982). *Men behind bars: Sexual exploitation in prison*. New York: Plenum Press.

Constitution as a Source for Prisoners' Rights, The

The rights and remedies available to prisoners have been greatly expanded over the past century and a half. Certainly, prison and jail administrators must know—and apply—the law in order to be in compliance with related rights and protections under the U.S. Constitution and per federal court decisions and legislative enactments. A collective body of rights is given to inmates in such areas as conditions of confinement, communications, access to law library and medical facilities, and so on—that provide inmates a minimum standard of living in order to survive and enjoy access to the courts and judicial process as needed.

DEMISE OF THE "HANDS-OFF" DOCTRINE

Historically, the courts followed what was termed the hands-off doctrine: the view that prison administrators should be given free rein to run their prisons as they deemed best. This view resulted in courts at one point in time regarding prisoners as little more than "slaves of the state." The judiciary, recognizing that it was not trained or knowledgeable in penology, allowed wardens the freedom and discretion to operate their institutions without outside interference, while being fearful of undermining the structure and discipline of the prison.

All of that has changed, however, in the contemporary era of the "hands-on" doctrine, or the belief by courts that inmates have certain constitutional rights that must be upheld and also be obeyed by prison administrators. This doctrine, beginning in the mid-1960s, brought about a sweeping change of philosophy in the courts regarding prisoners' rights. In sum, prison inmates now retain all the rights of free citizens *except* those restrictions necessary for their orderly confinement or to provide safety in the prison community. This latter point is important. Although prisoners now enjoy a vast array of rights (as compared to the era of hands-off), by virtue of their incarceration and the inherent dangers of correctional institutions, inmates do not and cannot enjoy the same panoply of rights reserved for free citizens. Indeed, by virtue of one's incarceration, the Constitution's equilibrium is necessarily shifted, and prison officials are granted a generous amount of discretion in deference to, and to preserve, their legitimate safety concerns.

SELECTED COURT DECISIONS

Several major U.S. Supreme Court decisions spelled the demise of the hands-off era, while also vastly improving the everyday lives of prison and jail inmates and reforming correctional administration.

A "Slave of the State"

The 1871 case of Woody Ruffin serves as an excellent beginning point for an overview of significant court decisions concerning inmates' rights. Ruffin, an inmate in Virginia, killed a correctional officer while attempting to escape and later challenged his conviction; the Virginia Supreme Court stated that Ruffin, like other prisoners, had "not only forfeited his liberty, but all his personal rights." The court added that inmates were "slaves of the state," losing all their citizenship rights, including the right to complain about living conditions (*Ruffin v. Commonwealth*, 1871). Therefore, under this philosophy, inmates essentially had no legal rights that had to be observed by prison administrators.

Legal Remedy and Access to the Courts

In *Cooper v. Pate* (1964), the Supreme Court first recognized the use of Title 42 of U.S. Code Section 1983 as a legal remedy for inmates. (Briefly, this section provides that "Every person who, under color of any statute, ordinance, regulation, custom, or usage, of any State or Territory or the District of Columbia, subjects, or causes to be subjected, any citizen of the United States or other person within the jurisdiction thereof to the deprivation of any rights, privileges, or immunities secured by the Constitution and laws, shall be liable to the party injured in an action at law, suit in equity, or other proper proceeding for redress.") An Illinois state penitentiary litigant claimed that he was unconstitutionally punished by being placed in a solitary confinement cell and being unable to obtain certain religious materials. The Supreme Court held not only that he should have been allowed to purchase the articles but that he also could use Section 1983 to sue the prison administration.

A significant case also involved the right of access to the courts. A Tennessee prisoner was disciplined for acting as what is termed a "writ writer"—one who assists other prisoners in preparing their legal arguments; doing so violated a prison regulation. The Supreme Court agreed that "writ writers" can become bothersome to prison administrators and are often a burden on the courts; however, because illiterate or poorly educated inmates were afforded no "reasonable alternative" for preparing their appeals, the court held that these so-called writ writers could not be prevented from giving such assistance to other prisoners (*Johnson v. Avery*, 1969).

In 1977, in another decision that concerned access to the courts, the Supreme Court held that prisoners must have access to adequate law libraries or at least assistance from persons trained in the law. To comport with this requirement, some methods for providing legal access might include hiring lawyers on a part-time consultant basis; providing training for inmates to serve as paralegals; using paraprofessionals and law students to advise inmates; and having programs through state and local bar associations, where attorneys can visit with and counsel inmates (*Bounds v. Smith*, 1977).

First Amendment: Freedom of Religion and Speech

The practice and exercise of religion by prison inmates has also been considered by the U.S. Supreme Court. In a landmark 1972 case, the plaintiff, a practicing Buddhist, was not only not allowed to use the prison chapel, but he was also placed in solitary confinement on a diet of bread and water for disseminating his religious materials among other prisoners. The court held that inmates with unconventional religious beliefs (i.e., not only those of Protestant, Catholic, and Jewish faiths) must also be given a reasonable opportunity to exercise those beliefs (*Cruz v. Beto*, 1972).

Regarding the freedom of speech, the court has also looked at mail censorship regulations that historically allowed and involved prison authorities to hold or censor mail that was either sent to or from prisoners. In an interesting line of reasoning, the court based its ruling not on the rights of the prisoner but rather on that of the free-world *recipient's* right to communicate with the inmate via the mail. The court held that mail censorship can be accomplished but only for the purposes of enhancing security, order, and rehabilitation; in other words, censorship must not be done merely to censor opinions or other expressions (*Procunier v. Martinez*, 1974).

Fourth Amendment: Search and Seizure

The U.S. Supreme Court's decision in *Estelle v. Gamble* (1976) represented its first foray into medical treatment for inmates. In *Estelle*, the court coined the phrase "deliberate indifference," defined as where the neglect of serious medical needs of prisoners involved the unnecessary and wanton infliction of pain. Here, Gamble, a Texas inmate, claimed that he was subjected to cruel and unusual punishment due to inadequate treatment of a back injury he sustained while engaged in prison work. The court, noting that medical personnel saw Gamble on 17 occasions during a three-month period and failed to treat his injury and related problems, demonstrated deliberate indifference to his medical needs, which thus constituted an "unnecessary and wanton infliction of pain."

Fourteenth Amendment: Due Process

A U.S. Supreme Court decision that instantly became landmark in nature was *Wolff v. McDonnell* (1974); here, the court acknowledged for the first time that inmates are entitled to certain due process rights during prison disciplinary proceedings. In what began as a grievance involving the use of mail and access to the prison law library (i.e., how many inmates could use the library, and for how long), McDonnell and other plaintiffs also complained that the disciplinary proceedings at their prison lacked procedural or substantive due process. The Supreme Court held that "prison officials must observe certain minimal due process requirements" during disciplinary proceedings: 24 hours' notice before a hearing, a written statement of the reason (charges) for the disciplinary hearing, the right to call witnesses and present evidence, an impartial prison disciplinary board, and counsel substitutes (they do not have the right to confront and cross-examine witnesses or to have the assistance of counsel). The court said that "there is no iron curtain drawn between the Constitution and the prisons of this country," that "a prisoner is not wholly stripped of constitutional protections." This statement has become known as the court's now-famous "iron curtain" speech: there is no iron curtain between the Constitution and the prisons of the United States.

Kenneth J. Peak

See also: Health Care in Prison Populations; Legitimate Penological Interests; Medical Experiments on Inmates; Pains of Imprisonment; Prison Law Libraries; *Ruffin v. Commonwealth*; Section 1983 Lawsuits; Sex Reassignment Surgery among Inmates; Solitary Confinement; Transgender Inmates; Use of Force in Prisons

Further Reading

Hudson, D., Jr. (2007). *Prisoners' rights*. New York: Chelsea House.

Human Rights Watch. (2015), *World report 2015: United States.* Retrieved from https://www.hrw.org/world-report/2015/country-chapters/united-states

Maass, D. (2015, December). *Defending prisoner rights in the digital world: 2015 in review.* Electronic Frontier Foundation. Retrieved from https://www.eff.org/deeplinks/2015/12/defending-prisoner-rights-digital-world-2015-review

Mushlin, M. B. (2017). *Rights of prisoners*. New York: Clark Boardman Callaghan.

Mushlin, M. B., & Galtz, N. R. (2009, January). Getting real about race and prisoner rights. *Fordham Urban Law Journal, 36*(1), 27–52.

Palmer, J. W. (2015). *Constitutional rights of prisoners* (9th ed.). New York: Routledge.

Continuum of Sanctions

The continuum of sanctions refers to a variety of sentencing, punishment, and supervision options that become more restrictive in a gradual process of civil liberty restriction, up to and just prior to actual imprisonment. Although not always true, in most circumstances, higher sanctions usually include the requirements of many or all of the lower sanctions as a type of combo package of requirements. Therefore, each sanction will usually include terms and conditions from lower-level sanctions. This series of sanction options gives the community supervision agency a fluid range of responses depending on the offender's sentence as well as his or her behavior while under supervision.

It is important to point out that the continuum of sanctions is not simply punishment oriented but is also intended to have a therapeutic benefit as well. Indeed, part of the requirements to a sanction level may be the necessity to attend various functions, such as peer support groups for drugs and alcohol, domestic violence groups for perpetrators, or speaking requirements at schools and/or other events. These enhancements to the requirements are intended to provide a productive element to the supervision requirement and to facilitate introspective thought and accountability in the offender.

SPECIFIC SANCTIONS WITHIN THE CONTINUUM

The first and least restrictive sanction that will be included is probation with community service and restitution. Offenders under this sanction are required to complete volunteer work, free of payment, for a defined set of hours that are determined by the court. When restitution is added, the offender must pay the state an identified amount of money that is, in turn, provided to the state's crime victim compensation fund. It is common for restitution to be required in violent crimes where a specific victim is harmed. In many cases, community service and restitution are used along with many of the other sentencing options that will follow.

The next progression in the continuum of sanctions is intensive supervised probation (ISP). This is a sentence that is considered the next-most-secure version of supervision just short of jail or prison. This type of supervision is usually utilized with the more serious offenders on community supervision and tends to emphasize public safety more than it does rehabilitation. Nevertheless, most often, in tandem with extensive security-oriented restrictions (i.e., strict curfew hours, multiple face-to-face visits with the probation officer each week, automated tracking, and so forth), a variety of treatment-related programs are often required as well.

The third sanction in the continuum is the use of the day/evening reporting center. This is a facility where the individual is required to attend daily treatment services, Monday through Friday, until completed. This type of sanction is usually given to offenders with histories of substance abuse. The goal of this type of programming is more therapeutic than punishment-based—the notion being that if the offender's drug issue can be ameliorated, recidivism will also be decreased. While in these programs, participants are under an 8-hour daily regimen of psychoeducation and prosocial activities. A less known option to the day reporting program is the evening reporting center. In this version of the program, the participant is required to engage in a 4-hour program during evening hours (e.g., from 5:30 p.m. through 9:30 p.m.) so as to allow participants to maintain employment while they continue their treatment. Naturally, because this type of programming is at half the pace of day reporting centers, the participant will need to continue the evening program for twice as many weeks.

The next step in the continuum of sanctions is home confinement with electronic monitoring. This sanction is an alternative to jail and is typically given when offenders commit some type of technical violation of their community supervision. This sanction is usually temporary with a duration of six months or less. Nevertheless, exceptions with problematic offenders, such as pedophiles or domestic violence perpetrators, may be given for prolonged periods of time to aid in maintaining community safety. The electronic monitoring feature helps to track the offender when outside of the house and also allows supervision staff to determine when the offender is heading to and from his or her home during home curfew.

The use of house arrest and electronic monitoring is often used along with ISP and a requirement that the offender attend either a day or a night reporting center. This combination of sanctions ensures that offenders are routinely watched through face-to-face contacts throughout the week and that they are under supervision of day/night reporting center staff during large segments of the day or evening as well. The use of house arrest and electronic monitoring over the weekend helps to provide a truly comprehensive program of supervision, which is restrictive yet also allows the offender to be productive while serving his or her sentence.

Another application to the sanctioning and supervision process is the global positioning satellite system (GPS). This system, unlike electronic monitoring by telephone contact, allows probation agencies to track probationers through real-time monitoring throughout any time of the day or night. This is far superior to other programs of supervision because it provides instant notification of an offender's location and also gives quick notice when they are in violation of their community supervision. This tracking technology can locate the offender in any area of the nation and can also determine when the offender is within the bounds of the jurisdiction's conditions or if he or she is in violation of those conditions. Therefore, if offenders enter an area that violates the terms and conditions of their supervision,

supervision personnel are instantly alerted. This sanction, when combined with previous sanctions discussed, provides for a seamless form of offender surveillance and supervision.

The next variation of sanctioning entails the use of residential treatment homes, which are very similar to day reporting centers but require that the offender stay at the facility overnight. When staying at a residential treatment home or center, the participant is also allowed to go to and hold a job, but the house or treatment staff will typically set the rules for when and how this is done. It is important to understand that, unlike a halfway house, these types of facilities are intended to be treatment-oriented, with fewer restrictions than would be encountered in a halfway house, jail, or prison. Most of these types of facilities focus on substance abuse treatment or other areas of treatment as well as changing criminal thinking and lifestyles.

The next progression in the continuum of sanctions is the halfway house, which is a residential setting for offenders who are court-ordered to stay in the facility while they complete their sentence. Conversely, some offenders who reside in halfway houses will be those who have recently been released from prison. The restrictions and curfews associated with these facilities are usually much greater than those associated with residential treatment facilities. In some cases, these facilities are used to house individuals who violate terms of their probation or parole requirements, particularly when jails or prisons are filled to capacity.

Moving further along the continuum of sanctions is the use of boot camps. These programs are usually short-term (90 days or so), which mimic the lifestyle, structure, and activities of army basic training. Usually, this sanction is used with youthful offenders and is designed to instill discipline in the offender. Although this intervention is short-term in duration, it is very intensive and challenging for offenders. This intensive form of intervention is intended to lay the groundwork for responsible living during the remainder of the probation sentence and beyond, and is, therefore, considered a reformative sanction.

Going further along the continuum of sanctions is the use of split sentencing. This sanction is implemented by a judge who sentences an offender to a defined term of jail or prison time that is followed by a specified period of community supervision. The specific ratio of time that is served in jail or prison versus time served on community supervision is often left up to the presiding judge to determine. In some states, however, specific guidelines exist where a minimum amount of jail or prison time is required, depending on the length of the sentence.

A similar form of sanction is shock probation. The key distinction between this sanction and split sentencing is that, where split sentencing provides a specified time frame during which the offender is incarcerated, shock probation leaves the length of imprisonment unknown to the offender. The logic behind this sentence is that the experience of incarceration will "shock" the offender, serving as a deterrent to future recidivism. The fact that the offender is left not knowing how long the prison term will ultimately last will help reinforce the displeasure of the experience, enhancing the deterrent effect.

The continuum of sanctions is a progressively restrictive set of conditions in the sentencing and supervision of offenders that is designed to provide sanctions that are commensurate with the crime and the characteristics of the offender. The particular set of sanctions given is also affected by the charge that the offender faces as well as his or her prior convictions. In the case of violent offenders, most will be given some type of jail or prison time. On the other hand, nonviolent offenders, particularly those who persist in offending, may find that they are processed and reprocessed through various levels of sanctions. Although this may not seem severe in approach, this continuum provides for a range of choices that can hold offenders accountable, reasonably aid in community safety, and provide a form of individualized supervision in a system that is often short on funds and resources. The continuum of sanctions, therefore, provides reasonable alternatives to prison that allow for public safety and potential offender rehabilitation. All of this is done at a fraction of the cost of prison.

Robert D. Hanser

See also: Inmates' Perceptions of Prison versus Alternative Sanctions; Presentence Investigation Reports

Further Reading

Barton, S., & Hanser, R. D. (2011). *Community-based corrections.* Thousand Oaks, CA: Sage.

Hanser, R. D. (2007). *Special needs offenders in the community.* Upper Saddle River, NJ: Pearson/Prentice Hall.

Hanser, R. D. (2014). *Community corrections* (2nd ed.). Thousand Oaks, CA: Sage.

Convict Criminology

Convict criminology or more formally, the New School of Convict Criminology, is represented in the American Society of Criminology (ASC), in the Division of Critical Criminology. Convict criminology is an informal organization of convicts, ex-convicts, and nonconvicts (who are also referred to as "enlightened practitioners"). Numerous ex-convicts (many with PhDs) are professors in universities, who along with convicts still in prison and noncons, write books, publish in journals, and present at academic and professional conferences about crime and corrections. The writing and conference presentations are an effort to foster a new perspective that challenges the entrenched policies, legislation, and correctional operations that have contributed to criminal justice failure and more specifically the failure of the ex-convict upon return to society.

Convict criminologists are focused on producing more humane practices that are helpful to those in prison and contribute to society through successful reentry. The convict criminologist represents the voice that has largely been absent in research and traditional sources of legislative and policy construction. In addition, that voice, is also absent from input about correctional operations.

The failure of correctional strategies to prevent crime and reform convicts has been addressed by convict criminologists in three major perspectives. First, there have been more than 200 years of failure to achieve the stated goals of prisons as a social institution. Second, the failure of convicts is not a reference to recidivism but includes those who, upon release from prison, are not allowed to regain societal inclusion due to repressive policies, legislation, labeling, collateral consequences, and other problems including myths about crime and those who commit crime. And third, the ineffectiveness of prisons to prepare convicts for release, and specifically in the areas of employment, drug treatment, and education, which have repeatedly been shown through research. There are substantial numbers of ex-convicts who do not reengage in crime and because of collateral consequences, bias, prejudice, and other instances of unfairness are not reclaimed and restored, and who cannot gain societal acceptance even though their debt to society has been paid.

Convict criminologists are included in this group as well. They have been discriminated against despite their academic standing (success as professors, writers, and social reform advocates) even though they have served their time and paid their debt. The discrimination includes the areas of academic employment, tenure, and promotions. In addition, there have been convict criminologists who have been dismissed from their academic positions because of their criminal past (even when it was known at the time of hiring) as the sole reason. These are some of the challenges that are accepted by convict criminologists as academics and through their mission as advocates for social reform of the prison.

Convict criminology is very emphatic that references to those in and out of prison should be referred to as convict and ex-convict. To call them inmates, offenders, or by other expressions is demeaning and insulting. For example, an inmate is one who follows the rules of the prison and may engage in inappropriate familiarity with guards or staff, thus betraying the trust of other convicts (for a more complete description of terms, see Ross & Richards, 2003, p. 13, note 1).

HISTORY

The first use of the term "convict criminology" appears to have occurred during a conversation between the late John Irwin (1929–2010) informally referred to as the original convict criminologist) and Chuck Terry who suggested a convict criminology session at the 1997 American Society of Criminology (ASC) conference. The term gained acceptance in the article "The New School of Convict Criminology" (Richards & Ross, 2001). Ross and Richards then published the book *Convict Criminology* (2003), which brought together nine ex-convict criminal justice professors and eight noncon (those not convicted of crime who are empathetic to the plight of convicts) criminal justice professors. This would be the first time that nine chapters by ex-convicts, as graduate professors, would discuss criminal convictions, prison experiences, and involvement in graduate school. Similarly, the noncons would discuss their research, personal experience with prisons, and perceptions of their role in society and the criminal justice system. The views of these nine ex-convicts and the nonconvict criminologists provide the personal experiences of being a convict, the prison's counterproductive effect on the convict, and corrections as detrimental to society.

Convict criminology was partially influenced by ex-convicts entering academia as students and professors. This was due in large part to the mass incarceration of those convicted of drug offenses. Offenders who, it is argued by convict criminologists, represent little risk to society because of low-level offenses. However, convict criminology as an informal group has not limited its membership to convicts with specific offenses; that is, convict criminology does not judge individuals because of their offense or use offenses to exclude someone from the group. In fact, convict criminology is quite emphatic that ex-offenders have paid their debt to society and that no crime shall be a reason to ban someone from participation. Convict criminology is inclusive in its membership, recognizing that the issues of crime and corrections are not the sole province of the criminal justice and academic communities but affects society as a whole. Men and women from government agencies, private foundations, private nonprofit agencies, and other community groups are active participants and contributors to convict criminology. Many convicts who have served time for other offenses similarly do not reoffend and do contribute to the effort to create a "new perspective" that is more pragmatic about the challenges of crime and its solutions.

The conventional presentations of crime and criminal justice containment models were wearisome, disappointing, and disturbing to convict criminologists who sought to overcome their frustration by arguing for new definitions and solutions to alleviate the myriad problems of the criminal justice system. Convict criminologists would begin to challenge such issues as mass incarceration and overcrowding as well as the harmful consequences of imprisonment to the detriment of society. The "new" convict criminologists would also challenge the legislation and correctional policies touted to reform existing and ongoing problems. Unfortunately, the alterations to existing practices did little to change the existing problems and merely ensnared the convict and ex-convict with new challenges that exacerbated age-old issues.

Convict criminologists were soon joined by nonconvict criminologists and sociologists, many with prominent academic standing at prestigious universities, who shared and also proposed the need for a critical perspective, a new analysis, from which to define crime and explore new social and legal responses to criminality. The group, informally referring to themselves as convict criminologists, saw their ranks increase and the issues expand challenging mass incarceration, prison conditions including overcrowding, lengthy sentences, inadequate programming both in and after prison, and other matters, including myths that have been promoted by the media and supported by legislation that fails socially and operationally. Significant to changing failed correctional practices is to reexamine the process of return to society and legislation affecting reentry and the damage of labeling ex-convicts.

CONVICT ETHNOGRAPHY

The late 1990s brought with it a new academic emphasis on convict ethnography. Ross and Richards (2003) argued for the authenticity of the convict voice, what and who represented that voice, and how to express what meaning would be derived from the voice. Part of the solution was that the study of prisons should be conducted from the inside out. Some of that authenticity would be achieved through a greater exposure to the exigencies of prison life and reentry, that is, the progression of personal experiences and conflicts faced by the individual as he or she advances from becoming a convict and engaging in the prison experience to emerging as an ex-convict who would endure the stigma and then fail again in society. Similarly, academic researchers are encouraged to humanize their research and results by entering the prison (i.e., leave the comfort of the academic office) to conduct hands-on personal analyses. Generalized statistical analyses detract or dehumanize the individual condition and distances the reality of the penal circumstance from a human and social issue. Convict ethnography, the "inside" study, would then produce a more robust understanding of the culture and its effects on convicts and society.

The ethnographic perspective as proposed by convict criminology would also take into consideration the past and present writing (autobiographies, novels, poetry, etc.) of convicts that details the personal prison experience and would add enhanced validity to the "new" criminology. The convict description of the correctional experience cuts across time and culture (and time and culture in which and during which other research has not been conducted or reports of which do not exist). The enhanced validity for convict criminology is the merging of the convict's past with their present. The academic study of convict criminology is based on perceptions, experiences, and critical analysis of ideas that originate from convicts and are developed by researchers (Ross & Richards, 2003).

Convict criminology encourages the revitalization of prisonization as a theoretical focal point of investigations. Prisonization, as a theory, has stood the test of time, and remains the theoretical perspective from which to investigate and understand the prison culture (Sheridan, 1991). Some would argue that the theory is dated since Clemmer's (1940) original definition. However, other theories that have sought to explain/explore the nature of the prison environment have failed to stand the test of time and to adequately provide a comprehensive understanding of the prison culture and prison experience. Clemmer, ironically, conducted his exploration from inside the prison and provides his interpretations of the convict community and the culture of the prison that influence the manner in which the convict must adapt to the environment. Clemmer's study led the way for others to explore prison survival—a topic that has currency today. Prisonization (Sheridan, 1991) remains the fundamental process that describes the convict's absorption into the prison environment by compelling the convict through a controlled process to discard the elements of his or her street identity in favor to the required and necessary prison identity of a convict.

John Irwin emerged from California's Soledad prison in 1957 after serving five years for armed robbery. In 1968, he received his PhD in sociology from the University of California. During his four decades in academia, he published many books and papers, which have become models for research, the methodology, and theoretical basis for convict criminology. For example, his book *The Felon* (originally his dissertation) was acclaimed for its genuineness and remains a classic of criminology. Irwin entered the prison, conducted interviews with convicts using their voice to explain the struggle of leaving prison to live with "straight" society. His themes, expressed in such work as *The Felon* (1970), *Prisons in Turmoil* (1980), and *The Warehouse Prison* (2004), have continued to maintain currency with prison issues.

Irwin has been a role model for many convict criminologists, including the unofficial leader for convict criminology, Dr. Stephen Richards.

EXPANSION OF CONVICT CRIMINOLOGY

The ranks of convict criminologists have increased as more convicts have emerged from prison, have been mentored by established academic members of the group to achieve their PhDs, have obtained faculty positions in academia, and have presented their research at conferences. Once the almost sole province of the United States (which continues to influence the most ex-convict and academic members) and Greg Newbold of New Zealand, convict criminology now claims many adherents from other parts of the world, including Great Britain, Canada, Australia, New Zealand, Finland, and European countries. Notably, it has been organized as convict criminology in Great Britain. In addition, there is an increasing number of men and women behind bars, some of whom have earned advanced degrees, who publish academic work about crime and corrections. Convict criminology has become increasingly more active at conferences, which include the American Society of Criminology (ASC), the Academy of Criminal Justice Sciences (ACJS), the American Correctional Association (ACA), the Midwestern Sociological Association Conference, and others. Often more than one panel presents at these conferences on a variety of topics. Conferences are opportunities for both established and emerging members of the group to propose topics, take the lead developing themes, and inviting panel members.

Emerging members of convict criminology have a wide variety of activities to choose from. They may take the lead on or contribute to academic articles. They may propose and submit research proposals and then conduct the research. The voice of the ex-convict is encouraged with the media to express ideas about current events, policy, and legislation. This is deemed critical to the mission of convict criminology, because it is in the media (books, newspapers, journalists, television, and movies) that the criminal justice system, and especially, the convict, ex-convict, correctional legislation, and policy are often misrepresented.

Different members of the group may voluntarily lead or take responsibility for assorted functions—for example, lead author on a conference paper, or academic article, research proposal, program assessment, mentoring students or junior faculty, or media contact. Ideally, the lead person invites one or more convict criminology colleagues to share the work and through this process attempts to generalize the discussion and socialize the membership into the norms of academia.

Matthew J. Sheridan

See also: Education in Prison; Prison Ethnography; Prisonization

Further Reading

Carceral, K. C. (2004). *Behind a convict's eyes: Doing time in a modern prison.* Belmont, CA: Wadsworth/Thompson Learning.

Carceral, K. C. (2005). *Prison, Inc.: A convict exposes life inside a private prison.* New York: New York University Press.

Clemmer, D. (1940). *The prison community.* New York: Rinehart.

Convict Criminology. Retrieved from www.convictcriminology.org

Hassine, V. (2011). *Life without parole: Living and dying in prison today* (5th ed.). New York: Oxford University Press.

Irwin, J. (1970). *The felon.* Englewood Cliffs, NJ: Prentice Hall.

Irwin, J. (1980). *Prisons in turmoil.* Boston: Little, Brown.

Irwin, J. (2004). *The warehouse prison.* New York: Oxford University Press.

Paluch, J. (2003). *A life for a life.* New York: Oxford University Press.

Richards, S., & Ross, J. (2001). The New School of Convict Criminology. *Social Justice, 28*(1), 177–190.

Rideau, W., & Wikberg, R. (1992). *Life sentences: Rage and survival behind bars.* New York: Times Books.

Ross, J., & Richards, S. (2003). *Convict criminology.* Belmont, CA: Wadsworth.

Sheridan, M. (1991). *An exploration of the personal experience of prisonization utilizing the concept of environmental press and the introduction of a concept of minor press to account for exceptional circumstances in the environment.* Unpublished dissertation, Rutgers University, New Brunswick, NJ.

Convict Lease System

The convict lease system was an institution of forced prison labor that took place most notably in the South from roughly 1846 to 1928. In this system, convicts were leased by the states to private contractors for an annual fee and made to work on farms, or in brickyards, lumber camps, coal and iron mining facilities, the turpentine industry, and railroad construction. Although legislators in the northern states also leased convicts to private contractors on occasion, these instances were different. Northern leasers never gave up complete control of their convicts.

Convict leasing was widespread in the South. It was practiced by all the southern states with the exception of Virginia. Alabama was the first to introduce leasing in 1846. In its footsteps were Mississippi and Texas, which began in 1866. Afterward came Arkansas in 1867, Georgia and Louisiana in 1868, Tennessee in 1871, the Carolinas in 1873, and, finally, Florida in 1877.

Although at least one state practiced convict leasing during the antebellum period, the system rose to popularity after the Civil War. At this time, the South faced hardship and dire economic issues. Prison officials were desperate for a solution to the destruction of penitentiary buildings during the war. There were also limited resources to handle overcrowding in those penitentiaries that did exist. Prison officials, state legislatures, and governors agreed that leasing convicts was the most practical pathway toward economic stability, since contractors would pay an annual fee to the state for leasing the convicts. But not all states were able to start the system with private contractors. Mississippi, Florida, and Arkansas initially paid lessees to take the convicts in order to get rid of an unwanted expense for the state.

Convict leases lasted anywhere between 1 and 20 years. The average length of a contract was 5 years. The longest contract was the 20-year lease, also known as the Great Lease of 1879 to 1899, and it existed only in the state of Georgia. This lease yielded $25,000 per year for the state. However, as with many leases, the state did not receive all of the money it was owed.

Convict oversight was handled by either the principal keeper of the penitentiary or the lessee. In Georgia, for example, many of the keepers were men with integrity, and they tried to shed light on the cruelty of the leasing system. However, the power of well-meaning officials was greatly limited. Usually, responsibility fell upon the lessees to feed, clothe, restrain, and control convicts as they saw fit. This meant that abuses were normally unseen by the public.

Not all convicts were leased to private contractors. Race played a big factor in determining who would be leased. In fact, many scholars have argued that the convict lease system was the "re-enslavement" of African Americans in the age of emancipation. With the adoption of the Thirteenth Amendment to the Constitution in 1865, slavery was formally abolished. Nonetheless, the amendment provided for involuntary servitude as a punishment for crime. This allowed for the inhumane treatment of mostly black convicts through the leasing system. Accordingly, the typical leased convict in the South was young, illiterate, male, and black.

Convicts played a huge role in railroad, mining, and coal industries despite their terrible working conditions. Tennessee, Georgia, Alabama, and the Carolinas all had convicts laboring in dark and dangerous mines, or in blistering heat to construct the railroad. One major contractor at the time was the Tennessee Coal, Iron and Railroad Company (TCI), owned by Thomas O'Conner. Another was the Georgia and Alabama Railroad, owned by William A. Fort.

While working on the railroad, convicts lived in rolling cages. Accounts of life in these cages illuminate a total disregard for the convict's life. Cages were small, and all convicts crammed into them had to relieve themselves in a bucket and bathe in the same filthy water. Sleep came at no avail because the cages did not have screens to keep insects out. Despite such conditions, hard labor was demanded from the convicts. In North Carolina alone, convicts laid almost all of the 3,500 miles of railroad tracks produced during the 1870s and 1880s. Private contractors saw tremendous profits from this system.

In mining, convicts were expected to extract a certain amount of coal each day. Most of them worked 16-hour shifts with only a short break for meals. If convicts did not meet their quota, they faced harsh punishment by the overseer. The most common form of punishment was whipping with a leather strap. This device was so common in Georgia that it became known as the "negro regulator." Convicts could receive up to 70 lashes at a time, which sometimes caused the skin to fall off their backs. Other forms of punishment were water torture, isolation in dark cells, dehydration, starvation, and shackles.

Convicts revolted against the system. They refused excessive work in mines and staged protests against the overuse of corporal punishment and bad food. They also engaged in everyday forms of resistance like filling the bottoms of coal cars with slate, feigning illness, and aiding the sick or injured to avoid labor. Convicts even tried to free themselves from the mines by setting fires and attempting to escape in the ensuing frenzy. Often, this plan did not go as predicted, and they died in the process. Overall, the principal keepers would not tolerate resistance. Protesters were often starved, forcing mutinies to collapse.

At the turn of the century, several factors combined to destroy the convict leasing system. These included the economic unsustainability of leases, shifting societal attitudes, and new opposition by middle-class reformers against abuses and the use of leases to influence political lobbyists. Formal abolition occurred in 1928, when the last convict left the Alabama mines. By this time, many states had already ended their systems. Although the convict lease system was abolished, the forced labor of convicts did not end. Southern states developed a new system in the form of convict road camps, also known as chain gangs.

Emelie Tang

See also: Convict Criminology; Prisons, History of

Further Reading
Blackmon, D. A. (2008). *Slavery by another name: The re-enslavement of black Americans from the Civil War to World War II.* New York: Doubleday.
Curtin, M. E. (2000). *Black prisoners and their world, Alabama, 1865–1900.* Charlottesville: University Press of Virginia.
Fraser, S., & Freeman, J. (2012). In the rearview mirror: Barbarism and progress: The story of convict labor. *New Labor Forum, 21*(3), 94–98.
Lichtenstein, A. (1996). *Twice the work of free labor: The political economy of convict labor in the new south.* London: Verso.
Mancini, M. J. (1996). *One dies, get another: Convict leasing in the American South, 1866–1928.* Columbia: University of South Carolina Press.
Oshinsky, D. M. (1996). *Worse than slavery: Parchman farm and the ordeal of Jim Crow justice.* New York: Free Press.
Shapiro, K. A. (1998). *A new South rebellion: The battle against convict labor in the Tennessee coalfields, 1871–1896.* Chapel Hill: University of North Carolina Press.

Cooking in Prison

In addition to prison facilities providing meals for daily consumption and prisoner nutrition, inmates may also be able to cook for themselves, or purchase food and ingredients from prison commissaries. Although the cafeteria is the main food source in prisons, the second major source of food comes from the prison commissary. The prison commissary sells a range of quick and convenient food products, as well as food seasonings. Examples include ramen-style prepackaged dried noodles, other packaged soups, raw spaghetti, rice, snack cakes, cookies, jellies, chips, pork-rinds/pork skin, pretzels, fruit-drink mixes, packets of hot cocoa mix; canned foods like tuna, mackerel, and herring; and dried items like beef jerky and meat sticks.

"Spreads" specifically refer to inmate created food. Prisoners often create spreads by transforming snack food, official rations, and items purloined from the cafeteria into more elaborate edible creations. These spreads are loosely based on cooked food dishes generally available outside of prison but rarely available within prison walls. Often, these spreads represent the culinary favorites and cultural variations of the inmates. These spreads may be designed to look like the standard dish, but the ideal taste is usually not replicated. Items that can be purchased in a prison commissary for use in a spread will vary, based on the types of products stocked, available, and allowed in each prison.

COOKING FOOD

Food purchased from the commissary (as well as food smuggled out of the cafeteria) can be cooked in their cells, housing units, and dayrooms. A prisoner's ability to cook is usually governed by prison regulations and guidelines. The "chefs" are generally untrained cooks who are making the most of their ingenuity and available ingredients. Methods of preparation include fermentation, brining, or dry salt rubs. However, the most prevalent method of cooking is by using heat. Some prison commissaries sell cooking supplies, such as "hot pots." There may also be the sanctioned use of microwave ovens in a prison. Overall, there are generally no stoves or ovens available to inmates to use for cooking, nor are there cooking utensils.

Those who do cook must improvise. Cooking tools and utensils are often created from repurposed items like hair dryers, old electrical items, nail clippers, and discarded tin cans. Plastic mirrors or plastic spoons can be repurposed for cutting needs. Food can also be cooked in "pots" made from clear plastic trash bags, similar to the "boil in a bag" food products in conventional grocery stores. When water is needed, it can be obtained from sinks in the cells or bathrooms. Water can then be heated using homemade "rigged" appliances called "stingers" made from repurposed electrical cords and wires, fingernail clippers or other sources of metal, and an electric charge. Towels can serve as insulation to keep heat in when using ambient heat to cook noodles.

Inmates cook various types of food, including soups, homemade desserts, spreads that mimic nacho salads, chicken-noodle dishes, pot stickers, paella, and fried jack mack, just a few examples. Inmates report using crushed potato or corn chips as a base for food, which can be mixed with water and used as a crust or tortilla for additional ingredients to cover. Condiments can also be prepared. Mixing grape jelly and hot sauce is an example of a condiment that can be prepared for use on a spread or other culinary creation. Transforming purchased prepacked items like snack cakes and honey buns with candy toppings or melted peanut butter is an example of an elaborate treat.

SOCIAL ASPECTS

Cooking in prison can be an individual endeavor or a collective effort. Although some inmates may cook only for themselves, inmate cooking in prison is more often a social activity. Often, these activities become essential to maintaining a sense of normalcy while behind bars, and builds community. When cooking is a collaborative effort, multiple people may contribute food items to be eaten and shared by the group. In this type of reciprocal environment, each person who eats is expected to have provided a contribution in some manner: obtaining food products, transporting contraband items from one location to another, providing cooking supplies, or serving as the chef cooking the food. Depending on the culture of the facility or the generosity of the contributors, the creations may be shared with other inmates.

POPULAR CULTURE

In recent years, the culinary creations of prison gourmet chefs have been the source of recipe collections in books, on websites, and shared through social media. Examples include the *Convict Cookbook*, a compilation of recipes from inmates housed in Walla Walla, Washington's Washington State Penitentiary; the *Jailhouse Cookbook: The Prisoner's Recipe Bible*, written by a chef-turned-inmate; and *From the Big House to Your House: Cooking in Prison*, featuring 200 recipes written by six female inmates at a prison in Gatesville, Texas.

More recent books include *Prison Ramen*, which showcases a collection of ramen noodle recipes as well as stories and anecdotes from inmates, including famous celebrities, who have spent time behind bars; and *Commissary Kitchen: My Infamous Prison Cookbook*, a 2016 book highlighting recipes and cooking resourcefulness by a former inmate. Prison cooking and socialization around food are also referenced or shown in movies, television shows, and web-produced media streaming.

CAREER SKILLS

Sometimes, prisoners are afforded the ability to develop cooking skills as part of social, rehabilitative, or community endeavors. Some prison facilities offer hands-on cooking classes to inmates utilizing prison kitchens, and meals are prepared from fresh food. In some instances, produce used for these classes are grown by inmates in on-site organic vegetable gardens. There is some research-based support validating the relaxing and therapeutic effect of working in prison gardens, and improved health outcomes among inmates. In addition to the benefits to inmates, growing and utilizing on-site gardens can support sustainability initiatives, capable of producing thousands of pounds of fresh vegetables annually.

While some programs offer traditional cooking classes, other programs offer rigorous culinary arts school-level training provided by nonprofit entities. A few of these programs are beginning to emerge in the United States. Outside of the United States, programs such as these have reported positive experiences with inmates. A prison in Padua, Italy, for example, has maintained a prison bakery since 2005 and in 2014 reported that recidivism for participants is at 1–2 percent, considerably lower than Italy's reported 70 percent national average recidivism rate.

Researchers in Denmark have described cooking in prison as a pathway inmates utilize for a system of self-catering, which in addition to providing food, is designed to assist in maintaining normalization between prison life and community life. The system allows prisoners to select the food of their choice and to prepare their own meals. Through this process, prisoners also develop the skills necessary to consider cooking as a professional vocation.

Moneque Walker-Pickett

See also: Cognitive-Behavioral Therapies in Prison; Education in Prison; Prison-Based Animal Training Programs; Prison Work Programs; Vocational Training and Education

Further Reading

Binnie, I. (2014, December 9). Italy's prison panettone offers sweet way to cut crime. *Reuters.com.* Retrieved from http://www.reuters.com/article/us-italy-prison-bakery -idUSKBN0JN0R920141209

Bomkamp, S. (2016, March 7). Jail culinary program preaches power of food. *Chicago Tribune.* Retrieved from http://www.chicagotribune.com/business/ct-jail-culinary -program-0306-biz-20160301-story.html

Cate, S. (2008). "Breaking bread with a spread" in a San Francisco county jail. *Gastronomica, 8*(3), 17–24.

Genis, D. (2015, July 9). The fine art of cooking in prison. *Thrillist.com.* Retrieved from https://www.thrillist.com/eat/nation/the-fine-art-of-cooking-in-prison-ingenious -jailhouse-cooking-hacks

Minke, L. K. (2014). Cooking in prison—from crook to cook. *International Journal of Prisoner Health, 10*(4), 228–238.

Pardes, A. (2015). The art of gourmet cooking in prison. *Vice.com.* Retrieved from https:// www.vice.com/en_us/article/the-art-of-gourmet-cooking-in-prison-511

Recipe for Change Project. (2017). Retrieved February 2017 from http://www.recipe forchangeproject.com

Rutt, D. (2015). FREE to grow. *Horticulture, 112*(4), 44–49.

Correctional Case Management

The term *correctional case management* refers to a job classification of an employee who is assigned a caseload of inmates to "manage" (it can also refer to a system by which paperwork associated with an inmate is managed). This term is used throughout prison systems in the United States. For an employee assigned a caseload, there is a wide variety of expectations both within systems and between systems. The primary issue with regard to the difficulty describing the job of a case manager is directly linked to the variety of expectations of stakeholders. Case managers themselves often find it difficult to succinctly describe their role, because it often depends on who is asking.

Case managers are pulled between the expectations of pushing paper and the expectations of guiding inmates through a change process. There is seldom time to do both because the caseloads can exceed 100 inmates. Many times the work of the case manager is judged by the quality and timeliness of the paperwork, so that is where their focus is often required. The paperwork includes vital documents such as earned/good time grants, classification actions, referrals to lower security facilities, and program placements. However, case managers often spend so much time on their computers in their offices that they have little time to work with their assigned inmates or even to find out what the individual inmate truly needs to progress. Additionally, the case manager is often the person that is held responsible (blamed) when an inmate is overlooked for progress, a program, and, in some states, for release.

The reality of the corrections system is that someone needs to be assigned to each individual inmate to ensure that he or she does not get lost in the process.

Ultimately, it would be ideal if that person who is assigned has the tools and time to help the inmate through a change process. Toward that end, many systems have implemented a series of important strategies to achieve this goal.

One of the first strategies implemented in a variety of corrections systems is to require some college or a college degree for entry into case management positions. The focus on the educational preparation implies that the system is serious about the level of work that is needed to assist individuals to change. This educational preparation is an important step if the expectation is that the case manager will be a part of the change process.

A second strategy in many jurisdictions is the adoption of evidence-based practices including motivational interviewing. Motivational interviewing is a style of "directive, client-centered counseling" that is aimed at behavior change of clients. This strategy requires individuals to be trained in the art of motivational interviewing, but it requires more than sending an employee to a couple days of training. Often at least two multiday trainings are required with follow-up coaching and monitoring for skill development throughout the process. The cost and time commitment to this strategy are significant, and it must be built within a system where the retention of case managers is a high priority. It does no good to send employees through this extensive process only to lose them to another agency or career opportunity.

An additional strategy that is in use is to focus on recruiting case managers who have education and experience in counseling and guidance. This seems to be a natural fit for the preferred outcomes of working with inmates. Systems that commit to this strategy can only be successful if the employee has the time to use these skills. When employees are specifically recruited for a "counseling" job, and then they find that they only have time for paperwork, their focus can quickly turn to finding a different job. These same college-educated case managers are also usually hired from outside the corrections system, so they have a very steep learning curve for working with inmates and working within the corrections culture. They may be great at counseling and even great at the paperwork, but the expectations of the corrections environment may not be a good fit.

In a perfect corrections system, the case manager would be the primary agent in guiding an inmate toward change. The case manager's work could focus on the reentry needs of the inmate, including housing, employment, and family support. Many imperfect systems have realized that this vital reentry piece is missing. Whether it is due to control, politics, or funding, one approach taken has been to develop another division of employees within the corrections workforce who do just reentry. Systems that have taken this approach have had some success in developing networks in the communities to support the inmates as they are released from prison. However, in such systems the end result can be a division between the reentry employees and all other employees. This can lead to a system where reentry is not the "job" of most correctional employees.

One study suggests that real change can only occur when all prison officials see the return of the inmate back to the community as part of their job (Petersilia, 2009). Although some systems have recently been successful in reducing recidivism of inmates, no system has been able to implement a complete culture change to where the job of reentry is shared by every employee.

As long as the recidivism rate is the standard by which success or failure of a corrections system is judged, then the case manager's work will continue to be a key part of this process. If the corrections systems could capitalize on the concept of reducing the caseloads of their case managers so that they could effectively guide each assigned inmate through the system, perhaps the result would be a reduction in inmates who return to prison.

If a case manager had the time and preparation to work with individual inmates, then a system could truly measure the effect of strategies like motivational interviewing. The case manager would then be in a position to ensure that the inmates are placed in the right program and facility, based on their needs and the safety and security needs of the jurisdiction. This case manager would also then be able to connect the individual inmate to the appropriate services and programs. In many cases, the program exists but often has the wrong inmate in it. In other instances, the "right" programming does not exist, so the case managers often get creative to try to fit the needs of their assigned inmates into the available program slots. This creativity is often not acknowledged and many times cannot be called an evidence-based programming choice.

Even with the right programs and a system that allows for inmates to be placed effectively, the individual inmates may not want to be rehabilitated. This type of resistance can be demoralizing and lead very quickly to burnout among all correctional employees, but the risk of burnout is perhaps higher among case managers.

The reality is that only on TV does the warden know the behavioral history of every inmate. If change is the goal, then the corrections system desperately needs someone who has connected to the individual inmate. One-to-one connections with individuals just might be the solution that the corrections system is searching for, and the case manager can be the person to be that connection. Case management is an idea that just might work to prepare individuals leaving prison for a productive life and keeping them out of prison.

Susan Jones

See also: Administration; Correctional Counseling; Inmates with Co-Occurring Disorders

Further Reading

Andrews, D. A., Bonta, J., & Wormith, J. S. (2006). The recent past and near future of risk and/or need assessment. *Crime & Delinquency, 52*(1), 7–27.

Clarkson, P., & Shaw, P. (1992). Human relationships at work and in organisations. *Management Education & Development, 23*(1), 18–29

Cullen, F. T., Link, B. G., Wolfe, N. T., & Frank, J. (1990). How satisfying is prison work: A comparative occupational approach. *Journal of Offender Counseling, Services & Rehabilitation, 14*, 89–108.

Finckenauer, J. O. (2005). The quest for quality in criminal justice education. *Justice Quarterly, 22*(4), 413–426.

Liou, K.-T. (1994). The effect of professional orientation on job stress. *Review of Public Personnel Administration, 14*(1), 52–63.

Motivational interviewing. (2016). *Motivational interviewing: What is MI?* Retrieved March 21, 2016, from http://www.motivationalinterview.net/clinical/whatismi.html

Petersilia, J. (2009). *When prisoners come home: Parole and prisoner reentry.* New York: Oxford University Press.

PEW Center on the States. (2011). *State of recidivism: The revolving door of America's prisons.* Washington DC: PEW Charitable Trust.

Sever, B., Coram, G., & Meltzer, G. (2008). Criminal justice graduate programs at the beginning of the 21st century. *Criminal Justice Review, 33*(2), 221–249.

Stinchcomb, J. B. (2004). Making the grade: Professionalizing the 21st century workforce through higher education partnerships. *Corrections Today.* Retrieved November 15, 2017, from https://www.thefreelibrary.com/Making+the+grade%3a+professionalizing+the+21st+century+workforce . . . -a0121150608

Correctional Counseling

"Correctional counseling" is a term that refers to any type of counseling, particularly counseling associated with mental health or substance abuse, occurring in a correctional institution or in a program aligned with a community corrections requirement. To be more specific, correctional counseling is the process whereby trained mental health professionals help offenders identify and incorporate adaptive behavioral, psychological, and emotional responses to life events so as to improve their quality of life and minimize their involvement in criminal activity. This process tends to occur in any environment where the clinician and the offender or offenders are able to gather in an attempt to set and achieve therapeutic goals that are set between the clinician and the offender client. The process of providing correctional counseling initially entails a process of screening, diagnosing, and assessing an offender in order to carry out a planned method of intervention that will help to replace dysfunctional behavior with adaptive and prosocial behavior.

Typically speaking, most types of correctional treatment programs have a process during which the offender is first examined, tested, diagnosed, and administratively classified for both supervision and treatment purposes. In one way or another, this process includes four key components: assessment, diagnosis, recidivism prediction, and classification. During assessment, both subjective clinical interviews and objective forms of test taking are conducted. This is followed by the diagnosis process where offenders' physical health, mental health, and life-course challenges are identified and usually coded using medical-based or *Diagnostic and Statistical Manual of Mental Disorders,* 5th ed. (DSM-5) criteria. After this, recidivism prediction requires a determination as to the level of risk that an offender may have for future offending. These predictions are often based on both subjective and objective information. Lastly, during classification, housing, job, and educational assignments are decided for offenders within correctional institutions, while treatment, vocational, and supervision levels are determined for offenders on community supervision.

Next, a treatment planning phase usually follows this four-stage process, whereby goals regarding mental health treatment, relapse prevention (for substance abusers), job acquisition, lifestyle choices, and other such issues are addressed. This goal-setting process is, in an ideal setting, a collaborative effort between the offender and the counselor. Next is the actual intervention program itself, which is often a manualized set of topics, assignments, and group discussions when in an institutional or court-mandated program. The last phase of this process is usually referred to as discharge planning. This is when the offender completes correctional programming, and plans are made for their future beyond treatment.

The aforementioned model of program delivery is taught to a variety of professionals in the mental health field, including counselors, social workers, psychologists, and psychiatrists. Counselors, particularly mental health counselors, usually have a master's degree in counseling and receive training in psychological interventions for life challenges as well as mental disorders. These individuals are then required to complete additional hours of supervised training for their licensure, ultimately being referred to as licensed professional counselors (LPCs). Social workers, particularly licensed clinical social workers (LCSW), have a master's degree in social work. Their training often includes psychological interventions and case management processes. They also must complete hours of supervised practice before obtaining their license. Psychologists who are independently licensed have doctoral degrees in psychology (having either a PhD or a PsyD), this usually being clinical psychology, along with extensive supervised practice. In addition, they typically have education and/or experience in both research and the administration of psychological tests and assessments. Lastly, psychiatrists have medical doctorates (MD) and serve as medical directors over many treatment programs, being responsible for delivering medications for inmates who are seriously disturbed or who need to be subdued. Their ability to prescribe medication for disorders like anxiety, bipolar and unipolar depression, and schizophrenia is what sets them apart from the other treatment providers.

COMMON THEORETICAL FOUNDATIONS

There are a number of theoretical approaches within the field of psychotherapy that might be employed by treatment providers. While this is the case, there are some approaches that are used more often than others within the correctional context. It is with this in mind that a brief overview of some of the more common therapeutic orientations found in prison and community corrections settings is provided. Thus, this list is by no means exhaustive but instead simply highlights the more common approaches that one might encounter within the correctional industry.

The first and most widely used approach is the use of cognitive-behavioral therapy, often referred to as CBT. A basic premise of this approach is that maladaptive behaviors, thoughts (cognitions), and emotions are learned and, by the same logic, can be unlearned, or modified by new learning. Though CBT is referred to as therapy, there is a strong educational component to this approach, as well. Participants are involved in a teaching-and-learning process whereby they challenge faulty thinking, cognitive distortions, catastrophic thinking, and they are required to practice more adaptive forms of thinking, feeling, and behaving.

Another common approach is reality therapy. This form of therapy contends that individuals have control over what they do. In this type of therapy, the counselor will usually reject irresponsible and unrealistic behavior, insisting that the client assume responsibility without offering denial or excuses for failing to be accountable. From this point the counselor teaches the offender-client how to fulfill his or her needs within the limits set by reality. More specifically, reality therapists first have offenders identify their wants and needs. Next, they have offenders examine their behavior to determine whether what they have been doing has provided them with these wants and needs. Next, the therapist will confront offenders with the consequences of their behavior and will require that offenders judge the overall effectiveness of their behavior. Lastly, when the offender fully evaluates his or her behavior and comes to the conclusion that a change is due, the therapist helps the offender-client to develop a plan for behavioral change.

Another counseling approach utilized in correctional systems is Adlerian therapy. This type of treatment is based on the belief that human behavior has a purpose, is goal oriented, and that the purposes and goals tend to exist within a fabric of social connections. Further, Alfred Adler (1870–1937) contended that many people suffer from emotional difficulties and suffer from feelings of inferiority. The counselor provides a reeducation approach that encourages greater social participation among offenders and also addresses root causes of inferiority. One key to this approach is that most of the problems facing offenders stem from their lack of social connections. Helping offenders to strive toward achieving social goals is a key aspect to this approach.

One last approach that is used frequently with correctional populations is family systems therapy. It should be noted that this approach is not often used in prisons but is most frequently used in community settings where offenders are provided treatment while on probation or parole. This is especially the case with juveniles and offenders who are parents seeking to resolve custody and/or parental fitness issues with state social services agencies. This is also a common adjunct therapy for individuals in substance abuse treatment. This type of counseling looks at the entire family as a system with its own customs, roles, beliefs, and dynamics that affect and routinely impact the offender. This type of therapy builds around individual counseling sessions and is effective in getting the family involved with the offender's treatment.

TWO GOALS

Correctional counseling is utilized in prisons and the community as a means of providing opportunities for change, should the offender be willing to do so. If offenders are motivated to change, it is presumed that their likelihood for recidivism will decrease, and it is also thought that their level of emotional functioning will increase. Both of these goals—the reduction of recidivism and the improvement of functioning—are simultaneously important. Indeed, while most correctional systems may place recidivism reduction as the chief priority, such reductions in the future commission of crime are unlikely to occur if the offender's overall level of functioning does not improve.

Many people, laypersons and professionals alike, fail to understand that correctional counseling programs are designed to improve public safety. Correctional counseling programs are almost universally intended to increase offender account-ability for their criminal behavior while giving them the insight and tools neces-sary to change that behavior. In this process, offenders are taught to identify persons, activities, and places that serve as risks to engaging in criminal behavior, and they are encouraged to identify persons, activities, and places that lead to law-abiding behavior. Obtaining law-abiding peer groups, attending prosocial functions, and frequenting places that have deterrents to the commission of crime all help to keep the offender focused on a life without crime.

The process of improving the offender-client's functioning involves an introspec-tive examination of how offenders rationalize their actions and also identifying the types of attributions that they make in relation to the intent and behavior of others. Often, the meaning and intent that offenders believe to be associated with other persons are simply projections that they make due to their own views of the world. Addressing criminogenic beliefs that justify criminal behavior (i.e., tech-niques of neutralization) are the result of distorted cognitions (i.e., all-or-nothing thinking) or lead to faulty expectations (i.e., unwillingness to delay gratification) that must be reworked so that offenders no longer seek to "get over" on society through hustling and conning. Rather, a change in their cognitive schema is the goal with moral views and perceptions of success emphasizing not only the out-come but the process by which a person makes his or her way through society.

Robert D. Hanser

See also: Correctional Case Management; Ethical Issues in Prison Counseling; Inmate Classification; Treatment Professionals in Prisons

Further Reading

Hanser, R. D. (2007). *Special needs offenders in the community.* Upper Saddle River, NJ: Pearson/Prentice Hall.

Hanser, R. D., & Mire, S. M. (2009). *Correctional counseling.* Upper Saddle River, NJ: Pearson/Prentice Hall.

Sun, K. (2013). *Correctional counseling: A cognitive growth perspective* (2nd ed.). Burl-ington, MA: Jones & Bartlett.

Correctional Employees and Administrators, Job Satisfaction of

Correctional officer job satisfaction is important to the success of prison operations as well as to the security of the inmates, personnel, and the facility. Job satisfac-tion refers to the extent to which an individual likes his or her job. Existing research has focused on many aspects of job dissatisfaction in order to identify procedures and practices that would likely increase job satisfaction and improve the efficiency of prison operations. Job stress and burnout, role conflict and ambiguity, lack of administration and supervisory support, work-family conflict, perception of job dangerousness, along with demographic variables such as age, work experience, education, race and ethnicity, and gender all play important roles in determining a correctional officer's level of job satisfaction. People who are satisfied with their jobs are more loyal, stay on the job longer, and handle pressure better.

Prison employees work in an environment that many would describe as stressful and often report higher levels of job dissatisfaction. Thus, stress and job dissatisfaction among correctional officers often occur together. Stress leads to high turnover among correctional officers, poor officer performance, costly errors, low morale, psychological tension, and a lack of pride or satisfaction in the job. Understaffing is a direct result of high turnover and may lead to mandatory overtime, which can be both physically and psychologically tiring for officers. It can also lead to conflict between the officer and his or her family.

Role conflict and role ambiguity are major contributors to job dissatisfaction among correctional officers. Role conflict refers to the ambiguous nature of the job where correctional officers are expected to maintain security in the prison and to treat or rehabilitate the inmates at the same time. This situation creates role conflict because what the officer might do to rehabilitate could conflict with requirements for safety. The policies, procedures, and responsibilities for operation are constantly changing, resulting in role ambiguity. Role ambiguity, lack of clarity in expectations of the job, is a source of stress that can lead to early termination or resignation of correctional officers.

Relationships matter for correctional employees. Correctional officers with good relationships with supervisors and their peers report greater job satisfaction. Correctional officers who view the administration as nonsupportive are more distrustful, have low morale, and experience higher levels of stress. A supportive administration assists in job satisfaction and a well-run, efficient prison operation. Positive relationships with coworkers also decrease stress and increase job satisfaction. Peer associations and clearly stated institutional policies greatly reduce stress and increase the level of job satisfaction of correctional officers far more than individual personal factors.

Another important factor when studying the effects of job satisfaction among correctional officers is the relationship between work-family conflict and its effect on the job. Growing incarceration rates, increasing officer turnover, mandatory overtime, and increased stress cause challenges for the correctional officer outside of the workplace. Job stressors such as shift work, exposure to dangers, lack of promotional opportunities, low pay, overtime, and lack of supervisor support may ultimately cause problems at home for the correctional officer and his or her family. The impact of work on family conflict can be ameliorated by the provision of supervisory support, education, and work-life balance programming.

Personal or demographic characteristics such as age, experience, and education have also been discussed for their impact on correctional officer job satisfaction. Research to date shows little support for age differences in levels of job satisfaction among correctional officers. However, the length of time employed, that is, experience on the job, may be an important determinate of correctional officer job satisfaction. In an attempt to reduce high employment turnover rates of correctional officers, many states are increasing educational requirements of their officers. Research to date shows mixed results regarding the relationship between education and job satisfaction of correctional officers. Thus, requiring correctional officers to be better educated has not necessarily led to greater job satisfaction.

Race and ethnicity are personal characteristics of officers that have been assumed to impact levels of job satisfaction. The research evidence has been inconclusive with some studies showing lower levels of job satisfaction among nonwhite officers, and race or ethnicity having limited impact in other studies. Geographic and cultural differences may have a bigger influence on job satisfaction than race or ethnicity alone. Studies conducted in southern states have shown a relationship between race, stress, and job satisfaction.

Prison policy and practices are often based on the belief that men are more effective correctional officers, and as a result females suffer from harassment from inmates, coworkers, and administration. Although the stress may be higher for female correctional officers than male correctional officers, the research on gender and job satisfaction has shown little or no relationship between the two. Educational background, perceptions of working conditions, job advancement and relations between inmates, attitudes toward peers, and supervisors impacted job satisfaction for both the males and females. Thus, while personal factors matter, job characteristics and organizational factors such as day-to-day duties and stressors, and social support, have a greater influence on correctional officer job satisfaction.

Existing research has focused mainly on stress and job satisfaction of correctional officers, but few studies have examined the levels of stress and its relationship to correctional supervisors and job satisfaction. Stress is an inherent part of the job, but stress may be higher for correctional officers than for their supervisors. Researchers found that among correctional agency supervisors, overall stress levels are low. Consequently, correctional supervisors experience less stress, report greater levels of social support, and are more satisfied with their jobs as supervisors. Research indicated that the higher level of job satisfaction among supervisors is related to a higher degree of locus of control. Correctional supervisors have significantly greater power to determine the nature, scope, and breadth of the daily work environment. Supervisors are the decision makers within the organization for themselves as well as for others. In contrast, correctional officers are more likely to perceive that their daily work experience is regulated by environmental factors that they cannot control. The result is that correctional supervisors are more satisfied with the job than the people they supervise.

It is critical for supervisors and prison administrators to assist officers by maintaining open lines of communication, increasing support, and reducing stressors that cause job dissatisfaction and job burnout. Correctional agencies characterized by high levels of stress, burnout, and dissatisfaction are less able to effectively monitor, supervise, and rehabilitate inmates. Thus, correctional agencies are encouraged to gather resources, develop programs, and implement more effective procedures to help lower and alleviate correctional officer stress. Clearly defining roles and duties, encouraging decision making and the use of discretion, working toward reducing staffing shortages and mandatory overtime, and providing adequate training are effective ways in which administrators can reduce job stress, increase correctional officer job satisfaction, and benefit the overall operation of the prison. A responsive administration, one that cares about the officers' concerns and needs, is a necessity for an efficiently functioning prison.

Correctional officers are an integral part of the prison community. The role of correctional officer is vital to the efficiency, stability, and security of prison operations. Demographic, organizational, and job characteristic factors play an important part in correctional officer job satisfaction. Increasing levels of satisfaction, decreasing stress, and providing ample supervisory and administrative support are essential to a well-run institution.

Brenda James and Martha Henderson Hurley

See also: Correctional Officer Subculture; Correctional Officers, Job Stress among; Inappropriate Correctional Employee–Inmate Relationships; Personnel

Further Reading

Armstrong, G. S., Atkin-Plunk, C. A., & Wells, J. (2015). The relationship between work-family conflict, correctional officer job stress, and job satisfaction. *Criminal Justice and Behavior, 42*(10), 1066–1082.

Blau, J., Light, S., & Chamlin, M. (1986). Individual and contextual effects on stress and job satisfaction: A study of prison staff. *Work and Occupations, 13*, 131–156.

Britton, D. (2003). *At work in the iron cage: The prison as a gendered organization.* New York: New York University Press.

Brough, P., & Williams, J. (2007). Managing occupational stress in a high-risk industry: Measuring the job demands of correctional officers. *Criminal Justice and Behavior, 34*(4), 555–567.

Camp, S., & Steiger, T. (1995). Gender and racial differences in perception of career opportunities and the work environment in a traditionally white, male occupation. In N. Jackson (Ed.), *Contemporary issues in criminal justice: Shaping tomorrow's system* (pp. 258–290). New York: McGraw-Hill.

Cheeseman, K. A., & Downey, R. A. (2012). Talking 'bout my generation: The effect of "generation" on correctional employee perceptions of work stress and job satisfaction. *The Prison Journal, 92*(1), 24–44.

Cheeseman, K. A., Kim, B., Lambert, E. G., & Hogan, N. L. (2011). Correctional officer perceptions of inmates and overall job satisfaction. *Journal of Crime and Justice, 34*(2), 81–102.

Cullen, F. T., Link, B. G., Cullen, J. B., & Wolfe, N. T. (1989). How satisfying is prison work? A comparative occupational approach. *Journal of Offender Counseling, Services and Rehabilitation, 14*, 89–108.

Cullen, F. T., Link, B. G., Wolfe, N. T., & Frank, J. (1985). The social dimensions of correctional officer tress. *Justice Quarterly, 2*, 505–533.

Grossi, E. L., & Berg, B. L. (1991). Stress and job dissatisfaction among correctional officers: An unexpected finding. *International Journal of Offender Therapy and Comparative Criminology, 35*(1), 73–81.

Grossi, E. L., Keil, T. J., & Vito, G. F. (1996). Surviving "the joint": Mitigating factors of correctional officer stress. *Journal of Crime and Justice, 19*(2), 103–120.

Hartley, D. J., Davila, M. A., Marquart, J. W., & Mullings, J. L. (2013). Fear is a disease: The impact of fear and exposure to infectious disease on correctional officer job stress and satisfaction. *American Journal of Criminal Justice, 38*, 323–340.

Jacobs, J. B., & Greer, M. P. (1977). Drop outs and rejects: An analysis of the prison guard's revolving door. *Criminal Justice Review, 2*(2), 57–70.

Jurik, N. C., & Halemba, G. J. (1984). Gender, working conditions and the job satisfaction of women in a non-traditional occupation: Female correctional officers in men's prisons. *The Sociological Quarterly, 25*, 551–566.

Lambert, E. G., Hogan, N. L., & Barton, S. M. (2002). Satisfied correctional staff. A review of the literature on the correlates of correctional staff job satisfaction. *Criminal Justice and Behavior, 29*(2), 115–143.

Lombardo, L. (1981). *Guards imprisoned: Correctional officers at work.* New York: Elsevier.

Owen, S. (2006). Occupational stress among correctional supervisors. *Prison Journal, 86,* 164–181.

Paoline, E. A., Lambert, E. G., & Hogan, N. L. (2006). A calm and happy keeper of the keys: The impact of ACA views, relations with coworkers, and policy views on the job stress and job satisfaction of correctional staff. *The Prison Journal, 86*(2), 182–205.

Triplett, R., Mullings, J. L., & Scarborough, K. E. (1996). Work-related stress and coping among correctional officers: Implications from organizational literature. *Journal of Criminal Justice, 24*(4), 291–308.

Van Voorhis, P., Cullen, F. T., Link, B. G., & Wolfe, N. T. (1991). The impact of race and gender on correctional officers' orientation to the integrated environment. *Journal of Research in Crime and Delinquency, 28,* 472–500.

Walters, S. (1993). Gender, job satisfaction, and correctional officers: A comparative analysis. *Justice Professional, 7*(2), 23–33.

Wright, K., & Saylor, W. (1992). Comparison of perceptions of the environment between minority and nonminority employees of the federal prison system. *Journal of Criminal Justice, 20,* 63–71.

Zimmer, L. (1986). *Women guarding men.* Chicago: University of Chicago Press.

Correctional Officer Subculture

Most professions, including corrections, create a subculture that identifies the values and norms that exist within the work environment. The type of work environment may dictate the extent and reach of these cultural rules. Corrections work is a very regimented and stressful environment; as a result, the subculture for corrections officers has evolved into a very rigid and unforgiving system. This culture is not formally taught to new employees, but it is learned very quickly and often very effectively. Both new and seasoned employees witness the impact of the culture when someone breaks one of the unwritten rules.

For instance, if an employee shares information with management personnel that results in another officer being disciplined, the backlash from the culture can be swift and daunting. This type of "ratting" does not have to be done with the intent to hurt another officer's career; it can be something as simple as truthfully detailing events of an incident. The naïve employee who does not think each part of the incident through to ensure that no one would be held accountable for wrongdoing is often ostracized by the group. Such a mistake or lapse in judgement can be something from which there is no recovery.

This subculture dictates expectations about how corrections staff treat each other, how they interact with management, and how they treat inmates. The nuances in this culture make allowances for differences between individual facility security levels and individual power. A corrections officer with a long family history in this line of work, or one who has paid the dues by working in corrections for over

30 years, may live by a slightly different set of rules than the new employee. For instance, such an employee may be supported in a decision to call in "sick" to work in order to play in a local golf tournament, but an employee with less power would be "punished" for such an affront to the people that they left to work short.

One of the most commonly communicated facets of this culture is that the corrections world is a family and that employees are part of that family whether they want to be or not. This family concept is communicated in such a fashion that many new employees believe that they will be supported and mentored into becoming a strong asset to the organization. Although this does sometimes occur, stories of how this "family" left a member alone or abandoned are also frequently communicated.

Another very common aspect of this culture is a clear idea of "us" versus "them." Agencies or facilities may differ about exactly how these groups are defined, but the need to identify the enemy is very strong in this culture. The term "them" is not always limited to the inmates. Some scholars have identified instances where corrections officers felt more aligned with the inmates than with their leadership.

This subculture is so powerful that it goes far beyond the perimeters of the correctional facilities and can be found in the surrounding communities. The strength of the culture's reach can be affected by the nature of the community. For instance, if the community has strong ties to the prison industry, the impact of the culture can be found within many facets of the community. In this type of community the use of prison slang is often found among people who do not directly work inside a corrections facility. Additionally, many community members may be able to describe with great detail particular emergency response protocols such as escape apprehension procedures.

This type of overflow into the local prison town is a direct result of a long history of living and working beside these institutions and corrections employees. The sound of the prison whistle at noon may be an ordinary part of the day, but the sound of three short bursts of this whistle may communicate that the search team has been called out and a variety of functions in the community will be affected. For instance, the schools may go on lockdown status without being specifically informed of an incident, and local convenience stores may hold over employees to staff the midnight shift because they know that this will impact their business.

The effect of this culture can also be seen when talking to the children of corrections officers. These children may learn some very valuable life skills, but they definitely learn some prison lingo. There is some anecdotal evidence that families and children of corrections employees may be more at risk of abuse or neglect, but this has not been thoroughly researched. Even so, the news media is quick to point out when a corrections officer has lashed out at his or her family.

This culture also fulfills a very important role by regulating the impact of change on its members. The correctional environment is constantly bouncing from one extreme to the other as the emphasis on rehabilitation and punishment changes. The effect on the people who work in this environment can be significant when the rules are altered dramatically. The subculture uses its power to make the responses to these orders for change more manageable. The primary tool in their arsenal is that of passive resistance. Waiting it out often includes an effort to make it look as if the new rules are being followed, but the reality is that very little below the surface actually changes.

The effect of this culture on the individuals who choose to work in this environment can be felt long after they leave corrections either by retirement, resignation, or termination. The impact of the corrections culture is often described as difficult to "shake." Some retired corrections workers have never really been able to remove themselves from the corrections world, and they may find themselves at one of two extremes: isolating from people or staying very connected to current employees so that they are very invested in the daily happenings within their former facility.

The corrections culture is similar to what might be found in large police agencies or military units. The need for a shared culture is an attempt to define boundaries and allegiances. This culture can bring a diverse group of people together to work toward a common and sometimes very difficult goal—keeping convicted criminals contained and controlled. This same culture can also be very harsh and cruel to its own members by failing to support individuals as they make mistakes in a very high stakes game.

Susan Jones

See also: Correctional Officer Unions; Correctional Officers and Discretion; Misconduct by Correctional Employees; Prisonization; Stanford Prison Experiment

Further Reading

American Correctional Association. (2012). *Public correctional policy on the term "correctional officer."* Public correctional policies. Alexandria, VA.

Armstrong, G. S., & Griffin, M. L. (2004). Does the job matter? Comparing correlates of stress among treatment and correctional staff in prisons. *Journal of Criminal Justice, 32*(6), 577–592.

Blau, J. R., Light, S. C., & Chamlin, M. (1986). Individual and contextual effects of stress and job satisfaction: A study of prison staff. *Work and Occupations, 13*(11), 131–156.

Britton, D. M. (1997). Gendered organizational logic. *Gender & Society, 11*(6), 796–818.

Britton, D. M. (2003). *At work in the iron cage: The prison as gendered organization.* New York: New York University Press.

Crawley, E. (2005). Prison officers and prison work. *Prison Service Journal, 3*(3), 3–10.

Esselstyn, T. C. (1966). The social system of correctional workers. *Crime & Delinquency, 12*(1), 117–126.

Gilmartin, K. M., & Davis, R. M. (2005). The correctional officer Stockholm syndrome: Management implications. In National Institute of Corrections (Ed.), *First Annual Symposium on New Generations Jails.*

Gordon, M. S. (2005). *Correctional officer control ideology: Implications for understanding a system.* Doctor of public administration, University of Baltimore, Baltimore, MD.

Jones, S. (2013). *A portrait of boundary violations: Former female employees of corrections who have established a relationship with an inmate.* Doctor of philosophy, University of Colorado, Colorado Springs.

Jones, S. (2015). Recommendations for correctional leaders to reduce boundary violations: Female correctional employees and male inmates. *Women & Criminal Justice, 25*(5), 1–19.

Lipsky, M. (1980). *Street-level bureaucracy: Dilemmas of the individual in public service.* New York: Russell Sage.

Micieli, J. (2008). *Stress and effects of working in a high security prison,* NCJ 224105. Rockville, MD: NCRS.gov. Retrieved from https://www.ncjrs.gov/App/Publications /abstract.aspx?ID=246060

Whitehead, J. T., & Lindquist, C. A. (1986). Correctional officer job burnout: A path model. *Journal of Research in Crime and Delinquency, 23*(23), 23–42.

Correctional Officer Training

The American criminal justice system is comprised of law enforcement, courts, and corrections. Corrections is a broad field that includes both community and institutional programs. The mission of institutional corrections has remained constant in recent history. Correctional agencies are charged with the care and custody of inmates and delivering various rehabilitative treatment programs, while focusing on public safety. Institutional corrections has experienced tremendous growth recently. More than half of the prisons in the United States have been built since the late 1980s. Also, 1 out of every 110 adults, more than 2.2 million, are incarcerated in jail or prison in the United States, at a cost of nearly $61 billion annually. Furthermore, there are nearly 750,000 correctional employees. Given the increasing inmate population, there is a need to recruit, train, and develop professional correctional officers (COs) to staff these facilities.

CORRECTIONAL OFFICERS

There are several levels of COs. The Federal Bureau of Prisons, within the Department of Justice, employs COs. All states have a department of corrections that is charged with operating facilities that employ COs. Sheriffs, or other county-level facilities, employ COs. Some municipalities hire COs to operate local facilities. There are many juvenile institutions that employ officers; however, they may have other job titles. Also, COs may work for private companies with contracts to operate facilities.

The role of the CO is to maintain public safety by managing institutional security and inmate accountability. Although specific job descriptions may vary depending on the level and jurisdiction, some common requirements include:

- Patrolling the facility
- Conducting searches
- Transporting inmates
- Using restraint equipment
- Maintaining proficiency with various weapons
- Counseling inmates

CO jobs offer competitive salaries, benefits such as retirement (often in a special risk classification), paid holidays, sick and annual leave, and opportunities to work overtime. Most agencies report staffing problems and are frequently recruiting new officers. Many states require that COs obtain and maintain certification. The process of certification is regulated by states.

Most CO positions require a high school diploma, GED, or equivalent. However, some scholars have called for COs to have college degrees. A college education may also provide an advantage for promotion and advancement within the agency.

BASIC RECRUIT TRAINING

The initial training of a CO is the basic recruit academy. The length, content, and requirements of the academy can vary. In some cases, academies may be residential. The COs will live in dormitories with meals provided at the academy cafeteria and have access to recreational or fitness facilities. The training is conducted in typical classrooms, labs that simulate the correctional institution setting, gymnasiums, and firearm ranges. Trainees will have examinations on the material that is presented. Furthermore, trainees may have to demonstrate certain skills through proficiency tests and role play. In some states, once trainees complete the academy, they will take a state-administered certification exam to complete the certification process. For example, in Florida, trainees who successfully complete the academy are eligible to take the Florida Department of Law Enforcement State Officer Certification Examination that is administered by the Standards and Training Commission. Candidates can have three attempts to pass the exam. If candidates fail to pass in three attempts, they must repeat basic recruit training.

Course Topic	Course Description	Clock Hours
Introduction to Corrections	This course introduces to the recruit the concepts and theories associated with the correctional side of the criminal justice system.	32
Correctional Communications	This course covers all aspects of communication within the correctional setting.	40
Correctional Officer Safety	This course covers all aspects of officer safety within the correctional setting.	16
Correctional Facility and Equipment	This course details and describes correctional facilities and equipment.	8
Correctional Intake and Release	This course details the intake and release requirements and processes.	18
Criminal Justice Defensive Tactics	This course provides skills development for the officer, appropriate for the threat level, within Florida law. Demonstration of proficiency is required.	80
Criminal Justice Firearms	This course develops proficiency with the semi-automatic pistol used by a law enforcement officer. Qualification with the weapon is required.	80

(*continued*)

Course Topic	Course Description	Clock Hours
CMS First Aid for Criminal Justice Officers	This course provides life-saving skills development in emergency medical situations appropriate for the law enforcement first responder, including CPR, communicable diseases, and hazardous materials.	40
Supervising in a Correctional Facility	This course details the supervision of inmates within a correctional facility.	40
Supervising Special Populations	This course details the special needs, requirements, and services for special population inmates within a correctional facility.	20
Responding to Correctional Incidents and Emergencies	This course details the procedures and requirements when dealing with critical incidents and emergencies within a correctional facility.	16
Correctional Officer Wellness and Physical Abilities	This course covers aspects of officer wellness and physical fitness training.	30
Total		420

Academy classes are taught by full-time academy instructors, adjuncts who have experience in the field, or topic experts. In Florida, academy instructors are required to be certified by completing an 80-hour instructor techniques course and a supervised internship. Furthermore, instructors of certain specialized topics like defensive tactics, firearms, and first aid must have additional training for certification.

FIELD TRAINING

Upon completion of the basic recruit academy, many agencies require COs to complete a formal field training program. Field training is an on-the-job training program where trainees are assigned to an experienced field training officer (FTO). Although the length of field training may vary, most programs utilize a multiphase approach. For example, during phase 1, the trainee may simply observe the FTO perform daily tasks. As these tasks are being performed, the FTO will provide continuous instruction to the trainee on policy and procedure. In phase 2, the FTO will gradually allow the trainee to perform some tasks under direct supervision. During phase 3, the trainee will be assigned additional tasks and responsibilities with little guidance from the FTO. In the final phase, the trainee performs the daily tasks of the job while the FTO only observes. The FTO makes written Daily Observation Reports (DORs) that evaluate the trainee's performance. Should a trainee fail to achieve satisfactory progress at any phase, the FTO may recommend an extension of training before the CO completes the field training program.

IN-SERVICE TRAINING

There are certain in-service training topics that can help COs perform job tasks more effectively and develop as professionals. One such topic is ethics training. The ethics of COs may be frequently tested by inmates. Prisoners are known to play "con-games" that attempt to compromise officers. COs must stay on guard for such attempts. Other topics that may assist COs in workplace include:

- Inmates with mental disabilities
- Prison Rape Elimination Act
- Juvenile and youthful offenders
- Sex offenders
- Elderly inmates
- LGBT inmates

Furthermore, many agencies require annual training in areas of high liability. In Florida, COs are required to train annually on the topics of human diversity, use of force, stun devices, and firearms qualification. Although not often required, many agencies offer stress reduction and wellness courses to help officers cope with stressors that are inherent to the occupation such as shift work, overtime, exposure to some of the worst members of society, and threats of violence. The world is rapidly changing, and the need for COs to keep up with technology and changes that impact corrections is paramount to perform job tasks well.

CONCLUSION

Corrections is a component of the criminal justice system that is experiencing tremendous growth. However, this growth has been challenged by shrinking operational budgets and intense public scrutiny. In order to operate efficiently and effectively, correctional agencies need to invest in their human resources by continuously evaluating the basic recruit, field, and in-service training programs that are provided for COs. Furthermore, training records of curriculum, attendance, instructors, and assessment of learning must be maintained to protect the agency from the torts of failure to train or negligent training and violations of Section 1983 of the federal Civil Rights Act. Likewise, corrections agencies must be sensitive to the Americans with Disabilities Act and its application to training. Agencies should ensure that training facilities and delivery comply with the requirement to make reasonable accommodations for officers with protected disabilities. Training and opportunities for professional development are essential for contemporary COs and correctional agencies to manage these institutions.

Jeffrey C. Lee

See also: Correctional Officers, Job Stress among; Personnel

Further Reading
Atherton, E., & Sheldon, P. (2012). Correctional training and technology: Keys to the future. *Corrections Today, 73*(6), 28–33.

Geiman, D. (2010). Enriching your staff's professional development. *Corrections Today*, *72*(3), 18–19.

Geiman, D. (2013). The Arkansas DOC's eCADEMY: A model program. *Corrections Today*, *75*(3), 22–29.

Geiman, D. (2016). Achieving significant return on investment with blended learning. *Corrections Today*, *78*(2), 64–66.

Peak, K. (2015). *Justice administration* (8th ed.). Upper Saddle River, NJ: Prentice Hall.

Schmalleger, F., & Smykla, J. (2015). *Corrections in the 21st century* (7th ed.). New York: McGraw-Hill.

Correctional Officer Unions

As democratic nations largely receptive to labor improvements, the United States and other Westernized countries provide fertile opportunities for union participation, including that by correctional officers. In general, unions exist to improve compensation, benefits and hours, and working conditions for organizational members. These entities protect employees from poor management, politics, and patronage. Representatives of correctional unions argue that organized labor is essential for these traditional goals, as well as to help protect members from the dangers of a prison environment.

Prison unionization is prevalent among countries in North America, Europe, and Australia. The Prison Officers Association grew from English unionization efforts in the early 20th century and is now the largest union in the United Kingdom, with more than 35,000 members. Correctional officers in Australia are represented by labor organizations including United Voice and the Western Australia Prison Officers' Union. In France, the General Confederation of Labour acts as a union for prison guards, while three primary Belgium labor unions represent prison workers. Unionized correctional officers in Belgium recently garnered national attention after striking due to accusations of poor working conditions. In response, government leaders mobilized the military to support prison operations during the work stoppage.

In the United States, prison unionization began locally in the early 20th century. Similar to organized labor in the manufacturing and service industries, many correctional unions are structured within local chapters that then interact at city, state, and/or regional levels. The California Correctional Peace Officers Association (CCPOA) was formed in 1957 after an officer, despondent over working conditions at San Quentin, committed suicide. In 1978, California legalized collective bargaining for state workers including correctional employees, and in 1982, CCPOA defeated the International Brotherhood of Teamsters for the right to represent prison officers.

The size and geographical strength of correctional unions vary. The New York State Correctional Officers and Benevolent Society, the National Correctional Employees Union (MA), and the CCPOA include thousands of members. Large national unions, including the American Federation of State, County, and Municipal Employees (AFSCME) and the Teamsters also represent thousands of prison personnel. The AFSCME reports correctional officer membership at 62,000, as well as having 23,000 other correctional employees at local, state, and federal correctional facilities. Union representation of correctional officers remains competitive, especially as larger entities like the AFSCME, AFL-CIO, and Teamsters compete to add membership. Recently, the Florida Police Benevolent Association launched a petition drive among correctional officers to challenge the current Teamsters union.

In lieu of the dangers faced by correctional officers, unions have obtained concessions for improved protections and compensation in the workplace. For instance, CCPOA negotiated with California officials to provide worker incentives that included a $520 annual uniform allowance, more vacation time than any other state employees, bilingual pay, and the issuance of improved safety equipment (e.g., OC spray and protective vests). Further and in 2015, the Teamsters Local 2011 threatened to file an unfair business practices complaint against the state of Florida regarding a proposed 12-month probationary requirement for newly promoted officers. State officials argued that the probation was a necessary trial period for new supervisors and protected the agency from unethical employees. Union officials countered that the practice was unfair as it deterred otherwise qualified candidates from applying due to the risk of losing employment.

Unlike most labor unions in the United States, prison unions do not automatically endorse Democratic Party candidates. Traditionally, Republicans have favored get-tough crime strategies that result in increased incarceration, thereby creating more prison jobs. For instance, CCPOA contributed almost $1 million in 1990 to help elect Republican Pete Wilson to governor of California. At that time, it was the largest one-time campaign donation in California history. Wilson served two terms as governor and in 1998 authorized a 12 percent pay increase for prison guards while vetoing similar increases for other state workers. In contrast, CCPOA contributed $2 million in 2010 to help Democrat Jerry Brown secure the governorship. Brown then offered officers a new contract with expanded vacation accumulations and lessened restrictions regarding physical fitness.

Despite the positive contributions of correctional unions, these entities are not without criticism. Some officials have accused union representatives of being self-serving instead of promoting what is best for society, and using overly aggressive negotiation tactics with prison management. Reports of inmate mistreatment and prison violence tend to generate significant negative reactions from the public. As such, modern correctional unions are more receptive to administrative efforts of reform. Three contemporary criticisms of U.S. correctional unions are that these entities contribute to mass incarceration, hinder effective prison management, and thwart efforts to privatize.

First, critics assert that CCPOA's push for job security of workers has led to mass incarceration in California. Union bargaining tactics, such as portraying inmates as extremely violent and incapable of rehabilitation, strengthened relationships with correctional officers and blended well with arguments for prison-funding increases. This approach of portraying inmates as dangerous also emphasized the need for more correctional officers, allowing union officials to resist efforts to close or combine California prison facilities. In 2011, the New York Correctional Officers & Police Benevolent Association campaigned against Governor David Paterson's proposal to close four minimum security facilities. The union argued that such action would endanger public safety and negatively impact local communities.

Adding to the unions and mass incarceration argument, critics have asserted that unions repeatedly support prison expansion. After two decades of propunitive policies, California was left with a bloated prison system. Despite the state's fiscal struggles, unions supported expansion and opposed efforts to reduce the number of secured facilities due to loss of member jobs. Also, CCPOA promoted California's three-strikes initiative that substantially increased imprisonment beginning in 1994 and then opposed subsequent efforts by legislators to limit the initiative's scope. In contrast, organized labor supporters argue that unionization and promoting member job security have had negligible effect on prison downsizing.

Second, unions have been condemned for the member benefits gained by battling management over control and work rules. Unions advocate for employee protections involving internal investigations and potential disciplinary actions, which can hamper effective correctional management. For instance, internal affairs investigators at New York's correctional department were recently accused of being reluctant to challenge the New York State Correctional Officers and Benevolent Association regarding individual personnel issues, thereby permitting abusive employees to continue working within the agency, even after guards were found guilty of inmate abuses. Specifically, one New York correctional officer had been sued 17 times for brutality, resulting in settlements of $650,000 paid by the government, yet was still employed with the state.

Another case involving management and union protections recently garnered national attention. In 2015, attorneys for the New York City Correction Officers' Benevolent Association filed a petition arguing the New York law that makes law enforcement records confidential should be extended to correctional officers. Referred to as Section 50a, the law was passed in 1976 to protect police officer personnel and misconduct files. Since then, court rulings have extended the scope of what is confidential, and union officials argued that previous court rulings should be protected as well. The issue involved a former New York City corrections officer who was investigated and then punished at a disciplinary hearing for abusing a juvenile offender. After an appeal, a judge cited a previous incident of abuse and recommended termination. Information on the previous abuse was available to the public via the jurisdiction's website, an aspect that union officials believe violated Section 50a. Advocates of open government dispute the union's position, arguing that public awareness of officer brutality is essential to effective law enforcement oversight.

Conversely, organized labor advocates argue that the lack of a strong prison officer union can result in an unprofessional workforce. For instance, in 2015, the U.S. Department of Justice took over Alabama's only prison for women after what investigators characterized as a workplace culture that supported inmate abuses. Union advocates argued that where union membership is absent, as with this women's prison in Alabama, professionalism suffers and the risk for inmate and employee injuries increases. For example, authorities in nonunionized Tennessee were criticized for reducing staffing levels to lower costs, a recent strategy that coincided with eight inmates being stabbed in one day at the reorganized facilities.

Finally, critics accuse correctional unions of stunting the growth of prison privatization. Recently, AFSCME advocated for state officials in Minnesota to close a private prison in Appleton, while expanding services at another public prison. Unionized correctional officers have higher wages than nonunionized peers, and this appeals to taxpayers in viewing private prisons as a less costly alternative. In 2008, less than 5 percent of Corrections Corporation of America's workforce, the largest private prison operator, was unionized. In some jurisdictions, collective bargaining by public employees is prohibited, thereby hindering the work of unions. In response, AFSCME and other unions have endorsed federal legislation that would increase opportunities for organized labor in corrections. In essence, prison privatization can be seen as a hindrance to correctional union expansion.

In conclusion, correctional unions are prevalent in Westernized countries. Prison officer unions intercede on the behalf of members and advocate for better pay and benefits. These labor organizations have been criticized for contributing to mass incarceration, hindering professional correctional management efforts, and hampering prison privatization. Union officials argue that actions benefit members and that prisons are dangerous workplaces. Moving forward, correctional unions will remain a strong voice as the immediate need for qualified officers continues.

Scott Thomas Duncan

See also: Administration; Australia, Prisons in; Correctional Employees and Administrators, Job Satisfaction of; Correctional Officer Subculture; England, Prisons in; Misconduct by Correctional Employees; Privatization; Use of Force in Prisons

Further Reading

American Federation of State, County, and Municipal Employees (AFSCME). (n.d.). *Our union: Jobs we do.* Retrieved from http://www.afscme.org/union/jobs-we-do/corrections

Bozelko, C. (2015, September 9). Correctional officer unions essential to criminal justice reform. *The Huffington Post.* Retrieved from http://www.huffingtonpost.com/chandra-bozelko/correction-officers-union_b_8083496.html

California Correctional Peace Officers Association (CCPOA). (n.d.). *Our history.* Retrieved from https://www.ccpoa.org/about-us/our-history

Carey, A. (2011, October 13). *The price of prison guard unions.* Capital Research Center. Retrieved from https://capitalresearch.org/2011/10/the-price-of-prison-guard-unions-2

Kilgore, J. (2013). Mass incarceration and working class interests: Which side are the unions on? *Labor Studies Journal, 37*(4), 356–372.

Kirchhoff, S. (2010). *Economic impacts of prison growth* (7-5700). Congressional Research Service. Retrieved from https://www.fas.org/sgp/crs/misc/R41177.pdf

Page, J. (2011). Prison officer unions and the perpetuation of the penal status quo. *Criminology & Public Policy, 10*(3), 735–770.

Thompson, H. (2011). Downsizing the carceral state: The policy implications of prison guard unions. *Criminology & Public Policy, 10*(3), 771–779.

Winerip, M., Schwirtz, M., & Robbins, T. (2016, April 11). NY State Corrections Dept. takes on union over brutality. *New York Times.* Retrieved from http://www.nytimes.com/2016/04/12/nyregion/new-york-state-corrections-dept-takes-on-guards-union-over-brutality.html

Zeman, N. (2016, April/May). Do corrections unions undermine reform? *Correction Managers Report, 88,* 96.

Correctional Officers, Job Stress among

Employment within the criminal justice system is generally considered stressful, and studies among police, probation, and correctional officers attest to this perception. Of course, stress within an organization can manifest itself in various ways, such as declining health of employees and inflated health care costs for organizations, absenteeism, and can lead to employee turnover. This in turn can also be costly for agencies as they have to train new employees to replace those who leave and place inexperienced workers in critical security-related positions. In fact, corrections has been found to be among the criminal justice occupations most prone to turnover.

As might be expected, job satisfaction has been found in criminal justice research to be a pivotal variable in assessing turnover intentions among employees, and corrections is no exception. The relationship is typically inverse. In other words, as thoughts of quitting (turnover intentions) increase job satisfaction decreases and vice versa. Likewise, increased job satisfaction is associated with decreased levels of job stress.

Surely one's health can have a positive or negative impact on his or her level of job satisfaction. With deteriorating health lower job satisfaction levels are likely to be found. Correctional personnel have been reported to have a propensity for various problems related to stress, including substance abuse, marital strife, ulcers, high blood pressure, heart attacks, suicide, and shorter life expectancies.

Research on measuring correctional job attitudes typically falls into three categories. These assessments are usually aimed at identifying personal, job, and organizational characteristics related to such things as stress. Thus, stress for correctional personnel can be classified as personal or occupational stress.

The personal or demographic characteristics that have been utilized in correctional research studies include age, race, gender, job tenure, position level within the organization of respondents, educational level, and marital status. Increases in age of employees have been found to be associated with declining occupational stress and increased job satisfaction. In other words, older employees have likely been around long enough to be more satisfied with their jobs and to have adjusted to the stressors affiliated with the jobs. Similarly, younger correctional employees have been found to be more likely to exhibit turnover intentions than their older colleagues. This very likely reflects that at this stage of their lives they have too much invested, possibly in terms of relationships, benefits, and potential retirement, to think about quitting their jobs and seeking employment elsewhere. Also, unlike some other criminal justice occupations, such as probation officers, individuals are typically not required to have a college degree to enter the workforce as correctional officers. This coupled with their longevity potentially makes it more difficult for correctional officers to find meaningful work elsewhere and negatively impacts their mobility.

While some researchers have not found a significant relationship between tenure (time in position) and turnover intention or job satisfaction, others have indicated that as time in position increases turnover intentions decrease but job stress increases. It seems that such correctional officers feel vested. The more time they have put into their careers, even in the face of increasing work stress, the less likely they are to report contemplating leaving their jobs. They appear to be desirous of holding on to what they have invested in and to what stability they have garnered.

The results in the research literature regarding the impact of supervisory status on correctional personnel are mixed. Some studies have not found a significant relationship between position level in correctional institutions and job satisfaction or turnover intention. Other studies have indicated that line correctional officers are more likely than supervisory personnel to exhibit turnover intentions and that supervisors had significantly lower levels of job stress and higher job satisfaction levels. Yet another study of correctional personnel reported that, in general, supervisors exhibit significantly higher levels of job stress than other workers.

Educational level of correctional officers has been found to be significantly related to both turnover intentions and job satisfaction. As educational levels of correctional officers increase, their job dissatisfaction increases and their thoughts of quitting their job increase. Likewise, those correctional officers with lower educational attainment tended to exhibit greater satisfaction with the job and lower turnover intention. Obviously, those workers who are not satisfied with their jobs and have thoughts of leaving their jobs tend to be more stressed than other employees. Again, correctional officers typically are not required to have college educations; but, when they do, they are often not satisfied with their work environment and more prone to think about quitting. Very possibly the more education one has within such a work culture may increase expectations in the workplace and enhance marketability external to the agency if expectations are not realized. This may influence their willingness to leave.

When correctional personnel have been analyzed in terms of race, no significant relationship has been found with job stress. However, mixed results have been found for race and correctional officer job satisfaction. Generally, there has not been a significant relationship identified in the research literature between gender and turnover intention among correctional personnel. However, male correctional employees have been found to exhibit greater levels of job satisfaction than females, and this is associated with lower job stress for male correctional officers. Similarly, female correctional officers are more prone than their male counterparts to report higher physical stress levels reflected in a culmination of health problems. It may be that their physical stress levels are no worse than male correctional employees, but females are more likely to reveal their maladies than male officers. This has been called by some the John Wayne syndrome, as men are more likely to keep a stiff upper lip and remain reluctant to acknowledge sicknesses that might show a sign of weakness.

As noted earlier, marital status has been a variable considered in correctional stress research. However, no significant relationship has been determined between marital status and correctional officer job stress.

A pivotal variable that has been identified from examinations of organizational, occupational, or job stress for correctional personnel is the atmosphere for participation in workplace decision making. Over several studies, correctional employees who perceive a positive atmosphere for participation in workplace decision making exhibit lower physical stress levels, lower workplace stress levels, greater job satisfaction, and are less likely to report thinking about quitting their jobs. However, those correctional officers who perceived the atmosphere for input into workplace decision making to be negative were more likely to exhibit higher stress levels and be more prone to contemplate quitting their jobs. Also, as might be expected, supervisors among correctional personnel have been found more likely than line officers to believe the atmosphere for participation in workplace decision making to be positive. In addition to correctional officer research, the atmosphere for participation in workplace decision-making variable has proven to be a critical variable in research involving police and probation officers.

Satisfaction with their jobs has been found to be a key variable with correctional personnel. Those correctional officers dissatisfied with their jobs are much more likely to experience job-related stress; furthermore, those correctional workers dissatisfied with their jobs are much more likely to think about quitting their jobs. This relationship regarding job dissatisfaction is also seen with probation officers and police officers. In fact, job satisfaction is considered an essential variable for inclusion when measuring turnover intention.

Salary has been identified as a potential means for leading to job dissatisfaction if it is inadequate. However, it has not been found in the research literature to lead to dissatisfaction for correctional personnel.

Job stress often emerges with persons who work with people in some capacity as with correctional officers. Long-term stress can develop into burnout and can manifest itself in increased turnover intention on the part of employees. Workplace centralization is associated with heightened job stress and job dissatisfaction. Therefore, as previously noted, a perceived lack of opportunities to meaningfully participate in workplace decision making has been identified as a significant contributor to job stress and turnover intention for correctional officers.

Unfortunately, long-term exposure to stress can lead to not only physiological illnesses but also to psychological and behavioral problems. As previously discussed, the emergence of these maladies is definitely present among correctional personnel.

Although some correctional organizations tend to focus on individual correctional officers by emphasizing employee wellness programs focusing on diet and exercise, the general agreement among researchers is that the vast majority of factors impacting job stress evolve from organizational or administrative sources and are not the fault of the individual. Thus, organizational interventions, such as increasing where possible opportunities for correctional employee input into the decisions that impact them, are warranted. It is believed such a participatory management strategy could lessen organizational stress, enhance job satisfaction, lessen physical stress, and reduce turnover intention. Correctional officers less hindered by organizational interference should prove to be healthier and able to willingly produce more for their employers.

Risdon N. Slate

See also: Economics of Crossing Over, The; Ethical Issues in Prison Counseling; Inappropriate Correctional Employee–Inmate Relationships; Personnel

Further Reading

Cheek, F. E. (1984). *Stress management for correctional officers and their families.* College Park, MD: American Correctional Association.

Cullen, F., Link, B., Wolfe, N., & Frank, J. (1985). The social dimensions of correctional officer stress. *Justice Quarterly, 2*, 505–533.

Dowden, C., & Tellier, C. (2004). Predicting work-related stress in correctional officers: A meta-analysis. *Journal of Criminal Justice, 32*(1), 31–47.

Griffin, M. L. (2006). Gender and stress: A comparative assessment of sources of stress among correctional officers. *Journal of Contemporary Criminal Justice, 22*(1), 5–25.

Griffin, M. L., Hogan, N. L., & Lambert, E. G. (2012). Doing "people work" in the prison setting: An examination of the job characteristics model and correctional staff burnout. *Criminal Justice and Behavior, 39*(9), 1131–1147.

Herzberg, F. (1966). *Work and the nature of man.* New York: Thomas Y. Crowell.

Lambert, E., & Hogan, N. (2009). The importance of job satisfaction and organizational commitment in shaping turnover intent: A test of a causal model. *Criminal Justice Review, 34*(1), 96–118.

Lambert, E. G. (1999). *A path analysis of the antecedents and consequences of job satisfaction and organizational commitment among correctional staff.* Doctoral dissertation, ProQuest Information & Learning.

Lambert, E. G. (2001). To stay or quit: A review of the literature on correctional staff turnover. *American Journal of Criminal Justice, 26*(1), 61–76.

Lambert, E. G. (2006). I want to leave: A test of a model of turnover intent among correctional staff. *Applied Psychology in Criminal Justice, 2*(1), 57–83.

Lambert, E. G., & Hogan, N. L. (2010). Wanting change: The relationship of perceptions of organizational innovation with correctional staff job stress, job satisfaction, and organizational commitment. *Criminal Justice Policy Review, 2*(2), 160–184.

Lambert, E. G., Hogan, N. L., & Allen, R. I. (2006). Correlates of correctional officer job stress: The impact of organizational structure. *American Journal of Criminal Justice, 30*(2), 227–246.

Lambert, E. G., Hogan, N. L., & Barton, S. M. (2002). Satisfied correctional staff: A review of the literature on the correlates of correctional staff job satisfaction. *Criminal Justice and Behavior, 29*(2), 115–143.

Lambert, E. G., Hogan, N. L., & Paoline, E. A. (2016). Differences in the predictors of job stress and job satisfaction for black and white jail staff. *Corrections: Policy, Practice and Research, 1*(1), 1–19.

Lambert, E. G., & Paoline, E. A. (2008). The influence of individual, job, and organizational characteristics on correctional staff job stress, job satisfaction, and organizational commitment. *Criminal Justice Review, 33*(4), 541–564.

Maahs, J., & Pratt, T. (2001). Uncovering the predictors of correctional officers' attitudes and behaviors: A meta-analysis. *Corrections Management Quarterly, 5*, 13–19.

Maslach, C. (1982). *Burnout: The cost of caring.* Englewood Cliffs, NJ: Prentice Hall.

Matz, A. K., Woo, Y., & Kim, B. (2014). A meta-analysis of the correlates of turnover intent in criminal justice organizations: Does agency type matter? *Journal of Criminal Justice, 42*(3), 233–243.

Moynihan, D. P., & Pandey, S. K. (2008). The ties that bind: Social networks, person-organization value fit, and turnover intention. *Journal of Public Administration Research and Theory, 18*(2), 205–227.

Paoline, E. A., Lambert, E. G., & Hogan, N. L. (2006). A calm and happy keeper of the keys: The impact of ACA views, relations with coworkers, and policy views on the job stress and job satisfaction of correctional staff. *The Prison Journal, 86*(2), 182–205.

Patterson, B. L. (1992). Job experience and perceived job stress among police, correctional, and probation/parole officers. *Criminal Justice and Behavior, 19*(3), 260–285.

Robinson, D., Porporino, F. J., & Simourd, L. (1997). The influence of educational attainment on the attitudes and job performance of correctional officers. *Crime & Delinquency, 43*(1), 60–77.

Schaufeli, W. B., & Peeters, M. C. W. (2000). *International Journal of Stress Management, 7*(1), 19–48.

Slate, R., & Johnson, W. (2012). Stressors experienced by state and federal probation officers. In M. K. Miller & B. H. Bornstein (Eds.), *Stress, trauma, and wellbeing in the legal system.* New York: Oxford University Press. Retrieved August 21, 2016, from http://www.oxfordscholarship.com/view/10.1093/acprof:oso/9780199829996.001.0001/acprof-9780199829996-chapter-9.

Slate, R. N. (1993). *Stress levels and thoughts of quitting of correctional personnel: Do perceptions of participatory management make a difference?* Doctoral dissertation, Claremont Graduate School. Ann Arbor, MI: University Microfilms International.

Slate, R. N., Johnson, W. W., & Colbert, S. S. (2007). Police stress: A structural model. *Journal of Police and Criminal Psychology, 22*, 102–112.

Slate, R. N., & Vogel, R. E. (1997). Participative management and correctional personnel: A study of the perceived atmosphere for participation in correctional decision making and its impact on employee stress and thoughts about quitting. *Journal of Criminal Justice, 25*(5), 397–408.

Slate, R. N., Vogel, R. E., & Johnson, W. W. (2001). To quit or not to quit: Perceptions of participation in correctional decision making and the impact of organizational stress. *Corrections Management Quarterly, 5*, 68–78.

Suurd Ralph, C. D., & Holmvall, C. M. (2016). Examining the relationships between the justice facets and turnover intent: The mediating roles of overall justice and psychological strain. *Military Psychology, 28*(4), 251–270.

Tewksbury, R., & Higgins, G. E. (2006). Prison staff and work stress: The role of organizational and emotional influences. *American Journal of Criminal Justice, 30*(2), 247–266.

Correctional Officers, Typology of

Correctional officers serve an important role in the criminal justice system. Correctional officers are responsible for the care, custody, and control of inmates in jails and prisons. Correctional officers must also ensure safety, security, and order within these correctional institutions. Naturally, correctional officers approach these duties in many different ways. Research indicates there are several types of correctional officers, with some who focus more on the strict rule enforcement aspects of the job, others who focus more on the caring aspects, and yet others still who fall somewhere along this continuum. The research on the typology of correctional officers often examines how staff and inmates perceive the role of the officer. This work also includes direct observations of the correctional officer and inmate interactions. Research suggests there are five main typologies of correctional officers: true carer, limited carer, old school, conflicted, and damaged.

A true carer, or people worker, is an officer who approaches the supervision of inmates with a caring and supportive attitude. These officers listen to inmates and try to assist and encourage inmates to behave prosocially. True carer officers seem to enjoy correctional work, and they easily form relationships with inmates. This type of officer seeks to gain inmate obedience and order through communication and respect.

A limited carer officer approaches inmate supervision with consistency. These officers meet inmate requests and show concern in complicated situations. Although limited carers are somewhat sympathetic to inmates, this sympathy is more limited than that of the true carer officers. The limited carer follows the rules but makes slight adjustments depending on the circumstances.

An old school officer, or rule enforcer, is less emotionally involved than a true carer. This group tends to consist of older, more seasoned officers. Old school officers approach inmate supervision in a uniform and emotional manner. These officers expect inmates to follow the rules, and they will respond to inmates' needs as long as they are in compliance. Old school officers are less sympathetic than limited carers and are not willing to bend the rules regardless of the circumstances. These officers are also more prone to use force and are quick to punish inmate misbehavior.

Conflicted officers consider "caring" for inmates as an important aspect of their job. This group of officers aspires to help inmates become better people; however, in contrast to the true carer, conflicted officers have unrealistic goals. Conflicted officers tend to view inmates as the problem to be solved rather than identifying an inmate's problems as situational and separate from them as people. Conflicted officers hold a negative perception of inmates and feel threatened by them. These officers derive job satisfaction from their relationships with colleagues and in protecting the public.

Finally, damaged officers are those who have been stigmatized by a negative situation on the job. This may include such things as being assaulted by an inmate or having a lack of support from administrators. Although members of this group may have initially cared for inmates, they are disgruntled and no longer interested in this role. This group of officers expresses the most negative views toward inmates and also feels the most threatened by them. Damaged officers often take a hardline approach toward the enforcement of institutional rules and are quick to punish even minor rule violations. These officers are likely to be more aggressive than is necessary when dealing with inmates, and they are also the most likely to be abusive.

Working in a correctional environment is a difficult task. Gaining compliance among inmates is complex, and officer's respond in a variety of ways. Although the evaluation research on the typologies of correctional officers is limited, it appears that better effects are achieved when officers adopt a caring role.

Megan M. King and Ryan M. Labrecque

See also: Correctional Officer Subculture; Correctional Officers and Discretion; Misconduct by Correctional Employees

Further Reading

Ben-David, S. (1992). Staff-to-inmate's relations in a total institution: A model of five modes of association. *International Journal of Offender Therapy and Comparative Criminology, 36*(3), 209–219.

Biggam, F. H., & Power, K. G. (1997). Social support and psychological distress in a group of incarcerated young offenders. *International Journal of Offender Therapy and Comparative Criminology, 41*(3), 213–298.

Farkas, M. A. (2000). A typology of correctional officers. *International Journal of Offender Therapy and Comparative Criminology, 44*(4), 431–449.

Gilbert, M. J. (1997). The illusion of structure: A critique of the classical model of organization and the discretionary power of correctional officers. *Criminal Justice Review, 22*(1), 49–64.

Klofas, J., & Toch, H. (1982). The guard subculture myth. *Journal of Research in Crime and Delinquency, 19*(2), 238–254.

Tait, S. (2011). A typology of prison officer approaches to care. *European Journal of Criminology, 8*(6), 440–454.

Correctional Officers and Discretion

Inmates live within a "total institution," where all their behaviors are closely monitored and regulated by correctional officers. As a result, they are subjected to the tendencies and habits of those supervising officers, insofar discretion remains permissible under the facility's policies and procedures. Discretion can be described as the ability to make a cognitive choice and choose to act or not act on those choices. In this regard, correctional officers are granted sworn authority to maintain order and security within an institution, manifested in various forms of institutional power and personal authority. Indeed, correctional facilities possess detailed and prescriptive policies that outline the appropriate response to prisoner misconduct, though deviations may occur or be permitted in extreme circumstances. Correctional officers are exposed to a listing of prohibited conduct early in their career through their department's training regimen, and prisoners are exposed to these same prohibitions, either through booking, orientation, or initial classification.

A disciplinary board or committee, in conjunction with a set disciplinary process, represents the formal authority responsible for the resolution of institutional conflicts, as empowered by the warden or superintendent. Misconduct can generally be divided among four broad categories: (1) minor (e.g., prisoners exchanging words, posturing), (2) low-moderate (e.g., prisoners shouting and drawing the attention of other inmates), (3) high-moderate (e.g., prisoners making physical contact by pushing or shoving), or (4) major (e.g., prisoner assault of another individual causing physical injury). For most institutions, all infractions, even minor, are to be documented using an incident report. That said, minor infractions are often resolved informally by the correctional officers reporting the incidents or by their direct supervisor. The rationale for this discretion for low-level infractions is simple: processing all incidents formally through a disciplinary committee would

Correctional Officers and Discretion

overwhelm the institution and impede its effectiveness. Disciplinary committees often struggle to keep pace with the rate of serious incidents alone, necessitating minor infractions be resolved informally by the reporting officers.

Institutional power concerns a range of punishments and rewards officers can utilize, in accordance with established policies and procedures. Examples include verbal reprimands, cell searches, urine tests, loss of good time credits, or even the use of solitary confinement. Unauthorized punishments may include violence, harassment, and threats. Official rewards may include recommendations to transfer an inmate to a lower-security-level facility, relocation to a facility closer to kin, access to congregate areas and recreation, or weekend leave. Finally, informal rewards may include granting inmates an extra hour of visiting time, not locking an inmate's cell door, or deliberately failing to document an inmate's infraction.

Although officers are unlikely to consciously mistake a major incident for that of a minor infraction, there is a tendency for some to inappropriately minimize events that occur, leading to a lower categorization of the misconduct than what is warranted. This may occur for a variety of reasons, but it is a pertinent concern among senior officers who have reportedly become desensitized to such conduct. Further, due to their role in shepherding new officers, these tendencies may inadvertently impact others' reporting habits as well, leading to a continual and gradual reduction of reported infraction seriousness that once fell under the purview of the disciplinary committee to now being placed under the informal discretion of line officers. Further, officers may also choose not to report an incident altogether, supported by a variety of rationalizations (e.g., not enough time in my shift, nothing will get done about it anyway, unclear what exactly occurred, fear of losing rapport with inmates, notion that one can handle discipline on his or her own).

It must be recognized that an officer's authority, similar to law enforcement's relations with the public through notions of legitimacy and procedural justice, can be enhanced if they appear just, impartial, honest, and respectful to the inmates. In other words, an officer's effective use of personal authority will depend, to some extent, on the inmates' degree of respect for the officer. Balancing the rules of the institution versus the needs and desires of the inmates may lead to role conflict. While an officer must maintain some distance or objectivity (i.e., to maintain the security of the institution), they must also exhibit some degree of empathy and consider the inmate's personal situation (i.e., to promote a rehabilitative environment; a.k.a. human service role). Officers that achieve a healthy balance between the security needs of the institution and the social welfare of the inmates will gain enhanced legitimacy, further preserving peace and order. Both correctional officers and inmates have been shown to agree that the qualities of a good officer include treating inmates fairly, not showing favoritism, not always following the rules to the letter, being professional, and treating inmates with respect.

Group solidarity with colleagues represents another variable that may impact how officers view and use discretion. Indeed, like police officers, correctional officers are dependent on their colleagues' support. This occupational subculture can function as a shield that insulates officers from outside criticism, recommendations, and new demands from either administration or the inmates, encouraging what may appear to be otherwise capricious discretionary decision-making behaviors to the outside observer.

Inmates have limited rights and legal protections while incarcerated. They are under the authority of the correctional personnel and therefore are subject to both their ethical and unethical behaviors. The work of correctional officials is done in isolation, far from public view. Interactions between correctional officers and inmates are often informal and are not always documented. Further, supervisors do not always have the time needed to thoroughly review the actions of their staff. The majority of correctional officers and inmates coexist peacefully, utilizing mutual respect to maintain order. However, the pains of imprisonment and the expectation of always supporting one's fellow officers can cause problems within a correctional institution. Those problems include a code of silence and officers' predisposition toward protecting their peers.

When correctional facilities fail in their mission, the judicial system is responsible for ensuring the adequate welfare of the inmate population. That said, the judicial system's willingness to intervene in the management of correctional institutions has fluctuated throughout history as reflected by the *hands-off period* from 1866 to 1963 and the general *deference period* in recent decades (1979–). The 1960s and 1970s are regarded as the *prisoners' rights period*, in which many basic protections were put into place, including challenges of confinement through writs of habeas corpus. That said, the U.S. Supreme Court recognizes that correctional departments must balance the rights of inmates against the security and order needs of the institution. Rather, constitutional protections relevant to the Eighth Amendment are primarily concerned with correctional officials doing something to inmates they should not, but also failing to do something that they should be doing (a.k.a. deliberate indifference), such as providing adequate health care. The American Bar Association has published *Criminal Justice Standards on the Treatment of Prisoners* that outlines specific standards relevant to all jails and prisons, including issues of classification, conditions of confinement, health care provision, solitary confinement, reentry planning, external oversight, and access to the courts.

Nicole Johanneson and Adam K. Matz

See also: Correctional Officer Subculture; Correctional Officer Training; Deliberate Indifference; Disciplinary Hearings; Good Time; Inmate Subculture; Misconduct by Prisoners; Respect

Further Reading

Arnold, H., Liebling, A., & Tait, S. (2009). Prison officers and prison culture. In Y. Jewkes (Ed.), *Handbook on prisons* (pp. 471–495). Devon, U.K.: Willan.

Bennet, J., Crewe, B., & Wahidin, A. (2008). *Understanding prison staff.* Devon, U.K.: Willan.

Faith, D. C. (2010). The challenge of prison oversight. *American Criminal Law Review, 47*(4), 1453–1462.

Freeman, R. M. (2003). Social distance and discretionary rule enforcement in a women's prison. *The Prison Journal, 83*(2), 191–205.

Hemmens, C., Belbot, B., & Bennett, K. (2013). *Criminal justice case briefs: Significant cases in corrections* (2nd ed.). New York: Oxford University Press.

Hemmens, C., & Stohr, M. K. (2000). The two faces of the correctional role: An exploration of the value of the correctional role instrument. *International Journal of Offender Therapy and Comparative Criminology, 44*(3), 326–349.

Kolind, T. (2015). Drugs and discretionary power in prisons: The officer's perspective. *International Journal of Drug Policy, 26*(9), 799–807.

Liebling, A. (2000). Prison officers, policing and the use of discretion. *Theoretical Criminology, 4*(3), 333–357.

Liebling, A. (2011). Distinctions and distinctiveness in the work of prison officers: Legitimacy and authority revisited. *European Journal of Criminology, 8*(6), 484–499.

McLellan, M. (2010). The trouble with officer discretion. *Corrections Today, 72*(5), 16, 23.

Schlanger, M., Love, M. C., & Reynolds, C. (2010). ABA Criminal Justice Standards on the Treatment of Prisoners. *Criminal Justice, 25*(2), 14–25.

Correctional Officers with Military Experience

Correctional officers in the United States often have mixed job histories. Many start a career in corrections following a turning point or after experiencing failure in other careers, such as the military. Prior research indicates that a large number of correctional officers and supervisory staff have previously served in the military: seven-tenths of caseworkers, nearly half of correctional officers, two-thirds of wardens, and one-third of juvenile facility directors have prior military experience. Studies on veteran employment characteristics demonstrate that veterans overall are more inclined to seek employment in corrections. In 2006, Gulf War–era II veterans were 9.8 percent more likely to seek employment in protective services, like police or correctional work, than nonveterans. Despite the large number of correctional officers with military experience, studies on their backgrounds and experiences are scant.

Although prior empirical research is limited, it is likely that former military officers have specific motivations toward entering a career in corrections. For instance, veterans may transition into corrections due to the paramilitary organization characterized by explicit lines of authority and control. Veterans often thrive in correctional environments because of the structured nature of correctional work similar to the military. Hence, the commonality in organizational structures between the military and correctional institutions is likely a major motivation for veterans' seeking employment in correctional agencies. Correctional agencies can recruit veterans to lessen employee turnover, which is a major organizational issue in corrections.

Further, the increased prevalence of veterans within corrections at the federal level may be due to certain incentives for former military members. For example, federal employment offers veterans the opportunity to receive "veterans' preference points" under certain conditions. Preference points allow veterans to be considered for employment ahead of other nonveteran applicants. In addition, veterans may be attracted to federal employment in prisons because they would receive partial credit from their time served in the military. Recently separated veterans who "roll over" their time served in the military into a federal corrections system often benefit from additional income at the point of retirement with prisons. Overall, a review of the literature suggests that correctional staff with prior military service demonstrate a clear preference for working in federal prisons rather than state and local institutions.

Research has shown that prior military experience may affect correctional officers' role orientation or which punishment ideology (i.e., rehabilitation, retribution, deterrence, punishment, or incapacitation) they most align with. However, such research provides mixed findings. Some research suggests that a background in military service was a significant predictor of a rehabilitative orientation. Conversely, another study found that correctional officers with prior military experience were less likely to support rehabilitation as a goal of corrections.

Similarly, prior research indicates that correctional staff with prior military experience may take a more hard-line approach to their job and interactions with inmates in which they are less likely to feel they have a responsibility to assist inmates in obtaining the proper medication or to help them gain access to programming. Consequently, correctional officers with prior military experience were less likely to be concerned with the welfare of inmates, subscribing to a "hack" orientation instead. Two additional studies indicated that veterans were also more likely than nonveterans to endorse the use of force as a means of gaining compliance with an order. However, another study did not find a significant relationship between military experience and role orientation.

Although the majority of the literature shows that veteran status is a significant factor in role orientation, one study noted that personal characteristics can only account for 10 percent or less of the variance in role orientation. Thus, further research is needed to understand how past experiences in the armed forces may impact correctional officers' attitudes and correctional orientation. In addition, more research beyond demographic factors as variables is needed to ascertain the attitudes of correctional staff.

Lastly, prior research also suggests prior military experience may affect their perceptions of female staff. One study found that veterans rated their female colleagues as less capable of performing their work duties when compared to male staff. On the other hand, nonveterans rated female staff more favorably. Researchers concluded that this finding is representative of the patriarchal attitudes also found in the military.

A large number of correctional officers indicate that they have previously served in the military. Although limited, prior research suggests that veteran status impacts correctional staff's attitudes toward treating correctional clients as well as how they view the capabilities of their fellow female officers. Nonetheless, as the field of corrections moves toward evidence-based practices that emphasize rehabilitation, it is imperative that correctional staff understand the value of rehabilitative goals. Accordingly, correctional agencies can provide additional training and incentives to veterans who are sometimes less apt to support rehabilitative efforts. Likewise, to counteract the tendency of correctional staff with prior military experience to devalue the contributions of female staff, administrators can implement further training to decrease sexist attitudes.

Cassandra Boyer and Breanna Boppre

See also: Correctional Officers, Typology of; Personnel

Further Reading

Caeti, T. J., Hemmens, C., Cullen, F. T., & Burton, V. S. (2003). Management of juvenile correctional facilities. *The Prison Journal, 83*(4), 383–405.

Carlson, J. R., & Thomas, G. (2006). Burnout among prison caseworkers and corrections officers. *Journal of Offender Rehabilitation, 43*(3), 19–34.

Cullen, F. T., Latessa, E. J., Burton, V. S., & Lombardo, L. X. (1993). The correctional orientation of prison wardens: Is the rehabilitative ideal supported? *Criminology, 31*(1), 69–92.

Hemmens, C., & Stohr, M. K. (2000). The two faces of the correctional role: An exploration of the value of the correctional role instrument. *International Journal of Offender Therapy and Comparative Criminology, 44*(3), 326–349.

Hemmens, C., & Stohr, M. K. (2001). Correctional staff attitudes regarding the use of force in corrections. *Corrections Management Quarterly, 5,* 27–40.

Hemmens, C., Stohr, M. K., Schoeler, M., & Miller, B. (2002). One step up, two steps back: The progression of perceptions of women's work in prisons and jails. *Journal of Criminal Justice, 30*(6), 473–489.

Kifer, M., Hemmens, C., & Stohr, M. K. (2003). The goals of corrections: Perspectives from the line. *Criminal Justice Review, 28*(1), 47–69.

Lambert, E. G., & Hogan, N. L. (2009). Exploring the predictors of treatment views of private correctional staff: A test of an integrated work model. *Journal of Offender Rehabilitation, 48*(6), 504–528.

Philliber, S. (1987). Thy brother's keeper: A review of the literature on correctional officers. *Justice Quarterly, 4*(1), 9–37.

Walker, J. A. (2008). Employment characteristics of Gulf War–era II veterans in 2006: A visual essay. *Monthly Lab Review, 131,* 3–13. Retrieved from https://www.bls.gov/opub/mlr/2008/05/art1full.pdf

Cost of Prisons

Over the past four decades, incarceration rates have continued to reach unprecedented levels. Currently, the United States has the highest documented incarceration rate in the entire world, imprisoning 754 persons per every 100,000 residents. Although the United States has approximately 5 percent of the world's population, it incarcerates almost 25 percent of the world's prisoner population. From changes in sentencing policies to new laws enacted by Congress to get tough on crime, the United States has increasingly relied on prisons to punish offenders and combat criminal activity. This enhanced dependence on incarceration has created issues ranging from inmate overcrowding to notable increases in correctional spending.

Prisons are very costly to operate and maintain. According to the Bureau of Justice Statistics, incarceration costs U.S. taxpayers an estimated $63 billion a year. The national average to lock up one inmate annually is a little over $31,000, although this cost varies from one state to another. Although some states like Indiana and Idaho pay an estimated $15,000 a year per inmate, other states like New York and Washington spend approximately $60,000 annually to incarcerate each inmate. Other states, such as Ohio and Florida, lie somewhere in the middle. Contributing factors to high incarceration costs include officer wages and benefits, prisoner heath care, and overhead costs like building maintenance and utilities. These costs are essential to daily prison operations and contribute largely to the amount of money spent each year on incarceration.

The high cost of incarceration in the United States is unmistakable. Since 1980, correctional spending has increased more than threefold, with billions of dollars each year now being spent on incarceration. These substantial increases in spending have occurred despite the fact that the overall crime rate in the United States has declined by more than 25 percent since the 1990s. This begs the question: if individuals are committing fewer crimes, why are prison expenditures continuing to rise? Despite fewer crimes being committed, the continued increase in prison expenditures can be attributed to state and federal policies, including mandatory minimum sentences, parole and probation practices, and punitive drug laws, which have inundated prisons with inmates and have driven up costs as a result.

Correctional institutions around the country have experienced major issues with inmate overcrowding and increasing prison expenditures. Since being adopted in the 1980s by government officials to address drug-related crimes, mandatory minimum sentences have vastly contributed to nationwide incarceration rates. Since this time, the amount of nonviolent drug offenders sentenced to lengthy prison terms has skyrocketed. As greater numbers of people are being locked up around the country, states are being forced to reprioritize their budgets and available resources in an effort to account for increased correctional expenditures. To this end, many states are now reassessing their correctional policies to address inmate overpopulation concerns. Certain states, such as Pennsylvania, have even shipped inmates to out-of-state correctional facilities to lessen serious overcrowding.

In addition to mandatory minimum sentences, parole and probation practices have been recognized as major factors that contribute to overcrowding and increased prison spending. Over the years, tighter restrictions have been placed on probationers and parolees, leading to widespread revocations and a greater number of prison admissions. Accordingly, prison and jail populations around the nation have become unbearable. In some states, activities and discretion of parole boards have been considerably restricted, while in other states such boards have been abolished completely. These factors have served as fundamental contributors to the ongoing growth of correctional populations and the exponential amount of money being spent on corrections.

Since a war on drugs was declared in 1971 by Richard Nixon, punitive drug laws have played a significant role in driving up incarceration rates and prison expenditures. More than half of prisoners are currently incarcerated for drug-related offenses, a percentage that has increased rather steadily over the past four decades. Money spent to enforce the war against drugs has also greatly increased. For instance, in 1982, more than $1.5 billion was spent at the federal level to fight the drug problem, while in 2010 the federal government spent $15 billion on the drug war. State expenditures have also extensively increased. For instance, in 1998, states spent nearly $40 billion on corrections, with 77 percent of this spending going toward the war on drugs. Current state corrections expenditures exceed $50 billion annually, far more than the amount of money spent on programs geared toward rehabilitation.

To address prison overcrowding and cost-related concerns of incarceration, the prison industry has turned to privatization for answers. Today, an estimated 10 percent of the corrections industry is controlled by for-profit privatized prisons, which have become the model for many state and federal penitentiaries, among other facilities. The largest private prison service provider, Corrections Corporation of America (CCA), constructs and manages the day-to-day operations of prisons, jails, detention centers, and residential reentry centers, housing nearly 70,000 inmates in more than 70 facilities throughout the United States. Privatized companies like CCA assert that they can operate prisons more effectively and more cheaply than government-run facilities, thus making prisons safer while saving taxpayer dollars.

Although privatized service providers can bring about short-term savings, such companies have been heavily criticized by opponents of prison privatization for allegedly transforming punishment into a very lucrative, profit-making enterprise. In 2013 alone, CCA brought in nearly $4 billion in revenue, while the GEO Group, the second largest privatized service provider, generated a little over $1.5 billion. To critics, private prisons really do not save money; instead, they are merely concerned with exploiting the prison industry to maximize their own profit. Compounding matters is the fact that the U.S. Department of Justice has recently maintained that private prisons are not cost-effective alternatives to government-run facilities, thereby distancing itself from such prisons.

The financial costs of prisons are quite distinct; however, there are other associated costs that run much deeper. There are, for instance, unique social costs of correctional confinement. While imprisoned, inmates lack the ability to be productive, contributing members of society. They are unable to maintain a legitimate job in the public sector and therefore cannot pay taxes. Inmates can also become more criminally sophisticated while locked up. Through their daily interactions with other convicted offenders, inmates can learn how to become better criminals, thereby increasing the chance they will recidivate at some point upon return to the community. When offenders return to criminal behavior after being released from prison, society becomes adversely affected and citizen safety is placed at risk.

Not only can prison be costly for the offender and society in general, it can also be quite expensive for the whole family. The devastating affect that incarceration can have on an entire family, especially when young children are involved, is well documented. On average, 1 in 43 U.S. children have at least one parent incarcerated every year. When a loved one is locked up behind bars, family members tend to suffer, often feeling disconnected, perhaps fearful, and even uncertain about the future. Additionally, parental incarceration can have a long-term impact on a child's growth and development, leading to adverse outcomes such as lower grades, fewer years of educational attainment, mental illness, and higher rates of antisocial and truant behavior.

The costs of American prisons are distinct and wide-ranging. The prison system itself is massive, with well over 2 million people currently incarcerated across the country. This has created a financial burden for communities and prisons that continue to operate at or beyond capacity. To cut costs and address overcrowding concerns, states have resorted to privatizing correctional facilities. However, this practice has endured widespread criticism, with the federal government and many states now moving away from privatization. To this end, there have been calls for extensive prison reform, accentuating the need to reduce overcrowding and expenditures while preserving community safety. Reform initiatives that create community-based alternatives to incarceration, especially for nonviolent drug offenders, have been emphasized. Such alternatives can help lessen mass incarceration and prison costs while improving the likelihood that inmates will live productive, law-abiding lives upon reentry to society.

Justin N. Crowl

See also: Incarceration Rates; Overcrowding; Privatization

Further Reading

American Psychological Association. (2014). Incarceration nation. *Monitor on Psychology, 45*(9). Retrieved from http://www.apa.org/monitor/2014/10/incarceration.aspx

Braman, D. (2002). Families and incarceration. In M. Mauer & M. Chesney-Lind (Eds.), *Invisible punishment: The collateral consequences of mass imprisonment.* New York: New Press.

CBS News. (2012). *The cost of a nation of incarceration.* Retrieved from http://www.cbsnews.com/news/the-cost-of-a-nation-of-incarceration

Friedmann, A. (2014). Apples-to-fish: Public and private prison cost comparisons. *Fordham Urban Law Journal, 42*(2), 503–568.

Henrichson, C., & Delaney. R. (2012). The price of prisons: What incarceration costs taxpayers. *Federal Sentencing Reporter, 25*(1), 68–80.

Lindsey, A. M., Mears, D. P., & Cochran, J. C. (2016). The privatization debate: A conceptual framework for improving (public and private) corrections. *Journal of Contemporary Criminal Justice, 32*(4), 308–327.

Lundahl, B. W., Kunz, C., Brownell, C., Harris, N., & Van Vleet, R. (2009). Prison privatization: A meta-analysis of cost and quality of confinement indicators. *Research on Social Work Practice, 19*(4), 383–394.

Pratt, T. C. (1999). Are private prisons more cost-effective than public prisons? A meta-analysis of evaluation research studies. *Crime & Delinquency, 45*(3), 358–371.

Custody Levels

Custody level is the assigned status of a convict and is generally referred to as maximum, medium, or minimum. Custody levels also designate the security level(s) assigned to a specific prison. There is a correlation between the level ascribed to the convict and the prison to which the convict is assigned. A specific prison may confine convicts with different custody levels. The custody level (called grade or the level of security in some prisons) is to minimize potential disruption while maintaining order in the prison through the appropriate assignment of custody level to the convict.

Classification determines the custody level according to the assessed degree of risk or threat the convict represents to the prison and others. Custody levels are named differently not only in the state and federal prison systems but also in different countries; nevertheless, the patterns are usually similar.

Custody Levels   147

The prison classification process utilizes both subjective and objective methodologies to assess risk. The mass incarceration of the past 45 years has altered the initial convict assignment from a specified wing in a prison to a prison specifically designated for reception and classification. Reception (also called quarantine) is the first prison encountered by a convict following sentencing. The reception facility is for the comprehensive evaluation of the convict.

Risk assessment takes into account the convict's criminal background and personal characteristics such as the offense, sentence, prior offense history, institutional adjustment, previous institutional experience, mental status, health, educational attainment, gang and other affiliations, and escape history. Subjective assessments rely on interviews with professional staff, observations by all staff, and personal knowledge of the convict. For example, correctional officers will report their interactions and observations of convicts during their respective shifts. These reports include assessments of the convict's interaction with other convicts, custody, adjustment and acceptance of the conditions of confinement, and especially tolerance for the cell. Other examples would be interviews and examinations with a psychological, medical, educational, or social service staff who report their impressions of the convict.

The objective assessment relies on a variety of tests that minimally include such instruments as the Minnesota Multiphasic Personality Inventory (MMPI), the Level of Service Inventory–Revised (LSI–R) or other risk assessment tool, and a test of educational attainment. These tests help determine security levels and programs as well as address other convict needs.

The convict appears before the classification committee (a group of ranking prison officials and department heads) at the conclusion of the reception period, to learn of the custody level, the appropriate level of prison and program eligibility that ensures that the prison meets its custody needs for security. Objective classification processes arrive at a score that establishes the custody level for the convict and concomitantly a prison with a similar designation. Prison administrators may exercise an override function to increase or decrease a committee's determination because of their perception of the needed level of custody for a convict.

Maximum security custody signifies that a convict represents the greater risk or threat. This often indicates a corresponding prison that houses that level of convict. There is an exception. The convict may receive an assignment of a medium custody prison within which there are different classifications of convicts including maximum custody level.

Maximum security prisons usually possess such features as tall walls, armed guards positioned on the walls, electronic sensors in or near the walls, roving patrols of armed guards, and locked gates that require clearances in order for a convict to pass. Trenton State Prison, New Jersey, is the oldest operating maximum security prison in the United States. ADX Florence is considered the most secure federal supermax prison. Convicts with a maximum custody level remain within the walls, have limited access to exercise yards (within the walls) and to visitors such as the use of confined space that separates visitor and convict and/or employs a telephone to avoid personal contact. Offenses for which the maximum custody level may be assigned would include those sentenced for multiple murders, terrorists, or escape.

Although escape is a lower level offense, it represents a higher level of threat for the prison and thus the more extreme custody status. Southern prison farms such as Angola in Louisiana are exceptions to the design. Maximum custody convicts do work outside the buildings but are constantly shielded by armed guards on horseback or in vehicles.

Although prisons have always had some sort of more secure prison within a prison called the hole, segregation, isolation, or protective custody, today there is the supermax prison. The forerunner of the modern supermax would be Alcatraz. The island prison was only accessible by boat, and the waters of the San Francisco bay are treacherous with cold currents and sharks. Al Capone, sentenced for income tax evasion, was sent to Alcatraz to avoid both racketeering influence and prison corruption such as had occurred during an earlier sentence to Eastern State Prison. Custody levels at Alcatraz were referred to as stages of being in grade. Those assigned the supermax custody status are often convicted of such crimes as terrorism, mass murder, organized crime, or gangs. Other convicts sent to the supermax are those found to be unmanageable under normal prison conditions and those whose perceived level of violence makes them a persistent threat. Individuals assigned to the supermax have their prison freedom greatly restricted. They often spend 23 hours a day in their cells with the remaining hour used for solitary recreation. All contact with others is avoided, and feeding is done in the cell with the food passed through a slot in the door called a wicket. Those assigned to supermax custody level seldom have that level reversed.

Medium security custody as the name indicates is an in-between level. That is, the convict is not deemed to be such a serious threat as to require maximum custody yet not such a minimal threat as to warrant minimum custody. Convicts with different custody levels may interact with each other in common settings such as for recreation, be assigned to the same cell blocks, or the same work assignments. In other circumstances medium and maximum facilities may be located on the same complex; however, convicts with different custody levels are restricted from contact with one another by physical restraints such as different buildings, fences, or walls. Convicts at medium security facilities, depending on their custody status, will be assigned different work and other assignments. For example, maximum custody convicts would only be allowed to work at inside assignments. Medium custody convicts may work outside but under the supervision of custody officials. Medium custody status does not (in all prison systems) require the use of armed guards on outside details.

Minimum security custody status is the least restrictive or for whom high levels of custody are unnecessary. Minimum custody status convicts may live, work, and have recreation and other privileges with little or no security coverage. There are minimum-level custody prisons. Such prisons often take the form of dormitory-like buildings that have no locked doors, armed guards, fences, or walls. Convicts with low-level offenses such as those who have committed white-collar crimes may be assigned this custody status upon arrival in the prison system. Others may begin with higher level custody status and be promoted after meeting specific requirements such as minimum amount of time served and demonstrating trust and acceptance of the prion rules and regulations. These changes in custody status represent

Inmate firefighters from Oak Glen Conservation Camp near Yucaipa, California, are transported to a work assignment under the authority of CAL FIRE, which maintains the camp and supervises the inmates while they are away from the minimum security facility. (David McNew/AFP/Getty Images)

an incentive offered by the prison as well as a reinforcement for adhering to prison conditions.

The lowest level of custody status is full minimum or what had commonly been referred to as trustee status. This level of status represents the greatest trust. A convict in this circumstance may be placed in situations of no supervision and be allowed to drive tractors or other vehicles. Although there have been reductions in the use of this status in recent years as prisons have adopted a more conservative posture, there remains some advanced applications. Convicts have been trusted to enter the community in a variety of capacities. These are often referred to as community release programs intended to help convicts with their preparation for release from prison. Community release programs include school and work release, furloughs, and halfway house participation. As the names indicate, convicts at this custody level are allowed to further their education or learn a vocational trade. Furloughs are opportunities to restore family ties and find a place to live and be employed. Work release enables convicts to work at a private enterprise to earn and save money for their return to society. Halfway house participation may begin prior to the actual release date from prison and acts as a step-down from prison prior to beginning full reentry from prison.

Mass incarceration has resulted in other innovations in custody level. The prison population is getting older, and we now see units in prisons for those who are geriatric and/or require hospice care. In another instance, convicts with mental health issues have resulted in the creation of mental health units and/or prisons for them.

Matthew J. Sheridan

See also: Alcatraz; American Prison Designs; Florence ADX; Halfway Houses; Inmate Classification; Maximum Security

Further Reading

Clear, T., Cole, G., & Reisig, M. (2013). *American corrections* (10th ed.). Belmont, CA: Wadsworth, Cengage Learning.

Irwin, J. (2004). *The warehouse prison.* New York: Oxford University Press.

Seiter, R. (2013). *Corrections: An introduction.* Hoboken, NJ: Pearson Education.

Death Penalty in the Middle East

The death penalty exists in the domestic law of most Middle Eastern countries, but the ways by which these states employ capital punishment are varied and inconsistent. With the advent of Islamic fundamentalism in the 1970s, more and more Middle Eastern countries began objecting to international norms for human rights and abolition of the death penalty, as being contrary to *sharia*, the historically formulated traditional law of Islam.

More than two-thirds of the countries in the world have now abolished the death penalty in law or practice. Out of 54 countries that have not, 26 are Islamic countries. In 11 Islamic countries, abolition is in practice. In 8 countries, Islamic laws do not provide for the death penalty for any crime (abolitionists for all crimes), and in one Islamic country laws provide for the death penalty only for exceptional crimes such as crimes under military law or crimes committed in exceptional circumstances (de facto abolition). Geographically, the majority of these Islamic countries are located in the Middle East.

It is estimated that there are more than 900 million Muslims in the world today. Many live in the Arab world, but many more live in countries such as Iran, Pakistan, Bangladesh, Indonesia, Malaysia, Nigeria, and Sudan. Although all Islamic countries are not retentionist (retain the death penalty), practice varies considerably from one to another. For instance, some Middle Eastern countries like Iran and Saudi Arabia are frequent practitioners, with thousands of executions, while others, such as Algeria, conduct executions in only the rarest of cases, or countries such as Israel and Turkey that have abolished capital punishment. The State of Israel is a death penalty free zone in the Middle East and has abolished capital punishment for all offenses other than genocide, war crimes, crimes against humanity, crimes against the Jewish people, and treason in wartime. The only execution that has taken place in Israel was the execution of Adolf Eichmann, in which the condemned man was hanged. The criminal justice system of Israel has been reluctant to inflict the death penalty even on traitors and terrorists. In Israel, after World War II, some traitors were sentenced only to imprisonment; the others were sentenced to death, but none were actually executed.

The diversity of practice suggests there is little consensus among Middle Eastern countries. For example, Sudan recently banned the juvenile death penalty and amended its laws in January 2010 to set 18 years as the firm age of majority nationwide, but still it is not clear whether the new 2010 law extends to Islamic offenses such as retaliation (*qisas*) and prescribed crimes (*hudud*).

Middle Eastern countries that practice *sharia* law as the source of their criminal justice system are associated with the use of capital punishment as retribution

Reformist students at Sharif University of Technology in Tehran, Iran, protest against the death sentence of Professor Hashem Aghajari. Aghajari was sentenced to death for apostasy after he gave a speech in which he counseled others not to "blindly follow" clerical rule. The sentence was commuted after an international outcry. (Kaveh Kazemi/Getty Images)

for a wide variety of crimes. Therefore, among Middle Eastern countries a distinction has to be made between Islamic states in which *sharia* law or Islamic law is practiced (e.g., Iran) with Islam as the official religion of a country and where Islamic courts may be used (e.g., Lebanon), and secular criminal justice systems in which government institutions are separate from religion (e.g., Turkey).

The death penalty in some Middle Eastern countries is applied to an overly broad range of crimes in addition to murder: incest, rape, sex between a non-Muslim and a Muslim female, adultery, sodomy, other homosexual acts after the fourth conviction, drinking liquor after three convictions, drawing arms to create fear, defamation to sanctities, drug trafficking above a certain amount, corruption on earth, fornication (fourth conviction), false accusation of unlawful intercourse (fourth conviction), and *had* theft (fourth conviction).

A major difficulty is how to distinguish between cruel and unusual punishment in the different Middle Eastern countries. The most dramatic differences are related to the proportionality doctrine. Penal proportionality based on religious proportionality in Islam is completely different from the secular proportionality in the Western countries or Israel. For example, the imposition of the death penalty for fornication between a non-Muslim man and a Muslim woman would not pass the secular proportionality doctrine. In the secular countries criminalizing sexual conduct is related to harm caused to the society rather than to the virtue of Muslims.

The Islamic criminal justice system of Middle Eastern countries recognizes four systems or categories of punishment. Under *had* or *hudud*, important crimes deemed to threaten the existence of Islam are punishable by penalties set by the *Quran*, or by the *Sunnah* (tradition of Prophet Muhammad). The following *hudud* crimes are punishable by death: adultery, sodomy, apostasy, and banditry (*Moharebeh* or resorting to arms to frighten people). Islamic jurists consider these sanctions immutable. The second system, *qisas*, concerns intentional crimes against the person. Its fundamental premise is the *lex talionis*, "eye for eye, tooth for tooth." *Lex talionis* is set out in the *Quran*, verse 5.32 (further developed by verse 17.33). According to the *Quran*, the victim or his or her heirs are to inflict the punishment, under the supervision of public authorities; the victims of such crimes may pardon the offender, in which case the death penalty set by *qisas* will not be imposed.

In cases where the offender is pardoned by victims, two other systems of crime and punishment come to play. These are the *diyat* (prescribes restitution or compensation for the victim) and the *taazir* (public authorities set their own punishment in which the judge has wide discretion). Under the *taazir*, public authorities may provide for capital punishment, but no religious text requires them to do so. Islamic penal codes in the Middle East use capital punishment for offenses such as defamation to sanctities, drug trafficking above a certain amount, and for the corruption on earth crimes.

Methods of execution in the Middle East vary and can include hanging, shooting, beheading, stoning, and dropping the convict from a high wall. In some Middle Eastern countries, public executions are carried out to heighten the deterrent effect of punishment. Hanging as an execution method is not in practice in the Western countries; however, some Middle Eastern countries routinely hang capital offenders.

The common method of execution in classical Islam was beheading by the sword, but in certain cases different methods are prescribed. For instance, in *Shiite* school, sodomy is punishable by beheading, stoning, burning, or dropping the convict from a high wall. In some Middle Eastern countries, governed by *sharia* law, stoning is still practiced. Stoning as a form of punishment is provided in the criminal codes of the following Middle Eastern countries: Iran, Pakistan, Saudi Arabia, Sudan, and the United Arab Emirates. The punishment of stoning to death (*rajm*) has a long tradition in Islam. When it comes to the practice of stoning adulterers, however, the traditions indicate that *Talmudic* law (Jewish law) primarily influenced Muhammad. The *hadith* present Muhammad as initially prescribing stoning explicitly for Jews who had been found guilty of adultery, then later referring to the Jewish law when imposing similar sentences on members of his own community. Muhammad even criticized the Jews for relaxing their adultery laws when Jewish people replaced stoning with smearing of coal on the face.

Some Middle Eastern nations with large Islamic populations have recently gone long periods without executions. Most of the Middle Eastern countries that are low-execution nations have a secular criminal justice system rather than religious criminal justice system. However, the tiny nation of Brunei Darussalam combined an Islamic theocratic regime with no execution until 2014.

Sanaz Alasti

See also: Capital Punishment, Collateral Consequences of; Death Penalty Legal Issues; Death Row Correctional Officers; Death Row Inmates

Further Reading

Alasti, S. (2007). Comparative study of stoning punishment in the religions of Islam and Judaism. *Justice Policy Journal, 4*(1), 1–38.

Anderson, J. N. D. (1951) Homicide in Islamic law. *Bulletin of the School of Oriental & African Studies, 13,* 811, 815.

Aslan, R. (2003–2004). The problem of stoning in the Islamic penal code: An argument for reform. *UCLA Journal of Islamic & Near Eastern Law, 3*(1), 91.

Cherif Bassiouni, M. (1988). *Introduction to Islam* (p. 8). Chicago: Rand McNally.

Ghomi, M. (1992). Jama al-Shetat, Volume 1, *Keyhan Publication* (p. 395) [In Farsi].

Hilli, A. (1999). Qawa'id al-ahkam, *Mu'assasat Nashr Islami, 3,* 521–523 [In Arabic].

Montazeri, H. A. (1998). Tozihol al-Masayel, *Fekr Publication* (p. 572) [In Farsi].

Mufid, M. (1990). *Mu'assasat Nashr Islami* (p. 789) [In Arabic].

Ownes, E. (2004). *Religion and the death penalty.* Grand Rapids, MI: William Eerdmans.

Peters, R. (2006). *Crime and punishment in Islamic law* (p. 36). Cambridge, U.K.: Cambridge University Press.

Schabas, W. A. (2000). Symposium: Religion's Role in the Administration of the Death Penalty: Islam and the Death Penalty, *William & Mary Bill of Rights Journal, 9,* 223.

Zimring, F., & Johnson, D. (2009). *The next frontier: National development, political change, and the death penalty in Asia* (p. 20). Oxford, U.K.: Oxford University Press.

Death Penalty Legal Issues

Since the 1960s, the U.S. Supreme Court has ruled on numerous death penalty cases, and the legal challenges to this sentence continue to evolve. Legal issues regarding the death penalty range from challenging the constitutionality of the sentence and methods of execution to challenging which crimes and offenders are eligible for the death penalty.

In *Trop v. Dulles* (1958), the U.S. Supreme Court held that the Eight Amendment's ban on cruel and unusual punishment must "draw its meaning from the evolving standards of decency that mark the progress of a maturing society" (p. 101). Since that decision, lawyers have argued that the death penalty is cruel and unusual punishment under modern standards of decency. And in several cases, the court has agreed with them.

Death penalty abolitionists received their first major victory in the case of *Furman v. Georgia* in 1972. The court held that giving jurors unrestricted discretion in deciding whether or not to impose the death penalty could result in arbitrary sentences in violation of the cruel and unusual punishment ban. The court's 5–4 decision was groundbreaking and unique. Each justice of the Supreme Court wrote separate opinions in this case. Justices Marshall and Brennan each wrote that the death penalty itself is cruel and unusual punishment. Justices Stewart, White, and Douglas wrote that the death penalty as applied in Georgia was unconstitutional. These combined five opinions comprised the majority position.

Justices Burger, Rehnquist, Powell, and Blackmun each wrote separate opinions stating that the death penalty did not constitute cruel and unusual punishment.

As a result of the *Furman* decision, death penalty statutes in 40 states were struck down because those statutes also gave unrestricted discretion to juries. Condemned inmates' death sentences were commuted to the most severe penalty provided for in each state. Because most states did not have life without parole statutes at that time, many of the 629 inmates with commuted sentences were later released on parole.

State legislatures responded to the *Furman* decision in three ways: (1) some passed statutes requiring the death penalty for all convicted of a capital offense; (2) some passed statutes providing guidance to juries; and (3) some took no action to potentially reinstate the death penalty. Of course, the new legislation would have to pass constitutional muster before any executions could occur.

North Carolina's new death penalty statute removed discretion entirely by requiring the death penalty if an offender was convicted of first-degree murder. The U.S. Supreme Court struck down North Carolina's mandatory death penalty law in *Woodson v. North Carolina* (1976). According to the court, there were three problems with this new law. First, it violated "modern standards of decency" because juries had already rejected the harshness of mandatory death penalty laws and legislatures replaced them with discretionary death penalty laws. Second, by eliminating all discretion, the new law did not provide an adequate response to *Furman*'s concern about unfettered jury discretion. Jurors still had no guidance to help them determine if an offender should receive a death sentence. Third, the court held that the decision in *Trop* requires that aspects of the character of the individual offender and the circumstances of the case be considered when considering a death sentence. The North Carolina statute treated all those convicted of first-degree murder, not as individual human beings, but as "members of a faceless, undifferentiated mass to be subjected to the blind infliction of the death penalty."

Georgia, Texas, and Florida passed legislation that guided jurors' discretion by requiring them to consider aggravating and mitigating factors. In the 1976 cases of *Gregg v. Georgia, Jurek v. Texas*, and *Proffitt v. Florida*, the U.S. Supreme Court upheld each state's guided discretion statute. The death penalty was ruled constitutional in these states because the statutes either explicitly (Georgia and Florida) or implicitly (Texas) required juries to consider aggravating and mitigating factors when deciding whether or not to impose the death penalty. These three cases, known collectively as *Gregg*, also upheld the use of separate hearings for determining guilt and sentencing; automatic appellate review of all death convictions and sentences; and proportionality reviews that compare cases on appeal with other death penalty cases in the state.

A series of U.S. Supreme Court rulings limited the crimes for which the death penalty could be a constitutional sentence. In *Coker v. Georgia* (1977), the court held 7–2 that the death penalty was a cruel and unusual sentence for the rape of an adult woman. In the plurality opinion, Justice White noted in this decision that Georgia was one of only three states to reinstate the death penalty after *Furman* that included rape as a capital offense and was the only state that still included rape as a capital offense at the time of the court's decision. Additionally, the court stated that juries in Georgia had refused to impose death for the conviction of rape in 90 percent of cases. Justices Burger and Rehnquist dissented. *Eberheart v. Georgia,* decided the same day as *Coker,* struck down the death sentence of John Wallace Eberheart Jr., who had been convicted of rape and kidnapping.

Louisiana v. Kennedy (2008) addressed the constitutionality of the death penalty for the rape of a child. Justice Kennedy wrote the majority opinion, which held that under the evolving standards of decency requirement of *Trop,* a death sentence is cruel and unusual punishment for the rape of a child where the child was killed or intended to be killed. The court wrote that there was a national consensus against the use of the death penalty for the rape of a child: only six states authorized the death penalty for the rape of a child, and although five states that had introduced legislation to authorize death for child rape, two of those bills had already failed at the time of the court's decision. Additionally, no state had executed anyone for the rape of an adult or child since 1964, no executions for any other offense that did not result in death had occurred since 1963, and Louisiana was the only state to have sentenced a person convicted of child rape to death. The majority of the court was also concerned that the death penalty for child rape cases could cause more harm to the victim and could result in the crime being underreported if the perpetrator is a family member. Moreover, the court was concerned about the possibility of wrongful conviction given the documented problems of child testimony and the fact that victims could exaggerate or fabricate the brutality of the crime. Finally, the court stated that allowing the death penalty for child rape would remove an offender's incentive not to kill the victim.

Another series of U.S. Supreme Court cases addressed who could lawfully receive the death penalty. Many of these cases involved juvenile offenders. In *Thompson v. Oklahoma* (1988), the U.S. Supreme Court held that it was unlawful to execute a person who was under the age of 16 at the time of the crime unless the legislature had specifically authorized the death penalty for such minors. The following year, the court held in *Stanford v. Kentucky* that there was no constitutional violation in imposing the death penalty on an offender who was 17 at the time of the offense. Likewise, the court in *Wilkins v. Missouri* (1989) held that the Eighth Amendment did not prohibit the execution of a person who was 16 at the time of the offense. In *Stanford* and *Wilkins,* the court held that there was no general consensus against permitting the death penalty for juvenile offenders because 22 states had laws that permitted such a sentence. The court would come to a different conclusion nearly 20 years later.

In *Roper v. Simmons* (2005), the U.S. Supreme Court reconsidered the issue of death sentences for juvenile offenders. Again using the *Trop* ruling regarding the application of "evolving standards of decency," this time the court held that executing offenders who were under 18 at the time of the offense was cruel and unusual punishment. In overturning *Stanford* and *Wilkins,* the court's 5–4 ruling noted that a review of modern standards of decency showed that now there was a general consensus against death sentences for juvenile offenders. Justice Kennedy wrote the majority opinion, finding that 30 states have rejected the death penalty for juveniles and that the execution of juvenile offenders was rare. The court also gave some weight to the global rejection of the death penalty for juvenile offenders, pointing

Death Penalty Legal Issues

out that the United States was the only country in the world that permitted such a sentence.

The U.S. Supreme Court has also addressed the use of the death penalty for "insane" and "intellectually disabled" offenders. In *Ford v. Wainwright* (1986), the court ruled that it was cruel and unusual punishment to execute an offender who is "insane" at the time of execution. Although Alvin Ford was competent at the time of the offense and trial, he became delusional after years of incarceration. In this 7–2 decision, Justice Marshall wrote: "For centuries no jurisdiction has countenanced the execution of the insane, yet this Court has never decided whether the Constitution forbids the practice. Today we keep faith with our common-law heritage in holding that it does." The opinion noted that English common law prohibited the execution of the insane as did every state in the United States. Such a punishment had no retributive or deterrent value because the offender could not comprehend why he was to be executed. Additionally, he stated that executing the incompetent offends humanity. The court struck down Florida's procedure for determining competency because it did not provide adequate assurance of accuracy, specifically noting that the condemned offender was denied a fact-finding hearing before a neutral body.

The issue of executing people with limited cognitive abilities was not as easily decided. In *Penry v. Lynaugh* (1989), the U.S. Supreme Court refused to hold that executing "mentally retarded capital murderers" violated the Eighth Amendment. The court reversed itself in 2002 when it decided the case of *Atkins v. Virginia* and held 6–3 that executing the intellectually disabled did constitute cruel and unusual punishment because it violated *Trop*'s evolving standards of decency standard. The majority opinion, written by Justice Stevens, noted that since the *Penry* decision, there had been a consistent change in state laws to ban the execution of the mentally retarded.

The public reaction to the execution of Jerome Bowden in Georgia in 1986 caused the Georgia legislature to pass a law to prevent the execution of a person with intellectual disability. Jerome Bowden had been declared mentally retarded when he was 14. He was granted a stay of execution by the Georgia Board of Pardons and Parole after public protests of his pending execution. During the stay, a state-selected psychologist conducted an intelligence test and determined that Bowden had an IQ of 65, which is firmly in the level to conclude that a person is mentally retarded. Despite the psychologist's findings, the board decided that Bowden knew right from wrong and lifted the stay. Bowden died in the electric chair on June 24, 1986. By April 1988, Georgia had passed a new law that gave juries the option to find a defendant guilty but mentally retarded in which case death would not be a possible punishment.

Other governments changed their laws as a result of the Bowden execution and the *Penry* decision. Between 1988 and the time of the *Atkins* decision, nearly 20 state and federal legislative bodies passed laws to prevent the execution of the mentally retarded. In at least two other states, Virginia and Nevada, similar legislation passed one house of the legislature. The Texas legislature unanimously passed legislation to exclude the mentally retarded from the death penalty, but Governor Rick Perry vetoed the bill. In the *Atkins* decision, Justice Stevens wrote that more important than the number of governments prohibiting the execution of the mentally retarded was the consistency in the direction of the legislation, the overwhelming support for the restrictive legislation, and the uncommon nature of executing mentally retarded offenders.

The issue of executing mentally retarded offenders continued to confront the courts. In *Schriro v. Smith* (2005), the U.S. Supreme Court held that states, not federal courts, were to establish a process to enforce the prohibition of the execution of the mentally retarded. Florida's mental retardation statute set a strict 70 IQ threshold requirement before the finding of mental retardation could be made. In 2014, the U.S. Supreme Court held in *Hall v. Florida* that the statute had been interpreted too narrowly by the Florida Supreme Court and stated that when an offender's IQ is within the margin of error, the offender must be able to submit other evidence of mental retardation.

The most recent legal issues confronting the courts have revolved around lethal injection. In *Baze v. Rees* (2008), the U.S. Supreme Court upheld 7–2 Kentucky's four-drug lethal injection protocol, holding that the state's use of lethal injection did not constitute cruel and unusual punishment. In recent years, many states have changed their lethal injection protocols because the drugs they had been using were becoming unavailable. Oklahoma revised its lethal injection protocol from the use of three drugs to the use of a new one-drug lethal injection of midazolam. In *Glossip v. Gross* (2015) the U.S. Supreme Court denied an injunction to stop the use of the new protocol stating that the petitioners failed to show that they could succeed on the merits of their case and to suggest an alternative method of execution. Another result of the lack of execution drugs has been legislation to keep the suppliers of the drugs and other parts of the execution protocols anonymous. Most such bills have passed the state legislatures; however, bills in Alabama and Louisiana failed. Lower courts have issued conflicting decisions regarding the constitutionality of these secrecy laws, so the U.S. Supreme Court may have another legal issue to face soon.

Stacy K. Parker

See also: Death Row Correctional Officers; Death Row Inmates; Execution Methods

Further Reading

Associated Press. (1988, April 12). Georgia to bar executions of retarded killers. *New York Times*. Retrieved from http://www.nytimes.com

Atkins v. Virginia, 536 U.S. 304 (2002).

Baze v. Rees, 553 U.S. 35 (2008).

Bohm, R. M. (2011). *Deathquest: An introduction to the theory and practice of capital punishment in the United States.* New York: Routledge.

Coker v. Georgia, 433 U.S. 584 (1977).

Court decisions reflect continuing ambivalence towards state lethal injection secrecy laws. (2015, October 12). Retrieved from http://www.deathpenaltyinfo.org/node/6324

Ford v. Wainwright, 477 U.S. 399 (1986).

Glossip v. Gross, 576 U.S. ___ (2015).

Hall v. Florida, 572 U.S. ___ (2014).

Jurek v. Texas, 428 U.S. 262 (1976).

Penry v. Lynaugh, 492 U.S. 302 (1989).
Proffitt v. Florida, 428 U.S. 242 (1976).
Roper v. Simmons, 543 U.S. 551 (2005).
Schriro v. Smith, 546 U.S. (2005).
Stanford v. Kentucky, 492 U.S. 361 (1989).
Thompson v. Oklahoma, 487 US 815 (1988).
Trop v. Dulles, 356 U.S. 86 (1958).
Wilkins v. Missouri, 492 U.S. 361 (1989).
Woodson v. North Carolina, 428 U.S. 280 (1976).

Death Row Correctional Officers

Condemned inmates are not the only people who spend a tremendous amount of time on death row. Across the United States, correctional officers are spending time on death row too. Death row correctional officers are charged with keeping the condemned inmate, other inmates and corrections employees, and the public safe until the time the death row inmate is moved to the execution facility. Because stays on death row can be quite lengthy—the average stay on death row is more than 15 years—correctional officers can develop personal relationships with inmates who are condemned to die. These officers have a unique perspective on the death penalty and those who inhabit death row, yet they have not been the subject of much research.

Researchers have found that almost 90 percent of those working on death row support the death penalty; nearly 61 percent consider the death penalty to be an important issue; and just over 87 percent report that their opinion of the death penalty was unlikely to change (Brown & Benningfield, 2008). Additionally, only 7 percent indicate that their experiences working on death row changed their opinion on the death penalty and that being a part of the life-taking process was not particularly problematic for them (Brown & Benningfield, 2008). Notably, only 30 percent of the death row officers required some participation in the execution process, and less than 8 percent of those studied had witnessed an execution (Brown & Benningfield, 2008).

Studies have also revealed that while the majority of death row correctional officers feel tense, frustrated, and under pressure at work, they also believe that working on death row is less stressful than working in the general population units. Many death row officers believe that general population inmates are more difficult to manage and get along with than those serving death sentences. They report that death row is very controlled and routine with copious rules that are strictly enforced.

Security is the main goal of death row correctional officers. This includes protecting others from the condemned inmates and also protecting the condemned inmates from others. When death row inmates are moved within the prison, they often wear waist chains, handcuffs, and leg irons. This leaves them exposed to other inmates in the facility who may wish to do them harm. Death row inmates must also be protected from one another. These inmates have shown that they can commit heinous crimes against other people, so violence among inmates must be prevented or responded to rapidly. Tactical units, rather than death row officers, are generally called on to quell any violence between inmates. Death row officers must also protect themselves from the possibility of harm and must be constantly concerned about their own security. Though relatively rare on death row, the potential for violence is a major cause of stress for death row correctional officers. It is this fear of potential violence that causes tension and concern for these officers. Such fear may not be rooted in the reality of the danger the officers face; rather, researchers have found that death row inmates are not more violent than those in general population.

Officers disagree about the most dangerous assignments on death row. Inmate counts, open areas, and escorting inmates to recreation were noted by some officers as the times they feel most vulnerable. Death row inmates have proved that they are capable of violence, but the restricted nature of the death row custody level limits physical interaction between inmates and officers. Unlike general population inmates who have more freedom and larger living spaces, many death row inmates are alone in their cells for up to 23 hours a day. Nonetheless, death row workers report fear of being killed or taken hostage by inmates who may believe they have nothing to lose. Likewise, they report concern about the ability of their colleagues to make no mistakes. All officers must do their job thoroughly and not become complacent because the consequences could be fatal, but some death row correctional officers report that they do not trust other officers to follow safety protocol.

Researchers have found that death row correctional officers believe that the work on death row is different from working in other units and that death row itself has a different overall feeling within a prison. This is in part because both the inmate and the officer understand that the inmate is there waiting to be executed. Officers have described death row as depressing, quiet, eerie, and even scary, which distinguishes it from the rest of the facility. Although most states have separate execution and death row facilities, partly in an attempt to lessen the negative emotional and psychological toll of executions on corrections officials, executions still affect both officers and death row inmates. Many inmates have been on death row together for many years and have developed close relationships. When an execution occurs, inmates may direct their anger, frustration, vulnerability, and loss of a fellow inmate on death row correctional officers. Death row workers often choose to focus on the procedural aspects of their jobs. This allows them to disengage from the condemned inmate and those who remain in death row and to maintain the professionalism that their jobs entail.

The fear of potential violence on death row may help to explain why death row correctional officers would choose to work on death row instead of other job assignments. Although the majority of officers studied reported that they would rather work with death row offenders than those in general population, only approximately 32 percent of those studied reported that they would choose death row over other assignments including cell houses (10.8 percent), supervising inmate workers (18.9 percent), and yard, wall, or perimeter duty (37.8 percent) (Brown & Benningfield, 2008).

Stacy K. Parker

See also: Death Penalty Legal Issues; Death Row Inmates; Execution Methods

Further Reading

Bohm, R. M. (2012). *Capital punishment's collateral damage.* Durham, NC: Carolina Academic Press.

Brown, K. L., & Benningfield, M. (2008). Death row correctional officers: Experiences, perspectives, and attitudes. *Criminal Justice Review, 33*(4), 524–540.

Gillespie, L. K. (2003). *Inside the death chamber: Exploring executions.* Boston: Allyn & Bacon.

Johnson, R. (1998). *Deathwork: A study of the modern execution process.* Belmont, CA: West/Wadsworth.

Death Row Inmates

The number of new death sentences and executions carried out has been declining since 1999. A growing number of states have abolished the death penalty altogether, but living on death row is still a reality for nearly 3,000 men and women throughout the United States.

At the end of 2013, there were 2,979 men and women facing death sentences in 35 states and in the U.S. federal system (Snell, 2014). This number is down 32 from the end of 2012 and marked the 13th year in a row where the number of people facing the death penalty decreased (Snell, 2014). The trend continued into 2015, which resulted in only 49 new death sentences, compared to 73 in 2014 and the all-time high of 315 in 1996 (Death Penalty Information Center [DPIC], 2016a). Likewise, the number of people executed has been decreasing from 39 in 2013 to 35 in 2014 and ending at 28 in 2015 (DPIC, 2016a).

Nine states had more than 100 inmates on their death rows as of December 31, 2013. California had the largest death row population with 735 inmates (Snell, 2014). Other states with more than 100 death row inmates were Florida (398), Texas (273), Pennsylvania (190), Alabama (190), North Carolina (151), Ohio (136), and Arizona (122) (Snell, 2014). The Federal Bureau of Prisons (BOP), which houses federal inmates, held 56 prisoners facing death (Snell, 2014).

Throughout 2013, 83 new death-sentenced inmates were received by 16 states and the BOP (Snell, 2014). California (25), Florida (15), and Texas (9) were responsible for 60 percent of new death sentences (Snell, 2014). During the same year, 115 inmates were removed from a death sentence in 22 states and the BOP (Snell, 2014). The largest category of inmates removed from a death sentence during this time (45) was because the convictions or sentences were overturned (Snell, 2014). Thirty-nine inmates were executed in 2013 while 31 others died from natural causes or suicide (Snell, 2014). The average stay on death row for inmates executed in 2013 was 15.5 years, which was four months shorter than 2012 (Snell, 2014).

There were 8,124 people sentenced to death between 1977 and the end of 2013 (Snell, 2014). Nearly three times the number of those executed received a different disposition at some point while awaiting execution (Snell, 2014). Approximately 17 percent of these inmates were executed, 6 percent died from a cause other than execution, and 40 percent received alternative dispositions (Snell, 2014). The federal government and 35 states have executed 1,359 inmates since 1977 (Snell, 2014).

Of those prisoners facing a death sentence at the end of 2013, 56 percent were white and 42 percent were black, 14 percent of those with a known ethnicity were Hispanic, and 98 percent were male (Snell, 2014). Those who were executed in 2013 included 26 white and 13 black prisoners, one of whom was a woman (Snell, 2014). The mean age of all those facing a death sentence in 2013 was 47 while the median age was 46 (Snell, 2014). Those who were sentenced to death in 2013 had a mean age of 39 and a median age of 38 (Snell, 2014). Nearly 48 percent of all those under a sentence of death had no education beyond the 11th grade; the same was true for 39 percent of those facing new death sentences (Snell, 2014). Marital status was consistent among all those facing a death sentence and those whose death sentence was handed down in 2013. The total death sentence population included 21.5 percent married, 20 percent divorced or separated, 3.6 percent widowed, and 54.8 percent never married (Snell, 2014). The new death sentence population comprised 22.4 percent married, 20.9 percent divorced or separated, 1.5 percent widowed, and 55.2 percent never married (Snell, 2014).

Criminal histories of those facing a death sentence in 2013 showed some variation by race. While 67 percent of all those under sentence of death had prior felony convictions, the percentage was higher among black (72.6 percent) and Hispanic (64.8 percent) than white (63.9 percent) (Snell, 2014). Hispanic inmates were less likely than white and black inmates to have a prior homicide conviction: 6.6 percent for Hispanics, 9 percent for white, and 9.6 percent for blacks (Snell, 2014). White people under a sentence of death were more likely to have charges already pending at the time of the capital offense (9.6 percent) than black (8.7 percent) and Hispanic (6.2 percent) prisoners, but they were less likely to have been on probation or parole at the time of the capital offense: whites (9.9 percent and 14.1 percent), blacks (12 percent and 18.5 percent), and Hispanics (13.8 percent and 18.3 percent), respectively (Snell, 2014). Finally, white people under a sentence of death in 2013 were more likely to have been incarcerated (3.5 percent) or escaped (1.8 percent) than black people (2.2 percent and 0.8 percent) and Hispanic people (2 percent and 1.1 percent), respectively (Snell, 2014).

In nearly every jurisdiction in the United States, inmates under a sentence of death are housed in a separate facility or unit of a facility that emphasizes isolation, controlled movement, tight security, and limited comforts. Corrections officials severely restrict those on death row because they presume that such inmates are inherently more dangerous to staff than those who did not receive a death sentence. This is not true for Missouri, however, where even inmates facing a death sentence have been housed with the general population since 1991. Researchers have found that death-sentenced inmates and those sentenced to life without parole (LWOP) are less likely to be involved in violent conduct than inmates who are eligible for parole. This was true even after researchers controlled for other variables that could relate to institutional violence such as age, race, education, prior imprisonment, and amount of time served.

Researchers have found that life on the traditional death row is harsh, regimented, and intimidating with severe and arbitrary restrictions on access to loved ones. To deal with the psychological issues, death-sentenced inmates use coping mechanisms similar to those with a terminal illness and may include denial, bargaining, and depression before acceptance. Inmates residing on death row may find their mental health deteriorating over time as a result of loss of support, loneliness, frustration, uncertainty, and hopelessness. It is not surprising, then, that suicide rates among death row inmates are much higher than that of men who have not been condemned to death. In lieu of suicide, many inmates under the sentence of death become "volunteers" for execution. That is, they waive all appeals in the hope to have the execution date moved sooner. Michael Ross of Connecticut provides an example of a volunteer. He attempted suicide three times while awaiting execution. His lawyers argued that he was not competent to waive his appeals and suggested that the conditions of his confinement led Ross to seek escape through death. They argued that he suffered from "death row syndrome" and was not capable of making a knowing choice to waive his appeals and be executed. Michael Ross was executed on May 13, 2005, after being found competent to waive his appeals and seek execution.

So-called "death row syndrome" has not been rigorously studied. Researchers state that condemned inmates may suffer from temporal, physical, and experiential components of this syndrome. The first, temporal, refers to the time between conviction and execution. Some researchers have found that condemned inmates adapt to life under a death sentence, while others have found that death row inmates' psychological states deteriorate over time. The physical component also relates to the amount of time spent awaiting death; however, this component focuses on the effects of the living conditions on death row on the psychological health of the condemned. The experiential component refers to living in fear of being forced to die by execution. Waiting for the execution to take place may be more of a punishment than death itself.

The delay between conviction and execution can lead to another issue: executing the elderly. Viva Leroy Nash was the oldest person to die on death row when he passed away at the age of 83 in Arizona in 2010 (DPIC, 2016b). Sentenced to death in 1983, Nash was deaf, nearly blind, wheelchair-bound, and suffering from dementia when he died of natural causes (DPIC, 2016b). Brandon Jones of Georgia served the longest time between conviction in 1979 and execution in 2016 and was the oldest person ever executed in the state at the age of 72 (DPIC, 2016b). Gary Alvord served 40 years on death row in Florida before dying of natural causes in May 2013 when he was 66 years old (DPIC, 2016b). He came close to execution twice, but severe schizophrenia prevented his execution from occurring. During his time on death row, 75 other inmates were put to death in Florida (DPIC, 2016b).

Stacy K. Parker

See also: Death Penalty Legal Issues; Death Row Correctional Officers; Execution Methods

Further Reading

Bohm, R. M. (2011). *Deathquest: An introduction to the theory and practice of capital punishment in the United States.* New York: Routledge.

Cunningham, M. D., Reidy, T. J., & Sorenson, J. R. (2005). Is death row obsolete? A decade of mainstreaming death-sentenced inmates in Missouri. *Behavioral Sciences and the Law, 23*(3), 307–320.

Death Penalty Information Center. (2016a). *The death penalty in 2015: Year end report.* Retrieved from http://deathpenaltyinfo.org/documents/2015YrEnd.pdf

Death Penalty Information Center. (2016b). *Time on death row.* Retrieved from https://deathpenaltyinfo.org/time-death-row

Johnson, R. (1979). Under sentence of death: The psychology of death row confinement. *Law & Psychology Review, 5*, 141–192.

Smith, A. (2008). Not "waiving" but drowning: The anatomy of death row syndrome and volunteering for execution. *The Boston University Public Interest Law Journal, 17*, 237–254.

Snell, T. L. (2014). *Capital punishment, 2013—Statistical tables.* Washington, DC: Bureau of Justice Statistics, U.S. Department of Justice. Retrieved from http://www.bjs.gov/content/pub/pdf/cp13st.pdf

Deliberate Indifference

Deliberate indifference is a legal standard used to determine whether corrections officials have violated an inmate's right to be free from cruel and unusual punishment under the Eighth Amendment. The Eighth Amendment prevents torture and physical punishments that lack any penological purpose. The Supreme Court extended the prohibition against cruel and unusual punishment beyond purposeful application of physical torture to situations where prison officials are deliberately indifferent "to a substantial risk of serious harm to an inmate" when "the official was subjectively aware of the risk" (*Farmer v. Brennan*, 511 U.S. 825, 828–829 [1994]).

The deliberate indifference standard is applied to cases arising out of a failure by prison officials to prevent harm to inmates. These cases are sometimes termed 1983 claims due to their reliance on 42 U.S.C. § 1983 that allows civil law suits for plaintiffs whose constitutional rights have been violated under color of law.

The deliberate indifference standard was first adopted by the U.S. Supreme Court in the 1976 case of *Estelle v. Gamble*. In *Estelle* the inmate suffered a back injury while working at the prison. After a series of medical examinations and prison staff disregard of necessary treatment, the inmate was cleared to return to work. The inmate claimed he was still injured but was placed in administrative segregation for refusing to work. While in segregation the inmate suffered chest pains, and a doctor diagnosed him with irregular cardiac rhythm. After the diagnosis the inmate complained of chest pains for two days. During this time the guards refused to let the inmate see a doctor. The inmate filed a lawsuit alleging violations of his right to be free from cruel and unusual punishment due to the insufficiency of his medical care.

At the time *Estelle* was decided the Supreme Court had a long history of defining Eighth Amendment cruel and unusual punishment claims as preventing torture and lingering death. Further extending this, the court recognized that the cruel and unusual punishments clause prevented punishments that are at odds with evolving standards of decency and include "the unnecessary and wanton infliction of pain" (*Estelle v. Gamble*, 429 U.S. 97, 103 [1976]).

Based on these precepts the court concluded that "deliberate indifference to the serious medical needs of prisoners" constitutes an actionable claim for a violation of the cruel and unusual punishments clause (*Estelle v. Gamble*, 429 U.S. 97, 104

[1976]). The deliberate indifference standard was expressly limited, however, by the court's assertion that inadvertent failures of care sufficient to sustain a medical malpractice claim do not meet the requirements of the deliberate indifference standard. Deliberate indifference requires more than just evidence of negligence.

Almost 20 years later in *Farmer v. Brennan*, the deliberate indifference standard was applied to cases outside the medical care arena to those where harm to the plaintiff came in the form of inmate violence. In this case a transgender inmate who presented as female but was biologically male was placed in the general population of the male prison; she was subsequently attacked and sexually assaulted by another prisoner in her cell. Prior to this occurrence the inmate spent a significant amount of time in administrative segregation due to both rule violations and concerns regarding her safety. However, prison officials claimed they did not know about a specific danger to this inmate and called attention to the fact that the inmate had not informed prison officials of any safety concerns.

A circuit split had arisen about the state of mind required to support an actionable claim based on the deliberate indifference standard. At the very minimum, as established in *Estelle*, more was required than a claim of mere prison official negligence. Some circuit courts adopted an objective test akin to the standard for recklessness in a civil action; the prison official either knew or should have known of "an unjustifiably high risk of harm" and failed to act (*Farmer v. Brennan*, 511 U.S. 825, 836 [1994]). Other courts, however, embraced a subjective test similar to the criminal law definition of recklessness; the inmate claimant needed to demonstrate that the prison official actually knew about the risk of harm and did nothing.

The Supreme Court rejected the objective test in favor of the subjective test. In doing so, the court noted that the mere presence of inhumane prison conditions alone did not create liability under the Eighth Amendment for prison officials. The court reasoned that prison officials were not inflicting punishment under the Eighth Amendment unless they knew specifically about a risk of harm. Thus, imputing liability to prison officials for what they should have known, but did not contemplate, was not sufficient for liability in the Eighth Amendment context. According to the Supreme Court, "An official's failure to alleviate a significant risk that he should have perceived but did not, while no cause for commendation, cannot under our cases be condemned as the infliction of punishment" (*Farmer v. Brennan*, 511 U.S. 825, 826 [1994]).

Despite requiring evidence of actual knowledge of an unjustifiable risk of harm, the court also held that the obviousness of a given risk of harm could allow a fact finder to attribute sufficient knowledge to prison officials to support a deliberate indifference claim. This prevents a defense for prison officials who choose to be willfully blind to unjustifiable risks or harm. An example of obviousness is found in *Hope v. Pelzer* (2002). In that case the inmate was twice shackled to a hitching post. The second occurrence lasted 7 hours; the inmate was in the sun with no shirt, and the guards gave him water no more than twice. The court held that the risk of harm was obvious under these conditions. Notwithstanding the court's language allowing for obviousness to stand in the place of evidence of actual knowledge, obviousness of risk can be a high bar for inmate plaintiffs to demonstrate.

Farmer v. Brennan also elaborated on the specifics of the type of knowledge required by prison officials. If there is actual knowledge about the risk, prison officials will still be held liable even if they do not have foreknowledge of the harm that ultimately befalls the claimant. For example, assume prison officials have notice of an increased risk of inmate violence toward Inmate A. The deliberate indifference standard does not require that officials know in advance that Inmate B will lead the attack. Furthermore, if it is known that a particular group of inmates is subjected to an increased risk of harm, then it is not necessary for prison officials to have explicitly considered the specific inmate to be at risk. It is enough that the claimant is a member of the group at heightened risk. Liability has been found under the deliberate indifference standard in cases where prison officials knew violence increased during periods of overcrowding yet did not alleviate the risk of harm to inmates.

If corrections officials do have actual knowledge of a serious risk of harm or knowledge is imputed to them due to the obviousness of the risk, they do not need to prevent the harm to escape liability; prison officials can discharge their duty by enacting a reasonable response to prevent the harm.

The requirement that correctional facilities to avoid deliberate indifference as to physical medical treatment, as in *Estelle v. Gamble*, has been extended to the delivery of services to address serious mental illness. This has profound implications due to evidence of widespread mental illness among inmates in correctional facilities.

Deliberate indifference in the provision of mental health services can result in increased risk of inmate suicide. Yet, liability is not a foregone conclusion in suicide cases. Courts have often required that the inmate present an apparent risk of suicide by telling staff or police they are suicidal or engaging in a recent suicide attempt. It is generally not sufficient that past inmates committed suicide in the same or similar manner as the plaintiff/decedent, absent information indicating that the she or he was specifically at risk of suicide; even if facility rules were not followed. However, officials claiming ignorance of suicide risk, yet actively evading facts that indicate such, have been deemed liable.

Use of solitary confinement has not generally been found to create liability, and courts appear willing to conclude that the psychological pain induced by solitary confinement is acceptable under the Eighth Amendment. However, placing mentally ill inmates in extended solitary confinement has been found to create liability under the deliberate indifference standard.

Todd C. Hiestand

See also: Evolving Standards of Decency; Health Care in Prison Populations; Mental Health Issues and Jails; Mentally Ill Prisoners; Overcrowding; Solitary Confinement; Suicide in Custody; Transgender Inmates; Use of Force in Prisons

Further Reading

Daniel, A. E. (2009). Suicide-related litigation in jails and prisons: Risk management strategies. *Journal of Correctional Health Care, 15*(1), 19–27.

Estelle v. Gamble, 429 U.S. 97 (1976).

Farmer v. Brennan, 511 U.S. 825 (1994).

Hafemeister, T. L., & George, J. (2012). The ninth circle of hell: An Eighth Amendment analysis of imposing prolonged supermax solitary confinement on inmates with a mental illness. *Denver University Law Review, 90,* 1–54.

Hope v. Pelzer, 536 U.S. 730 (2002).

Tartaro, C. (2015). What is obvious? Federal courts' interpretation of the knowledge requirement in post–*Farmer v. Brennan* custodial suicide cases. *The Prison Journal, 95*(1), 23–42.

Deprivation Model

The deprivation model is one of the most tested theories of institutional behavior and inmate subculture development. The basic tenet of the model is that social interaction, and specifically social roles within the inmate subculture, are a response to the five "pains of imprisonment" as described by Gresham Sykes.

Based on his 1950s study of a male maximum security prison, Sykes found that inmates felt extremely deprived and frustrated with the conditions of their confinement. These pains of imprisonment, or deprivations, may be seen as part of the punishment being inflicted on the offender. Sykes described each of the five deprivations with attention to how they threaten an inmate's personality and self-worth and how they work to create the inmate social system within the prison.

The first pain of imprisonment is the deprivation of liberty. Sykes described this as a double loss to the inmate; the inmate is not only confined to the institution but confined within the institution. The inmate may feel rejected by the free world and is isolated from family, a condition that is rarely mitigated by visitation, mail, or phone conversations. The inmate's movement is restricted within the institution by strict schedules. These rejections and restrictions are thought to impact the ego of inmates and occur both inside and outside of the institution. The stigma of being an ex-inmate and the associated loss of opportunity are carried beyond the prison walls and can result in a lack of employment and secure living arrangements and, in some states, civil death.

The second pain of imprisonment, as described by Sykes, is the deprivation of goods and services. Although basic material needs, such as food and shelter, are being met by the institution, it is the deprivation of amenities, such as free-world clothing, food, furnishings, and privacy, that the inmate feels the most, as these often define the inmate in the free world. Although this deprivation could be in part addressed by the use of commissary for snack foods, clothing items, and other amenities, many inmates are indigent and cannot afford these prison luxuries.

The third pain of imprisonment faced by inmates is the deprivation of heterosexual relationships. Very few states allow conjugal or family visits for inmates. The vast majority of inmates are therefore subject to what Sykes called "involuntary celibacy." Even masturbation has been curbed by the limiting or banning of pornographic literature and art. The lack of outlets to relieve heterosexual frustration can lead inmates to engage in homosexual acts to fill the void. These acts may be forced, coerced, or brought on by latent homosexual tendencies, any of which may lead inmates to question their masculinity as measured by heterosexual prowess.

The fourth pain of imprisonment is the deprivation of autonomy. This deprivation relates to dependent status, or the inability of inmates to make individual choices about what they do, where they go, who they interact with, and the like. The inmate world is governed by the rules and regulations of the prison administration. An inmate may feel hostility toward the administration and officers who are tasked with enforcing the rigidness of the prison as a total institution.

The fifth and final pain of imprisonment within the deprivation model is the deprivation of security. Inmates face increased anxiety due to living with other inmates and may lack the psychological fortitude to cope with their new surroundings. The reality of being housed with other offenders, including those with extensive histories of violence, and the expectation that, at some point, an inmate may be tested, creates fear among new inmates and recidivists alike. Inmates perceived as weak may be taken advantage of by inmates or inmate groups looking to coerce or informally control other inmates by force.

In response to these deprivations, inmates rely on their connection to similarly affected others. A system of social interaction forms with certain argot roles developing in response to the various pains of imprisonment. As described by Sykes, Rats and Center Men align with or aid the prison administration. Gorillas and Merchants use force or participate in the black market to obtain amenities. *Wolves* and *Punks* participate in homosexual behavior in prison. Ball Busters and Real Men are known for how they respond to prison authority, and Toughs and Hipsters are named for either being potentially threatening to other inmates or pretending to be that way. Sykes also addressed how riots erupt in response to deprivation and related frustrations. These deprivations, as described by Sykes, thus shape prison subculture and impact how inmates perceive the social aspects of their lives.

Ashley G. Blackburn

See also: Prisonization; Sykes, Gresham

Further Reading

Clemmer, D. (1958). *The prison community.* New York: Holt, Rinehart, & Winston.

Cooley, D. (1993). Criminal victimization in male federal prisons. *Canadian Journal of Criminology, 35,* 479–495.

DiIulio, J. (1991). *No escape: The future of American corrections.* New York: Basic Books.

Dye, M. H. (2010). Deprivation, importation, and prison suicide: Combined effects of institutional conditions and inmate composition. *Journal of Criminal Justice, 38,* 796–806.

Gaes, G. (1994). Prison crowding research re-examined. *Prison Journal, 74,* 329–363.

Gaes, G., & McGuire, W. J. (1985). Prison violence: The contribution of crowding versus other determinants of prison assault rates. *Journal of Research in Crime and Delinquency, 22,* 41–65.

Hochstetler, A., & DeLils, M. (2005). Importation, deprivation, and varieties of serving time: An integrated-lifestyle-exposure model of prison offending. *Journal of Criminal Justice, 33,* 257–266.

McCorkle, R. C., Miethe, T., & Drass, K. A. (1995). The roots of prison violence: A test of the deprivation, management, and not-so-total institutions models. *Crime and Delinquency, 2,* 197–221.

Sykes, G. M. (1958). *The society of captives: A study of a maximum security prison.* Princeton, NJ: Princeton University Press.

Thomas, C. W. (1977). Theoretical perspectives on prisonization: A comparison of the importation and deprivation models. *Journal of Criminal Law and Criminology, 68*(1), 135–145.

Useem, B., & Piehl, A. M. (2006). Prison buildup and disorder. *Punishment and Society, 8,* 87–115.

Determinate versus Indeterminate Sentencing

The use of determinate sentencing is a relatively new phenomenon within the United States justice system. Determinate sentencing refers to the requirement that a sentence be defined and final—not subject to amendment by a judicial or parole board official. Over the past three decades, determinate sentencing has hindered judges' ability to use discretion when imposing sentences, and parole boards have essentially vanished with the elimination of early release for good behavior.

Prior to determinate sentencing, the public's trust in the justice system's capacity to impose a reasonable sentence made the use of discretion and indeterminate sentencing an acceptable practice. Judges were granted wide discretionary powers and, in order to justly and reasonably sentence the defendant, were expected to consider facts outside of the offender's crime and criminal characteristics, such as their likelihood of reoffending or rehabilitating into a productive member of society.

Early on, minimum and maximum sentences began to appear in statutes, specifying the range in possible incarceration for crimes. However, this scheme still granted significant discretion to judges. Often judges imposed harsh sentences on the convicted, anticipating that a parole board would grant early release to those who behaved. Judges could rest assured that a sentence would not be overturned through appellate review, as providing reasons for sentences was not required so long as they were within the bounds of sentencing requirements. In practice, there was little to no appellate review of sentencing, and overly harsh sentences were expected to be corrected through the parole review process.

As crime rates rose in the 1980s, and data failed to prove that the federal system was rehabilitating its inmates, liberals and conservatives alike began demanding determinate sentences. Liberal critics argued that indeterminate sentencing bred sentence disparity and fueled racial bias, pointing to data that showed unacceptably high variability between the sentences given for similar crimes. Conservatives, on the other hand, claimed that indeterminate sentencing and "soft-on-crime" judges were responsible for rising crime rates and repeat offenders. Fundamentally, both ends of the political spectrum were vying for less discretion and discrimination, and more uniformity in sentencing and punishment.

These critiques combined with declining public support for a rehabilitative criminal justice philosophy as the answer to crime, especially as published reports seemed to suggest that criminals could not be rehabilitated. With more punitive criminal reform gaining support, and momentum through the use of ballot initiatives, judges and politicians alike felt great pressure to conform to public opinions on crime and enact determinant sentencing laws that might not otherwise have stood review by experts in criminology and sentencing.

With the advent of mass incarceration under determinate sentencing, prisons became overcrowded. Research suggests that prison facilities have turned more disorderly, as inmates sentenced under determinate sentencing guidelines break rules and commit infractions more often than others. In addition to neglecting to consider the actual capacity of the prison system, these policies also fail to account for strains in budgets and financial resources, social services, and maintaining high standards for facility conditions.

In *United States v. Booker,* the U.S. Supreme Court sought to settle a number of issues involving sentencing in the federal system, including determinate and indeterminate sentencing. The court determined that federal sentencing had greatly shifted sentencing authority from judge to prosecutors, who have enormous ability to influence potential sentencing through selecting which charge to bring against a defendant (i.e., "charge-bargaining'). The court also found that judges had sunk into the role of "fact finder," traditionally a jury's duty, where their primary efforts were to create a factual record to which they applied preset outcomes. As such, in *Booker*, the court ruled that sentencing guidelines were advisory only and that judges could diverge from them whenever there exists a sound reason to do so.

The ability to depart from mandatory sentencing allowed for judges to reassert some discretion but left in place determinate sentencing once a sentence was reached. Moreover, some 20 states also adopted some form of determinate sentencing regime. If the criminal justice system is to be the subject of meaningful review and reform, the dissolution of parole board and judicial discretion is one area prime for reconsideration.

Yandeli Cabrera and Kwan-Lamar Blount-Hill

See also: Federal Sentencing Guidelines; Sentencing Disparities and Discrimination in Sentencing; Truth in Sentencing

Further Reading

Aharonson, E. (2013). Determinate sentencing and American exceptionalism: The underpinnings and effects of cross-national differences in the regulation of sentencing discretion. *Law and Contemporary Problems, 76,* 161–187.

Bales, W. D., & Courtney, M. H. (2012). The impact of determinate sentencing on prisoner misconduct. *Journal of Criminal Justice, 40,* 394–403.

Bureau of Justice Assistance. (1996). *National assessment of structured sentencing.* Washington, DC: U.S. Department of Justice.

Driessen, M. A., Durham, W., Jr., and Durham, C. (2002). Sentencing dissonances in the United States: The shrinking distance between punishment proposed and sanctions served. *The American Journal of Comparative Law, 50,* 623–641.

Gertner, N. (2006). What Yogi Berra teaches about post-*Booker* sentencing. *The Yale Law Journal, 115.* Retrieved from http://www.yalelawjournal.org/forum/what-yogi-berra -teaches-about-post-booker-sentencing

Gertner, N. (2010). A short history of American sentencing: Too little law, too much law, or just right. *The Journal of Criminal Law and Criminology, 100*(3), 691–708.

King, R. S., Mauer, M., & Young, M. C. (2005). *Incarceration and crime: A complex relationship*. Washington, DC: Sentencing Project. Retrieved from http://www.sentencingproject.org/wp-content/uploads/2016/01/Incarceration-and-Crime-A-Complex-Relationship.pdf

Lahn, J. (2009). The demise of the law-finding jury in America and the birth of American legal science: History and its challenge for contemporary society. *Cleveland State Law Review, 57*, 553–578. Retrieved from http://engagedscholarship.csuohio.edu/clevstlrev/vol57/iss3/6

United States v. Booker, 543 U.S. 220 (2005).

Yellen, D. (2005). Reforming the federal sentencing guidelines' misguided approach to real-offence sentencing. *Stanford Law Review, 58*, 267–276.

Disciplinary Hearings

Although correctional institutions have multiple goals, including providing treatment and rehabilitation to inmates, they are secondary to maintaining order and security. Prisoner conformity to the rules is essential for the daily running and maintenance of the institution. When prisoners violate the rules of the institution, they threaten the physical safety and emotional well-being of staff and inmates. Prisoner misconduct further hinders the organizational management of the institution. However, maintaining order in a prison setting is arguably paradoxical, as we expect coercively confined prisoners to abide by the rules of the institution when they have demonstrated their inability to adhere to the rules of the larger society.

Prisoner misconduct is behavior that violates the rules of the correctional institution that may result in minor (e.g., suspension of privileges) or serious (e.g., loss of good time credits, segregation) sanctions. Although similar to the laws in the larger society, prison misconduct may include acts that would otherwise not be deemed illegal, such as disobeying orders, leaving one's cell without permission, or failing to maintain proper hygiene. Thus, institutional rules are designed to regulate inmate behavior that threatens the welfare of staff and inmates, while also maintaining security and order within the facility.

Inmate rules of conduct and the disciplinary procedures for rule violations are established by the individual states through prison directives and are provided to inmates during the intake process. Correctional agencies are mandated to provide inmates with clear and explicit written policies and procedures as established in case law and national accreditation standards. Correctional policies must be designed to serve a legitimate institutional outcome, such as institutional safety, security, and sanitation, as well as inmate rights, welfare, and due process protections. Inmate handbooks provide notice of prohibited behaviors, outline the hearing process for inmates charged with misconduct, and provide a list of sanctions that correspond to specific violations.

Similar to those who break the laws of the larger society and receive punishment, inmates who engage in prison misconduct are subject to institutional sanctions, such as removal from work assignments, cell restriction, loss of privileges, or reprimands. Inmates may also be placed in restricted housing units isolated from the general population, with loss of privileges and possible removal from treatment programs. The impact of disciplinary records for inmates may also have long-term consequences beyond the immediate sanction, including removal of good time credits and denial of prerelease or parole. Within the institution, prison misconduct is also a consideration when determining inmate classification, custody level, and work assignments. Thus, the outcome of disciplinary hearings can result in the loss of institutional liberty, as well as traditional liberty.

Although charges of prisoner misconduct can have serious implications, due process protections under the Fourteenth Amendment to challenge institutional rules, charges of misconduct, or disciplinary procedures were generally not afforded to inmates prior to the 1960s. Prior to this time, the "hands-off" policy of the courts allowed the disciplinary policies of correctional administrators to go essentially unchallenged, with many judges citing the holding in *Ruffin v. Commonwealth* (1871). In this case, the Virginia Supreme Court held that convicted felons were "slaves of the state" and afforded only those rights given them by the state. Moreover, because the judiciary considered the administration of corrections an executive agency, interference by the judiciary was viewed as a violation of the separation of powers.

Starting in the 1960s, however, we began seeing the courts put an end to their hands-off policy. Most notably, in the 1964 case, *Cooper v. Pate*, the U.S. Supreme Court ruled that prisoners have the right to file lawsuits against correctional officials using the federal Civil Rights Act. Soon after, the courts were inundated with prisoner lawsuits. It was, at this time, that the court began to lay the foundation of procedural due process rights afforded prisoners charged with serious misconduct. Although several cases between 1970 and 1973 addressed the due process rights of inmates in administrative hearings, it was in the 1974 case of *Wolff v. McDonnell* that the court specifically addressed the question of whether due process requirements applied to prison disciplinary hearings and if so, what rights would be afforded inmates.

The holding of the court in the *Wolff* case was critical in establishing the rights of prisoners to not be wholly stripped of their constitutional protections. However, the court also clearly stated that the due process requirements of prisoners must be balanced with the needs of the correctional institution. Specifically, the court established certain mandatory rights afforded all prisoners: (1) the right to a fair disciplinary hearing; (2) written notice of the charges no less than 24 hours prior to their appearance in the disciplinary hearing; (3) a statement of the evidence used to determine the reason for the disciplinary action; and (4) the right to call witnesses and provide evidence in their defense, if doing so does not interfere with the safety or goals of the institution. The court did not extend the procedural protections of confronting or cross-examining adverse witnesses or the right to retained or appointed counsel. The court did, however, provide for representation and/or counsel by another inmate or staff member if the charged inmate is incapable of effectively representing himself or herself or is unable to understand the complexity of the issues (e.g., mentally ill, illiterate, language barrier). This decision was reaffirmed by the court in 1976 in *Baxter v. Palmigiano*.

The due process rights afforded inmates by the courts have addressed the protection of inmates charged with serious misconduct that may result in the deprivation of liberty. However, not all charges of prisoner misconduct result in formal disciplinary hearings. Minor misconduct charges (e.g., lying to an employee, disobeying orders, loaning or borrowing property, unauthorized use of the mail or phone) are resolved informally and carry less serious sanctions such as warnings or reprimands, loss of privileges, additional work assignments without compensation, or loss of commissary privileges.

Although disciplinary hearing procedures vary from state to state, the following procedures are practiced in Pennsylvania. Serious violations (e.g., assaults, riots, escape) that may result in the deprivation of institutional or traditional liberty must be resolved through formal disciplinary hearings by a hearing examiner. An inmate may choose to waive his or her right to attend the hearing, but failure to do so will typically forfeit the right of the inmate to appeal the hearing examiner's decision. Hearings will be held no less than 24 hours or typically more than one week following notification of charges to the inmate unless specific cause for the delay has been approved by the examiner (e.g., the inmate is not available to attend the hearing on the scheduled date). Inmates with mental illness or other barriers (e.g., language, literacy) that may impede their ability to effectively represent themselves at the hearing will be provided assistance in procuring the necessary documents and preparing needed materials. During the hearing, a correctional officer is typically present to ensure the security of the proceeding and will be instructed to remove anyone who is deemed disruptive, including the inmate. At the outset of the hearing, the inmate will be formally notified of the charge(s) and asked to enter a plea. Similar to a trial proceeding, individuals providing testimony at the hearing will be sworn in and testify under oath. Determination of guilt is based on the preponderance of the evidence (the evidence is weighted in favor of a particular side), as compared with the stricter standard of proof "beyond a reasonable doubt" used in criminal proceedings.

At the completion of the hearing process, and within a designated period of time, according to institutional policy, the inmate will be provided a written summary of the hearing examiner's findings. If the inmate is found guilty, the notification of decision will include the evidence/facts considered in the case and the rationale for the decision. Inmates may request an appellate review of the hearing examiner's decision on specific grounds (e.g., the hearing procedures violated the law, the sanction was disproportionate to the offense, or the facts of the case were not sufficient to support the decision).

Over the past half century, courts have recognized the need of inmates to have certain fundamental procedural due process protections when charged with serious misconduct. However, the courts further recognized the importance of balancing the rights of the inmate with the needs of the correctional institution to maintain security and order. Thus, certain rights afforded defendants in criminal proceedings, such as the right to counsel or confront witnesses, have not been extended to inmates because the adversarial nature of these rights may be disruptive to the institution. In sum, inmates have been granted many protections in the disciplinary hearing process since the 1960s, but disciplinary proceedings are still primarily in the control of the correctional institution.

Kimberly A. Houser and Evan Fry

See also: Constitution as a Source for Prisoners' Rights, The; Misconduct by Prisoners; Treatment in Prisons

Further Reading

Cao, L., Zhao, J., & Van Dine, S. (1997). Prison disciplinary tickets: A test of the deprivation and importation models. *Journal of Criminal Justice, 25*(2), 103–113.

Flanagan, T.J. (1982). Discretion in the prison justice system: A study of sentencing in institutional disciplinary proceedings. *Journal of Research in Crime and Delinquency, 19,* 216–237.

Hartney, C. (2006). *U.S. rates of incarceration: A global perspective.* Washington, DC: National Council on Crime and Delinquency.

Houser, K.A., Belenko, S., & Brennan, P. (2012). The effects of mental health and substance use disorders on institutional misconduct among female inmates. *Justice Quarterly, 29*(6), 799–828.

Houser, K.A., & Welsh, W. (2014). Examining the association between co-occurring disorders and seriousness of misconduct by female prison inmates. *Criminal Justice and Behavior, 41*(5), 650–666.

Kaeble, D., Glaze, L., Tsoutis, A., & Minton, T. (2015). *Correctional populations in the United States, 2014* (NCJ249513). Washington, DC: Bureau of Justice Statistics, U.S. Department of Justice.

Lovell, D., & Jemelka, R. (1996). When inmates misbehave: The costs of discipline. *The Prison Journal, 76*(2), 165–179.

Martin, J. L., Lichenstein, B., Jenkot, R. B., & Forde, D. R. (2012). They can take us over any time they want: Correctional officer's responses to prison overcrowding. *The Prison Journal, 92*(1), 88–105.

Millemann, M. A. (1971). Prison disciplinary hearings and procedural due process—The requirement of a full administrative hearing. *Maryland Law Review, 31*(1), 27–59.

National Institute of Corrections. (n.d.). *Correctional policy and procedure.* Washington, DC: U.S. Department of Justice.

Pew Charitable Trusts. (n.d.). *One in 31 U.S. adults are behind bars, on parole or probation.* Washington, DC: Author.

Wright, K. N. (2000). The evolution of decision-making among prison executives, 1975–2000. In J. Horney (Ed.), *Criminal Justice 2000* (Vol. 3, pp. 177–224). Washington, DC: U.S. Department of Justice.

DNA Exonerees

Persons may find themselves wrongly convicted for a number of reasons. The cause for these incorrect decisions may be the result of inaccurate eyewitness identifications, misused/applied forensic science, false/coerced confessions, government misconduct, motivated informants, and ineffective assistance of defense counsel. Of course, many defendants forego their ability to challenge these potential violations in a trial court by pleading guilty. Although there are some who argue that modifications for intervention should be made to the plea-bargaining process and its aftermath, these recommendations are beyond the scope of this treatise.

Several organizations have been devoted to the exoneration of the wrongly convicted and, in addition to the United States, can be found in the Netherlands,

Taiwan, South Africa, New Zealand, Italy, Israel, Ireland, France, Canada, Australia, and Argentina. In some instances, students with specialized training have been involved in providing meaningful assistance to identify the wrongly convicted and seeking justice for them as seen, for example, with the Northwestern University School of Law. Barry Scheck and Peter Neufeld, who established the Innocence Project at the Benjamin Cardozo Law School in New York in 1992 realized the value of engaging students in the process of establishing innocence for those wrongly convicted. It is the Innocence Project and its network that has been involved in a number of DNA exonerations in the United States.

First of all, DNA is known as "deoxyribonucleic acid [and has been defined as] an extremely long macromolecule that is the main component of chromosomes and is the material that transfers genetic characteristics in all life forms, constructed of two nucleotide strands coiled around each other in a ladder-like arrangement with the sidepieces composed of alternating phosphate and deoxyribose units and the rungs composed of the purine and pyrimidine bases adenine, guanine, cytosine, and thymine: the genetic information of DNA is encoded in the sequence of the bases and is transcribed as the strands unwind and replicate." Through what is termed DNA fingerprinting characteristics that are unique to a particular individual, unless one is an identical twin, these can be pinpointed and used to distinguish the presence of one individual from another.

Calculating the exact number of wrongly convicted individuals is not possible, but estimates are that it is anywhere from 2.3 percent to 5 percent of all inmates in the United States who are actually innocent. With say 2.2 million persons incarcerated in prisons and jails in the United States annually, that would suggest that at an error rate of 1 percent in felony convictions that roughly 22,000 of those incarcerated are actually innocent. Further, it is reported that DNA exists in fewer than 10 percent of all felony convictions; DNA exonerations for wrongful convictions are just the "tip of the iceberg" since DNA analysis is available in only a minute number of cases.

According to the Innocence Project, the first DNA exoneration in the United States transpired in 1989. DNA exonerations have proven successful in 37 states. Of 344 people exonerated in the United States, 20 of them served time on death row; Kirk Bloodsworth was the first death row inmate to be exonerated on the basis of DNA evidence; 36 of the 344 exonerees pleaded guilty. The average length of time served by DNA exonerees was 14 years with the total number of years served by all of them in excess of 4,600 years. The average age at which they were wrongly convicted was 26 and one-half years, and the average age they were exonerated was 42 years old. In terms of how the DNA exonerees were wrongly convicted, more than 70 percent were found guilty based on incorrect eyewitness identification, almost half were convicted based on faulty science, more than one in four falsely confessed to the crime that they were sentenced for having committed, and 17 percent of the wrongful convictions involved informants. Of the 344 DNA exonerations, the Innocence Project was involved in 180 of them.

Of the 344 DNA exonerations, more than half (212) were African Americans, 105 were Caucasians, 25 were Latinos, and 2 were Asian Americans. The longest

Kirk Bloodsworth was the first American sentenced to death row who was exonerated by DNA fingerprinting. Bloodsworth was wrongly convicted in 1985 for the rape and murder of a nine-year-old girl and was released in 1993. (Mladen Antonov/AFP/Getty Images)

amount of time served in prison by an individual wrongly convicted who went on to be exonerated by DNA testing is 35 years. James Bain, from Florida, an African American, who had been sentenced to life in prison, was released from prison in 2009. He had been convicted on the basis of faulty eyewitness testimony. James Bain did receive $1.7 million from the state of Florida, $50,000 for every year he was wrongly incarcerated.

A number of states, however, do not provide for compensation to the wrongly convicted. Exonerees in Wyoming, South Dakota, South Carolina, Rhode Island, Pennsylvania, Oregon, North Dakota, New Mexico, Nevada, Michigan, Kentucky, Kansas, Indiana, Idaho, Hawaii, Georgia, Delaware, Arkansas, Arizona, and Alaska offer no such possibilities for compensation to those wrongly convicted. Thus, as high as 40 percent of persons wrongly convicted receive no compensation whatsoever upon being exonerated and returning to society. Many justly convicted inmates released on parole might be offered more assistance with reentry into the community, such as access to health services, transportation, and housing, than those who are exonerated and returning to free society.

Of course, a problem with wrongly convicting someone for the commission of a particular crime is that the actual perpetrator likely remains free. In fact, the Innocence Project identified 148 actual perpetrators that continued on to be convicted of committing 146 violent crimes, which included 77 sexual assaults and 34 murders, while remaining free in the community when they should have been incarcerated if someone else had not been wrongly convicted.

Some states are more prone to having inmates who are wrongly convicted exonerated than others. The leading states in terms of the number of exonerations since January 1989 through December 2013 are New York, California, Texas, Illinois, Michigan, Florida, Pennsylvania, Louisiana, and Ohio.

Although DNA testing can free those wrongly convicted, sometimes it comes too late. For example, Frank Lee Smith was sentenced to death for murder and rape; he died on death row from cancer almost a year before the state agreed to DNA testing that demonstrated that he did not commit the offenses he had been sentenced to death for in Florida.

The use of DNA testing to free those wrongly convicted can also result in others being apprehended and brought to justice through DNA analysis. Furthermore, while DNA testing has not been used as frequently of late for exonerations, DNA evidence is not infallible and can lead to both false incriminations and convictions.

Risdon N. Slate

See also: Innocence Project; Prison Reform, Intended and Unintended Consequences of; Sentencing Disparities and Discrimination in Sentencing

Further Reading

Acker, J. R. (2012). The flipside of wrongful convictions: When the guilty go free. *Albany Law Review, 76*(3), 1629–1723.

Blume, J. H., & Helm, R. K. (2014). The unexonerated: Factually innocent defendants who plead guilty. *Cornell Law Faculty Working Papers* (Paper 113). Retrieved September 25, 2016, from http://scholarship.law.cornell.edu/clsops_papers/113

Gross. S. R., & Shaffer, M. (2012). *Exonerations in the United States, 1989–2012.* Report by the National Registry of Exonerations. Retrieved September 26, 2016, from https://www.law.umich.edu/special/exoneration/Documents/exonerations_us _1989_2012_full_report.pdf

Innocence Project. (2016). *DNA exonerations in the United States.* Retrieved September 25, 2016, from http://www.innocenceproject.org/dna-exonerations-in-the-united-states

Knowles, N. N. (2015). Exonerated, but not free: The prolonged struggle for a second chance at a stolen life. *Hastings Race & Poverty Law Journal, 12,* 235–259.

Loevy, J., Ainsworth, R., Horn, G., & Thompson, T. (2016). *The Exoneration Project.* University of Chicago Law School. Retrieved September 26, 2016, from http://www .law.uchicago.edu/clinics/exoneration

The National Registry of Exonerations. (2016). *Known exonerations in the United States as of January 1, 2014.* Retrieved September 26, 2016, from https://www.law.umich .edu/special/exoneration/Documents/Exonerations_in_2013_Report.pdf

Pendergrass, M. L. (2014). Maryland repeals the death penalty, but leaves five on death row: What has the state learned from Kirk Bloodsworth? *University of Baltimore Law Forum, 44*(2), 109–134.

Ricciardelli, R., Bell, J. G., & Clow, K. A. (2011). Now I see it for what it really is: The impact of participation in an Innocence Project practicum on criminology students. *Albany Law Review, 75*(3), 1439–1466.

Schler, R., Kaplan, A. B., & Beety, V. (2015). Contemporary perspectives on wrongful conviction: An introduction to the 2015 Innocence Network Conference, Orlando, Florida. *Texas A&M Law Review, 3,* 179–187.

Thompson, W. C. (2016). The potential for error in forensic DNA testing. *GeneWatch.* Council for Responsible Genetics. Retrieved September 26, 2016, from http://www .councilforresponsiblegenetics.org/genewatch/GeneWatchPage.aspx?pageId=57

What is a DNA fingerprint? Wellcome Genome Campus. Retrieved September 25, 2016, from http://www.yourgenome.org/facts/what-is-a-dna-fingerprint

Drug Use in Prison

The presence of drugs in the prison system is just one of the many problems the criminal justice system faces. Despite efforts to reduce the prevalence of drugs, drug use is inherently linked to crime and criminal behavior. Therefore, it is not uncommon for inmates to use drugs. Problems associated with drug use in the prison system incorporate inmate violence, psychological issues, and the prison black market. The smuggling and the subsequent use of drugs are a matter of concern among all prisons, although some facilities may have a higher prevalence rate. An increased focus of treatment and rehabilitation of offenders with drug problems could reduce the prevalence of unwarranted substances, as well as lower recidivism rates.

Drugs enter the prison system through a number of ways. In fact, the exploitation of prison staff is one of the most common methods drugs are smuggled into prison. Most officers use discretion on the allowance of drugs, and some believe drugs contribute to a more stable atmosphere. This leniency of behavior facilitates drug use as officers may purposefully turn a blind eye or physically carry in the supplies themselves. Such influences of cooperation by correctional officers include monetary bribes, threats to family, or personal corruption and willingness. Inmates also use cell phones illegally to arrange "drug drops," in which the inmate in charge of the phone details the exact location where someone from the outside would be free to throw drugs over the fence. Drones can also be used for drug drops, in which the apparatus is wirelessly controlled (by a smartphone outside the prison boundaries) and drops supplies over the prison yard. However, drones are not often instrumental to a drug dealer's smuggling tactic because prisons typically monitor air traffic, though breaches may occur. Drone use is still a relatively new phenomenon but is becoming a growing matter of concern for prison officials in controlling smuggling of drugs and other illegal objects. After the drug drop, an inmate mule collects and prepares the package.

The distribution of the supply chain continues to the users—with the main prison dealer never having to physically associate with the drugs. A final popular method of smuggling involves prison visits. This has often been highlighted in fictional depictions of prison life. Despite some prisons increasing precaution with the allowance of visitors, such as mandating metal detectors, drugs are not metal and, therefore, have the ability to pass undetected. It is a violation to strip search every visitor in the way most inmates are searched and this, as a result, allows for the susceptibility of drugs. Drugs are hidden in the mouth (passed through kissing and swallowed by the inmate), in women's bras, or other body cavities.

Drug dealers are given a tremendous amount of power, resting at the top of the prison hierarchy system, with many people at their disposal. Drug dealers often

Drug Use in Prison

find themselves living comfortably in jail. In fact, the desire to feel safe and secure, and maintain a position of power, are popular reasons drug dealers deal. Inmates often get caught up in the drug-smuggling business without any intent on doing so, simply for associating with one wrong person, or having a favorable prison job that a dealer can exploit.

Drug use is not strictly limited to one gender or race, with certain characteristics that provide for potential predictors of drug use. Some of the most common predictors in males include prior drug history, recidivists in prison, and those with longer prison sentences; with females, these include prior drug history, same-sex relationships, history of childhood sexual abuse, and earlier onset of criminal activities.

Social, environmental, and personality factors may also influence prisoners' use of illegal narcotics. Persistent pressures from fellow inmates, pure boredom of prison life, mandatory drug testing (MDT) by the prison, and impulsivity are some of the major causes leading to drug use in prisons. Loss of friends and family may lead to associations with other inmates connected to the prison drug markets. Long prison sentences, coupled with insufficient prison programming, may lead to boredom and, in turn, time may be spent engaging in illegal activities. Inmate users substantiate their claims with a desire to fill the void of prison life or a desire to escape reality. The assumption that MDT would deter prisoners from utilizing illegal substances, inmates claim, may lead to opposite effects. Since heroin is less likely to be detected due to a shorter detectable period, some drug users transitioned from cannabis to hard drugs during the duration of their sentence. A final contributing characteristic to drug use is the personality trait of impulsivity. Persistent drug users have significant correlations of using within one month prior to incarceration and a self-proclaimed dependence on drugs.

Popular drugs within prisons are often similar to common drugs outside prisons. Drugs commonly found in prisons include alcohol, marijuana, methamphetamines, heroin, and crack. In most prisons, drug use among inmates is as low as the general population but, with some low-security facilities, can be as high as 20 percent of the inmate population. Those caught typically receive time added or certain privileges revoked.

Drug use affects prisoners' health and well-being. There is a positive correlation of inmate drug use and testing positive for HIV, especially because many inmates share needles. Additionally, prisons have seen a number of deaths by overdose, an increase of attempts in suicide while under the influence of drugs, and a correlation of drug use with self-harming behaviors. Prisons promote a dangerous setting for both prior addicts to relapse and first-time users to experiment.

The prison black market creates an increase of violence. Also known as the informal economy, this system involves a trade of contraband goods and services, not limited to weapons, sex, protection from other inmates, housekeeping, and illegal drugs. Correctional officers may ignore the prison black market, letting inmates trade among themselves so long as the correctional atmosphere is not disrupted or destroyed. Drugs on the prison black market are exceedingly inflated, costing three or four times more than the community street value. As a result, consistent drug use during incarceration can become costly. If inmates do not have money to buy drugs, they may use cigarettes as a form of payment or enlist the aid of someone outside the prison to financially secure the payment with the dealer's outside contacts. Many prisons' informal economies are operated by street gangs. As a result, violence is employed as a method of punishment when problems with payment occur.

Institutional means to combat drug use in prisons vary. Substance abuse treatment programs are used primarily to alleviate the problem. Roughly a quarter of crimes are committed by someone under the influence of drugs, which means many prisoners have a substance abuse history. As a result, providing programming to target these users may limit their desire to continue use. Opioid substitution therapy is a drug treatment that substitutes medicinal opioids for illegal drugs, effectively reducing drug use in sample studies, the cost compared to other treatments (e.g., similar costs to community programming), and infectious diseases. It would also be beneficial to provide psychological interventions alongside substance abuse treatments. A nonmedicinal treatment option is Narcotics Anonymous (NA), which provides a support group for those who recognize they have an issue and would like to take steps to improve their well-being in a positive setting. Narcotics Anonymous provides those with prior drug history or addiction the opportunity for a safe haven, which is especially important when drugs severely impact inmate behavior. The program is a volunteer-based, low-cost opportunity that reduces recidivism rates.

Lisa M. Carter and Destiny Zunic

See also: AIDS/HIV among Inmates; Methadone Maintenance for Prisoners; Misconduct by Prisoners

Further Reading

Baltieri, D. A. (2014). Predictors of drug use in prison among women convicted of violent crimes. *Criminal Behaviour & Mental Health, 24*(2), 113–128.

Bernstein, M. H., McSheffrey, S. N., van den Berg, J. J., Vela, J. E., Stein, L. R., Roberts, M. B., & . . . Clarke, J. G. (2015). The association between impulsivity and alcohol/drug use among prison inmates. *Addictive Behaviors, 42*(1), 140–143.

Caravaca-Sánchez, F., Falcón Romero, M., & Luna, A. (2015). Prevalence and predictors of psychoactive substance use among men in prisons. *Gaceta Sanitaria/S.E.S.P.A.S., 29*(5), 358–363.

Crewe, B. (2006). Prison drug dealing and the ethnographic lens. *Howard Journal of Criminal Justice, 45*(4), 347–368.

Dolan, K., Moazen, B., Noori, A., Rahimzadeh, S., Farzadfar, F., & Hariga, F. (2015). People who inject drugs in prison: HIV prevalence, transmission and prevention. *International Journal of Drug Policy, 26*(1), S12–S15.

Levan, K. (2012). *Prison violence: Causes, consequences, and solutions.* Burlington, VT: Routledge.

Roger, D. (2016). Drones. *Corrections Forum, 25*(1), 14–18.

Stöver, H., & Michels, I. I. (2010). Drug use and opioid substitution treatment for prisoners. *Harm Reduction Journal, 7*(1), 17–23.

Economics of Crossing Over, The

Although prisons and jails have explicit rules that forbid any type of familiarization between correctional officers and prisoners, some officers cross the line and engage in inappropriate relationships with the very inmates they are paid to protect and supervise. Inappropriate relationships are best defined as "personal relationships between employees and inmates/clients or with family members of inmates/clients." This behavior is usually sexual or economic in nature and has the potential to jeopardize the security of a prison institution or compromise the integrity of a correctional employee (Worley, Marquart, & Mullings, 2003, p. 179).

In order to examine why inappropriate relationships occur, Professors Robert and Vidisha Worley (2016) developed the "economics of crossing over" theory. In this theory, the authors draw on the sociological theory of relative deprivation and certain aspects of Jungian clinical psychology. They argue that a type of crossing over or "coutertransference" occurs when a correctional officer projects his or her own feelings and emotions on the prisoner he or she is supposed to be supervising. Worley and Worley contend that this countertransference can lead to "compassion fatigue," where an officer, because of being highly involved, experiences secondhand the trauma suffered by the inmate resulting in stress and burnout Worley and Worley contend that one of the earliest references to the cost of caring for others can be traced to Jung's (1907) struggle with countertransference. This is usually a reaction to "transference," where clients project on the counselor traits or characteristics of others in their lives. While these feelings of empathy for the patients in clinical psychology can lead to compassion fatigue manifested in stress and burnout, within correctional facilities, it can lead to inappropriate relationships with inmates.

The economics of crossing over theory also contends that sociologists Judith Blau and Peter Blau's (1982) notion of "relative deprivation" provides insights into why some prison staff engage in inappropriate relationships with offenders. Worley and Worley surmise that correctional officers who feel relatively deprived, compared to other professionals, are likely to turn to those who are further relatively deprived, in this case the inmates, thus feeling closer to those they have power and control over. They argue that these feelings are aggravated when correctional officers lack the support of their supervisors or families and are often not clear about what their role entails, thus feeling constantly undermined and undervalued. Worley and Worley contend that these negative feelings about themselves, coupled with stress from role conflict, and a feeling of hostility toward their supervisors and others in society in general who do not have similar experiences, make them feel relatively deprived and be more drawn toward the inmates they are guarding than the rest of society.

Robert Worley, who is also a former correctional officer, later expanded on the burgeoning economics of crossing over theory in an autoethnographic work where he provided real-life examples of how some staff members use other correctional employees who work in the same facility as a reference group to whom they compare themselves. Professor Worley argues that if a correctional employee feels particularly deprived when making a comparison to other professionals or even his or her coworkers, this may lead to feelings of professional inadequacy. When correctional officers experience a state of deprivation and low self-image, the economics of crossing over theory demonstrates how the badge of honor holds no meaning anymore. Worley and Worley contend that correctional officers who find themselves in this state of deprivation are at a higher risk, compared to their coworkers, of going down a slippery slope of boundary violations in order to boost themselves and feel wanted. Thus, the economics of crossing over emerges from a cost-benefit analysis that allows deprived professionals to seek comfort from those over whom they exercise power and control.

Robert M. Worley

See also: Inappropriate Correctional Employee–Inmate Relationships

Further Reading

Beck, A. J., Berzofsky, M., Caspar, R., & Krebs, C. (2013). *Sexual victimization in state and federal prisons reported by inmates, 2011–2012* (NCJ 241399). Washington, DC: U.S. Department of Justice.

Blackburn, A. G., Fowler, S. K., Mullings, J. L., & Marquart, J. W. (2011). When boundaries are broken: Inmate perceptions of correctional staff boundary violations. *Deviant Behavior, 32,* 351–378.

Blau, J. R., & Blau, P. M. (1982). The cost of inequality: Metropolitan structure and violent crime. *American Sociological Review, 47,* 114–128.

Dial, K. Cheeseman, & Worley, R. M. (2008). Crossing the line: A quantitative analysis of inmate boundary violators in a southern prison system. *American Journal of Criminal Justice, 33,* 69–84.

Freud, S. (1910). The future prospects of psychoanalytic therapy. In *The standard edition of the complete psychological works of Sigmund Freud, 11,* 141–151. London: Hogarth Press.

Gentry, J. E. (2002). Compassion fatigue: A crucible of transformation. *Journal of Trauma Practice, 1,* 37–61.

Jung, C. G. (1907). *The psychology of dementia praecox.* London, U.K.: Routledge & Kegan Paul.

Ulberg, R., Aardal Falkenberg, A., Buran Nærdal, T., Johannessen, H., Olsen, J. E., Klokseth Eide, T., Hersoug, A. G., & Johnsen Dahl, H.-S. (2013). Countertransference feelings when treating teenagers: A psychometric evaluation of the feeling word checklist-24. *American Journal of Psychotherapy, 67,* 347–358.

Worley, R. M. (2016). Memoirs of a guard-researcher: Deconstructing the games inmates play behind the prison walls. *Deviant Behavior, 37,* 1215–1226.

Worley, R. M., & Cheeseman, K. A. (2006). Guards as embezzlers: The consequences of non-shareable problems in prison settings. *Deviant Behavior, 27,* 203–222.

Worley, R. M., Marquart, J. W., & Mullings, J. L. (2003). Prison guard predators: An analysis of inmates who established inappropriate relationships with prison staff, 1995–1998. *Deviant Behavior, 24,* 175–198.

Worley, R. M., Tewksbury, R., & Durant Frantzen, D. (2010). Preventing fatal attractions: Lessons learned from inmate boundary violators in a southern penitentiary system. *Criminal Justice Studies, 23,* 347–360.

Worley, R. M., & Worley, V. B. (2011). Guards gone wild: A self-report study of correctional officer misconduct and the effect of institutional deviance on care within the Texas prison system. *Deviant Behavior, 32,* 293–319.

Worley, R. M., & Worley, V. B. (2013). Games guards play: A self-report study of institutional deviance in the Texas Department of Criminal Justice. *Criminal Justice Studies, 26,* 115–132.

Worley, R. M., & Worley, V. B. (2016). The economics of crossing over: Examining the link between correctional officer pay and guard-inmate boundary violations. *Deviant Behavior, 37,* 16–29.

Education in Prison

Information about American prison education programs dates back to the 1790s. Commonly known as "Sabbath schools," these early education programs were implemented by Quakers and were founded on the ideals of evangelical humanitarianism. Sabbath school classes were usually taught by chaplains or better-educated inmates. Although writing, spelling, and history were taught in the early 19th century, Quakers argued that reading took precedent over any other subject. Developing reading skills allowed the inmates to comprehend biblical text, the word of God—thus leading offenders on a path of righteousness and eventually into morally righteous Christians.

The rise in the prison rehabilitative perspective in the mid-19th century led to an increase of prison education programs in the northern states, and by the 1870s, prison education programs were not just focused on religious and moral instructions. Both juvenile reformatories and adult prisons began to implement subjects such as astronomy, geography, phonography, and arithmetic. The Elmira Reformatory led the way for this new approach of prison education. Zebulon Brockway, the Elmira Reformatory superintendent, worked with a group of educational specialists, which led to the use of community professionals to educate inmates in a variety of educational subjects including arts and humanities classes, as well as the development of a vocational training program that included plumbing, tailoring, telegraphy, and painting.

Between the 1880s and 1930s most penitentiaries followed Elmira Reformatory's education model. However, many political leaders despised the idea of spending public money on educating prisoners, leading to poorly operated education programs with inefficient resources and inadequate educators. Rather than focusing on education, many penitentiary superintendents in the late 19th century preferred using inmates as cheap labor to pay for prison operations or even turn a profit.

The late 1920s marked the beginning of a new era of prison education. The discovery of systematic abuse and of prison industries in the early 20th century led to a decrease in support and resources of prison industries and an increase in vocational training resources. Additionally, the development of the federal prison system produced properly funded education facilities. Lastly, prisons began to rely heavily on counselors and psychologists to develop individual rehabilitative plans for each inmate. Even though prison education programs were commonly seen as tools to help inmates better understand society and obtain employment, psychologists saw education as a tool to improve an inmate's psyche, therefore commonly referring inmates to these programs.

Prison education programs survived the prison reform of the 1960s, caused by the system-wide corruption and the abundance of discretionary power throughout the criminal justice system. Prior to the 1960s higher education programs offered in prison were rare; however, once Congress passed the Higher Education Act in 1965, the number of higher education prison programs exponentially increased, marking the start of the "golden era" of prison higher education programs. The Higher Education Act included Pell Grants, which offered founding assistance for qualified citizens who were attending postsecondary education courses. Three key requirements were needed for citizens to qualify for these federally funded grants. First, citizens must be enrolled in an approved postsecondary education program. Second, the applicant must not possess a bachelor's degree or higher. Lastly, to receive funding, applicants must fall below a specific household income level.

Prison inmates are some of the most disadvantaged individuals in U.S. society. The majority of the inmates come from impoverished households. Additionally, these already impoverished individuals are unable to acquire wealth while in prison, placing the majority of them well below the household income threshold set forth by the Pell Grant. Inmates, on average, have a much lower education level, with many not possessing a high school or equivalent degree and even fewer obtaining postsecondary certificates or degrees prior to incarceration. Therefore, the Pell Grant became the primary source of funding for prisoners attending higher education.

The "golden era" of prison education experienced a mass increase in public attention, leading to a plethora of research centering on the evaluation of educational programs. The effectiveness of these programs became a widely debated topic, with researchers and politicians both supporting and refuting the positive influence these programs have on offender postrelease success. The majority of research conducted between 1960 and 1990 found that prison education at all levels reduced recidivism and increased postrelease employment. Not all research was positive during this period. The extremely popular and frequently cited study, known as the Martinson Report, refuted the idea that educational programs lead to postrelease success. The Martinson Report was a review of more than 200 studies covering rehabilitation programs in prison. The reports concluded by stating that the methods used to evaluate prison education programs are flawed, and thus there is no evidence that suggests prison education programs, in general, reduce recidivism.

Support for educational programs continued throughout the 1970s and 1980s. Many prisons began to require inmates who had not received a high school degree or equivalent to participate in educational programs that would lead to them receiving one of these degrees. The practice of forced participation in educational programs continues today, and like the 1970s and 1980s, many practitioners have conflicting views of this practice. Proponents of forced participation argue that since

Inmates serving time at San Quentin State Prison learn computer skills that can help them obtain good-paying jobs when they are released. (Melanie Stetson Freeman/ The Christian Science Monitor via Getty Images)

95 percent of inmates will be released from prison, inmates who do not have a high school degree or equivalent need to improve their education level to help increase their employability. Refuters of these policies often argue that forcing inmates who do not want to participate in these programs will impede the learning process of inmates who want to participate.

The tough-on-crime stance was peaking in the 1990s and helped lead to the passage of the 1994 Violent Crime Control and Law Enforcement Act. Even though prisoners received only sixth-tenths of 1 percent of the $6 billion of Pell Grants funds in 1993, legislators included a prison Pell Grant exclusionary provision within the act. Although high school and general education degree programs continued to operate in prison, many of the prison higher education programs were eliminated in the 1990s and 2000s, with the remaining programs usually operating with privately funded grants.

The extremely high prison population coupled with national recidivism rates in the 60 percent range has rekindled the discussion of prison education. Perhaps this is why prison education is one of the oldest correctional programs, surviving many reforms. The majority of research has found prison education programs to greatly reduce recidivism rates and increase postrelease employment rates. Moreover, cost-benefit analyses have continually shown that prison education programs, by reducing recidivism and increasing employment, more than pay for themselves and actually save taxpayer money.

Wesley Bruce Maier

See also: Evidence-Based Practice in Corrections; Prisons, History of; Vocational Training and Education

Further Reading

Gehring, T. (1997). Post-secondary education for inmates: An historical inquiry. *Journal of Correctional Education, 48*(2), 46–55.

Pillsbury, S. H. (1989). Understanding penal reform: The dynamic of change. *The Journal of Criminal Law and Criminology, 80*(3), 726–780.

Pisciotta, A. W. (1994). *Benevolent repression: Social control and the American reformatory-prison movement.* New York: NYU Press.

Roberts, A. R., & Lejins, P. P. (1971). *Sourcebook on prison education: Past, present, and future.* Springfield, IL: Charles C. Thomas.

Schlossman, S., & Spillane, J. (1992). *Bright hopes, dim realities: Vocational innovation in American correctional education.* Santa Monica, CA: RAND.

Wilson, D. B., Gallagher, C. A., & MacKenzie, D. L. (2000). A meta-analysis of corrections-based education, vocation, and work programs for adult offenders. *Journal of Research in Crime and Delinquency, 37*(4), 347–368.

Zoukis, C. (2014). *College for convicts: The case for higher education in American prisons.* Jefferson, NC: McFarland.

Elderly Offenders in Prison

Elderly offenders are the fastest-growing population in United States prisons and are considered to be one of the most challenging groups to manage because of their special needs. Elderly offenders, those older than 55 years old sentenced to more than one year in state prison, represented only 3 percent of the total state prison population in 1993 and increased to a full 10 percent of the population in 2013 (Carson & Sabol, 2016). According to the Bureau of Justice Statistics, the actual number of elderly offenders increased from 26,300 in 1993 to 131,500 in 2013. In 2013, approximately 66 percent of elderly offenders were incarcerated for a violent offense, compared to 58 percent for the other age groups. The majority of elderly offenders in the United States are male, whereas females represent only about 6 percent. Forty-two percent of elderly offenders are Caucasian, 33 percent are African American, and approximately 15 percent are Hispanic. Because Americans are living longer than ever, by the year 2030, elderly offenders are expected to represent a full third of prison populations across the nation (Ollove, 2016).

Aside from living longer lives, policy reform since the 1970s, such as mandatory minimums, "truth in sentencing," abolition of federal parole, "three-strikes laws," the war on drugs, and an overall reduction in compassionate release, has caused the elderly prison population to grow at a dramatic rate. Because of these policies, the number of elderly offenders has increased, and many are serving life sentences (Maschi, 2012). Between 1984 and 2008, life sentences quadrupled from approximately 34,000 to 140,610. In a growing trend across the nation, more people in their thirties and forties are being arrested and convicted of felonies; thus the young "punk" offender stereotype has evolved into a more mature offender, representing those who will require additional services as they age in the system (Carson & Sabol, 2016).

Elderly Offenders in Prison

Offenders who suffer from physically or mentally debilitating illnesses, who are advanced in age and are incapable of harming society, are eligible for compassionate release in 15 states and the District of Columbia, as long as they have served at least half their sentence. In a 2010 study by the Vera Institute of Justice, however, the majority of states offering compassionate release for the above reasons did not exercise it for offenders meeting the qualifications (Chiu, 2010).

When housing an elderly offender, special issues need to be taken into consideration, such as prison design, the cost of housing the elderly, specialized training for staff, additional staffing positions (such as nursing assistants and occupational therapists), how to care for an elderly offender with a terminal illness, assuring human rights are not violated, moving the elderly offender from independent living to assisted care accommodations, assuring the elderly are not victimized by other offenders, and emergency management response.

When housing elderly offenders, prison administrators must address prison design. The elderly offender should reside on the ground floor, have bathrooms equipped with handicapped bars, and have access to ramps, canes, walkers, and wheelchairs, all of which present various safety risks for staff. Housing the elderly on any floor but the ground floor presents a safety risk as well. In an emergency situation, moving the elderly offender to the ground floor can put both the offender and the staff at risk. Failure to address structural issues for the elderly offender is a violation of federal law. Historically, prisons did not accommodate the special needs of elderly inmates; prison administrators across the nation struggle with how to generate funding to ensure prisons are structurally compliant for elderly offenders.

The cost of care, custody, and control for an elderly offender is higher than that of a younger offender. The average cost to house a healthy offender under the age of 55 years old is approximately $30,000 a year. Elderly offenders, however, cost approximately $70,000, and if they have a serious condition such as cancer, the cost to the taxpayers skyrockets. When factoring in additional health problems, the cost to care for the elderly offender continues to rise (Henrichson & Delaney, 2012).

Because each elderly offender presents unique health issues, prison administrators must handle his or her needs on a case-by-case basis. Just as with the elderly living in any community, some will be incontinent, have memory problems, suffer from chronic illnesses, be physically challenged, require portable oxygen, wear eyeglasses, and wear hearing aids. Some will require help bathing, getting dressed, and even moving themselves enough in bed so they don't develop bedsores. Additionally, many elderly offenders suffer from a variety of medical problems, such as arthritis, high blood pressure, mental illness, heart problems, ulcers, diabetes, hepatitis, and cancer. Failure to address the needs of the elderly offender can lead to neglect, and if the neglect is severe enough, it may result in death.

Prison administrators need to assure their staff have specialized training in how to properly care for the elderly offender. Prison staff must treat elderly offenders with dignity and respect, and because of their increased need for services, prison administrators must address each of the offender's needs to assure the offenders are not neglected. Additional staff positions, such as occupational and physical therapists, nurses, nursing assistants, and specialized doctors, must work as a team and address each offender individually, as his or her health care needs are often complex. Additional care is necessary for elderly offenders with osteoporosis, dementia, and terminal illnesses, as they can cause the offender to fall ill more frequently than the younger offenders. Additionally, because of the stress of incarceration, the death rate of the elderly offender is much higher than that of an elderly person in the community.

Because most are vulnerable, the elderly offender can become a target for a younger predatory offender. Prison staff must assure the elderly offenders are protected, and because of their special needs, they can easily become targets for the younger predatory offenders to bully and victimize.

At the Department of Rehabilitation and Correction in Ohio, offenders older than 50 years old are housed at the Hocking Correctional Facility. Of the 407 offenders at the facility, 398 of them qualified for special housing, which automatically doubles the daily average cost per offender, from $6.79 to $14.75. Staff at Hocking Correctional Facility receive special training on how to care for elderly offenders, which includes sensitivity training. This specialized training provides staff with a deeper understanding of what elderly offenders face as they live day to day in prison. During training, staff have their fingers taped together in order to assimilate arthritis; then they attempt to feed themselves or to count medication tablets. Staff also train by using blindfolds and thick gloves, which allow them to understand how lack of vision and nerve sensation can affect your perception. In a program called "Don't Forget," staff learn how to provide elderly offenders who suffer with dementia ways to improve their memory. And in the grandparents program, staff learn how to work with elderly offenders so they can increase and enhance their family connections on the outside.

Historically, prisons did not take many steps to assist elderly offenders with their special housing and health care needs. Today, however, states across the nation are implementing programs and special activities for elderly offenders so they have more to do than sit around playing cards, as is so often portrayed in prison movies. In a 2001 survey by the Criminal Justice Institute, about 15 of the 44 states had some form of recreational program in place for elderly offenders (Human Rights Watch, 2012). Some of the states surveyed had special educational programs on health care and wellness, with the goal of keeping elderly offenders healthy and strong as they age. Activities such as aerobics, shuffleboard, bingo, horseshoes, walking programs, basic adult education, and GED classes are available at numerous prisons across the nation. Some prisons even provide healthier meal choices for the elderly offender, with features such as heart healthy options, low fat, high fiber, and low sugar food options. In 16 states, separate housing facilities are available for elderly offenders, which provide physical aids, such as assistance bars on bathroom walls, and an added layer of security, so younger offenders can no longer prey upon the elderly offenders. Many states offer licensed nursing care, to include nurses who specialize in elderly health issues, and licensed nursing assistants, who assist the offenders with walking, going to the bathroom, bathing, eating meals, and getting dressed. Eight states even offer hospice care for offenders who are gravely ill (Human Rights Watch, 2012).

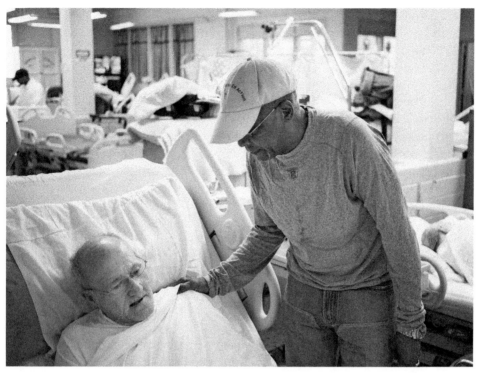

Prisoners over the age of 50 are one of the fastest growing segments within the general inmate population. Some correctional facilities occasionally permit a few select inmates to take care of other aging prisoners. (Annie Flanagan for The Washington Post via Getty Images)

Once known as the bloodiest and most violent prison in the United States, Angola State Prison in Louisiana offers hospice care to offenders facing their final stage of life because of a terminal illness. Younger offenders at Angola participate in a program that builds the burial caskets for offenders who die while in prison. They also participate in burial services, which include digging the graves for the deceased.

California Penal Code § 6267 provides the California Department of Corrections and Rehabilitation (CDCR) the ability to contract with both public and private facilities in order to establish care for offenders who have a limited ability to perform activities of daily living, and who are in need of skilled nursing care on a daily basis. Whether public or private, the facility must provide for the long-term care of offenders, as well as the offenders' personal security, the security of the facility, and the safety of the outside community. All facilities with contracts for long-term skilled nursing care for offenders in California must be licensed, and if the facility is noncompliant in any way, CDCR may revoke the facility agreement.

In Stockton, California, the California Health Care Facility specializes in providing medical care and mental health treatment for offenders who have severe, long-term needs. The 54-building complex provides treatment for 2,951 offenders and employs a staff of 2,500. Although it was designed as a medium security prison, the facility houses offenders of all security levels. It provides offenders with acute medical and mental health treatment, rehabilitation services, academic training, vocational programs, and substance abuse treatment.

In the California Men's Colony, CDCR provides all offenders with programs for self-improvement, academic and vocational education, work skills in prison industry, and participation in self-help groups. The facility also provides offenders with cognitive behavior therapy, substance abuse counseling, and both anger management and family classes. Of particular interest is the hospice program, which has 100 community volunteers and 61 offender volunteers. All volunteers must complete the necessary training and be willing and able to assist any terminally ill offender. In addition to hospice care, the facility runs a dementia program. Both prison staff and trained offenders assist offenders who suffer from dementia with daily living tasks, such as showering, shaving, changing adult diapers, brushing teeth, combing hair, and applying deodorant. Classes are also offered to stimulate the offender's memory with the goal of decreasing his or her disorientation from dementia. Offenders who work in the program are trained by the Alzheimer's Association and are paid $50 per month for their work.

In 1996, Laurel Highlands, a Pennsylvania state prison, began housing elderly offenders and younger offenders requiring nursing home care. Laurel Highlands was originally a state psychiatric hospital but was converted to care for the increase in elderly offenders and others requiring nursing care. Although correctional officers are not dealing with the more aggressive offenders at Laurel Highlands, they receive special training on how to properly manage the care, custody, and control of the elderly offender and others requiring nursing home care.

Specialized prison facilities are scattered across the nation, many specifically geared toward elderly offenders. Florida, Nevada, New York, Pennsylvania, Virginia, and Washington have all either converted prisons or built new ones to accommodate the special needs of the elderly offender. Aside from offering special programs geared to care for the special needs of the elderly offender, these states have raised the bar for other states that do not currently offer special facilities for this population.

In order to care for elderly offenders, some states are considering outsourcing their care to nursing homes. To accomplish this, the state would transfer elderly offenders, or offenders requiring skilled nursing care, to a more age-appropriate facility, designed to specifically manage the special needs of the elderly. If offenders require 24-hour skilled nursing care and no longer pose a threat to society, they may be transferred to a private nursing home. There, they are placed on a parole officer's caseload. If the offender's condition improves, he or she may be returned to the prison. In most cases, however, elderly offenders with severe health issues have conditions that are terminal; thus they will likely never return to prison.

Solutions for caring for elderly offenders vary from transferring them to a nursing home if skilled nursing care is required, to relaxing get-tough-on-crime legislation, especially in light of the continual increase in the overall human life expectancy in the United States. Additional licensed, specialized, secure facilities need to be built, and implementation of accredited training programs for staff must be uniformly adhered to across the nation. An increase in the number of states offering specialized facilities is suggested, as elderly offenders in states with no special facilities will suffer. Although not frequently used, states should revisit compassionate release. Although the process is lengthy, compassionate release was created for offenders who were no longer a danger to society, and most of those offenders are elderly offenders with terminal illnesses.

As with any social issue, there are two sides. Many argue that compassionate release, a reduction of sentences from the get-tough-on-crime era—and sending elderly and terminally ill offenders to nursing homes and building specialized facilities—is a waste of time and money. They believe giving special treatment to a specific population of offenders makes it unfair to others. They believe the punishment should fit the crime, and sentences should be completed, no matter the cost. Supporters also believe giving special treatment to elderly offenders and offenders with terminal illnesses is contrary to victims' rights, and punishment should be meted out equally and not conditioned according to the age or health of the offender. Another argument as to why elderly offenders and those with terminal illnesses should not be released early through compassionate release is that the offenders were convicted of a crime (or crimes), and releasing them from the facility would provide negative publicity, as that action would be perceived as being "soft" on crime and punishment. They also argue that releasing elderly offenders and those who are terminally ill would give society, and particularly children and teenagers, the wrong message and show them that people really can get away with crimes if they are old or sick enough. And finally, they argue that if released due to their age or illness, offenders would be returned to society where they would have the opportunity to commit further crimes.

As people continue to live longer in the United States, the aging prison population will continue to grow. While incarcerated, a person ages more quickly due to the lifestyle and prison conditions he or she must endure. Budgetary requirements to accommodate longer sentences at both the state and federal level will continue to rise, particularly if the nation continues to sentence harshly through get-tough-on-crime legislation. Although some states are addressing the special needs of the elderly offender, experts warn that more planning and action must take place, or prisons will soon be faced with a crisis that has the potential to threaten the lives of elderly offenders across the nation.

Kim Schnurbush

See also: Angola; Compassionate Release; Cost of Prison; Incarceration Rates and Race; Three-Strikes Laws; Truth in Sentencing

Further Reading

Auerhahn, K. (2002). Selective incapacitation, three strikes, and the problem of aging prison populations: Using simulation modeling to see the future. *Criminology, 1,* 353–388.

Barnes, M. (1999, June 21). Aging offenders present problems: Prison population grays with nation. *Fayetteville Observer,* p. 6.

Bouplon, R. A. (1999). *1999 annual report.* Tallahassee: Florida Corrections Commission.

Carson, E. A., & Sabol, W. J. (2016, May 19). *Aging of the state prison population.* Bureau of Justice Statistics, 1993–2013.

Chaneles, S. (1987). Growing old behind bars. In K. C. Haas & G. P. Alpert (Eds.), *The dilemmas of corrections: Contemporary readings* (pp. 548–554). Prospect Heights, IL: Waveland Press.

Chiu, T. (2010, April). *It's about time: Aging prisoners, increasing costs, and geriatric release.* New York: Vera Institute of Justice.

Doughty, P. (1999). *A concern in corrections: Special health needs.* Oklahoma City: Oklahoma Department of Corrections.

Duckett, N., Fox, T. A., Harsha, T. C., & Vish, J. (2001). *Issues in Maryland sentencing—The aging Maryland prison population.* College Park: Maryland State Commission on Criminal Sentencing Policy.

Durham, A. M. (1994). *Crisis and reform: Current issues in American punishment.* New York: Little, Brown.

Exploding number of elderly offenders strains system, taxpayers. (2013, June 30). WRCBtv.com. Retrieved from http://www.wrcbtv.com/story/22725460/exploding-number-of-elderly-prisoners-strains-system-taxpayers

Formby, W. A., & Abel, C. F. (1997). *Elderly men in prison.* In J. I. Kosberg & L. W. Kaye (Eds.), *Elderly men: Special problems and professional challenges* (p. 317). New York: Springer.

Goetting, A. (1983). The elderly in prison issues and perspectives. *Journal of Research in Crime and Delinquency, 20,* 291–309.

Henrichson, C., & Delaney, R. (2012, January 20). *The price of prisons: What incarceration costs taxpayers.* New York: Vera Institute of Justice.

Hooyman, N., & Kiyak, H. A. (1999). *Social gerontology: A multidisciplinary approach.* Needham Heights, MA: Allyn & Bacon.

Human Rights Watch. (2012). *Old behind bars: The aging prison population in the United States.* Human Rights Watch. Retrieved from https://www.hrw.org/sites/default/files/reports/usprisons0112webwcover_0.pdf

Maschi, T. (2012, August 23). The state of aging: Prisoners and compassionate release programs. *Huffington Post.*

Morton, J. (1992). *An administrative overview of the older offender.* Washington, DC: U.S. Department of Justice, National Institute of Corrections.

Neeley, C. L., Addison, L., & Craig-Moreland, D. (1997). Addressing the needs of elderly offenders. *Corrections Today, 59*(5), 120–123.

Ollove, M. (2016, March 17). Elderly offenders burden state prisons. *Stateline.* Pew Charitable Trusts.

Price, M. (2015, May 6). *America's elderly prison population boom is becoming a nightmare.* MSNBC. Retrieved from http://www.msnbc.com/msnbc/americas-elderly-prison-population-boom-becoming-nightmare

Rikard, R. V., & Rosenberg, E. (2007). Aging offenders: A convergence of trends in the American criminal justice system. *Journal of Correctional Health Care, 13*(3), 150–162.

Schreiber, C. (1999, July 19). Behind bars: Aging prison population challenges correctional health system. *NurseWeek,* p. 3.

Terry, W. C., III, & Entzel, P. (2000). Police and elders. In M. B. Rothman, B. D. Dunlop, & P. Entzel (Eds.), *Elders, crime, and the criminal justice system* (pp. 3–18). New York: Springer.

Vaughn, M. S., & Carroll, L. (1998). Separate and unequal: Prison versus free-world medical care. *Justice Quarterly, 3*(3).

Yates, J., & Gillespie, W. (2000). The elderly and prison policy. *Journal of Aging & Social Policy, 11*(2–3), 167–175.

Zimbardo, P. (1994). *Transforming California's prisons into expensive old age homes for felons: Enormous hidden costs and consequences for California's taxpayers.* San Francisco: Center on Juvenile and Criminal Justice.

England, Prisons in

England and Wales's prison system consists of 133 facilities spread across the two nations; two of these are immigration removal centers. Fourteen of these facilities are private prisons, designed, constructed, managed, and financed by private companies, the first opening its doors in 1997. The country's prison population is 85,130 for a prison population rate of 146 per 100,000 populations. England's prisons are overcrowded with a 111 percent occupancy rate. Those imprisoned in remand (pretrial or presentencing) make up 13.3 percent; compared to other countries this percentage is low and is lower than in the recent past. For example, in 2000, the remand percentage was 17.5 percent of the total prison population (World prison brief).

In the last two decades, U.K. imprisonment rates have increased from the 1990s, 93 per 100,000 to the current 146 per 100,000. The increase in imprisonment rates is due to several simultaneous factors. First, the average prison sentence handed down by the courts has increased from about 15 months in 1995 to almost 19 months in 2015. From 1993 to 2016, the proportion of offenders convicted of violence against the person (VATP), sexual offenses, and drug offenses has increased from 40 percent to 60 percent of those sentenced to prison. These offenses carry longer, sometimes indeterminate, sentences than other offenses. Third, the number of "life sentences" has increased by 40 percent since 2002. Lastly, due to new, more conservative legislation, the number of parolees recalled for breaking the conditions of their parole has greatly increased from about 150 in 1995 to 6,600 in 2016 (World prison brief).

Several of these changes in the criminal justice system contributing to increased imprisonment rates are due to a turn to tougher "law and order" policies long advocated by the Conservative Party since the late 1970s such as 1993's Conservative Party's home secretary's populist slogan "prison works," but also adopted by the New Labour Party with the party's 1994 slogan: "tough on crime, tough on the causes of crime." The slogan "prison works" was intended to mean prison works as a deterrent to crime and to incapacitate criminals from committing other crimes, and the policy included tougher sentencing laws and the building of new prisons.

While the Conservative Party was in control until 1997, the newly illiberal New Labour Party controlled the government from 1997 to 2010. At the same time, although the incarceration rate for England and Wales is higher than it was in the past, it does not compare to that of the United States' incarceration rate of more than 700 per 100,000, where tough "law and order" policies have greatly affected the prison system (World prison brief).

After the abolition of the death penalty in England and Wales in the mid-1960s and the spectacular and high-profile escapes from five different prisons also during the mid-1960s, two high-level studies of how to best provide security to prevent future escapes were produced: the Mountbatten Report (1966) and the Radzinowicz Report (1968). The Mountbatten Report prescribed a single very high security prison, which would hold all the prisoners at the highest security risk. However, a single concentration of high-risk prisoners was seen as almost an invitation to a mass breakout or even a mass rescue (perhaps of Irish political prisoners).

The Radzinowicz Report recommended, instead, dispersal prisons. England has six maximum security dispersal prisons that hold the most high-risk prisoners,

"Category A," who are serving long sentences for the most serious crimes such as murder, manslaughter, attempted murder, and rape. Category A prisoners are considered to pose an extreme danger to the public should they escape. Not all the prisoners are Category A in the dispersal prisons. In fact, the majority held in these prisons are the less dangerous Category B prisoners. Nevertheless, in the maximum security dispersal prisons as conceived in the 1960s through the 1990s, it was also recognized that constructive and humane treatment of prisoners would provide a disincentive to escape and repressive prison conditions would likely lead to violence. Unfortunately, following a series of escapes in the early 1990s from two of the maximum security dispersal prisons, new security measures and a relatively harsh and austere security regime were imposed from about 1995 onward.

The British are among the pioneers of creating local houses of correction or "bridewells" to house and exploit the labor of "vagrants" and debtors from the mid-16th century. A further mission of the bridewell was reform through labor. King James I made it mandatory that each county have its own house of correction in 1609. In addition, after 1615 King James I introduced transportation as an indentured servant to the American colonies, and after 1718 transportation became an important judicial penalty. However, due to the Revolutionary War, by 1776, England was no longer able to use transportation as a punishment. Instead, they slowly developed a more formal prison system within their own country after first temporarily using old ships or hulks as prisons.

In 1777, John Howard published *The State of Prisons in England and Wales*. As sheriff of Bedfordshire, he had investigated conditions at the county jail and was shocked by the harsh conditions and lack of Christian charity. The book led to some prison reform with the Penitentiary Act of 1779, but enthusiasm at the national level soon waned. At the county level, however, there was enthusiasm as some 45 prisons were rebuilt through the 1770s and 1780s. There was a second wave of prison building in the 1820s.

Samual Romilly, another reformer, proposed in 1810 in Parliament that the Penitentiary Act of 1799 be resurrected. He and other prison reformers thought that prisons should not inflict needless and excessive pain but that they should employ a minimal level of severity in order to reform the prisoner. During the 1810s, the Quakers also became very active in calling for prison reform asserting that prisoners should be ruled by kindness to produce rehabilitation. The Quaker influence was successful through the creation of the Society for the Improvement of Prison Discipline (SIPD) founded in 1816 that was able to wield political influence through the 1840s. The idea of early parole (called *remission* or *ticket of leave*, at the time) was born in the 1850s where prisoners served five-sixths to two-thirds of their sentence and could be released, subject to recall, early.

The Prison Act of 1865 consolidated Britain's prison system with local prisons. One hundred and twenty-six local prisons still served as the main centers for remand but also for offenses where the sentence was up to two years. The national system consisted of nine convict prisons, an asylum for the criminally insane, and a refuge for women prisoners. Through the 20th century, England's prisons declined in quality due to higher levels of demand and inadequate funding. However, at the same time in the early 20th century, England adopted the Borstal system—training youth (ages 17–21) prisoners through personal relations, trust, and responsibility. This program of rehabilitation was partially transplanted to the adult system in the 1930s. Elements persisted into the 1980s.

Another positive development of the 20th century was the elimination of penile servitude in 1948. By the 1970s, however, the efficacy of prisons to reform and rehabilitate was called into question. Events in the late 1970s, such as a major riot at Hull prison in 1976 that destroyed about two-thirds of the facility, hardened attitudes and led to hard-line penal populism and prison policies of coercion, discipline, and austerity.

In 2016, the English prison system is in crisis due to a combination of prison officer shortage and overcrowding. The recidivism rate is now almost 50 percent. The root cause of the shortage of prison officers is government austerity. Since the Great Recession of 2008–2012, the Conservative-controlled government's (since 2010) prescription for fixing the U.K. economy and deficit spending has been to cut government spending. This has meant a 25 percent budget cut for the Ministry of Justice.

Furthermore, the cuts have led to staffing cuts of about one-third, which has meant more difficult and dangerous working conditions for prison officers, which has led to very high turnover and labor unrest in the prison system. This has also, in turn, meant a prison system that does have a goal of rehabilitation in addition to deterrence and incapacitation but has insufficient staff to allow rehabilitation programs such as education or job training to operate. In some prisons, inmates spend only 2 hours a day outside their cells due to prison officer shortages. There are numerous outbreaks of violence. Riot squads are routinely dispatched 30 to 40 times a month. In 2015, there were 100 suicides, 2,000 fires, and a 20 percent rise in assaults. The government of the United Kingdom recognizes these limitations and has suggested "in-cell" technology such as iPads to allow prisoners to use online education and keep in contact with their families. Furthermore, the government has suggested building six new "reform" prisons that will emphasize rehabilitation.

James A. Norris

See also: Education in Prison; Escapes; Incarceration, Factors Contributing to the Growth in; Incarceration Rates; Inmate Classification; Maximum Security; Overcrowding; Political Prisoners; Prison Populations, Trends in; Prison Reform, Intended and Unintended Consequences of; Prisons, History of; Privatization; Punishment Philosophies; Recidivism; Riots; Self-Injury in Prison; Suicide in Custody; Violence in Prison

Further Reading

Allen, R. (2013). Paying for justice: Prison and probation in an age of austerity. *British Journal of Community Justice, 11*(1), 5–18.

Drake, D. H. (2014). *Prisons, punishment and the pursuit of security.* New York: Palgrave Macmillan.

Emsley, C. (2007). *Crime, police, & penal policy: European experiences, 1750–1940.* Oxford, U.K.: Oxford University Press.

Howard, M. (2011). *Carlton University lecture: Does prison work?* Retrieved from http://michaelhoward.org/political

Matthews, R. (2005). The myth of punitiveness. *Theoretical Criminology, 9*(2), 175–201.

Ryan, M., & Sim, J. (1998). Power, punishment and prisons in England and Wales, 1975–1996. In R. P. Weis & N. Smith (Eds.), *Comparing prison systems: Toward a comparative and international penology* (pp. 175–205). Amsterdam, Netherlands: Gordon and Breach.

Turner, L. (2014). Penal populism, deliberative methods, and the production of 'public opinion' on crime and punishment. *The Good Society, 23*(1), 87–102.

World prison brief. United Kingdom: England & Wales. Retrieved from http://prisonstudies .org/county/united-kingdom-england-wales

Enlightenment and Punishment

The religious philosophy or setting for the Age of Reason or the Enlightenment was that God directly controlled all human behavior, and the authority of the Catholic Church, which dominated Europe, should be accepted—absolutely. Enlightenment philosophers such as René Descartes, Jean-Jacques Rousseau, and John Locke instead felt that God had left people to govern their own affairs through the exercise of free will and reason. The Age of Enlightenment is the era in Western philosophy and intellectual, scientific, and cultural life, in which reason was advocated as the primary source and legitimacy for authority.

The Enlightenment started in 17th-century England and eventually became a worldwide movement. The term "Enlightenment," historically taken as a skeptical view of traditional dogma and belief systems, stands in stark contrast to the dark superstition that pervaded the Middle Ages. The Enlightenment focused on the power of rationality. Some of the doctrines of the Enlightenment include the following: (1) Reason is the most significant and positive capacity of people—it has liberating potential; (2) reason enables one to break free from dogmatic and superstitious beliefs holding one in the traditional bonds of irrationality and ignorance; (3) through philosophical and scientific progress, reason can lead humanity as a whole to a state of earthly perfection; (4) reason makes all people equal and, therefore, deserving of equal liberty and treatment before the law; and (5) all beliefs should be accepted only on the basis of reason and not on any type of traditional authority.

The Scientific Revolution, also occurring during this period, fostered the Age of Reason or Enlightenment. Inventions gave people the freedom to reject long-standing biblical beliefs, as science could explain much of the natural world. The Enlightenment saw itself as rejecting medieval beliefs and moving away from religion. In terms of crime, the Enlightenment resulted in newly evolved ideas of individual rationality and free will, which would become the cornerstone of the classical school of criminology. Eventually the growth of science would affect criminology when Auguste Comte founded the positive school. Comte argued that human behavior is determined by forces beyond the individual's control. This, indeed, will mitigate free will.

Cesare Beccaria (1738–1794) and Jeremy Bentham (1748–1832) were the founders of the classical school. They saw individual conduct being determined by the self-centered quest for pleasure or the need to avoid pain. In attempting to fulfill these desires, people sometimes turn to crime. Crime, in turn, needs punishment.

Enlightenment and Punishment

According to the Enlighteners, punishment should not be an act of vengeance. The only just role for punishment is as a protective element in society, carried out lawfully, with the aim of preventing recidivism and future crimes. The classicists describe the criminals as fully rational, exercising free will when they commit crimes.

Cesare Beccaria argued that people should only be punished when they violate laws. In addition, individual citizens must understand societal laws as rational and made with the intention of achieving societal equality. The laws and punishments for breaking the laws would be closely aligned, ensuring that, in essence, the punishment fit the crime. Beccaria argued for a renewed penal system that might enact punishments with the aim of encouraging a positive future for both criminals and society at large. Punishments would be chosen so that criminals would be discouraged from committing further crimes, and so that other citizens would be dissuaded from committing similar offenses. The punishments chosen and inflicted on offenders must make a lasting impression on both the criminal and others who might consider crime. Physical punishments could not be imposed.

The classical movement encouraged just, rational punishments, and Beccaria introduced the idea that punishment should be proportionate to the seriousness of the crime. Before this period in history, a citizen who stole a small item would be dealt the same punishment as a murderer. Beccaria believed that prison should be better utilized and that prison conditions should be altered to ensure the best chance of rehabilitation. He further believed that offenders should be separated based on factors such as age and degree of criminality.

In colonial America punishment was not designed to rehabilitate criminals. Instead, physical punishment/pain was publicly inflicted on convicted criminals. The purpose was to humiliate them and to deter other people from crime. The ideas of the Enlightenment led Americans to see people as rational beings who could control their own behavior, in contrast to the idea that they were sinful beings. As a result, theories of punishment began to change. This idea led to a reevaluation of punishment and the beginning of a search for causes of criminal behavior. Prison was being seen as a method to punish criminals, leading to repentance, but not yet as a way to rehabilitate them.

Society believed that the industrial revolution had disrupted the American social order and crime was a symptom. Reforms were aimed at creating orderly prisons, training inmates in religion and requiring hard work and strict discipline. This orderly environment would affect their reform by furnishing them with a strong moral foundation needed to resist the corrupting influences in society.

Beccaria and Bentham influenced the creation of the modern prison. Before their ideas took hold, long-term incarceration did not exist; jails were intended only for the short-termed stay—for suspects awaiting torture, trial, or execution. The development of the prison thus represented a major change in the punishment of criminals. Critics of the classical reformers said their views were too simplistic; crimes were also the result of people acting emotionally. Beccaria's ideas are reflected in debates over the rationality of criminals and the deterrent effect of law. Throughout the whole of his writings, Beccaria develops his position by appealing to two central philosophical theories: utility and social contract. Beccaria advocates for punishments that serve the greater good, leading to the most beneficial outcome for the criminal and the public at large.

Beccaria suggested reforms to an array of criminal justice practices. For example, he suggested that public duels might come to an end if laws were enacted to protect a person's honor. He felt that laws forbidding suicide might be best omitted, as punishment for that crime could be left to God. Beccaria saw bounty hunting as unhelpful and outdated, as it encouraged immorality and conveyed a weakness in the government. He believed that laws should be written clearly, making a judge's role that of a decision maker rather than interpreter, and that treason was the worst crime a person could commit, as it damages the social contract.

His book, *On Crimes and Punishments,* was also the first full-scale work of penology to tackle criminal law reform and suggest that criminal justice should conform to rational principles. The principles to which Beccaria appealed were *reason,* an understanding of the state as a form of contract, and *utilitarianism,* the greatest happiness for the greatest number.

Beccaria authored some of the first modern arguments against the death penalty. He was firmly against the death penalty, finding capital punishment useless and unnecessary, and he also contended that the state had no right to take a life. Beccaria is credited with the development of a number of principles: "punishment should be proportionate to the crime committed; the probability of punishment, not its severity, would achieve the preventive effect; punishment has a deterrent, not a retributive effect; procedures of criminal convictions should be public; and punishment should be prompt."

Three principles served as the basis of Beccaria's theories on criminal justice: manipulability, free will, and rational manner. Manipulability describes the way that a criminal might be discouraged from committing a crime if the severity of the punishment outweighs the benefits of getting away with the crime. According to Beccaria, citizens will use free will and rational thought when making choices that might result in personal gratification, leading him to support laws that upheld the social contract and benefited society.

Many improvements in the penal codes of the European nations can be traced back to Beccaria's writings. In addition, his ideas eventually helped shape the rights listed in the U.S. Constitution and the Bill of Rights. His theories, as expressed in his work *On Crimes and Punishments* (1764), continue to be discussed today as nations continue to consider topics such as truth in sentencing and the death penalty.

Craig J. Forsyth and Britain Bailey Forsyth

See also: Beccaria, Cesare; Incarceration, Impact of Social Progressives on; Prisons, History of; Punishment Philosophies

Further Reading

Beccaria, C. (1963). [1764]. *On crimes and punishments.* Indianapolis: Bobbs-Merrill.

Fridell, R. (2004). *Capital punishment.* New York: Benchmark Books.

Taylor, I., Walton, P., & Young, J. (1973). *The new criminology: For a social theory of deviance.* London: Routledge & Kegan Paul.

Vold, G. B., & Bernard, T. J. (1986). *Theoretical criminology.* New York: Oxford University Press.

Environmentally Friendly ("Green") Prisons

Environmentally friendly, or "green," prisons represent various efforts to reduce the environmental harms and operating costs of housing convicted criminal offenders inside correctional institutions. By transforming prisons into "greener" facilities that are more energy and resource efficient, the idea is that places of confinement may be less damaging to society and more likely to provide inmates with prosocial opportunities. As incarceration continues to serve as a primary form of punishment for lawbreakers in the United States, green institutions and environmentally friendly prison programs are expanding.

At present, approximately 2.2 million people are incarcerated inside federal and state prisons and local jails in the United States. This figure is four times the number of individuals who were locked up in 1980. Much of this increase may be attributed to sentencing policies associated with the war on drugs, including mandatory minimum prison sentences for certain crimes and truth-in-sentencing legislation that limits the early release of inmates to community supervision. At the same time, the limited availability of correctional programming may play a role in the growing number of individuals behind bars. Nonetheless, higher prison populations mean higher financial costs. State correctional expenditures, for instance, cost nearly $50 billion each year. As American prisons and jails approach physical and financial capacity, their survival has been called into question, and policy makers across the nation have looked for ways to sustain them. The "greening" of correctional institutions is one approach toward prison sustainability.

WHAT IS GREENING?

Sustainability efforts have been widespread in many sectors across the United States, and prisons are no different. Because correctional institutions often provide inmates with education, food, housing, laundry, recreation, and other services, they require a considerable amount of resources. Therefore, it may be crucial for prisons to engage in sustainability efforts or greening that include reducing energy consumption, enhancing recycling efforts, and investing in composting and gardening. These sustainable solutions are likely to help save taxpayers' money and may also assist inmates. If people learn sustainable job skills while incarcerated, they may be more marketable upon returning to society. Ninety-five percent of inmates will exit prisons at some point in their lives and return to free society. If they are able to find gainful employment, they may be less likely to recidivate.

In an effort to create green standards for companies, organizations, and other entities to follow, the United States Green Building Design Council established a rating system in 2000. These Leadership in Energy and Environmental Design (LEED) certifications are the most widely used third-party verification of green structures. LEED certifications may be made at one of four levels (i.e., certified, silver, gold, or platinum), which represent a continuum of resource efficiency. Ratings are based on the location, transportation required to access the site, environmental sustainability, water efficiency, energy use and atmospheric output, material use, and quality of the indoor environment.

WHO IS GREENING?

Currently, there are several greening initiatives across the United States that provide inmates with marketable skills through labor and training opportunities while simultaneously reducing carceral spending. These initiatives may be found in many states, such as California, Illinois, Maryland, New York, Ohio, and Washington. Not only are individual states examining their own correctional practices and how they may be creating environmental and financial harms, but national organizations, such as the National Institute of Corrections, have also become involved in these initiatives.

Many greening programs owe their successful operations to the cooperation of several agencies. The Maryland Green Prisons Initiative, for instance, involves a collaboration between the state's Department of Public Safety and Correctional Services and a research program (i.e., Baltimore Ecosystem Study) dedicated to the study of ecological systems. The Sustainability in Prisons Project, as another example, is a partnership between the Washington State Department of Corrections and The Evergreen State College. Collaborators across the country span the professional spectrum of researchers, scientists, educators, vocational specialists, and others. Greening programs often match their team of professionals to specific prisons and inmate populations to maximize their success with sustainability efforts. At the federal level, the Federal Correctional Institution (FCI) in Hazelton, West Virginia, has recently earned the LEED gold certification rating. The first federal institution to receive LEED certification, however, was the FCI in Butner, North Carolina.

WHY GREEN?

The impetus to pursue greening in the correctional field, at least at the federal level, likely stems from two executive orders (EOs). In order to reduce environmental harms, limit energy consumption, and improve fiscal situations, George W. Bush signed EO 13423, and Barack Obama signed EO 13514. In March 2015, however, Obama signed EO 13693, which rescinded and revoked the previous orders by outlining specific guidelines and desired outcomes for greening at the federal level.

As a result of these executive orders and related federal guidelines, Federal Prison Industries (FPI) has altered its structure and the ways in which inmates manufacture goods in federal prisons. The goods that are manufactured by federal inmates utilize a variety of approaches to improve environment impacts, decrease energy use, and reduce costs associated with such production. Materials used in the manufacturing process include fibers recycled at a high rate (sometimes as high as 100 percent), foam that is entirely recyclable, and adhesives and paints that are water-based, nontoxic, and otherwise chemically inert. Inmates also copy paper documents to electronic formats, creating digital data and recycling by-products, which is a practice found across FPI programs. More recently, inmates have started to manufacture solar panels to be used by government agencies.

The financial savings associated with greening efforts are perhaps the most commonly asserted reasons for starting, continuing, or expanding such operations, policies, and programs inside correctional institutions. The California Department of Corrections reports annual savings in the millions of dollars after adopting greening initiatives. To be sure, with prison operational expenses at record levels, correctional agencies and systems are looking for ways to reduce financial costs. Under many environmentally friendly prison strategies, resources that would otherwise be wasted are repurposed, reused, and recycled. At the same time, prison greening allows institutions to use less costly alternatives to traditional practices. For example, greening initiatives to reduce waste and harness available energy may include water conservation, the use of solar panels and wind turbines, recycling, and composting.

The positive outcomes associated with green prisons are not limited to their favorable economic impacts. Some institutional greening programs, in addition to or in conjunction with sustainability efforts, offer various forms of nature-based therapy for inmates. Such therapy is a practice that may be unavailable without the implementation of greening initiatives. Activities, such as gardening and landscaping, are often combined with programming that is focused on social skills, cognitive reorientation, and interpersonal communication skills. Offenders who are involved in greening programs, specially such curriculums that offer therapy, are often found to be at a lower risk of reoffending in comparison to other similarly situated offenders who are not involved in greening programs. In some cases, individuals who participate in greening programs have recidivism rates that are 50 percent lower than individuals outside of the programs.

Inmates at Solano State Prison in Vacaville, California, install a drought-tolerant garden as part of the Insight Garden Program, which teaches inmates environmental and gardening skills. The garden is irrigated using reclaimed water from the prison's kitchen. (Justin Sullivan/Getty Images)

Psychological research has consistently shown that psychosocial improvements are found when inmates are offered activities that involve interaction with the physical landscape and environment, such as those provided by many greening programs. The psychosocial benefits that have been revealed from inmate work and other activities that incorporate nature in greening initiatives may be reinforced by accompanying therapeutic programs. Inmates who participate in combined greening and therapeutic curriculums commonly report improved feelings of self-worth and purpose, self-efficacy, and relaxation, as well as decreases in aggression and depression. At the same time, they often indicate reduced substance use and less risk taking. These negative emotions, stresses, and behaviors routinely have been linked to criminal behavior, and prison programs that utilize greening may be promising for curbing additional offending.

Although greening may be a relatively new phenomenon, especially in carceral settings, it is increasingly popular for a number of reasons. Green prisons and correctional institutions that implement greening initiatives are likely to cost much less to operate in comparison to other prisons. At the same time, green prisons typically incorporate sustainable practices that have little to no adverse effect on the environment. What is more, offenders who are involved in greening programs inside these institutions generally recidivate at lower rates due to improved psychosocial skills, enhanced emotional and behavioral regulation, and timely acquisition of practical skill sets.

David Patrick Connor and Philip D. McCormack

See also: American Prison Designs; Cost of Prisons; Education in Prison; Prison Industries; Prison Work Programs; Recidivism; Second Chance Act

Further Reading

Davidson, S. (2013). *The Green Corrections Project: Action plans and lessons learned.* Washington, DC: National Institute of Corrections.

Feldbaum, M., Greene, F., Kirschenbaum, S., Mukamal, D., Welsh, M., & Pinderhughes, R. (2011). *The greening of corrections: Creating a sustainable system.* Washington, DC: National Institute of Corrections.

Lynch, M. J., & Stretesky, P. B. (2003). The meaning of green: Contrasting criminological perspectives. *Theoretical Criminology, 7*(2), 217–238.

Moran, D., & Jewkes, Y. (2014). "Green" prisons: Rethinking the "sustainability" of the carceral state. *Geographica Helvetica, 69*(5), 345–353.

Equine-Facilitated Prison-Based Programs

Prisons and correctional institutions often use animal-based intervention programs as part of their efforts to rehabilitate inmates. The philosophy behind equine-facilitated prison-based programs derives from the general idea that animal-facilitated interventions in institutional settings reinforce the bonds that humans share with animals, while teaching respect and responsibility. Examples in the United States trace back to 1919, where dog-facilitated interventions are reported to have been used. Although many programs include domestic animals such as dogs, interventions have included other domesticated animals, farm animals, and wild animals.

Equine-Facilitated Prison-Based Programs   203

Numerous countries operate prison-based animal programs, including Australia, Austria, Canada, South Africa, the United Kingdom, and the United States. These programs are designed around eight different program types: (1) visitation programs, (2) wildlife rehabilitation programs, (3) community service programs, (4) vocational programs, (5) service animal socialization programs, (6) livestock care programs, (7) pet adoption programs, and (8) programs incorporating multiple programmatic components.

Correctional institutions in the United States began using equine-facilitated intervention programs starting in the 1980s. Two models of equine-facilitated prison-based programs are utilized in the United States: the Thoroughbred Retirement Foundation's Second Chances program and the Wild Horse Inmate program. Both types of programmatic models consist of a vocational component that provides career training and a community service component. Career training offered under the prison-based animal program's vocation component involves training and/or certifying participants in animal handling, animal grooming, and animal care. The community service program component involves participants in the training and care of animals that are then adopted out to the community. The prison-based animal programs that utilize the dual vocational and community service program components are referred to as multimodal programs.

Since 1984, the U.S.-based Thoroughbred Retirement Foundation's Second Chances program has provided vocational training on horse care and maintenance of retired race horses. The Second Chances program has been implemented in correctional facilities serving men and women, as well as juvenile offenders, in nine states. Their programs primarily teach inmates horse care through theoretical and practical application, which is assessed through a structured, tested curriculum. Participants demonstrate competence in horse anatomy, and advanced horsemanship skills including horse handling, general stable procedures, racetrack procedures, horse behavior and psychology, tack care, grooming, horse examination and health checks, hoof care, and horse nutrition. Once released, graduates of these types of programs can work at horse farms and pursue other careers working with horses. In addition to the career preparation aspects of this training, the program is also designed to promote productive citizenship and social responsibility in released inmates.

The other existing model of equine-facilitated prison-based programs is the Wild Horse Inmate Program, which began in 1986, partnering departments of corrections with the U.S. Department of the Interior Bureau of Land management. Unlike the Second Chances program, which uses retired thoroughbred racehorses, the Wild Horse Inmate Program utilizes wild horses and burros that are "gentled" and then made available to the public. The Wild Horse Inmate Program is a rehabilitative-type program that provides training to inmates in a growing number of states, including Arizona, Colorado, Kansas, Nevada, Utah, and Wyoming. The Wild Horse Inmate Program provides halter training and saddle training to "gentle" or domesticate the wild horses and requires inmates to feed and provide care for all of the wild horses and burros at the facility. Here, too, inmates gain work experience that may prove useful upon release. These skills include farrier services, animal husbandry, and horsemanship. The program is also designed to instill in

An inmate poses with one of many horses he has trained as part of the Wild Horse Inmate Program in Cañon City, Colorado. (John Leyba/The Denver Post via Getty Images)

inmates a sense of respect for both people and animals. The Wild Horse Inmate Program sells the trained horses and burros to members of the community, which alleviates the concern for costs, time, or facilities needed to train an equine off site. Horses are also provided to therapeutic riding organizations, youth riding organizations, riding stables, government agencies, and are sold to law enforcement agencies.

Programmatic costs involved with equine-facilitated prison-based programs include the value of inmate labor, currently estimated at an average 50 cents per hour per inmate. Additional costs include the salaries of program directors, harnesses, saddles, feed, medicine, and the equipment used to maintain pastures. However, monies from the sale of trained horses may be utilized to support the prison facility.

Little research exists that empirically examines the effects of equine-facilitated prison-based programs on recidivism rates. U.S.-based researchers have reported a 25 percent recidivism rate among male participants in New Mexico, less than the state average recidivism rate of 38 percent. Countries outside of the United States have also experienced positive results from similar equine-facilitated prison-based programs. In one 2015 report from the United Kingdom, the 12-month postrelease recidivism rate among participants was at 36 percent, which is 27 percentage points lower than the predicted recidivism rate of 63 percent. Adjudications went down 74 percent, and negative entries (e.g., chits) were also down 72 percent (Laurie &

Noble, 2015). Positive behavior choices have also been reported. Although much of the evidence of success in equine-facilitated prison-based programs is anecdotal, empirical research does support the overall positive results garnered from animal-based prison programs specifically, and inmate training and education programs in general.

Moneque Walker-Pickett

See also: Cognitive-Behavioral Therapies in Prison; Education in Prison; Prison-Based Animal Training Programs; Prison Work Programs; Vocational Training and Education

Further Reading

Arizona Correctional Industries. *Wild horse program.* Retrieved from https://www.aci.az.gov/wild-horse-program

Bachi, K. (2013). Equine-facilitated prison-based programs within the context of prison-based animal programs: State of the science review. *Journal of Offender Rehabilitation, 52*(1), 46–74.

Bureau of Land Management. (2016). *Colorado Wild Horse Inmate Program.* Retrieved August 2016 from http://www.blm.gov/co/st/en/BLM_Programs/wild_horse_and_burro/Wild_Horse_Inmate_Program_Colorado.html

Bureau of Land Management. (2016). *Saddle-Trained Wild Horse & Burro Inmate Training Program.* Retrieved August 2016 from http://www.blm.gov/nv/st/en/prog/wh_b/saddle_horse_training.html

Burgon, H. (2011). "Queen of the world": Experiences of "at-risk" young people participating in equine-assisted learning/therapy. *Journal of Social Work Practice, 25*(2), 165–183.

Cushing, J. L., Williams, J. D., & Kronick, R. F. (1995). The Wild Mustang Program: A case study in facilitated inmate therapy. *Journal of Offender Rehabilitation, 22*(3/4), 95–112. doi:10.1300/J076v22n03_08

Dalke, K. (2008). At the threshold of change: The inmates and wild horses of Cañon City, Colorado. *Reflections, 14*(4), 12–16.

Hemmingway, A., Meek, R., & Hill, C. E. (2015). An exploration of an equine-facilitated learning intervention with young offenders. *Society & Animals, 23*(6), 544–568.

Jensen, E. L., & Reed, G. E. (2006). Adult correctional education programs: An update on current status based on recent studies. *Journal of Offender Rehabilitation, 44*(1), 81–98.

Laurie, H., & Noble, J. (2015, February). *TheHorseCourse: Working with offenders: Evidence review: Theory of change and contribution analysis.* Retrieved September 2016 from http://www.thehorsecourse.org/docs/TheHorseCourse_Evidence_Review_2015_web.pdf

Meek, R. (2012). *TheHorseCourse at HMP/YOI Portland: Interim evaluation findings.* 2015 Update. Retrieved September 2016 from http://www.thehorsecourse.org/docs/Eval-THC.pdf

Moreau, L. (2001). Outlaw riders: Equine-facilitated therapy with juvenile capital offenders. *Reaching Today's Youth: The Community Circle of Caring Journal, 5*(2), 27–30.

Strimple, E.O. (2003). A history of prison inmate-animal interaction programs. *American Behavioral Scientist, 47*(1), 70–78.

Thoroughbred Retirement Foundation. (2016). *TRF's Second Chances program.* Retrieved September 4, 2016, from http://www.trfinc.org/trf-second-chances-program

Wild Horse Inmate Program (W.H.I.P.). Retrieved from https://www.coloradoci.com/serviceproviders/whip

Escapes

On any given day in the United States, there are more than 2.2 million adult offenders incarcerated in prison. One of the major responsibilities of prison administrators is to prevent these inmates from escaping from custodial supervision. Correctional policies often consider escape risk to be an important consideration during the inmate classification process. Criminal statutes also provide additional prison terms to those individuals who are convicted of escaping or attempting to escape from custody. Escapes are a popular topic in the media, likely because they invoke fear and intrigue among members of the public. A prison escape can be as simple as walking away from a minimum security institution or as complex as breaking out of a maximum security facility. Escapes can also include failing to return from an authorized release or fleeing during a transport.

Research shows that escapees and nonescapees differ on a number of demographic and criminal history variables. For example, escapees are more likely to be younger and have convictions for property, rather than violent, offenses than nonescapees. When considering race and gender, escapees are more likely to be white and male than nonescapees. Escapees also tend to have more extensive criminal records, past incarcerations, parole violations, institutional violations, and prior escapes compared to nonescapees. Escaping is also linked to several situational variables, including family problems, not receiving mail or visits from family members, being placed in facilities that are a great distance from home, and feeling threatened by correctional officers or other inmates.

There are also facility-level characteristics that make some prisons more susceptible to escapes than others. For example, inmates are more likely to escape from minimum security institutions than maximum security facilities. Escapes are also more likely to occur from older facilities rather than newer institutions. Other aggregate-level correlates of escape include younger overall age of prison population, lower rate of treatment staff to inmates, less supervision of inmates, and fewer resources provided to inmates. There is also some evidence to suggest that inmates may be more likely to escape from prisons that are not accredited by the American Correctional Association (ACA) than those that are accredited by the ACA. Finally, crowded living conditions in prison may also contribute to increases in escapes.

Escapes appear to be driven by both motivation and opportunity. There are several circumstances that could potentially lead an inmate to an attempt at escape. Although media accounts of these incidents often depict escapes as complex and sensational acts, many escapes involve little or no planning at all. For example, the most common types of escape involve an inmate simply walking away from a nonsecure area and failing to return as instructed from an authorized leave of absence. Time is also an important factor in prison escapes. Research shows that escapes are most likely to occur during the warmer months of the year and on the weekends. Furthermore, escapes are most likely to occur in the early morning or late evening hours of the day when there is less supervision and oversight.

Far fewer escapes actually involve breaking out of a secure area. Secure areas include some type of physical barrier that the inmate must overcome to escape, such as a fence, gate, wall, or locked door. In order to escape from these more secure settings, inmates must cut through, climb over, tunnel under, or otherwise overcome the physical obstacles. Seldom do escapees use force against correctional staff or other inmates in the commission of an escape. In rare situations, escape attempts involve the assistance of an individual from within or outside the prison walls such as a family member, friend, or staff member. On rare occasions, an escapee may impersonate a correctional officer or hide in a vehicle during an escape.

There is no doubt that escapees pose a potential threat to communities and its members. It is important to note, however, that escapes are a fairly low occurring event in the United States. For example, there were only 611 inmates who were involved in 503 documented escape incidents in 2009. Even when inmates are successful in escaping, justice authorities are often able to recapture and return these individuals to custody within a year of the escape. A common misconception regarding prison escapes is that escapees universally go on to commit heinous criminal acts once in the community. Although some escapees do engage in such criminal behaviors and efforts should certainly be taken to reduce the probability of these events from occurring, the typical escapee infrequently commits any serious or violent offenses while on the run.

One way for prison officials to reduce escapes is to target both inmate opportunities and motivations for escaping. This strategy for better controlling escapes should include improving offender classification protocols, increasing security measures for higher risk inmates, and ensuring proper inmate observation and accountability. This strategy should also include offering more counseling and treatment services to inmates, allowing and even promoting visits with family and friends (both in the prison and in the community), and protecting inmates when they feel their safety is in jeopardy.

Megan M. King and Ryan M. Labrecque

See also: Misconduct by Prisoners; Riots; Treatment in Prisons

Further Reading

Anson, R. H., & Hartnett, C. M. (1983). Correlates of escape: A preliminary assessment of Georgia prisons. *Criminal Justice Review, 8*(1), 38–42.

Carlson, K. A. (1990). Prison escapes and community consequences: Results of a case study. *Federal Probation, 54*(2), 36–43.

Culp, R. F. (2005). Frequency and characteristics of prison escapes in the United States: An analysis of national data. *The Prison Journal, 85*(3), 270–291.

Culp, R. H., & Bracco, E. (2005). Examining prison escapes and the routine activities theory. *Corrections Compendium, 30*(3), 1–5, 25–27.

Fisher, S., Allan, A., & Allan, M. M. (2004). Exploratory study to examine the impact of television reports of prison escapes on fear of crime, operationalised as state anxiety. *Australian Journal of Psychology, 56*(3), 181–190.

Kaeble, D., Glaze, L. Tsoutis, A., & Minton, T. (2016). *Correctional populations in the United States, 2014.* Washington, DC: Bureau of Justice Statistics.

Peterson, B. E. (2014). Newsworthiness of prison escapes: Content analysis of factors influencing print media coverage, 2006–2010. *American International Journal of Social Science, 3*(1), 174–187.

Peterson, B. E., Fera, A., & Mellow, J. (2016). Escapes from correctional custody: A new examination of an old phenomenon. *The Prison Journal, 96*(4), 511–533.

United States Sentencing Commission. (2008). *Report on federal escape offenses in fiscal years 2006 and 2007*. Washington, DC: Author.

Wortley, R. K. (2002). *Situational prison control: Crime prevention in correctional institutions*. Cambridge, U.K.: Cambridge University Press.

Ethical Issues in Prison Counseling

Ethical guidelines and requirements are in place to protect the consumer and the public at large. The process of governing ethical behavior among prison counselors is also considered important because, to some extent, inmates are at a disadvantage when compared to individuals in the broader society. Indeed, inmates must be allowed to engage in the process without force or coercion, and stringent efforts should be made to protect their confidentiality despite the fact that prisons have numerous individuals kept in close quarters with one another.

In many cases, ethical standards of behavior and service delivery are provided to help counselors determine a best course of action in difficult or ambiguous situations. In such situations, the key concern should always be the welfare of their client. This underlying concern is, of course, something that can also run counter to the objectives of other prison staff, namely security staff, who may not understand the need for confidentiality given that security is expected to keep a watchful and suspicious eye over inmates who are in their custody. Because of this, there is sometimes tension between treatment staff and security staff. However, the seasoned prison counselor will be able to navigate this in a manner that is conducive to both therapeutic objectives and security concerns.

When conducting prison counseling, it is important that the clinician consider a number of ethical safeguards. Among these are ensuring that the client has informed consent, which simply means that the offender is made aware of what to expect from the counseling process and what it is likely to entail first, before engaging in the counseling process. Also, confidentiality is a key issue that should be covered, meaning that prior to divulging information to the counselor, the offender understands what information can and will remain confidential and that they understand what information the counselor cannot keep confidential. These and other ethical considerations for prison counselors will be discussed in more detail throughout the remainder of this entry.

INFORMED CONSENT

Informed consent is a critical component of all counseling programs. It is important to note that there are ethical guidelines that inform the proper process and circumstances in which consent should be obtained from clients. In addition, informed consent is often obtained in separate circumstances that may fall under the umbrella of counseling. For example, offenders will often be asked to provide consent for the completion of their initial assessment. Further, it is common to have an evaluation component attached to many of the correctional counseling programs, which also requires informed consent. Evaluation studies are primarily aimed at

Ethical Issues in Prison Counseling

measuring selected variables at different points in time to determine if progress is being made by the offender. It is important that clients know the nature of the data that will be collected and how the data will be used. For these types of activities, informed consent must be obtained.

Prior to assessing a client, counselors should provide an explanation as to the scope and purpose of the assessment and the specific use of results in language the client (or other legally authorized person on behalf of the client) can understand, unless an explicit exception to this right has been agreed upon in advance. This must be done prior to engaging in these activities in a manner that ensures that the offender client understands what will take place.

Further, the prison counselor should make sure that offender clients understand that they have the freedom to choose whether to enter into a counseling relationship, and they must be made aware that they are able to desist from counseling whenever they desire. In doing this, prison counselors should review the process of counseling, both verbally and in writing, so that they understand their rights and responsibilities during the therapeutic relationship. Informed consent continues to apply and is ongoing throughout the counseling relationship and should be revisited intermittently, particularly when appraisals, topics, or goals change or are modified as the professional relationship progresses.

Clients need to be given clear and distinct information regarding the counselor who delivers therapeutic services. Beyond matters of confidentiality, clients have a right to know other parameters related to their counselor and their perspective, before any counseling begins. Clients should be informed of the counselor's qualifications and credentials, the parameters related to those credentials, the nature of the counseling relationship, the counselor's areas of expertise, fees and services offered, the boundaries of privileged communication, the limits of confidentiality, client responsibilities, and any potential risks that may occur as a result of the counseling process. Each of these points of information are important because they educate the client on the process and they ensure that no feelings of betrayal emerge from the client as the counselor administers services and/or ensures compliance with the agreed-upon treatment plan.

CONFIDENTIALITY

Confidentiality is a concept that describes the process of keeping private information disclosed by a client to a counselor during a counseling session. The essence of confidentiality is very important to the success of counseling. This point was highlighted in the U.S. Supreme Court case of *Jaffee v. Redmond* (1996). In its opinion, the court clearly articulated that an atmosphere of confidence and trust is necessary for a client to feel comfortable enough to make disclosures relating to emotions, memories, and fears. The court further reasoned that because of the nature of the problems for which clients seek the assistance of counselors, embarrassment or disgrace may be endured if information is not properly contained, and is likely to impede the confidential relationship necessary for effective treatment.

Nevertheless, issues with confidentiality and the need to release information without the offender's consent are not as stringent as they are for persons who are

210   **Ethical Issues in Prison Counseling**

not incarcerated. Indeed, some prison counselors may falsely believe that the Health Insurance Portability and Accountability Act of 1996, otherwise known more commonly as HIPAA, prohibits them from releasing information. In fact, correctional facilities (and prison counselors) can disclose information about an offender without that offender's authorization for the following:

• To provide health care to an inmate
• To ensure the health and safety of the inmate-victim or other inmates
• To ensure the health and safety of inmates, officers, or individuals who transport inmates
• To provide law enforcement officials who are at the correctional facility
• To advance the administration and maintenance of the safety, security, and order of the correctional facility

From the above noted guidelines, it can be seen that the general theme is that an inmate's right to privacy or confidentiality is balanced against the correctional agency's need to maintain safety and security of those in its charge. Even when examining various ethical codes such as that for the American Counselor's Association (ACA), disclosure may be necessary to protect a client or others who are specifically identified from serious and foreseeable harm or when the law requires that such information be revealed. Thus, the overarching issue is ultimately the safety and security of the correctional institution.

Beyond these, however, the issue of confidentiality becomes much less clear, especially within the domain of prison counseling. Usually, confidentiality will be maintained unless the offender presents a danger to self or others. In addition, it is important to note that confidentiality is not as easy to maintain in group counseling settings, as other inmates can also end up being responsible for leaking information discussed within the therapy session. In such cases, the prison counselor has few options as to preventing this type of a violation of confidentiality as inmates cannot be held legally responsible for maintaining such expectations. Naturally, this may discourage other participants of a group from sharing their information as they may fear that their disclosures will get back to the dorm or cell block where they live among other inmates. This is a reality behind counseling within the prison environment.

PROFESSIONAL BOUNDARY SETTING

To ensure that the counseling relationship maintains a sense of upstanding professionalism, certain boundaries must be established and not breeched. Prison counselors must be careful if they use self-disclosure in therapy and must also ensure that the relationships they develop with offender clients do not go beyond the bounds of counselor-client. This can be a particularly serious concern when the counselor and the offender are of opposite gender as offenders can be quite manipulative, engineering a relationship over time, that goes beyond the professional boundaries considered acceptable. Thus, prison counselors who are having problems (i.e., family, marital, financial, or otherwise) must be careful to not let these issues enter into the counselor-client relationship lest they find that they are exploited by the very persons they are attempting to help.

Gift giving is another common boundary issue that can emerge in prisons. It is important that prison counselors not take gifts from inmates, whether expensive or otherwise, as this can be perceived as a scenario where the counselor might be "on the take," or might provide preferential treatment to clients who provide gifts. In fact, many prison counselors find that, over time, offenders in their programs will ask for letters verifying their improvement in programs and/or letters that verify their attendance. Offenders may be tempted to provide gifts to influence the counselor's overall appraisal and/or to build some other rapport to gain an advantage in requesting such services. Prison counselors must be wary of these and other means whereby their sense of ethical boundaries can be tested and potentially breached.

Robert D. Hanser

See also: Correctional Case Management; Correctional Counseling; Inmate Classification; Treatment Professionals in Prisons

Further Reading

American Counseling Association. (2014). *ACA code of ethics.* Retrieved January 27, 2017, from https://www.counseling.org/resources/aca-code-of-ethics.pdf

Hanser, R. D., & Mire, S. M. (2009). *Correctional counseling.* Upper Saddle River, NJ: Pearson/Prentice Hall.

Masters, R. (2004). *Counseling criminal justice offenders* (2nd ed.). Thousand Oaks, CA: Sage.

Evidence-Based Practice in Corrections

The term "evidence-based practice" first emerged in the field of medicine in the 1990s. Since that time, application of this term has expanded to many disciplines that involve client care, including the field of corrections. The term "evidence-based practice" involves making decisions about what treatment strategies to use based on the current body of research on effective practice; practitioner expertise is also considered so that treatment can be individualized to the unique needs of the client. In the field of corrections, effective practices are typically measured by that intervention's success at reducing recidivism (tendency to reoffend). Beginning in the late 1970s, a large body of research emerged related to what works in reducing offender recidivism. This research can be summarized into three core principles of effective intervention—the risk-need-responsivity (R-N-R) principles.

A group of Canadian researchers paved the way for decades of study on the principles of effective intervention, commonly known as R-N-R. These researchers were able to provide research-based guidelines on effective treatment and supervision practices in corrections. Briefly described, the risk principle focuses on who to target for various correctional interventions; the need principle suggests what offender characteristics or needs should be targeted to reduce reoffending; the responsivity principle is the how principle—this principle informs practitioners as to what model is most effective in changing behavior as well as how to address

212   **Evidence-Based Practice in Corrections**

differences in learning styles and barriers to learning that often impede successful completion of supervision or treatment. Adherence to the R-N-R model has been associated with improved program outcomes in both prison and community-based interventions as well as improved management of an inmate population.

RISK PRINCIPLE

The risk principle suggests that intensive correctional treatment and supervision programs target those offenders who are at highest risk of criminal recidivism. The reason for this is that higher risk offenders seem to benefit most from such interventions (via reduced reoffending). Further, research on this principle finds that low-risk offenders do poorly when exposed to intensive correctional treatment and supervision services. The risk principle requires that correctional entities accurately assess the risk level of the offenders being served. Risk assessments examine a series of risk factors associated with criminal offending, such as drug and alcohol use, neighborhood, criminal attitudes and associates, and criminal history. The risk assessment produces a composite risk score that allows offenders to be classified into risk categories—typically high, moderate, or low risk for recidivism.

According to evidence-based practices, the risk level (along with other factors) should be used to determine what type of program or services the offender needs. Intensive correctional programs such as a residential treatment program or, in a prison, a therapeutic community would be reserved for moderate to high-risk offenders. Low-risk offenders would be diverted when appropriate, or would be assigned to nonreporting or low-risk community supervision caseloads.

NEED PRINCIPLE

The need principle asserts that correctional services should target the offender needs that are associated with recidivism. The following eight risk factors consistently emerge in research as being strongly correlated with recidivism: (1) criminal history, (2) antisocial (or procriminal) attitudes, (3) antisocial peers, (4) antisocial personality characteristics, (5) family relationships, (6) substance use, (7) educational achievement and employment, and (8) leisure time. This list includes both static and dynamic risk factors. Static risk factors are those that cannot be changed, such as prior arrests, prior misconduct in an institution, or past drug use. Dynamic risk factors are amenable to change and are also referred to as criminogenic needs. Examples of criminogenic needs include current substance use, unemployment, spending time with antisocial peers, attitudes conducive to law-violating behaviors, poor problem-solving ability or coping skills, and lack of a supportive family.

The need principle stipulates that correctional interventions, from a treatment provider or a parole officer, target criminogenic need areas. This can be witnessed in the topics covered during treatment groups, in treatment or case plans, or in the types of interventions offered by a treatment program or prison. It may be necessary to also target noncriminogenic needs (or needs that are not associated with recidivism), such as mental health issues; however, according to evidence-based practices, when working with a moderate to high-risk offender population, the bulk of treatment and supervision time should be spent addressing criminogenic need areas.

RESPONSITIVITY PRINCIPLE

The final principle of effective interventions is the responsivity principle. The responsivity principle is divided into two areas: specific responsivity and general responsivity. Specific responsivity suggests that offenders come to programs with barriers that can impede the likelihood of that client being successful. Often, these barriers are not criminogenic in nature (i.e., not directly correlated with recidivism) but can impact the likelihood that the client can successfully meet his or her goals. Examples of specific responsivity factors include mental health instability, transportation issues, language barriers, cultural factors, child care issues, victimization histories, and lack of motivation to change. Although these factors alone are not directly linked to increased risk for reoffending (i.e., offenders with mental illness are no more likely to engage in criminal behavior than offenders without mental illness), possessing such barriers could certainly impact an offender's ability to engage in and successfully complete supervision or a treatment program. Beyond barriers, the specific responsivity principle suggests that issues such as gender, culture, and learning styles be considered when matching offenders to services and staff.

The general responsivity principle looks more broadly at what therapeutic model seems to have the greatest impact on decreasing criminal behavior. This principle suggests that behavioral interventions are most effective. This recommendation is made because research indicates that behavioral and cognitive-behavioral models are superior at reducing offender recidivism for a number of justice-involved populations.

APPLICATION IN A PRISON SETTING

Many would argue that prison is not the ideal place to provide treatment. While not ideal, prison is an opportunity to offer services to inmates to help prepare them for reentry to the community. As noted, the risk principle relies on accurate classification of offenders by risk to appropriately match them to services. Many state and federal systems use risk levels to determine eligibility for programming in the prison. Risk for recidivism is also sometimes considered when placing offenders on specialized treatment units, such as in therapeutic communities.

Evidence of the need principle emerges when examining what treatment programs administrators elect to offer within the prison system. Adherence to the need principle is evident when programs target areas such as criminal attitude; substance abuse; social, coping, and emotion-regulation skills; or healthy family relationships. Specialized programs are often offered in prisons, such as sex offender or domestic battery treatment programs.

Finally, the responsivity principle would be assessed by examining how the programs operate—exploring what strategies are used to change offender behavior.

Cognitive-behavioral models would include regular use of role play, thinking reports, and homework to help generalize the skills being used. Likewise, there would be evidence that mental health, victimization concerns, language barriers, medical needs, female-specific necessities, and other barriers are being addressed.

Although offering evidence-based practices in prison can be a challenge, it is an important component of reentry. Following prison programs with a community-based aftercare component tends to produce the best results.

Lori Brusman Lovins

See also: Cognitive-Behavioral Therapies in Prison; Correctional Counseling; Inmate Classification; Prisoner Reentry/Family Integration; Punishment Philosophies; Treatment Professionals in Prisons

Further Reading

Andrews, D. (2006). Enhancing adherence to risk-need-responsivity: Making quality a matter of policy. *Criminology and Public Policy, 5,* 595–602.

Andrews, D., & Bonta, J. (2010). *The Psychology of Criminal Conduct* (5th ed.). Cincinnati: Anderson.

Andrews, D., Zinger, I., Hoge, R., Bonta, J., Gendreau, P., & Cullen, F. (1990). Does correctional treatment work? A clinically relevant and psychologically informed meta-analysis. *Criminology, 28*(3), 369–404.

Burgeon, G., & Armstrong, B. (2005). Transferring the principles of effective intervention into a "real world" prison setting. *Criminal Justice and Behavior, 32*(1), 3–25.

French, S., & Gendreau, P. (2006). Reducing prison misconducts. *Criminal Justice and Behavior, 33*(2), 185–218.

Gendreau, P., French, S., & Gionet, A. (2004). What works (what doesn't work): The principles of effective correctional treatment. *Journal of Community Corrections, 13,* 4–30.

Landenberger, N., & Lipsey, M. (2005). The positive effects of cognitive-behavioral programs for offenders: A meta-analysis of factors associated with effective treatment. *Journal of Experimental Criminology, 1*(4), 451–476.

Lowenkamp, C. T., Latessa, E., & Smith, P. (2006). Does correctional program quality really matter? The impact of adhering to the principles of effective intervention. *Criminology and Public Policy, 5,* 201–220.

Evolving Standards of Decency

"Evolving standards of decency" is a legal framework that is used to judge cases that concern an Eighth Amendment question. The Eighth Amendment, in part, prohibits "cruel and unusual punishment." It also includes an implied proportionality clause that relates to how the sanction lines up with or fits the seriousness of the crime. The evolving standards of decency framework used in Eighth Amendment litigation applies to both the cruel and unusual clause and the proportionality clause. So the question that evolving standards of decency helps to answer in a case is: How is one to judge whether a punishment is proportionate and/or cruel and unusual?

The evolving standards of decency framework was established by the Supreme Court of the United States (SCOTUS) in *Trop v. Dulles* (1958). Chief Justice Earl

Warren in his opinion asserted that the Eighth Amendment must be interpreted on the basis of the "evolving standards of decency that mark the progress of a maturing society." The salient terms in what the chief justice wrote are the word "evolving" and the phrase "progress of a maturing society." Decency, in the context of punishment, may change over time. A case nearly two decades later, *Coker v. Georgia* (1977), provided an impetus that the framework be judged on objective evidence to the extent possible. To date, the objective evidence criterion used to judge evolving standards of decency in a maturing society include a review of current legislative practices across state jurisdictions, trends in decisions of case outcomes, and the views of experts with subject-matter expertise (American Bar Association, 2004). Importantly, the *Coker* decision also established that while objective evidence is important, it cannot "wholly determine" the questions of proportionality and cruel and unusual punishment in cases that invoke the Eighth Amendment.

The evolving standards of decency criterion has been used to resolve a number of Eighth Amendment issues. Most notable, because of how recent the cases are and due to their cultural significance, are the cases that applied the death penalty to either a juvenile or an intellectually challenged offender, and cases that concern application of life without parole (LWOP) sentences to juvenile offenders. The juvenile and mentally challenged offender death penalty cases and the juvenile LWOP cases are used here to illustrate the meaning behind evolving standards of decency because they demonstrate how standards of decency were determined to have changed over time on the question of how mental capacity of the offender relates to appropriateness of very severe forms of punishment.

In a pair of cases from 1988 and 1989 the SCOTUS drew the line of 16 years of age at the time of the offense as the marker to judge the death penalty as applied to a juvenile offender. The case *Thompson v. Oklahoma* (1988) resulted in a ruling that the death penalty used for an offender 15 years old or younger at the time of the offense violates the Eighth Amendment. One year later in *Stanford v. Kentucky* (1989) the court permitted the execution of an offender 16 years of age at the time of the offense. A major distinction between the *Thompson* and *Stanford* case outcomes was that all of the states that specified an age that a person can be considered for the death penalty set the age at 16 or higher, thus there was not strong evidence that execution of a 16-year-old violated a national consensus against it. In the same year as the *Stanford* case, the court in *Penry v. Lynaugh* (1989) ruled that the execution of an intellectually disabled offender does not violate the Eighth Amendment. (The term "retarded" was used in the SCOTUS cases; in 2010, the term "intellectually disabled" was mandated as a replacement term for the federal government.) The court eventually overruled the decisions in *Stanford* and *Penry*. The basis for the changes in direction was the criterion of evolving standards of decency.

In 2002 the SCOTUS was asked to reconsider in *Atkins v. Virginia* whether the death penalty could be carried out in a case where the offender meets the accepted definition of intellectually disabled. The SCOTUS concluded that the sanction of death for intellectually disabled individuals is against the evolving standards of decency and therefore violated the Eighth Amendment. In this instance, the court utilized each of the three elements of the objective criterion to evaluate whether standards of decency had evolved.

The court noted that at the time of the *Penry* decision, 14 states prohibited the death penalty for all offenders and an additional 2 states authorized the death penalty but expressly prohibited it in cases of an intellectually disabled offender. By the time that *Atkins* was decided by the court, an additional 16 states prohibited the sanction for intellectually disabled offenders. Three other states had a bill that would prohibit the sanction for this class of offenders to either pass through both chambers of the state legislature and get vetoed by the governor (Texas) or pass one chamber of the state legislature (Virginia and Nevada). It was not simply that change in state laws had occurred but rather that these changes were considered in conjunction with a clear pattern of consistency in the direction of the changes. The states that had made changes to their statutory provisions since the *Penry* case had consistently altered their laws in the direction of greater protection for the intellectually disabled offender.

Current practices across the states were also a foundational component of the court's decision. At the time of the *Atkins* case, it was exceedingly rare that a person with an IQ (intelligence quotient) below 70 was executed. The majority opinion also relied on the views of subject-matter experts in intellectual functioning and adaptive skills. Intellectual disability reduces one's capacity to process information, communicate, learn from experience, logically reason, control impulses, and understand interpersonal reactions, which, the court reasoned, diminishes personal culpability of the offender. The court's opinion further asserted that owing to diminished capacity of these offenders, the deterrent and retributive functions of the death penalty, if the sanction is applied, are more limited.

Opponents of the juvenile death penalty seized on the opportunity provided by the *Atkins* ruling to ask the court to revisit the constitutionality of the juvenile death penalty. The court in *Roper v. Simmons* (2005) struck down state laws that permitted the death penalty for offenders under the age of 18 at the time of the offense. Similar to the court's opinion in *Atkins*, it applied the objective criterion of the evolving standards of decency framework to juvenile offenders. The court advanced the fact that 30 states had either rejected the death penalty altogether or had prohibited its application to juvenile offenders, and that in the 20 states without a statutory exclusion of juveniles from the reach of the death penalty the sanction was rarely used for juvenile offenders. Consistency of change in the direction of alterations in state law toward greater protection of youth offenders was also noted by the majority opinion. The court additionally delved into the realm of international law in its elaboration of the point that standards had evolved and noted that the United States was the only country in the world with a juvenile death penalty.

In *Roper* the court cited scientific empirical evidence to support its conclusion that there is an emerging consensus among subject-matter experts that there are important differences between adults and juveniles that render juveniles less culpable. Juveniles were described in the opinion as less mature, having an "underdeveloped sense of responsibility," impulsive, more risk-seeking, susceptible to peer pressure, having little control over their environmental conditions, and influenced by personality traits that are more transitory and less fixed. The court extended its argument on the diminished relevance of deterrence and retribution justifications of punishment from *Atkins* to the juvenile death penalty question.

The rationale that the court set forth in both *Atkins* and *Roper* was subsequently extended to two cases that concerned the constitutionality of a life without parole (LWOP) sentence for a juvenile offender. In *Graham v. Florida* (2010) the SCOTUS considered whether an LWOP sentence for a juvenile offender convicted in a nonhomicide case is permissible under the Eighth Amendment. The court ruled that such a sanction is a violation of the Constitution. The majority opinion in this case conducted a similar evolving standards analysis and noted that although there was no clear statutory consensus against LWOP in nonhomicide cases (based on a counting of state codes from what is written in the relevant law), there is a consensus that emerges when one considers the actual practices in the states. At the time there were 123 juvenile offenders serving an LWOP sentence for a nonhomicide offense, but all of these offenders were sentenced in 11 states. Twenty-six of the 39 states did not in practice extend their actual case decision making to what their statutory provisions technically allowed.

Two years later in *Miller v. Alabama* (2012), the court addressed the constitutionality of mandatory LWOP sentences for juvenile offenders convicted of homicide. More importantly, its decision in this case is a firm illustration of the principle from *Coker* that while the objective evolving standards of decency criterion are important, the SCOTUS retains the authority to limit the criterion's determinative power in a case and venture into more subjective aspects in arriving at a decision. Twenty-nine states authorized a mandatory LWOP sentence for offenders in homicide cases. The court illustrated that this fact alone cannot be viewed as determinative of the outcome because it was impossible to determine whether the state legislature actually endorsed mandatory life terms for juveniles in homicide cases. A number of the states permitted the mandatory sanction because they allowed the transfer of certain juveniles into adult court, not due to a state law that specifically endorsed mandatory LWOP sentences for juvenile homicide offenders. The court ruled that mandatory LWOP sentences for juvenile homicide offenders violate the Eighth Amendment.

Kevin G. Buckler and Elizabeth L. Gilmore

See also: Constitution as a Source of Prisoners' Rights, The; Death Penalty Legal Issues; Juveniles in Corrections, Landmark Cases Involving

Further Reading

American Bar Association. (2004, January). *Cruel and unusual punishment: The juvenile death penalty evolving standards of decency.* Washington, DC: Juvenile Justice Center.

Atkins v. Virginia, 536 U.S. 304 (2002).

Coker v. Georgia, 433 U.S. 584 (1977).

Graham v. Florida, 560 U.S. 48 (2010).

Miller v. Alabama, 132 S. Ct. 2455 (2012).

Penry v. Lynaugh, 492 U.S. 302 (1989).

Roper v. Simmons, 543 U.S. 551 (2005).

Stanford v. Kentucky, 492 U.S. 361 (1989).

Thompson v. Oklahoma, 487 U.S. 815 (1988).

Trop v. Dulles, 356 U.S. 86 (1958).

Execution Methods

There are five legal methods of execution available in the United States: lethal injection, electrocution, gas chamber, hanging, and firing squad.

Lethal injection is the primary method of execution in all 31 states that still have capital punishment. Lethal injection is also authorized for use by the U.S. military and federal government. Oklahoma passed the first legislation to permit executions by lethal injection in 1997, but Texas was the first state to utilize this method of execution when Charles Brooks was put to death in 1982. Since that time more than 1,200 people have died by lethal injection.

Most states with lethal injection used a three-drug protocol until the 2010s when some of the drugs were no longer readily available. The drugs are administered intravenously through long tubes that extend from the execution chamber to a separate room where the drugs, executioner or lethal injection machine, and other personnel are located. The condemned inmate is generally strapped to a gurney or table by execution team members before needles are inserted into the inmate's veins. Saline is the first fluid to flow through the tubes and into the condemned. After the saline solution, the first drug, sodium thiopental or sodium pentothal, is administered.

These drugs are very short acting anesthetics that relax the condemned inmate into a state of unconsciousness. The lines are cleared with saline before each new

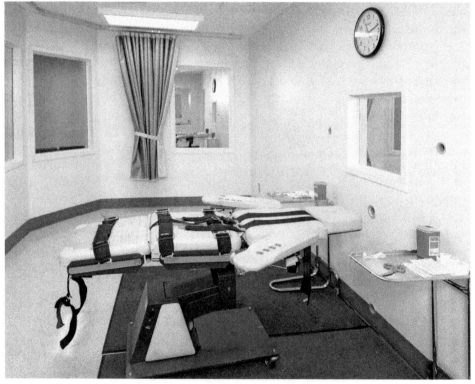

The lethal injection room used for executions at San Quentin State Prison in California. (California Department of Corrections)

drug is administered to ensure that the drugs do not crystallize before entering the inmate's bloodstream. The second drug, pancuronium bromide, paralyzes the inmate's muscle system resulting in the inability to breathe. This is to prevent the condemned inmate's body from moving or convulsing when the third drug, potassium chloride, is administered. Potassium chloride causes cardiac arrest, which stops the heart and results in death.

Lethal injection is not without risk, and botched executions have occurred when needles were not properly inserted, leaked, or became dislodged. If the anesthetic is not properly administered, a condemned inmate could remain conscious but paralyzed when the pancuronium bromide causes cardiac arrest. This would cause the inmate to suffer extreme pain, but the body would be unable to react. Of the 1,054 lethal injection executions conducted before 2011, 75 were reported as botched—the highest botched execution rate of any execution method in the United States.

Electrocution is a permissible form of execution in eight states—Alabama, Arkansas, Florida, Kentucky, Oklahoma, South Carolina, Tennessee, and Virginia—but lethal injection remains the primary method. The Georgia and Nebraska supreme courts have found this method to violate their state constitutions. New York was the first state to use the electric chair when it executed William Kemmler in 1890, and it became the most-used execution method in the 20th century. Since the reintroduction of the death penalty in 1976, 158 people have been executed by electrocution.

Execution by electrocution generally involves shaving the head of the condemned inmate and strapping him or her to a specially built wooden chair. Electrodes are secured to the scalp and forehead of the condemned over a moist, natural sponge. An additional electrode is secured to the inmate's shaved leg. The hair of the head and leg is removed to reduce electricity resistance. The executioner pulls a handle to connect the power supply of the electric chair to administer a series of electric jolts. When the first series of electrical jolts are completed, the body is permitted to cool before it is checked for a heartbeat. If the inmate's heart is still beating, the process will be repeated until death is confirmed.

Electrocution has been described by witnesses as causing the inmate to move violently, defecate, urinate, and vomit blood and drool. Bodies turn red and the flesh swells. Witnesses smell burning flesh while hearing the sound of the electrical current. The body suffers from third-degree burns at the electrode sites, and the brain has been described as appearing cooked. Death by electrocution does not result in immediate death, and botched executions have occurred from its early uses into the modern death penalty age. It has been reported that 84 of the 4,374 electric chair executions between 1890 and 2010 were botched.

The gas chamber is a method of execution available in five states. Arizona, California, Missouri, and Wyoming permit cyanide gas executions, while in 2015 Oklahoma became the first state to authorize the use of nitrogen gas. Oklahoma's law allows the use of nitrogen gas if lethal injection drugs are unavailable or if lethal injection is found to be unconstitutional, but it does not provide information about how such executions would be carried out. Nitrogen gas would cause hypoxia and death from oxygen deprivation. Nevada was the first state to authorize lethal gas as a method of execution and carried out its first execution using cyanide gas in

1924. Officials originally intended to administer lethal gas in the condemned inmate's prison cell without warning while the inmate was sleeping. This idea proved impracticable, though, so the first execution chamber was built. Only 11 people have been executed using the gas chamber since the reintroduction of the death penalty in 1976.

The gas chamber in California is an octagonal, airtight enclosure with windows on all sides so witnesses can view the execution. Condemned inmates have a stethoscope strapped to their chest and are secured to a chair inside the gas chamber. The stethoscope can be accessed by a doctor outside of the chamber to determine if the inmate's heart continues to beat. To cause death, cyanide crystals are released using a lever outside of the chamber into a container of sulphuric acid and distilled water that are stored under the chair in the gas chamber.

When the ingredients are mixed, cyanide gas fumes are released and fill the gas chamber. The inmate dies from oxygen deprivation. The body of the deceased inmate remains in the gas chamber after death while the poison gas is removed and water flushes the gas's residue from the chamber. The body is also sprayed with liquid ammonia to neutralize any remaining gas before workers wearing gas masks and rubber gloves remove the deceased.

Condemned inmates are advised to take deep breaths when the gas is released so they will lose consciousness more quickly and potentially avoid choking, but most hold their breath and struggle. Witnesses have described seeing evidence of horror, pain, and strangling; popping eyes, purpling of skin, and drooling; as well as anxiety. Research indicates that the pain felt by the condemned would be similar to that of a person experiencing a heart attack. Between 1924 and 2010, 32 of the 593 lethal gas executions have been reported as botched. This rate is second to that of lethal injection.

Hanging was technically a legal method of execution in three states—Washington, New Hampshire, and Delaware—until the Delaware Supreme Court found the death penalty to be unconstitutional in August 2016. Delaware dismantled its gallows in 2003, though, because none of the people on death row at that time were eligible to choose execution by hanging, which had been supplanted by lethal injections. Only three people were executed by hanging since the reintroduction of the death penalty in 1976, but hanging accounts for more than 70 percent of all executions in U.S. history.

Execution by hanging requires an approximately 1-inch rope that has been boiled and stretched. The condemned inmate's hands and legs are secured and a noose placed around his or her neck. The executioner releases a trapdoor through which an inmate falls. This is supposed to cause the inmate's neck to break and death to occur. The length of the rope is determined by the weight of the condemned and is tested using a sandbag that is the same weight as the inmate.

Selecting the correct rope length is not an exact science, and selecting the wrong size can have unintended results. An inmate could be decapitated from a rope that is too long and strangled by a rope that is too short. Strangulation causes the person's face to become engorged, tongue to protrude, and eyes to pop. Death is caused by slow oxygen deprivation. It has been reported that 85 of the 2,721 executions by hanging between 1890 and 2010 were botched.

Two states currently allow execution by firing squad. Oklahoma authorizes this method if lethal injection and electrocution are found to be unconstitutional. In 2015, Utah reauthorized firing squad executions if the drugs needed for lethal injection are unavailable. Three people have died from firing squad executions since the death penalty was reinstituted in 1976.

In Utah, execution by firing squad involves securing the condemned inmate to a chair that is surrounded with sandbags. After a black hood is pulled over the head of the condemned, a doctor locates the inmate's heart and marks it as the target. Five shooters stand 20 feet away from the inmate holding .30 caliber rifles. All of the marksmen fire at the target through a slot located in the canvas wall that separates them from the condemned, but one of them has been provided a blank round of ammunition. Death results from blood loss.

Execution by firing squad can be botched if the shooters do not hit the heart, which would cause the condemned to bleed to death more slowly. Only 34 people were executed by firing squad between 1890 and 2010, and none were reported as botched.

Stacy K. Parker

See also: Capital Punishment, Collateral Consequences of; Death Penalty in the Middle East; Death Penalty Legal Issues; Death Row Correctional Officers; Death Row Inmates

Further Reading

Bohm, R. M. (2012). *Deathquest: An introduction to the theory and practice of capital punishment in the United States*. New York: Routledge.

Hillman, H. (1992). The possible pain experienced during executions by different methods. *Perception, 22*(6), 745–753.

Sanburn, J. (2015, April 17). The dawn of a new form of capital punishment. *Time*. Retrieved from http://time.com/3749879/nitrogen-gas-execution-oklahoma-lethal-injection

Sarat, A. (2014). *Gruesome spectacles: Botched executions and America's death penalty*. Palo Alto, CA: Stanford University Press.

Weisburg, J. (1991, July 1). This is your death. *The New Republic*.

Fathers behind Bars

According to the most recent data available, in 2007, an estimated 809,800 prisoners of the approximately 1.5 million held in prisons across the country were parents of minor children. Ninety-two percent of these parents were fathers. Despite the fact that there are substantially more incarcerated fathers than mothers, the majority of the research on parenting in prison has focused on mothers. Partly responsible for this trend is the widespread belief that the mother-child bond is stronger, and thus, more important, than the father-child relationship as well as the fact that mothers are more likely to be living with their minor children prior to incarceration than fathers. In recent years, however, there has been an increasing interest in incarcerated fathers. As a result of this growing interest, researchers, nonprofit groups, and prison administrators alike have been working toward developing and implementing programs designed to provide support for incarcerated fathers and their children.

The most recent national data available on incarcerated fathers come from personal interviews with prisoners who participated in the Bureau of Justice Statistics' 2004 Survey of Inmates in State and Federal Correctional Facilities (SISFCF). As noted above, in 2007, approximately 53 percent of inmates held in prisons across the United States indicated being parents of minor children. In total, these inmates reported having approximately 1.7 million children, representing 2.3 percent of minor children in the United States. These numbers have been steadily increasing since 1991, though the rate of growth has decreased. Fathers represent the majority of incarcerated parents, reportedly having 1.5 million minor children. Minorities represent the largest category of incarcerated fathers, with more than 40 percent being black and approximately 20 percent being Hispanic. In regard to age, incarcerated fathers tend to be relatively young with 63 percent of fathers in state facilities and 74 percent in federal facilities being between the age of 25 and 34.

In order for incarcerated fathers to continue to play an active role in their child(ren)'s lives, they must be allowed to have contact. In prisons, there are typically three ways to contact outsiders—through telephone, mail, and personal visits. According to data from the 2004 SISFCF, mail is the most common way to maintain contact in state facilities, with approximately 50 percent indicating that they received mail at least once a month from their minor children. Telephone use is much less common, however, with only 37 percent indicating at least monthly phone calls with their children. Interestingly, 47 percent of fathers in state facilities indicated never talking on the phone with their minor children. In contrast, in federal facilities telephone use is the main form of contact, with almost 75 percent indicating talking on the phone with their children at least once a month.

An inmate spends quality time with his children during a family visit at the Kit Carson Correctional Center in Burlington, Colorado. (Joe Amon/The Denver Post via Getty Images)

Mail contact was used less frequently but was still relatively common with approximately 65 percent indicating having mail contact with their children at least once a month. In both federal and state facilities, personal visits were less common. In state facilities, only 18 percent of fathers reported having personal visits with their minor children at least once a month. Almost 60 percent of fathers in state prisons reported never having a personal visit from their minor children. In federal facilities, the numbers are relatively similar with 19 percent of fathers indicating at least monthly visits and 45 percent of inmates reporting never having a personal visit.

Numerous factors have been found to play a role in the amount of contact between a child and their incarcerated father including distance, limited financial resources, level of preprison involvement with the child, relationship with current guardian, and institutional policies and procedures.

Distance is one factor that has been attributed to limiting the number of personal visits between a father and their minor child(ren). Often, incarcerated fathers are held in facilities more than 100 miles from their last residential location, making it difficult for minor children to visit on a regular basis. In a study conducted in 2010 by the Department of Health and Human Services, distance was reported to be the top barrier to contact by incarcerated fathers. Limited financial resources also limit father-child contact. Prior to incarceration, many prisoners lived in impoverished conditions. Further, in many cases, incarcerated fathers were the financial providers for their minor children. Thus, upon incarceration, their families took a financial hit, decreasing their ability to be able to afford phone calls or in-person visits. Another factor found to play a role in the likelihood of child contact is the level of preprison involvement.

Research has found that contact between the incarcerated father and his minor child is more likely when the child lived with the father prior to incarceration. Similarly, research has found that father-child contact is contingent on the father's relationship with the current guardian. Many incarcerated fathers report the caregiver of the child, often the mother, engaging in gatekeeping, or attempting to restrict the father from seeing the child. However, fathers indicate that if the child's mother has a favorable attitude toward them, then it is more likely that mothers will help to maintain the father-child relationship.

Lastly, institutional policies and procedures represent an additional barrier to father-child contact. Often, prison systems schedule visiting hours only on the weekends and only for a few hours. This may limit the feasibility of children visiting their fathers. Additionally, many prisons only allow limited contact visits in which minimal physical contact is allowed between the father and the child. Further, the visitation process itself may be a barrier. Often, fathers are forced to visit with their children in large, crowded, and loud open visiting areas. Many times these facilities lack adequate seating, bathrooms, healthy food in vending machines, and toys and activities for children. It has also been noted that prison staff often treat the visitors poorly. These unpleasant experiences often lead to incarcerated fathers and/or current caregivers being hesitant to bring the child(ren) for visitation.

Recent research has found father-child contact to be beneficial for both the incarcerated father and the child. Specifically, it has been found that children who continue to have a close relationship with their incarcerated father are less likely to engage in delinquent behavior. Additionally, fathers have been found to exhibit better behavior while incarcerated as well as have a reduced likelihood of reoffending once released. Recognizing the benefits of maintaining father-child contact, several programs have been developed and implemented in facilities across the country aimed at encouraging and strengthening father-child bonds. Most prisons provide parenting education courses that focus on a range of topics including, but not limited to, parenting skills, child development, problem solving, nonviolent discipline, and legal issues. These courses are often facilitated by either prison staff, nonprofit groups, or even inmates. Parenting Inside Out is one example of an evidence-based parenting program that has been implemented in a number of prison facilities. Additional programs have also been implemented in prisons across the country. One program entitled the Storybook Project allows incarcerated parents to record themselves reading a children's book. The recording and the book are then sent to the incarcerated parents' child to enjoy. Similar programs like this exist nationwide. Other programs take the idea of reading to children one step further and have the children visit the facility to read with their incarcerated parent. One such program is Reading Unites Families. Other programs/policies that have been implemented include allowing contact visits, providing transportation to prison facilities, and hosting Father's Day celebrations.

Fathering behind bars is not an easy task and has been found to have negative effects on both the father and the child. With the increased focus on parents behind bars, particularly fathers, there is hope that programs and policies will continue to be put in place to reduce the negative impact of parental incarceration. However, more research needs to be conducted.

Riane M. Bolin

See also: Inside-Outside Relationships; Pains of Imprisonment; Pregnancy and Motherhood in Prisons; Prisoner Reentry/Family Integration; Sentencing of Mothers and Parental Rights; Visitation

Further Reading

Arditti, J. A., Smock, S. A., & Parkman, T. S. (2005). "It's been hard to be a father": A qualitative exploration of incarcerated fatherhood. *Fathering: A Journal of Theory, Research, and Practice about Men as Fathers, 3*(3), 267–288.

Dallaire, D. H. (2007). Incarcerated mothers and fathers: A comparison of risks for children and families. *Family Relations, 56*(5), 440–453.

Glaze, L. E., & Maruschak, L.M. (2008). *Parents in prison and their minor children.* Washington, DC: U.S. Department of Justice.

Jeffries, J. M., Menghraj, S., & Hairston, C. F. (2001). *Serving incarcerated and ex-offender fathers and their families: A review of the field.* Washington, DC: Vera Institute of Justice.

LaRosa, J. J., & Rank, M. G. (2001). Parenting education and incarcerated fathers. *Journal of Family Social Work, 6*(3), 15–33.

Lee, C., Sansone, F. A., Swanson, C., & Tatum, K. M. (2012). Incarcerated fathers and parenting: Importance of the relationship with their children. *Social Work in Public Health, 27*(1/2), 165–186.

Magaletta, P. R., & D. P. Herbst. (2001). Fathering from prison: Common struggles and successful solutions. *Psychotherapy: Theory/Research/Practice/Training, 38*(1), 88–96.

Pierce, M. B. (2015). Male inmate perceptions of the visitation experience. *Prison Journal, 95*(3), 370–396.

Roy, K. M., & Dyson, O.L. (2005). Gatekeeping in context: Babymama drama and the involvement of incarcerated fathers. *Fathering: A Journal of Theory, Research, and Practice about Men as Fathers, 3*(3), 289–310.

Swanson, C., Lee, C., Sansone, F. A., & Tatum, K. M. (2013). Incarcerated fathers and their children: Perceptions of barriers to their relationships. *The Prison Journal, 93*(4), 453–474.

Federal Sentencing Guidelines

The Sentencing Reform Act was passed in 1984, shifting responsibility for federal sentencing policies from Congress to the U.S. Sentencing Commission. The crowning achievement of the commission has been the promulgation of the federal sentencing guidelines, a set of instructions that serve as a reference for judges when providing sentences. The purpose of these guidelines was to standardize the types and nature of sentences for similar charges, reducing disparities that arose from such extralegal factors as the preferences of a federal circuit or a judge's personality.

The guidelines further sought to provide truth in sentencing. Heretofore, it was possible for a convicted offender, sentenced to 10 years of imprisonment, to remain incarcerated for the entire term or for 4 years and paroled for 6, dependent merely on the whim of the Parole Commission. The guidelines abolished parole and required that those convicted actually served the sentences they were given.

Though the intention of the guidelines was to create equal and honest sentencing through standardization, they were criticized for giving too much power to prosecutors through sentence bargaining, hindering judges' discretion in sentence determination, and conflicting with the role of mandatory minimums. Moreover, the guidelines created tension between trial and appellate courts. Trial courts hold the power to issue initial sentences according to the guidelines, but appellate courts might overturn those sentences because of differences in interpretation. Variant interpretation of the guidelines detracted from their purpose by creating a new cause of disparity.

In 2005, the U.S. Supreme Court took up *United States v. Booker*, a consolidated case concerning whether sentence enhancements based on facts not presented to a jury violated the Sixth Amendment to the Constitution. The court held that enhancement of sentences solely based on judicial discretion is a violation of the Sixth Amendment. However, the court went beyond that. In its opinion, the court also declared the guidelines advisory, as opposed to mandatory.

Nevertheless, most judges continue to rely on the guidelines today, giving them the same effect as if they were still mandatory. Due to this, some have criticized the import of the *Booker* case. In response, several recommendations have been made to address ongoing issues with the guidelines. The doctrine of alternate variance sentences, established by the Fourth Circuit Court in *United States v. Savillon-Matute* (2011), holds that, if the guidelines did not influence a trial court judge's ultimate decision on a sentence, appellate courts cannot override a decision made by the trial court based on error in interpreting the guidelines. Instead, in such cases, the courts of appeal can only reverse a sentence if it is unreasonable. A second doctrine—strict textualism—would read the guidelines in such a strict manner as to greatly diminish judicial manipulation by interpretation, eliminating the likelihood of interpretive disputes. Finally, repealing mandatory minimums, which tend to conflict with the sentences that the commission proposes, would do much to enhance the effectiveness of the commission.

The goal of fairness in sentencing is a laudable one. Nevertheless, however praiseworthy the goal, the nation's continued experiment with federal sentencing guidelines demonstrates the complexity in approximating a precise formula for justice.

Naomi Gulama and Kwan-Lamar Blount-Hill

See also: Determinate versus Indeterminate Sentencing; Sentencing Disparities and Discrimination in Sentencing; Truth in Sentencing

Further Reading

Bowman, F. O. (2014). Dead law walking: The surprising tenacity of the federal sentencing guidelines. *Houston Law Review, 51,* 1227–1270.

Breyer, S. (1999). Federal sentencing guidelines revisited. *Federal Sentencing Reporter, 11*(4), 180–186.

Edwards, E. (2017). Eliminating circuit-split disparities in federal sentencing under the post-*Booker* guidelines. *Indiana Law Journal, 92*, 817–844.

Harlow, J. W. (2015). Does the calculation matter? The federal sentencing guidelines and the doctrine of alternative variance sentences. *South Carolina Law Review, 66*, 987–1009.

United States v. Booker, 543 U.S. 220 (2005).

United States v. Savillon-Matute, 636 F.3d 119 (4th Cir. 2011).

Florence ADX

Often referred to as "the terrorist's lockup," Florence ADX is located in Colorado and is often considered the United States' toughest prison. Nicknamed the "Alcatraz of the Rockies," Florence ADX began operating in 1994. In order to build the prison, more than 600 acres of property were donated to the federal government for the construction of the federal correctional complex. This includes a minimum security federal correctional camp, a medium security federal correctional institution, as well as a high-security institution that features both detention and general population units. The administrative security max (ADX) institution houses inmates deemed extremely dangerous, prone to escape, those with possible terrorist links, high-level gang members, and those requiring the highest security measures possible. Although there are supermax prisons all over the country, Florence ADX is considered to be among the most extreme within the United States.

Supermax prisons have been utilized since the 1980s when a series of tough criminal penalties (such as the three-strikes laws) were implemented. The first supermax prison was constructed in Marion County, Illinois. Increased popularity has brought about more than 45 supermax prisons housing more than 25,000 of the United States' inmates. The practice of solitary confinement and lack of recreation time has been seen to severely affect inmates, including inmates inflicting self-harm or even death. Due to the severe mental impact of solitary confinement, the practice has been brought into question, and some have challenged it based on the Eighth Amendment prohibition from cruel or unusual punishment. Solitary confinement follows the Pennsylvania model, based on Pennsylvania's system of the early 1800s that approached incarceration as a time for solitude and seeking penance. Many inmates who have been in solitary confinement have increased episodes of mental breakdowns that include self-harm, suicides, and suicide attempts.

As with a typical supermax facility design, inmates at Florence ADX are held in solitary confinement for 23 hours a day. Florence ADX features 7×12 feet cells outfitted with a concrete bed and a small window that illuminates the cell, but the window is deliberately built too high for the inmate to view outside. A lack of contact from the outside world creates an environment of complete isolation. Inmates housed in Florence ADX's solitary confinement are allowed two 15-minute phone calls per month and visits only from immediate family and legal counsel. Visitation with family occurs using a thick sheet of plexiglass between the inmate and the visitor and communication through a telephone system. Inmates in the general population of Florence USP have the opportunity to utilize the "step-down" program, a program designed to reward good behavior with more privileges. These

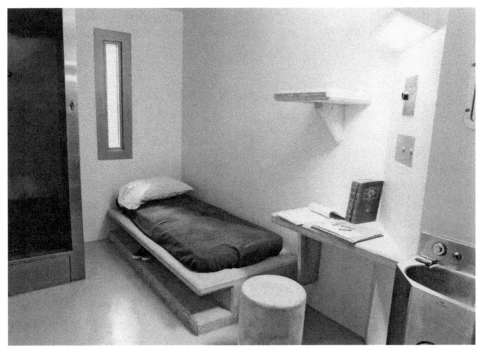

The ADX (administrative maximum) Supermax Prison in Florence, Colorado, is a state-of-the-art isolation prison for repeat and high-profile felony offenders. (Lizzie Himmel/Sygma via Getty Images)

inmates have the privilege of a small black-and-white television featuring educational and religious programming, increased phone calls, 10 hours of recreation time weekly, and the opportunity to work in the prison conducting cleaning tasks.

Although some inmates incarcerated at Florence ADX do have high-profile cases with ample amounts of media coverage, 95 percent of the inmates at ADX Florence are transfers from other prisons. These inmates may have been convicted of serious crimes while incarcerated that may include the murder of another inmate or correctional officer, multiple assaults on other inmates in a short period of time, known gang leadership positions, or an inmate may have made an escape attempt. Some inmates incarcerated at Florence ADX include Zacarias Moussaoui, the conspirator behind the September 11 attacks; Terry Nichols, one of the Oklahoma City bombers; Michael Swango, a doctor who murdered more than 60 of his patients; Richard Reid, the "shoe bomber"; and Dzhokhar Tsarnaev, one of the Boston bombers. In the instance of Tsarnaev, Florence ADX is currently incarcerating him until his execution is set. Once an execution date is set, Tsarnaev will be transferred to a federal prison in Terre Haute, Indiana, the prison that holds the federal government's death row inmates. There he will be executed by lethal injection.

Controversial issues at Florence ADX include the practice of solitary confinement. Perhaps due to complete isolation and harsh conditions of Florence ADX, a number of inmates have attempted or committed suicide. Additionally, many inmates engage in self-harm such as cutting, tattooing, and consuming their feces.

One inmate, Jack Powers, cut off his earlobe and a testicle, and committed numerous other acts of self-harm. Another inmate, David Shelby, ate his own finger.

Several lawsuits have been brought against supermax prisons, in general asserting inmates' Eighth Amendment right, which grants freedom from cruel and unusual punishment, as well as lawsuits alleging that inmates' mental health needs have been neglected through the denial of psychotropic medications. In 2012, an Illinois senator hosted a congressional hearing regarding the use of solitary confinement at Florence ADX. Joining him was a psychologist, Dr. Craig Haney, who found that about half of the prisoners were suffering from a mental illness. Another psychologist estimated that up to 70 percent of the prisoners at Florence ADX were suffering from at least one serious mental illness. Additionally, it was discovered that most of the patients had been taken off their medications and denied specialized treatment. Eventually, a federal magistrate oversaw a settlement, and implementations of additional psychiatrists and mental health programming became available to inmates at Florence ADX.

Lisa M. Carter and Kaitlin M. Hearthstone-Leroux

See also: Maximum Security; Solitary Confinement

Further Reading

Binelli, M. (2015, March 28). *Inside America's toughest federal prison.* Retrieved August 24, 2016, from http://www.nytimes.com/2015/03/29/magazine/inside-americas-toughest-federal-prison.html?_r=0

Pilkington, E. (2012). *ADX Florence supermax prison: The Alcatraz of the Rockies.* Retrieved August 24, 2016, from https://www.theguardian.com/world/2012/apr/10/abu-hamza-isolation-supermax-prison

Tsarnaev arrives at Colorado prison. (2015). Retrieved August 24, 2016, from http://edition.cnn.com/2015/06/25/us/tsarnaev-prison-colorado

What's life like in Supermax prison? (2015). Retrieved August 24, 2016, from http://www.cnn.com/2015/06/25/us/dzhokhar-tsarnaev-supermax-prison/index.html

Folsom State Prison

Folsom State Prison (FSP) is a state-operated corrections facility under the administration of the California Department of Corrections and Rehabilitation. One of numerous 19th-century U.S. prison environments still in operation, the prison exists as a representation of the rich history of American corrections.

The facility, located within the city of Folsom, California, is the state's second oldest prison environment. Folsom State Prison was initially opened as one of the country's first maximum security prisons and is widely known for its harsh conditions in the decades following the California gold rush. The facility was conceived in 1858 as the answer to the overcrowding problems occurring at the state's first prison, San Quentin. Construction of the facility began in 1878 on the site of the Stony Bar mining camp along the American River. The site of the facility was carefully selected based on its close proximity to the river and to vast deposits of granite that could be quarried to complete the prison's construction.

Folsom State Prison is a California state prison located 20 miles northeast of the state capital of Sacramento. It is one of America's most famous penal institutions, thanks to a song of that name performed by country singer Johnny Cash. Opened in 1880, Folsom is the second-oldest prison in the state and was the first in the country to have electricity. (Library of Congress)

In July 1880, Folsom prison recorded receipt of its first 44 prisoners. The original facility opened with a capacity of 1,800 inmates. The early facility, which lacked any electricity and plumbing, housed prisoners behind solid boiler plates in stone cells measuring 4 by 8 feet (1.2 by 2.4 meters) with 6-inch (15-centimeter) eye slots. In 1884, plumbing was installed at the facility. In 1890, Folsom prison began construction of a hydroelectric power house and in 1893 became the first prison in the nation to have electric power. For the first 40 years of its operation, Folsom lacked an outer perimeter wall due to limited construction funding. Referred to as the "prison without walls," the institution maintained perimeter security by means of six armed gun towers positioned outside of the prison buildings. In 1907, work began on the granite walls that would surround the prison. It would take more than four decades for the prison to be surrounded by solid walls, being brought to the final stage of completion in 1923. In 1916, prisoners completed the construction of an additional housing unit. The unit, documented as the largest single-cell housing unit in the nation, has a capacity of nearly 1,200 inmates on four five-tiered sections. Presently, the facility operates five housing units within the secure perimeter, including the original two-tiered structure. Prison facilities also include two dining halls, a large central prison exercise yard, and two smaller exercise yards.

Operations at Folsom prison throughout its early operation reflected primitive living conditions. Inmates were managed through the use of corporal punishments and solitary confinement. Social events, including an annual Fourth of July picnic, were held, which invited members of the community to visit the institution and be spectators to numerous inmate athletic events and theatrical presentations. Folsom State Prison was one of two state prison locations in California to administer the death sentence after the state took sole control of the death penalty in 1891. The method of execution at FSP was hanging. Between 1895 and December 1937, a total of 93 prisoners were hanged at Folsom. Following its final execution in 1937, the use of the gas chamber at San Quentin State Prison was established as the state's location for the administration of the sentence of death.

The use of inmate labor was fundamental to both the initial construction of FSP and the ongoing operation of the institution. The prison completed construction of an ice plant in 1894 and a rock crushing plant in 1895. The quarry at FSP provided granite for the foundation of the state capitol building and much of the gravel used in the early construction of California's roads. Folsom prison ultimately established itself as a model for prison industry. Contemporary translations of prison industry at Folsom prison include metal fabrication and a print shop, as well as the manufacturing of California's vehicle license plates.

Although opened as a maximum security institution, Folsom State Prison now primarily houses medium security general population inmates. Folsom also houses minimum security inmates within a minimum security facility located just outside of the main security perimeter. In 2013, the administration of Folsom State Prison activated Folsom Women's Facility (FWF), a 523-bed stand-alone unit that provides housing, rehabilitative and reentry programming, substance abuse treatment, and job training to the medium and minimum security female population.

The prison has housed some of the most notorious criminals in California, including convicted murderer Charles Manson and mafia kingpin "Little Pete" Fong Ching. Folsom has also been home to numerous celebrities, including actor Danny Trejo and record producer Marion "Suge" Knight. The most infamous celebrity visitor of Folsom prison was Johnny Cash. Cash performed numerous concerts at the prison, the most notable being his January 1968 concert. This concert recording was later translated into one of his most popular albums, *At Folsom Prison*.

Folsom State Prison has long stood as an example of the unique and ever-changing manner in which inmates are held and supervised in the United States. The application of the antiquated environment to contemporary corrections practice further illustrates the progressive nature of American corrections practice.

Katrina Cathcart

See also: Maximum Security; Prisons, History of

Further Reading

Ardaiz, J. (2012). *Hands through stone: How Clarence Ray Allen masterminded murder from behind Folsom's prison walls.* Fresno, CA: Linden.

Beley, G. (2005). Folsom prison blues. *Virginia Quarterly Review, 81*(1), 218–227.

Bradley, M. (2015). *Dirty tears: An anthology of Folsom prison writings*. CreateSpace Independent Publishing Platform.

Brown, J. (2008). *Folsom Prison*. San Francisco, CA: Arcadia.

Ginoza, M., Ruano, R., Woodford, J., & Butler, D. (2003). Renovating historic structures: Seismic retrofits at Folsom and San Quentin state prisons. *Corrections Today, 65*(4), 78–117.

Moore, A. (2013). *Folsom's 93: The lives and crimes of Folsom prison's executed men*. Fresno, CA: Linden.

Streissguth, M. (2005). *Johnny Cash at Folsom prison: The making of a masterpiece*. Cambridge, MA: De Capo Press.

France, Prisons in

The French prison system has a long and storied past that has evolved and developed through some of the world's most tumultuous historical periods. Given its lengthy history, it is perhaps not surprising that the French prison system has undergone a series of dramatic and substantive changes since its inception. Some of the world's most recognized and infamous penal institutions have been located within France itself or within its many territories. Throughout its history, the French prison system has reflected the larger social, economic, and political events and concerns of the national culture in which it is immersed. To a certain extent then the history of France is intertwined with the advent, growth, and development of its prison system and its prison institutions. Perhaps even more significantly, many of the most significant developments in Western European history are further mirrored in the institutions and practices of the French penal system. The French correctional system shares a number of important commonalities with its Western European and North American counterparts. However, it is also characterized by its own unique features and characteristics that serve to differentiate it from the correctional systems of other countries around the globe. Today, the French penal system continues to grow and develop in a manner conducive to meeting the many changing needs of the nation that it serves.

The current French prison system has its earliest roots in the 13th century, although it did not develop into a more recognizable version of its current self until sometime later. Originally, the system was intended to both house and punish criminal offenders and those who opposed the ruling class. Later, additional prisons were constructed to accommodate still more offenders and to accommodate prisoners of war and revolutionaries who advocated casting aside the existing French state. The conditions within these early prisons were frequently atrocious by contemporary standards and the harsh physical punishments quite brutal.

In spite of this, a number of French penal institutions have secured prominent places in the historical imagination of contemporary society. For instance, due to extensive media portrayals, Devil's Island remains one of the most prominently known penal colonies in the history of the world. This particular penal institution is representative of the French correctional system's historical tendency to rely on inmate transportation as one means of removing individuals that were viewed as being dangerous or undesirable from French society. Another prominent example is the Bastille, which remains one of history's most iconic prisons long after its destruction as a result of some of the prisoners it held and the important role that it played in the development of Western Europe with regard to the French Revolution.

Today the French prison system has transformed itself in response to contemporary changes in the standards that are associated with modern penal design and current correctional practice. Change has also come to the French penal system in the form of the increasing size of the correctional population. This population in the French penal system has continued to grow over time as has the scope of systemic responsibility resulting from a more diverse set of public expectations. In response to changes of this nature, a variety of different types of penal institutions have developed within the French correctional system. Each of these different types of correctional institutions fills a niche within the larger penal system, is thought to contribute to the achievement of France's overriding correctional goals and objectives, and houses a different classification of inmates. The *maison d'arrêt* is a correctional facility that might best be thought of as the rough equivalent of a North American jail. These institutions house offenders awaiting legal processing, those being transferred to other penal institutions better able to serve their needs, and convicted offenders who are in the process of serving relatively short correctional sentences. The *maison centrale* is a type of correctional facility that houses France's more dangerous offenders and others that have been convicted and are serving longer sentences. These types of institutions would be roughly comparable to an American prison. A French *centre de détention* houses a variety of different types of offenders who are collectively believed to be amenable to treatment and capable of successfully reintegrating back into larger society at some point in the future. Finally, the *centre de semi-liberté* is a type of correctional institution that is similar in many respects to a work release or transitional housing center in that they provide offenders with an opportunity to continue their educational pursuits or maintain employment while still under correctional monitoring or supervision.

The vast majority of correctional inmates housed within the French prison system are adult males. However, this does not mean that women and juveniles are completely absent. Juvenile offenders can be incarcerated in institutions commonly referred to as *éstablissement pénitentiaire pour mineurs*. The comparatively small numbers of female and juvenile inmates are likely a reflection of the fact that the French justice system tends to use imprisonment as a last resort with these populations.

One of the major contemporary challenges facing the French prison system has to do with the changing nature of its inmate population in part as a result of the global fight against terrorism. France has experienced a number of significant terrorist attacks within the last several decades. These attacks have resulted in enhanced efforts to target individuals thought to be associated with extremist organizations that might sanction or support terrorism. At least some of the recent increases in the French inmate population have occurred as part of efforts to target individuals associated with terrorist organizations. Accompanying changes in the nature and makeup of the French prison population have undermined traditional ideals and practices that previously characterized its penal system.

At the same time that changing prison populations have underscored the need for a revised understanding of the mission and purpose of the French prison system, the recent terrorist attacks have resulted in both increased public awareness and additional scrutiny of the French prison system resulting in increased calls for both enhanced responsibility and greater transparency.

In addition to the evolving nature of its inmate population, French correctional officials have found themselves confronting an increasingly crowded and more violent penal culture. Although the French prison system remains much less crowded than its American counterpart, the number of inmates that it incarcerates has been steadily growing during the course of the past several decades. As a result, French prisons have become both more crowded and more dangerous for both the inmates that reside in them and the staff that operate them.

Violence of both an individual and communal nature has become increasingly common, creating a growing challenge that will likely not be easy for system officials to quickly ameliorate. Moving forward, the correctional institutions of France will have to search for more effective ways of managing larger numbers of increasingly violent inmates that are substantively different than those that they have traditionally incarcerated. The success of the system in this regard will likely influence both its reputation among the public and the professional perceptions regarding its efficacy in relation to its ability to achieve its systemic objectives. Given the complexity of the tasks before it, the French prison system will certainly face a challenging future that must be undertaken with no small amount of understanding and respect for its roots along with critical reflection and optimism regarding its future.

Jason R. Jolicoeur

See also: Incarceration Rates in the United States Compared to Other Countries; Inmate Classification; Inmates, Transportation of; Prisons, History of; Violence in Prison

Further Reading

Beken, T.V. (2016). *The role of prison in Europe: Traveling in the footsteps of John Howard.* London: Palgrave MacMillan.

Berneman, C. (2013). A French perspective on culture in prison. *The Journal of Arts Management, Law, and Society, 43*(4), 191–202.

Chantraine, G. (2009). French prisons of yesteryear and today: Two conflicting modernities: A socio-historical view. *Punishment and Society, 12*(1), 27–46.

Cliquennois, G. (2013). Which penology for decision making in French prisons? *Punishment and Society, 15*(5), 468–487.

Kazemian, L., & Andersson, C. (1987). *The French prison system: Comparative insights for policy and practice in New York and the United States.* New York: Research and Evaluation Center, John Jay College of Criminal Justice, City University New York.

Mandhouj, O., Aubin, H.J., Amirouche, A., Perroud, N. A., & Huguelet, P. (2014). Spirituality and religion among French prisoners: An effective coping resource? *International Journal of Offender Therapy and Comparative Criminology, 58*(7), 821–834.

Milhaud, O., & Moran, D. (2013). Penal space and privacy in French and Russian prisons. In D. Moran, N. Gill, & D. Conlon (Eds.), *Carceral spaces: Mobility and agency in imprisonment and migrant detention* (pp. 167–182). New York: Ashgate.

Miras, A. (2010). Interpersonal inmate violence in French prisons: Results of the TAR-TARE survey. *Injury Prevention, 12*(1), 27–46.

O'Brien, P. (1982). *The promise of punishment: Prisons in 19th century France.* Princeton, NJ: Princeton University Press.

Simon, R. J., & De Wall, C. A. (2009). *Prisons the world over.* Lanham, MD: Lexington Books.

Furloughs

A furlough is a prison program that permits a low-risk prisoner's temporary leave from the correctional institution for emergency, educational, or work purposes. Furloughs have also been referred to as temporary release, day release, or work release, and have been widely used by prisons since the 1960s. While a prison official authorizes the prescribed amount of time of release into the community on a furlough, furloughs are statutory measures that allow the inmate an unsupervised leave from the prison for specific purposes. A furlough is essentially a type of prison release program active in most states, the District of Columbia, and the federal system. Furloughs typically range from several hours during weekdays to a period of a few days. Not all prisoners are eligible for furloughs, and correctional authorities establish written policies that delineate eligibility requirements, furlough types, and release procedures. These policies are developed in accordance with the law. A common correctional goal with a furlough program is to assist the inmate with reintegration into the community. Research shows that by slowly being reintegrated into the community, prisoners are better able to adjust to society when they are released from the institution.

Home visits are one type of furlough that has been permitted by institutions for many years. These types of visits permit inmates to maintain relationships with family members and strengthen the ties between inmates and the family. Inmates with strong relationships with family members may be less likely to return to prison once released. Home visits may also benefit the family of those incarcerated who seek to maintain close relationships. However, home visits can be challenging for some inmates who may not be prepared for the emotional or structural changes that may have occurred within the family, or the distress of having to return to the facility at the end of the furlough. But the most common reason for a home furlough is an emergency crisis. An eligible inmate may be granted a furlough to attend the family member's funeral services or visit the critically ill family member. Likewise, furloughs have been granted to ailing inmates to receive medical treatment. These furloughs are time-limited and may be further restricted based on distance from the prison facility or other aspects of correctional policy.

Furloughs for educational purposes may also be part of an agency's correctional policy. Although much of the educational programming is provided directly in the prison facility, some inmates may be permitted to temporarily leave the institution to attend high school, vocational/technical-related training, or college classes during day hours. The prisoner then returns to the prison facility or other site at night. This type of furlough expands the educational options to a much greater variety of training and course work not available in a correctional facility. Although the number of inmates participating in an educational furlough tends to be smaller than other types of furloughs, evaluations show that inmates tend to be successful in these programs. However, with small numbers participating in educational furloughs, prisons are still challenged by the numbers of undereducated persons in custody. But this furlough is similar to one that may be granted for work-related reasons.

In a work furlough, an offender close to his or her release from prison may be able to temporarily leave the prison to seek employment or perform other tasks necessary for reentry into the community once released from corrections. As a result, prospective employers are an important component of work furloughs. Correctional administrators work collaboratively with community businesses and other professionals to identify employment opportunities. Although inmates may have assistance from prison officials in seeking employment, they also use typical methods of want ads and personal contacts to help in locating employment opportunities. In some cases, potential employers are apprehensive of hiring convicts as they are deemed more of a risk to the community. Inmates may even receive negative attention from community residents. However, research indicates that many community members, particularly employers, want to learn more about furlough programs and have expressed readiness to hire those who are participating in a furlough program. Some inmates may utilize the furlough program to work in the community. Such employment could permit establishing a work history, or contributing to child support or victim restitution. Furloughs have also been used for participating in civic, religious, and social activities that facilitate a positive transition to the community. Thus, furloughs are one mechanism to achieve common correctional goals.

In both federal and state prisons, eligibility for furloughs depends on a number of factors, and an inmate generally makes an application for a furlough. Inmates typically become eligible for furloughs when they are nearing time that they may be eligible for release through the parole process. Security classification is also a factor, as inmates that may pose a danger to the community are not eligible for a furlough. Prison officials may evaluate an inmate's criminal history, escape history, as well as the inmate's behavior while incarcerated to help determine suitability for a temporary release. Inmates with a history of violent behavior are usually not permitted to participate in a furlough program. Many state prison officials also consider the views of victims of crime as well as law enforcement personnel when considering an inmate for furlough participation. The drawback to furlough programs is obvious, as the program does present some degree of risk to the local community. When furloughs are revoked, it is more likely to be for rule violations, such as the failure to return to the facility or site at the designated time. Revocations also occur for drug and alcohol violations, as well as the commission of a new criminal offense.

The effectiveness of furlough programs has been empirically measured through analysis of the recidivism rates of participants. This includes measurement of the rearrest, reconviction, or reincarceration in the future, or by comparing these measures for inmates who have received a furlough to similar inmates who did not receive a furlough. Thus, recidivism rates can provide a measure of rehabilitation of offenders, since effective rehabilitation is linked to the lack of future involvement in the criminal justice system. Recent research studies indicate that furlough programs may be an effective tool in rehabilitating inmates. For example, a study of inmates who were granted temporary release from prison for vocational purposes and home visits indicated that in both types of furloughs the inmates were significantly less likely to return to prison. In another study, researchers found that work release programs were effective in improving postrelease employment skills as well as achieving reductions in recidivism. Researchers caution that furlough programs should not be viewed in isolation as inmates earn furloughs through time and through a series of events, such as maintaining good behavior while incarcerated and earning the trust of prison officials. When correctional officials decide to temporarily release an inmate into the community, it indicates a measure of confidence in the inmates, which can be viewed positively by the inmate's family and some community members. However, when furlough programs are viewed negatively, it can impact their administration in correctional facilities.

Public perception of the furlough program is an important aspect in its continued use. Over the years, media reports of incidents that demonstrate problems with the furlough program can impact public perception. This was the case in 1986, when the furlough of inmate William Horton made national headlines, when he failed to return to his Massachusetts prison at the end of his furlough. Horton had been serving a prison sentence for rape and murder but was participating in a weekend furlough program when he absconded. Nine months later while still out of prison, he committed another rape and murder. The incident was widely reported in the media, impacting public perception of furloughs. In fact, the Horton case was the impetus for new restrictions and limitations on furlough programs throughout the country. Studies show that there were thousands fewer furloughs granted, and some jurisdictions revised the eligibility for furlough participation, or even discontinued the furlough program altogether. The incident brought the issue of furloughs to the forefront of American politics and the correctional system. Although the case is viewed as an example of the failure of the furlough program, much research shows that inmates that are granted furloughs not only return to the facility at the end of the furlough but also are less likely to commit further crimes.

Lynn M. Barnes

See also: Compassionate Release; Leaving Prison; Prison Work Programs; Prisoner Reentry/Family Integration; Vocational Training and Education

Further Reading

Anderson, D. C., & Enberg, C. (1995). Crime and the politics of hysteria: How the Willie Horton story changed American justice. *Journal of Contemporary Criminal Justice, 11*(4), 298–300.

Cheliotis, L. K. (2008). Reconsidering the effectiveness of temporary release: A systematic review. *Aggression and Violent Behavior, 13*(3), 153–168.

LeClair, D. P., & Guarino-Ghezzi, S. (1991). Does incapacitation guarantee public safety? Lessons from the Massachusetts furlough and prerelease programs. *Justice Quarterly, 8*(1), 9–36.

Marlette, M. (1990). Furloughs tightened: Success rates high. *Corrections Compendium*, *14*(1), 1–21.

Perk Davis, S. (1991). Number of furloughs increasing—Success rates high. *Corrections Compendium*, *16*, 10–21.

U.S. Department of Justice, Federal Bureau of Prisons. (2014). *Inmate admission & orientation handbook.*

General Strain Theory and Incarceration

General strain theory is attributed to the work of Robert Agnew as a way to explain why juveniles offend. His original work, published in 1992, expanded earlier classical strain theories, which mainly focused on the blockage of economic goals. Agnew believed that there were multiple sources of more immediate strain that could impact youth behavior. In addition, his theory incorporated research on stress from the medical sociology and social psychology research to explain how delinquency is the result of three types of deviance-producing strain. They are the failure to achieve positively valued goals, the absence of positively valued stimuli, and the presentation of negatively valued stimuli. Agnew claimed that these conditions might lead a person to experience strain, which in turn, would manifest into negative affect, such as frustration, disappointment, and anger. Thus, if a juvenile lacked emotional, behavioral, or cognitive coping skills to resolve the strain, the juvenile would be inclined to turn to delinquency.

Strain (or objective strain), one of the central concepts of Agnew's theory, can be defined as unfavorable situations or events that are experienced by the individual. For juveniles, the strains that increase the likelihood of crime include parental rejection, inconsistent parental supervision or discipline and/or harsh discipline, child abuse and neglect, negative experiences in secondary school, and rejection by peers or abusive peer relations. For adults, sources of strain are generally different, such as unemployment, marital problems, and menial work in the service sector. However, there are strains that are experienced by both juveniles and adults. These include the failure to achieve one's goals, criminal victimization, residency in an underprivileged community, homelessness, and racial/ethnic discrimination.

Clearly, general strain theory has been widely tested with the juvenile population, yet it has been extended to adult offending populations. Although the examples of strains mentioned earlier take place in the "free world" and can contribute to juvenile delinquency or adult deviance, researchers have also found that these external strains can be brought into the prison and influence an inmate's behavior. Researchers have also found that inmates are presented with additional strains or noxious stimuli while on prison grounds. Here, researchers who have used Agnew's theory to examine adult prisoner behavior hinge their work on Donald Clemmer's concept of prisonization. Essentially, the notion is that once inside prison, inmates will assimilate to prison norms and culture. In turn, when an inmate adopts the values, norms, and mores of the penitentiary, they are less likely to be influenced by conventional culture, even upon release. Another concept that is linked to applying Agnew's theory to inmate populations is the pains of imprisonment by Gresham Sykes. The pains of imprisonment are numerous as inmates are subjected to a loss of privacy, deprivation of freedom and autonomy, deprivation of a hetero-sexual relationship, loss of material goods, and fewer resources, just to name a few.

Two different theoretical perspectives are used best by researchers when it comes to the patterns of response to imprisonment. The first is called the deprivation model. This model states that the prison experience alone is known to produce depersonalizing, stigmatizing, and alienating effects where an inmate may cope or respond to the pains of imprisonment by acting out violently or aggressively. Second, prison research also suggests that newcomers can influence the prison culture and environment as they inherently bring with them deviant values, attitudes, and experiences inside the prison. In brief, the deprivation model is one that explains how the oppressive nature of prison leads to inmate violence, whereas the importation model explains how inmates bring with them a culture of toughness and physical exploitation, so much so that violent behavior permeates the prison environment.

Current research suggests that overcrowded and high-security prisons, coupled with exposure to prison gang activity and members, and a threatening or hostile living prison environment, for example, are likely to contribute to violent inmate misconduct. Notably, criminal victimization such as a physical or sexual assault while incarcerated has been linked to violent behavior inside the prison as well as depression and substance abuse. Based on Agnew's theoretical framework, it is clear that what complicates matters is that prisoners lack positive cognitive coping skills and the ability to escape these strains given that they exist within a captive society. This places a greater burden on correctional administrators to ensure the safety of the inmate population and to provide appropriate responses to inmate victims so that inmates can manage anger and other negative emotions.

Other research has turned attention to the strains and stressors experienced by female inmates, many of whom are mothers. For example, female inmates experience deprivation stressors as they are separated from their children, and they lack frequent contact visits with their children. Female inmates also may import stressors such as past sexual abuse and physical abuse from childhood or preprison adult relationships. These sources of strain have been found to affect the physical and mental health of the inmate. Moreover, research has found that women who have younger children while they are incarcerated experience more worry and stress than if they have older children. Aside from the mother's point of view, children of incarcerated parents are subject to their own set of strains that make them vulnerable to negative coping strategies. Research has shown that children of incarcerated parents have a higher likelihood of being imprisoned themselves, especially minority children and children from low-income households.

Aside from the research that has demonstrated how strain such as physical assault during incarceration will result in negative emotions and produce hostility, it is equally important to recognize that once the inmate is released, there may be a carryover effect where the inmate continues to commit violent or deviant acts. For instance, in one research study, inmates who reported a negative and hostile prison environment had a higher likelihood of recidivism (i.e., returning to prison after release or reoffending). Furthermore, theft, physical altercations, and verbal/emotional victimization were also related to an increased likelihood that the inmate

General Strain Theory and Incarceration 243

would reoffend. In addition, inmates who reported a fearful prison living environment had higher chances of being rearrested.

Results from these studies demonstrate the utility of Agnew's general strain theory as a principal explanation for prison violence, misconduct, recidivism, substance abuse, and poor mental and physical health conditions among male and female inmates and bring forth the potential to shape prison policy. First, inmates who experience criminal victimization as well as other deprivations may be more likely to commit violent acts while incarcerated, posing a danger to other inmates or correctional staff. Mechanisms should be in place to ensure the safety of prison staff and other inmates. Second, researchers have argued that making the prison environment more hostile or harsh, may in turn, reduce the deterrent effect that prisons are intended to have, and inmates may return to society with unfavorable criminogenic risk factors. Third, a framework needs to be developed that considers the pains of imprisonment in a gender-specific context. For mothers behind bars, the stressors of imprisonment may contribute to depression and drug abuse. Children of incarcerated parents are subject to numerous stressors that may impact their own behavior and lead to future offending as well. Providing social support by encouraging family and child visitations may reduce negative affect among female inmates and their children. For male inmates, increasing social support can ameliorate negative emotions too, thereby reducing inmate-to-inmate and inmate-to-staff assaults, and lowering the temptation to turn to drugs or alcohol. Last, correctional education and vocational programs may also serve as a conventional way to reduce stress and misconduct.

Kimberly A. DeTardo-Bora

See also: Deprivation Model; Importation Model; Misconduct by Prisoners; Prisonization; Sykes, Gresham

Further Reading

Agnew, R. (1992). Foundation for a general strain theory of crime and delinquency. *Criminology, 30*, 47–87.

Agnew, R. (2006). *Pressured into crime: An overview of general strain theory.* Los Angeles: Roxbury.

Blevins, K. R., Listwan, S. J., Cullen, F. T., & Johnson, C. L. (2010). A general strain theory of prison violence and misconduct: An integrated model of inmate behavior. *Journal of Contemporary Criminal Justice, 26*(2), 148–166.

Clemmer, D. (1958). *The prison community.* New York: Holt, Rinehart & Winston.

Foster, H. (2012). The strains of maternal imprisonment: Importation and deprivation stressors for women and children. *Journal of Criminal Justice, 40*, 221–229.

Listwan, S. J., Sullivan, C. J., Agnew, R. A., Cullen, F. T., & Colvin, M. (2013). The pains of imprisonment revisited: The impact of strain on inmate recidivism. *Justice Quarterly, 30*(1), 144–168.

Morris, R. G., Carriaga, M., Diamond, B., Piquero, N. L., & Piquero, A. R. (2012). Does prison strain lead to prison misbehavior? An application of general strain theory to inmate misconduct. *Journal of Criminal Justice, 40*, 194–201.

Sykes, G. M. (1958). *The society of captives: A study of a maximum security prison.* Princeton, NJ: Princeton University Press.

Wulf-Ludden, T. (2016). Pseudofamilies, misconduct, and the utility of general strain theory in a women's prison. *Women and Criminal Justice, 26,* 233–259.

Zweig, J. M., Yahner, J., Visher, C. A., & Lattimore, P. K. (2015). Using general strain theory to explore the effects of prison victimization experiences on later offending and substance use. *Prison Journal, 95*(1), 84–113.

Genetics in Sentencing, Role of

The field of criminology has historically been dominated by sociological explanations that focus almost exclusively on the criminogenic (likely to cause criminal behavior) effects of environmental factors, ranging from neighborhoods and peers to parents and poverty. Relatively recently, however, there has been a small movement away from only focusing on environmental effects toward estimating the role of genetic influences on the development of criminal behavior. The output of these studies has provided a great deal of information regarding the genetic architecture of violence, aggression, and antisocial behaviors in general.

To understand how genetic effects are estimated, it is important to understand the twin-based methodology. The twin-based methodology is the most common research design used to estimate the role of genetic influences. With this design, monozygotic (MZ) twins are compared to dizygotic (DZ) twins. MZ twins share 100 percent of their DNA and thus are genetically identical. DZ twins, in contrast, share 50 percent of their distinguishing DNA and thus are just as similar genetically speaking as regular biological siblings. At the same time, the environments that MZ twins share are assumed to be no more similar as the environments that DZ twins share. Mathematical evidence supports this assumption and, as a result, the only reason that MZ twins from the same twin pair should be more similar to each other (on any measure of interest, such as crime, delinquency, or violence) than DZ twins from the same twin pair is because they share twice as much genetic material. And, as the similarity of MZ twins increases relative to the similarity of DZ twins, the genetic effect also increases.

The results of twin-based research provide detailed and accurate estimates of genetic effects and environmental effects. Specifically, the genetic effect is referred to as a heritability estimate, and heritability estimates reveal that proportion of variance (in the measure of interest) that is accounted for by genetic variation. Although there tends to be the belief that twin-based studies only provide information about genetic effects, this is an erroneous belief. The variance that is not accounted for by heritability is accounted for by environmental factors. The twin-based method, however, makes the distinction between two types of environments: shared environmental factors and nonshared environmental factors. Shared environments are environments that are the same between siblings and that make them similar to each other. Socioeconomic status, for instance, is an environmental factor that is shared between siblings from the same household, and exposure to it should make the siblings more similar to each other. Nonshared environments, in contrast, are environments that are dissimilar between siblings and that make them different from each other. Differential exposure to peer groups, for example, is an environmental factor that is unique to each sibling and, therefore, should result in the siblings being more different from each other. Collectively, the effects of heritability, the shared environment, and the nonshared environment account for 100 percent of the variance in the measure that is being studied.

As with all research designs in the social sciences, there are some potential weaknesses with the twin-based methodology. Fortunately, there are alternative research designs that can be used to estimate genetic and environmental influences. Perhaps one of the most straightforward of these alternative designs is the adoption-based research design. With this research design, adoptees are compared to their biological parents and to their adoptive parents. If the adoptees were adopted early in life and had no contact with their biological parents, then the only reason they should resemble them (e.g., similar in behaviors or personality traits) is because of the genetic material that they share with them. At the same time, the only reason that theadoptees should resemble their adoptive parents is because of the environment and socialization experiences that they were exposed to during their upbringing.

There are alternatives to both the twin-based methodology and the adoption-based research design (e.g., the blended-family design, the MZ reared apart design), but the results of these alternative designs all converge on the same findings in regard to heritability, shared environmental, and nonshared environmental influences. Across hundreds of studies that analyzed thousands of twins, siblings, and adoptees, the results reveal that antisocial behavior tends to be about 50 percent heritable, meaning that about one-half of the variance in antisocial outcomes is the result of genetic variation. The remaining 50 percent of variance is accounted for by environmental factors. The effects of shared and nonshared environments, however, are far from equal. Shared environmental effects tend to range between 0 percent and 20 percent, while nonshared environmental effects tend to hover around 40 to 50 percent. These findings are highly robust as they have been garnered in no less than five separate meta-analyses.

Given that antisocial behavior has been found to be highly heritable, a wave of research has attempted to identify the specific genes that might be involved in increasing the propensity to engage in criminal and delinquent behavior. The results of these efforts have been met with mixed success, as only a small handful of genes have been found to be consistently linked to antisocial behaviors across studies. Most of the genes that have been identified are involved in the process of neurotransmission. For example, dopaminergic (related to dopamine) genes and serotonergic (related to serotonin) genes have been shown to increase the likelihood of violent and aggressive behaviors across a wide range of samples. But perhaps the gene that has most consistently been tied to criminal behaviors is the monoamine oxidase A (MAOA) gene.

The MAOA gene is partially responsible for regulating levels of neurotransmitters. If neurotransmitter levels are too high or too low, then there is the possibility that maladaptive outcomes, such as aggression, might emerge. Research has revealed that individuals who carry a particular variant of the MAOA gene are at heightened risk for a wide range of violent behaviors, including using a weapon in a fight and being part of a violent gang. The link between MAOA and violence has been replicated so consistently that it is considered one gene that likely has a causal influence on antisocial behaviors (in some capacity).

Against this backdrop, there has been a great deal of interest in figuring out how the results of genetic research studies should be integrated into the criminal justice system, particularly in regards to criminal trials and sentencing decisions. On the one hand, if an offender is found to have a genetic predisposition for antisocial behavior, then that information could be used to help justify longer and more punitive sanctions. On the other hand, there is the possibility that such findings could be used to help justify more lenient sentences as genetic influences could be viewed as removing some of the personal culpability of offenders.

One study explored these two possible ways in which genetic research would be used in sentencing decisions by studying judges' view of testimony regarding biological and genetic influences using vignettes. The results of the study revealed that the judges viewed this type of information as an aggravating factor (as opposed to a mitigating factor). Despite viewing genetic information in this light, judges significantly reduced the sentences of offenders who had a biological liability versus those who did not have such a liability.

The use of genetic information in courtroom trials does not just have to be viewed through hypothetical studies as genetics is beginning to more frequently be incorporated into actual courtroom trials. Virtually of the cases that have used such information use it as a mitigating factor in sentencing decisions. For example, after the defendant is found guilty of whatever crime he or she was on trial for, evidence that the offender possesses a genetic liability is often introduced in hopes that it is viewed by the judge as a mitigating factor. The end result is a more lenient sentence because the genetic component removes some personal responsibility.

The success rate of the genetics-as-mitigation approach is somewhat mixed. There have been a number of high-profile cases where the defense team has successfully argued that a reduced sentence is appropriate because the offender had a genetic predisposition for violence. For instance, in Tennessee in 2009, Bradley Waldroup was found guilty of murdering his estranged wife in 2006. His defense team argued that he should not be found guilty of murder and be sentenced to the death penalty as he possessed the variant of the MAOA gene that has been found to increase violence, aggression, and impulsive acts. Apparently, the jury agreed as they did not convict him on first-degree premeditated murder (but rather on lesser charges), and the judge sentenced him to 32 years in prison. In another case in Italy, the judge shaved one year off the sentence of a convicted murderer because of evidence that he also possessed the variant of the MAOA gene related to violence. Numerous other cases have also had the findings from genetic, biological, and neurobiological studies used as part of the defense strategy. The outcomes associated with these attempts have been variable, and thus there is no clear-cut indication as to the true success rates of genetic defenses.

There is little doubt that as more and more research is published uncovering the genetic and biological influences related to the etiology of antisocial behaviors that defense teams will attempt to use this information to help their clients. The question, of course, is whether a genetic defense is appropriate or whether it should be shut out of the court system. In many ways, this is a legal or philosophical question. After all, the available evidence clearly indicates that criminal behaviors are about 50 percent heritable. These findings are perhaps the most replicated in all of the social sciences, and thus they are not likely due to a methodological or statistical artifact. Whether these findings should be used to justify more lenient sentences, however, is perhaps one of the most pressing issues that the U.S. court system will have to deal with in the next decade. It will be interesting and instructive to examine various court's rulings when it comes to the applicability and legality of genetic research in criminal cases.

Kevin M. Beaver

See also: DNA Exonerees; Federal Sentencing Guidelines; Sentencing Disparities and Discrimination in Sentencing; Truth in Sentencing

Further Reading

Aspinwall, L. G., Brown, T. R., & Tabery, J. (2012). The double-edged sword: Does biomechanism increase or decrease judges' sentencing of psychopaths? *Science, 337,* 846–849.

Beaver, K. M. (2016). *Biosocial criminology: A primer* (3rd ed.). Dubuque, IA: Kendall/Hunt.

Benet, W., Vnencak-Jones, C. L., Farahany, N., & Montgomery, S. A. (2007). Bad nature, bad nurture, testimony regarding MAOA and SLC6A4 genotyping at murder trials. *Journal of Forensic Science, 52,* 1362–1371.

Denno, D. W. (2011). Courts' increasing consideration of behavioral genetics evidence in criminal cases: Results of a longitudinal study. *Michigan State Law Review, 967,* 968–1028.

Ferguson, C. J. (2010). Genetic contributions to antisocial personality and behavior: A meta-analytic review from an evolutionary perspective. *Journal of Social Psychology, 150,* 160–180.

Mason, D. A., & Frick, P. J. (1994). The heritability of antisocial behavior: A meta-analysis of twin and adoption studies. *Journal of Psychopathology and Behavioral Assessment, 16,* 301–323.

Miles, D. R., & Carey, G. (1997). Genetic and environmental architecture of human aggression. *Journal of Personality and Social Psychology, 72,* 207–217.

Pinker, S. (2002). *The blank slate: The modern denial of human nature.* New York: Penguin Books.

Polderman, T. J. C., Benyamin, B., de Leeuw, C. A., Sullivan, P. F., van Bochoven, A., Visscher, P. M., & Posthuma, D. (2015). Meta-analysis of the heritability of human traits based on fifty years of twin studies. *Nature Genetics, 47,* 702–709.

Rhee, S. H., & Waldman, I. D. (2002). Genetic and environmental influences on antisocial behavior: A meta-analysis of twin and adoption studies. *Psychological Bulletin, 128,* 490–529.

Good Time

Good time is a policy that permits inmates to reduce their prison sentences by earning credits. These credits are also commonly referred to as gain time, sentence remission, diminution of sentence, time off for good behavior, good conduct time, and meritorious time. Although the sentence deduction is at the discretion of the prison administration, good time credits can be earned for good behavior, participation in vocational, educational, or treatment programs, extra work, or other statutory policies. The number of credits that can be earned and the procedure for earning those credits vary from state to state. The amount of the deduction is predicated on the number of credits earned. Most states and the federal prison system have provisions for good time.

Good time policies may serve a number of purposes. Since the amount of prison time may be reduced, good time is valuable to inmates. The possibility of earning good time credit provides an incentive for prisoners to follow institutional rules. Rule compliance improves safety and helps the correctional facility operate more smoothly. Furthermore, good time may provide an incentive to inmates to participate in institutional programming such as work, educational, or other types of programs. Correctional officials deem program involvement positively, as it may enhance rehabilitation and improve the overall climate of the institution. Good time has also been used as a management tool to reduce overcrowding in prison facilities. This tactic aids correctional officials in securing space for additional prisoners by releasing those who have demonstrated good conduct while incarcerated.

States define and administer good time policies differently. The eligibility for good time, as well as the amount of good time days that may be subtracted from the prisoner's sentence, is stipulated by law and generally calculated by prison authorities. Although all prisoners may not be eligible for good time credits, the amount of days to be subtracted from the prison sentence usually varies between 5 to 10 days a month. However, in most cases, one good time credit is the equivalent to one day of a prison sentence. Good time may be credited as it is earned on a monthly, quarterly, or yearly basis, or it may be credited at the beginning of the prison sentence. In some states, once a specific number of days of good time is earned, it is vested. This means that the good time credit earned, once vested, cannot be taken away as a means of institutional punishment. Thus, inmates who violate prison rules risk losing only those credits not vested.

There are four general types of good time policies used by states. Statutory good time is granted automatically when an inmate complies with prison rules, avoids disciplinary infractions, and demonstrates overall good behavior in the institution. Once the inmate is classified, potential credits are accrued but can be revoked based on behavior. When good time is credited at the beginning of the prisoner's sentence, it appears that the credit is not a reward for good behavior but a punishment because it may be revoked after a disciplinary hearing. Earned time is normally defined as credits earned as a result of participation in vocational or educational programs. Credits can also be earned during work or prison industry assignments. Since most inmates are required to work, good behavior exhibited during their work performance could lead to good time credits. The awarding of earned time is not automatic like statutory time; it must be earned. Meritorious time credit provides inmates with the opportunity to be awarded credit for performing exemplary acts or outstanding service in the prison. For example, an exceptional act of service during an emergency situation could quality for additional credit. Most often, meritorious time credit is a one-time credit, and a state will normally specify the maximum that can be awarded as part of meritorious time. The emergency credit good time may be used by some states to reduce prison overcrowding. The release date and parole hearing for a prisoner could be accelerated in order to relieve an institution that has reached or is over capacity. In this case, good time credits would typically be awarded to those who have displayed good behavior and a good work history in the prison. Prison officials may use the inmate's security classification and criminal history as determining factors in whether emergency credits should be authorized. States vary in the administration of good time, and most impose restrictions and may deem prisoners ineligible, particularly if they are serving death or life sentences. The nation's largest prison system, the Federal Bureau of Prisons, also administers a good time credit policy.

Within the Federal Bureau of Prisons, good time of up to 54 days per year can be earned per year imprisoned (prorated for a partial year). The good time credit earned is in addition to any credit the prisoner receives for time served. Since the implementation of the Prison Litigation Reform Act (1997), the amount of good time eligible to be earned is based on whether the prisoner has earned or is pursuing a high school diploma or its equivalency. Those who have not earned a high school diploma or its equivalency may earn up to 42 days of good time credit for each year incarcerated. Inmates serving life sentences are not eligible for good time credits, and the inmate must be sentenced to at least a year in prison. In many cases correctional officials can reduce good time for institutional infractions. The federal law governing good time credits can be found at 18 U.S.C. § 3624(b).

In the United States, good time polices have been in effect since the early 1800s. New York was the first state to implement a good time policy, and 100 years later, all states of the Union and the District of Columbia had some form of prisoner good time law. Over the years, correctional officials considered the policies necessary for maintaining order in the facility, and in many cases for reducing prison crowding. Critics of the policy maintain that it gives correctional personnel too much discretion in the amount of time a convicted offender may spend incarcerated and that it is not a strong predictor of future recidivism. Conversely, proponents of good time maintain that the policy may mitigate sentence severity and encourage rehabilitation. Studies have shown that inmates that receive good time credits present a low risk to public safety once released. Research also indicates that inmates released under good time are no more likely to reoffend than those who are released through parole or serve their entire sentence. Today, many in the criminal justice system think about good time policies in terms of the actual amount of time an offender may serve. Since most criminal court cases are not resolved by trial, prosecutors and defense attorneys may take good time into consideration during the plea-bargaining process.

Lynn M. Barnes

See also: Overcrowding; Prison Populations, Downsizing of; Prison Work Programs; Prisoner Reentry/Family Integration; Vocational Training and Education

Further Reading

Demleitner, N.V. (2009). Good conduct time: How much and for whom—the unprincipled approach of the Model Penal Code: Sentencing. *Florida Law Review, 61,* 777–796.

Emshoff, J. G., & Davidson, W. S. (1987). The effect of "good time" credit on inmate behavior: A quasi-experiment. *Criminal Justice and Behavior, 14*(3), 335–351.

James, N. (2014). *Early release for federal inmates: Fact sheet.* Washington, DC: Congressional Research Service.

Larkin, P. J. (2013). Clemency, parole, good-time credits, and crowded prisons: Reconsidering early release. *Georgetown Journal of Law & Public Policy, 11*(1), 1–44.

Parisi, N., & Zillo, J. A. (1983). Good time: The forgotten issue. *Crime & Delinquency, 29*(2), 228–237.

Weisburd, D., & Chayet, E. S. (1989). Good time: An agenda for research. *Criminal Justice and Behavior, 16*(2), 183–195.

Gossip and Rumors

The topic of prison rumors and gossip can be distinguished by population and by topic. There are three populations that primarily participate in prison rumors and gossip: correctional officers, the public, and inmates. The differences of gossip between genders exist, in part, due to the fact that female inmates enter same-sex relationships voluntarily at a higher rate than male inmates. Gossiping in prison serves several purposes, such as progressing within one's subculture or promoting one's interests; it may also serve as a form of entertainment, or a coping mechanism.

Two populations—the correctional officers and the public—most commonly conduct and disseminate relatively minor gossip. Correctional officers discuss the high-profile inmates and the administration, while the public focuses on the high-profile inmates, and administration is not commonly discussed. The topic of high-profile inmates varies by the level of information that these two populations possess. Correctional officers tend to discuss high-profile cases that have appeared in the media; the staff do not discuss an "everyday" inmate whose crimes are not perceived to be extraordinary or whose conduct within the facility is appropriate. Because the correctional officers interact with these inmates, their level of knowledge is not constrained by their media portrayal. On the contrary, the public's information on high-profile cases comes almost exclusively from the media; hence, their perception may be biased depending on their personal choices of media outlets. A topic that draws attention from the correctional officers is changes in administration, which are issues that directly affect them and their job. Thus, this topic is rarely discussed among civilians even at visitation.

The gossip primarily pursued by the inmates is more convoluted; this phenomenon results from male and female inmates talking about sensitive topics and using distinctive jargon while gossiping. Both genders hold a conversation face to face or utilize "cadillacs" to convey information to other inmates. Given the nature of "cadillacs," which is a string connecting inmates' doors through which messages can be passed on "cars," this method is rarely used for gossiping as there is written proof that may be obtained by others.

Both female and male inmates avoid the term "gossip" or "rumor" due to its negative connotation as such actions are perceived to be feminine. The slang phrases "talk" or "chop it up" are used among male inmates in order to discuss unconfirmed information. The main topics of their conversations include other inmates, administration, contraband, and family. In connection to other inmates, male inmates will discuss others' crimes mainly in one of these instances: first, their crimes are not confirmed; second, they have appeared in the media extensively; and third, their crimes are deemed to be low on the hierarchy. The crimes and reputation obtained by other inmates are categorized within the hierarchy that is universally accepted among inmates. The status of murderers will be relatively high within the subculture given the magnitude of this crime. Individuals convicted of child molestation ("chomos"), severe sexual assaults ("rapo"), and inmates who cooperate with law enforcement or prison staff ("snitches" or "rats") inhabit the lowest ranks of this hierarchy. Hence, the gossip about low-ranking inmates reflects their position.

Rumors about other inmates often result in the individual being shunned from their group. Individuals of the same race usually form prison groups, and each group has either one or more spokespersons. Hence, if an individual in one group "snitches" on a person in another group, the spokespersons in both groups tend to get together, clarify the situation, and create the plan of action. This situation commonly results in the "snitch" being shunned from their group due to the group's risk of a problematic relationship with the affected group by association. Further, the individual is at risk of being "jumped" or "smashed" by the members of the affected group, who have cleared this intention with the spokesperson of the perpetrator's group.

Inmates also discuss unconfirmed changes in administration that could affect them, such as new wardens, correctional officers, and changes in rules and privileges. It is noted that given the strong working of prison subcultures, inmates are sometimes better informed than the staff. One of the most widespread topics of rumors is drugs and contraband. Inmates discuss who is able to provide interested individuals with drugs, which inmates were apprehended for having contraband, or whether the correctional officers are conducting unit searches for contraband. The last significant topic of gossip is holding a conversation about other inmates' personal lives and families, such as do they have significant others, whether someone visits them, or if they receive mail or packages. Nevertheless, malicious gossip pertaining to one's relationship is more frequent in female institutions where same-sex relationships are more prevalent. There are two off-limit topics with regard to gossip about contraband and inmates' personal lives. First, the method of bringing contraband inside of the prison is not inquired, because inmates inquiring about these techniques may start being perceived as "snitches." Second, if male inmates witness another inmate displaying emotions during visitations, such occurrences are not discussed back in their groups.

Tereza Trejbalova

See also: Drug Use in Prison; Prison Argot; Snitches; Underground Prison Economy; Visitation

Further Reading

Huggins, D., Capeheart, L., & Newman, E. (2006). Deviants or scapegoats: An examination of pseudofamily groups and dyads in two Texas prisons. *The Prison Journal, 86*(1), 114–139.

Ireland, J. L. (2000). "Bullying" among prisoners: A review of research. *Aggression and Violent Behavior, 5*(2), 201–215.

McPherson, M., Smith-Lovin, L., & Cook, J. M. (2001). Birds of a feather: Homophily in social networks. *Annual Review of Sociology, 27*, 415–444.

Phillips, C. (2012). *The multicultural prison: Ethnicity, masculinity, and social relations among prisoners*. Oxford, U.K.: Oxford University Press.

Reiter, K. A. (2012). Parole, snitch, or die: California's supermax prisons and prisoners, 1997–2007. *Punishment & Society, 14* (5), 530–563.

Tomer, E., & Chen, G. (2012). Gossip in a maximum security female prison: An exploratory study. *Women & Criminal Justice, 22*(2), 108–134.

Guantanamo Bay

The United States established the Naval Station Guantanamo Bay in 1903 in the Oriente Province of Cuba, as a coaling—or fueling—station and naval base. The purpose of the naval station is to provide a base of operations for the U.S. Navy's Atlantic Fleet, as well as for the U.S. Navy and allies operating in the Caribbean. The George W. Bush administration established the Guantanamo Bay detention camp in January 2002 as a temporary facility to house detainees in the war on terror following the terrorist attacks of September 11, 2001.

The detention camp facility is comprised of seven camps. Camp Delta holds six of these camps, a total of 612 units. Camp Delta was completed in April 2002, and the facility includes detainees from Camp X-Ray, which was the original temporary holding facility established in January 2002. The seventh camp, which was appropriately named Camp Seven, is the highest security facility in the detention camp, housing the highest risk detainees, including conspirators of the 9/11 attacks. For the first two years of its operation, the existence of Camp Seven was not acknowledged, and detainees held there are transferred using hoods and windowless vans to prevent them from knowing exactly where they are on the military base.

The land for the base was leased from the Cuban government by the U.S. government for the gold equivalent of $2,000, but this was renegotiated in 1934 with a treaty that changed the price to about $4,085. Although diplomatic relations with Cuba had remained relatively stable through both World War I and World War II, the 1950s saw a strain in this relationship as the Cuban Revolution began and Fidel Castro came into power. Officially, diplomacy with Cuba ended in 1961 during the Dwight D. Eisenhower administration. However, the military base remains in place due to a stipulation in the original lease agreement that states that both the Cuban government and the U.S. government must agree to terminate the lease. This way, despite Cuban protest, the United States is able to maintain the naval station, as well as the detention camp on the military base.

There is an important distinction at Guantanamo Bay, which is that the individuals imprisoned there are called "detainees," not "prisoners of war," because to call them prisoners of war would imply that the terrorist organizations they claim allegiance to are legitimate governmental institutions, rather than illegal groups. A prisoner of war is an individual who has been captured during an armed conflict and has been endorsed by a recognized country. Another term for detainees at the Guantanamo Bay detention camp is unlawful combatants, or those who engage in armed conflict with U.S. forces without endorsement from a legitimate government's armed services.

Under international laws of war, enemy combatants, whether lawful or unlawful, may be detained until the end of hostilities. However, armed conflict with terrorist groups often does not follow the laws of war, and there is usually not a clear end to hostilities; therefore, there is no clear indication of when detainees may be released, nor to whom they may be released. As a result, many detainees at the Guantanamo Bay detention camp spend nearly a decade at the facility, if not longer.

Initially, as unlawful combatants, detainees were not protected by the Geneva Convention; however, this was appealed in 2006. The U.S. Supreme Court ruled in *Hamdan v. Rumsfeld* that detainees at the Guantanamo Bay detention camp were allowed minimal protections under Common Article 3 of the Geneva Convention, which requires humane treatment and prohibits cruel and unusual punishment. This ruling prompted interest in investigating operations at the detention camp by organizations such as the International Committee of the Red Cross.

The Guantanamo Bay detention camp has faced criticism from a number of organizations, including Amnesty International and Human Rights Watch, along with criticism from governmental organizations, such as the European Union and the United Nations Commission on Human Rights. These groups have criticized the detention camp for alleged mistreatment of detainees, calling for the permanent closure of the facility.

The International Committee of the Red Cross inspected the Guantanamo Bay detention camp in 2004, and a report leaked to *The New York Times* alleged that

U.S. Army military police escort a detainee to his cell in the Guantanamo Bay detention camp in Guantanamo Bay, Cuba. (U.S. Department of Defense)

the detainees were subject to cruel and unusual punishment, degradation via social and cultural humiliation, solitary confinement, stress positions, exposure to loud music, sleep deprivation, and waterboarding.

On January 22, 2009, his second full day in office, President Barack Obama issued Executive Order 13492, which established the Guantanamo Review Task Force. President Obama had proposed the closure of the Guantanamo Bay detention camp during his campaign and created the Guantanamo Review Task Force with the purpose of determining which detainees could be prosecuted, released, or transferred to other facilities. The task force was coordinated by the U.S. Department of Justice and included experts from the U.S. Department of State, U.S. Department of Defense, and U.S. Department of Homeland Security.

Traditionally with the anticipated closure of a facility housing enemy combatants, the detainees are classified into either of the aforementioned groups; however, with Guantanamo Bay, the task force determined there was another category of detainees, the indefinite detention group. This group is comprised of those detainees who have been deemed too dangerous and high risk to transfer or release but for whom prosecution is not a viable option. Additionally, some detainees could not be transferred to their home countries, due to an unstable political climate, so negotiations needed to be held with other nations who could potentially accept them.

Some countries were allowed to accept detainees with origins there but soon lost that privilege—a notable example is Kuwait, who assured the United States that the unstable political climate would not affect the rehabilitation center they had built in anticipation of receiving detainees. Despite this promise, of the four detainees that Kuwait was allowed to receive in 2009, two were acquitted almost immediately after a cursory trial. This followed an incident during the Bush administration, in which eight detainees were transferred to Kuwait and then were almost immediately released in Kuwait. Of those eight, one recidivated and drove a truck bomb onto an Iraqi military base, killing 13 Iraqi military personnel.

The final report from the Guantanamo Review Task Force indicated that of the 240 detainees at the facility, 126 could be transferred to prisons either in their home countries or somewhere that would agree to take them; 36 could be prosecuted, either in federal court or at a military tribunal; 48 could be held under laws of war; and 30 Yemenis could be transferred to Yemen if the security situation in their country improved.

Since being established in January 2002, 780 detainees have passed through the Guantanamo Bay detention camp. Of those detainees, 242 remained in January 2009, when President Barack Obama took office and began marshaling efforts to permanently close the facility. President Obama oversaw the release of more than 200 detainees, with the last 4 being transferred on January 19, 2017, his last full day in office. As of January 20, 2017, there are 41 detainees remaining.

The Donald Trump administration does not intend to close the facility and actively plans to expand its detainee population. Additionally, Trump advocates for the renewed implementation of previously frowned on enhanced interrogation techniques, including waterboarding and torture, which sets back the progress made by the previous administration significantly.

Vrishali Kanvinde

See also: Custody Levels; Maximum Security; Prison Industries

Further Reading

Bruck, C. (2016, August 1). Why Obama has failed to close Guantánamo. *The New Yorker.* Retrieved June 19, 2017, from www.newyorker.com/magazine/2016/08/01/why -obama-has-failed-to-close-guantanamo

DoD news briefing—Secretary Rumsfeld and Gen. Pace. (2002, January 22). U.S. Department of Defense. Retrieved from archive.defense.gov/transcripts/transcript.aspx ?transcriptid=2254

Finn, P. (2010, January 22). Justice task force recommends about 50 Guantanamo detainees be held indefinitely. *Washington Post,* WP Company. Retrieved from www .washingtonpost.com/wp-dyn/content/article/2010/01/21/AR2010012104936.html

The Geneva Conventions of 1949 and their additional protocols. (2010, October 29). International Committee of the Red Cross. Retrieved from www.icrc.org/eng/war-and -law/treaties-customary-law/geneva-conventions/overview-geneva-conventions .htm

Hamdan v. Rumsfeld, 548 U.S. 557, 126 S. Ct. 2749 (2006).

Koren, M. (2016, May 12). Who is left at Guantanamo? *The Atlantic,* Atlantic Media Company. Retrieved from www.theatlantic.com/politics/archive/2016/05/guanatanamo -bay-forever-prisoners/482289

Lewis, N. A. (2004, November 30). Red Cross finds detainee abuse in Guantánamo. *New York Times.* Retrieved from www.nytimes.com/2004/11/30/politics/red-cross-finds -detainee-abuse-in-guantanamo.html

Naval Station Guantanamo Bay, U.S. Navy. Retrieved from www.cnic.navy.mil/regions /cnrse/installations/ns_guantanamo_bay.html

Savage, C. (2017, January 19). Obama transfers 4 from Guantánamo, leaving 41 there as term ends. *New York Times.* Retrieved from www.nytimes.com/2017/01/19/us /politics/obama-transfers-4-from-guantanamo-leaving-41-there-as-term-ends.html

Vogel, S. (2002, January 9). Afghan prisoners going to gray area; military unsure what follows transfer to U.S. base in Cuba. HighBeam research, newspaper archives and journal articles. *Washington Post.* Retrieved from www.highbeam.com/doc/1P2 -320927.html

Habeas Corpus Writs

Known as the Great Writ of Liberty, the writ of habeas corpus is a legal device for challenging the government's basis for imprisoning an individual. The power of a government to lock up a person represents one of the greatest single threats to individual freedom. When an agent of the government takes such an action—confining a person in jail, prison, a mental institute, or an airport—the writ of habeas corpus entitles the prisoner to be physically (in Latin habeas corpus means "have the body") brought into court to contest the legality of his or her detention, and if a judge finds it to be unlawful to be released without delay. In this way, the Great Writ of Liberty serves as a vital check against the abuse of government power and a safeguard of civil liberty.

The writ of habeas corpus originated in the English common law and can be traced as far back as the founding document of Anglo-Saxon jurisprudence, the Magna Carta. As early as 1215, the Magna Carta provided that "no free man shall be arrested or imprisoned" in the absence of the "lawful judgment of his peers" or "the law of the land." By the time of the American Revolution, the right to habeas relief had become so deeply ingrained in the common law that the drafters of the U.S. Constitution presupposed its existence; though they did narrowly define the justifications for its suspension, a rebellion or invasion.

Even so, to dispel any remaining doubts, the First Congress codified the writ with the Judiciary Act of 1789, requiring the federal courts to grant habeas relief to federal prisoners. Yet because the early denizens of the several states remained wary of federal powers, access to habeas relief in the federal courts was limited to these individuals, preventing federal judges from second-guessing state court decisions concerning state prisoners. Eventually, each of the 50 states would pass their own constitutional guarantees, under which state prisoners could file habeas challenges vis-à-vis the state.

Throughout history access to habeas corpus has undergone periods of expansion and contraction. During the Civil War (1861–1865), President Abraham Lincoln suspended the writ so as to allow his generals to detain members of the rebel army without having to answer for their actions in court. Following the war, Congress moved in the opposite direction with the passage of the Habeas Corpus Act of 1867, which opened the doors of the federal court to writs filed by state prisoners. This was partly to ensure that, if the state courts refused to vindicate the constitutional rights of the recently emancipated slaves, then recourse in the federal courts would still be available. However, since the scope of habeas review in federal courts was circumscribed to jurisdiction matters, it would take another century for the Warren Court to fully realize these protections for state prisoners.

Just as the Warren Court increased the range of procedural due process protections to which the state courts could be held, so too did it expand access to habeas relief in federal courts for failure to meet these same requirements. More recently, access to habeas relief was significantly curtailed under the controversial Antiterrorism and Effective Death Penalty Act (AEDPA) of 1996, which places a number of restrictions on the claims that can be reviewed by federal courts—most notably, a one-year statute of limitations and a more stringent standard for demonstrating that a state court's decision violated federal law.

For example, a person tried and convicted of murder in a state court can see habeas relief. As a matter of right, postconviction such individuals could appeal their case up to the highest court in the state, generally a supreme court, on any number of constitutional grounds: evidence from a warrantless search was admitted (Fourth Amendment), a confession was forced (Fifth Amendment), counsel was ineffective (Sixth Amendment), and so on. If these direct appeals fail, then the defendant could still appeal to the Supreme Court, although review is unlikely as it is granted in only a small fraction of cases. In addition, the defendant could use the Great Writ of Liberty to level a so-called collateral attack in federal court, giving a federal judge another crack at uncovering procedural problems in the case.

Stephen Koppel

See also: Access to the Courts; Antiterrorism and Effective Death Penalty Act of 1996; Innocence Project

Further Reading

Hartman, M. J., & Nyden, J. (1996). Habeas corpus and the new federalism after the antiterrorism and effective Death Penalty Act of 1996. *John Marshall Law Review, 30,* 337.

Hertz, R., & Liebman, J. S. (2015). *Federal habeas corpus practice and procedure.* New Providence, NJ; San Francisco: LexisNexis.

Mayers, L. (1965). The Habeas Corpus Act of 1867: The Supreme Court as legal historian. *The University of Chicago Law Review, 33*(1), 31–59.

Oaks, D. H. (1966). Legal history in the High Court: Habeas corpus. *Michigan Law Review, 64*(3), 451–472.

Turner, R. V. (2003). *Magna Carta: Through the ages.* Harlow, England; New York: Pearson/Longman.

Halfway Houses

Halfway houses were originally developed due to the ineffectiveness of traditional prison programs, as a cost-effective strategy to keep prisoners in the community, to reduce prison overcrowding, and to help prisoners find and maintain employment. Halfway houses provide a secured and structured residential setting that allows residents to participate in the community by working and maintaining family relationships. Also referred to as community correction facilities, community correction centers, residential reentry centers, and prerelease centers, these facilities serve as both a "halfway in" and/or "halfway out" program. Halfway houses are often used for people leaving prison ("halfway out" for those on parole supervision) and for people who are in need of an alternative to prison ("halfway in" for probationers or technical parole violators). Usually halfway house facilities serve one specific population (parolees or probationers); however, some states house both offender types in the same facility.

Many states operate their halfway houses by contracting with independent groups. For example, many states contract with the nonprofit Volunteers of America (VOA) and Correctional Education Centers (CECs). Other states, including the federal government, contract with private companies such as the GEO Group or Corrections Corporation of America (CCA). Regardless of facility type, most halfway house programs operate on a level system that allows residents to gradually earn privileges such as later curfews, family visitation, and furloughs (i.e., unsupervised time away from the facility). Most halfway house programs serve as work release facilities and often have a range of other services onsite. These services may include substance abuse treatment, mental health services, individual and group counseling, anger management, and case management support. Many halfway houses refer clients to services that they do not have available on-site.

Halfway out programs become a crucial reentry tool that allows offenders to receive services to address their immediate needs. For example, many returning offenders need to secure housing. Although some offenders will live with family once released from prison, or a halfway house, others do not have family to support them. Living in a halfway house facility eliminates the emergency need to find a place to live. Having several months to search and save money for housing helps to alleviate the stress of securing housing while in prison.

The ability to obtain employment while living at a halfway house is also a benefit for individuals without family financial support. Many returning prisoners need immediate employment to take care of other basic needs. Halfway house programs typically require offenders to obtain work while residing in the facility. The stigma of a criminal record is a major reentry barrier when returning prisoners begin the employment search. To alleviate this stigma, some halfway houses assist offenders with job readiness skills, job leads, and placement services.

Evaluations on the effectiveness of halfway house programs are not very common. Some states have evaluated their systems and find some level of effectiveness. Often researchers find that offenders who participate in halfway house programs are less likely to recidivate, or reoffend at a slower rate, than those who do not participate. Programs are more likely to be successful if they incorporate evidence-based practices (e.g., targeting criminogenic needs, serving high-risk offenders, and providing services based on cognitive behavioral treatment).

Andrea Cantora

See also: Evidence-Based Practice in Corrections; Furloughs; Prisoner Reentry/Family Integration

Further Reading

Bonta, J. (1996). Risk/needs assessment and treatment. In A. T. Hartland (Ed.), *Choosing correctional options that work: Defining the demand and evaluating the supply* (pp. 18–32). Thousand Oaks, CA: Sage.

Hamilton, Z. K., & Campbell, C. M. (2014). Uncommonly observed. The impact of New Jersey's halfway house system. *Criminal Justice & Behavior*, *41*(11), 1354–1375.

Latessa, E. J., Travis, L. F., & Lowenkamp, C. T. (2016). Halfway houses (updated). In E. J. Latessa & A. Holsinger (Eds.), *Correctional contexts: Contemporary and classical readings* (5th ed., pp. 310–319). New York: Oxford University Press.

Lowenkamp, C. T., Latessa, E. J., & Smith, P. (2006). Does correctional program quality really matter? The impact of adhering to the principles of effective intervention. *Criminology and Public Policy, 5*(3), 201–220.

Travis. J. (2005). *But they all come back: Facing the challenges of prisoner reentry.* Washington, DC: Urban Institute.

Health Care in Prison Populations

All American prisoners are entitled to health care while in a state or federal correctional facility according to the Eighth Amendment. This includes medical, dental, and mental health care. Although the quality of health care varies from state to state, *Estelle v. Gamble* (1976) made clear that deliberate indifference to the health care needs of incarcerated persons with serious medical conditions is a violation of the Constitution and constitutes cruel and unusual punishment. However, prison administrators must continually update the standards to which they hold themselves as *Rhodes v. Chapman* (1981) explained that evolving standards of decency must guide the consideration of what is an acceptable standard of health care. As Wright (2008) explains, what was acceptable in 1972 may not necessarily be acceptable in 2009. For instance, doctors now manage HIV and AIDS as a chronic illness rather than viewing the disease as a death sentence. Prisons must not only follow the same guidelines as the general population for preventive care, but the addition of new medications, forms of treatment, and immunizations must all be taken into consideration when trying to assess the evolving standards of decency.

Because prisons cannot ignore the health condition of their inmates, health care has become a large portion of the budget. Since 1976, the total annual prison spending has increased over tenfold to $77 billion, more than 10 percent of which is for health care (Stephan, 2001). In Washington, DC, for example, inmate medical services cost about $33 million, which in 2012 was a quarter of its corrections budget. This does not include the cost of sending corrections officers to guard prisoners who receive medical treatment outside the jail or prison (Schaenman et al., 2013). In order to recover some of the money spent on health care, prisoners may be asked to make an annual copayment for their health care, or a copay for each medical service required. A survey of jails in 2005 found that approximately 60 percent assess a copay for pharmacy, usually about $5, and medical office/physician visits, usually about $10 (Krauth, Stayton, & Clem, 2005). About half (45 percent) of the jails surveyed assess a copay for dental examinations/care (usually $10), while a quarter of jails charge a fee for eye care examinations and prescriptions, with exams usually costing $10 and prescriptions $15. Charging a copay is also thought to keep the number of prisoners who malinger to a minimum; however, it may also discourage those prisoners who have real illnesses from visiting the clinic if they cannot afford the copay. Though the payment is relatively small in comparison to fees for those in the general population, many prisoners may still not be able to afford it. The money often comes from the prisoners' commissary account, which is funded by the prisoners' families or earnings from prison jobs (Andrews, 2015).

In general, most prisons have a clinic for which prisoners must send in a written request. It can take from up to three to five days to receive permission to visit the medical facility, which consists of various medical staff including a combination of doctors, nurse practitioners, or physician assistants. Patients who are in the clinic for routine checkups or minor illnesses will likely be seen by the nurses, leaving the doctor more time for serious illnesses. Larger prisons have physical and/or occupational therapists as well as a phlebotomist and the ability to conduct X-rays on-site. For specialized treatment of maladies like cancer or cardiac or emergency care, the prison may have an agreement with a local hospital or specialist to provide such care. Importantly, many prisons also have psychologists or psychiatrists on staff to help with the omnipresent mental illness in the prison population.

Although there are some similarities across correctional facilities, the size, quality, and distribution system of health care vary widely depending on who manages the facility. Several private prison companies have been cited for endangering inmates by providing inadequate health care services (Mason, 2012). Mattera, Khan, and Nathan (2003) believe failure to provide proper medical care in some private prisons may be due to the attempt to maximize profits at the expense of employee training. A large disparity in health care needs has also been noted for prisoners in comparison to the surrounding community (Marshall, Simpson, & Stevens, 2001). For example, male prisoners consult doctors six times per year—three times more frequently than a demographically equivalent community population. Female prisoners, on the other hand, consult doctors 14 times per prisoner year—3 times more frequently than a demographically equivalent community population.

Despite being a minority of the population, female prisoners are differentiated not only from those in the general population, but they also enter correctional facilities with more critical and unique needs. They often come from deprived backgrounds and experience problems related to alcohol and drug dependencies, infectious diseases, reproductive diseases, and histories of physical and sexual abuse (Van den Bergh, Gatherer, & Moller, 2009). Being a victim of prior sexual abuse puts them at greater-than-average risk for high-risk pregnancies and life-threatening illnesses such as HIV/AIDS, hepatitis C, and human papillomavirus infection, which may increase risk for cervical cancer (Braithwaite, Treadwell, & Arriola, 2008). High rates of mental health problems such as post-traumatic stress disorder, depression, anxiety, a tendency to self-harm, and suicide have been reported in the women prison population as well (Van den Bergh et al., 2009). Despite the increase in the number of female inmates, little attention has been given to their unique health concerns. The gynecological needs of female inmates are often dismissed as not important by prison officials. Furthermore, medical concerns that relate to reproductive health and to psychosocial matters are often overlooked (Braithwaite et al., 2008).

Though females have more special needs than their male counterparts, much of the increased spending on health care may be attributed to the growing number of elderly prisoners who are serving life sentences without parole (Fifer, 2012). Although these inmates exhibit many of the same ailments as the general population such as Alzheimer's disease, cancer, and pulmonary disorder (Moraff, 2012), health care costs for this specific population are so high that prison officials often cannot provide them with adequate care (Cohen, 2015). Under federal law, the Bureau of Prisons has authority to release prisoners who meet specific criteria. This program is known as the federal Compassionate Release/Reduction in Sentence (CR/RIS) program. In addition to health and age criteria, the prison must believe that the inmate does not pose a threat to society once released.

Carla Lewandowski and Vanessa D'Erasmo

See also: AIDS/HIV among Inmates; Cognitive-Behavioral Therapies in Prison; Elderly Offenders in Prison; Inmate Dental Care; Mental Health Issues and Jails; Mentally Ill Prisoners; Overcrowding; Pregnancy and Motherhood in Prisons; Treatment in Prisons

Further Reading

Andrews, M. (2015, September 30). Even in prison, healthcare often comes with a copay. *NPR.* Retrieved from http://www.npr.org/sections/health-shots/2015/09/30/444 451967/even-in-prison-health-care-often-comes-with-a-copay

Braithwaite, R. L., Treadwell, H. M., & Arriola, K. R. (2008). Health disparities and incarcerated women: A population ignored. *American Journal of Public Health, 98*(Suppl. 1), S173–S175.

Cohen, A. (2015, May 7). Older prisoners, higher costs. *The Marshall Project.* Retrieved from https://www.themarshallproject.org/2015/05/06/older-prisoners-higher-costs# .MAFjWUKmk

Fifer, B. (2012). The graying of Pennsylvania's prisons. *Correctional Forum.* Retrieved from http://media.wix.com/ugd/4c2da0_a1a9113f3f73fb58c3d36c0adbd65209.pdf

Krauth, B., Stayton, K., & Clem, C. (2005). *Fees paid by jail inmates: Fee categories, revenues, and management perspectives in a sample of US jails.* National Institute of Corrections, Jails Division.

Marshall, T., Simpson, S., & Stevens, A. (2001). Use of health services by prison inmates: Comparison with the community. *Journal of Epidemiology and Community Health, 55*(5), 364–365.

Mason, C. (2012). *Too good to be true: Private prisons in America.* Washington, DC: Sentencing Project.

Mattera, P., Khan, M., & Nathan, S. (2003). *Corrections Corporation of America: A critical look at its first twenty years.* Charlotte, NC: Grassroots Leadership. Retrieved from http://www.grassrootsleadership.org/_publications/CCAAnniversaryReport .pdf

Moraff, C. (2012, February 19). The graying of America's prison population. *The Philadelphia Tribune.* Retrieved from: http://www.phillytrib.com/news/graying-of -america-s-prison-population/article_aa5d6414-e2f9-5612-ba63-97d69cfbc2e9.html

Schaenman, P., Davies, E., Jordan, R., & Chakraborty, R. (2013). *Opportunities for cost savings in corrections without sacrificing service quality: inmate healthcare.* Washington, DC: Urban Institute. Retrieved from http://www.urban.org/Uploaded PDF/412754-Inmate-Health-Care.pdf

Stephan, J. (2001). State prison expenditures. *Bureau of Justice Statistics.* Retrieved from http://www.bjs.gov/index.cfm?ty=pbdetail&iid=1174

Van den Bergh, B. J., Gatherer, A., & Moller, L. F. (2009). Women's health in prison: Urgent need for improvement in gender equity and social justice. *Bulletin of the World Health Organization, 87*(6), 406–406.

Wright, L. N. (2008). Healthcare in prison thirty years after *Estelle v. Gamble. Journal of Correctional Healthcare, 14*(1), 31–35.

Health Promotion in Prison Settings

Prisons are vulnerable to health issues, and prison health care must compensate for a variety of unique conditions including overcrowding, high turnover rates, poor hygiene, and/or previous medical conditions. Moreover, some health issues are more prevalent among the prison population, such as mental health issues (schizophrenia to bipolar disorder), suicidal tendencies, substance abuse, addiction and/or secondary medical issues often linked to previous drug use. Physical and mental health issues aside, prisons experience higher rates of infectious diseases such as HIV/AIDS, viral hepatitis, tuberculosis, and sexually transmitted diseases than the general population (Steele et al., 2007, p. 5). These vulnerabilities can be exacerbated when treatment suffers from an inherent lack of resources and underequipped prison facilities. Recent indications suggest that prisons faced with these deficits simply cannot provide effective care, which has ushered in a new era of prison health care relying on privatized aid or contracted health care (Austin & Coventry, 2001, p. 9).

Correctional health care has undertaken a settings-based environment shift, dedicated to promoting health in prisons (Standard minimum rules for the treatment of prisoners, 1957). This design extends broad medical care to cover an active promotion of health within the prison setting. This settings-based approach to promoting health in prisons draws on prison policies that promote health, making sure the prion environment is supportive to heath and initiatives that are specific to individual prisons (Whitehead, 2006). A philosophy spearheaded by the World Health Organization's (WHO) Health Promoting Prisons Project (HPP), also called Health in Prisons Project (HIPP), extends to 30 member states. HPP ushered in a facelift to the prisoners/health debate by acknowledging the inequality between public health and prison health. This settings approach attempts to close this gap by highlighting prison policies, prison environment, and personalizing prisoner care. Ultimately, the goal of this project is to improve public health by addressing health care in prisons, implementing a settings approach that addresses prison policies, prison environments, and health issues specific to individuals (Woodall et al., 2014, p. 115). The WHO's Health in Prisons Project's main purpose is to support the European Union's 28 member states by improving public health and health care in prisons at national and international levels.

There are multiple region-based health care implementations and rights that pertain to prisoners. For example, region-based policies include the Southern Center for Human Rights, which "ensures adequate medical care for people who are incarcerated, SCHR brings class action lawsuits" and is a for-profit health care provider for people in prisons whose medical needs have suffered. The offender health research network is focused on health care research innovations and aims to develop a pathway of research between the criminal justice system and the University of Manchester. The National Commission on Correctional Health Care's (NCCHC) mission is to also improve the quality of health care in jails, prisons, and juvenile facilities (NCCHC, 2002). Each state has a Department of Health Services that provides for correctional institutions.

Corrections is accustomed to a system reform approach; however, the health-promoting prison model has experienced resistance. As such, the WHO's health-promoting model has been reconceptualized and has begun to solidify over the last decade. Woodall, in a 2014 study, supports a social model approach that facilitates a wider appreciation of social determinants that often affect health. In order to promote prisoner health there must be a push past a restorative medical model and toward a "preventative perspective" design (Woodall et al., 2014, p. 114). Philosophical changes must be accommodated alongside changes in the groundwork. Specifically, areas of concern often expose a triage suffering from routine deficits, individualized medical care, education, and adequate health care upon release.

Adopting a social model that focuses on a preventative approach assists within individualizing prisoner treatment. Another study points toward a *Survey of Inmates in Local Jails*: the research indicates that a vast majority of prisoners do not receive adequate care during their incarceration, even for the most serious chronic physical illnesses (Wilper et al., 2009). The research is data-driven showing "13.9% of federal inmates, 20.1% of state inmates, and 68.4% of local jail inmates with a persistent medical problem hadn't received a medical examination since beginning their prison term" (Wilper et al., 2009, p. 20). Drawing on recommendations from the HPP model outlined above, litigations from the Snake River Correctional Institution exposed inadequate mental health care when a prisoner died in the Disciplinary Segregation Unit in this Oregon prison resulting in the opening of a health promotion unit in 2016. Prison staff and administration addressed the program's efficacy, noting how inmates are able to work with other inmates who are also working on similar goals. Moreover, these individualized programs with real-time monitoring supports a proactive approach allowing inmates to change their own mind-sets.

Educational programs may be key to promoting health within an institutionalized prison setting. Specifically, offenders who are educated about diseases, illnesses, and mental disorders can begin to acknowledge warning signs themselves, furthering the possibility for seeking treatment. The National Commission on Correctional Health Care (2002) promotes this approach and sponsors transitional health care to include continuation of support services and health care treatments as well as planning activities. Flanagan (2004) addresses the goals for transitional health care planning in *Health Care Needs of Inmates Leaving U.S. Prisons, and Recommendations for Improving Transitional Health Care*, which includes: "accurate assessment of offender health care needs, seamless transfer from the prison health care provider to the community provider to ensure continuity of care, and interagency collaboration and communication." Long-term goals consist of "maintenance of the health care treatment regimens, promotion of health for the individual and community and reduction of recidivism related to health care problems such as mental illness or substance abuse" (Flanagan, 2004, p. 26). Educational programs were exiled in the 1990s by President Clinton's Violent Crime Control and Law Enforcement Act of 1994 that denied Pell Grants and other educational resources to prisoners. This void in educational programs severely crippled the rehabilitation efforts within correctional institutions. Some researchers argue that the lack of job skills, diminishing self-esteem, and diminishing social modeling relationships shape the social world of incarcerated individuals when education is supposed to be a democratic right (Watts, 2016). Both individualized treatment and education programs adhere to the goals of HPP.

Moreover, the HPP standards also support the larger correctional philosophy serving the reduction of recidivism. Health care, or aftercare, for prisoners upon release, is very sporadic and unreliable. Many prisoners experience a variety of strains that are tightly linked to health. Disadvantaged circumstances augment a range of health and social needs that weaken prisoner health. A 2004 study argued that the needs of prisoners are often lost, simply due to the lack of an adequate information system, which includes data collection and record-keeping, and can potentially transition offenders following release and establishing treatment plans for postrelease programs (Flanagan, 2004). Later research reveals that prisoners receive, on average, a 22-day total supply of medication and often have difficulty getting access to the rest (Flanagan, 2004). Moreover, only 28 states report referrals to community health agencies. Postrelease care is central to offenders' physical and mental health issues. For instance, Yellowstone County Jail and Montana Women's Prison are researching the idea of enrolling all of their inmates with Medicaid. According to Larry Mayer, writer of the local *Gazette*, the county and the state corrections department want to use Medicaid to reduce the costs and recidivism because the majority of their inmate population are incarcerated for drug-related problems.

Individualized treatment, education, and solid documentation upon release continue to be areas correctional facilities must foster within the HPP model. Prisoner health relies on tailored treatments, self-promotion, and accurate data collection. Treatment and education are areas that are gaining focus in correctional facilities. However, correctional facilities may be lacking in technological advances such as record-keeping, in-house data, storage of inmate information, and protocols with differing computer systems. For the WHO's HPP model to take root, reliance on accurate and valid information must be adopted to assist in developing a promising correctional health care system. A prisoner health care reform that not only studies and monitors diseases will also track the health issues alongside well-known recidivism trends.

Emily A. Hayden

See also: AIDS/HIV among Inmates; Education in Prison; Mentally Ill Prisoners; Overcrowding; Recidivism

Further Reading

Austin, J., & Coventry, G. (2001). *Emerging issues on privatized prisons* (NCJ 181249). Washington, DC: Bureau of Justice Assistance.

De Viggiani, N. (2006). Surviving prison: Exploring prison social life as a determinant of health. *International Journal of Prisoner Health, 2*(2), 71–89.

Flanagan, N. A. (2004). Transitional health care for offenders being released from United States prisons. *Canadian Journal of Nursing Research, 36*, 38–58.

Green, J., Tones, K., Cross, R., & Woodall, J. (2015). *Health promotion: Planning & strategies.* Thousand Oaks, CA: Sage.

Herbert, K., Plugge, E., Foster, C., & Doll, H. (2012). Prevalence and risk factors for noncommunicable diseases in prison populations worldwide. *The Lancet, 397*, 1975–1982.

National Commission on Correctional Health Care. (NCCHC). (2002). *The health status of soon-to-be-released inmates: A report to Congress* (Vols. I and II). Chicago: Author. Retrieved from http://www.ncchc.org/health-status-of-soon-to-be-released-inmates

Standard minimum rules for the treatment of prisoners. (1957). Adopted by the First United Nations Congress on the Prevention of Crime and the Treatment of Offenders, held at Geneva in 1955, and approved by the Economic and Social Council by its resolutions 663 C (XXIV) of 31 July 1957 and 2076 (LXII) of 13 May 1977. Retrieved from http://www.ohchr.org/EN/ProfessionalInterest/Pages/TreatmentOfPrisoners.aspx

Steele, C. B., Meléndez-Morales, L., Campoluci, R., DeLuca, N., & Dean, H. D. (2007, November). *Health disparities in HIV/AIDS, viral hepatitis, sexually transmitted diseases, and tuberculosis: Issues, burden, and response, a retrospective review, 2000–2004.* Atlanta: Department of Health and Human Services, Centers for Disease Control and Prevention. Retrieved from http://www.cdc.gov/nchhstp/healthdisparities

United Nations. (1990). *Basic principles for the treatment of prisoners.* Adopted and proclaimed by General Assembly resolution 45/111 of 14 December 1990. Retrieved from http://www.ohchr.org/EN/ProfessionalInterest/Pages/BasicPrinciplesTreatmentOfPrisoners.aspx

Watts, A. (2016). Education in prison: A spiritual revolution America needs. *The Blog, HuffPost.*

Whitehead, D. (2006). The health promoting prison (HPP) and its imperative for nursing. *International Journal of Nursing Studies, 43,* 123.

Wilper, A. P., Woolhandler, S., Boyd, J. W., Lasser, K. E., McCormick, D., & Bor, D. H. (2009). The health and health care of US prisoners: Results of a nationwide survey. *American Journal of Public Health, 99*(4), 666–672.

Woodall, J., de Viggiani, N., Dixey, R., & South, J. (2014). Moving prison health promotion along: Toward an integrative framework for action to develop health promotion and tackle the social determinants of health. *Criminal Justice Studies, 27,* 114–132.

Hunger Strikes

The concept of hunger strikes is defined as the intentional self-deprivation of food and nutrition during a significant interval, characteristically for political purposes. They are most often accomplished in prison environments or other types of detention facilities, thus contributing to complex concerns such as the physical and psychological well-being of those incarcerated and the potential for legal and ethical debate. Further, hunger strikes are generally not perceived as a method of suicide but as an avenue to have specific demands met and for bringing alleged injustices to a national or global audience.

From a historical perspective, hunger strikes are not a new phenomenon. Their account dates back to pre-Christian Ireland when they were used as a means of protest within the Brehon law system. Civil codes were interpreted by *Brehons* (jurists), who served as intermediaries and made oral decisions pertaining to the fate of those who harmed others. Fasting developed as a common choice in objection to those verdicts. This custom of self-deprivation was also seen in India during ancient times as a communal request for fairness. It became banned by the government in the mid-19th century. In more contemporary times, hunger strikes have evolved as a technique of bringing awareness to actual or perceived injustices by the reigning political administration. This practice became prevalent in

Northern Ireland during the "Troubles," by ostensive political prisoners, most noted by the 1981 starvation of Irish republican detainee Bobby Sands inside the HM Maze Prison located 9 miles southwest of Belfast. Nine others who were serving a prison sentence on H block with Sands also died over a period of four months.

Although often associated with Irish history and folklore, hunger strikes have more recently been realized in North American, Europe, and parts of the Middle East. In 2005, while being held at the military prison at Guantanamo Bay, Cuba, 50 detainees were reported to be participating in hunger strikes in protest of their custody and indeterminate confinement. The following year, a 69-day hunger strike occurred in Turkey when inmates demonstrated against harsh physical conditions, extended periods of isolation, and being incarcerated in remote prisons, far removed from their families and legal advocates. The protest led to the death of a dozen prisoners and questions about human rights issues against the Turkish government. A second and more devastating demonstration occurred between 2000 and 2003 when hundreds of prisoners across Turkey began fasting and pronouncing their willingness to die in order to stop the construction of F-type prisons. These prison styles created seclusion and limited communal interaction. They further allowed for unreported acts of violence and potential human rights violations. At the conclusion, more than 100 lives were lost, and continued questions were raised about government policies on the moral treatment of prisoners and whether or not they should be permitted to starve to death.

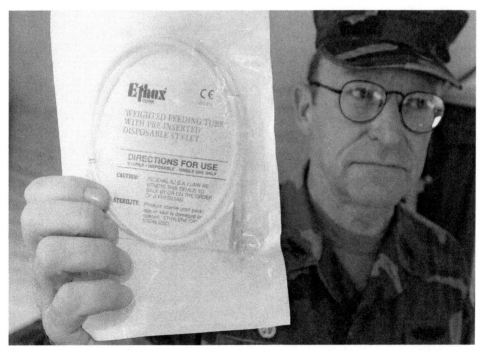

Occasionally, some inmates use hunger strikes to disrupt the prison regime. Officials have used feeding tubes on inmates who conduct hunger strikes to ensure they receive the proper nutrition. (Chris Hondros/Getty Images)

Other noted hunger strikes occurred in 2012 when nearly 2,000 Palestinian prisoners incarcerated in Israeli jails protested against their conditions of confinement and policies surrounding family visitation privileges. In 2013, one of the largest hunger strikes ensued throughout the California prison system when almost 30,000 inmates refused meals. Like many other prison demonstrations, California prisoners condemned the punitive conditions of solitary confinement and how it was widely used as an indiscriminate method of retribution. The strike ended after two months when a California judge permitted the force-feeding of the protesters.

In many cases, incidents such as these present concerns about ethics and the legality of force-feeding prisoners. This process frequently embraces the use of restraint chairs, coercive techniques, and the introduction of nasogastric tubes as a procedure to get nutrition and sustenance into the prisoner through the nasal cavity. Policies such as force-feeding are often designed to preserve life and can be perceived as a medical procedure that sustains the safety of the inmate. However, human rights activists propose the methods used are abusive and the nasogastric tubes used to induce feeding are seen as barbaric. The World Medical Association suggests that physicians who examine those on hunger strikes assess the individual's mental capacity and ensure their actions are knowingly and voluntarily undertaken, with a clear understanding of their potential harm and possible death.

Darren K. Stocker

See also: Health Care in Prison Populations; Political Prisoners; Solitary Confinement

Further Reading

Anderson, P. (2004). 'To lie down to death for days': The Turkish hunger strike, 2000–2003. *Cultural Studies, 18*(6), 816–846.

Annas, G. J. (1995). Hunger strikes. *BMJ: British Medical Journal, 311*(7013), 1114.

Crosby, S. S., Apovian, C. M., & Grodin, M. A. (2007). Hunger strikes, force-feeding, and physicians' responsibilities. *Journal of the American Medical Association, 298*(5), 563–566.

Fessler, D. M. (2003). The implications of starvation induced psychological changes for the ethical treatment of hunger strikers. *Journal of Medical Ethics, 29*(4), 243–247.

Gross, M. L. (2013). Force-feeding, autonomy, and the public interest. *New England Journal of Medicine, 369*(2), 103–105.

Scanlan, S. J., Stoll, L. C., & Lumm, K. (2008). Starving for change: The hunger strike and nonviolent action, 1906–2004. *Research in Social Movements, Conflicts and Change, 28*, 275–323.

Sweeney, G. (1993). Irish hunger strikes and the cult of self-sacrifice. *Journal of Contemporary History, 28*(3), 421–437.

Yuill, C. (2007). The body as weapon: Bobby Sands and the Republican hunger strikes. *Sociological Research Online, 12*(2), 1–11.

Importation Model

The importation model is a theoretical model that explains inmate behavior in prison. It is thought that inmates import behaviors or characteristics into the prison from the outside. Any traits an individual possesses will be mirrored in prison if those traits are present prior to incarceration. For example, if a person has a tendency for violence outside of prison, then that person will likely behave violently in prison. In order to cope with their new prison environment, inmates will rely on their attitudes, beliefs, values, experiences, and social norms to acclimate themselves to prison life.

The importation model views the characteristics of the inmate, rather than characteristics of the prison environment, as being at fault for misconduct, violence, suicide, and other maladjustments. Inmates' demographic, social, and psychological characteristics best explain adjustment or behavior in prison. One's norms and values will facilitate how one reacts to incarceration. Common measures of the importation model include age, gender, race, marital status, education, employment, mental illness, substance abuse, violence, and previous criminal history. The individuals' preprison socialization, experience, and lifestyle will greatly influence how they respond to incarceration, which social groups they become a part of, whether or not they comply with prison rules, if they will resort to drug use, if they will require mental health care, and other considerations.

Individual inmates who adapt to prison life may subscribe to a certain subculture within the prison setting. The characteristics that get imported will affect the type of subculture created. If the inmates belong to a gang outside of prison walls, those inmates will import the norms and values of their gang into how they conduct themselves in prison. These individuals will likely be aggressive, violate rules, and get involved with extortion or other illegal activity inside prison walls, much like they would outside of prison in their street gang. They may find others with similar mind-sets or behaviors and recruit individuals into their subculture or clique, similar to recruiting gang members on the outside.

The importation model is limited in scope as it does not address the prison context or the role of the prison environment in inmates' behavior. The model does not consider the conditions, culture, or deprivations that prisons present. It is too simplistic to dismiss situational factors and has difficulty in explaining how to intervene in prison adjustment or behavior. It discredits how various situations, influences, and experiences within prison can affect how individuals deal with their new environment.

The importation model cannot be discussed without mention of its counterpart, the deprivation model. This model stems from the pains of imprisonment.

Specifically, inmates develop a culture to adapt to being deprived of autonomy, privacy, property, safety, freedom, basic goods and services, and family contact. The deprivation model theorizes that the conditions, environment, culture, or restrictions of the prison itself influences how inmates adjust to incarceration. Situational factors are at the core of this model. Limitations exist in the deprivation model as well. The deprivation model lacks insight on individual inmate characteristics, propensities, and lifestyles and how these factors can contribute to prison behavior.

Although both models exhibit limitations, the importation and deprivation models may not be mutually exclusive. Another branch of thought is that a combined model exists to explain inmate behavior or adjustment. In the combined model, both personal characteristics and prison characteristics influence how an individual adapts to prison life. Inmates react differently to prison conditions based largely on their individual characteristics. However, these characteristics may be hard to separate from the influences of the prison environment in promoting or limiting how inmates cope. For instance, prisoners who have demographic, social, or psychological characteristics that influence their behavior may be more likely to adapt positively to the prison environment when conditions are less depriving. On the other hand, prisoners with such characteristics may experience heightened responses if prison conditions are more depriving.

Overall, the importation model suggests that behaviors such as aggression are not products of the prison but instead the dispositions of the individuals housed there. This has grave implications for how society views criminal offenders when the sole blame is placed on the personal characteristics of inmates. However, if adjustment to prison is solely influenced by the predisposition of inmates, then intervention with high-risk inmates may be simplified by assessing their personal characteristics without consideration of the prison environment. If it is known how an offender behaves in the outside world, prison staff and officials can project potential behavior in the prison.

Maria M. Buchholz-Kerzmann

See also: Deprivation Model; Pains of Imprisonment

Further Reading

Cao, L., Zhao, J., & Van Dine, S. (1997). Prison disciplinary tickets: A test of the deprivation and importation models. *Journal of Criminal Justice, 25*(2), 103–113.

DeLisi, M., Berg, M. T., & Hochstetler, A. (2004). Gang members, career criminals and prison violence: Further specification of the importation model of inmate behavior. *Criminal Justice Studies, 17*(4), 369–383.

DeLisi, M., Trulson, C. R., Marquart, J. W., Drury, A. J., & Kosloski, A. E. (2011). Inside the prison black box: Toward a life course importation model of inmate behavior. *International Journal of Offender Therapy and Comparative Criminology, 55*(8), 1186–1207.

Dye, M. H. (2010). Deprivation, importation, and prison suicide: Combined effects of institutional conditions and inmate composition. *Journal of Criminal Justice, 38*(4), 796–806.

Hochstetler, A., & DeLisi, M. (2005). Importation, deprivation, and varieties of serving time: An integrated-lifestyle-exposure model of prison offending. *Journal of Criminal Justice, 33*(3), 257–266.

Irwin, J., & Cressey, D. R. (1962). Thieves, convicts and the inmate culture. *Social Problems, 10*(2), 142–155.

Jiang, S., & Fisher-Giorlando, M. (2002). Inmate misconduct: A test of the deprivation, importation, and situational models. *The Prison Journal, 82*(3), 335–358.

Sorensen, J., Wrinkle, R., & Gutierrez, A. (1998). Patterns of rule-violating behaviors and adjustment to incarceration among murderers. *The Prison Journal, 78*(3), 222–231.

Sykes, G. M. (2007). *The society of captives: A study of a maximum security prison.* Princeton, NJ: Princeton University Press.

Thomas, C. W. (1977). Theoretical perspectives on prisonization: A comparison of the importation and deprivation models. *Journal of Criminal Law & Criminology, 68*, 135.

Thomas, C. W., & Foster, S. C. (1973). The importation model perspective on inmate social roles: An empirical test. *The Sociological Quarterly, 14*(2), 226–234.

Inappropriate Correctional Employee–Inmate Relationships

In the United States, more than 2.3 million prisoners are currently incarcerated at a cost of approximately $80 billion per year. Given the tremendous amount of resources that are invested in the mass incarceration movement, researchers have begun to examine inappropriate staff-inmate relationships—the boundary violations between correctional staff members and inmates that are often economic or sexual in nature as well as illegal. Although it is true that the guard subculture discourages overfamiliarity between prison staff and inmates, some correctional employees still cross over the sacrosanct border and become overly familiar with the very prisoners they are paid to supervise. If this goes unchecked, the deviant correctional officer may even assist an inmate in an escape. Indeed, this occurred in 2015, when Joyce Mitchell, a 51-year-old grandmother, made international headlines after pleading guilty to helping two convicted murderers escape from the Clinton Correctional Facility in New York.

Sadly, the above case is not an anomaly within the world of institutional corrections. On the contrary, every day staff members put not only themselves but also their coworkers at risk by behaving inappropriately with the inmates. Correctional administrators are fully aware of this, and as a result, virtually every jail and prison agency in the United States provide employees with specialized training specifically designed to prevent inappropriate staff relationships from occurring. In fact, Bud Allen and Diana Bosta's *Games Criminals Play* (1981), a book which warns correctional employees of the dangers of overfamiliarity with inmates, was once required reading for all newly hired correctional officers within the Federal Bureau of Prisons.

In spite of the preventive measures that administrators take to reduce inappropriate relationships, many individuals who work behind the prison walls know that inappropriate relationships occur with surprising regularity. Robert M. Worley, a self-described "guard-researcher," describes in his autoethnographic account how inmate manipulators identify the weak links among the guards, subtly feel them out, and then untiringly persist in establishing these inappropriate relationships.

272   Inappropriate Correctional Employee–Inmate Relationships

He notes that when sexual relationships between inmates and staff occur, they tend to take place in semiprivate areas such as kitchens, laundry rooms, commissaries, and workshops. There is also research which indicates that when offenders willingly have sexual relationships with correctional employees, they typically attempt to conceal this behavior not only from staff members but also from their fellow prisoners who have incentives to inform on them.

Although it is true that an offender cannot legally consent to a sexual relationship of any kind by virtue of the fact that he or she is incarcerated, a growing body of research suggests it is not unusual for male inmates to initiate interactions with female staff for the purpose of establishing an inappropriate relationship. It is noteworthy that the correctional facilities of today are no longer sexually segregated places. Female correctional officers are free to work in male prisons and constitute roughly 40 percent of the guard workforce. Even though the sexual integration of the correctional officer workforce has undoubtedly assisted females in making much-needed strides toward gaining equality in the workplace, it has had the unintended consequence of creating new opportunities for male inmates to have sexual relationships with staff.

In a Bureau of Justice Statistics (BJS) analysis of aggregate level data, Allen J. Beck, Ramona R. Rantala, and Jessica Rexroat (2014) discovered that offenders appeared to be willing participants in 84 percent of the cases of sexual misconduct between male inmates and female correctional employees. In an additional governmental study, conducted by Allen J. Beck, Marcus Berzofsky, Rachel Caspar, and Christopher Krebs (2013), commonly referred to by prison researchers as the National Inmate Survey, 2.3 percent of inmate respondents reported to be a willing participant in a sexual relationship with a staff member within the past 12 months. In a similar yet significantly smaller study, Kelly Cheeseman Dial and Robert M. Worley (2008) administered questionnaires to male inmates within the Texas Department of Criminal Justice and found that 14 percent (50 of the 367 respondents) reported engaging in a sexual act with a prison staff member.

Though it is true that some offenders are motivated to have sexual relationships with correctional employees, they also seek to establish inappropriate relationships with prison staff to obtain dangerous contraband, such as, tobacco, illicit drugs, weapons, and cell phones. Prisoners may additionally initiate relationships with correctional employees to gain "creature comforts," such as gum, fast food, or even sexually oriented magazines—which are prohibited by some correctional agencies.

It is possible that some prison employees who cross the line with inmates have psychological problems or are even afflicted with a disorder known as *hybristophilia*, the love of criminals. Nevertheless, there is a strong indication that broader environmental variables often permit inmate-staff inappropriate relationships to flourish. For instance, poor supervision practices, low hiring standards, dangerous working conditions, abysmal pay, and a perceived lack of public support may increase the prevalence of boundary violations throughout correctional facilities. There is also research that suggests correctional employees who view their supervisors as unsupportive are more likely than their coworkers to engage in acts of deviance, including behaving inappropriately with inmates. Given that inappropriate relationships can wreak havoc on correctional facilities and compromise

Inappropriate Correctional Employee–Inmate Relationships 273

institutional security, researchers will continue to conduct academic investigations of the various ways by which social distance is diminished between the keeper and the kept.

Robert M. Worley

See also: Baltimore City Detention Center; Consensual Sex between Inmates; Economics of Crossing Over, The; Mitchell, Joyce

Further Reading

Allen, B., & Bosta, D. (1981). *Games criminals play.* Susanville, CA: Rae John.

Beck, A. J., Berzofsky, M., Caspar, R., & Krebs, C. (2013). *Sexual victimization in state and federal prisons reported by inmates, 2011–2012* (NCJ 241399). Washington, DC: U.S. Department of Justice.

Beck, A. J., Rantala, R.R., & Rexroat, J. (2014). *Sexual victimization reported by adult correctional authorities, 2009–11* (NCJ 243904). Washington, DC: U.S. Department of Justice.

Blackburn, A. G., Fowler, S. K., Mullings, J. L., & Marquart, J. W. (2011). When boundaries are broken: Inmate perceptions of correctional staff boundary violations. *Deviant Behavior, 32,* 351–378.

Dial, K. C., & Worley, R. M. (2008). Crossing the line: A quantitative analysis of inmate boundary violators in a southern prison system. *American Journal of Criminal Justice, 33,* 69–84.

Marquart, J. W., Barnhill, M. B., & Balshaw-Biddle, K. (2001). Fatal attraction: An analysis of employee boundary violations in a southern prison system, 1995–1998. *Justice Quarterly, 18,* 878–910.

Ross, J. I. (2013). Deconstructing correctional officer deviance: Toward typologies of actions and controls. *Criminal Justice Review, 38,* 110–126.

Worley, R. M. (2011). To snitch or not to snitch, that is the question: Exploring the role of inmate informants in detecting inappropriate relationships between the keeper and the kept. *International Review of Law, Computers, and Technology, 25,* 79–82.

Worley, R. M. (2016). Memoirs of a guard-researcher: Deconstructing the games inmates play behind the prison walls. *Deviant Behavior, 37,* 1215–1226.

Worley, R. M., & Cheeseman, K. A. (2006). Guards as embezzlers: The consequences of non-shareable problems in prison settings. *Deviant Behavior, 27,* 203–222.

Worley, R. M., Marquart, J. W., & Mullings, J. L. (2003). Prison guard predators: An analysis of inmates who established inappropriate relationships with prison staff, 1995–1998. *Deviant Behavior, 24,* 175–198.

Worley, R. M., Tewksbury, R., & Frantzen, D. (2010). Preventing fatal attractions: Lessons learned from inmate boundary violators in a southern penitentiary system. *Criminal Justice Studies, 23,* 347–360.

Worley, R. M., & Worley, V. B. (2011). Guards gone wild: A self-report study of correctional officer misconduct and the effect of institutional deviance on care within the Texas prison system. *Deviant Behavior, 32,* 293–319.

Worley, R. M., & Worley, V. B. (2013). Games guards play: A self-report study of institutional deviance in the Texas department of criminal justice. *Criminal Justice Studies, 26,* 115–132.

Worley, R. M., & Worley, V. B. (2013). Inmate public autoerotism uncovered: Exploring the dynamics of masturbatory behavior within correctional facilities. *Deviant Behavior, 34,* 11–24.

Worley, R. M., & Worley, V. B. (2016). The economics of crossing over: Examining the link between correctional officer pay and guard-inmate boundary violations. *Deviant Behavior, 37*, 16–29.

Worley, R. M., Worley, V. B., & Hsu, H. (2018). Can I trust my co-worker? Examining correctional officers' perceptions of staff-inmates inappropriate relationships with a southern penitentiary system. *Deviant Behavior, 39*, 332–346.

Worley, V. B., Worley, R. M., & Mullings, J. L. (2010). Rape lore in correctional settings: Assessing inmates' awareness of sexual correction in prisons. *Southwest Journal of Criminal Justice, 7*, 65–86.

Incarcerated Veterans

More than 180,000 veterans were inmates of U.S. correctional facilities in 2011–2012. While comprising roughly 8 percent of the total inmate population in our nation's prison and jails, these veterans represent men and women who have served in various conflicts including World War II, Korea, Vietnam, Persian Gulf, Iraq, Afghanistan, and other regional conflicts. The relationship between military service and criminality is complex, and for many years criminality was simply considered a by-product of war, a preexisting propensity, or an unexplained phenomenon for a few unfortunate service members. However, today with more attention placed on the role of post-traumatic stress disorder (PTSD), traumatic brain injury (TBI), depression, and suicide, the relationship between military service and criminal activity has received renewed, interdisciplinary attention (Culp et al., 2013).

One of the most accessible sources of data for justice-involved veterans is the U.S. Department of Justice (DOJ). The Bureau of Justice Statistics (BJS), an integral data clearinghouse of the DOJ, conducts a national survey of federal and state inmates and periodically reports on incarcerated veterans. In 2015, military veterans comprised 9 percent of the U.S. population, 8 percent of the state and federal inmates, and 7 percent of the jail population (Bureau of Justice Statistics, 2015). The number of incarcerated veterans in prisons and jails across the United States has declined over the last 30 years. During the 1970s and 1980s veterans were more likely to be incarcerated than nonveterans; however, this trend reversed in the 1990s. By 2004, veterans made up about 10 percent of the inmate population, down from 20 percent in 1986.

In comparison to the general population, veterans had a lower rate of incarceration (855 per 100,000) than nonveterans (968 per 100,000), were more likely to be convicted of a violent offense (64 percent) than their nonveteran counterparts (48 percent), and were older (43 percent) than nonveterans (32 percent). Veterans were more likely than nonveterans to be married, divorced, male, and Hispanic. Incarcerated veterans were more likely to have fewer prior arrests, violent sexual offense convictions, sentences longer than five years, or a life sentence. Veterans sentenced to our prisons and jails generally are better educated than their nonveteran counterparts (BJS, 2015). The majority of incarcerated veterans were honorably discharged, and about half served at least three years in the military. At least half of all veterans in prisons and jails have been diagnosed with a mental disorder, and a large percentage had four or more prior arrests. Nearly 75 percent of

A Vietnam veteran and inmate of the medium-security Federal Correctional Institution near Coleman, Florida, is serving a 50-year prison sentence for engaging in various drug offenses. In some cases, veterans, especially those who are accustomed to combat and bored with civilian life, may commit crimes to heighten their adrenaline levels. (Nikki Kahn/The Washington Post via Getty Images)

incarcerated veterans did not see combat during their military service. More than 50 percent of the incarcerated veterans served in the U.S. Army, while 2 percent served in the Coast Guard. Only 1 percent of veterans serving time in jail or prison were female.

As previously noted, concern about the relationship between military service and criminality is not unique to veterans of contemporary conflicts. Although concern over "battle fatigue," "shell shock," "combat fatigue," or "combat stress" can be found across the psychology, social work, and psychiatry literature, examination of the nexus between military service and involvement in the criminal justice system is not as abundant. Over time with the softening and distancing of the negative attitudes toward the Vietnam War and the advancement of our understanding of mental health issues among veterans, it became important to determine why so many of our men and women in uniform were winding up behind bars. Some studies examined incarcerated Vietnam veterans and found a relationship between combat exposure and criminality (Shaw et al., 1987). Others examined mental health and criminality, while some focused extensively on the relationship between substance abuse and crime.

Veterans often lose or have their Veterans Administration (VA) benefits significantly reduced while they are incarcerated. To assist justice-involved veterans, many federal, state, and local agencies have developed programs to assist veterans during and after their incarceration. Self-help groups within prison and jails are often established to provide peer support, safe zones, and information to incarcerated veterans. These self-help groups consist of veterans helping other veterans deal with issues such as obtaining veterans benefits, correcting military records, and discharge upgrades. In 2007, the VA established the Health Care for Re-entry Veterans (HCRC) targeting issues facing veterans as they are released from prison or jail. The VA focuses their efforts on transition and permanent housing, access to community-based substance abuse treatment and mental health services, community readjustment, employment, and veterans benefits.

In one study on the impact of HCRC outreach services using data from the 2010 National Survey of Incarcerated Veterans, researchers noted that in a sample of more than 30,000 incarcerated veterans, those with service in Operation Enduring Freedom (OEF), Operation Iraqi Freedom (OIF), or Operation New Dawn (OND) were less likely than other veterans to be incarcerated yet were more likely to have combat exposure and PTSD. Further, these veterans were less likely to report substance abuse issues, were homeless, and without recent income than older veterans. Alcohol abuse or dependence was common among all veterans, although OEF, OIF, and OND veterans were more likely to seek VA services (Tsai et al., 2013b).

In a similar study using the same data from the 2010 National Survey of Veterans, researchers found that African American and Hispanic males are overrepresented in the incarcerated veteran population across all age groups, although the rate is lower than that of the general population. The authors suggest that veteran status could be viewed as a protective or insulating factor (e.g., military training and other educational opportunities) against incarceration, while veteran race could elevate the risk of incarceration (Greenberg & Rosencheck, 2011; Tsai et al., 2013a). Others suggest that the armed forces recruitment and retention policies (e.g., draft, all-volunteer force) may be a factor in the quality of personnel serving in the armed forces and their propensity to engage in criminal activity before, during, and after military service (Greenberg & Rosencheck, 2011).

A study of incarcerated veterans found that individuals with combat experience are less likely than those without combat exposure to be in prison or jail (Culp et al., 2013). That is, combat service decreases the likelihood of incarceration and military-related factors lack sufficient explanatory power, especially for draft-era veterans, to account for veteran criminality. Instead, demographic and social factors are more relevant, thereby debunking the myth of the violent, mentally unstable combat veteran (Blodgett et al., 2015; National Institute of Corrections, 2016).

State and local government across the county have established programs for at-risk veterans. One such program that is growing exponentially is the veterans treatment court (VTC). Veterans treatment courts are a hybrid, problem-solving court based on existing drug and mental health court models. The first VTC was established in 2008 in Buffalo, New York, by Judge Robert Russell. By 2012 there were 168 VTCs across the country and more than 7,500 participants (Frederick, 2013). The VTCs try to divert justice-involved veterans from jail or prison by offering evidence-based programming, supervision, and support that are tailored to meet the unique needs of the offender. The key components of VTCs include early identification and placement of participants, integrated substance abuse treatment and mental health services, nonadversarial courtroom work groups, frequent screening for drugs and alcohol, continuum of care, judicial involvement, coordinated strategies of graduated responses, partnerships with the VA, community-based agencies and other local resources, ongoing interdisciplinary educational opportunities, and the use of veteran mentors to provide essential peer support to the justice-involved veteran. The final component is ongoing monitoring and evaluations of program effectiveness and modification.

Elizabeth L. Grossi

See also: Mentally Ill Prisoners; Recidivism

Further Reading
Black, D. W., Carney, C. P., Peleso, P. M., Woolson, R. F., Letuchy, E., & Doebbeling, B. N. (2005). Incarceration and veterans of the first gulf war. *Military Medicine, 170* (7), 612–618.

Blodgett, J. C., Avoundjian, T., Finlay, A. K., Rosenthal, J., Asch, S. M., Maisel, N. C., & Midboe, A. M. (2015). Prevalence of mental health disorders among justice-involved veterans. *Epidemiologic Reviews, 37*(1), 163–176.

Bureau of Justice Statistics. (2007). *Veterans in state and federal prison, 2004.* Washington, DC: U.S. Department of Justice.

Bureau of Justice Statistics. (2015). *Veterans in prison and jail, 2011–12.* Washington, DC: U.S. Department of Justice.

Culp, R., Youstin, T. J., Englander, K., & Lynch, J. (2013). From war to prison: Examining the relationship between military service and criminal activity. *Justice Quarterly, 30*(4), 651–680.

Frederick, A. (2013). Veterans treatment courts: Analysis and recommendations. *Law & Psychology Review, 38,* 211–230.

Greenberg, G. A., & Rosencheck, R. A. (2011). Incarceration among male veterans: Relative risk of imprisonment and differences between veteran and nonveteran inmates. *International Journal of Offender Therapy and Comparative Criminology, 56,* 1–22.

National Institute of Corrections. (2016). *Veterans treatment courts: A second change for vets who have lost their way.* Washington, DC: U.S. Department of Justice.

Saxon, A. J., Davis, T. M., Sloan, K. L., McKight, K. M., McFall, M. E., & Kivlahan, D. R. (2001). Trauma, symptoms of posttraumatic stress disorder, and associated problems among incarcerated veterans. *Psychiatric Services, 52,* 959–964.

Shaw, D. M., Churchill, C. M., Noyes, R., Jr., & Loeffelholz, P. L. (1987). Criminal behavior and post-traumatic stress disorder in Vietnam veterans. *Comprehensive Psychiatry, 28*(5), 403–411.

Sigafoos, C. E. (1994). A PTSD treatment program for combat (Vietnam) veterans in prison. *International Journal of Offender Therapy and Comparative Criminology, 38*(2), 117–130.

Tsai, J., Rosencheck, R. A., Kasprow, W. J., & McGuire, J. F. (2013a). Risk of incarceration and clinical characteristics by race/ethnicity. *Social Psychiatry and Psychiatric Epidemiology, 48,* 1777–1786.

Tsai, J., Rosencheck, R. A., Kasprow, W. J., & McGuire, J. F. (2013b). Risk of incarceration and other characteristics of Iraq and Afghanistan veterans in state and federal prisons. *Psychiatric Services, 64*(1), 36–43.

Yager, T., Laufer, R. S., & Gallops, M. S. (1984). Some problems associated with war experience in men of the Vietnam generation. *Archives of General Psychiatry, 41,* 327–333.

Incarceration, Factors Contributing to the Growth in

The United States has only 5 percent of the world's population, yet it houses 25 percent of the world's prisoners, giving it the dubious distinction of having the highest incarceration rate. Over the past 47 years, numerous factors have contributed to the growth of incarceration in the United States. Political factors are those that fall under politicians' influences on penology. Social factors create inequalities that increase the chances of individuals becoming involved with the criminal justice system. Economic inequalities make it difficult for those within the lower strata of U.S. society to avoid criminalization. These factors present a complex myriad of consequences for one of the United States' biggest penal problems. The high number of persons under correctional supervision in the United States creates a unique phenomenon worthy of discussion, examination, and reevaluation. Research shows that the U.S. incarceration rate of 698 out of every 100,000 people is the highest among developed countries. When compared to China's rate of 119, there is a huge discrepancy; the U.S. rate is more than five times that of China despite the fact that China's total population is more than four times that of the United States (Walmsley, 2016).

An upward trend in incarceration in the United States became noticeable in 1973. Prison numbers were stable until about 1973–1974, when the numbers started to rise. This upward trend is attributed to changes in penal policies. Increases in crime during a period of political conflict met with more severe criminal sanctions, making incarceration a tool to control criminal behavior. Prison sentences became longer and harsher for violent crime, and less violent crimes began to require prison time. Mandatory and truth-in-sentencing punishment policies were enacted into law while drug offenses were criminalized. Researchers concluded that the best explanation for rising incarceration was the government's harsher policies rather than rising crime.

According to the Bureau of Justice Statistics (BJS), the number of people in prison in the United States grew from 503,600 in 1980 to 1,910,400 in 2015. The data show that the U.S. total correctional population reached an all-time high of 7,339,600 individuals in 2007. This number includes both people under community supervision as well as those incarcerated. Of the total 7,339,600 incarcerated, 2,297,700 individuals resided in local, state, or federal jails and prisons. However, in examining the actual numbers of people incarcerated, 2006 had the highest all-time number of incarcerated people at 2,310,300. It is noteworthy that the beginning of a decline became evident in 2009. Although there have been fluctuations over the last nine years, there has generally been a downward trend ever since (BJS, n.d.). Nonetheless, the United States still has the highest incarceration rate in the world as of 2016.

The United States, along with Canada and the United Kingdom, are major contributors of help to other nations through foreign aid, refugee assistance, and economic alliances. However, while other Western countries have been able to keep their crime and incarceration rates down by using alternatives to incarceration, crime rates in the United States fell while incarceration rates continued to rise. The United States uses incarceration as its primary source of crime control even for individuals who are not a serious threat to the community. These individuals, once incarcerated, find it difficult to become productive members of society.

The Vera Institute of Justice conducted a survey in 2012 through distribution to all the states in the country. The study examined the true cost of incarceration to the United States. Information was collected from 40 states on their 2010 correctional spending. According to the results of this study, Texas spent 50 percent more ($3.3 billion) than its correctional budget of $2.2 billion. The unbudgeted costs were for capital expenditures and for financing retirement benefits and health care expenses for correctional staff. Even though the highest cost of incarceration to most states is compensation paid to correctional staff, other expenses, such as prisoners' health care overheads, associated expenses of treatment, and educational and vocational programs for prisoners, are all beginning to increase the overall cost of incarceration (Vera Institute for Justice, 2012).

In the United States, incarceration rates have continued to rise despite the drop in crime rates, a phenomenon for which the United States stands alone among Western countries. Specific policies that have led to the growth in incarceration include the war on drugs and changes in sentencing policies. Also, the politicization of crime is a major contributing factor to the growth of incarceration. Politicians, in seeking election or reelection, bow to the urges and wishes of the populace, whom they perceive want to be tough on crime. However, research on crime policy and the public has shown that while the public favors harsher sentences, a deeper look at the public's opinions does not show people to be more in favor of punitive measures than court and penal administrators, thereby calling into question the influence that public opinion has on legislators and their crime policies. Consequently, when examined closely, individuals polled do not support harsher sentences than the average member of the judiciary. Public opinion does not have as strong an effect on politicians being elected as previously thought. Nevertheless, the literature reflects that politicians create an atmosphere of fear to build platforms for election and reelection and subsequently support policies that will appear to be tough on crime to appeal to the public.

Sentencing policies have given rise to high imprisonment rates spanning from the 1970s to 2010. Sentencing policies changed in two phases. The first phase targeted fairness and consistency, while the second phase targeted drug crimes by increasing certainty and severity of punishments, a just deserts solution for the problem of increasing drug use and drug crimes. The sentencing structure changed from indeterminate to a determinate structure to ensure fairness and consistency between sentences. Some advocates opposed judges having the power to determine sentences and therefore allowing some people to go free or receive lighter sentences while others received harsher sentences for the same crime. This opposition led to the era of determinate sentencing and other such policies, which eventually became crueler. The second phase also ushered in mandatory minimum sentences like the truth-in-sentencing policies, which ensured that convicted individuals serve a minimum prescribed percentage of their sentence, and the "three strikes, and you're out" policies, which guaranteed that habitual offenders serve longer prison sentences. Sentencing policies, especially when applied to drug offenses, widened the net of the justice system's effect on individuals.

The war on drugs is a major contributor to high incarceration rates. The war on drugs was first introduced in 1970 when the Controlled Substance Act was passed into law. The law was passed to regulate the use of particular drugs and controlled substances given that many controlled substances have medical uses and a consequential potential for abuse. The result was that the war on drugs became a major policy with far-reaching consequences for mass incarceration. In the 1980s, even though drug use was in decline, sentencing policies became more punitive, consequently increasing the number of individuals arrested and convicted of drug crimes. Gallup polls have shown that the number of Americans favoring the legalization of marijuana has increased from 16 percent between 1972 and 1975 to 64 percent in 2017. Recent polls also show that people's views about the seriousness of illegal drug use has dropped from 83 percent in 2000 to 65 percent in 2016 (Gallup News, n.d.). It is important to note that some states have recently changed their sentencing policies in a bid to reduce punitive policies on drug crimes, especially for nonviolent drug offenders.

High recidivism rates have hampered reentry efforts and prevented individuals from reintegrating into society. When ready to be released from prison after serving long sentences, many ex-prisoners face numerous challenges, like housing, employment, and the negative stigma of being a convicted criminal. These negative forces cause some of them to reoffend and return to prison, keeping imprisonment rates high. While some individuals recommit crimes because of unemployment, others find it difficult to reintegrate into an unfamiliar society after being imprisoned. They reoffend or violate the conditions of their parole deliberately to go back to where they call "home." In addition, many of these individuals lack the necessary education or means to get an education to find opportunities to begin a new life after prison. This continuous recycling of felons in and out of prisons has increased incarceration rates.

The school-to-prison pipeline is also another phenomenon that negatively affects racial minority juveniles. Zero-tolerance policies in schools across the United States have channeled youths into detention centers, where their fate is ultimately decided. The schools that practice zero tolerance are often located in minority and disadvantaged neighborhoods. Once students are transferred to alternative schools and juvenile detention centers, their chances of graduating from high school diminishes while their chances of becoming involved in the juvenile justice system increases. A majority of these youth subsequently become involved with the criminal justice system as adults. Research has also shown a link between low levels of education and the possibility of prison; consequently, a high percentage of prisoners have a high school education or less. Indeed, if an African American male does not graduate high school, there is a 50 percent chance that he will spend some time in a correctional facility during the course of his life.

All the factors discussed have had far-reaching consequences for incarceration rates in the United States. Economic downturns leading to scarce resources, the need for an efficient system that solves the mass incarceration problem, and penology researchers' evaluation of the social consequences of mass incarceration have made penal policy changes necessary. The problem of funding, as well the United States' status as an example to other countries, makes it important for penology policies to be reexamined and mass incarceration reduced. Therefore, the excessiveness of already tight budgets is an issue that must be addressed. Reducing prison costs is a priority for the United States. The Fair Sentencing Act (2010), which reduces disparities of federal sentences on crack and powder cocaine arrests, is an example of welcome policy changes aimed at reducing incarceration. It is also critical for the United States to strive to reduce its high incarceration rates and recidivism through evidence-based practices proven to save taxpayers funds across all levels of government. Finally, reinvesting the funds saved from lower incarceration rates into alternatives like probation within communities would be crucial to ensure judicious use of taxpayers' funds.

Lucy K. Tsado

See also: Incarceration Rates in the United States Compared to Other Countries; Prison Populations, Trends in

Further Reading

Brown, B. S., & Courtless, T. F. (1968). The mentally retarded in penal and correctional institutions. *American Journal of Psychiatry, 124*(9), 1164.

Brown, E. K., & Socia, K. M. (2017). Twenty-first century punitiveness: Social sources of punitive American views reconsidered. *Journal of Quantitative Criminology, 33*(4), 935–959.

Bureau of Justice Statistics. (n.d.). *Key statistics: Estimated number of persons under correctional supervision in the United States, 1980–2015.* Retrieved from https://www .bjs.gov/index.cfm?ty=kfdetail&iid=487)

Gallup News. (n.d.). *Illegal drugs.* Retrieved from http://news.gallup.com/poll/1657/illegal -drugs.aspx

Gonsoulin, S., Zablocki, M., & Leone, P. E. (2012). Safe schools, staff development, and the school-to-prison pipeline. *Teacher Education and Special Education, 35*(4), 309–319.

Jones, J. (2016, October 28). In U.S., 65% say drug problem 'extremely' or 'very serious.' *Gallup News, Social Issues.* Retrieved from http://news.gallup.com/poll/196826/say -drug-problem-extremely-serious.aspx?g_source=MARIJUANA&g_medium =topic&g_campaign=tiles

Mallet, C. (2016). The school-to-prison pipeline: A critical review of the punitive paradigm shift. *Child and Adolescent Social Work Journal, 33*(1), 15–24.

Nelson, M. S., Gabbidon, S. L., & Boisvert, D. (2015). Philadelphia area residents' views on the disproportionate representation of blacks and Hispanics in the criminal justice system. *Journal of Crime and Justice, 38*(2), 270–290.

Roberts, D. (2004). The social and moral cost of mass incarceration in African American communities. *Stanford Law Review, 56*(127), 1271–1305.

Roberts, J. V. (1992). Public opinion, crime, and criminal justice. *Crime and Justice, 16,* 99–180. Chicago: University of Chicago Press. Retrieved from http://www.jstor.org /stable/1147562

The Sentencing Project. (n.d.). *U.S. state and federal prison population, 1925–2015.* Retrieved from http://www.sentencingproject.org/criminal-justice-facts

Skiba, R. J., Michael, R. S., Nardo, A. C., & Peterson, R. L. (2002). The color of discipline: Sources of racial and gender disproportionality in school punishment. *Urban Review, 34*(4), 317–342.

Tonry, M. (1994). Race and the war on drugs. *University of Chicago Legal Forum 1994* (4). Retrieved from http://chicagounbound.uchicago.edu/uclf/vol1994/iss1/4

Tonry, M. (1995). *Malign neglect: Race crime and punishment in America.* New York: Oxford University Press.

Tonry, M. (2004). *Thinking about crime: Sense and sensibility in American penal culture.* New York: Oxford University Press.

Tonry, M., & Farrington, D. (2005). Punishment and crime across space and time. *Crime and Justice, 33,* 1–39.

Travis, J., Western, B., & Redburn, S. (2017). *Growth of incarceration in the United States: Exploring causes and consequences.* Washington DC: National Academies Press/ National Academy of Sciences.

Unnever, J. D. (2008). Two worlds far apart: Black-white differences in beliefs about why African-American men are disproportionately imprisoned. *Criminology, 46*(2), 511–538.

Unnever, J. D., & Cullen, F. T. (2010). The social sources of American's punitiveness: A test of three competing models. *Criminology, 48*(1), 99–129.

Vera Institute of Justice; Center on Sentencing and Corrections. (2012). *The price of prisons: What incarceration costs taxpayers.* Retrieved from http://archive.vera.org /sites/default/files/resources/downloads/the-price-of-prisons-40-fact-sheets -updated-072012.pdf

Walmsley, R. (2016). World prison population list. *Institute of criminal policy research: World prison brief* (11th ed.). Retrieved from http://www.prisonstudies.org/highest -to-lowest/prison_population_rate?field_region_taxonomy_tid=All.

Western, B., & Pettit, B. (2010). Incarceration & social inequality. *Daedalus, 139*(3), 8–19.

Incarceration, Impact of Social Progressives on (1900s–1920s)

Central to all progressive social movements is the belief that the people do not have to wait for change from the top. Individuals can be catalysts for change from the bottom up. Many social movement activists came from middle- or working-class backgrounds and possessed organizing skills. In colonial America the criminal justice system was not designed to rehabilitate criminals. Instead, physical punishment/ pain was publicly inflicted on convicted criminals. The purpose was to humiliate them and to deter other people from crime. Imprisonment was rarely used for punishment; jails existed as wait stations for those awaiting a beating, torture, or execution.

The ideas of the Enlightenment led Americans to see people as rational beings who could control their own behavior, in contrast to the idea that they were sinful beings. As a result, theories of punishment began to change. This idea led to a reevaluation of punishment and the beginning of a search for causes of criminal behavior. Prison was being seen as a method to punish criminals but not yet as a way to rehabilitate them. Ideas such as prison as a method to cure offenders or as a period of reflection on their life would lead them to repentance.

Society believed that rapid industrialization had disrupted the American social order, and crime and other social problems were a symptom. Reforms were aimed at creating orderly prisons—training inmates in religion, requiring hard work, and strict discipline. The orderly prison environment would affect their reform by furnishing them with a strong moral foundation needed to resist the corrupting influencing that were rampart in society. This was the foundation the Progressives reacted to. The Progressives were also reacting to the large number of immigrants who had entered/were entering the country. These groups had mores that clashed with other Americans; they were also the targets of abuse from both American industry and its criminal justice system.

The Progressive Era of the early 20th century was characterized by the belief in the states' ability to improve society through liberal reform. Progressivism as reform has always focused on social injustice, corruption, and inequality. The various Progressive movements believe in the empowerment and equality of the less privileged in society, democracy, and the idea that government should guard the population from abuse.

They challenged government to eliminate its own legal injustices. Progressivism began as a social movement and grew into a political movement. Progressives have always been urban, more educated than the rest of society, and believed that government could be a tool for change. They concentrated on exposing the evils of corporate greed, combating fear of immigrants, and urging Americans to use democracy to improve it.

Progressivism gained a strong voice when Theodore Roosevelt became president in 1901. Progressives used the ideas promoted by the new penology suggested in the 1870s—rehabilitation as the basis of their approach to crime. They relied on the indeterminate sentence to foster rehabilitation, advocated for community corrections rather than prison, empowered parole boards to release those offenders, who seemed likely to stay away from crime, supported the idea of probation or supervised release of offenders, and suggested that probation officers investigate the backgrounds of offenders and provide judges with presentence reports to be used to individualize sentences.

Social movements, by definition, arise from a minority of citizens working together to shape public consciousness about injustices. Social movements have invariably advanced moral and political causes surrounding gender, racial, and class equality with much greater force and consistency than those in mainstream politics. The ideas of social movements often become the focus of mainstream politics after prolonged struggles. Some social movements band together to create new political institutions to challenge the partisan status quo from the outside as seen with social reformers and dissident Republicans of the early 1900s who formed the Progressive Party.

The idea of rehabilitation as put forth by the Progressives had the greatest effect on the juvenile justice system. The child-saving movement, which was part of this Progressive Era, should be credited with the first juvenile court in 1899; by 1920 all but three states had juvenile courts. In spite of the success of the Progressive movement for the American criminal justice system, the rehabilitation model was never truly implemented. Criminals have never been treated solely as being sick and able to be cured under the guise of a medical model. But the idea of rehabilitation remains the ideology of the system but not the practice. The system sees rehabilitation as a required function of punishment. In practice the work of the Progressives remains in place structurally. Criminals are routinely sentenced to long sentences and must demonstrate to parole boards they have been rehabilitated.

The best way to do that is the convict's participation in and completion of treatment programs while in prison. Whether the treatment has any effect or not, the convict knows what criteria the parole board will use in making a judgement.

The rehabilitation model introduced by the Progressives is different from the deterrence and retribution perspectives. Those supporting retribution claim that penalties should be just and specific. This allows criminals to retain their dignity by paying for their crimes. Retributivists claim that to be subjected to rehabilitation or to be cured when the criminal is not sick is an insult. Criminals do not consider themselves sick, and the public does not either. Retributivists further claim that to be treated kindly for what most criminals feel is rational behavior is to be considered childlike. However, to be punished, because the person deserved it, is to be treated as a rational human being. Retribution does not always lead to longer sentences than rehabilitation. The rehabilitation model may actually produce longer sentences, which can be justified by the need to cure the inmate. The deterrence perspective sees both potential offenders and criminals as rational individuals. These individuals will stay away from crime if the threat of punishment outweighs the perceived reward of crime. Both the retribution and deterrence models of punishment regard individuals who break the law as rational decision makers who knowingly take risks when they break the law. The rehabilitation model of the Progressives regard individuals who violate the law as defective and in need of treatment.

The evaluation of a particular rehabilitation program to examine its effectiveness is typically measured using the recidivism rate—whether the released offender gets into trouble and/or breaks the law again. An additional method of evaluation is the measurement of improved social functioning such as holding a job and/or supporting your family. Rehabilitation programs are generally seen as ineffective. Defenders of these programs most often claim the failure to implement the program properly is the flaw. Critics suggest that the rehabilitative model has intrinsic flaws that make it ineffective; as a result there is no clear pattern to indicate the efficacy of any particular method of treatment. Rehabilitation programs of any type cannot overcome or even appreciably reduce the potent penchant for offenders to continue in criminal behavior. Treatment programs are based on a theory of crime as a disease that can be cured. This perspective is/was considered flawed in that it denies the normality of crime in society. It also overlooks the personal status quo or ordinariness of crime in a very large proportion of offenders, who are merely responding to personal circumstances and the conditions of society.

Craig J. Forsyth and Britain Bailey Forsyth

See also: Determinate versus Indeterminate Sentencing; Enlightenment and Punishment; Evolving Standards of Decency; Innocence Project; Prison Reform, Intended and Unintended Consequences of; Prisons, History of

Further Reading

Conrad, P., & Schneider, J. W. (1992). *Deviance and medicalization: From badness to sickness*. Philadelphia: Temple University Press.

Cornish, D. B., & Clarke, R. V. (1986). *The reasoning criminal: Rational choice perspectives on offending*. New York: Springer.

Cullen, F. T., & Gilbert, K. E. (1982). *Reaffirming rehabilitation*. Cincinnati: Anderson.

Durlak, J. A., & DuPre, E. P. (2008). Implementation matters: A review of research on the influence of implementation on program outcomes and factors affecting implementation. *American Journal of Community Psychology, 41,* 327–350.

Grupp, S. E. (1971). *Theories of punishment.* Bloomington: Indiana University Press.

Kassebaum, G., Ward, D. A., & Wilner, D. M. (1971). *Prison treatment and prison survival: An empirical assessment.* New York: Wiley.

Lipton, D., Martinson, R., & Wilks, J. (1975). *The effectiveness of correction treatment: A survey of evaluation studies.* New York: Praeger.

Martinson, R. (1974). What works? Questions and answers about prison reform. *The Public Interest, 35*(Spring), 22–54.

Miller, J. M., & Miller, H. V. (2015). Rethinking program fidelity for criminal justice. *Criminology & Public Policy, 14*(2), 339–349.

Platt, A. M. (1977). *The child savers: The invention of delinquency.* Chicago: University of Chicago Press.

Rothman, D. J. (1971). *The discovery of the asylum: Social order and disorder in the New Republic.* Boston: Little, Brown.

Rothman, D. J. (1980). *Conscience and convenience: The asylum and its alternatives in progressive America.* Boston: Little, Brown.

Incarceration, Social Costs of High Rates of

Monetary cost is just a small component of a much larger impact incarceration has on society. There are countless additional factors contributing to the social costs of incarceration. Society itself is impacted by the necessary removal of a citizen from the pool of positive societal contributors. Incarcerated persons not only fail to contribute to societal effectiveness, but they place a deficit on the rest of society.

The Bureau of Justice Statistics (BJS) estimates that more than 75 percent of former inmates are rearrested within five years of being released from prison (BJS, 2014). In light of the dismal instrumental value of incarceration as a means of meeting correctional goals, the benefit of incarceration as a correctional tool in the area of crime reduction is questionable at best. Incarceration must be a last imperative option due to the direct costs of incarceration in addition to the incalculable societal consequences.

WORLD LEADER

Without high rates of incarceration, there cannot be a high social cost of incarceration. Historically, incarceration has been reserved for common-law crimes. Common-law crimes are acts like battery, rape, murder, and theft. Regardless of any written law, these acts are considered immoral and require a response. In a civilized society, the response is punishment decided by the government.

Incarceration incapacitates offenders for the duration of their imprisonment. Offenders cannot steal or hurt people outside the prison walls during their imprisonment. Incarceration has been expanded to many other areas such as those who cannot pay a traffic citation and drug offenses. In many cases, personal and property criminals are incarcerated for less time than nonviolent drug offenders. By statute, some states require less time in prison for rape than for possession of a small amount of illicit drugs. The war on drugs has filled U.S. prisons, built more, and filled them as well. The impact of treating drug use and abuse with a jail cell will be felt for decades. The dramatic increase in monetary and social costs of U.S. incarceration is explained solely by the war on drugs.

MONETARY COSTS

Incarceration costs are easy to identify from the simplistic perspective of measuring state and federal governmental correctional budgets. All 50 states and the federal government have a budget dedicated to corrections. The correctional budget is spread across many areas such as incarceration, probation, parole, work release, rehabilitation, etc. The average cost of incarceration per offender per year in the United States is $31,286, meaning the estimated annual cost is more than $70 billion (Henrichson & Delaney, 2012). Once inmates are released or if they are given probation, there are additional costs for probation and parole.

The United States has the highest incarceration rate in the world with over 2.3 million people incarcerated in prisons and jails in 2014 (BJS, 2016). There is an ethical component for mass incarceration. Every dollar spent on incarceration could be used for effective investment strategies such as education, drug treatment, and job training. Incarcerated persons place a burden on society due to costs, but they also are removed from the employed population. Free people are more likely to be employed, support their families, and pay taxes. Lost revenue due to removal from the taxpayer population is massive but incalculable.

The majority of incarcerated persons are men, although there has been an increase in female incarceration in recent decades. Many are parents who are unable to provide financial support for their families. Many children of offenders are on governmental assistance. They are further more likely to become incarcerated in adulthood. Incarceration disproportionately impacts poor and minority populations, which are often one in the same. This further impacts the ability to influence the political process through lack of capital and exclusion from voting in elections.

COSTS IMPACTING THE OFFENDER

There are several applicable labels for those who were or are incarcerated. Some are criminals, drug dealers, convicts, deviants, etc. Many if not most employers ask about criminal history on job applications. These labels prevent many employers from offering employment after incarceration. Some states are exploring legislative remedies to discontinue asking applicants about criminal history. These efforts are known as banning the box, referring to the check box for a criminal conviction. Prior offenders with a criminal conviction are often overlooked by employers who subscribe to labeling ex-offenders as permanent deviants. Offenders who cannot obtain adequate employment are more likely to return to criminality. Often, the only available employment is in low-wage positions without opportunities for advancement. Society is understandably skeptical of ex-offenders.

Many argue against giving offenders a second chance at employment because there are plenty of people in the workforce who remained crime-free.

Education is an effective method of preventing criminality and reducing recidivism. There was a time when "drug offender" was the worst label a criminal could receive. It became politically popular to label such offenders and create legislation targeting them. One such piece of legislation excluded certain drug offenders from accessing federal aid for higher education. Other laws eliminated driving privileges for drug offenders. No such laws existed for released sex offenders or murderers. Some argue against using taxpayer dollars to fund educating ex-offenders. When looked at from a budgetary perspective, $5,000 for tuition is much cheaper than over $30,000 per year for incarceration.

Offenders who cannot access prosocial opportunities such as employment or education are more likely to return to illicit activities. Societal treatment contributes to the social costs of incarceration. Proponents of restorative justice argue that released offenders should have an attainable path to earn his or her way back into the good graces of society. Restorative justice proponents argue it is counterproductive to continue the punishment long after release. They note that society benefits when an offender effectively becomes a contributing member of society through his or her own prosocial achievement.

SOCIAL IMPACTS

Children of incarcerated offenders often end up being cared for by the government in one way or another. They are more likely to be involved in crime themselves, thereby further increasing the correctional budget. Many are cared for by foster parents or publicly funded group homes. Many are raised in single-parent homes, which carries higher risk for delinquency and criminality. Single parents are less able to provide basic necessities for children, adequate supervision, or curricular support. Some needs of children are supplemented by the government in the form of food stamps, welfare, subsidized housing, or other such services. This further increases the costs of incarceration.

Many offenders are excluded from the voting process, which is a reduction in the ability to influence the political process. Some speculate certain laws have been written to exclude minorities and the poor from voting. This speculation is difficult to debate when considering the sentences for crack versus powder cocaine. Cocaine in crack form has less of the actual drug in it, although cocaine in a concentrated state is punished with less severity in some jurisdictions. Crack is more popular with poor and minority groups, whereas powder cocaine is more expensive and therefore is most used by the affluent.

Poor communities have large clusters of their population serve time in prison. The collateral damage goes far beyond the punishment of the offender. Most offenders will be released from prison, and many will return to their preincarceration area. They can influence the culture of the area resulting in higher crime rates and therefore perpetuating the cycle of crime, incarceration, and victimization.

A major goal of incarceration is to rehabilitate the offender. With drug offenders, a jail cell fails to effectively stop offenders from returning to drug use after release. Criminal justice reform is transitioning to a more evidence-based approach, and we are seeing small steps in reducing incarceration rates through more effective methods such as drug courts and drug treatment. Drug abuse can be effectively treated with research-proven methods outside a jail cell. Drug treatment is significantly less expensive than incarceration. Effective treatment results in an immediate savings from a reduction in incarceration costs in addition to long-term savings from a reduction in recidivism.

MITIGATING SOCIAL IMPACTS

The correctional system has several main goals. Some are retribution/punishment, rehabilitation, deterrence, incapacitation, and restoration. The current focus has been on retribution and incapacitation. Incapacitation can be effective as long as there are unlimited funds for filling and expanding the prison system. Recent fiscal problems have resulted in an imperative focus on effectiveness and efficiency. The focus has shifted to restorative justice methodologies. Restoration is more victim focused. Crime victims are made whole through restitution and victim services. Offenders are rehabilitated with a specific focus on research-proven best practices to reduce recidivism. Ideally, the offender contributes to the restoration of the victim, which contributes to the offender gaining the respect of society.

Incarceration costs go far beyond the correctional system operating budget. There are countless unintended or ignored consequences impacting society. People are impacted directly and indirectly. The offender is directly impacted. Families and communities are also impacted. Children learn from their incarcerated parents resulting in similar behavior. Communities and families suffer by the removal from the workforce, leading to dilapidation and increased poverty. Every incarceration decision must include a consideration of the immediate budgetary impact, external budgetary impact, and the societal impact. Incarceration is a necessary component of the criminal justice system. Incarceration directly serves society through the incapacitation of offenders. Every offender who is incapacitated should need such removal based on evidence-based correctional practices.

Wayne Steve Thompson

See also: Education in Prison; Evidence-Based Practice in Corrections; Fathers behind Bars; Incarceration Rates and Race; Overcrowding; Prison Reform, Intended and Unintended Consequences of; Prisoner Reentry/Family Integration; Recidivism; Restoration of Rights after Conviction; Restorative Justice; Sentencing Disparities and Discrimination in Sentencing; Stigmatization versus Reintegrative Shaming; Truth in Sentencing; Vocational Training and Education

Further Reading

Bureau of Justice Statistics. (2014). *Recidivism of prisoners released in 30 states in 2005: Patterns from 2005 to 2010 correctional populations in the United States.* Retrieved at http://www.bjs.gov/content/pub/pdf/rprts05p0510.pdf

Bureau of Justice Statistics. (2016). *Correctional populations in the United States, 2014.* Retrieved at BJS http://www.bjs.gov/content/pub/pdf/cpus14.pdf

Henrichson, C., & Delaney, R. (2012). *The price of prisons: What incarceration costs tax payers.* Center on Sentencing and Corrections. Retrieved from http://www.vera.org/sites/default/files/resources/downloads/price-of-prisons-updated-version-021914.pdf

Incarceration of Undocumented Immigrants

The incarceration of undocumented immigrants involves the apprehension, prosecution, and detainment/incarceration via holding in detention centers, jails, or public or private prisons for committing a crime. Whereas many countries have banned the practice of incarcerating undocumented immigrants in jails or prisons, this practice is common in the United States most likely because many private prisons benefit from its practice. Within the United States, many immigrants are held in jails or prison cells for committing minor offenses (e.g., traffic violations or immigration-related offenses) as opposed to detention centers designed for detaining immigrants after illegal entry into a country. In fact, though immigration is generally viewed as a federal government concern, many state level officials with arresting powers (state and local police) have arrested individuals because of illegal immigration suspicions.

Although the breadth of immigrant incarceration statistics is often contested, data supplied by the United States Department of Homeland Security report that, for the fiscal year 2015, a total of 337,117 illegal immigrants were "apprehended" or arrested (United States Department of Homeland Security, 2015). In 2015, the United States charged approximately 75,000 undocumented immigrants with immigration-related offenses (Global Detention Project, 2016). However, studies show that prosecutions for illegal entry are on the rise, from 4,000 cases in 1993 to 91,000 in 2013 (Global Detention Project, 2016). Scholars have attributed these increases to programs designed to reduce undocumented immigration, such as Operation Streamline (2005–), Secure Communities (2008–2014), and Priority Enforcement Program (2015–), and to an overall negative sentiment toward immigrants that resulted, in part, from the September 11 terrorist attacks in 2001.

Even though the intended purpose of these programs was to reduce crime, many of the programs have violated human rights of both citizens and noncitizens. Although Operation Streamline's goal was to deter illegal entry and recidivism by prosecuting first-time illegal offenders for crossing the border, it has resulted in a process by which masses of immigrants are sentenced with federal felonies of illegal reentry without due process protections. Secure Communities was designed to create safer communities by allowing police to use their discretion to identify noncitizens and report their whereabouts and status to the federal government. However, this program resulted in police racial and ethnic profiling and targeting of both noncitizens and citizens for minor offenses, such as traffic or immigration-related crimes, which created distrust of police, particularly among immigrant communities.

The most recent program, Priority Enforcement Program (PEP), replaced the Secure Communities program. This new program requires law enforcement to fingerprint arrested individuals and submit biometric data to federal agencies. The program and its operation were designed to redirect attention to immigrants with a history of committing serious criminal offenses or those who pose a threat to public safety. To date, less is known about how this program affects the detainment and incarceration processes of immigrants.

Aside from fear and safety concerns, proponents of immigrant deportation tend to cite overall costs as a driving factor in the need for removal of undocumented immigrants. Incarceration costs of undocumented immigrants are undertaken by the federal government. Although some state and local governments also incarcerate immigrants in nonfederal detention centers, a percentage of the cost is reimbursed by the federal government. Even so, spending on immigration enforcement steadily increased from 2005 to 2010. According to statistical figures, approximately $5.05 million is spent per day for undocumented immigrant operations and custody. This budget results in taxpayers paying upward of $159 per day per immigrant detainee (National Immigration Forum Staff, 2013).

Several departments participate in the incarceration and removal processes of undocumented immigrants in the United States. Nestled under the Department of Homeland Security, the U.S. Immigration and Custom's Enforcement (ICE), U.S. Customs and Border Protection (CBP), and the U.S. Citizenship and Immigrations Services (USCIS) together are responsible for enforcement of immigration law. Along with the removal of undocumented immigrants, these government organizations are given the authority to handle any issues concerning immigration, citizenship, and citizenship status.

Newer programs, such as the Priority Enforcement Program, instruct ICE and CBP agents to target immigrants who can be categorized as "priority aliens." Priority aliens are undocumented immigrants who include, but are not limited to, undocumented immigrants who are perceived to be threats to border security, threats to national security, threats to public safety, and criminal aliens who have been convicted of crimes, such as felonies and misdemeanors. These agencies reported that 59 percent of those deported immigrants in fiscal year 2015 were convicted criminals, while 41 percent of those deported that same year were noncriminal immigration law violators (United States Department of Homeland Security, 2015).

Individuals detained for violation of immigration laws tend to be apprehended by CBP while attempting to enter the United States illegally at one of its northern or southern land borders or via a port of entry (air, land, and sea ports), or by ICE when caught in the interior United States. ICE can arrest individuals suspected of breaking immigration law by responding to reports of possible undocumented immigrants living in the United States, by way of incarceration by local and state law enforcement during their investigations, or by targeting of employers who hire undocumented immigrants. In circumstances where undocumented immigrants are arrested by state and/or local police, ICE will then issue a detainer so that the individual, when released by state or local authorities, will be released into ICE custody within 48 hours of detainer issuance. Once released into federal custody, officials must then determine whether the individual poses a threat to public safety and/or qualifies as a priority alien. Future handling depends on an immigrant's priority status and the state in which the individual was apprehended.

After initial arrest or transfer into ICE/CBP custody, immigrants are processed. Processing not only registers identity, fingerprints, and a photograph of the immigrant, but it allows agencies to issue background checks to determine if the immigrant has any prior order of removal (deportation) on record and any prior criminal convictions. Immigrants with any prior criminal conviction(s) are often subject to mandatory detention in an ICE immigration holding facility. These immigrants are often those that fit priority 1 (threats to national security, border security, and public safety), priority 2 (misdemeanants and new immigration violators), or priority 3 (other immigration violations) status. Although ICE's newest immigration enforcement policies have redirected their focus to apprehending and removing criminal immigrants, many noncriminal immigrants face deportation if their deportation serves important federal interest.

Reportedly, 26 percent of undocumented immigrants left ICE custody via deportation, in November–December of 2012 (Transnational Records Access Clearinghouse, 2013). However, many are often mandatorily detained without due process until removal because of their criminal status, because they appeal removal decisions, or because they apply for relief from removal. Occasionally, some undocumented immigrants (those not deemed a danger to security) may be released on bond or on their own recognizance until they are summoned to court for immigration proceedings. Expedited removals, which stipulate that an immigrant cannot return to the United States, can occur without an immigration hearing. Those immigrants who are permitted removal hearings are allowed to voluntarily return to their country of origin, plead guilty to the charged criminal offense and continue detainment until removal completion, or continue to appeal the court's decision.

Immigrants are held in prisons, jails, and private correctional facilities, with criminal offenders, when waiting for asylum and deportation hearings. Although statutes are in place that limit detainment time to approximately five months, many immigrants are incarcerated for elongated periods ranging from several months to several years awaiting case decisions. Of those immigrants apprehended, the largest portion are arrested at or near a border or port of entry. In the year 2015, 75,829 undocumented immigrants deported by ICE were apprehended at a border or port of entry compared to the 63,539 removed individuals arrested inside the United States (United States Department of Homeland Security, 2015). Once apprehended, individuals suspected of holding undocumented immigrant status proceed through a series of steps that, many times, end with prolonged detention.

It is not unusual for undocumented immigrants to face increasingly inhumane detention conditions. Immigrants who are detained or incarcerated often receive inadequate care (i.e., poor medical care, insufficient food), are transferred across prisons or detainment centers with little notice, and many female immigrants are reportedly sexually abused, thereafter, receiving no mental or physical health treatment. Detained or incarcerated immigrants are also likely to lose contact with their families, including their children. Further, between 2003 and 2011, 126 immigrant deaths were reported to have occurred while under supervision of ICE (Immigration and Customs Enforcement, 2011).

Undocumented immigrants were once housed in "Tent City," a temporary outdoor jail in Phoenix, Arizona. The controversial jail was run by former Maricopa County sheriff Joe Arpaio, an outspoken critic of illegal immigration. (John Moore/Getty Images)

Many of these deaths have been attributed to the harsh conditions in prison as well as the lack of medical care and attention for individuals with chronic diseases. Although many agencies, such as civil rights organizations (e.g., Amnesty International, Human Rights Watch, and the American Civil Liberties Union), continue to protest the uncivil and inhumane conditions experienced by detained or incarcerated immigrants, many of these harsh conditions remain.

Sierra L. Nelson and Megan Stubbs-Richardson

See also: Access to the Courts; Incarceration, Factors Contributing to the Growth in; Incarceration, Social Costs of High Rates of; Incarceration Rates and Race; Rights Are Lost versus Rights Are Retained; Sentencing Disparities and Discrimination in Sentencing

Further Reading

ACLU IRP Issue Brief. (2009). *Prolonged immigration detention of individuals who are challenging removal.* Retrieved from https://www.aclu.org/files/images/asset_upload_file766_40474.pdf

Anonymous. (2009). Some barriers detained migrant women face. *Social Justice, 36*(2), 104–105.

Bernstein, N., & Williams, M. (2009, April 2). Immigration agency's revised list of deaths in custody. *New York Times.* Retrieved from https://www.nytimes.com/2009/04/03/nyregion/03detainlist.html

Bosworth, M., & Kaufman, E. (2011). Foreigners in a carceral age: Immigration and imprisonment in the United States. *Stanford Law & Policy Review, 22*(2), 429–454.

Global Detention Project. (2016, May). *United States Immigration detention profile.* Retrieved from https://www.globaldetentionproject.org/countries/americas/united-states

Immigration and Customs Enforcement. (2011). *List of deaths in ICE custody.* Washington, DC: Author. Retrieved from www.ice.gov/doclib/foia/reports/detaineedeaths 2003-present.pdf

National Immigration Forum Staff. (2013). *The math of immigration detention.* Retrieved from https://immigrationforum.org/blog/themathofimmigrationdetention

No More Deaths. (2008). *Crossing the line: Human rights abuses of migrants in short-term custody on the Arizona/Sonora border.* Tucson, AZ: Author. Retrieved from http://forms.nomoredeaths.org/wp-content/uploads/2014/10/CrossingTheLine-full.compressed.pdf

Reasoner, W. D. (2011). *Deportation basics.* Retrieved from http://cis.org/deportation-basics

Transnational Records Access Clearinghouse. *Decisions on ICE detainees: State-by-state details (fiscal year 2013).* Retrieved from http://trac.syr.edu/immigration/reports/320

Transnational Records Access Clearinghouse. *Immigration prosecutions for September 2015 (fiscal year 2015).* Retrieved from https://trac.syr.edu/cgi-secure/product/login.pl?+SERVICE=express9&_DEBUG=0&_PROGRAM=interp.annualreport.sas&p_month=dec&p_year=15&p_topic+40&p_agenrevgrp=&p_distcode=&p_trac_leadcharge=&p_progcat+&p_stat=fil

United States Department of Homeland Security, Immigration and Customs Enforcement. *Delegation of Immigration Authority Section 287(g) Immigration and Nationality Act.* Retrieved from https://www.ice.gov/factsheets/287g

United States Department of Homeland Security, Immigration and Customs Enforcement. *ICE immigration enforcement and removals operations report (fiscal year 2015).* Retrieved from https://www.ice.gov/sites/default/files/documents/Report/2016/fy2015removalStats.pdf

United States Department of Homeland Security, Office of Inspector General. (2013). U.S. Immigration and Customs Enforcement's Management Letter for FY 2012 DHS Consolidated Financial Statements Audit. Retrieved from https://www.oig.dhs.gov/assets/Mgmt/2013/OIG_13-66_Apr13.pdf

United States Department of Homeland Security, United States Border Patrol. *Total nationwide apprehensions fiscal year 1925–2017.* Retrieved from https://www.cbp.gov/document/stats/us-border-patrol-total-apprehensions-fy-1925-fy-2017

Weiss, H. E., & Vasquez, L. M. (2012). Immigrants under correctional supervision: Examining the needs of immigrant populations in a penal environment. Invited chapter in L. Gideon (Ed.), *Special needs offenders in correctional institutions.* Thousand Oaks, CA: Sage.

Incarceration Rates

Prisons and jails serve a variety of functions in society. Typically discussed are goals such as punishment, retribution, deterrence, or incapacitation. The ability of prisons to meet any of these goals is the subject of much debate. Prisons are federal or state-run facilities designed for those convicted and sentenced to more than a year of incarceration; jails are designed for short-term incarceration. Discussions of trends in incarceration are often talked about in terms of rates per 100,000 in the population. The incarceration rate is measured as the estimated number of inmates under the jurisdiction of state or federal prisons or held in local jails per 100,000 of the total U.S. population or the U.S. population of residents over the age of 18. This is very different from the imprisonment rate that refers to the estimate of inmates held in state or federal prisons sentenced to a period of incarceration of one year or more. Because the imprisonment rate is a subset of the total number of those held in prison, the incarceration rate is always larger than the imprisonment rate. The United States has one of the highest incarceration rates in the world.

The U.S. prison population has been relatively stable for the last century. However, starting in the late 1970s, the number of incarcerated individuals increased dramatically. A review of data from 1925 through 1973 from the Bureau of Justice Statistics reveals that the correctional population mirrored the increase in the population of the United States overall. Between 1973 and 2008, the correctional population increased 705 percent, contributing to overcrowding and the prison population explosion. At the same time the number of prisons increased by 70 percent during this time. Thus, since 1980, the number of people incarcerated in American prisons quadrupled over a 30-year period. Between 1990 and 1998, the state prison population increased by an amazing 77 percent due to an increase in parole violators, longer sentences, an increase in violent offenders, and new court commitments and policies. By the end of the 1990s, state prisons were operating at or as much as 17 percent above capacity, and federal institutions were 32 percent above capacity. The increase in incarceration has resulted in states that now spend nearly $52 billion per year on corrections compared to the $6.7 billion spent in 1985. For many states this is more money than is spent on education.

In 2014, there were more than 6.8 million individuals or 1 in 36 adults under some form of correctional sanction in the United States. State and federal prisons held 1,561,500 prisoners, and local jails held more than 744,000 individuals. The incarceration rate has declined an average of 1 percent per year since 2007. Despite the decrease in the use of incarceration and the crime rate drops experienced, the United States continues to incarcerate more people, with 2 million behind bars, than many Western industrialized nations.

According to the World Prison Brief, no Western nation comes close to matching the U.S. incarceration rate. The countries with the highest incarceration rate per 100,000 of the national population are Seychelles (799 per 100,000), followed by the United States (698), St. Kitts and Nevis (607), Turkmenistan (583), U.S. Virgin Islands (542), Cuba (510), El Salvador (492), Guam—U.S.A. (469), Thailand (461), Belize (449), Russian Federation (445), Rwanda (434), and British Virgin Islands (425). The rates for the United States are three times higher than Australia (152), Spain (131), China (118), Canada (114), and France (103). The result is that an individual who commits a crime in the United States has a greater chance of going to prison and receiving a longer sentence than in more than 100 other countries in the world (Walmsley, 2016).

The rise in the utilization of incarceration can be traced back to changes in correctional policies dating back to the birth of the nation. Prior to the 1800s, offenders were housed in a facility only until their sentence or punishment was delivered. Sentences such as branding, flogging, whipping, or execution were common forms of punishment. Incarceration facilities, primarily jails, were used merely as a temporary place to detain the offender while awaiting punishment. With the Age of

Incarceration Rates

Enlightenment, confinement became the primary method of punishment, and the penitentiary was born. In the latter part of the 1900s changes in legislation such as the "war on drugs," "three-strikes" legislation, "get tough" policies, determinate sentencing, and strict sentencing guidelines also had an impact on the United States. There are more than 2 million individuals in state or federal prison or jails. The types of offenses committed that led to incarceration differ between the federal and the states. The federal prison population is primarily driven by drug offenses. More than half (50.1 percent) of all federal prisoners were incarcerated for drug offenses, and another fourth were incarcerated for public order offenses such as immigration violations, weapons possession, or other nonviolent offenses. Furthermore, those convicted of drug offenses in the federal system are held in prison nearly three times longer than those convicted of other offenses. In contrast, those incarcerated in state correctional facilities primarily committed violent crimes (53.2 percent), drug offenses (15.7 percent), or property crimes (19.3 percent).

The incarceration rate varies across the U.S. states. Prison populations decreased in several state prisons. Mississippi, Texas, Louisiana, and New York each experienced a decrease of at least 1,000 prisoners in 2015. Southern states such as Louisiana, Texas, Mississippi, Alabama, Georgia, and South Carolina have typically had the highest incarceration rates. California, Pennsylvania, and Ohio also have traditionally housed large numbers of prisoners. In contrast, Maine, Minnesota, North Dakota, Rhode Island, and New Hampshire have continued the lowest incarceration rates in the nation. The variability in incarceration rates between the states is typically ascribed to differences in sentencing practices rather than to the crime rate for each state. A stark reality is that there are approximately nine states that have higher incarceration rates than any other nation in the world. High incarceration rates cause overcrowding in both state and federal prisons. At present 18 states and the Bureau of Prisons are all above maximum capacity. One result of the overcrowding has been the increased use of private prisons to house prisoners.

The high incarceration rate in the United States has disproportionately impacted minorities. Despite comprising only 13 percent of the U.S. population, African Americans make up nearly 40 percent of the state and federal prison population. When people of color (African Americans and Hispanics) are added together, the figure rises to more than 60 percent of the prison population. A comparison of incarceration rates for African American males is even more startling. In 2014, more than 515,000 African American males were in custody. African American males of all ages had the highest imprisonment rate and were incarcerated more often than white or Hispanic men. African American males are six times more likely to be incarcerated than white males and nearly two times more likely than their Hispanic male counterparts to reside in prison. The lifetime likelihood of going to prison for African American men born in 2001 is 1 in 3 compared to 1 in 17 for white men and 1 in 6 for Latino men. The results for African American males between the age of 18 and 19 are even more disturbing.

The number of women in prison has been increasing at a rate that is 50 percent higher than for males since 1980. In 1980, there were 13,258 women held in federal and state prisons. By 2014, the figure had increased nearly tenfold. The states with the highest incarceration rates for women are Oklahoma, Idaho, Kentucky,

Arizona, and Missouri. The states with the lowest rates of incarceration for women are Rhode Island, Massachusetts, Maine, New Jersey, and New York. Female prisoners comprise nearly 7 percent of the total prison population.

The disproportionality in incarceration is also evidenced for women of color in comparison to other racial and ethnic groups. The rate of imprisonment for African American women at 109 per 100,000 in the population is nearly two times higher than the rate for white women (53 per 100,000). Latina women with an imprisonment rate of 64 per 100,000 falls between the two groups. A white female born in 2001 has a 1 in 11 lifetime likelihood of imprisonment compared to an African American woman where 1 in 18 has a lifetime likelihood of imprisonment.

With nearly 600,000 inmates released from prison each year, advocacy groups and the general public have become increasingly concerned about the impact of incarceration on citizens. They allege that incarceration is costly, inefficient, and does not deter future criminality. Incarceration is also linked to negative consequences such as loss of the right to vote, restricted access to student loans, inability to hold public office, restricted access to public housing, inability to own a firearm, and loss of parental rights. Still others argue that success in reducing incarceration relies on reducing the barriers to reentry. Thus, in order to reduce the rate of incarceration, the correctional system would need to address employment, housing, substance use issues, and a host of other problems associated with returning prisoners to the same communities that helped initiate and support criminal activity.

Brenda James and Martha Henderson Hurley

See also: Incarceration, Factors Contributing to the Growth in; Incarceration, Social Costs of High Rates of; Incarceration of Undocumented Immigrants; Incarceration Rates and Race; Incarceration Rates in the United States Compared to Other Countries; Incarceration Rates, Trends in the United States; Prisoner Reentry/Family Integration; Sentencing Disparities and Discrimination in Sentencing; Three-Strikes Laws; Truth in Sentencing

Further Reading

Bureau of Justice Statistics. (1980, May). *Prisoners in state and federal institutions.* Washington, DC: U.S. Department of Justice.

Bureau of Justice Statistics. (1996). *Sourcebook of criminal justice statistics, 1996.* Washington, DC: U.S. Department of Justice.

Bureau of Justice Statistics. (2000, August 9). *The nation's prison population growth rate slows.* Washington, DC: U.S. Department of Justice.

Bureau of Justice Statistics. (2001, August 12). *Correctional population in the U.S., 2000.* Retrieved from bjs.gov/index.cfm?ty=pbdetal&iid=927

Bureau of Justice Statistics. (2015, September). *Prisoners in 2014: Summary.* Washington, DC: U.S. Department of Justice.

Bureau of Justice Statistics. (2015, September 17). *Correctional population in the U.S., 2014.* Retrieved from bjs.gov/index.cfm?ty=pbdetal&iid=5387

Enns, P. K. (2014). The public's increasing punitiveness and its influence on mass incarceration in the United States. *American Journal of Political Science, 58*(4), 857–872.

Haney, C., & Zimbardo, P. (2016). The past and future of U.S. prison policy. In E. J. Latessa & A. M. Holsinger (Eds.), *Correctional contexts: Contemporary and classical readings* (pp. 136–158). Los Angeles: Oxford University Press.

Latessa, E. J., & Holsinger, A. M. (2016). Introduction. In E. J. Latessa & A. M. Holsinger (Eds.), *Correctional contexts: Contemporary and classical readings* (pp. 1–3). Los Angeles: Oxford University Press.

Walmsley, R. (2016). *World prison population list* (8th ed.). London: International Centre for Prison Studies. Retrieved from http://www.prisonstudies.org/sites/default/files /resources/downloads/world_prison_population_list_11th_edition.pdf

Weiss, D. B., & MacKenzie, D. L. (2010). A global perspective on incarceration: How an international focus can help the United States reconsider its incarceration rates. *Victims and Offenders, 5,* 268–282.

Incarceration Rates, Trends in the United States

The U.S. incarcerated population has been increasing dramatically over the past few decades. According to the Bureau of Justice Statistics, the U.S. prison population has increased by 500 percent in the past 40 years, peaking in 2008 with 740 out of every 100,000 American citizens behind bars, or 24.79 percent of the world's incarcerated population. The ever-increasing incarceration rate in the United States can be explained by a number of reasons. Policy changes such as three-strikes laws and mandatory sentencing greatly contribute to the rising incarceration rate. Additionally, the ramifications of these policies can lead to longer prison terms, and a considerable number of the prison population are now considered geriatric and require specialized facilities.

STATISTICS

The Prison Policy Initiative, a nonprofit with a research focus on mass incarceration, released a report in 2017 about the statistical breakdown, which indicated that there were 2.3 million people currently incarcerated in the United States, which is 0.71 percent of the total population in the United States. Of that 2.3 million, 1.3 million were in state prisons, 197,000 in federal prisons (of those, 97,000 were serving time for nonviolent drug-related convictions), 630,000 in local jails, 13,000 in territorial prisons, 41,000 in immigration detention centers, 6,400 under civil commitment, 2,500 in Indian country prisons, 1,400 in military prisons, and 34,000 youths in juvenile detention facilities. Of the 34,000 youths, 600 were incarcerated for status offenses, 6,600 for technical violations of existing parole or probation, 1,900 for drug-related offenses, 8,100 for property offenses, 3,700 for public order offenses, and the remaining 13,600 for direct personal victimization offenses. However, when an individual is incarcerated, only his or her most serious offense is recorded, so someone with a recorded violent offense might have also had a drug offense in the same incident that was not recorded.

Disparities

The Prison Policy Initiative also noted racial disparities in the incarcerated population. Whereas whites make up 64 percent of the total U.S. population, they are

39 percent of the prison and jail population. For African Americans, who make up just 13 percent of the total U.S. population, this disparity grows, as the group makes up 40 percent of the prison and jail population. The Hispanic and Latino population is 16 percent of the U.S. population overall but 19 percent of the prison and jail population, and the Native American population is 0.9 percent of the U.S. population but 1 percent of the prison and jail population. This indicates that minorities are represented at a disproportionately high rate in prisons and jails, as every group except for whites has a higher percentage of the prison population than the total population.

There is also a vast disparity with gender representation in prisons and jails. Men make up 49 percent of the U.S. population but 91 percent of the prison and jail population. Meanwhile, women, who make up 51 percent of the U.S. population, are 9 percent of the prison and jail population. The disparity between men and women in prison might indicate a disparity in how men and women are treated in the criminal justice system from arrest to conviction.

When compared to similar nations, the incarceration rate in the United States looks especially astronomical. Remember, the U.S. incarceration rate is 740 out of 100,000 people behind bars. The country most similar to the United States, both geographically and ethically, is Canada, with an incarceration rate of 106 people out of 100,000 behind bars. That means the United States has just about seven times as many people in prisons or in jails as Canada. Other comparable nations include England with an incarceration rate of 148 out of 100,000 people in prison or jail, Australia with 151 out of 100,000 incarcerated, Spain with 141 out of 100,000 incarcerated, Greece with 120 out of 100,000 in prison or jail, Norway with 71 locked up, the Netherlands with 75 behind bars, and finally Japan, with one of the lowest incarceration rates in the world, with 49 out of 100,000 people serving time in prisons and jails.

One reason that the United States has such a high incarceration rate might be due to the length of each individual sentence. Sentencing guidelines in the United States call for longer lengths of time incarcerated than many other developed nations. This leads to a large degree of overlap in the prison and jail system, so at any given time there might be more people in prisons and jails in the United States.

EXPLAINING THE RISE IN INCARCERATION

Retributive Model of Criminal Justice

During the 1970s through the 1990s, the criminal justice system transitioned into an increasingly punitive model, as a result of the highly politicized war on drugs and crime. Prison populations started increasing dramatically in the late 1970s, as states started adopting mandatory sentencing policies and three-strikes laws after criticisms about indeterminate sentencing. Three-strikes laws are laws that state that upon a third conviction, the offender would be sentenced to at least 25 years in prison and would be required to serve all 25 due to truth-in-sentencing laws also enacted at the time, as an effort to incapacitate the most dangerous offenders.

In general, three-strikes laws had three goals: (1) to reduce sentencing disparities by limiting judicial discretion, (2) to increase fairness in sentencing, and (3) to act as a deterrent against future offending with the threat of increased incarceration. The laws first appeared in the early 1990s, during the war on drugs, when the state of Washington passed Initiative 593, which is considered the first official three-strikes law. Initiative 593 had four main purposes. First, it was intended to improve public safety. Second, it was supposed to reduce repeat offending through tougher sentencing. Third, it was to simplify sentencing practices in drug cases. Finally, it was to restore public trust in the criminal justice system.

After Washington passed Initiative 593 and the phrase "three strikes" was lobbed around by politicians playing into the media-fueled fears of the general public, California passed Proposition 184, which was their version of the three-strikes law. Proposition 184 was considered the most controversial of the three-strikes laws, due to the ambiguous wording of the document, which included a wider scope of offenders than the Washington law, and was called the toughest in the nation. California's Proposition 184 mandates a 25-year sentence for an offender's third conviction, which for some offenders can mean life in prison.

Once California passed the proposition in 1994, other states followed in the next two years. Currently, there are 24 states and the U.S. Department of Justice with three-strikes laws in place. The federal three-strikes provision was designed specifically for violent offenders, who are required to serve three-strikes sentences consecutively, not concurrently.

Although three-strikes laws are touted as a method of crime reduction, they do very little to actually reduce crime. Although the general crime rate had been gently declining since before any three-strikes laws were implemented, the overall percentage of violent and property crimes has been gradually increasing since 1992. Three-strikes laws also do not serve as an effective deterrent from criminal behavior, as many offenders are not aware of their existence. And aside from Proposition 184 in California, three-strikes laws have a very narrow scope, so most offenders are not even affected by them. Additionally, offenders who do know about three-strikes laws might take extreme, potentially violent, measures to avoid capture and that third conviction that would lock them away for the rest of their lives.

Implications

An unforeseen effect of these mandatory sentencing and three-strikes laws is the aging prison population, which brings a host of problems for the already overwrought prison system, such as increased costs due to health care needs of older prisoners. Due to such laws, the prison population has increased dramatically since the 1970s, leading to prison overcrowding and the advent of the "penal harm movement," which was the conscious effort to make prisons extra unpleasant by making everything from the physical facilities to the food even worse. These were passed as cost-cutting measures, which included reducing health care services for elderly prisoners, which can total around $70,000 per year. Prisons try offsetting this cost by restricting access to medications or physicians and by charging inmates copays for services received, which is especially hard on elderly patients who are less likely to be employed within the prison due to physical constraints, as well as less likely to have family to provide monetary support outside of prison.

As mandatory sentencing laws led to the quadrupling of the prison population since the early 1980s, offenders born in the 1960s, who would have been coming of age—old enough to be tried as adults—in the 1980s would be the first group really affected by mandatory sentencing laws. Additionally, as the overall population in the United States ages, due to the baby boomer generation, the average age in prison rises as well. Another reason the population of prisoners aged 50 or older has doubled since 2001, making up 10.38 percent of the U.S. prison population, is that the aforementioned tough-on-crime movement limited judicial discretion, so judges could not consider advanced age a mitigating factor during sentencing, even though older prisoners are much less likely to recidivate.

It is hard to define a universal age at which an inmate can be considered elderly; however, the general consensus is that the cutoff is much younger than the general unincarcerated population, due to a lower life expectancy behind bars (Maschi et al., 2014). Additionally, the onset of serious health problems is typically sooner and more likely than in the general population, because a lot of prisoners grew up without access to adequate health care, having come from a disadvantaged background.

Aging in Prison

Many prisons consider the old age cutoff to be around 50 years old, which is when age-related functional decline starts to occur. Psychologically, incarcerated individuals act and feel 10 years older than a comparable nonincarcerated group, due to previous lifestyle choices as well as environmental factors within the prison. Around 85 percent of aging prisoners face a major health issue, such as arthritis, back and other musculoskeletal problems, cardiovascular issues, dementia and senility, as well as hearing and vision problems associated with aging (Maschi et al., 2014).

Housing an elderly inmate can cost up to three times as much as housing a younger inmate, with the cost of an elderly inmate's housing and health care reaching up to $70,000 a year, while a younger, healthier inmate only costs the system around $20,000 a year. Prison health care facilities are often designed with the needs of the younger, healthier inmate population in mind, which presents problems for older inmates. Geriatric inmates often need assistance with activities of daily living (ADLs), much like their nonincarcerated peers, which include eating, bathing, or using the toilet; however, they do not have the same standard of care applied to their needs. This group could also include inmates who need some, but not as much, assistance, such as ramps or mobility aids. These individuals are housed in separate facilities, which prisons have to retrofit to allow geriatric inmates to move around safely.

In addition to retrofitting their facilities, prisons also have to spend money on services such as physical therapy, nurses, health care services such as dialysis, and mobility aids such as walkers and wheelchairs. The cost of housing aging inmates is going to continue to grow as individuals who have been sentenced to long prison terms age, and more and more need assistance or mobility aids in their daily lives. Moreover, since incarcerated individuals are not eligible to apply for social benefits such as Medicare or Medicaid, the cost of housing them is not mitigated through those programs as it would be for elderly individuals in the nonincarcerated U.S. population.

Vrishali Kanvinde

See also: Elderly Offenders in Prison; Incarceration Rates; Incarceration Rates and Race; Incarceration Rates in the United States Compared to Other Countries; Prison Industries; Prison Populations, Trends in; Sentencing Disparities and Discrimination in Sentencing; Three-Strikes Laws; Truth in Sentencing

Further Reading

Aday, R., & Farney, L. (2014). Malign neglect: Assessing older women's health care experiences in prison. *Journal of Bioethical Inquiry, 11*(3), 359–372.

Highest to lowest—Prison population rate. World Prison Brief, Institute for Criminal Policy Research. Retrieved from www.prisonstudies.org/highest-to-lowest/prison _population_rate?field_region_taxonomy_tid=All

Kaeble, D., & Glaze, L. E. (2016, December 29). *Correctional population in the United States, 2015.* Bureau of Justice Statistics (BJS). Retrieved from www.bjs.gov/index .cfm?ty=pbdetail&iid=5870

Maschi, T., Viola, D., Harrison, M. T., Harrison, W., Koskinen, L., & Bellusa, S. (2014). Bridging community and prison for older adults: Invoking human rights and elder and intergenerational family justice. *International Journal of Prisoner Health, 10*(1), 55–73.

Mauer, M. (2016, June 28). *Incarceration rates in an international perspective.* Sentencing Project. Retrieved www.sentencingproject.org/publications/incarceration-rates -international-perspective

Miller, H. (1981). Projecting the impact of new sentencing laws on prison populations. *Policy Sciences, 13*(1), 51–73.

Porter, L., Bushway, S., Tsao, H., & Smith, H. (2016). How the U.S. prison boom has changed the age distribution of the prison population. *Criminology, 54*(1), 30–55.

Rabuy, B., & Wagner, P. (2017, March 14). *Mass incarceration: The whole pie 2017.* Prison Policy Initiative. Retrieved from www.prisonpolicy.org/reports/pie2017.html

Reddington, F. P., & Bonham, G., Jr. (2012). *Flawed criminal justice policies.* Durham, NC: Carolina Academic Press.

World Prison Brief. An online database comprising information on prisons and the use of imprisonment around the world. Retrieved from www.prisonstudies.org

Zhang, Y., Maxwell, C. D., & Vaughn, M. S. (2009). The impact of state sentencing policies on the U.S. prison population. *Journal of Criminal Justice, 37*(2), 190–199.

Incarceration Rates and Race

Race is extremely relevant to the discussion of incarceration rates in the United States. Incarceration rates have shown a disparity based on the race of the offender. This disparity most often has a negative impact on African Americans and Hispanics/Latinos. Recent data demonstrate that black males have a higher imprisonment rate than inmates of any other race. Recent numbers have also shown that black females have a higher imprisonment rate than white and Hispanic females.

It is important to attempt to identify why these disparities in incarceration rates exist. Politics and policies have been credited with creating a mass increase in the number of people in the United States who are incarcerated. Getting tough on crime, espousing the need for "law and order," and attempting to please constituents, particularly those who are conservative, played a role in policies and practices that helped create the increase in the prison population over the past approximately 40 years. The increase in the number of incarcerated individuals in the United States also contributed to the increasing number of people of color who are behind bars in the United States.

A primary source of the disparity seen in imprisonment rates in the United States is drug arrests largely based on the war on drugs. Research has found that during a 27-year-period, blacks were arrested on drug charges at rates as much as five times higher than rates for whites nationwide (Fellner, Manning, & Mukpo, 2009). Further, at the state level, blacks were arrested on drug charges at rates as much as 11 times higher than the arrest rate for whites (Fellner et al., 2009). Due to the higher arrest rates of blacks for these types of offenses, conviction rates are also higher, contributing to the disparity in incarceration rates. In spite of the differences seen in arrest rates, it has been argued that this is not due to the fact that blacks use or sell drugs more often than whites.

In addition to arrests for drug offenses, research has also shown that racial differences in arrest rates for violent crimes also contribute at least somewhat to racial disparities in incarceration rates. Sentencing has also played a role in the disparities seen in incarceration rates based on race. For instance, three-strikes laws may have an impact on this disparity. Research has demonstrated that three-strikes laws may have a disproportionate impact on African Americans and Latinos, thereby having an impact on the disparity seen in incarceration rates. In addition, because sentences for drug offenses are often longer than those for most other offenses, this can lead to blacks and Latinos serving longer sentences, thereby influencing disproportionate incarceration rates, again based on race.

Another sentencing issue that may be related to race and incarceration rates is the previous 100-to-1 disparity applied in sentencing for crack versus powder cocaine offenses in the federal courts. This had a disproportionate impact on people of color, primarily black males. Black males were more likely to be in possession of crack cocaine, whereas whites were more likely to possess powder cocaine. Due to the Fair Sentencing Act of 2010, the disparity is now 18 to 1, but the application of sentencing for these offenses is still not equal.

Although there is limited data available on other racial/ethnic groups, the numbers indicate that Native Americans also have higher incarceration rates than whites. On the other hand, data also indicate that the racial/ethnic group with the lowest incarceration rate is Asian Americans/Pacific Islanders.

Based on the trends, scholars have predicted that 1 in every 3 black males and 1 in every 6 Latino males born in 2003 can expect to be sent to prison during his lifetime (Bonczar, 2003). This demonstrates yet another glaring disparity, as 1 in

17 white males born in the same year can have the same expectation (Bonczar, 2003). Black females also face a greater chance of being sent to prison during her lifetime. As with black males, the expectations for black females are higher than those for Latino and white females (Bonczar, 2003).

It has been suggested that in order to combat the disparities in incarceration rates, changes need to be made in terms of how laws are enforced in different communities. The argument is that arrests for drug offenses are concentrated primarily in communities of color, even though whites are also using and selling drugs at similar rates. In addition, researchers and politicians argue that sentencing policies that negatively impact people of color and contribute to the racial disparities in incarceration rates need to be revised. Lastly, researchers argue that politics/partisanship needs to be removed from the process, and evidence-based policies need to be created and implemented.

Rashaan A. DeShay

See also: Incarceration Rates; Incarceration Rates, Trends in the United States; Sentencing Disparities and Discrimination in Sentencing; Three-Strikes Laws

Further Reading

Alexander, M. (2012). *The new Jim Crow: Mass incarceration in the age of colorblindness.* New York: New York Press.

Bonczar, T. (2003, August). *Prevalence of imprisonment in the U.S. population, 1974–2001.* Washington DC: U.S. Department of Justice, Bureau of Justice Statistics.

Brownsberger, W. N. (2000). Race matters: Disproportionality of incarceration for drug dealing in Massachusetts. *Journal of Drug Issues, 30,* 345–374.

Carson, E. A. (2015). *Prisoners in 2014.* Washington, DC: Bureau of Justice Statistics.

Ehlers, S., Schiraldi, V., & Lotke, E. (2004). *Racial divide: An examination of the impact of California's three strikes laws on African-Americans and Latinos.* Washington, DC: Justice Policy Institute.

Fellner, J., Manning, R., & Mukpo, A. (2009). Decades of disparity: Drug arrests and race in the United States. New York: Human Rights Watch.

Frase, R. S. (2009). What explains persistent racial disproportionality in Minnesota's prison and jail population? *Crime and Justice, 38,* 201–280.

Hartney, C., & Vuong, L. (2009, March). *Created equal: Racial and ethnic disparities in the U.S. criminal justice system.* Oakland, CA: National Council on Crime and Delinquency.

Keen, B., & Jacobs, D. (2009). Racial threat, partisan politics, and racial disparities in prison admissions: A panel analysis. *Criminology, 47,* 209–238.

Mauer, M. (2011). Addressing racial disparities in incarceration. *The Prison Journal, 91,* 87S–101S.

Nellis, A. (2016). *The color of justice: Racial and ethnic disparity in state prisons.* Sentencing Project. Retrieved from https://www.sentencingproject.org/wp-content/uploads/2016/06/The-Color-of-Justice-Racial-and-Ethnic-Disparity-in-State-Prisons.pdf

Radosh, P. F. (2008). War on drugs: Gender and race inequities in crime control strategies. *Criminal Justice Studies, 21,* 167–178.

Schoenfeld, H. (2012). The war on drugs, the politics of crime, and mass incarceration in the United States. *The Journal of Gender, Race & Justice, 15,* 315–352.

Tighe, S. (2014). 'Of course we are crazy': Discrimination of Native American Indians through criminal justice. *Justice Policy Journal, 11*, 1–38.

Tonry, M. (2011). *Punishing race: A continuing American dilemma.* New York: Oxford University Press.

Incarceration Rates in the United States Compared to Other Countries

The latest estimates put the worldwide prison population at 10.4 million. However, due to missing data from countries such as North Korea and incomplete records from China, there are believed to be well over 11 million individuals incarcerated across the globe. The World Prison Brief database, maintained by the Institute for Criminal Policy Research at Birkbeck at the University of London for over a decade, collects statistics on prison populations from 223 countries. By continent, Asia contains 3.9 million prisoners, the Americas 3.8 million, Europe 1.6 million, and Africa another 1 million. Oceania, in reference to Australia and the surrounding islands, contains a prisoner population of 55,000. The United States leads all countries with a total prison population of 2,217,000, followed by China (1,657,812), Russia (642,470), Brazil (607,731), India (418,536), Thailand (311,036), Mexico (255,138), Iran (225,624), Turkey (172,562), and Indonesia (161,692). Other notables with much lower prisoner populations include England (85,843), France (66,864), and Japan (60,486). The United States, China, Russia, and Brazil contain about half of the world's total prison population.

Incarceration rates provide a greater measure of depth in terms of imprisonment use in relation to population size, represented as the ratio of individuals incarcerated per 100,000. Seychelles, an island within the Indian Ocean roughly 1,000 miles from the coast of East Africa, possesses the highest incarceration rate at 799 per 100,000. Note the actual population of Seychelles is 92,000, with 735 prisoners. The United States possesses the second-highest incarceration rate at 698 per 100,000, followed by St. Kitts and Nevis (607), Turkmenistan (583), U.S. Virgin Islands (542), Cuba (510), El Salvador (492), Guam (469), Thailand (461), and Belize (449). India, which has one of the larger populations of prisoners, has one of the 10 lowest incarceration rates at 33 per 100,000. Other notable countries with lower incarceration rates include England (146), Canada (114), France (103), Sweden (53), Japan (48), Iceland (45), Nigeria (31), Pakistan (43), and Bangladesh (43).

Examining incarceration rates by region, Bahrain possesses the highest rate in the Middle East at 301 per 100,000. Mentioned previously, the United States possesses the highest rate in North America at 698, Turkmenistan possesses the largest rate in Asia at 583, Seychelles the highest rate in Africa at 799, and St. Kitts and Nevis of the Caribbean at 607. El Salvador possesses the highest incarceration rate for Central America at 541, French Guiana for South America at 326, the Russian Federation at 450 and Belarus at 306 in Europe, and Guam at 469 in terms of Oceanic representation.

The World Prison Brief also collects data on a country's occupancy level, which considers the total capacity of the country's prison system in relation to its total prisoner population. Such results provide a general indicator of the level of

Comparative Incarceration Rates 305

overcrowding that may exist in a given nation. For the 204 nations from which data were obtained, a little more than half (116) possess occupancy rates in excess of 100 percent. These rates do not speak to any standardized considerations of physical space but rather are set by each country independently. The United States, specifically, possesses a reported occupancy rate of 103 percent, ranking 109th out of the 204 nations providing occupancy data. The United States' northern neighbor, Canada, possesses a near identical occupancy level at 102 percent while its southern neighbor, Mexico, is at 118 percent. Although these figures indicate, at an aggregated level, that the United States has an issue of overcrowding, it is far from the worst, or the best, in the world. Haiti possesses an astonishing 454 percent occupancy rate, followed by Benin (354 percent), Philippines (316 percent), El Salvador (310 percent), Guatemala (296 percent), Uganda (273 percent), Venezuela (270 percent), Bolivia (269 percent), Antigua/Barbuda (258 percent), and Sudan (255 percent). Three of the top 10 highest occupancy level nations are from Africa (Benin, Uganda, Sudan), two from Central America (El Salvador and Guatemala), two from South America (Venezuela and Bolivia), two from the Caribbean (Haiti and Antigua/Barbuda), and one from Asia (Philippines). Clearly, these are nations that have extremely limited capital for correctional institutions. On the other hand, countries such as Japan (67 percent) and Sweden (84 percent) possess more modest occupancy levels. Other Western nations possess rates similar to the United States including France (119 percent), New Zealand (106 percent), and Turkey (103 percent) despite much lower incarceration rates.

Data in terms of pretrial detention (also known as remand prisoners) further reveals that for several countries the majority of their prison populations comprised individuals yet to be formally convicted and sentenced. The World Prison Brief estimates that roughly 3 million prisoners are under some form of remand or pretrial custody, about a quarter of all prisoners. For nations in Central Africa, Western Africa, and Southern Asia more than 50 percent of their prisoner populations are on remand. This excess in pretrial detainees has been attributed, in large part, to resource constraints that prohibit a more efficient processing of justice-involved individuals. This is a prevalent issue for nations with low economic development. In contrast, about 20 percent of U.S. prisoners are being held under pretrial custody. For Canada, the rate is 35 percent.

There exists little comparative research pertaining to demographical features of prisoner populations across the globe. Currently, only data pertaining to gender have been actively and accurately recorded for comparison. Females make up a small proportion of prisoners at an estimated 700,000 worldwide, less than 7 percent of the entire prisoner population. The United States, however, possesses the 17th highest percentage of female prisoners at 9.3 percent. Canada ranks 73rd at 5.6 percent, while the highest percentage comes from Hong Kong (China) with 20.5 percent. By continent, the Americas possess the highest proportion of female prisoners at 8.0 percent, followed by Oceanic nations at 7.0 percent, Asia at 6.8 percent, Europe at 6.4 percent, and Africa at 3.0 percent.

Worldwide, the prison population has increased from an estimated 8.7 million in 2000 to 10.4 million in 2015—a 20 percent increase in the prisoner population compared to 18 percent growth of the general population. By continent the

Americas increased from 2.7 million in 2000 to 3.8 million by 2015 (41 percent), from about 900,000 to 1.0 million in Africa (15 percent), 3.0 to 3.9 million in Asia (29 percent), and from 34,000 to 55,000 for Oceanic nations (59 percent). Interestingly, Europe experienced a decline in its prisoner population from 2.0 million in 2000 to 1.6 million in 2015 (–21 percent). Europe also experienced the smallest population growth of all continents at an estimated 3 percent increase, while Africa experienced the greatest change in population growth at 44 percent. The Americas' population growth of 17 percent was comparable to Asian and Oceanic regions at 18 and 25 percent, respectively. These results suggest the increased use of imprisonment is *not* driven by population growth.

Interestingly, the United States was not the primary driver of increased imprisonment population in the Americas over the past 15 years, which had experienced much of its imprisonment boom through the 1990s. If removed, the percentage increase in the prisoner population of the Americas increases to 108 percent, suggesting the use of imprisonment has increased greatly in other countries in the Americas after the mass incarceration experience of the United States began to plateau. An examination of incarceration rates beginning in the 1980s further demonstrates this trend with the United States starting just above 200 per 100,000 in 1980, increasing to 300 by 1985, up to 450 by 1990, jumping to 600 by 1995, and settling in the 700s through the 2000s before declining to 698 in 2015. On the other hand, El Salvador, for example, held a steady incarceration rate of around 100 per 100,000 through the 1980s and 1990s before beginning a distinct uphill climb at the start of the 2000s. Beginning in 2000, El Salvador's incarceration rate increased steadily to 500 by 2015. Though less pronounced, Colombia exhibits a similar trend as well with a rate of 100 per 100,000 through the 1980s and 1990s before increasing in the 2000s to about 250 in 2015. Brazil, which has the fourth-highest number of prisoners in the world, also possessed an incarceration rate of about 100 per 100,000 in 1995 before experiencing a marked increase in the 2000s, reaching 300 in 2014. The increase in El Salvador's incarceration rate has been attributed to new antigang laws introduced in the 2000s and the lengthening of sentences more broadly. Colombia and Brazil have experienced the introduction of tougher drug laws. Colombia and Brazil also possess a high proportion of remand prisoners at 38 percent and 39 percent, indicating issues of efficiency with judicial processing.

The United States comprises 21 percent of the world's prisoners yet only 4.4 percent of the world's general population. It currently possesses the second-highest incarceration rate at 698 per 100,000, a decrease from a peak of about 750 in the mid-2000s. The growth of imprisonment in the United States has stabilized and in recent years has begun to recede after a lengthy imprisonment boom dating back to the 1970s. Today, there are more than 3,000 jails and 1,000 state and federal prisons.

The growth of the penal institution in the United States has been largely attributed to the punitive, lengthy, sentencing of drug offenders, including the implementation of mandatory minimum and truth-in-sentencing policies geared toward reducing or eliminating parole release opportunities. The recent declines in the prisoner population have been a function of governmental fiscal constraints, sentencing reform, and the greater acceptance of community alternatives. However, the

United States remains the leader in terms of its raw prisoner population and the second highest in terms of incarceration rate.

Adam K. Matz

See also: Australia, Prisons in; Canada, Prisons in; China, Prisons in; England, Prisons in; France, Prisons in; Incarceration Rates, Trends in the United States; Norway, Prisons in; Peru, Prisons in; South Africa, Prisons in

Further Reading

Barry, M., & Leonardsen, D. (2012). Inequality and punitivism in late modern societies: Scandinavian exceptionalism revisited. *European Journal of Probation, 4*(2), 46–61.

Byrne, J. M., Pattavina, A., & Taxman, F. S. (2015). International trends in prison upsizing and downsizing: In search of evidence of a global rehabilitation revolution. *Victims and Offenders, 10*(4), 420–451.

Coyle, A., Fair, H., Jacobson, J., & Walmsley, R. (2016). *Imprisonment worldwide: The current situation and an alternative future.* Chicago: Policy Press.

DeMichele, M. (2014). A panel analysis of legal culture, political economics, and punishment among 15 western countries, 1960–2010. *International Criminal Justice Review, 24*(4), 360–376.

Downes, D. (2001). The macho penal economy: Mass incarceration in the United States: A European perspective. *Punishment & Society, 3*(1), 61–80.

Garland, D. (2001). *The culture of control: Crime and social order in contemporary society.* Chicago: University of Chicago Press.

Li, E. (2016). China's urban underclass population and penal policy. *Criminology & Criminal Justice, 16*(1), 80–98.

Neapolitan, J. L. (2001). An examination of cross-national variation in punitiveness. *International Journal of Offender Therapy and Comparative Criminology, 45*(6), 691–710.

Snacken, S. (2015). Punishment, legitimate policies and values: Penal moderation, dignity and human rights. *Punishment & Society, 17*(3), 397–423.

Informal Methods of Control Utilized by Correctional Officers

Control may be defined as the means by which one guides, directs, or redirects the behavior of another (or, in the case of self-control, themselves). To say that an authority has control over a subordinate is to say that the authority has the capability of directing, redirecting, or, at the least, guiding the behavior of that subordinate. The ability to control may be termed power, and authorities obtain compliance with their directives through the purposive and strategic use of power. Correctional officers are no different than any other authority figure in this regard—they rely on various forms of control to exercise power over the behavior of inmates and goings-on within the correctional facility.

Theories of control vary in their explication of the nature of control, though it is possible to organize their insights in such a way as to present a comprehensive view of the concept. First, control may be either formal or informal. Formal control is characterized primarily by standardization and structure, based on guidelines and regulations established by prison or jail administrators and designed to dictate the methods by which correctional officers control inmates with the least reliance on officers' own discretion. Informal methods of control are those that do not rely on agency-based rules and are utilized by guards to give them a measure of power that maximizes their own discretion.

Both formal and informal controls can be seen as rewards-based (remunerative) or punitive (coercive). Correctional authorities guide or direct inmate behavior both by satisfying inmate desires or by imposing unpleasant conditions on them. Because correctional facilities are institutions of total control, nearly every aspect of inmates' lives are subject to influence by their overseers and, thus, opportunities abound for their conduct to be controlled through offering rewards ("carrots") or punishments ("sticks"). Taking phone privileges as an example, inmates may be rewarded when officers "extend" their allotted time by only leniently enforcing telephone talk-time limitations. Prisoners may also be punished by denying them the ability to use the telephones.

Alternative explanations of institutional controls hold that controls consists of four types, each of which may be either formal or informal, remunerative or punitive. Controls may be physical, that is, characterized by imposing pain or bodily discomfort, or by physically constraining the controlled. Resource controls are designed to guide or direct behavior by manipulating one's access to material or nonmaterial tools used to enhance one's quality of life. Controls may be social in nature. Social controls have been researched extensively in criminology and are based on the persuasiveness of affective interpersonal relationships. Social controls are founded on humans' need for social companionship, offering acceptance through approval or threatening isolation through rejection. Finally, an oft forgotten class of controls arise from the impact of personal moral codes. Individuals seek to view themselves in a positive light—as valuable, worthy of respect, and exemplary— and a primary way to judge oneself is against standards of "rightness" that promote how one believes people should conduct themselves.

Correctional officers utilize a bevy of social, resource, and moral controls outside of formal processes. Literature has indicated at least five bases of power, first proposed by John French and Bertram Raven: (1) coercive, (2) reward, (3) expert, (4) legitimate, and (5) referent. These "bases of power" are always not entirely clear in their contours, but controls of each type—social, resource, or moral—can be founded on one or more of them. For example, correctional officers often offer resource, social, and moral rewards to establish rapport, and subsequent degrees of control, over prisoners. Investigations into the nature of officer-inmate relations have shown that correctional officers have the ability to enhance inmates' ability to improve their quality of life by supporting their assignment to coveted work opportunities, allowing them access to exercise equipment, extending their time outside of their cells, or providing material benefits such as foodstuffs, entertainment materials, and other accommodations. Officers may also overlook violations of prison codes restricting inmates' possession of valuable items and underground market activity. By making the direct provision of resources or the granting of leniency contingent on inmate compliance with officer requests, officers redirect inmate behavior from intolerable to tolerable activities.

Officers also have the ability to reward inmates socially or morally. From allowing certain inmates to congregate together and carry on social relationships with each other, to permitting inmates to communicate with intimates outside the prison walls (e.g., the lenient enforcement of phone restrictions), to developing cordial relationships with inmates themselves, correctional officers have, and use, ways of influencing the quality of inmates' social lives to encourage compliance, even outside of formal processes. Moreover, officers may be able to provide moral rewards, especially for inmates who demonstrate a desire to transition to more conventional value systems. For these, the respect of prison guards and the recognition of positive progress toward change can be as important a motivation as anything.

Expertise as a basis of power develops as inmates see correctional officers as competent and reliable resources in the institutional context. An officer's ability to resolve problems or address inmate concerns expeditiously will serve as a source of influence for the officer. Prisoners also see correctional officers as having authority simply on the basis of their position (legitimacy, according to French and Raven) or by virtue of respect held for certain officers as individual personalities. Expertise seems mostly tied to an officer's ability to resolve requests for material resources. Social and moral controls tend to be more associated with legitimate and referent power. Demonstrating the efficiency and fairness of the institution and its operations enhances the legitimacy of the organization and sets the stage for inmates to accept correctional authorities as legitimate. In such cases, officers' social pressures and moral appeals can carry weight. Germinating an authentic personal—albeit, professional—connection to inmates creates the environment where officers' expressions of approval or disapproval matter and where those expressions can even have an impact on how the inmate views himself or herself.

Physical control is also a form of control, though, in prison, the use of physical force by correctional officers is nearly always a matter of formal control. There are reports of officer-on-inmate abuse outside of formal channels. What is more, excessive use of force may be seen as an informal control if, by informal, one means the portion of force that is not justified by the situation. Yet, as even excessive force is typically initiated in connection with otherwise legitimate uses of force supported and sanctioned by formal rules and regulations, and is usually documented in official records, it is difficult to call these purely informal methods of control. Coercive physical controls are also closely associated with officers holding more punitive perspectives on the purpose of corrections. As the field embraces more rehabilitative goals, the use of less punitive, more informal controls should be expected to increase. Still, it should be noted that, as prison systems opt for decreasing recreational and educational opportunities combined with greater levels of restriction, officers will be forced to rely more and more frequently on these least effective methods of control.

Kwan-Lamar Blount-Hill

See also: Administration; Correctional Officer Subculture; Correctional Officers, Typology of; Correctional Officers and Discretion; Misconduct by Correctional Employees; Personnel; Punishment Philosophies; Total Institutions; Treatment in Prisons; Use of Force in Prisons

Further Reading

French, J. R. P., Jr., & Raven, B. (1959). The bases of social power. In D. Cartwright (Ed.), *Studies in social power* (pp. 259–269). Ann Arbor: University of Michigan Press.

Gordon, J. A., & Stichman, A. J. (2016). The influence of rehabilitative and punishment ideology on correctional officers' perceptions of informal bases of power. *International Journal of Offender Therapy and Comparative Criminology*, *60*(4), 1591–1608.

Ibsen, A. Z. (2013). Ruling by favors: Prison guards' informal exercise of institutional control. *Law & Social Inquiry*, *38*(2), 342–363.

Ricciardelli, R., & Sit, V. (2016). Producing social (dis)order in prison: The effects of administrative controls on prisoner-on-prisoner violence. *The Prison Journal*, *96*(2), 210–231.

Inmate Classification

In correctional theory and practice, classification has traditionally been conceptualized as a process by which a correctional agency determines differential care in the handling of offenders. It is the system that assesses the needs and requirements of incarcerated offenders, and then assigns them to facilities and programs in accordance with their needs and the resources of the correctional institution to which they are assigned. Classification has two competing purposes: (1) to enhance security and control of inmates so that a safe environment is maintained, and (2) to assign inmates to treatment programming that will best lead to rehabilitation.

When inmates first enter the correctional system, they are assessed and matched to a facility with an appropriate security level and housing assignment to reduce risks of rule infractions, violence, and escape. Additionally, the decisions consider a prisoner's needs with respect to medical, mental health, vocational, and educational services. Following the initial assessment, a classification committee will periodically review the inmates' classifications. Adjustments may be made to the initial classification as needed, taking into account rule infractions and other problems or any other development that might indicate a need for changes in security, custody, or programming.

Historically, classification meant separating inmates based on such characteristics as age, race, sex, prior criminal history, and the offense of conviction. Behavior at the institution, past and present, was also used in decisions. Based on these criteria, inmates are placed in maximum, medium, or minimum security levels, with maximum security denoting the most intense supervision and minimum the least intensive supervision. Most prisons, or corresponding state statutes, indicate some of the criteria used. For example, first offenders, young offenders, or offenders with less than a two-year sentence would be classified as minimum security risks, while recidivist property offenders would be classified as medium security risks. Violent offenders, inmates with long sentences or those believed to be escape risks, would be classified as requiring maximum security.

There have been several criticisms of the traditional system. Offense of conviction, a primary component of decision making, has not been particularly predictive of behavior. Many offenders commit a wide variety of crimes, and offense of conviction, the offense for which they were caught, might or might not be reflective of their typical pattern of behavior. In addition, the traditional classification scheme does not address individual treatment needs. Finally, a common problem is overclassification, when prisoners are assigned to a higher security level than is needed. Overclassification results in greater expenditures because greater security costs more than lower levels of security, and prisoners are subjected to conditions that are usually harsher and more restrictive than is necessary.

Although the traditional system dates back to the early penitentiaries, the process of classification is becoming more sophisticated, particularly with the development of better psychological tests and statistical techniques. The National Institute of Corrections (NIC) issued 14 principles for classification, including the development of written policies and procedures and the use of measurements and testing instruments demonstrated to be reliable, valid, and objective. Care must be taken to ensure that the classification method is constitutional, as a number of prisoner lawsuits have challenged particular systems. The NIC also recommended that administrative and line staff have input in the development of classification systems.

Most of the systems that have been developed are based on risk and other behavioral assessments. Clinical methods involve interviews with offenders using checklists formulated by professionals to gauge behavioral indicators. Actuarial techniques rely on statistically based instruments grounded in theory, research, and factors identified from empirical studies to be related to criminal behaviors, which are then used to develop a predictive model. The Megargee typology, based on MMPI (Minnesota Multiphasic Personality Inventory) subtest scores to differentiate behavioral patterns among groups of inmates, is an example of this technique.

Actuarial risk assessment instruments have been demonstrated to be more accurate in predicting future behavior, compared to clinical methods. However, actuarial assessment methods still have limitations. In particular, they are based on generalized linear models, and thus they tend to assume a one-size-fits-all approach, without individual considerations. This approach does not take into account the possibility that different factors might apply to different subgroups when predicting behavior, and relationships between behavior and test scores might not be linear. Thus, these methods have some predictive ability, and are promising, but the ability to predict behavior, especially dangerous behavior, is still limited, presenting challenges to the classification of prison inmates.

Carol A. Veneziano

See also: Maximum Security; Treatment in Prisons

Further Reading

Aegisdotter, S., White, M. J., Spengler, P. M., Maugherman, A. S., & Anderson, L.A. (2006). The meta-analysis of clinical judgment project: Fifty-six years of accumulated research on clinical vs. statistical prediction. *The Counseling Psychologist, 34,* 341–382.

Berk, R. A., & Bleich, J. (2013). Statistical procedures for forecasting criminal behavior: A comparative assessment. *Criminology and Public Policy, 12,* 513–544.

Bonta, J. (1996). Risk needs assessment and treatment. In A. T. Harland (Ed.), *Choosing correctional options that work: Defining the demand and evaluating the supply* (pp. 18–22). Thousand Oaks, CA: Sage.

Clements, C. B., McKee, J. M., & Jones, S. E. (1984). *Offender needs assessment: Models and approaches.* Washington, DC: National Institute of Corrections.

Gendreau, P., Goggin, C. E., & Law, M. A. (1997). Predicting prison misconduct. *Criminal Justice & Behavior, 24,* 414–431.

Hanson, R. K. (2005). Twenty years of progress in violence risk assessment. *Journal of Interpersonal Violence, 20,* 212–217.

Megargee, E. I., & Bohn, M. J. (1979). *Classifying criminal offenders.* Thousand Oaks, CA: Sage.

National Advisory Commission on Criminal Justice Standards & Goals. (1973). *Report on corrections.* Washington, DC: U.S. Department of Justice.

Ngo, F. T., Govindu, R., & Agarwal, A. (2015). Assessing the predictive utility of logistic regression, classification and prediction tree, chi-squared automatic interaction detection, and neural network models in predicting inmate misconduct. *American Journal of Criminal Justice, 40,* 47–74.

Singh, J. P., & Fazel, S. (2010). Forensic risk assessment: A meta-review. *Criminal Justice & Behavior, 37,* 965–988.

Welch, M. (2011). *Corrections: A critical approach.* New York: Routledge.

Inmate Dental Care

Inmates have more dental problems than people in the general public. They are statistically more likely to enter prison with poor dental health, to be missing teeth, to have periodontal disease, and to have unfilled cavities. Inmates with histories of substance abuse, particularly users of crystal methamphetamines and ecstasy, are more likely than other subsets of inmates to have profound dental health problems due to the gum decay and tooth damage associated with these drugs. Minority inmates also tend to have worse dental health than their white counterparts, perhaps due to lack of access to preventive care in their home communities.

Correctional facilities, as extensions of the government, have significant legal and medical responsibilities to provide a baseline of dental care. Legally, these obligations are governed by the Constitution's due process clauses, civil rights law, and relevant case law. Clinically, prison dental care must comply with the medical communities' standards of care and must be "constitutionally adequate." Specific guidance on best practices can be found in standards promulgated by the Bureau of Prisons, state departments of corrections, the American Dental Association, the National Commission on Correctional Health Care, and the American Correctional Association. These organizations provide targets for optimal care, which are helpful for policy development and clinical guidance.

However, these entities do not define or enforce law. Instead, the courts define the law on inmate dental care. The law in this area, on the whole, describes conduct that is prohibited, but it does not state what is expected. The law on inmate dental care derives from a famous case, *Estelle v. Gamble* (1976), that says that prisons must not be "deliberately indifferent" to a "known or obvious" dental condition. Proscribed conduct is decided on a case-by-case basis by the courts. Thus, prison dental care providers can look to the courts to identify practices that are unconstitutionally insufficient, but there are no comprehensive standards on what is constitutionally sufficient.

With that said, a few directives have been established. For example, prisons are not required to provide advanced or cosmetic dentistry, but they must provide basic tools for prophylactic care (toothpaste, toothbrushes). They also cannot allow prolonged suffering from oral disease. Prisons are encouraged to fill cavities instead of extracting teeth because of the established stigma associated with missing teeth, and they are expected to conduct dental screenings every 6 to 12 months.

Most inmates seek dental care at some point during their incarceration, more than almost any other form of health care. Inmate dental care includes prophylactic, remedial, and emergency dental services. These services are adapted from practices within the community to accommodate the prison setting. Providing prison dental care entails several risks and obstacles. The logistical challenges of providing dental care in a carceral setting are many: the risk of disease transmission via saliva or blood; the risk that inmates will use dental equipment as weapons during exams to injure clinicians; and the risk that inmates will steal dental equipment and use it against guards or other inmates. Additionally, many dental professionals prefer not to work in correctional institutions. Many prison clinics lack a full complement of appropriate equipment and suffer from poor record-keeping. To address clinicians' reluctance to provide care in prisons settings, some communities are partnering with universities to allow dental students to receive academic credit for working in prisons and loan forgiveness programs for dentists who agree to work within prisons upon graduation. In light of these risks and rewards of inmate dental care, dental providers continue to seek innovative ways of delivering dental care in institutional settings. Many institutions are using electronic dental records, some are assigning inmate health identification numbers to facilitate record transfers as inmates move throughout the criminal justice system, while others are implementing "teledentistry."

From a public policy perspective, prison dental care is a key component of preserving the general public health, of promoting prosocial behaviors among inmates during times of incarceration, and maximizing

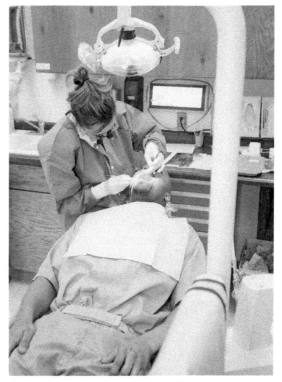

An inmate receives dental care from a prison dentist at the Nebraska Department of Corrections. (Mikael Karlsson/Alamy Stock Photo)

postprison reintegrative success when inmates transition back into society. For many inmates, their time of incarceration may be their only opportunity to receive dental care. Social science research has demonstrated that good dental care and remediation of dental problems can improve inmates' likelihood of success as they leave prison and seek employment. Having poor dental health or missing teeth can impede peoples' ability to find good jobs or complete academic programs. Perhaps relatedly, poor dental health and missing teeth also adversely impact former inmates' interpersonal interactions. Inmates who leave prison with missing teeth or noticeably compromised dental health experience increased levels of shame, decreased self-esteem, and increased problems interacting with friends and family. Failure to address physical deficits such as impaired teeth can increase antisocial behavior and increase criminal activity. Inmates who receive restorative care and return home report increased self-confidence, increased job performance, and increased ability to set good examples for their children.

Anne S. Douds and Eileen M. Ahlin

See also: Health Care in Prison Populations; Health Promotion in Prison Settings

Further Reading

Albright, D., Gonzalez, A., Willis, D., Bridy, L., & Lyons, C. (2011). *Reducing barriers to re-entry: Assessing the implementation and impact of a pilot dental repair program for parolees.* Albuquerque, NM: Institute for Social Research, University of New Mexico.

Clare, J. H. (2002). Dental health status, unmet needs, and utilization of services in a cohort of adult felons at admission and after three years incarceration. *Journal of Correctional Health Care, 9*(1), 65–75.

Douds, A. S., & Ahlin, E. M. (2015). Prisoners' constitutional right to dentures. *Correctional Health Care Report, 16*, 39–41.

Douds, A. S., Ahlin, E. M., Kavanaugh, P. R., & Olaghere, A. (2016). Decayed prospects: A qualitative study of prison dental care and its impact on former prisoners. *Criminal Justice Review, 41*(1), 21–40.

Glassman, P., & Subar, P. (2010). Creating and maintaining oral health for dependent people in institutional settings. *Journal of Public Health Dentistry, 70*(s1), S40–S48.

Mack, K., & Collins, M. (2013). Access to oral health care in the Georgia prison system. *Journal of Dental Hygiene, 87*(5), 271–274.

Makrides, N. S., & Shulman, J. D. (2002). Dental health care of prison populations. *Journal of Correctional Health Care, 9*(3), 291–306.

Moran, D. (2014). Leaving behind the 'total institution'? Teeth, transcarceral spaces and (re)inscription of the formerly incarcerated body. *Gender, Place and Culture, 21*(1), 35–51.

Treadwell, H. M., & Formicola, A. J. (2005). Improving the oral health of prisoners to improve overall health and well-being. *American Journal of Public Health, 95*(10), 1677–1678.

Walsh, T., Tickle, M., Milsom, K., Buchanan, K., & Zoitopoulous, L. (2008). An investigation of the nature of research into dental health in prisons: A systematic review. *British Dental Journal, 204*(12), 683–689.

Woods, L. N., Lanza, S., Dyson, W., & Gordon, D. M. (2013). The role of prevention in promoting continuity of health care in prisoner reentry initiatives. *American Journal of Public Health, 103*(5), 830–838.

Inmate Subculture

Prisons are considered total institutions, as described by Erving Goffman. Inmates have all aspects of life controlled and decided for them and spend relatively long periods of time within this system of control. The confining and restrictive nature of correctional institutions provides an ideal environment for inmates to develop their own subculture. Just as in general subculture of crime theories, transgressions against individuals may be viewed as disrespectful and may be met with retaliation, including acts of violence.

Subcultures exist among both male and female correctional institutions, and the degree to which these subcultures are formed depends on the types of institutions in which the inmates are housed. Inmates housed in maximum and medium security institutions are more likely to ascribe to inmate subcultures than those housed in minimum security facilities. These subcultures are characterized by distinct roles, norms, and values that are generally oppositional to those in mainstream society. Some examples of the inmate subculture include a greater reliance on violence for problem resolution, exertion of toughness or masculinity, participation in the black market for goods and services, adherence to the prison hierarchy, and the potential existence of the convict code.

Relationships between inmates vary by type and security level of the institution, as well as by whether the inmates housed there are male or female. Past indications are that female inmates are prone to create pseudofamilies with their fellow inmates, which includes designating various traditional familial roles to individual inmates. Within these pseudofamilies, women may carry out stereotypical household duties within the institution, such as laundry, for each other, or may engage in sexual relationships with one another. More recent research reveals that female inmate subcultures may be evolving to more closely mimic those of male inmate populations. Some explanations for this shift include female correctional facilities are less likely to be structured like cottages, female inmates serve longer prison sentences than in previous years, and females in the free society have more expansive roles than prior years.

Male inmates are more likely than females to participate in prison gangs in order to display power over one another and achieve a higher status in the prison hierarchy. Gang affiliation is primarily determined by an inmate's race and ethnicity. Gang affiliation in the community also contributes to prison gang affiliation. In some institutions the neighborhood from which an inmate originates also can determine their affiliation with a particular gang. Gangs, and subsequently the prison hierarchy, can serve multiple functions for inmates, including providing protection, and access to goods and services on the black market to their members. Because membership in a prison gang is often met with severe consequences, including administrative segregation or assignment to higher security institutions, gang membership is relatively secretive.

In prison, many of the goods and services that are readily available in the community are either restricted or completely disallowed. Through black market networks, some inmates have access to contraband, including drugs, weapons, or cigarettes. Items from the prison commissary, such as snack foods, also may be traded in the black market economy. Inmates who hold legitimate employment in the prison, such as in the kitchen, can gain access to wanted goods more easily. Others are able to perform a wanted service such as tattooing. Other activities, such as gambling, are also part of the black market economy. Access to these types of goods and services often give inmates additional leverage to secure a higher status among the inmate population. In the hierarchical system, this leverage equates to power and control among the inmates.

Another feature of the inmate subculture is prison argot (jargon or slang). Argot serves as a language between inmates, with some terms being used for objects, such as a "shank" or "shiv" to describe a self-crafted knife, and other terms used to describe individuals and their roles within the subculture. For instance, inmates who target other inmates for sexual assault may be called "wolves," "aggressive wolves," or "nonaggressive wolves." Inmates who are newly admitted and more prone to being victimized are referred to as "fish." Prison argot serves as an important communication tool for the inmate subculture.

Researchers have historically discussed whether the violence and subculture among inmates is a product of inmate importation or institutional deprivations. Importation theory assumes that prisoners import characteristics that are conducive to violence into the prison environment. Individuals in prison are continuing to live as they did prior to their sentence, with an emphasis on aggressive and criminogenic values. In contrast, deprivation theory states that it is being deprived of certain things (such as autonomy, heterosexual relationships, access to goods and services, safety and liberty) that can create tension and violence among inmates. Other perspectives, such as the situational model, combine perspectives of these two theories. The situational model focuses on the complexities of the factors involved in perpetration of violence among inmates and can be used to explain why inmates have differential prison experiences. Some factors to consider include the location of the institution, family visitations, and the complex relationships between the inmates and correctional officers.

Adherence to an inmate code, or convict code, is also an essential element of the inmate subculture. Most of the tenets of the code display inmate solidarity against the correctional staff. For instance, it emphasizes not "snitching" on each other and that correctional officers are not considered trustworthy, creating further division between the staff and inmates. The power differential between inmates and correctional staff can contribute substantially to the emergence and continuation of the inmate subculture on an institutional level. Moreover, because inmates may be viewed as nonpersons, their individual needs may be ignored, or they may become privy to correctional officer conflicts relatively unnoticed.

Inmates range in their level of adaptation to prison life. Although some inmates are primarily interested in completing their sentence and returning to the free community, others engage in as many programs as possible for rehabilitation and reintegration. Some other inmates are deeply engrained in the prison subculture and have more easily adjusted to being incarcerated.

Assimilation into the prison culture occurs over time in a process called prisonization. Over a period of years, inmates become acclimated to the subculture. Some may have few, if any, visits from family members or little participation in prison programming. The longer inmates are incarcerated, the more likely they are to be more prisonized or assimilated into the subculture. Consequently, inmates serving longer sentences are likely to have more difficulty reintegrating into society and leaving the inmate subculture. This is especially true if the inmates have not participated in any of the above-mentioned programs or received quality visitation time with their family members.

There are also some inmates who opt not to engage in the inmate subculture and adhere to conventional norms and values. Inmates who are less likely to adhere to subculture are those who maintain social connections with family, attend rehabilitation sessions, and participate in vocational and educational programming. Even seemingly minor attachments to the outside world, such as wearing clothing styles of the free community and having television privileges, can prevent some from becoming immersed in the inmate subculture.

Inmate subcultures may vary across time and space. Although there are some relatively consistent factors, many of the issues discussed here differ according to the location of the institution, the type of institution, and the inmates who are being housed within the facility.

Kristine Levan

See also: Consensual Sex between Inmates; Cooking in Prison; Drug Use in Prison; Gossip and Rumors; Masturbation in Prison; Prison Argot; Prison-Brewed Alcohol; Prison Gangs; Prisonization; Protective Pairing in Men's Prisons; Pseudofamilies in Women's Prisons; Rapelore in Prisons; Respect; Sexuality in Women's Prisons; Sexually Explicit Materials in Prisons; Snitches; Tattooing in Prison; Total Institutions; Underground Prison Economy; Violence in Prisons

Further Reading

Cheeseman, K. (2003). Importing aggression: An examination and application of subculture theories to prison violence. *The Southwest Journal of Criminal Justice, 1*(1), 24–38.

Clemmer, D. (1940). *The prison community.* New York: Rinehart.

Goffman, E. (1961). Essays on the social situation of mental patients and other inmates. Garden City, NY: Anchor Books.

Greer, K. R. (2000). The changing nature of interpersonal relationships in a women's prison. *The Prison Journal, 80*(4), 442–468.

Hassine, V. (2011). *Life without parole: Living and dying in prison today.* New York: Oxford University Press.

Hensley, C., Wright, J., Tewksbury, R., & Castle, T. (2003). The evolving nature of prison argot and sexual hierarchies. *The Prison Journal, 83*(3), 289–300.

Irwin, J. (1980). *Prisons in turmoil.* Boston: Little, Brown.

Irwin, J. K., & Cressey, D. (1962). Thieves, convicts, and the inmate culture. *Social Problems, 10,* 142–155.

Steinke, P. (1991). Using situational factors to predict different types of prison violence. *Journal of Offender Rehabilitation, 17,* 119–132.

Sykes, G. M. (1958). *The society of captives.* Princeton, NJ: Princeton University Press.

Sykes, G. M., & Messinger, S. L. (1960). The inmate social code and its functions. *Social Science Research Council, 15,* 401–405.

Trammell, R. (2012). *Enforcing the convict code: Violence and prison culture.* Boulder, CO: Lynne Rienner.

Trammell, R., & Rundle, M. (2015). The inmate as the nonperson: Examining staff conflict from the inmate's perspective. *The Prison Journal, 95*(4), 472–492.

Inmate-on-Inmate Sexual Abuse

A male's foremost concern during his first day of confinement is being raped (Jones & Schmid, 1990). This concern is well founded in that, as Holmberg (2001) observed, "New [male] convicts are almost instantly sized up as dominant and submissive, penetrator or penetrated" (p. 89). However, recent studies indicate that female inmates are at greater risk of inmate-on-inmate sexual victimization than their male counterparts (Beck et al., 2010, 2013).

DEFINITION

Historically, the lay term "prison rape" denoted coerced, penetrative sex between inmates of the same sex but otherwise went undefined. The enactment of the Prison Rape Elimination Act, 42 U.S.C. § 15609 (PREA) by the U.S. Congress in 2003, provided the first comprehensive, multijurisdictional definition of prison rape. It defines prison rape as follows:

A. the carnal knowledge, oral sodomy, sexual assault with an object, or sexual fondling of a person, forcibly or against that person's will;

B. the carnal knowledge, oral sodomy, sexual assault with an object, or sexual fondling of a person not forcibly or against the person's will, where the victim is incapable of giving consent because of his or her youth or his or her temporary or permanent mental or physical incapacity; or

C. the carnal knowledge, oral sodomy, sexual assault with an object, or sexual fondling of a person achieved through the exploitation of the fear or threat of physical violence or bodily injury. 42 U.S.C. § 15609[9]

Controversially, some commentators have argued that inmates' working concept of prison rape diverges from the lay definition as well as the PREA's (Fleisher & Krienert, 2009). Upon interviewing more than 500 inmates, Fleisher and Krienert (2009) concluded that the inmate society imparts a "sexual worldview" that narrowly defines prison rape by excluding incidents in which the victim fails to fight hard or other "blame-the-victim" scenarios as defined by hypermasculine norms (p. 84). Likewise, Fowler (2007) found that "rape-supportive beliefs led inmates to excuse perpetrators, blame victims, and prevent inmates from accepting legally defined incidents of sexual assaults. . . ." (p. 4870).

In implementing PREA through the issuance of Standards to Prevent, Detect, and Respond to Prison Rape, the U.S. Department of Justice (2012) determined that "sexual abuse is a more accurate term [than prison rape] to describe the behaviors that Congress aimed to eliminate" than prison rape (p. 21). The Justice Department's definition of sexual abuse is as follows:

Sexual abuse of an inmate, detainee, or resident by another inmate, detainee, or resident includes any of the following acts, if the victim does not consent, is coerced into such act by overt or implied threats of violence, or is unable to consent or refuse:

1. Contact between the penis and the vulva or the penis and the anus, including penetration, however slight;
2. Contact between the mouth and the penis, vulva, or anus;

Inmate-on-Inmate Sexual Abuse

3. Penetration of the anal or genital opening of another person, however slight, by a hand, finger, object, or other instrument; and

4. Any other intentional touching, either directly or through the clothing, of the genitalia, anus, groin, breast, inner thigh, or the buttocks of another person, excluding contact incidental to a physical altercation. (U.S. Department of Justice, 2012, p. 195)

FREQUENCY

Buchanan (2010) observed that "[u]ntil about 2007, empirical evidence of the prevalence and dynamics of prison rape was relatively scanty, and methodologically unreliable" (Buchanan, 2010, p. 1645). In 2007, the Bureau of Justice Statistics undertook the first of several large-scale prison and jail sexual victimization surveys as mandated by the Prison Rape Elimination Act (Beck & Harrison, 2007, 2008). The most recent national survey was administered to some 92,000 inmates aged 18 or older, querying inmates if they had been sexually victimized in the preceding 12 months—May 2011 to May 2012—or since admission if they arrived prior to May 2011 (Beck et al., 2013) (NIS-3). Overall, NIS-3 estimated that 4 percent of state and federal prisoners and 3.2 percent of jail inmates reported being sexually victimized by fellow inmates or staff during May 2011–May 2012. Regarding inmate-on-inmate sexual victimization, NIS-3 estimated that 2 percent of state and federal prisoners and 1.6 percent of jail inmates reported one or more incidents of sexual victimization.

Importantly, NIS-3 revealed distinct patterns of inmate-on-inmate sexual victimization:

- 1.7 percent of males in prisons and 1.4 percent of males in jails reported one or more sexual victimizations, compared to 6.9 percent of females in prison and 3.6 percent of females in jails.

- 1.2 percent of heterosexuals in prisons and 1.2 percent of heterosexuals in jails reported one or more sexual victimizations, compared to 12.2 percent of nonheterosexuals in prisons and 8.5 percent of nonheterosexuals in jails.

- 0.5 percent of incarcerated males and 3.4 percent of incarcerated females with no indication of mental illness per NIS-3 criteria reported one or more sexual victimizations, compared to 5.6 percent of males and 12.9 percent of females experiencing serious psychological distress per NIS-3 criteria.

- 1.8 percent of juveniles ages 16 to 17 held in prisons and jails reported one or more sexual victimizations, compared to 2 percent of adults in prisons and 1.6 percent of adults in jails.

CAUSATION

Male Inmates

Explanations for prison sexual abuse have evolved. The middle of the 20th century was a watershed period in which the etiology of sex among male inmates changed from the prison as an institution that "collect[ed] perverts" to the prison "play[ing] an active part in producing them" (Kunzel, 2008, p. 8). For example, Sykes, writing in 1958, portrayed the prison as a distinct subculture, with prison sex being a response to the deprivations of imprisonment, one being the loss of heterosexual sexual activity. The "dominance-enforcement model" is the prevailing explanation of inmate-on-inmate sexual abuse (Robertson, 2016; Sabo, Kuppers, & London, 2001; Wooden & Parker, 1982). This model posits that intermale sexual victimization is part and parcel of a "hierarchical process of inter-male dominance in which groups of elite males subjugate and dominate groups of lesser-status males" (Sabo et al., 2001, p. 5).

The controlling principle of the dominance-enforcement model is hypermasculinity, that is, the exaggerated performance of heterosexual norms such as aggressive, toughness, exploitation, and resilience (Harris, 2000; Holmberg, 2001). Hypermasculine status in the prison society is thus privileged but also conditioned upon dominating other men. In the prison gender system, inmates affirm their hypermasculine status by engaging in the ultimate act of domination, raping another inmate. As Donaldson (2001) observed, "The sexual penetration of another male prisoner by a man is sanctioned by the subculture, is considered a male rather than a homosexual activity, and is seen as validation of the penetrator's masculinity" (Donaldson, 2001, p. 119). Prospective victims have a dichotomous choice: "fight or f***" (Weill-Greenberg, 2005, para. 8).

The sexual victimization of inmates has structural context: a hierarchical system of gender roles that are either voluntarily embraced or imposed (Ridgeway, 2011). The *real man* is "the model of heterosexual masculinity" (Ristroph, 2006, p. 152) and the embodiment of hypermasculinity (Holmberg, 2001; Lockwood, 1980). The longer his incarceration, the more likely that he will engage in same-sex relationships (Fleischer & Krienert, 2009). To maintain his real man status, this inmate must be the dominant sexual actor (i.e., the "inserter").

Out-of-closet gays represent "true" homosexuals because they entered prison as openly gay. By contrast, *closet gays* entered prison with a heterosexual orientation, only to transition to a gay or bisexual orientation (Castle, Hensley, & Tewksbury, 2002).

Queens, sometimes labeled sissies, voluntarily assume a female persona through dress and makeup (Ross & Richards, 2002). They submit to a passive role in sexual encounters. Robertson (2016) observed that "[t]heir scarcity requires that wolves look for sexual partners among the vulnerable heterosexual men who can be transformed into punks" (Robertson, 2016, p. 371).

Ladies are the transgender male-to-female prisoners housed in men's prisons. They desire to be "authentically female" (Jenness & Fenstermaker, 2014, p. 14), and as such they are among those inmates most likely to experience sexual victimization.

The *punk* typically begins his imprisonment as heterosexual but is "turned"—that is, coerced into assuming a female persona for sexual purposes. He is thus seen by inmates and staff as weak and therefore unmanly, consigning him to the bottom of a hierarchical system of gender roles (Robertson, 2016).

Female Inmates

Historically, sex between female inmates was understood as a desire for affection and companionship of a situational nature (Kunzel, 2008). In turn, contemporary explanations speak of the "affectional starvation" of daily life in confinement (Ward & Kassebaum, 1964, p. 73); the quest for "romantic love" (Giallombardo, 1966, p. 141); and a longing for the preimprisonment roles of father, mother, and daughter (Owen, 1998). On the other hand, Greer's (2000) interviews with female prisoners suggest a transformation in their interpersonal relationships distinguished by the disappearance of pseudofamilies, with same-sex sexual behavior motivated by a host of individualized factors such as economic gain, loneliness, and game playing.

As with their male counterparts, the sexual activity between female prisoners is in large part expressed through gender roles. The *play family,* the principal and most enduring gender role in women's prisons (Owen, 1998), finds expression in the sexually dominant and protector father, sexually passive and comforting mother, and sexually inactive children (Waterson, 1996). However, contemporary research suggests that the sexual subculture in women's prisons is less familial and more coercive and exploitive (Greer, 2000; Owen, 1998).

The *stud broad,* also known as "the "husband, butch, and little boy" (Owen, 1998, p. 143), assumes a male role and exercises dominance over the play family (Ward & Kassebaum, 1964). Her persona is expressed in attire, hairstyle, and walk (Diaz-Cotto, 2006; Owen, 1998; Watterson, 1996). *Femmes* assume traditional, passive female roles and are typically situational homosexuals in that most enter prison with a heterosexual orientation and assume the same when they reinter society (Owen, 1998).

SCENARIOS

The "bad man" portrait of a prison rape, in which the aggressor is "an evil and brutal character," is the prototype of prison sexual victimization but not the rule (Ristroph, 2006, p. 183). In a survey of former inmates on parole, 51.7 percent of sexually abused inmates reported that they had been coerced by means other than "force/threat" such as blackmail and settling debts (Beck & Johnson, 2012, p. 12).

Victor Hassine's typology captures the wide range of inmate-on-inmate sexual victimization scenarios:

- *Strong arm rape* where sexual predator violently assaults an often weak or otherwise vulnerable inmate.

- *Extortion rape* where a hustler, such as drug dealer or loan shark, assaults a deeply indebted mark, punishing him for failure to pay up.

- *Date rape* where a con artist targets a physically and psychologically weak inmate by being in his constant presence, thereby identifying them as a "couple" to inmates and staff.

322   **Inmate-on-Inmate Sexual Abuse**

- *Confidence rape* where a con artist targets a young, frightened inmate, convincing his mark that he is his only true friend and protector.

- *Drug rape* where the assailant targets a fellow drug user by developing a relationship with his mark. (Hassine, 2009)

PREVENTION

Until recently, prison sexual victimization was considered the "the most closely guarded secret activity of America's prisons" (Weiss & Friar, 1974, p. x). Prison officials generally did little to prevent it, claiming that it was a rare occurrence (Human Rights Watch, 2001). The public exhibited indifference to this scourge (Sontag, 2015).

Yet prison rape is not inevitable:

> One of the most pernicious myths about prisoner rape is that it is an inevitable part of life behind bars. This is simply wrong. . . . In well-run facilities across the country it is being prevented—and this shouldn't be surprising. After all, the government has extraordinary control over the lives of those it locks up. Stopping sexual abuse in detention is a matter of using sound policies and practices, and passing laws that require them. (Kaiser & Stannow, 2010, para. 3)

In the new millennium a broad coalition of religious, business, and human rights groups successfully lobbied the U.S. Congress to enact PREA. Its provisions included the drafting by the U.S. Department of Justice (2012) of National Standards to Prevent, Detect, and Respond to Prison Rape Standards, which were published in the Federal Register on June 20, 2012.

Broadly, PREA adopts one of two models for combating inmate-on-inmate sexual abuse. The model PREA embraced emphasizes control over prisoner sexuality through intensified surveillance, classification, and punishment (Ristroph, 2006). The other model expands a prisoner's sexual autonomy by permitting conjugal visits, condom distribution, consensual sex between inmates, and "any measures which can give prisoners a feeling of more control over their own life without breaching institutional security" (Ristroph, 2006, p. 182).

James E. Robertson

See also: Consensual Sex between Inmates; Prison Rape Elimination Act; Sexual Abuse of Inmates by Correctional Staff

Further Reading

Beck, A. J., & Harrison, P. M. (2007). *Sexual victimization in state and federal prisons reported by inmates, 2007.* Washington, DC: Bureau of Justice Statistics.

Beck, A. J., & Harrison, P. M. (2008). *Sexual victimization in local jails reported by inmates, 2007.* Washington, DC: Bureau of Justice Statistics.

Beck, A. J., Harrison, P. M., Berzofsky, M., & Caspar, R. (2010). *Sexual victimization in prisons and jails by inmates, 2008–09.* Washington, DC: Bureau of Justice Statistics.

Beck, A. J., Harrison, P. M., Berzofsky, M., & Caspar, R. (2013). *Sexual victimization in prisons and jails reported by inmates, 2011–12.* Washington, DC: Bureau of Justice Statistics.

Beck, A. J., & Johnson, C. (2012). *Sexual victimization by former state prisoners, 2008.* Washington, DC: Bureau of Justice Statistics.

Buchanan, K. S. (2010). Our prisons, ourselves: Race, gender and the rule of law. *Yale Law and Policy Review, 29,* 1–82.

Castle, T., Hensley, C., & Tewksbury, R. (2002). Argot roles and prison sexual hierarchy. In C. Hensley (Ed.), *Prison sex: Practice and policy* (pp. 13–26). Boulder, CO: Lynne Rienner.

Diaz-Cotto, J. (2006). Gender, sexuality and family kinship networks. In R. Solinger, P. C. Johnson, M. L. Raimon, T. Reynolds, & R. C. Tapia (Eds.), *Interrupted life: Experiences of incarcerated women in the United States* (pp. 131–144). Berkeley: University of California Press.

Donaldson, S. (2001). A million jockers, punks, and queens. In D. Sabo, T. A. Kupers, & W. London (Eds.), *Prison masculinities* (pp. 118–126). Philadelphia: Temple University Press.

Fleisher, M. S., & Krienert, J. L. (2009). *The myth of prison rape: Sexual culture in American prisons.* Lanham, MD: Rowman & Littlefield.

Fowler, S. K. (2007). *Prison rape-supportive cultural beliefs and inmate perceptions of sexual assault: A Texas inmate sample.* ProQuest Digital Dissertations (AAT 3288391).

Giallombardo, R. (1966). *Society of women: A study of a women's prison.* New York: Wiley.

Greer, K. (2000). The changing nature of interpersonal relationships in a women's prison. *The Prison Journal, 80,* 442–468.

Harris, A. P. (2000). Gender, violence, race, and criminal justice. *Stanford Law Review, 52,* 777–806.

Hassine, V. (2009). *Life without parole* (4th ed.). Los Angeles: Roxbury.

Holmberg, C. B. (2001). The culture of transgression: Initiations into the homosociality of a midwestern state prison. In D. Sabo, T. A. Kupers, & W. London (Eds.), *Prison masculinities* (pp. 78–92). Philadelphia: Temple University Press.

Human Rights Watch. (2001). *No escape: Male rape in U.S. prisons.* New York: Human Rights Watch.

Jenness, V., & Fenstermaker, S. (2014). Agnes goes to prison: Gender authenticity, transgender inmates in prisons for men, and pursuit of "the real deal." *Gender & Society, 28,* 5–31.

Jones R. S., & Schmid, T. S. (1990). Inmates' conceptions of prison sexual assault. *The Prison Journal, 69,* 53–61.

Kaiser, D., & Stannow, L. (2010, March 25). The way to stop prison rape. *New York Review of Books.* Retrieved from http://www.nybooks.com/issues/2010/03/25

Kunzel, R. (2008). *Criminal intimacy: Prison and the uneven history of modern American sexuality.* Chicago: University of Chicago Press.

Lockwood, D. (1980). *Prison sexual violence.* New York: Elsevier North-Holland.

Owen, B. (1998). *In the mix: Struggle and survival in a women's prison.* Albany: State University of New York Press.

Prison Rape Elimination Act of 2003, Pub. L. No. 108–79, 117 Stat. 972 (2003, September 4), codified as amended at 42 U.S.C. §§ 15601-15609 (2015). AB34 (2012, May 16).

Rideau, W., & Wikberg, R. (1992). *Life sentences: Rage and survival behind bars.* New York: Random House.

Ridgeway, C. L. (2011). *Framed by gender: How gender inequality persists in the modern world.* New York: Oxford University Press.

Ristroph, A. (2006). Sexual punishments. *Columbia Journal of Gender and Law, 15,* 139–184.

Robertson, J. E. (2016). Sex in jails and prisons. In H. Fradella & J. Sumner (Eds.), *Sex, sexuality, law, and (in)justice* (pp. 367–401). New York: Taylor & Francis/ Routledge.

Ross, J. I., & Richards, S. C. (2002). *Behind bars: Surviving prison.* New York: Alpha/ Penguin Group.

Sabo, D., Kupers, T.A., & London, W. (Eds.). (2001). *Prison masculinities.* Philadelphia: Temple University Press.

Sontag, D. (2015, May 12). Push to end prison rape loses earlier momentum. *New York Times.* Retrieved from https://www.nytimes.com/2015/05/13/us/push-to-end-prison -rapes-loses-earlier-momentum.html

Sykes, G. M. (1958). *The society of captives: The study of a maximum security prison.* Princeton, NJ: Princeton University Press.

U.S. Department of Justice. (2012, May 6). *Standards to prevent, detect, and respond to prison rape.* 28 CFR Part 115, Docket No. OAG131; AG Order No. RIN 1105. Society, 3, 95–133.

Ward, D. A., & Kassebaum, G. G. (1964). *Women's prison: Sex and social structure.* Chicago: Aldine.

Watterson, K. (1996). *Prison: Inside the concrete womb.* Boston: Northeastern University Press.

Weill-Greenberg, E. (2005, October 7). Gay man sues over Texas prison rapes. *Washington Blade.* Retrieved from http://www.justdetention.org/en/jdinews/2005/1007.aspx

Weiss, C., & Friar, D. (1974). *Terror in the prisons.* New York: Bobbs-Merrill.

Wooden, W. S., & Parker, J. (1982). *Men behind bars: Sexual exploitation in prison.* New York: Plenum.

Inmates, Transportation of

The term "inmate transportation" refers to the historical penal practice of relocating offenders from the jurisdiction where their original offense was committed to an alternative location where a sentence, often involving indentured servitude or hard labor, would be served. Often, these sentences would be served in isolated penal colonies, such as England's Norfolk Island or France's Devil's Island. Although most of the offenders subject to transportation were males, females and children were also transported, albeit with lesser frequency. Where employed, inmate transportation provided a historical alternative to the harsh physical punishments that were commonplace for criminal offenders. Although specific standards and requirements varied, offenders were typically subject to transportation for felonious offenses that could have otherwise resulted in their eligibility for the death penalty. As a result, transportation was used by public officials to demonstrate a measure of compassion and concern for the public. This was especially true when inmate transportation was contrasted with those offenses that qualified for capital punishment. The public perception that transportation offered a humane alternative was further underscored when countries began restricting the secular use of the benefit of clergy, which had previously provided offenders with one possible means of seeking leniency through ecclesiastical courts.

The practice of inmate transportation, while commonly associated with England, was widely practiced to differing degrees in a number of countries, including Russia, France, and Scotland. Those countries that relied on the practice of inmate transportation typically viewed it as a means of populating their territories, providing the labor necessary to develop their colonies, controlling their prison populations, and removing individuals thought to be troublesome or dangerous from within their borders. Additionally, since the transportation process itself was believed to be perilous, the relocation destinations viewed as undesirable, and the awaiting years of forced labor seen as dangerous and demeaning, it was thought that penal transportation acted as a deterrent to future criminal offending. As a formal penal sanction, inmate transportation had its origins in the historical practices of exile and banishment, which were widely employed by many of the world's earliest civilizations. However, transportation, unlike exile and banishment, was not fundamentally viewed as a terminal punishment as the possibility of the offenders returning after having served their sentence was rare in many instances.

The inmate transportation practices of many countries remained fluid and dynamic over time as context and environment continued to influence evolving penal practices. For instance, England initially transported large numbers of offenders to its American colonies. However, this practice was discontinued with the onset of the Revolutionary War. At the conclusion of the Revolutionary War, England had to look elsewhere in an attempt to find another suitable location for the future transportation of its inmates. After a temporary decline in its reliance on inmate transportation, England began to again relocate significant numbers of inmates; however, this time it was to its Australian colonies. Regardless of the specific characteristics of the destination, inmate transportation often contributed to the growth and development of permanent human settlements. This occurred partly because resettled inmates increased the size of local populations and partly because these inmates brought the skills and abilities necessary to ensure the growth and development of the penal colonies to which they were transported. The permanent settlements that developed in and around the former English penal colonies in Australia provide a good example of the influence that transportation had in this regard.

A variety of systems were established for underwriting the costs associated with inmate transportation. In many instances these costs were the responsibility of either the state or the individual being sentenced to transportation. When funding transportation, the state would often pay a private merchant a set amount for each individual offender that they transported. When the sentenced individuals were responsible for transportation costs, it was typically for their return trip in instances when such a trip was allowed after their sentence had been served. For those offenders who could not afford these costs, transportation could become a permanent sanction. Although an increasingly popular sentence throughout the course of the 17th and 18th centuries, reliance on inmate transportation began to decline after this period. By the latter half of the 19th century inmate transportation was no longer in widespread use as a criminal sanction either due to explicit prohibitions or through an informal lack of use.

Jason R. Jolicoeur

See also: Australia, Prisons in; Benefit of Clergy; England, Prisons in; France, Prisons in; Maconochie, Alexander; Prisons, History of

Further Reading

Adams, B. (1996). *The politics of punishment: Prison reform in Russia, 1863–1917.* DeKalb, IL: Northern Illinois University Press.

Bowker, L. H. (1980). Exile, banishment, and transportation. *International Journal of Offender Therapy and Comparative Criminology, 24*(1), 67–80.

Coldham, P. W. (1992). *Emigrants in chains: A social history of forced emigration to the Americas of felons, destitute children, political and religious non-conformists, vagabonds, beggars, and other undesirables, 1607–1776.* Baltimore: Genealogical.

Ekirch, A.R. (1987). *Bound for America: The transportation of British convicts to the colonies, 1718–1775.* New York: Oxford University Press.

Kercher, B. (2003). Perish or prosper: The law and convict transportation in the British Empire, 1700–1850. *Law and History Review, 21*(3), 527–584.

Reece, B. (2001). *The origins of Irish convict transportation to New South Wales.* Basingstoke, England: Palgrave.

Rees, S. (2001). *The floating brothel: The extraordinary true story of an eighteenth-century ship and its cargo of female convicts.* London: Headline.

Robson, L. L. (1965). *The convict settlers of Australia, Carlton, Victoria.* Melbourne, Australia: Melbourne University Press.

Shaw, A. G. (1971). *Convicts and the colonies: A study of penal transportation from Great Britain and Ireland to Australia and other parts of the British Empire.* London: Faber and Faber.

Shore, H. (2002). Transportation, penal ideology and the experience of juvenile offenders in England and Australia in the early nineteenth century. *Crime History and Societies, 6*(2), 81–102.

Willis, J. J. (2005). Transportation versus imprisonment in eighteenth- and nineteenth-century Britain: Penal power, liberty, and the state. *Law and Society Review, 39*(1), 171–210.

Inmates and Freedom of Religion

The freedom to decide one's own religious beliefs and to engage in activities based on those beliefs are foundational to the notion of liberty enshrined in the U.S. Constitution. After all, religious freedom was among the primary concerns motivating colonial emigration to America. Accordingly, the First Amendment to the Constitution states:

> Congress shall make no law respecting an establishment of religion, or prohibiting the free exercise thereof; or abridging the freedom of speech, or of the press; or the right of the people peaceably to assemble, and to petition the government for a redress of grievances.

The first of these two clauses is called the "establishment clause," guaranteeing that U.S. citizens are in no way compelled to believe in, hold membership in, or support a state-endorsed religion. The second is the "free exercise clause," guaranteeing that no citizen is denied the right to choose and practice her own religion. Although these two clauses most directly address religious freedom, the First

Amendment also protects one's right to proclaim her beliefs (e.g., religious speech), publish her beliefs (e.g., religious press), gather together with those sharing her beliefs (e.g., religious assembly), and to challenge her government when it infringes on these rights.

Meriam-Webster's dictionary defines religion as (1) "the belief in a god or in a group of gods," (2) "an organized system of beliefs, ceremonies, and rules used to worship a god or a group of gods," or (3) "an interest, a belief, or an activity that is very important to a person or a group." Thus, the First Amendment, specifically the free exercise clause, can be said to protect an individual's freedom to believe in God or otherwise hold a set of beliefs as important to them as is typically attributed to belief in God. Furthermore, the clause protects one's ability to practice in accordance with the belief. To determine whether a set of beliefs is protected within the ambit of free exercise, courts have looked to "whether the alleged religion addresses fundamental life questions, is comprehensive, and has a formal organizational structure." This protection is not forfeited just because an individual is incarcerated.

Of course, all constitutional guarantees are bounded by implied limitations, and nowhere are those guarantees more limited than in the context of prison. The Supreme Court ultimately carries the authority to interpret the Constitution, and it has stated that the freedoms provided by the free exercise clause are limited by correctional institutions' "legitimate penological interests" regarding the safety, security and welfare of their staff, inmates, and the general public. Specifically, the court has signaled that the First Amendment protects the religious freedom of inmates only to the point where prison officials irrationally limit the free exercise of one's faith. Prison administrators need only express a rational justification for their decisions and they will have satisfied the demands of the First Amendment. A vague reference to the need to maintain order has, in some cases, been enough to sustain institutional practices denying individuals from attending religious services, possessing religious paraphernalia, or engaging in certain religious ceremonies.

Moreover, even nonincarcerated persons may have their religious practices curtailed where it violates a generally applicable law. In this case, a law that does not specifically target religion and applies across the board may permissibly burden the practice of an individual's religion. Health laws that require vaccination, for example, may be enforced against everyone even if some religious faiths object to this form of medical treatment. The same is true of lawful institutional policies. Prison inmates have exceedingly little guarantee that they will be free to practice the religion of their choice in the way that they choose.

The court, however, has permitted the political branches of government (i.e., the legislative and executive branches, Congress, and the president, respectively) to enhance the religious protections of the incarcerated. Twice, they have chosen to do so. In 1993, the Religious Freedom Restoration Act (RFRA) was passed. Originally, RFRA applied to all governments, including state and local. Its reach was limited after the court's decision in *City of Boerne v. Flores* (1997), which held that the Fourteenth Amendment was insufficient to support its application to the states. Still applicable to the federal government, RFRA prohibits any action that "substantially burden[s] a person's exercise of religion even if the burden results from a rule of general applicability" unless the government can demonstrate that the burden "(1) is in furtherance of a compelling governmental interest; and (2) is the least restrictive means of furthering that compelling governmental interest." Inmates may vindicate their rights in court by showing a promulgated restriction deficient in either of these respects. This law, then, raises the level of protection for federal prisoners, providing a claim against prison policies that negatively impact one's religion, even when generally applicable.

In 2000, the Religious Land Use and Institutionalized Persons Act (RLUIPA) was enacted, applying the same restriction on state and local government actions concerning "a person residing in or confined to an institution" where the activity was funded by the federal government or caused a "substantial burden" affecting "commerce with foreign nations, among the several States, or with Indian tribes." Virtually all state prison systems receive federal funding and are, therefore, covered by the dictates of RLUIPA. This act was designed then to fill the gap made by RFRA's limited applicability, including extending RFRA's protections to that majority of the nation's prisoners who are housed in state—as opposed to only federal—prisons. Under RLUIPA, it is no longer sufficient for correctional officials to assert a rational, reasonable, and legitimate interest is being protected by limiting religious practice in prison. Instead, the institution must be acting to protect a "compelling" interest.

It should be noted, however, that, despite the act's promise of greater protection for religious inmates, courts have generally found that prison administrators meet the compelling-interest test. The Supreme Court had presaged this in its *Cutter v. Wilkinson* (2009) decision which, while holding RLUIPA to be constitutional, also gave the caveat that "an accommodation must be measured so that it does not override other significant interests" and that those interests include, broadly, excessiveness, undue imposition on others, or jeopardy to the "effective functioning of an institution." Moreover, in recognition that "prison security is a compelling state interest," courts are instructed that "deference is due to institutional officials' expertise in this area." This is seemingly done in two ways—first, by accepting prison administrators' arguments that a restriction is not a "substantial burden" to religious exercise, and, failing that, by accepting that the institution's compelling interest in the effectual operation of the facility justifies any burden endured. The question of whether a regulation puts a burden on religious practice, prison administrators may further question the sincerity of a prisoner's religious conviction. Where the prisoner is insufficiently religious, the argument goes, impeding her practice is not burdensome. Lodging any of these arguments has seemed to grant prison officials carte blanche in determining where to draw the line on acceptable restrictions concerning the religious practice of inmates.

Recognizing the apparent weakness of the First Amendment to assure inmates' religious rights, some legal scholars have begun to look for other avenues to support liberal free exercise in correctional settings. Due process challenges are based on the Fifth and Fourteenth Amendments and protect citizens from unfair procedures and governmental denials of their fundamental rights, for example, the free exercise of religion. In the prison context, due process claims are governed under the test announced in *Turner v. Safley* (1987). Unfortunately, they have not had much success in courts, though such claims might succeed if the weight of religious concerns occasioned a more searching and less lenient application of *Turner*'s strictures. Jeffrey Welty argues that the Eighth Amendment regulations regarding permissible conditions of confinement provide a rich source of religious protection. By arguing that prison administrators evince willful indifference to inmates' religious needs and that these violate present-day standards of decency, inmates might prevail. Still, Eighth Amendment claims have not typically been successful short of egregious actions on the part of prison officials resulting in physical harm. The Fourteenth Amendment's equal protection clause prohibits governments from denying citizens "equal protection of the laws." Prisoners may assert equal protection claims where officials discriminate against them based on their religiosity or where prison administrations are more hostile to minority or stigmatized religions relative to other faiths. The equal protection clause will provide little recourse, however, where administrators are generally restrictive or apply restrictions equally across faiths. Finally, even in cases where the court has held the right to free exercise of religion insufficient to overturn prison restrictions on its own, it has expressed support for greater scrutiny where multiple constitutional rights are implicated. Prisoners may find redress when showing that prison regimes have denied them freedom of religious exercise in addition to some other right, such as freedom of expression, press, or assembly—though these have also been limited by Supreme Court precedents in the context of the prison environment and may not provide the added heft desired.

A rich religious life may reduce the likelihood of continuing in criminal behavior. It would appear that no class of individuals would be more in need of the prosocial influence of religious faith than those the criminal justice system has already found guilty of criminal acts in the past. Among the myriad of ways that society may direct or guide the behavior of its members—including physical, resource, or social controls—none are so potent as morality, and no source so generally effective as religion in cultivating moral norms. From a policy perspective, allowing inmates the freedom to worship as they please may add to the safety of correctional facilities, encourage prisoners to be more compliant, and facilitate the rehabilitative process so that recidivism is less likely upon release. It may be that the more efficacious route to protecting inmates' religious freedom is to convince the political branches of government to continue what they began with the passage of RFRA—for the courts, at present, provide inmates with little refuge.

Kwan-Lamar Blount-Hill

See also: Benefit of Clergy; Constitution as a Source for Prisoners' Rights, The; Deliberate Indifference; Evolving Standards of Decency; Fathers behind Bars; Judicial Involvement in Prison Administration; Legitimate Penological Interests; Muslim Inmates; Prison Ministry; Religious Programs Outreach

Further Reading

Brady, K. L. (2011). Religious sincerity and imperfection: Can lapsing prisoners recover under RFRA and RLUIPA? *The University of Chicago Law Review, 78,* 1431–1464.

City of Boerne v. Flores, 521 U.S. 507 (1997).

Cutter v. Wilkinson, 544 U.S. 709 (2009).

Employment Division, Department of Human Resources of Oregon v. Smith, 494 U.S. 872 (1990).

McMullin, J. B. (2005). Incarceration of the Free Exercise Clause: The Sixth Circuit's misstep in *Cutter v. Wilkinson. BYU Journal of Public Law, 19,* 413–435.

O'Lone v. Estate of Shabazz, 482 U.S. 342 (1987).

Sowa, J. L. (2012). Gods behind bars: Prison gangs, due process, and the First Amendment. *Brooklyn Law Review, 77*(4), 1593–1631.

Turner v. Safley, 482 U.S. 78 (1987).

United States Library of Congress. (n.d.). *America as a religious refuge: The seventeenth century.* Retrieved September 22, 2016, from https://www.loc.gov/exhibits/religion /rel01.html

Welty, J. (1998). Restrictions on prisoners' religious freedom as unconstitutional conditions of confinement: An Eighth Amendment argument. *Duke Law Journal, 48*(3), 601–628.

Inmates with Co-Occurring Disorders

When an individual has two disorders or illnesses that occur simultaneously, treatment professionals diagnose the individual with a co-occurring disorder (COD). Co-occurring mental health and substance abuse disorders are common among both jail and prison populations. In prison, about 30 percent of individuals who have a substance abuse disorder also have a mental health issue. Estimates indicate the rates are higher in jails with approximately 72 percent of inmates reporting a co-occurring substance abuse and mental health disorder (Plotkin & Coombs, 2012). Earlier research also demonstrates that the prevalence of CODs is greater among jail inmates (60.5 percent) compared to state prison inmates (49.2 percent) (James & Glaze, 2006).

Inmates with CODs often have a difficult time adjusting to incarceration. For example, the symptoms associated with mental illness and substance abuse disorders may affect an inmate's ability to understand and follow instructions given by correctional staff. Research indicates conditions of confinement, such as overcrowding and the use of solitary confinement, exacerbate symptoms of mental illness and increase the odds of psychiatric decompensation (Fellner, 2007). In addition, conditions of confinement increase the likelihood of developing new symptoms of psychotic (hallucinations and delusions) and mood (mood swings and mania) disorders. Research also shows that inmates with CODs are at an increased risk for victimization, including physical and sexual assault and financial exploitation (Peters, Wexler, & Lurigio, 2015). Therefore, it is important for correctional administrators and personnel to be vigilant in addressing the needs of offenders with CODs.

Inmates with CODs often have behavioral issues and are more likely to engage in institutional misconduct (Slate, Buffington-Vollum, & Johnson, 2013). Misconduct may include actions such as refusing to leave a cell, self-harming behaviors, poor hygiene, vandalism, and assault. Intake screening is crucial for identifying inmates with CODs to reduce the likelihood of institutional misconduct and aggressive behavior among inmates with CODs. Correctional officers and medical staff should receive training to identify inmates with CODs, and they should understand that the misconduct of inmates with CODs is typically related to inmate symptomology and not a deliberate refusal to comply with correctional staff instructions. Correctional staff should keep this in mind and, when possible, avoid the use of solitary confinement. In addition, correctional staff should minimize the use of force in dealing with inmates with CODs because these inmates cannot fully appreciate the wrongfulness of their behavior.

Treatment and correctional staff should be aware that individuals with CODs frequently suffer from impaired memory and deficits in cognitive functioning. As a result, offenders may not be the best resource for gathering information about their prior mental health and substance use histories. Inaccurate self-reports complicate the ability of treatment professionals to diagnose and provide proper treatment. When possible, correctional treatment professionals should seek out medical records from community treatment providers to increase the likelihood of proper diagnosis and treatment.

There are several effective treatment strategies for inmates with CODs, including Illness Management and Recovery (IMR), integrated group treatment, therapeutic communities, social skills training, cognitive-behavioral therapy, and medications to treat both substance use and mental health disorders (Peters et al., 2015). Treatment programs for CODs include orientation, strategies for service motivation and engagement, structured treatment and supervision services, supportive as opposed to confrontational therapeutic philosophies, crisis care, medication monitoring, extended assessment and program duration, and cross training of staff (Edens, Peters, & Hills, 1997; Lurigio, 2011). Correctional counselors and mental health professionals also should receive training to address the gender-specific needs of incarcerated women. For example, women offenders often have suffered physical and sexual abuse, been diagnosed with post-traumatic stress disorder (PTSD), and need intensive services related to education, literacy, employment, parenting, family reunification, and health care.

Correctional facilities can take steps to improve the delivery of services to inmates with CODs. Integrated treatment strategies should be developed and implemented whenever possible because they address a wide variety of treatment needs for inmates with CODs. Barriers to treatment also should be identified in an effort to reduce or eliminate them. Finally, improved screening and assessment instruments and procedures, especially those that assess an individual's risks and needs, are critical to ensuring that inmates with CODs receive appropriate treatment and services.

Kimberly D. Dodson and Jerrod Brown

See also: Correctional Counseling; Drug Use in Prison; Inmates with Intellectual Disabilities; Mentally Ill Prisoners; Treatment in Prisons; Treatment Professionals in Prison

Further Reading

Brown, J., Haun, J., & Wartnik, A. (In press). Offenders with co-occurring disorders: Mental illness and substance abuse treatment. In K. D. Dodson (Ed.), *Handbook on offenders with special needs.* New York: Routledge.

Edens, J. F., Peters, R. H., & Hills, H. A. (1997). Treating prison inmates with co-occurring disorders: An integrative review of existing programs. *Behavioral Sciences and the Law, 15*, 439–457.

Fellner, J. (2007, July 19). Keep mentally ill out of solitary confinement. *Huffington Post.* Retrieved from http://www.hrw.org/news/2007/07/19/keep-mentally-ill-out-solitary-confinement

James, D. J., & Glaze, L. E. (2006). *Mental health problems of prison and jail inmates.* Washington, DC: U.S. Department of Justice, Bureau of Justice Statistics.

Lurigio, A. J. (2011). Co-occurring disorders: Mental health and drug misuse. In C. Leukefeld, T. P. Gullotta, & J. Gregrich (Eds.), *Handbook of evidence-based substance abuse treatment in criminal justice settings* (pp. 279–292). New York: Springer.

Peters, R. H., Wexler, H. K., & Lurigio, A. J. (2015). Co-occurring substance use and mental disorders in the criminal justice system: A new frontier of clinical practice and research. *Psychiatric Rehabilitation Journal, 38*(1), 1–6.

Plotkin, M., & Coombs, R. (2012). *Adults with behavioral health needs under correctional supervision: A shared framework for reducing recidivism and promoting recovery.* New York: Council of State Governments Justice Center.

Slate, R. N., Buffington-Vollum, J. K., & Johnson, W. W. (2013). *The criminalization of mental illness: Crisis and opportunity for the justice system* (2nd ed.). Durham, NC: Carolina Academic Press.

Sung, H.-E., & Mellow, J. (2010). Jail inmates with co-occurring mental health and substance use problems: Correlates and service needs. *Journal of Offender Rehabilitation, 49*, 126–145.

Van Voorhis, P., & Salisbury, E. J. (2014). *Correctional counseling and rehabilitation.* New York: Routledge.

Wood, S. R., & Buttaro, A., Jr. (2013). Co-occurring severe mental illness and substance abuse disorders as predictors of state prison inmate assaults. *Crime & Delinquency, 59*(4), 510–535.

Inmates with Intellectual Disabilities

Inmates with intellectual disabilities are overrepresented in U.S. prisons and jails today. However, significant disagreement exists in the research about the prevalence rate of intellectual disabilities (IDs) in prison populations, and the actual number of inmates with ID is unknown. It has repeatedly been reported that differences in methods used to identify ID, weak research designs, nonrepresentative samples, and inconsistent use of terminology make it difficult to reach a consensus on the actual number of inmates with ID in prisons (Lindsay et al., 2002; McAfee & Gural, 1988).

Significant definitional inconsistencies exist in the research on intellectual disability, and these definitional disagreements pose considerable disadvantages for inmates with ID within U.S. prisons. It is, therefore, important to explore varied definitions and terminologies of ID employed by the criminal justice system.

The terms used within the research to define intellectually disabled persons include the following: mentally retarded, mentally challenged, mentally disabled, mentally disordered, mentally handicapped, mentally impaired, intellectually challenged, intellectually handicapped, handicapped, developmentally disabled,

Inmates with Intellectual Disabilities

low-functioning, and intellectually deficient. Over five decades the term "intellectual disability" replaced some of the pejorative terms, such as mental retardation. For example, the American Association on Mental Retardation, the leading nonprofit organization in the field of intellectual and developmental disabilities, eliminated the term "mental retardation" and changed its name to American Association on Intellectual and Developmental Disabilities (AAIDD) in 2007. An intellectual disability is defined by AAIDD as "characterized by significant limitations both in intellectual functioning and in adaptive behavior, which covers many everyday social and practical skills. This disability originates before the age of eighteen" (Schalock et al., 2010). According to AAIDD, to consider an individual as intellectually disabled, he or she must receive an intelligence quotient (IQ) score under 70.

The prevalence of ID in the United States is estimated to be around 1 percent to 3 percent of the population (Moeschler & Shevell, 2014). However, the rate of inmates with ID in U.S. prisons is between 1 percent and 30 percent, with most of the evaluations being between 4 percent and 10 percent (Scheyett et al., 2009). For example, in a landmark study, Brown (1968) estimated that prevalence rates ranged from 2.6 percent to 24.3 percent, with a national average of 9.5 percent in the United States. Denkowski and Denkowski (1985) found that the prevalence of inmates with ID ranged from 1.5 percent to 19.1 percent, with an average of 6.2 percent, depending on the testing method used. In another study, Veneziano and Veneziano (1996) sampled inmates in both federal and state prisons, and they found the prevalence of intellectual disabilities at 4.2 percent in U.S. prisons.

More recently, similar research was conducted by the Bureau of Justice Statistics among state prisoners, federal prisoners, and local jail inmates and reported that 19 percent of prisoners and 31 percent of jail inmates had cognitive disabilities, such as intellectual disabilities, Down syndrome, autism, attention-deficit/hyperactivity disorder, and traumatic brain injury (Bronson, Maruschak, & Berzofsky, 2015). Davis (2006, p.13) remarked on the overrepresentation of inmates with ID in prison that "this does not mean people with disabilities are more likely to commit crimes, but they are more likely to get caught if they become involved in a criminal act (they may or may not realize the act they are involved in is actually a criminal offense)."

Inmates with intellectual disability face considerable problems in the prison system. Compared with the general population, people with ID are often not aware of their legal rights, quickly accept charges against them, are more likely to plead guilty, and receive harsher punishments than people without ID (Denkowski & Denkowski, 1985; Scheyett et al., 2009). The ID prisoners may have difficulty in obtaining bail or own recognizance release, perhaps because these prisoners are unemployed or have previous violations of bail conditions or lack access to stable accommodation, which are fundamental criteria when determining whether or not bail is granted. When they are incarcerated, they are more likely to receive longer sentences. They may also have greater difficulty fully comprehending rules when in prison; therefore, inmates with intellectual disabilities are less likely to receive good time credits, be eligible for probation or parole, and tend to serve longer sentences than other inmates incarcerated for the same offenses.

While they are in prison, they are frequently victimized and exploited by other inmates, such as having them assist in illegal activities as they are not aware of the prison rule violations. Inmates with ID are also isolated because of limited rehabilitative services in prison. Considering their weaknesses, predicting their vulnerability to physical, emotional, sexual violence, and financial abuse within the prison system will not be shocking.

Because of the adversity in the prison system, early identification of incarcerated persons with ID is crucial. Once they are imprisoned, early identification of prisoners with ID provides treatment opportunities, social services, and educational resources and facilitates a diversion from prison. The Hayes Ability Screening Index (HASI) and the Wechsler Adult Intelligence Scale–Revised (WAIS–R) are the most widely used tools for full psychological assessment of intellectual disabilities for identifying offenders. However, there are no well-established procedures and rules for conducting screening during jail intakes.

Steelman (1987, pp. 46–47) described the process of identification of incarcerated persons with ID within New York's prisons in the following manner:

1. All inmates receive a group intelligence test, upon arrival at a reception/classification center.

2. Those scoring less than 70 on the group I.Q. test are sent to the Extended Classification Unit for further testing and assessment.

3. Those identified as mentally retarded, and requiring special services, remain in Extended Classification until an opening becomes available in the required program.

During the intake process, inmates with ID may be stressed out, and they may have difficulty in understanding the questions directed to them in a chaotic prison setting. Besides, inmates with ID may be uncomfortable to talk about their disability in front of other inmates, and they may conceal their situation out of fear of being stigmatized and victimized. Therefore, it is essential to interview individual ID inmates within a private setting during intake to obtain accurate information about their disability. In addition, adequate training of correctional officers and criminal justice mental health teams is essential in the appropriate determination of an ID.

Durmus Alper Camlibel

See also: Mental Health Issues and Jails; Mentally Ill Prisoners

Further Reading

Bronson, J., Maruschak, L. M., & Berzofsky, M. (2015, December). *Disabilities among prison and jail inmates, 2011–12.* U.S. Department of Justice, Bureau of Justice Statistics. Retrieved from https://www.bjs.gov/content/pub/pdf/dpji1112.pdf

Brown, B. S. (1968). The mentally retarded in penal and correctional institutions. *American Journal of Psychiatry, 124*(9), 1164.

Davis, L. A. (2006). *The arc's justice advocacy guide: An advocate's guide on addicting victims and suspects/defendants with intellectual disabilities.* Silver Spring, MD: Arc of the United States.

Denkowski, G. C., & Denkowski, K. M. (1985). The mentally retarded offender in the state prison system: Identification, prevalence, adjustment, and rehabilitation. *Criminal Justice and Behavior, 12*(1), 55–70.

Ellis, J. W., & Luckasson, R. A. (1985). Mentally retarded criminal defendants. *George Washington Law Review, 53*, 414–493.

Holland, S., & Persson, P. (2011). Intellectual disability in the Victorian prison system: Characteristics of prisoners with an intellectual disability released from prison in 2003–2006. *Psychology, Crime & Law, 17*(1), 25–41.

Lindsay, W. R., Smith, A. H., Law, J., Quinn, K., Anderson, A., Smith, A., Overend, T., & Allan, R. (2002). A treatment service for sex offenders and abusers with intellectual disability: Characteristics of referrals and evaluation. *Journal of Applied Research in Intellectual Disabilities, 15*(2), 166–174.

McAfee, J. K., & Gural, M. (1988). Individuals with mental retardation and the criminal justice system: The view from states' attorneys general. *Mental Retardation, 26*(1), 5.

Moeschler, J. B., & Shevell, M. (2014). Comprehensive evaluation of the child with intellectual disability or global developmental delays. *Pediatrics, 134*(3), e918.

Petersilia, J. (1997). Justice for all? Offenders with mental retardation and the California corrections system. *The Prison Journal, 77*(4), 358–380.

Schalock, R. L., Borthwick-Duffy, S. A., Bradley, V. J., Buntinx, W. H., Coulter, D. L., Craig, E. M., Gomez, S.C., Lachapelle, Y., Luckasson, R., Reeve, A., Shogren, K. A., Snell, M. E., Spreat, S., Tassé, M. J., Thompson, J. R., Verdugo-Alonso, M. A., Wehmeyer, M. L., & Yeager, M. H. (2010). *Intellectual disability: Definition, classification, and systems of supports* (11th ed.). Washington, DC: AAIDD.

Scheyett, A., Vaughn, J., Taylor, M., & Parish, S. (2009). Are we there yet? Screening processes for intellectual and developmental disabilities in jail settings. *Intellectual and Developmental Disabilities, 47*(1), 13–23.

Steelman, D. (1987). *The mentally impaired in New York's prisons: Problems and solutions.* New York: Correctional Association of New York.

Veneziano, L., & Veneziano, C. (1996). Disabled inmates. In M. McShane & F. Williams (Eds.), *Encyclopedia of American prisons.* New York: Garland.

Inmates' Perceptions of Prison versus Alternative Sanctions

Practices and policies regarding how to best punish individuals who violate the law have long been debated. Historical and contemporary thought regarding levels of chastisement have received a general consensus among criminal justice practitioners and a major segment of the public. It is commonly believed that the most severe sanction that can be imposed, excluding capital punishment, is prison. The least severe is unsupervised probation. The logic associated with this severity scheme is that the fewer freedoms one has, the more severe the punishment. This graduated sanctions model was the prevailing paradigm for centuries and continues to drive sentencing decisions. Only recently, however, have researchers begun to investigate incarcerated persons' perceptions regarding the continuum of punishment severity.

The early 1990s were when some of the first published studies regarding inmates' views of punishments began to surface. Survey results revealed evidence that contradicted commonly held views of punishment. In quantitative and qualitative studies, some inmates explained that they preferred the restrictive environment of prison over an opportunity to be on intensive supervised probation. This may be the case because inmates view community supervision as extremely strict and the supervisors as abusive. With similar justification, some incarcerated persons revealed that no amount of alternative sanctions would be considered less punitive than prison. Possible explanations for this finding include the predictability of incarceration and the opportunities for counseling, treatment, educational, and employment services. Despite the relatively consistent findings regarding prisons, perceptions of jail tend to vary.

Following the graduated sanctions model, the public tend to think that because jail is typically reserved for short-term incarceration, it is less punitive than prison but more intensive than alternative sanctions. Some inmates have expressed that the severity of jail varies as a function of the length of their stay. For instance, shorter jail sentences are considered to be more punitive than longer stays. It has been hypothesized that this may be true for some inmates because when they are incarcerated, they are likely to experience economic and social consequences that extend beyond the carceral environment (e.g., job loss, loss of the home, loss of child custody). Other inmates view jail as having a relatively consistent severity, regardless of the length of incarceration, because the economic and social consequences are often discrete moments and do not vary over time.

Despite the nearly 4 million individuals on probation in 2013, electronic monitoring and house arrest are widely thought to be some of the more severe community-based punishments. These sanctions are considered by inmates to be punitive but not as punitive as prison. An explanation for this includes the increased physical freedom associated with electronic monitoring. This sanction remains relatively severe because there is an increased perception of freedom combined with a lack of physical mobility due to consistent monitoring and strict boundaries. Many jurisdictions require that persons on house arrest do not exit their home except during a designated time block within the week. During this time, there tend to be restrictions on what can be done and where one can go. The relative consistency of this data can be misleading, however, if one fails to examine how the findings are affected by various inmate demographics and their individual histories.

Perceptions of the criminal justice system are known to vary based on one's race. Additionally, data have illuminated that people of color, especially blacks, have greater amounts of contact with the criminal justice system and higher rates of incarceration than whites. Thus, it would hold that one's race would influence one's perception regarding sentence severity. Findings have supported this notion.

Blacks tend to be the racial group that has the least positive views of the criminal justice system. Interestingly, they do not view imprisonment as punitive as whites do. In fact, it has been found that blacks prefer incarceration over community alternatives. Some studies have found that nearly one-quarter of black individuals would prefer 12 months in a medium security prison as opposed to any amount of time released to the community with a mandate of day reporting. Nearly 98 percent of whites, however, would prefer the community-based alternative. Some authors have suggested that this relationship may hold true because black individuals are disproportionately affected by the criminal justice system. Thus, they would prefer not to risk reincarceration after a term of probation. Similarly, they have reasoned that black individuals are more likely to violate the term of their probation that mandates that they not be associated with felons. Because the black individuals released on probation would return to a community that disproportionately has felonies, the risk of a probation violation is heightened. In both of these cases, these individuals would prefer the predictability of prison and the removed risk of more prison time added for a violation of probation. Some other studies have identified blacks, when compared to whites, to perceive prison as less severe than regular probation, intensive supervised probation, and electronic monitoring. Despite the seeming salience of race as a factor that affects perceptions, some research suggests that race does not influence one's view of sentence severity.

Perceptions of punishment severity as a function of race have been denied by some researchers. Although it is acknowledged that perceptions differ among persons, the differences may be accounted for by other factors. For instance, socioeconomic status may affect one's perceptions about punishment more than race. This is one of the primary hypotheses because black individuals are disproportionately of a lower socioeconomic status and, thus, the aforementioned studies may have problems with internal validity. Other factors affecting perceptions have not faced such scrutiny.

Research utilizing gender as a variable that affects perceptions on sentences has displayed some unexpected results. Gender does not affect one's preference for incarceration or community-based programs, but it does appear to affect the length of time one would be willing to participate in an alternative program to avoid jail or prison. Women have been found to be willing to serve more time in alternative sentences than men to avoid imprisonment. This may be true because females have stronger social bonds to their communities. Women are also more likely to avoid incarceration if they are parents. This appears to be true regardless of race. Men and women, however, tend to respond similarly if they are married and employed.

Studies have found that married persons often prefer community sanctions over incarceration. It is hypothesized that this is a result of marriage being a source of positive support during times of crisis. The physical proximity of the couple reassures the person being punished and eases the psychological burden associated with criminal justice involvement. The carceral environment, however, may cause increased hardship on marriages, which may fail due to the severe communication and physical restrictions of prisons and jails. Additionally, removal from the community strains a marriage's economic well-being.

Employment is commonly considered to be a reason why individuals would prefer to avoid incarceration. This is not always the case, however. Individuals in jail or prison do not often have strong emotional or social bonds to their employment, regardless of part- or full-time status. The opposite is true for educational attainment, however. The more educated one is, the less likely one is to desire prison over alternative sentences. It is hypothesized that this is true because these individuals want to avoid any social stigma that may be placed on them for being institutionalized.

338 Inmates' Perceptions of Prison versus Alternative Sanctions

Age has largely been expected by researchers to encourage people to prefer community-based sanctions in lieu of incarceration. Contrary to this, some studies have found that the older a person is, the more likely he or she would prefer prison. A possible explanation for this finding is that the individuals who are incarcerated at older ages may be in need of the services that prison offers. Additionally, they may not have access to the services they need outside of the institution.

As has been explained, laypersons who follow the graduated sanctions model have perceptions that differ greatly from those who have been incarcerated. This model, in which unsupervised probation is considered the least severe and prison the most severe, has begun to receive criticism as more research is conducted utilizing inmates as the population of interest. Incarcerated persons have a different perception of what graduated sanctions look like, which may change based on their demographic characteristics.

As a result of the above information, policy makers may begin to abandon the graduated sanctions model for one based on inmate perceptions. If the goal of punishment is personal deprivation, perceptions of various communities should be measured and outlined as meso-level, graduated sanctions. Certainly, more research should be forthcoming regarding various sanctions that have been underexamined, such as those that are therapeutically orientated. One study conducted by Eric J. Wodahl and colleagues suggested that inpatient treatment is viewed as overall more punitive—approximately twice as punitive—as jail. Despite this, further research is needed to make a more definitive claim about the perceived severity of this type of sanction. As this body of literature expands, one may expect to see sentencing practices and correctional facilities change.

Andrew C. Michaud

See also: Fathers behind Bars; Inside-Outside Relationships; Prisoner Reentry/Family Integration

Further Reading

Applegate, B. K. (2013). Of race, prison, and perception: Seeking to account for racially divergent views on the relative severity of sanctions. *American Journal of Criminal Justice, 39*(1), 59–76.

Crouch, B. M. (1993). Is incarceration really worse: Analysis of offenders' preferences for prison over probation. *Justice Quarterly, 10*(1), 67–88.

Irizarry, Y., May, D. C., Davis, A., & Wood, P. B. (2016). Mass incarceration through a different lens: Race, subcontext, and perceptions of punitiveness of correctional alternatives when compared to prison. *Race and Justice, 6*(3), 236–256.

May, D. C., Applegate, B. K., Ruddell, R., & Wood, P. B. (2014). Going to jail sucks (and it really doesn't matter who you ask). *American Journal of Criminal Justice, 39*(2), 250–266.

May, D. C., & Wood, P. B. (2005). What influences offenders' willingness to serve alternative sanctions? *The Prison Journal, 85*(2), 145–167.

May, D. D., & Wood, P. B. (2010). *Ranking correctional punishments: Views from offenders, practitioners, and the public.* Durham, NC: Carolina Academic Press.

Payne, B. K., May, D. C., & Wood, P. B. (2014). The 'pains' of electronic monitoring: A slap on the wrist or just as bad as prison? *Criminal Justice Studies, 27*(2), 133–148.

Williams, A., May, D. C., & Wood, P. B. (2008). The lesser of two evils? A qualitative study of offenders' preferences for prison compared to alternatives. *Journal of Offender Rehabilitation, 46*(3), 71–90.

Wodahl, E. J., Ogle, R., Kadleck, C., & Gerow, K. (2009). Offender perceptions of graduated sanctions. *Crime & Delinquency, 59*(8), 1185–1210.

Wood, P. B., & May, D. C. (2003). Racial differences in perceptions of the severity of sanctions: A comparison of prison with alternatives. *Justice Quarterly, 20*(3), 605–631.

Innocence Project

The Innocence Project is a national organization founded in 1992 by Barry Scheck and Peter Neufeld, two attorneys who had significant experience in civil rights litigation. Through both litigation and public policy, the Innocence Project aims to exonerate innocent individuals who have been wrongfully convicted yet remain incarcerated. An additional goal of the organization is to reform the criminal justice system in ways that will prevent future injustice. Originally founded as part of the Cardozo School of Law at Yeshiva University, New York, the Innocence Project became an independent nonprofit organization in 2003. Once funded completely by the Cardozo School of Law, it is now funded almost entirely by individual and foundation donations. In 2014, the operating revenue for the organization was over $16 million.

Scheck and Neufeld founded the Innocence Project after closely following a case that involved the first DNA exoneration in the United States in 1989. At the time of founding, the main goal of the organization was to exonerate wrongfully convicted people through DNA testing. To this day, that goal remains central to the mission of the Innocence Project, though the organization is also involved in advocacy and criminal justice policy reform as well.

LEGAL WORK

Through full-time staff attorneys and the support of law school students, the Innocence Project provides direct legal representation or other forms of critical assistance to clients. The process typically begins with an incarcerated individual filling out an application for assistance, which will then be reviewed by students or other volunteers. The Innocence Project receives around 3,000 letters each year from people seeking help, and at any given time, they are evaluating between 6,000 and 8,000 cases (The Innocence Project, 2012). This evaluation involves an in-depth evaluation of each case to determine whether DNA testing could be conducted to prove a client's innocence. Of those, some cases will be selected and then taken on by the Innocence Project's full-time staff and affiliated law school students. According to Innocence Project cofounder, Peter Neufeld, about half the time that the organization tests DNA evidence, it confirms their innocence of the crime for which they were convicted.

POLICY DEPARTMENT

In addition to direct legal representation and other direct service work to clients, the Innocence Project has a policy department that works with the federal and state governments as well as local policy makers to implement legislation that will prevent wrongful convictions and to enable those who have been wrongfully convicted to receive justice.

The Innocence Project recognizes six common avenues by which wrongful convictions can occur: (1) eyewitness misidentification, (2) invalid and improper forensic science, (3) false confessions, (4) informants, (5) government misconduct, and (6) inadequate defense. Therefore, the policy department seeks to support state and federal reforms that address these problems that contribute to wrongful conviction. Additionally, the policy department advocates for the development of laws that adequately compensate those who have experienced harm as the result of a wrongful conviction, recognizing that exonerees have significant needs upon release from prison, including housing, transportation, and medical needs.

INNOCENCE NETWORK

The Innocence Project is a founding member of the Innocence Network, which is an affiliation of other independent organizations that similarly work to overturn wrongful convictions and to reform the criminal justice system. Although the Innocence Project is a national organization, many of the affiliated organizations involved in the Innocence Network serve a more focused geographic area.

These organizations focus generally on three main goals that are central to the mission of the Innocence Project. First, they seek to provide pro bono legal and investigative services to individuals seeking to prove they are innocent of the crimes for which they have been convicted. Second, they work to address the consequences of wrongful convictions. Lastly, they work to support exonerated individuals after they are released from correctional supervision.

There are currently 69 organizations around the world that make up the Innocence Network, including institutions in the United States, Canada, Argentina, Israel, Ireland, New Zealand, Australia, the United Kingdom, Taiwan, Italy, and the Netherlands. Many of these organizations, particularly those in the United States, are run out of law schools.

IMPACT

Although the total number of innocent people behind bars is unknown, as of June 2016, there have been 342 known cases in which wrongfully convicted people have been exonerated for crimes due to DNA evidence. The Innocence Project has been involved in more than half (56 percent) of these exonerations. Of the total known cases involving a wrongful conviction, the real perpetrator was eventually identified in nearly half of them (163 cases). Among the known population of the wrongfully convicted, individuals spent an average of 14 years incarcerated before they were exonerated. Of the 342 known cases of wrongful conviction in which defendants were exonerated by DNA evidence, there were 20 defendants who had spent time on death row after receiving a capital conviction.

By providing solid evidence that our criminal justice system has wrongly accused these 342 individuals, the Innocence Project has demonstrated that our system is flawed, indicating that there are likely many other innocent people who have been wrongfully convicted. When each of the stories of wrongfully convicted individuals are aggregated, as the Innocence Project has done, they expose that our criminal justice system is failing its most important tasks: distinguishing between the innocent and the guilty, and protecting the rights of the innocent.

Additionally, data collected from these cases demonstrate that there are systemic racial disparities in wrongful convictions. More than 60 percent of the wrongfully convicted were African American, while almost 60 percent of the victims in these cases were Caucasian (The Innocence Project, 2012). The racial disparities seen among the wrongfully convicted demonstrate that race can affect the experience of an innocent individual throughout the criminal justice process, from arrest to conviction.

Rebecca Pfeffer

See also: DNA Exonerees; Prison Reform, Intended and Unintended Consequences of; Sentencing Disparities and Discrimination in Sentencing

Further Reading

Drizin, S. A., & Leo, R. A. (2004). The problem of false confessions in the post-DNA world. *North Carolina Law Review, 82,* 891–1004.

Gross, S. R., Jacoby, K., Matheson, D. J., Montgomery, N., & Patil, S. (2005). Exonerations in the United States, 1989 through 2003. *The Journal of Criminal Law & Criminology, 95*(2), 523–560.

Gross, S. R., O'Brien, B., Hu, C., & Kennedy, E. H. (2014). Rate of false conviction of criminal defendants who are sentenced to death. *Proceedings of the National Academy of Sciences of the United States of America, 111*(20), 7230–7235.

The Innocence Project. (2012). *What wrongful convictions teach us about racial inequality.* Retrieved from https://www.innocenceproject.org/what-wrongful-convictions -teach-us-about-racial-inequality

Rizer, A. L., III. (2003). The race effect on wrongful convictions. *William Mitchell Law Review, 29*(3), 845–867.

Scheck, B., Neufeld, P., & Dwyer, J. (2001). *Actual innocence: When justice goes wrong and how to make it right.* New York: Penguin.

Zalman, M., & Carrano, J. (2014). *Wrongful conviction and criminal justice reform: Making justice.* New York: Routledge.

Inside-Out Prison Exchange Program

The Inside-Out Prison Exchange Program was founded by Lori Pompa, an instructor of corrections courses, at Temple University, Pennsylvania, in 1995. The inspiration for the program began three years prior, in 1992, when Pompa was on a field trip to a state prison in Pennsylvania. Rather than structure the field trip as a traditional facility tour, Pompa arranged for her Temple University students to engage in dialogue with a panel of incarcerated men from the facility to get a real-world perspective of the criminal justice system. The dialogue and learning that ensued during that session led one of the incarcerated men, Paul, to approach Pompa afterward. He suggested that they coordinate more of these conversations in the form of a semester-long course involving both incarcerated (inside) and university (outside) students.

The program was piloted in the Philadelphia Prison System in 1997 to a class of 15 inside and 15 outside students. Since then, under the leadership and direction of Lori Pompa, who has provided training to educators across the country, the program has expanded significantly. Paul, who is credited with coming up with the idea for the program, was eventually able to take part in the program when it was implemented in Graterford Prison, Pennsylvania. He remains involved to this day.

Interested instructors seeking to facilitate this program must attend a rigorous week-long training before they are able to offer their own Inside-Out courses. As of 2016, there are more than 300 trained instructors from more than 150 colleges and universities in the United States, Canada, Australia, and the United Kingdom who have been trained to implement the program in their home regions. More than 10,000 inside and outside students have taken an Inside-Out course in more than 60 correctional facilities, including county jails, state prisons, federal prisons, juvenile facilities, and community correctional facilities.

MISSION AND PHILOSOPHY

Inside-Out's mission is to "create opportunities for people inside and outside of prison to have transformative learning experiences that emphasize collaboration and dialogue and that invite them to take leadership in addressing crime, justice, and other issues of social concern" (Inside-Out Center, 2016, Mission). Although the course subject matter can vary across disciplines, from sociology to philosophy to literature and beyond, it is the collaborative dialogue and learning at the heart of the program implementation that distinguishes this program and what all Inside-Out courses share in common, no matter what subject focus.

Importantly, this program is structured for inside and outside students to find common ground in learning and thinking about critical social issues. The program is not an advocacy or activism program, nor is it an avenue for university students to learn about incarcerated populations. It is also not structured as a community service project or in any way designed for the outside students to provide help to the inside students. It is strictly an educational program, which some might consider a community-based learning experience. Similarly, Inside-Out is not a traditional prison educational program, in that it embodies experiential learning and the incorporation of traditional college students.

Since programs are run as individual partnerships between colleges or universities and prisons and jails, the model for programs varies between partnerships and locations. Although there are some components of the program that are standardized across sites—such as expectations for participants—there are other components that vary depending on site. Course credit for inside students, for example, varies based on the agreement between the correctional institution and the college or university. Other variable factors include size of classes, inside and outside student recruitment and screening processes, course topics, and more.

CLASS STRUCTURE

Inside-Out is an atypical, transformative learning experience that breaks down the walls of both classrooms and prisons. There is a facilitator instead of a professor. There are discussions instead of lectures. There is no campus, no lecture hall, and no PowerPoint. For outside students, using your smartphone during class could mean a felony charge. For inside students, the topics, assignments, and colleagues provide a glimpse of a university life that seemed unattainable for many.

In class, outside (college) and inside (incarcerated) students become one student body—usually composed of 20–40 students with an equal number of inside and outside individuals. The content of each course is less important than the method, and Inside-Out courses have been offered in a wide range of disciplines from criminal justice to philosophy to theater to nursing. What is nonnegotiable across classes is learning through "the prism of prison" in the form of a circle. Experiential learning takes place through dialogue that often begins in a small group setting and evolves when that content is brought back to the larger group.

Students are challenged in Inside-Out, and they often find that the course has a therapeutic aspect embedded in it that helps them understand the past while planning for the future. Each student's voice is important. The honest dialogue that the course inspires is governed by rules and guidelines that are developed by the students. Whenever possible, no correctional staff are present in the learning environment, which encourages a safe space to explore the difficult topics surrounding incarceration.

There is typically no final exam. Instead, students work collaboratively to identify a need that is addressed through a group project. These projects are organic to that particular class, but they commonly seek to improve the criminal justice system and sometimes are implemented by practitioners and policy makers. Past projects have included a design template for a new women's prison, plans to make a prison more environmentally friendly, and a program designed to educate incarcerated individuals on the impact of victimization. In this sense, Inside-Out classes are structured so that students "learn by doing," and the class experience often goes beyond students to positively impact the communities in which they live.

The culmination of the class is a celebration, often marked by a graduation ceremony in which certificates are awarded to program graduates. Outside guests such as university and correctional administrators are invited. Speeches are given. Food and music are shared. Projects are presented. Once the public celebration ends, a more intimate graduation ceremony takes place among only facilitators and students. Given the no-further-contact expectation of the course, this is often the last time that inside and outside students will speak to one another. It can be an emotional time, which truly speaks to the power of the transformative learning experience of Inside-Out.

Inside-Out courses are so meaningful and so impactful that they often do not end when the semester is over. A number of "think tanks" have been developed across the nation that bring together interested outside and inside individuals to continue the ideals of Inside-Out. The first of these—the Graterford Think Tank—was created after a summer 2002 Inside-Out class and has met weekly ever since. The group acts as an advisory committee for the national organization and is a critical component to the Inside-Out Training Institute that takes place in Philadelphia. Think tanks everywhere ensure that the impact of Inside-Out is not limited to the time and space of individual courses.

CHALLENGES FOR TEACHING INSIDE-OUT

Instructors seeking to implement the Inside-Out program may encounter varied levels of support for the program from their own educational institutions, the potential correctional institutions, and from the community at large. Some may work in areas with limited social support for correctional education generally, which may also be reflected in legislative initiatives and resources available for correctional programming. Additionally, the partnership between the university and the correctional facility involves a great deal of legal concerns from both institutions, and institutional support can shift with changing administrators and administrative priorities.

A common concern from the perspectives of both the college or university and the correctional institution is for the safety of inside and outside student participants. The National Inside-Out Program, which trains every single Inside-Out instructor, has very specific safety rules and policies about such topics as the ban of inside-outside student contact after the program, which must be followed at any Inside-Out implementation site. Above and beyond these stringent baseline rules, individual universities and correctional facilities may also implement their own policies.

PROGRAM IMPACT

Limited research has been conducted on the impact of the program on participants and has mostly focused on the impact on outside students. One 2014 study sought to better understand the impact of the Inside-Out program on outside participants based on data from weekly reflection papers they composed during the course of the program. The findings from this study indicated that students highly valued this unusual educational opportunity, citing the course as one of the most valuable they had taken and as a once in a lifetime opportunity. This analysis also found that the program shifted the way students thought about crime and justice. The authors note that throughout the semester, students began to critically assess their own values and beliefs about punishment and the criminal justice process (Hilinski-Rosick & Blackmer, 2014).

Other studies have found that inside students are typically better prepared for the class sessions than outside students in terms of doing the required readings ahead of time. Some research found that the structure of the class sessions—typically composed of a dynamic and quickly changing mix of ice breakers, small-group discussions, large-group brainstorming, and other methodologies—not only helped students learn the course content but also facilitated individual "serendipitous discoveries" (such as the common humanity between the inside and outside students) and the breaking down of preconceived notions about other people in the room or the groups they represented, whether incarcerated persons or college students.

Rebecca Pfeffer and Kevin Wright

See also: Education in Prison

Further Reading

Allred, S. L. (2009). The Inside-Out Prison Exchange Program: The impact of structure, content, and readings. *The Journal of Correctional Education, 60*(3), 240–258.

Davis, S. W., & Roswell, B. S. (Eds.). (2013). *Turning teaching inside out: A pedagogy of transformation for community-based education.* New York: Palgrave Macmillan.

Hilinski-Rosick, C. M., & Blackmer, A. N. (2014). An exploratory examination of the impact of the Inside-Out Prison Exchange Program. *Journal of Criminal Justice Education, 25*(3), 386–397.

Inside-Out Center. (2016). Retrieved from http://www.insideoutcenter.org

Pompa, L. (2004). Disturbing where we are comfortable: Notes from behind the walls. *Reflections, 4*(1), 24–34.

Pompa, L. (2013). One brick at a time: The power and possibility of dialogue across the prison wall. *The Prison Journal, 93*(2), 127–134.

Van Gundy, A., Bryant, A., & Starks, B. C. (2013). Pushing the envelope for evolution and social change: Critical challenges for teaching inside-out. *The Prison Journal, 93*(2), 189–210.

Werts, T. (2013). Tyrone Werts: Reflections on the Inside-Out Prison Exchange Program. *The Prison Journal, 93*(2), 135–138.

Inside-Outside Relationships

The original purpose for incarceration was to temporarily house inmates until they could be sentenced for punishment. Later, imprisonment was used as the actual method of punishment. However, more recently, the purpose of incarceration has taken on multiple attributes such as a means for rehabilitating prisoners, deterrence of unlawful behavior, and a means by which the public might be protected from harm brought about by such behaviors. The evolution of the purposes for incarceration has given rise to social questions that look into the effectiveness of the practice of imprisonment, the short- and long-term impacts these practices have on familial and community relationships, and reentry issues experienced upon release. The impact on relationships need to be examined and understood, as it is through relationships that identities, familial bonds, support systems, commitment to self-improvement, and a sense of "greater good" are established.

Because humans are highly social in nature, being connected to others or affiliated to a group is essential to the process of establishing one's identity, self-esteem or value, and commitment to others. This social nature makes incarceration a paradigm of social impediment and/or impotence that affects not only prisoners but also those who are in relationship with them, including spouses, children, parents, and custodial guardians.

The war on drugs, economic fluctuations, and lengthy prison sentences all serve to fortify the U.S. standing in having the largest incarceration rate in the world. It was in the mid-1970s that the U.S. incarceration rate increased as much as five-fold—a phenomenon commonly called mass imprisonment or the prison boom. One study claimed that the majority of this increase can be found among "fragile families," including poor, uneducated, and minority men. It is the nature of relationships found within these groups that increase the risk of past, present, and future familial generations also being incarcerated.

Cross-sections of prisoners, family members, friends, and communities offer multidimensional views of how relationships between those inside corrections and those outside are impacted. From preincarceration to prisoner reentry into a free society, "struggles are real" and suggest additional, and significant, adverse implications for the ability to sustain strong, healthy, and palatable relationships during incarceration. This is especially concerning, as relationships are important to decreasing and deterring future unacceptable social behaviors and their weakness a key obstacle to rehabilitation. Since relationships are among the core building blocks of human character and self-actualization, looking at imprisoned persons and their bonds with others offers an opportunity to see the real effects of suppressed or limited socialization.

Most prisoners have a history of unemployment, drug abuse, and neglect that fragment the family even before imprisonment. During imprisonment, stressors placed on each member of the family serve to weaken already faltering bonds and stifle prisoner rehabilitation. Since most inmates are from lower economic classes, stressors caused by incarceration often exacerbate economic and social needs. Although there are multiple stressors that impact the family, for prisoners with personal issues, being incarcerated can be a reprieve for their families. Parents with past addiction struggles and bouts of mental illness often neglect or abuse their children and significant other. In turn, children affected by such abuse take an apathetic attitude toward the parent once imprisoned. This attitude adversely affects interactions between parent and child. The incarcerated parent often becomes frustrated due to guilt for subjecting his or her family to added stress.

Policies placed on facilities restrict the ability prisoners have to see their families. As early as the 1990s, video calls began to supplant face-to-face visits, and privatization of prisons allowed them to charge exorbitant rates for video and phone calls. With harsher restrictions on physical visitation, all members of the family suffered. When visitation is allowed, the sitting room becomes the primary environment families are allotted to nurture complex relationships. Whether the parent incarcerated is trying to carve a niche in his or her children's lives or attempting to reconcile with a spouse, the inmate focuses this time to bond, make amends, and plan for the future. The caregiver/spouse and child also utilize this time to voice concerns and expectations for their collective futures.

Spousal inmate relationships are among the most complex and most researched, at least in the heterosexual context. After a partner's incarceration, the nonincarcerated spouse takes on the additional responsibilities of becoming the primary breadwinner, and, where there are children, caregiver for the family. In typical relationships, partner roles are intertwined, regardless of gender. However, when one spouse is imprisoned, the other takes on a blended role, acquiring the responsibilities previously shared with the incarcerated partner. This can stretch the nonincarcerated spouse thin and becomes a significant stressor.

When a paternal parent is incarcerated, the children are more likely to be in the care of the mother. Although the maternal parent often has a tumultuous past with the father, the father is still essential to create a sense of normalcy, and relationships often continue, at least in part, for this reason. The mother is also the more likely to take proactive steps, that is, initiate visitation, to maintain the marriage. One phenomenon that often occurs is relationship "reset." This is especially true in relationships where the now-incarcerated partner had been a substance abuser. The prisoner is given the opportunity to tackle personal issues through forced sobriety. Given time, the prisoner reciprocates the visiting spouse's effort to either strengthen or rekindle the relationship.

The role of spouse and caregiver are not mutually exclusive but can be taken on by other maternal figures, such as the grandparents. In fact, when the inmate is the maternal parent, caregivers are more likely to be grandparents. Although the dynamics of having a caregiving grandparent is more straightforward than spouses, the role can be equally burdensome. The stress placed on those who take the parental role in the care of the children is stressful due, in part, to inadequate resources and physical attrition, which can be aggravated by a higher number of children or children with greater needs. Under these more stressful circumstances, visitation is used to berate and chastise the inmate for bad choices and the lack of support they provide the family from prison. Caregivers have complications in providing the proper support for children, but many times children's relationship with the imprisoned parent is that of a stranger. Control over whether or not the child gets to see an incarcerated parent adds another dimension. Only through healthy caregiver/prisoner relationships are positive relationships with the children maintained.

The relationship between children and imprisoned parents is often equivocal. When the parent is incarcerated before the child is born, the parent is considered a stranger. Since the relationship has not been established, visitation rooms become the only place to connect with a parent. The dubiousness of creating a bona fide relationship can be seen during those times of visitation. On the other hand, children who have an established relationship with the inmate are often victims of parental neglect. For others, the impact of the vacant role causes mental health issues, delinquency, and an increase in the chance of imprisonment. Still, much like the resetting of a spousal relationship, there is a chance that the parent can build or reconcile relationships splintered by imprisonment.

It has been noted that caregivers play a significant role in the healing process faced by children and imprisoned parents, largely because they determine the "when," "if" and "how often" visitation takes place. Children also often look for the approval and support of the caregiver in building the relationship with the prisoner. These rekindled relationships help rehabilitation by allowing the prisoner to focus on his or her relationships and responsibilities to the child. Mothers tend to have closer relationships with their children for a variety of reasons, including the fact that communication is not as restricted in female facilities, relationships between mother and child are often closer in nature, especially during formative years, and women are likely to carry a lighter sentence, which causes fewer problems during visitation.

The dynamics and changes that occur in relationships of prisoners, spouses, and caregivers in the context of an environment used to punish and seclude prisoners are testament to the enduring resilience of human affection and the drive for social connection and esteem. The challenges also alert to the difficulty of maintaining the core relationships whose bonds would usually restrain individuals from committing more crime upon release. Still, more studies are required to fully comprehend both adverse and positive effects that incarceration has on inmates and their outside relationships.

Zavan A. Blount-Hill, Juan C. Ghiorzo, and Kwan-Lamar Blount-Hill

See also: Conjugal Visits; Pregnancy and Motherhood in Prisons; Prisoner Reentry/Family Integration; Privatization; Recidivism; Visitation; Women in Prison

Further Reading

Beckmeyer, J. J., & Arditti, J. A. (2014). Implications of in-person visits for incarcerated parents' family relationships and parenting experience. *Journal of Offender Rehabilitation, 53*(2), 129–151.

Christian, J., & Kennedy, L. W. (2011). Secondary narratives in the aftermath of crime: Defining family members' relationships with prisoners. *Punishment & Society, 13*(4), 379–402.

Fathi, D. (2013). An endangered necessity: A response to prison visitation policies: A fifty-state survey. *Yale Law & Policy Review, 32*(1), 205–209.

Mitchell, M. M., Spooner, K., Jia, D., & Zhang, Y. (2016). The effect of prison visitation on reentry success: A meta-analysis. *Journal of Criminal Justice, 47*, 74–83.

Tasca, M., Mulvey, P., & Rodriguez, N. (2016). Families coming together in prison: An examination of visitation encounters. *Punishment & Society, 18*(4), 459–478.

J

Jailhouse Lawyers

A jailhouse lawyer often isn't a lawyer at all. They have no formal legal training, yet they dispense legal advice in a jail or a prison setting. Jailhouse lawyers are inmates of a correctional institution who have acquired the skills needed to demonstrate a level of competence in legal work, and, in particular, have the skills and knowledge needed to file federal lawsuits (Feierman, 2006). The most known jailhouse lawyer is Mumia Abu-Jamal, who is serving a life sentence for a murder of a Philadelphia police officer in the 1980s. In *Jailhouse Lawyers: Prisoners Defending Prisoners v. the USA* (2009), Abu-Jamal discussed the important distinctions between an official lawyer and a jailhouse lawyer, with the latter lacking formal legal training, and beginning the acquisition of legal knowledge at very rudimentary stages (literacy skills). A jailhouse lawyer is not, however, left entirely to his or her own devices to practice this sort of lawyering. The *Columbia Human Rights Law Review* has published several editions of a *Jailhouse Lawyer's Manual* to assist jailhouse lawyers. The manual contains more than 40 chapters with comprehensive information pertinent to legal matters relevant to inmates.

Most of the lawsuits filed by inmates with the assistance of jailhouse lawyers are either civil suits that deal with poor prison conditions and/or allege improper treatment, or habeas corpus petitions that challenge the legality of an inmate's confinement on constitutional grounds (Roots, 2002). Notably, some of the most historically important prisoners' rights cases were originally filed by jailhouse lawyers (Feierman, 2006). These include cases that concern abuse by other inmates, excessive force utilized by correctional staff, and the right to medical care while under a period of incarceration. Prison and jail administration have taken steps to limit the capability of jailhouse lawyers to aid other inmates in the legal process. This prompted inmates to initiate legal filings to claim that these administrative efforts violate the Sixth Amendment right to counsel or the Fifth and Fourteenth Amendments' protections of due process.

As such, there are several U.S. Supreme Court decisions that have laid a foundation for inmates' legal rights to access the courts while incarcerated. An important concept in access to the courts is that the available options are "meaningful" (Feierman, 2006). In *Ex Parte Hull* (1941) the court affirmed the notion that an inmate may engage in self-representation in a petition for habeas corpus review. Just as important as the self-representation component of the case, the Supreme Court also established that the inmate has a right to advance the petition to a court and be free from any prison administration screening or censuring of the document.

Seven years later, in *Price v. Johnston* (1948), the Supreme Court considered whether a federal circuit court had made an error in its conclusion that the district court need not direct an inmate's presence in court to determine why an allegation made in a fourth habeas corpus petition was not made in three earlier petitions. Also of importance is that in this case the court gave credence to the notion that an inmate's deficiency in legal knowledge has the potential to inhibit the inmate's ability to effectively argue the case; thus access to the courts matters a great deal.

Subsequent court access cases decided by the U.S. Supreme Court also led the justices to consider more directly how literacy of the inmate impacts access to the courts. *Johnson v. Avery* is a 1969 case where an inmate was disciplined for providing assistance to another inmate in preparation of a court filing. Here, the court balanced the rights of inmates who have literacy challenges to get assistance to access the courts against the state's interest in limiting the practice of law to qualified attorneys. The court concluded that if a correctional institution is to limit the capability of an inmate to obtain assistance with legal filings from another inmate, the institution must provide a reasonable alternative that assists inmates who have literacy challenges or are too undereducated to effectively navigate the legal system. Absent such an alternative, the institution may not obstruct more knowledgeable inmates from providing legal assistance.

The U.S. Supreme Court considered the adequacy of legal research material available to inmates in a 1977 case, *Bounds v. Smith*. In the case, the North Carolina Department of Corrections maintained control of 100,000 inmates housed in 80 units spread over 67 counties. Yet the only adequate law library was located at the central unit in Raleigh, North Carolina. The court concluded that legal material and assistance are essential to meaningful access to the courts to frame habeas corpus and civil rights court filings. Importantly, the court rejected the argument of the state that inmates are not equipped to utilize legal material.

In *Lewis v. Casey* (1996), the U.S. Supreme Court provided a clearer framework for the outcome of the *Bounds* decision nearly 20 years earlier. The court in *Lewis* concluded that an inmate does not have an independent right to access legal material. Rather, to prevail in a claim as to the inadequacies of legal material, an inmate would necessarily need to show that actual injury occurred. This set of five cases generally established that inmates may self-represent without counsel, and that absent a mechanism to provide inmates with legal advice from trained attorneys, an institution may not prevent jailhouse lawyers from providing assistance to other inmates and has some obligation to provide legal material to inmates.

The "get tough" era of criminal justice that was initiated in the 1970s and extended into the 1980s and 1990s, as it relates to inmate-initiated litigation, severely limited the capability of inmates to file lawsuits. The movement, with respect to prison litigation, culminated with two pieces of legislation signed during the administration of President Bill Clinton. The Antiterrorism and Effective Death Penalty Act of 1996 limited the circumstances in which a judge may grant habeas corpus relief to an inmate. The Prison Litigation Reform Act, also signed in 1996, is designed to reduce the incidence of frivolous filings by inmates and limit the ability of judges to initiate costly reform mandates on state corrections systems. These efforts created complex rules and technical hurdles that inmates who file habeas corpus and civil rights lawsuits must understand, and has, by default, solidified the need for jailhouse lawyers to aid those inmates who are unfamiliar with legal procedure.

Today, jailhouse lawyers remain an important resource for inmates, but they also face retaliation from prison staff, particularly when cases they assist with allege violation of civil rights of an incarcerated inmate (Hudson, 2017). In an American Bar Association article, David L. Hudson noted that a district judge in 2017 asserted that "the use of jailhouse lawyers is one recognized avenue available to ensure that non-English-speaking and/or illiterate inmates have meaningful access to the courts" (Hudson, 2017). In a different 2017 case, a circuit court concluded that it was not proper for an institution to remove an inmate from a particular job as retaliation for having provided legal assistance to an inmate or for helping the inmate to file a grievance. Even after a series of cases that have spanned 55 years, jailhouse lawyers continue to experience institutional practices to limit their effectiveness. Regardless of this, the courts show few signs of reversing a course that has legitimated their importance.

Elizabeth L. Gilmore and Kevin G. Buckler

See also: Judicial Involvement in Prison Administration; Prison Law Libraries

Further Reading

Abu-Jamal, M. (2009). *Jailhouse lawyers: Prisoners defending prisoners v. the USA*. San Francisco: City Lights Books.

Antiterrorism and Effective Death Penalty Act, 18 U.S.C. § 101–108 (1996).

Bounds v. Smith, 430 U.S. 817 (1977).

Ex Parte Hull, 312 U.S. 546 (1941).

Feierman, J. (2006). "The power of the pen": Jailhouse lawyers, literacy, and civic engagement. *Harvard Civil Liberties Civil Law Review, 41*, 369–389.

Hudson, D. L. (2017, August). Jailhouse attorneys fill vital need for inmate access to the courts. *ABA Journal*. Retrieved from http://www.abajournal.com/magazine/article/jailhouse_lawyers_inmate_access_court

Johnson v. Avery, 393 U.S. 483 (1969).

Lewis v. Casey, 516 U.S. 804 (1996).

Price v. Johnston, 334 U.S. 266 (1948).

Prison Litigation Reform Act, H.R. 3019, 104th Congress (1996).

Roots, R. (2002). Of prisoners and plaintiffs' lawyers: A tale of two litigation reform efforts. *Williamette Law Review, 38*, 221–222.

Jails Compared to Prisons

Perhaps the most distinct difference between jails and prisons is the amount of time that individuals in each correctional facility serve. Jails are meant to house offenders that have been sentenced to a term of one year or less. Prisons on the other hand, are facilities that house offenders with convictions of one year or more. The offenders serving time in jails are mostly misdemeanor offenders, while prisons house mainly felony offenders. This can vary some from state to state. For example, Texas has state jails that are prison facilities meant to be used for low-level drug offenders who may benefit more from treatment than from pure incarceration. Those individuals sentenced to a state jail serve no more than two years in these special facilities.

Another basic distinction between jails and prisons is the agencies that operate them. Jails are operated by county and/or city governments, whereas state and federal governments operate prisons. In part, because of the difference in authority, jails on average have a smaller population of inmates compared to prisons. There are some extremely large jails, such as Rikers Island in New York, the L.A. County Jail, and the Cook County Jail in Chicago, but most jails are smaller and established in more rural counties and cities.

The fact that jails house individuals with mainly misdemeanor convictions does not mean that there are no violent offenders in these facilities. A large majority of persons who are housed in jails have not even been to trial or pleaded guilty to the crimes for which they have been accused. Besides housing convicted misdemeanor offenders, jails are also responsible for holding those who have been arrested and are being held while they await trial for the crimes for which they have been accused. Jails are also responsible for holding individuals who have violated their probation or parole, those waiting to be transferred to state jails or prisons, and even holding persons for the U.S. Marshals Services or U.S. Immigration and Customs Enforcement (ICE). This creates a very complex population to manage that can also lead to an interesting dynamic when handling classification.

The classification issue leads to one similarity between jails and prisons: the security level. All prisoners must enter through the jail system prior to being convicted and sentenced to a prison facility, so the security level of offenders in both jails and prisons is basically the same. The charges for pretrial jail inmates can run the spectrum from a very minor misdemeanor, like a public intoxication, to a major felony, such as capital murder. In turn, jails must operate under the assumption that some of the accused will be tried and convicted of these major felonies, so the level of security must be that of a maximum security prison facility.

Prison facilities are a bit more segregated based on security classification, as the inmates are usually separated by minimum, medium, and maximum custody levels. The typical guidelines for classification maintain that minimum and medium inmates can be housed together, and medium and maximum inmates may be housed together, but minimum and maximum level inmates can never be mixed in the same unit. This type of segregation may be attempted in a jail facility, but it is not always guaranteed both because of space and the fact that prior to being convicted, the actual security threat may not truly be known.

In jail facilities, mostly because of space limitations, a typical classification that is done at prison transfer facilities is basically impossible. There are not enough places to segregate all the special population inmates, including gang members, those with chronic illnesses, the elderly, and inmates suffering from mental illness. Dealing with these special populations is typically feasible in the larger prison facilities, but it is extremely difficult to properly manage these populations in smaller jails. For instance, it is much harder to separate rival gangs in jails than prisons because of limited space. Prisons have more space to separate

Jails Compared to Prisons

gangs and can even send gang leaders to different units across the state to prevent gang activity in the prison.

Rates of tuberculosis, suicide, and mental illness are all higher in local jails than state prisons. This is especially unfortunate because jails tend to have higher percentages of special needs inmates compared to prisons, even though they are less capable of taking care of these groups. Treatment of inmates with chronic illnesses such as tuberculosis can be significantly different in jails versus prisons. Tuberculosis rates are nearly four times higher in local jails than in state prisons.

Most prisons are large enough that the facility has proper staff and equipment in place to meet the needs of special needs offenders. Jails, on the other hand, lack the tools needed to deal with these special populations. A negative air quarantine unit is ideal when working with an inmate who has active tuberculosis. Most prisons do not have the resources to provide this treatment option, so it is obvious that small-scale jails would be even less likely to provide these types of special services.

Some prisons have designated units within the facility for elderly inmates or others with special health needs. Some state prison systems even have stand-alone psychiatric or geriatric facilities where inmates can be sent, from throughout the state for specialized care. In contrast, jails struggle with having enough staff or specialized medical teams to properly accommodate special needs. Another component of this is cost. Small jails are often incapable of providing certain services just because of the expense that it takes to do so. State prison facilities have much more revenue that they can use to cover medical expenses for inmates.

Suicide rates are more than three times higher in jails than prisons, with smaller jails having the highest suicide rates. Suicides are higher in jail facilities because suicides are most common amongt people who are having their first experience with being incarcerated. Nearly half of all jail suicides occur in the first week of being in custody (Mumola, 2005). This is also exacerbated by the fact that jails tend to encounter more individuals who suffer from a mental illness.

Mental health is problematic for both prisons and jails. Even large prison facilities struggle with having proper mental health staff and space to properly deal with inmates who suffer from mental illnesses. This problem is worse in jails, however, because there is an even higher percentage of individuals with mental illness in jails than prisons. Local jails are estimated to have as many as 64 percent of inmates suffering from a mental illness compared to 53 percent in the state prison system and 45 percent in the federal system. Once again, this is unfortunate because smaller jail facilities are often not prepared for proper psychiatric care, especially at this magnitude.

A less recognized item of contrast between jails and prisons is the population turnover. Due to the function of a jail being the initial house of arrest for every criminal who gets arrested, the jail has a much higher rate of turnover than a prison. Many people are a quick book and release that may take less than an hour, while there are others who may be serving a full-year sentence. The average length of stay for 85 percent of all new admissions to jail is four to five days, with small jails having higher turnover than larger jails. The prison population is much more stable,

354   **Judicial Involvement in Prison Administration**

since inmates are currently serving out their sentences, leading to an average length of stay of about three years.

The length of stay in the institution plays a role in what programs are offered at a facility as well. There are usually more program options for prison inmates due to their having more time available to complete them. Also, prison inmates are often expected to work in some capacity if they are physically able. A jail setting has some work options for those who are convicted, but the greater number of inmates will not be there long enough to even bother trying to get into a program or on a work detail.

Prison inmates, since they are convicted felons, have a lesser expectation of privacy and fewer freedoms. Jail inmates who have not yet been convicted have more rights than the convicted felons in a prison. It is crucial that officers who work with jail inmates who have not been convicted of a crime yet are careful not to violate any of the inmate's rights, because it is possible that this person may be innocent, depending on the outcome of a trial. Overall, there are many items that are similar or related between jails and prisons, but the type of facility, the availability of resources, and the type of inmates who reside within each facility all create differences in how things are managed.

Nick Terry Harpster

See also: Custody Levels; Education in Prison; Incarceration Rates; Inmate Classification; Mental Health Issues and Jails; Mentally Ill Prisoners; Overcrowding; Prison Gangs; Suicide in Custody

Further Reading

James, D. J., & Glaze, L. E. (2006). *Mental health problems of prison and jail inmates.* Washington, DC: Bureau of Justice Statistics. Retrieved from https://www.bjs.gov /content/pub/pdf/mhppji.pdf

Lambert, L. A., Armstrong, L. R., Lobato, M. N., Ho, C., France, A. M., & Haddad, M. B. (2016). Tuberculosis in jails and prisons: United States, 2002–2013. *American Journal of Public Health, 106*(12), 2231–2237.

Mumola, C. J. (2005). *Suicide and homicide in state prisons and local jails.* Washington, DC: Bureau of Justice Statistics. Retrieved from http://www.bjs.gov/index.cfm?ty =pbdetail&iid=1126

Judicial Involvement in Prison Administration

For the entire 19th century and much of the 20th century, inmates of the correctional system were closed off from filing grievances with courts. The U.S. Supreme Court in *Pervear v. Commonwealth* (1867) ruled that an Eighth Amendment claim could not be filed by a state inmate because "the article of the Constitution relied upon in support of it does not apply to State but to National legislation." In *Ruffin v. Commonwealth* (1871) the Supreme Court of Virginia provided a different rationale that foreclosed the use of courts by inmates: that inmates are slaves of the state. The Virginia court wrote of the defendant in the case that, "He has, as a consequence of his crime, not only forfeited his liberty, but all his personal rights except those which the law in its humanity accords to him. He is for the time being the slave of the State. He is *civiliter mortuus*; and his estate, if he has any, is administered like that of a dead man."

The salient implication of both cases was that inmates had no standing to assert rights and liberties granted to citizens by the U.S. Constitution and its amendments. This stance on inmates changed in the 1960s with two U.S. Supreme Court decisions: *Jones v. Cunningham* (1963) and *Cooper v. Pate* (1964). Each case opened the door for correctional inmates convicted by the state to seek legal relief in the federal court system. These cases collectively initiated a shift from a "hands-off" approach to judicial involvement in prison administration to an open door policy for inmates to file lawsuits in federal courts.

The *Jones* case (1963) was the first instance where a state inmate (a parolee at the time) was permitted to proceed in a habeas corpus filing to challenge the merits of the detention. In a habeas corpus petition the correctional inmate sets forth reasons to show that the detention is illegal and generally seeks either release or a new trial or proceeding. In *Cooper* (1964), the court for the first time permitted a correctional inmate to file a lawsuit under the Civil Rights Act of 1871 to challenge the conditions of the confinement. In a civil rights lawsuit, the correctional inmate asserts that there has been a specific violation of a right or liberty granted by the U.S. Constitution and its amendments and generally asks for a declaratory judgment that a constitutional violation has occurred and either corrective action or a monetary judgment.

Following these two cases state correctional agencies had to respond to inmate filings in a manner that they did not have to in the past. Correctional inmates filed lawsuits on a whole host of issues, including, but not limited to, access to mail and publications, access to the courts and to legal materials, conditions of confinement (such as overcrowding), search and seizure and general privacy rights, excessive force, and the availability of and quality of medical and mental health care. Generally speaking, the courts have approached inmate lawsuits by weighing the rights of the inmate against the interests of the state and the institution to effectively manage the facility, recognizing that a correctional inmate does not have the same quality and degree of constitutional protections as free citizens.

Courts have typically steered clear of broad-based pronouncement of rights, while maintaining that some attention must be extended by the institution to protect basic rights of inmates. To illustrate, the court recognized the need to have legal material (*Bounds v. Smith*, 1977) and legal advice (*Johnson v. Avery*, 1969) available to inmates, but has granted prisons the discretion to choose how to do so and has said that to be successful in a claim the inmate must show actual damages owing to the lack of legal material available (*Lewis v. Casey*, 1996). In other areas, such as civil rights lawsuits filed alleging inadequate medical care (an allegation of an Eighth Amendment violation), the court has made it extremely difficult for the correctional inmate to prevail. An inmate in such a case must show that the prison staff acted with "deliberate indifference," which is a very difficult legal standard to meet.

Amid growing concern that correctional inmates file too many "frivolous" lawsuits and apprehension that federal judges were going too far in the direction of inmate rights, in 1996, the federal government passed two pieces of legislation known, respectively, as the Antiterrorism and Effective Death Penalty Act (AEDPA) and the Prison Litigation Reform Act (PLRA). The AEDPA placed limits on the circumstances in which a judge may grant habeas corpus relief to an inmate. Specifically, following passage of the act, a judge may grant relief only when a ruling by a lower court violates "clearly established law" or when a lower court decision is based on an "unreasonable determination of facts." The AEDPA also put in place very strict statutes of limitations. An inmate who loses a direct appeal (an appeal that follows the conviction) or who has new evidence discovered must file a habeas corpus petition within one year.

The PLRA sought to limit the capacity of federal judges to issue injunctions and to set in motion remedies that states and prison institutions must follow. The PLRA requires that before a federal judge may act: (1) the relief proposed must be narrowly drawn, (2) the relief must go no further than necessary to correct the violation of the federal right, and (3) the relief must be the least intrusive means available to correct the violation. The PLRA also placed limitations on judges in injunctive relief (to make a prison stop doing something), initiated a requirement that administrative remedies be exhausted prior to a lawsuit, requires a showing of physical injury in federal civil lawsuits, limits the possibility of a reward of attorneys' fees paid by the prison when the inmate prevails in a lawsuit, and placed filing fee penalties on inmates who have filed prior lawsuits that were subsequently dismissed by a court.

The Supreme Court has begun to carve out exceptions to some of the provisions of these acts and has found favorably that certain processes respect the spirit of the acts while also provide protections to correctional inmates. It has in essence started to strike a necessary balance in the need for courts to oversee corrections but also prevent judges from proceeding too far in the proscribed solutions to address constitutional violations. In *McQuiggin v. Perkins* (2013) the court ruled that claims of "actual innocence" are an exception to the statutes of limitations in the AEDPA. The court acknowledged the miscarriage of justice and fundamental unfairness of a statute that would allow an innocent citizen to remain incarcerated all due to technicalities that were not followed in the time to file the claim.

Brown v. Plata (2011) is a case that raised a question about whether a court order from a three-judge panel that required the state of California to reduce its prison population to 137.5 percent of capacity violates the provisions of the PLRA. The court ruled that the order was not a violation of the act. It noted that prior court decisions on remedies had not been followed and that the state had ample time to take steps to reduce the prison population to address medical and mental health problems evident in the state prison system. The court concluded that the three-judge panel did not make an error when it found that overcrowding is the primary cause of the violation, and that the evidence supported a finding that no other relief would remedy the violation, and that the relief was narrowly tailored and was the least intrusive means to remedy the violation.

Kevin G. Buckler and Elizabeth L. Gilmore

See also: Access to the Courts; Antiterrorism and Effective Death Penalty Act of 1996; Constitution as a Source for Prisoners' Rights, The; Deliberate Indifference; Habeas

Corpus Writs; Legitimate Penological Interests; Prison Litigation Reform Act; *Ruffin v. Commonwealth*; Section 1983 Lawsuits

Further Reading

Antiterrorism and Effective Death Penalty Act, 18 U.S.C. § 101–108 (1996).

Bounds v. Smith, 430 U.S. 817 (1977).

Brown v. Plata, 563 U.S. 493 (2011).

Cooper v. Pate, 378 U.S. 546 (1964).

Johnson v. Avery, 393 U.S. 483 (1969).

Jones v. Cunningham, 371 U.S. 236 (1963).

Lewis v. Casey, 516 U.S. 804 (1996).

McQuiggin v. Perkins, 133 S. Ct. 1924 (2013).

Pervear v. Commonwealth, 72 U.S. 475 (1867).

Prison Litigation Reform Act, H.R. 3019, 104th Cong. (1996).

Ruffin v. Commonwealth, 62 Va. 790 (1871).

Juvenile Detention Centers

Juvenile detention centers are responsible for holding juvenile offenders whose conduct is subject to court jurisdiction. Detention centers are equivalent to adult jails in which the main purpose is for temporarily holding youth who are likely to commit another crime prior to adjudication or who are likely to fail to appear at an upcoming court date. As with jails, detention centers also hold adjudicated juveniles who have been given short-term sentences (typically less than six months). Detention centers may be administered by city, county, or state governments. However, in most cases, the county, in conjunction with the juvenile court and the probation department, is responsible for the daily administration.

Theoretically, juvenile detention centers are supposed to be reserved for serious juvenile offenders who pose a serious threat to either themselves or society; however, research has found that most detained youth do not fit this criteria. In fact, in 2013, only 26 percent of detained youth had committed a person offense. The other nearly two-thirds of youth being held were charged with nonviolent offenses including property, drug, and public order offenses as well as technical probation violations and status offenses (noncriminal acts considered law violations solely because of a juvenile's status as a minor).

Detention rates not only vary by offense but by multiple demographic characteristics as well, including gender, age, and race. Male offenders tend to be more likely to be detained than female offenders. Additionally, older youth (16 or older) are more likely to be detained than younger youth (15 or younger). Race represents the greatest variation among delinquency cases. Black juvenile offenders are detained at a disproportionately higher rate than white juvenile offenders for all types of offenses. To illustrate, in 2004, black juvenile offenders accounted for 29 percent of delinquency cases handled by the court; however, the proportion of detained youth who were black was 37 percent. This trend has been consistent since at least 1985. These findings are not unique to detention decisions as it has been found that blacks are overrepresented in all stages of the juvenile justice system.

The idea of detaining youth separately from adults came about during the 19th century when society's perception of children and their criminal responsibility began to shift. Specifically, in 1822, the Society for the Prevention of Pauperism, a group that was influential in the reformation of the treatment of juveniles, issued a report recommending the establishment of a separate penitentiary for juvenile offenders. The New York House of Refuge was created three years later, representing the first institution to deal solely with the care and confinement of juvenile offenders. Following its creation and a good reception by the public, numerous other cities followed suit, building their own houses of refuge.

Municipal and state governments began to play an increasing role in the creation and administration of juvenile institutions during the mid-19th century. As part of this shift, there was an increased emphasis on formal education, as it was believed that educating and properly training youthful offenders could help to offset the numerous factors contributing to their delinquent behavior, such as poverty and a poor family environment. To illustrate this new emphasis, houses of refuge were renamed reform schools. With the exception of the South, by 1890, almost every state had developed some type of reform school for boys, and many even had separate institutions for girls.

Although the initial intent of reform schools was to rehabilitate youth and prepare them to be productive members of society, this idea took a blow during the mid-1970s when Robert Martinson published his infamous study "What Works?—Questions and Answers about Prison Reform," which concluded that nothing works when it came to rehabilitating offenders. Following this report, detention centers began to more closely resemble adult jails, emphasizing punishment as opposed to rehabilitation. The erosion of rehabilitation continued throughout the 1980s and 1990s as juvenile crime increased and the public feared the rise of "juvenile superpredators."

Also during this time, detention rates more than doubled. From 1985 to 1995, there was a 68 percent increase in the one-day detention rate. Detention rates continued to increase until they peaked in 2002. Since that time, they have been steadily decreasing. As of 2013, detention rates were at their lowest level since at least 1985. In conjunction with the growing emphasis to reduce the number of detained youth, there has also been a renewed interested in rehabilitation, which has resulted in the implementation of various types of programming.

The majority of programming available within detention facilities is focused on education and mental health. Educational programming is required in all facilities due to compulsory education laws. The first of these laws was enacted by Rhode Island in 1840, and by 1918 every state had enacted similar statutes. These laws require that state legislatures provide free education for all juveniles, including juvenile delinquents, residing within the state. Although states are required to provide educational services in detention centers, in many cases, little attention is paid to the quality of education provided. Institutions vary on the educational services available and the quality of such services. In some cases, facilities lack designated classrooms, instructional technology, libraries, and even books. Further, teachers within detention facilities are often poorly trained and incapable of dealing with the needs of detained youth.

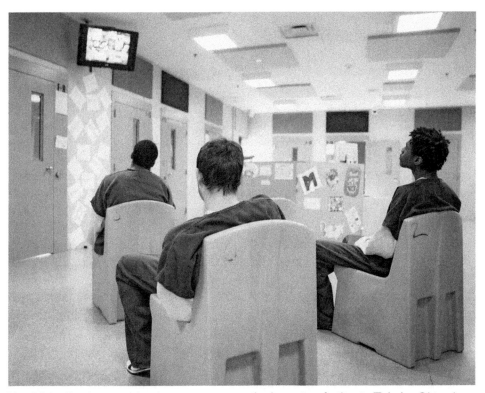

Youthful offenders watch television at a juvenile detention facility in Toledo, Ohio. As is the case with adult incarceration, the vast majority of inmates in juvenile detention facilities are male. (Melanie Stetson Freeman/The Christian Science Monitor via Getty Images)

In order to try to combat these problems, the federal No Child Left Behind Act of 2001 required states receiving federal funding for education to monitor and improve correctional education services. However, states violating the requirements of the act have failed to face major consequences, thus giving states little incentive to make changes. Although the quality of educational programming available in juvenile detention centers is still lacking, hopefully, with the renewed focus on rehabilitation, efforts will be made to improve the quality of educational services provided to detained youth.

Many detained juveniles have been diagnosed with a mental health illness. Research has found that approximately 65 to 70 percent of youth in the juvenile justice system have a diagnosable mental illness. Additionally, more than 60 percent of youth with a mental health disorder also have a substance use disorder. Recognizing that in order to rehabilitate youth their illnesses must be addressed, detention centers have implemented a variety of different programs focused on mental health and substance use issues. Minimal data exist on available mental health programming in detention centers; however, according to a study conducted during the 1990s by the Office of Juvenile Justice and Delinquency Prevention (OJJDP) on conditions of confinement in juvenile justice facilities, mental health professionals were available in 87 percent of facilities with detained youth. The majority of services available during this time focused on individual and family counseling, substance use and abuse, and suicide prevention.

A relatively new emphasis has been on implementing trauma-informed care in juvenile detention centers. Trauma-informed care is a treatment framework that involves understanding the effects of trauma and how to appropriately respond to it. Thus, for a detention center, trauma-informed care would involve implementing strategies and policies aimed at minimizing the effects of institutional trauma as well as addressing prior traumatic experiences. Strategies that have been implemented to reduce trauma include front door screening and orientation, staff training, behavioral interventions, and reforming institutional values. Trauma-informed care has achieved some success, but the practice is not yet universal and further research needs to be conducted in order to determine the most effective practices.

Despite the renewed emphasis on programming and rehabilitation, research has found that detention has a negative impact on multiple areas of a juvenile's life, including the likelihood of reoffending, mental health, and education. One of the main arguments for detaining youth is that it will keep them from engaging in additional crimes. It has been found, however, that detaining youth may actually increase the likelihood of reoffending. In fact, one study of incarcerated youth in Arkansas found that prior commitment was the most significant predictor of recidivism. Researchers have cited social learning theory to explain this phenomenon. It is argued that congregating delinquent youth together allows them the opportunity to learn antisocial attitudes and behaviors from their peers.

Detention can also negatively impact a youth's mental health. As noted above, the majority of detained youth enter detention with some mental health issue. Often, the conditions of confinement, such as overcrowding, enhance one's condition. Further, it has been found that some youth develop a mental illness while being detained. One study found that one-third of incarcerated youth diagnosed with depression developed the condition during their detention stay.

Finally, detention has been found to impact detained youths' education. Studies have found that many detained youth fail to return to school upon release. A study conducted by the Department of Education found that 43 percent of youth receiving remedial education services in detention failed to return to school after release. An additional 16 percent enrolled in school but ultimately dropped out. Due to the potential negative effects of detention, its use should be reserved for the most serious offenders.

Detaining juveniles in facilities separate from adults has been a common practice in the United States for almost two centuries, with its main purpose fluctuating between treatment and punishment. In recent decades, there has been a shift toward reducing the number of youth detained as well as increasing the available programming in detention facilities. As society continues to change, so too will the role and purpose of juvenile detention centers.

Riane M. Bolin

See also: Juveniles in Corrections, Landmark Cases Involving; Sight and Sound of Juvenile Offenders; State-Raised Youths

Further Reading

Burrell, S. (2013). *Trauma and the environment of care in juvenile institutions.* Los Angeles: National Center for Child Traumatic Stress.

Desai, R. A., Goulet, J. L., Robbins, J., Chapman, J. F., Migdole, S. J., & Hoge, M. A. (2006). Mental health care in juvenile detention facilities: A review. *Journal of the American Academy of Psychiatry and the Law, 34*(2), 204–214.

Holman, B., & Ziedenberg, J. (2006). *The dangers of detention: The impact of incarcerating youth in detention and other secure facilities.* Washington, DC: Justice Policy Institute.

Pickett, R. S. (1969). *House of refuge: Origins of juvenile reform in New York State.* Syracuse, NY: Syracuse University Press.

Platt, A. M. (1969). *The child savers: The invention of delinquency.* Chicago: University of Chicago Press.

Twomey, K. (2008). The right to education in juvenile detention under state constitutions. *Virginia Law Review, 94*(3), 765–811.

Juveniles in Corrections, Landmark Cases Involving

During the 1960s and 1970s, the Supreme Court decided a number of juvenile court cases. However, the majority of these cases dealt with due process proceedings in the juvenile court. The court heard relatively few cases dealing with juvenile corrections; of these cases, they have focused largely on the sentencing of juveniles in adult courts. While the Supreme Court has heard few cases involving juvenile corrections, federal circuit courts have made many important rulings regarding juvenile corrections, specifically juveniles' right to treatment and conditions of confinement.

One issue that the Supreme Court has dealt with three separate times is the constitutionality of the juvenile death penalty. The Supreme Court first ruled on this issue in *Thompson v. Oklahoma* (1988). Thompson, a 15-year-old boy, was charged, along with three other individuals, with murdering his brother-in-law because he had been physically abusing Thompson's sister. Though Thompson was considered a juvenile under Oklahoma law, the prosecutor decided to charge Thompson as an adult. Ultimately, Thompson, along with his codefendants, were found guilty of first-degree murder and were sentenced to death. In this case, the Supreme Court was charged with deciding whether it was constitutional to execute offenders who committed their crimes while under the age of 16.

The court analyzed the constitutionality of this practice by assessing whether it aligned with "evolving standards of decency that mark the progress of a maturing society." Utilizing a broad range of criteria to measure national standards, the court held that the national consensus did not support the imposition of death for juveniles under the age of 16. Although this case did help to clarify the age limit at which juveniles may not receive a sentence of death, it left open the question of whether it was constitutional to sentence any juvenile to the death penalty. The court clarified their stance a year later in *Stanford v. Kentucky* (1989).

Stanford v. Kentucky involved two separate, but similar, cases that had been consolidated by the court when granting certiorari. The first case involved a

17-year-old, Kevin Stanford, who was charged with a number of crimes including first-degree murder, sodomy, robbery, and receiving stolen property. Though he was still eligible based on his age for prosecution in juvenile court, the seriousness of the crimes coupled with previous failed attempts of rehabilitation by the juvenile system, led to him being tried in adult court. At trial, Stanford was sentenced to death.

The second case involved Heath A. Wilkins, a 16-year-old, who was charged with first-degree murder, armed criminal action, and carrying a concealed weapon. Prosecutors sought to try Wilkins in adult court due to the nature of the crimes. Wilkins pleaded guilty to all the charges, and both the prosecutor and Wilkins asked for the death penalty, which was granted. In this case, the Supreme Court was to decide whether it was cruel and unusual punishment to sentence juveniles, who were between the ages of 16 and 17 when they committed their crimes, to death. In a 5–4 decision, the court held that it was constitutional for states to impose a death sentence on individuals who were aged 16 or 17 at the time of their crimes. With this decision, the court made clear that the minimum age at which juveniles may constitutionally be sentenced to death is 16 years old.

Following the decision in *Stanford*, the issue of the death penalty for juveniles remained untouched by the Supreme Court until 2005 in the case of *Roper v. Simmons*. In 1993, 17-year-old Christopher Simmons, along with a 15-year-old accomplice, were charged with brutally murdering a woman with whom Simmons had recently been involved in a car accident. Simmons was tried and convicted in adult court and received a death sentence. In 2002, asserting that the Supreme Court's decision in *Atkins v. Virginia* (2002), which eliminated the death penalty for offenders with intellectual disability, established the same constitutional prohibition against the death penalty for juveniles, Simmons filed a habeas corpus petition with the Missouri Supreme Court. The Missouri Supreme Court agreed with Simmons and converted his sentence to life without the possibility of parole.

In order to revisit the question of the death penalty for juveniles, the Supreme Court decided to hear the case. In order to make their decision, the court once again looked at the national standards of decency. They found that as of 2005, 30 states had already eliminated the death penalty for juveniles, and in the states where it remained a sentencing option, executions were rare. The Supreme Court also referenced the research on the development of the human brain, which concluded that juveniles cannot be cognitively compared to adults. Unlike adults, the research argued, juveniles lack the ability to be in complete control of their emotions and behavior. In other words, like intellectually disabled individuals, juveniles have diminished capacity. A final factor that impacted the court's decision was the international stance on the death penalty for juveniles. Of all the democratic nations, the United States was the only one left that allowed for the execution of juveniles. Based on the above factors, the court held that it was unconstitutional to execute individuals who committed their crimes while under the age of 18.

With the elimination of the death penalty for juveniles, the next most severe punishment available to juveniles was life without the possibility of parole. Due to this fact, it is no surprise that the court soon was asked to assess the constitutionality of these sentences for juveniles. The first case dealing with life without the

Juveniles in Corrections, Landmark Cases Involving   363

possibility of parole for juveniles was *Graham v. Florida* (2010). This particular case dealt with whether a sentence of life without the possibility of parole could be imposed on a juvenile who committed a nonhomicide offense.

In this case, Terrence Graham, a 16-year-old, was convicted in adult court of armed home robbery. This conviction occurred six months after having served a yearlong sentence for another armed burglary and attempted armed robbery. Graham was sentenced to life without the possibility of parole. Graham appealed his sentence, arguing that it constituted cruel and unusual punishment. Although both the Florida District Court of Appeals and the Florida Supreme Court both disagreed with Graham's assertion, the Supreme Court held that Graham's sentence did represent cruel and unusual punishment. The court held that juveniles can only be sentenced to life without the possibility of parole for cases involving homicide.

Two years after the ruling in *Graham*, the issue of life without the possibility of parole for juveniles once again made its way to the Supreme Court. In *Miller v. Alabama* (2012), the court assessed whether the imposition of a sentence of life without the possibility of parole for juveniles violated the Eighth Amendment prohibition against cruel and unusual punishment. This case was decided alongside another case, *Jackson v. Hobbs*. In both cases, 14-year-old boys who had been convicted of murder were granted mandatory sentences of life without the possibility of parole. The court ruled that mandatory sentences of life without the possibility of parole were unconstitutional. However, they failed to eliminate life without the possibility of parole sentences for juveniles altogether. Due to the court's failure to provide specific criteria for how to determine when life without the possibility of parole is an appropriate sentence for juveniles, it is likely that the court will one day again have to revisit this issue.

These cases are the only cases involving juvenile corrections for which the Supreme Court has granted certiorari. However, federal circuit courts have been influential in cases involving juvenile corrections. The majority of these cases have dealt with conditions of confinement and the right to treatment for incarcerated juveniles. The first federal circuit court case to deal with either of these issues was *Creek v. Stone* (1967). In this case, the court held that under the principle of *parens patriae*, juvenile correctional facilities should provide similar environments to what a child should have received at home. In *Martarella v. Kelly* (1972), a federal district court expanded the requirements of *Creek* by specifying elements that should be available in juvenile facilities including education and recreation programs, caseworkers, and access to psychiatric services.

Another federal court case dealing with conditions of confinement was *Inmates of Boys Training School v. Affleck* (1972). In this case, a district court in Rhode Island set minimum standards in a variety of different areas of juvenile institutional life including clean bedding, personal hygiene supplies, appropriate clothing and clothing changes, daily showers, access to books, and nursing staff on duty 24 hours a day. The courts in these decisions concluded that the main purpose of the juvenile justice system is rehabilitation, and as such juveniles had a statutory right to treatment.

A final landmark case involving juveniles' right to treatment was *Nelson v. Heyne* (1974). Citing the *Martarella* case, the court ruled that juveniles do not just have a statutory right to treatment but a constitutional right to treatment. Based on the current shift toward rehabilitation in juvenile justice, it is likely that in the upcoming decades both the federal courts and the Supreme Court will be asked to review cases involving some of the more punitive practices that were implemented during the get tough era.

Riane M. Bolin

See also: Constitution as a Source for Prisoners' Rights, The; Death Penalty Legal Issues; Evolving Standards of Decency; Habeas Corpus Writs; Juvenile Detention Centers

Further Reading

Borra, J. E. (2005). Roper v. Simmons. *Journal of Gender, Social Policy & the Law, 13*(3), 707–715.

Feld, B. C. (2008). A slower form on death: Implications of Roper v. Simmons for juveniles sentenced to life without parole. *Notre Dame Journal of Law, Ethics, & Public Policy, 22,* 9–65.

Frisch, M. (1974). Constitutional right to treatment for juveniles adjudicated to be delinquent—Nelson v. Heyne. *American Criminal Law Review, 12,* 209.

Hemmens, C., Steiner, B., & Mueller, D. (2013). *Significant cases in juvenile justice* (2nd ed.). Oxford, U.K.: Oxford University Press.

Lerner, C. S. (2012). Sentenced to confusion: Miller v. Alabama and the coming wave of Eighth Amendment cases. *George Mason Law Review, 20*(1), 25–40.

Scott, E. S. (2012). Miller v. Alabama and the (past and) future of juvenile crime regulation. *Law & Inequality, 31,* 535–541.

Smith, R. J. (2010). Redemption song: Graham v. Florida and the evolving Eighth Amendment jurisprudence. *Michigan Law Review First Impressions, 108,* 86–94.

L

Leavenworth

The U.S. Penitentiary, Leavenworth, is located in Leavenworth, Kansas, and is a medium security federal penitentiary. As of 2016, there were 1,440 inmates living in the prison and an additional 400 in a minimum security satellite camp, which is next to the prison.

Federal funding was authorized for the building of three federal penitentiaries in 1891. The land for the penitentiary was deeded to the Justice Department by the War Department in 1897. The purpose of the site was to build a U.S. federal penitentiary.

Inmates who were being housed in the U.S. Disciplinary Barracks (a military prison located at Fort Leavenworth) worked on the first phase of the construction project and were later the first inmates housed in the new prison. Work started on the prison in 1897, but crews did not complete the facility for 25 years. Cell houses officially opened in 1906, but some inmates were housed in the prison while it was being finished.

Leavenworth was built in the Auburn prison style, which emphasized the use of single cells, large concrete walls, and imposing prison buildings. The walls of the Leavenworth penitentiary are 80 feet high, 40 feet being below the ground. The walls enclose 22.8 acres of land and all the buildings. Leavenworth was the largest maximum security prison in the United States until 2005. It lost this designation as the security level was changed from maximum to medium security.

Leavenworth was the first penitentiary in the world that was completely self-contained. Everything needed to operate the prison is contained in the grounds. The prison has a large domed building, known as the "Big House" or "Big Top." There are four cell houses that radiate from the Big Top and one additional "spoke," which contains offices and the school. Leavenworth had the first school to be built inside a prison.

Although progressive in some areas such as education, the prison practiced several 19th-century inmate-control techniques such as the use of lockstep marching and hard labor. Classification of inmates was not a concern in the early prison, and the inmates had few privileges or comforts. The focus of the prison staff was to control the inmates and keep them from escaping the institution.

The Leavenworth penitentiary took the lead in the use of fingerprints to identify inmates. One story suggests that this interest in fingerprinting was inspired by a problem with inmates' identification, which took place in Leavenworth. In 1903, the prison administration discovered that they had two men in the prison with the same name, Will West. When the second man entered the prison, he denied a prior incarceration, although the person checking him in insisted he had already served

The United States Penitentiary, Leavenworth (USP Leavenworth), located in northeast Kansas, houses medium-security male offenders. (Harperdrewart/Dreamstime.com)

time in Leavenworth. The records clerk found a file for Will West, and the man matched the photo and other measurements. It was then discovered that two William Wests were in the prison at that time. At approximately the same time, the prison was learning of the fingerprint system of identification and made a request to the U.S. attorney general to be given permission to install the fingerprint system at the Leavenworth penitentiary. This request was approved, and Leavenworth led the nation in the collection of inmate fingerprints. In 1905, the two William Wests were fingerprinted and found to have distinctly different prints.

Leavenworth was the site of several executions in the early 1930s. One of the men hanged was Carl Panzram. Panzram was described as a murderer, rapist, burglar, and sodomist. He never apologized for his crimes and seemed to take pride in what he had done, describing himself as "rage personified." Panzram was serving a 25-year sentence at Leavenworth when he killed a laundry foreman with a metal bar. Although not all crimes were verified, Panzram claimed to have killed 21 men and to have raped 1,000 young men and boys. He was executed for the murder he committed in the prison.

Many famous criminals have been housed in the Leavenworth penitentiary. The offenders have included Robert Stroud, Machine Gun Kelly, James Earl Ray, Leonard Peltier, and in more recent years, former National Football League star Michael Vick.

Robert Stroud, the Birdman of Alcatraz, had a long prison history and was known for violence. He had originally been sentenced to prison for a murder he committed in Alaska. He was first housed at McNeil Island but was transferred to Leavenworth after assaulting an orderly. While at Leavenworth, Stroud attacked and killed an officer. He was sentenced to death, but due to his mother's lobbying and her appeals to Edith Wilson, then-wife of President Woodrow Wilson, Stroud's sentence was changed to life in isolation. While in Leavenworth, Stroud accumulated almost 300 birds and wrote two books on bird care. Stroud was transferred to Alcatraz in 1942, after already serving 33 years in prison. His work on birds has been of value to the field of ornithology. Two of his books, focusing on the diseases of birds, are particularly well known.

George Kelly, better known as Machine Gun Kelly, was a Prohibition era gangster, who was involved in armed robbery and bootlegging. He was sentenced to life in prison for the 1933 kidnapping of Texas oilman Charles R. Ruschel. Kelly was in Leavenworth from 1933 to 1934, and from 1951 until he died in 1954.

A number of men, involved in well-publicized, political crimes, have also been sent to Leavenworth. James Earl Ray was held in Leavenworth from 1955 to 1958, after being convicted of a forgery charge. He later assassinated Dr. Martin Luther King Jr. in 1968. Leonard Peltier, a Native American activist, and leader of the American Indian Movement, served time in Leavenworth for murder. Peltier was convicted in 1977 for the murder of two FBI agents during the shootout at Pine Ridge Indian Reservation in 1975.

Several well-known sports figures have been held in Leavenworth for a variety of crimes. Randy Lanier was a racecar driver who won the 1986 Indy 500 Rookie of the Year award. He was convicted on a number of drug offenses and for running a criminal enterprise. In 1988, he was sentenced to life in prison. Michael Vick, an NFL quarterback, was convicted of running a dog-fighting ring. He spent 23 months in custody in Leavenworth before being released in 2009.

Pete Earley wrote the book *The Hot House*, which describes Thomas Silverstein's incarceration. Silverstein was a leader of the Aryan Brotherhood and was convicted of four murders while in prison (one murder was later overturned). He is serving three life sentences plus 45 years, which means he will never complete the sentence. After the 1983 killing of a federal prison guard, he was placed on a "no human contact" status that lasted for decades. Silverstein spent 18 years in Leavenworth but was moved to another maximum security prison in 2005 when Leavenworth was changed to a medium security prison. The book of his time in prison is an interesting history of living in long-term solitary confinement in federal prisons.

The U.S. Penitentiary, Leavenworth, remains a classic example of a traditional prison designed to control inmate behavior and present a foreboding image. The prison continues to have a reputation of being harsh, and officers have often been accused of abusing inmates. Prison gangs are reported to be active and cause numerous acts of violence on other inmates. Female officers have also been accused and convicted of having sexual relations with inmates. These problems are not unique to Leavenworth, but they are unfortunately a common occurrence in many U.S. prisons.

Paige Heather Gordier

See also: Alcatraz; Attica; Maximum Security; Prison Reform, Intended and Unintended Consequences of; Violence in Prison

Further Reading

Earley, P. (2011). *The hot house: Life inside Leavenworth prison.* New York: Bantam.

Johnston, J. H., & E. F. Reilly. (2005). *Leavenworth penitentiary: A history of America's oldest federal prison.* J. H. Johnston.

LaMaster, K. M. (2008). *U.S. Penitentiary Leavenworth.* Charleston, SC: Arcadia.

U.S. Bureau of Prisons. (2014). *USP Leavenworth inmate handbook.* Retrieved from https://www.bop.gov/locations/institutions/lvn/LVN_aohandbook.pdf

Leaving Prison

Because prison is often seen by the convicted as a traumatic experience, being released to return home is typically viewed as a new beginning. Coming home—an individual's release from prison, presumably into the community from which the person was taken—is the process of reentering familial and other intimate relationships and reacclimating to the norms of the larger society. People stagnate in prison, being without the resources to keep up with technological advances or changes in culture and typical day-to-day activities. In their intimate relations, family members continue their patterns and routines that are noninclusive of the missing family member. In the larger societal context, barriers are put in place on housing, ability to find meaningful work, educational opportunities, and participatory practice in the electoral process. The reentry process is further hindered by the individual's need to counter the prisonization process undergone during incarceration.

The authoritarian nature of prison regimes—arguably, necessary to maintain control and safety—develops a unique culture among inmates, acculturation to which is known as prisonization. As a person enters prison, the prisoner is forced to be subordinate to the hierarchy of a paramilitary system where he or she is the lowest member. In this system, the prisoner is expected to follow all correctional staff orders and, even if they are not legal, the required course is to obey (so long as they do not put the prisoner in immediate danger) and then file a complaint afterward. Even intensely invasive events, such as strip and body cavity searches, are carried out at an officer's discretion, without input from the inmate. Communication with family or friends is monitored, and materials sent to the inmate can be denied as contraband at the discretion of a correctional officer. To survive in this environment, inmates develop ways of promoting normalcy and acceptability within their constrained parameters. Over time, these practices change normative behavioral patterns. The longer the sentence and harshness of the facility conditions, the more deeply embedded the pattern of behavior becomes. Still, while helping an individual to cope with prison, adopting a prisonized perspective makes the reentry challenging, creating psychological barriers to more typical outside ways of thought and social interaction.

During the period that individuals are incarcerated, their family develops patterns of daily life without them. Spouses find avenues to support their family without the assistance of the incarcerated spouse. Furthermore, spouses find alternative sources of emotional support. Children develop attachments and expectations of present authority figures that do not include distant, incarcerated parents. Thus, when the incarcerated individual returns to the family, expecting to resume the role he or she left, this causes disruption. Children and their spouse may not accept the change in dynamics. The instability of the returning loved one does not lend itself to trust in the ability of the individual to navigate within the parameters of the new world. Reestablishing respect and a role in the family depends on developing trust, stability, and demonstrating one's worth through positive contributions to the family, as well as having a consistent presence in the family's life.

Policies in various states and the practices of several private organizations create barriers to everything from housing and employment, to social services and participation in the electoral process. Today's technological advancements allow a person's criminal record to be accessed by virtually anyone—though the record may not always be complete and accurate. Barriers to reentry essentially "silence" the voices of those who were incarcerated, and thus results in creating a permanent underclass. Being unable to gain meaningful employment and housing creates the need for alternative strategies to meet basic survival needs like financial resources and housing. Things like putting rental leases in the names of family, or acquiring them under aliases, are illegal but are often resorted to. Ex-convicts find jobs under assumed names or seek cash-based employment. Other—less than legal—means of gaining financial stability are also commonly considered.

Even assuming that the formerly incarcerated individual has tenable employment and housing, the state of mind caused by prisonization will likely hinder a smooth transition. Incarceration is a traumatic event, and many of previously incarcerated individuals leave prison with mental illnesses or suffering from substance addiction. Where people import these conditions into prisons, the correctional environment exacerbates them, and the prisoners reenter society in a worse position than when they left. Prisons have proven to be poor spaces for treating mental illness. When mentally ill prisoners are released (an, admittedly, rarer event than for those considered of sane mind), they are given a limited supply of medications and let go with minimal, or no, supervision. The recidivism rate for these individuals is higher than for the average prisoner. After-incarceration adjustment makes for a difficult transition under the best of circumstances; for those with mental incapacities, this is incredibly hard. Those with substance abuse issues are rarely given the treatment needed within the prison environment, though statistics indicate a correlation between incarceration and drug abuse. Studies have found a considerable number of substance abuse victims began their substance use while incarcerated. The likelihood of success for someone with substance abuse issues is reduced, and returning home can be a veritable death sentence for many substance abusers attempting to resume their use at levels that they had tolerated before but to which their bodies cannot accommodate after months of sobriety or reduced use. Many who suffer from substance abuse have victimized their family and friends. Trust having been broken, many find this avenue of support is no longer available. These individuals often find their reentry process beginning in high drug areas, residing in homeless shelters or welfare hotels.

Financial barriers are a factor when coming home. Incarcerated individuals earn little, if any, money during their incarceration. Some states do not compensate their prisoners for labor performed while incarcerated, and others provide negligible compensation. Few states provide a wage that would allow a prisoner to develop the savings to have the financial resources to smoothly reenter society. Most prisoners report little financial resources upon release. One study showed that prisoners are released with an average of between $3 and $2,340, with a median of approximately $40. Financial instability factors into problems such as housing, transportation, and the ability to seek employment. With limited resources available and less knowledge on how to access them, these individuals struggle to gain a foothold in their new environment.

Individual accounts express, and studies support, that while the degree of disorientation experienced when being released from prison vary, most will undergo a period of discomfort with the change in setting. The process of reentry has stages that are dependent on the stability of key factors. The factors include but are not limited to housing, employment, and feelings of community inclusiveness. Studies demonstrate that the length of sentence and degree of custody status are contributing factors to this phenomenon. Nevertheless, over time, ex-convicts tend to adapt, to varying degrees, examples of the human ability to cope with all manner of conditions. Like their adaptation to prison, settling into life on the outside is a process.

Ronald W. Pierce and Kwan-Lamar Blount-Hill

See also: Inmate Subculture; Mental Health Issues and Jails; Mentally Ill Prisoners; Prisoner Reentry/Family Integration; Prisonization; Recidivism

Further Reading

Chung, J. (2017). *Felony disenfranchisement: A primer.* Washington DC: Sentencing Project.

Halkovic, A., Fine, M., Bae, J., Campbell, L., Evans, D., Gary, C., Greene, A., Ramirez, M., Riggs, R., Taylor, M., Tebout, R., & Tejawi, A. (2013). *Higher education and reentry: The gifts they bring.* New York: Prison Reentry Institute, John Jay College of Criminal Justice, City University of New York.

Travis, J., Solomon, A. L., & Waul, M. (2001). *From prison to home: The dimensions and consequences of prison reentry.* Washington, DC: Urban Institute.

Visher, C., Kachnowski, V., La Vigne, N., & Travis, J. (2004). *Baltimore prisoners' experiences returning home.* Washington, DC: Urban Institute. Retrieved from https://www.opensocietyfoundations.org/sites/default/files/baltimore_prisoners.pdf

Legitimate Penological Interests

The U.S. Supreme Court established the concept of "legitimate penological interests" in a 1987 case related to inmates' constitutional rights. *Turner v. Safley* (482 U.S. 78, 1987) clearly established a new standard for determination of whether prison actions violated inmates' constitutional rights. The development of the "legitimate penological interests" standard dispelled confusion about the proper standards lower courts should use when balancing inmates' rights and the prison authority. This decision gave prison administrators more power and authority to manage the prisons. It was easier to establish the requirements of a legitimate penological interest than some of the earlier standards. This conservative decision limited the constitutional rights of the inmates and expanded the authority of the prisons. The *Turner v. Safley* decision has been used throughout the years and continues to be viewed as the proper test in recent cases.

Inmate rights have often been the subject of much debate in the United States. Although many believe that a person who is incarcerated should have few if any

Legitimate Penological Interests

legal rights, others have argued that constitutional rights should still apply to this unique population. The U.S. Supreme Court has often been called upon to set the standards that prison administrators must use when determining how to apply constitutional protections to the inmate population and at the same time maintain control of the prisons.

Prior to the 1960s, the prisons were operated under the concept of the hands-off doctrine. This doctrine was based on the belief that prisons were under the control of the wardens, and the inmates had little legal recourse to complain or attempt to bring attention to their conditions of confinement. The courts viewed inmates as "slaves of the state" and therefore did not interfere with the rights of incarcerated inmates.

In the 1960s and 1970s, the extremely poor conditions in several southern states brought attention to the plight of the inmates. Inmates were being denied medical care, were not allowed to practice their religions, and were often beaten as part of prison discipline. Constitutional rights were then applied to inmates, and the courts were active in ending abuse and hardships, which had been commonplace in prisons across the country.

As the courts became more involved, different standards were applied to determine if policies and procedures used in the prisons violated inmate rights. "Compelling state interest," "least restrictive means," and "rational relationship" were all standards used by the courts to determine if inmates' rights were being violated by prison regulations. Each court case seemed to bring a new definition of what standard of treatment was constitutional. As each term could be interpreted differently, by the judges involved, a clearer standard was needed.

The *Turner v. Safley* case involved the Missouri Division of Corrections and two regulations that related to First Amendment rights. The first regulation permitted inmates to marry only if they had permission of the superintendent of the prison. This permission was only granted if there were compelling reasons to allow the marriage (the only reason that was accepted was the pregnancy or birth of an illegitimate child). The second regulation related to mail privileges. Prison policy did not allow mail to be sent from one inmate to another, unless the inmates were related, or the correspondence related to legal matters.

The case went to the U.S. Supreme Court, which issued a decision on June 1, 1987. The court unanimously struck down the restrictions on inmate marriages but upheld the inmate-to-inmate correspondence regulations. In the decision, the court set a standard for review for prisoner constitutional claims. "When prison regulation impinges on inmates' constitutional rights, the regulation is valid if it is reasonably related to legitimate penological interests."

In the court decision written by Justice Sandra Day O'Connor, several factors were established to determine if a prison regulation met this standard:

1. Whether there is a valid, rational connection between the prison regulation and the legitimate government interest used by the prison to justify the regulation. The objective of the prison must be legitimate and neutral.

2. The presence of another means of exercising the right that is available to the inmates.

372   **Legitimate Penological Interests**

3. Whether accommodating the inmates' constitutional rights will infringe on the rights of the guards or other inmates. Also, the use of prison resources needed to be considered in the accommodation given to the inmates.
4. The presence of an easy and lower cost alternative to the inmates' rights.

The court did not see how allowing inmates to marry would infringe on any penological interests. This regulation was not related to the safety of the institution and limited the rights of those people who were not incarcerated, if they wanted to marry an inmate. However, the sending of mail between inmates was viewed as a security problem, as information could be transmitted between prisons, which could relate to escapes, uprisings, and other problem behaviors. Communication between gang members and other groups is a legitimate threat to prison safety and control.

Although the original court case focused primarily on First Amendment rights, inmates are now provided with many more constitutional rights. The federal courts will take action, to remedy violations of those rights, which are retained by prisoners. Prison regulations may infringe on prisoners' constitutional rights, only if they are related to legitimate penological interests.

Penological interests are those held by the prison administrations, which are necessary for operating the prison. Legitimate penological interests include "the preservation of internal order and discipline, the maintenance of institutional security against escape or unauthorized entry, and the rehabilitation of the prisoners" (*Procunier v. Martinez,* 416 U.S. 396, 1974). Therefore, the prison administrators have the legal right to impose regulations that help them maintain safety and security of the prisons.

In an effort to maintain safety and security, prison officials may search inmates' cells and bodies for weapons and contraband. Mail restrictions are often very strict, and visitation can be limited or stopped if there are actual risks to the prison personnel or other inmates. In many prisons, inmates are allowed very limited phone usage, and the people they can communicate with, often, must be approved, by the prison administration. All these regulations help prevent threats to prison security.

In the case of *Beard v. Banks* (548 U.S. 521, 2006), the court applied the legitimate penological interest standard to the issue of a prison denying newspapers, magazines, and photographs to a group of inmates. The inmates were a very dangerous group of men, housed in solitary confinement. The prison argued that the material was being withheld, in an effort to provide an incentive for the inmates to behave better and get out of solitary confinement. The court ruled that this action on the part of the prison was legitimate, and the regulation was not a violation of the inmates' rights.

Although it has often taken multiple court cases to define inmates' rights, there are many constitutional rights that are provided to them. Inmates have the constitutional right to access the courts, and prison regulations cannot restrict that right. Inmates must be provided with access to legal documents and assistance in the preparation of legal petitions.

Inmates have maintained their First Amendment rights of free speech, religion, and association, limited though by some legitimate penological interests (e.g., inmate-to-inmate mail). Inmates are allowed to send and receive mail, with restrictions that prevent harmful items or illegal material from entering the prisons. Mail can be screened and scanned for security reasons. Inmates are free to practice their religion if the rituals do not cause security risks or legitimately disrupt the operation of the prison.

Fourth Amendment rights related to a reasonable expectation of privacy have been very limited in the prisons as there are obvious legitimate penological interests that require the searching of cells and property in the institutions. The court has provided some protections against unreasonable strip searches and body cavity searches.

The use of the legitimate penological interest standard has not been limited to prisons; jail regulations have also been held to this standard. In the case of *Florence v. Board of Chosen Freeholders of County of Burlington et al.* (566 U.S.__, 2012), the Supreme Court ruled that the use of a strip search on a person arrested for a nonviolent offense was allowed. The court ruled that jails had the right to enforce rules that helped them maintain the security of the facility. Even though some arrestees are unlikely to have concealed weapons or contraband, it is for the safety of the jail personnel and other inmates, that incoming arrestees are strip searched.

Paige Heather Gordier

See also: Access to the Courts; Constitution as a Source for Prisoners' Rights, The; Prisoner Handbooks

Further Reading

Eaglin, J., Cordisco, M., Wheeler, R., & McKenna, J. (1997). *Resource guide for managing civil rights litigation.* Collingwood, PA: Diane.

McGuinn, S. C. (2014). *Prison management, prison workers, and prison theory: Alienation and power.* Lanham, MD: Lexington Books.

Palmer, J. W. (2014). *Constitutional rights of prisoners.* New York: Taylor and Francis.

Sigler, R. T., & Shook, C. L. (1995). The federal judiciary and corrections: Breaking the "hands-off" doctrine. *Criminal Justice Policy Review, 7*(3–4), 245–254.

Zick, T. (1991). *Prisoner rights.* Faculty Publications, Paper 1151. William and Mary Law School Scholarship Repository.

Lockups

A lockup is a facility where criminal suspects are initially confined following their arrest until their initial court appearance when formal criminal charges are filed and bail is set. A lockup can also house arrestees during their transfer from jail to a pretrial hearing or criminal trial.

Because they have been infrequently studied, lockups are in the "netherworld" of the criminal justice system. Even the precise number of lockups is unknown, with estimates ranging from 13,500 to 16,000. Lockups are usually operated by local police departments and less commonly by the courts. It has been estimated that 10 million admissions to lockups occur yearly, with some arrestees being admitted several times. The length of confinement in a lockup is typically just under 22 hours or, in other words, the median time-lapse between arrest and the arrestee's initial appearance in court. In some jurisdictions that time-lapse is up to 72 hours.

Inhospitable-to-inhumane conditions of confinement are a reoccurring theme in the history of lockups. Notably, a 1993 report by the Visiting Committee of the Correctional Association of New York was highly critical of New York City's main lockups, where arrestees could expect to be "jammed for many hours, sometimes for more than a day, in open cells with one toilet, which may be stopped up, one sink, which may not operate, for everyone to use" (p. 3). Lockups in New York City and around the nation have until recently operated free of standards addressing conditions of confinement such as hygiene, health care, and safety.

Since the demise of the hands-off doctrine in the 1960s, federal courts have entertained civil rights lawsuits alleging the operation of lockups violate constitutional guarantees. To prevail, lockup detainees must usually show that they were deprived of at least one basic human need and that the officers responsible for their care exhibited deliberate indifference to their welfare. Such a showing is challenging largely because judges hearing civil rights lawsuits brought by detainees have deferred in varying degrees to explanations offered by lockup administrators.

To reduce the negative consequences of lockups the National Conference of State Legislatures (2013) as well as the Vera Institute of Justice (2015) recommend increased use of citations in lieu of transportation to lockups for nonviolent offenses, including certain drug offenses. A complementary strategy advocated by Hounmenou (2012) calls for the monitoring of lockups by nongovernmental, community-based organizations.

James E. Robertson

See also: Jailhouse Lawyers; Jails Compared to Prisons

Further Reading

Garcia, V. (2005). Lockups. In M. Bosworth (Ed.), *Encyclopedia of prisons and correctional facilities* (pp. 57–59). Thousand Oaks, CA: Sage.

Hounmenou, C. (2010). *Standards for monitoring human rights of people in police lockups.* Chicago: Jane Addams Center for Social Policy and Research. Retrieved from https://socialwork.uic.edu/wp-content/uploads/bsk-pdfmanager/Standardsfor MonitoringHumanRightsforPeople_2_127.pdf

Hounmenou, C. (2012). Monitoring human rights of persons in police lockups: Potential role of community-based organizations. *Journal of Community Practice, 20,* 274–292.

Leigh K., & Tait, S. (2008). *Protecting human rights for people in police custody.* Retrieved from http://www.ibac.vic.gov.au/docs/default-source/reports/opi-report/protecting -human-rights-ahrpc2008-paper—dec-2008.pdf?sfvrsn=6.pdf?sfvrsn=2

National Conference of State Legislatures. (2013). *Citation in lieu of arrests.* Retrieved from http://www.ncsl.org/research/civil-and-criminal-justice/citation-in-lieu-of-arrest .aspx

Robertson, J. E. (2017). Conditions of confinement in lockups. *Correctional Law Reporter, 29*(3), 41–44.

Vera Institute of Justice. (2015). *Incarceration's front door: The misuse of jails in America*. Retrieved from http://www.safetyandjusticechallenge.org/wp-content/uploads/2015/01/incarcerations-front-door-report.pdf

Visiting Committee of the Correctional Association of New York. (1993). *Crisis in the court pens: A report of the Visiting Committee of the Correctional Association of New York*. Retrieved from http://www.ncjrs.gov/pdffiles1/Photocopy/146095NCJRS.pdf

Maconochie, Alexander (1787–1860)

Alexander Maconochie was an academic, a British naval officer, and a penal reformer who is best remembered for a mark system that he championed and to some degree implemented. Specifically, Maconochie is credited with the creation of a progressively staged process by which an offender transitioned between captivity and freedom that was contingent on reformation and work.

Although he had written previously on geography, commerce, and punishment, Maconochie's foray into penal reform started in 1836 during a time in which Maconochie was assigned to be the private secretary to Lieutenant Governor Sir John Franklin in Tasmania. Under Sir Franklin, he wrote *A Report on the State of Prison Discipline in Van Diemen's Land*. This paper was not only a critique of the current transportation practices but also put forth several reformatory recommendations that continually reemerged as themes in Maconochie's career. The Molesworth committee on transportation (1837–1838) in its final evaluation of that correctional practice, ultimately decided that a new initiative should move forward—one that would allow the person in charge to be more reactive to medical and morale needs of inmates in their charge. In 1840, Alexander Maconochie became commandant superintendent of the Norfolk Island penal settlement to oversee his correctional vision.

Maconochie implemented a progressive system called the "Mark system" that was fundamentally different than a "time" sentence based on years, in that it imposed a punishment based on a predetermined amount of labor. In addition to the labor, the system forced the inmates to purchase any goods and services beyond the basic survival needs of food, water, and shelter. The only form of currency within the institution were Maconochie's marks, which could be earned through behavior and achievements, rewarded for behaviors, taken for misconducts, and used to purchase goods and services or reduce labor requirements. According to Maconochie's vision, inmates could—hypothetically—reduce the amount of time in prison through industrious behavior, compliance, and spartan living. Although historians question the degree to which Maconochie had the authority or power to grant an earlier release, the true contributions of the Mark system were the clear stages differentiating punishment and reform. These stages have been loosely identified as (1) a brief punishment phase, (2) collaborative labor, (3) extended freedom of movement, and ultimately (4) liberty.

The first stage consisted of a brief duration of punishment, which was needed to accentuate society's rebuke of bad behavior and to subdue any obstinate refusals to engage in meaningful reform. Punishment was a mechanism that forced the inmates to contemplate their own actions, and the subsequent remorse prepared the mind and soul for reform. Contrary to some accounts, Maconochie did use corporal punishment, but he found such strategies distasteful and counterproductive to reform.

Maconochie viewed that a person's individual flaws could only be remedied through treatment, training, and mentorship. His writings posited that the failure of the current system in reducing criminal behavior was a result of a correctional system attempting to simultaneously deter and reform while actually achieving neither. To Maconochie, an example of this futility was the early ticket-of-leave program he witnessed firsthand upon arrival in Tasmania.

The ticket-of-leave system allowed a modicum of freedom to convicts but imposed severe housing restrictions, a night curfew, and commerce restrictions that subjected the offender to intrusive surveillance at the whim of local law enforcement who operated with great autonomy. Ultimately, Maconochie viewed the whole process as an overly coercive disciplinary program that used humiliating and often debilitating punishments that did little but to inspire fear and harbor resentment. He saw no opportunity for moral growth or the ability of the owner of a ticket to become progressively more comfortable in the exercise of restraint that is needed in a free society.

The second stage of the Mark system was the fundamental core of the system, where Maconochie advocated that the inmates' fates should be placed in their own hands, allowing the offenders the opportunity to work toward their own reformation. He viewed that any failure to take advantage of this system was an indication that the offender was not yet ready to reintegrate back into society. To this end, hard labor acted as both a preparation for employment outside of the facility and as a cautionary warning to offenders who chose to spend their time in idle contentment. Reform could not be avoided by the individual by merely enduring a length of punishment.

Offenders were allowed to self-select themselves into groups of a half a dozen men who were held accountable for their own actions and that of all within the group. The purpose of the group dynamics was the belief that reformation was a social experience and peers could either be an aid or a hindrance toward that end. As marks for an entire group could be awarded and lost depending on any one individual's actions, this put tremendous pressure for peers to monitor the behavior of members within their own group. Maconochie believed this would, eventually, encourage individuals to think about the collective as well as their own individual needs.

Theoretically, this collective concern could be generalized to thinking about societal needs when an individual was finally released from the institution. When groups were unresponsive to reform and disbanded, individual members were forced to find another group in which to work if they wanted to progress toward increased freedom of services. This process served not only to institutionally punish troublesome inmates but to provide social pressure for any to be as productive as possible. With the accumulation of marks and good behavior came increased attitude, services, and eventually freedom.

Interestingly enough, two aspects of the Mark system may have been outside of Maconochie's purview. Scholars have suggested that he may have taken advantage of the significant autonomy that the remote post afforded him to enact policies before formal approval was given from his supervisor. Specifically, there was question whether he had the capability to unilaterally reduce sentences and whether such newly granted freedom extended to the point that the offenders could leave the island as free men. Secondly, while Maconochie wanted the interchangeability of marks for currency, the approval of such exchange had never been formalized, nor had it been clarified whose coffers that money would be drawn from. It had not been decided prior to the dismissal from his post in 1844.

Despite the scholarly debate to the degree which Maconochie successfully implemented many of the proposed correctional reforms in his career, his ideas laid the intellectual groundwork for later reforms. Among those were Sir Walter Crofton's Irish convict system, the declaration of principles by the American Prison Association in 1870, and the Elmira Reformatory in New York State from 1876.

Richard Lemke

See also: Leaving Prison; Parole, History of

Further Reading

Barry, J. (1958). *Alexander Maconochie of Norfolk Island.* Melbourne: Oxford University Press.

Maconochie, A. (1853). *Penal discipline: Three letters suggested by the interest taken in the recent inquiry in Birmingham and published in the Daily News.* Retrieved from https://ia902709.us.archive.org/25/items/penaldiscipline00macogoog /penaldiscipline00macogoog.pdf

Moore, J. (2011). Alexander Maconochie's mark system. *Prison Service Journal, 198*, 38–46.

Stephan, W. (1976). Alexander Maconochie and the development of parole. *Journal of Criminal Law and Criminology, 67*, 72–88.

Ward, G. (1960). Captain Alexander Maconochie, R.N., K.H., 1787–1860. *Geographic Journal, 126*(4), 459–468.

Male Prisoners' Perceptions of Female Officers

Inmates tend to have perceptions of female correctional officers that differ from those of female correctional officers, and those perceptions differ from those of administrators who handle the organizational operations of the correctional facility. At Curran-Fromhold Correctional Facility, Philadelphia, Pennsylvania's largest correctional facility, about 40 percent of the approximate 500 correctional officers are female. To accurately determine male prisoners' perceptions of female correctional officers, the first step is examining how female correctional officers present themselves and operate.

Female correctional officers operate with the overwhelming mind-set to treat prisoners firmly but fairly and consistently. They view their role as not solely an enforcer of order and structure but also as a social worker, therapist, or caregiver. This is especially significant in smaller facilities if they are assigned to a specialty unit, such as the medical wing. If female correctional officers are consistent and show no fear toward their inmates, the instances where inmates try to antagonize the correctional officers, or "push their buttons," fail to evoke the desired negative reaction.

Female correctional officers experience a variety of responses from their male inmates. They have encountered inmates who view them as inferior based solely on their gender, and, therefore, behave in a defiant and difficult manner, almost for sport. These same inmates have accused some female officers of being too author-itative and controlling, which results in officers maintaining their firm, but fair and consistent, application of the rules. Despite the occasional problematic inmate, female correctional officers reported that male inmates seem to prefer their pres-ence and believe the female officers to be more lenient than their male counter-parts. As a result, male inmates will occasionally try to take advantage of an officer's sympathies. Although the officers are aware that their presence is preferred, they insist on maintaining a professional and distant relationship with inmates. Main-taining that professional demeanor is imperative, but showing human emotions can soften the posture of a hardened offender.

Male inmates express an overwhelming preference for female correctional offi-cers. Despite complaints that female officers may occasionally "pick at them," or nag and refuse to let issues rest, male inmates find female officers more empathetic to their plight. They enjoy the normalcy of being around females as part of their daily interactions, since female guards remind them of their own female family members. Although inmates accept the reality that female officers hold the author-ity in their relationship, their presence is still an unexpected comfort. As a result, inmates become protective of the female officers and even have their favorites. While officers conduct their daily duties, it may be common for inmates to make officers' jobs easier by getting out of their way or exhibiting small acts of chivalry accompanied by "go ahead, ma'am."

Since much of prison language includes profanity, male inmates are comfort-able with female correctional officers cursing at them to gain compliance. They do not feel that profanity increases tension or aggravation; in fact, inmates prefer loud cursing over the use of pepper spray to end a conflict. Another reason male inmates prefer female officers is due to their inclination to listen and counsel. Female offi-cers are willing to give inmates advice, and "tell them like it is," using their level headedness to apply tough love.

Although not as frequent, male inmates described an overly tough female offi-cer. This officer was delineated as unnecessarily strict and rule binding, more apt to write up infractions, and incite aggravation and annoyance among the popula-tion. However, even with the overly strict female officers, the male inmates are still less inclined to physically assault a female correctional officer. The aversion to striking a female holds true, even in prison. So long as the correctional officer has established herself as being level headed, she is less likely to be met with name calling and defiance.

Prison administrators have observed their female officers taking a maternal inter-est in the inmates under their watch. Officers relate to offenders in the role as a mother, aunt, or sister and therefore tend to repeat verbal commands more fre-quently, as opposed to escalating toward physical confrontation to ensure compli-ance. The result is the male inmate treating the female correctional officer with more reverence and less likely to physically challenge her. What prison officials find as a benefit within the facility is the ability for female officers to deescalate altercations with their presence. Not every infraction requires a hands-on resolution, and often the female officers are able to calm tense situations upon their arrival. Even an inmate behaving in a loud and obnoxious manner may settle down and cease on his own accord in the presence of a female officer.

Prison officials see less of an ego, from both officer and inmate, when the two sexes are intermingled. However, a concern with females overseeing males is the potential for undue familiarity within the facility. Male inmates try to flirt and woo officers, overstepping the boundaries, no matter how slight, to request preferential treatment. The request may come in the form of free goods, but requiring officers to act in a firm, fair, and consistent manner negates this concern. However, some inmates, as a way of harassment, masturbate in the presence of female officers, even those who are very professional in their interactions with offenders.

Male inmates express a strong preference for female correctional officers. Male inmates behave better in the presence of females, making a safer environment for all. Whether due to the maternal instinct of the officers, or the calming presence of a female, or the respect shown to a level-headed authority figure, males are responding in a positive way. Inmates appreciate the time female officers are willing to give to them, especially if the guards have proven themselves as reasonable. Not only are these women working in defense of law and order, but they are helping to guide and counsel for a more positive outcome.

Beth J. Sanborn

See also: Correctional Officer Subculture; Correctional Officers, Typology of; Inappropriate Correctional Employee–Inmate Relationships; Inmate Subculture; Masturbation in Prison; Personnel

Further Reading

Cheeseman, K., & Worley R. (2006). Women on the wing. *Southwest Journal of Criminal Justice, 3*(2), 86–106.

Farkas, M., & Rand, K. (1997). Female correctional officers and prisoner privacy. *Marquette Law Review, 80*, 995–1030.

Juirk, N. (1985). An officer and a lady: Organizational barriers to women working as correctional officers in men's prisons. *Society for the Study of Social Problems, 32*(4), 375–388.

Murphy, D. S., Terry, C. M., Newbold, G., & Richards, S. C. (2008). A convict criminology perspective on women guarding men. *Justice Policy Journal, 4*(2), 1–36

Worley, R. M., & Worley, V. B. (2013). Inmate public autoerotism uncovered: Exploring the dynamics of masturbatory behavior within correctional facilities. *Deviant Behavior, 34*(1), 11–24.

Masturbation in Prison

Most inmates within the United States lack legitimate opportunities for sexual gratification by virtue of their incarceration. Not surprisingly, these actors often seek relief by way of alternative outlets, and masturbation behind the prison walls is often seen as a viable solution to this dilemma. In one of the earliest scholarly examinations of inmate autoerotism, Wayne S. Wooden and Jay Parker (1982) collected questionnaires from 200 male inmates in a California prison. The researchers found that every offender in the sample admitted to masturbating during his incarceration, with 14 percent masturbating daily, 46 percent masturbating three to five instances per week, 30 percent masturbating one to two times weekly, 5.5 percent masturbating one to three times per month, and 4 percent reported masturbating less than once a month. In a related study, Christopher Hensley, Richard Tewksbury, and Jeremy Wright (2001) found that 99.3 percent of a sample of 142 inmates admitted to masturbating while incarcerated. In the above study, it was discovered that educated inmates were more likely to be frequent masturbators than less educated inmates.

Although masturbation can be a healthy form of sexual release for offenders who are confined to prisons and jails, researchers have recently made a distinction between "public" and "private" acts of inmate autoerotism. Acts of private inmate autoerotism tend to go unnoticed by correctional officials, and therefore cause few problems for other inmates or staff members. Public acts of autoerotism, however, occur whenever an inmate intentionally exposes himself to another person. In the hypermasculine environment of male prisons, it is likely that female correctional officers could find themselves to be victims of "inmate public autoerotism," an aggressive form of behavior where prisoners expose themselves to female staff and violently masturbate in their presence. In a study by Robert M. Worley and Vidisha Barua Worley (2013), the lead author interviewed 15 inmates who admitted to masturbating in the presence of female prison staff. Some inmate-masturbators justified their behavior as a way to seek revenge on a female officer who they believed had wronged them.

In a self-report study, administered across four male prisons in Texas to 367 inmates, Kelly Cheeseman Dial and Robert M. Worley (2008) found that inmate boundary violators who successfully established inappropriate relationships with correctional employees were statistically more likely than other prisoners to masturbate in the presence of female staff. Given the above finding, it is plausible that some inmates use masturbation as a strategy to "test" a female employee to ascertain whether or not she might be interested in engaging in a sexual relationship. Although some inmates may appear to be outraged by this behavior, it is likely that many offenders revel in hearing tales of inmate public autoerotism and are specifically curious as to which female employees permit this type of behavior.

Even though the layperson might believe that inmate-on-officer masturbation is exceedingly rare or uncommon, research has confirmed that this behavior occurs frequently and has the potential to create a hostile work environment. Given this, it is essential that male correctional employees take the lead in condemning acts of inmate public autoerotism, as inmates might look to these individuals for subtle cues as to what type of behaviors will be tolerated, regardless of the official rules. Female correctional officers must also do their part and promptly write a disciplinary case for any inmate who uses masturbation as a weapon to antagonize his captors. It is especially important for this behavior to be reported, for if it goes unchecked, the inmate may perceive (incorrectly) that the employee-victim is amenable to engaging in boundary violations, or even worse, having an inappropriate relationship with an offender.

Robert M. Worley

See also: Economics of Crossing Over, The; Inappropriate Correctional Employee–Inmate Relationships

Further Reading

Beckford v. Department of Corrections. 605 F.3d 951 (2010).

Dial, K. C., & Worley, R. M. (2008). Crossing the line: A quantitative analysis of inmate boundary violators in a southern prison system. *American Journal of Criminal Justice, 33,* 69–84.

Hensley, C., Tewksbury, R., & Wright, J. (2001). Exploring the dynamics of masturbation and consensual same-sex activity within a male maximum security prison. *Journal of Men's Studies, 10,* 59–71.

Trammell, R., Raby, J., Anderson, A., Hampton, S., & Stickney, T. (2014). Maintaining order and following the rules: Gender differences in punishing inmate misconduct. *Deviant Behavior, 34,* 805–821.

Trammell, R., & Rundle, M. (2015). The inmate as the nonperson: Examining staff conflict from the inmate's perspective. *Prison Journal, 95,* 472–492.

Wooden, W. S., & Parker, J. (1982). *Men behind bars: Sexual exploitation in prisons.* Cambridge, MA: Da Capo Press.

Worley, R. M., & Cheeseman, K. A. (2006). Guards as embezzlers: The consequences of non-shareable problems in prison settings. *Deviant Behavior, 27,* 203–222.

Worley, R. M. & Worley, V. B. (2013). Inmate public autoerotism uncovered: Exploring the dynamics of masturbatory behavior within correctional facilities. *Deviant Behavior, 34*(1), 11–24.

Worley, R. M., & Worley, V. B. (2016). The economics of crossing over: Examining the link between correctional officer pay and guard-inmate boundary violations. *Deviant Behavior, 37,* 16–29.

Maximum Security

"Maximum security" is a term used in corrections to define those inmates who are held at the highest or most secure custody level. It is also frequently used to describe facilities that hold such inmates. This custody level is also sometimes called close confinement. Another colloquial term for maximum security confinement is "supermax," which is a term generally used to indicate facilities that were built in the last 40 years that were specifically engineered and designed to hold maximum security inmates. Another form of maximum security confinement is often called administrative segregation, or "AdSeg," and is reserved for those offenders who are persistent or violent transgressors of prison rules.

Maximum security cells are nothing new in the United States. According to Matthew Meskell, in 1790 when Pennsylvania passed the first law in the United States establishing a prison system, the law provided for 16 cells to be used for solitary confinement. Those cells were the first attempt by a state to separate more hardened from less hardened prisoners within a facility (Meskell, 1999).

Soon, the idea of taking a few cells and using those cells for maximum security placement expanded to designing an entire facility for maximum security inmates. The best known early example of this was the construction and use of the federal penitentiary on Alcatraz Island in San Francisco Bay. Taking land and buildings that had been used as a fortress and a military jail, the U.S. Department of Justice took over the site in 1933, and the Federal Bureau of Prisons established the federal penitentiary there in 1934.

Colloquially known as "The Rock," from 1934 until its closure in 1963, Alcatraz consistently held more than 200 of the most dangerous, notorious, and escape-prone inmates in the federal system. It almost immediately became associated in the public consciousness with the worst of the worst of American crime. Alcatraz housed such inmates as Al Capone, George "Machine Gun" Kelly, Meyer "Mickey" Cohen, Arthur "Doc" Barker, Alvin "Creepy" Karpis, and Robert "The Birdman" Stroud, some of whom were sent directly to Alcatraz after sentencing. Alcatraz quickly captured the imagination of the public, and even today it attracts 1.5 million visitors per year as a tourist attraction.

Alcatraz also showed the difficulty in maintaining maximum security facilities. First, since it was on an island, everything used by the prison had to be brought in by boat from San Francisco, thereby increasing the costs of operating the institution dramatically. Studies conducted in the years before its closure showed that it cost more than three times as much to house a prisoner at Alcatraz than it did to house the same inmate elsewhere in the federal system.

The other pernicious enemy of the institution was the damp sea air. Salinated wind and rain battered and weakened the concrete structure and rusted the bars. This led to the most famous escape in the history of the prison in 1962. Frank Morris and brothers John and Clarence Anglin cut holes through the concrete at the back of their cells, then escaped into a utility corridor and out onto the roof of the prison. They subsequently climbed down to the bay and paddled out to sea in a raft made from rubber raincoats, leaving behind papier maché dummy heads in their bunks to convince the guards that they were still in their cells. They have never been found and are presumed dead by the Bureau of Prisons, though no remains have ever been found. This embarrassment to the Bureau of Prisons led then Attorney General Robert F. Kennedy to order that the prison be closed in 1963. This necessitated the construction of a new facility to hold the "worst of the worst," and although this facility would not be on an island, it would still have problems of its own.

To replace Alcatraz, the Bureau of Prisons built USP Marion in the southern part of Illinois, 300 miles south of Chicago and 120 miles east of St. Louis near the town of Marion, which has a population of a little over 17,000 and serves as the county seat of Williamson County, Illinois. The site was chosen for both its rural nature and its relative proximity to major cities and the center of the country. The facility was primarily built to house the most troublesome and incorrigible inmates in the federal system, not necessarily those who had committed the most serious crimes. In this sense, Marion can be considered the Federal Bureau of Prisons' first attempt at a "supermax" facility. In other words, if people are convicted of a federal crime, they are sent to a federal prison. If they then cannot follow the rules of the federal prison, they are sent to Marion.

Few inmates today are assigned directly to Marion after sentencing. The exception to this general rule is those inmates that are convicted of espionage, terrorism, or crimes of a political nature. Those inmates are often sent to Marion immediately after their conviction and sentencing.

At Marion, all of the cells are disciplinary isolation cells. No inmates are allowed to go to the dining hall or elsewhere as a group. There is a prison yard, but no inmates have been allowed to go there since the famous Marion lockdown of 1983. On October 22, 1983, two correctional officers at Marion were killed in separate incidents. One of the incidents involved former Aryan Brotherhood leader Thomas Silverstein. Silverstein was sent to Marion after killing an inmate at Leavenworth. While Silverstein was escorted to a shower, he was handed a "shank," or homemade prison knife, by another inmate. He then killed Officer Merle Clutts by stabbing the officer more than 40 times. Silverstein was then placed on a "no human contact" status, a status he has been kept on for more than 30 years, even though he is now 65 years old.

Since that day in 1983, Marion has been on permanent lockdown. The vast majority of inmates are locked in their cells 23 hours a day, and some are kept in their cells 24 hours a day. The majority of inmates never leave the cell block, although some are allowed noncontact family visits or are taken off the block for legal visits or for medical reasons.

After 18 months without a disciplinary write-up, a select few inmates are allowed to work in the UNICOR federal prison industries shop. The shop at Marion produces telecommunication cables for the military. This model of treating the entire facility as an administrative detention facility has been challenged by prison activists and in lawsuits, but has generally been upheld by the courts.

The states have also experimented in building their own stand-alone maximum security, or "supermax," facilities. The trendsetter among state institutions is California's Pelican Bay State Prison. The facility was built in 1989 in the northwest corner of California near the Oregon border. The facility contains the Security Housing Unit (SHU), which has a similar lockdown policy as USP Marion. Prisoners are housed in 8×10 single-person, windowless cells with steel doors containing food ports. The openings in the cell doors look out onto blank concrete walls. All movement is electronically controlled through a control booth that can open and close any of the cell doors. Only one door is opened at a time, and like Marion, there is no group movement of prisoners at any time.

This sterile design has caused problems for the institution. Notably, there have been many lawsuits filed by inmates and advocates alleging that these conditions produce symptoms of mental illness, such as severe depression, hallucinations, extreme anger, anxiety, and increased risk of suicide. These complaints have largely been rejected by the courts as well. However, the inmates at Pelican Bay have responded to these denials by staging several well-publicized hunger strikes. One strike in 2011 was so well publicized that inmates at other California prisons, most notably Folsom and Corcoran, joined in the strike as well. More than 2,000 inmates refused food for several days to protest the conditions in the Secure Housing Unit.

This action led to a policy change by the California Department of Corrections. Previously, inmates who were perceived to be a risk at classification were sent directly to Pelican Bay. After 2015, however, the state agreed to keep only those offenders who had committed crimes inside the institution in permanent isolation in the SHU. The state also agreed to review the files of the inmates who had already been held in solitary confinement for years to see if some of them could be moved to less restrictive housing facilities.

Continued confinement of offenders in maximum security facilities at the state and federal level will be an issue of concern for correctional officials for as long as there are prisons. The process to determine which inmates truly are the "worst of the worst" and how to house them will continue to be a challenge. An even greater challenge will be determining the process by which offenders who are placed in maximum security are allowed to leave for less restrictive prison environments.

John H. Weigel and Henda Y. Hsu

See also: Cost of Prisons; Inmate Classification; Solitary Confinement

Further Reading

Mears, D. (2013). Supermax prisons: The policy and the evidence. *Criminology and Public Policy, 12*(4), 681–719.

Meskell, M. (1999). An American revolution: The history of prisons in the United States from 1777 to 1877. *Stanford Law Review, 51*, 839–865.

Reiter, K. (2014). The Pelican Bay hunger strike: Resistance within the structural constraints of a US supermax prison. *The South Atlantic Quarterly, 113*(3), 579–612.

Richards, S. (2008). USP Marion: The first federal supermax. *The Prison Journal, 6*(22), 6–22.

Van Raphorst, D. (2011). *Alcatraz—the history of an island prison: From the development to an American myth.* Lewiston, NY: Edwin Mellen Press.

Medical Experiments on Inmates

Inmates have been used in scientific, medical, and social experiments throughout history, and contemporary protections of human subjects are based on the abuses of which prisoners were historically subjected. The use of prisoners for medical experiments is most notoriously associated with Nazi Germany. During World War II (1939–1945), thousands of concentration camp prisoners were subjected to unethical and deadly experimentation without their consent. Ultimately, post–World War II, the Nuremberg trials were held in which Nazi doctors and scientists were tried, and most were convicted for murder. The result with regard to studies of humans was the Nuremberg Code, which outlines human subject research requirements, including the necessity of participant consent, a cost-benefit analysis of the research, and codified the "do no harm" adage. The Nuremberg Code, along with the Belmont Report, is meant to prevent the exploitation and abuse of human research subjects. The Declaration of Helsinki was developed by the World Medical Association as a set of ethical principles regarding medical research involving human subjects. In addition, the U.S. Code of Federal Regulations, 45 CFR 46 subpart C, identifies and provides for additional protection of prisoners as they are seen as a vulnerable population. In 1991, the U.S. federal government adopted the Federal Policy for the Protection of Human Research Subjects (i.e., the Common Rule), which limits the use of prisoners in studies to research that poses no more than minimal risk and is related to incarceration or criminal behavior.

Although medical experimentation on inmates occurred under Nazi rule, the United States is not without its own issues in this arena. Researchers in the United States have engaged in medical research using inmates for purposes ranging from medically relevant studies on the transmission and infection of various illnesses and testing of potential treatments to what may be surmised as pure curiosity. In a time when infectious diseases killed many more people than today (e.g., pandemic flu in the early 1900s), some studies heralded the promise of prevention and intervention; however, none truly reported on the treatment of the test subjects before, during, or after the study.

In 2010, the United States under the Barack Obama administration apologized to Guatemala for U.S. federal doctors infecting its prisoners and mental patients with syphilis from 1946 to 1948 to determine the efficacy of penicillin. This event prompted more investigation by media and others regarding the exploits of medical scientists and researchers in using inmates for medical advancement. It also opened the door for a more rigorous bioethical perspective. Although most questionable experimentation took place in the early 20th century, specifically with an increase in health care interests and drug clinical trials taking place in the 1940s and 1950s, issues still existed in the latter part of the 20th century, and the lessons and concerns must be mitigated for current research conducted in prisons. A brief review demonstrates the concern regarding ethical treatment of inmate participants and why they are, today, a vulnerable research population.

In 1942, inmates in Stateville Prison, outside of Chicago, were infected with malaria so that doctors could study the disease and develop a treatment for military personnel fighting in World War II. In the 1950s, inmates in Atlanta were infected with gonorrhea to study transmission and eventually provided antibiotics to treat the disease. The most egregious medical experimentations occurred at Holmesburg Prison in Philadelphia. For more than 20 years, under the direction of Dr. Albert Kligman, inmates were paid to participate in medical studies where they were exposed to various chemicals (e.g., foot powder, shampoo, mind-altering drugs, and dioxin, the main ingredient in Agent Orange) that caused pain and permanent damage. The exploits and consequences of this medical/dermatological research are documented in *Acres of Skin*. The use of inmates, as well as those with mental impairment, was seen as more acceptable, historically speaking, given these individuals were seen as having fewer rights than fully functional, capable, and free persons. Ultimately, in response to Holmesburg, the Bureau of Prisons barred all research conducted by drug companies and outside research agencies within federal prisons.

Although prisoners are still utilized today for research, they are a highly protected subject group due to their vulnerabilities, which includes their ability to make an informed and voluntary decision given the literacy issue and other intellectual disabilities within the prison population. With the limitations provided under the Common Rule, medical research involving prisoners has decreased, although it still does occur, and advocates for and against relaxing human subject research standards have continued to debate the utility and ethics of prisoners in experimentation.

Deborah T. Vegh

388   Mental Health Issues and Jails

See also: Inmates with Intellectual Disabilities; Mental Health Issues and Jails; Mentally Ill Prisoners; Stanford Prison Experiment

Further Reading

Cislo, A. M., & Trestman, R. (2013). Challenges and solutions for conducting research in correctional settings: The US experience. *International Journal of Law and Psychiatry, 36*(3), 304–310.

Hornblum, A. M. (2013). *Acres of skin: Human experiments at Holmesburg Prison.* New York: Routledge.

Johnson, M. E., Brems, C., Mills, M. E., & Eldridge, G. D. (2016). Involving incarcerated individuals in the research process: Perspectives of key stakeholders. *Action Research.* doi:1476750316661397

Mitscherlich, A., & Mielke, F. (1949). *Doctors of infamy: The story of the Nazi medical crimes.* New York: Henry Schuman.

Obasogie, O. K., & Reiter, K. A. (2011). Human subjects research with prisoners: Putting the ethical question in context. *Bioethics, 25*(1), 55–56.

Reiter, K. (2009). Experimentation on prisoners: Persistent dilemmas in rights and regulations. *California Law Review, 97*(2), 501–566.

Valapour, M., Paulson, K. M., & Hilde, A. (2013). Strengthening protections for human subjects: Proposed restrictions on the publication of transplant research involving prisoners. *Liver Transplantation, 19*(4), 362–368.

Mental Health Issues and Jails

Local community jails in the United States have a long and troubled history. Drawing on the British *gaol* model, colonial county governments in the 1800s authorized sheriffs to run a variety of poorly constructed edifices financed by an unpredictable fee system. American jails, similar to their European counterparts, were used to confine all types of offenders and social "miscreants," typically in the same space. Men, women, and children were lodged together in unhealthy and inhumane conditions—a breeding ground for disease, abuse, and corruption. Even as 300 years of reform movements have focused on addressing issues of jail funding, quality of staff and services, overcrowding, prisoner separation, safety, and health, the jail as an institution of incarceration has been largely impervious to improvement. A current report on American jails retains the label of "warehouse" to describe the ongoing "misuse" of "incarceration's front door." And more than ever, today's jails, whether large or small, urban or rural, are serving as asylums for the mentally ill.

Early colonial records support the notion that families and communities did their best to care for "mad" and "crazed" individuals among them. In 1756, Philadelphia completed the building of the Hospital for the Relief of the Sick Poor and the Reception and Cure of Lunatics. Although the descriptions of treatment methods for the mentally disturbed seem barbaric at best, community leaders recognized that "insane" individuals needed special care, especially those who were poor and dependent. Dr. Benjamin Rush, known as the founder of American psychiatry and one of the founding members of today's Pennsylvania Prison Society, initiated more humane and compassionate practices for patients in the Philadelphia Hospital where he began work in 1783. Nonetheless, as colonial populations grew and the American Revolution left many local governments lacking in financial resources, workhouses and jails began to fill with mentally ill who had no other place to go.

In Massachusetts, the Reverend Louis Dwight, a Massachusetts congregation-alist minister and the founder of the Boston Prison Discipline Society in 1825, lob-bied for the removal of the mentally ill from jails. A report issued by a committee of the Massachusetts legislature resulting from Dwight's work recommended that confining the mentally ill in jails be made illegal. Similarly, Dorothea Dix, a teacher and writer, encountered the mentally ill living in deplorable conditions in the East Cambridge, Massachusetts, jail in 1841. Dix then began a research tour of all the jails, almshouses, and houses of corrections in Massachusetts. Her findings were reported to the legislature and created public interest via newspapers and a pub-lished pamphlet. Dix lobbied for the creation of state mental hospitals, going on to play a role in the founding of 32 of them across the country.

That, 175 years later, jails are once again considered the new asylums that pri-marily house the mentally ill in the United States is directly linked to two failed national policy initiatives of the last 50 years—deinstitutionalization and the war on drugs. Social historians have identified three major historical cycles in U.S. mental health care reform. The first cycle introduced by the 19th-century asylum model of Dorothea Dix focused on "moral treatment." Next came the mental health movement and the establishment of the psychopathic hospital in the early 20th century. Deinstitutionalization and the replacement of state psychiatric hos-pitals with community mental health centers were set in motion from the mid-1950s. It is this third cycle that has resulted in transinstitutionalization, placing the men-tally ill back in jails.

Most accounts of the five previous decades during which deinstitutionalization has been unfolding emphasize changes in ideology and medicine, as well as civil rights movements that called attention to the plight of institutionalized mentally ill patients and rallied for their more humane treatment. With the post–World War II introduction of narcoleptic drugs in large mental hospitals, the door was opened to a community care model for treating mental illness. Congress, responding to lob-bying by community mental health care advocates, passed the Mental Health Study Act of 1955, which led to the passage of the Community Mental Health Care Cen-ters Act of 1963.

The initial era of "emptying" state hospitals, 1955 to 1965, resulted in a 15 percent patient population decrease. The real impact was to come between 1965 and 1975 when 60 percent of mental health hospital residents were released. Civil commit-ment law changes and the passage of Medicare, Medicaid, and Supplemental Secu-rity income laws allowed states to transfer the deinstitutionalized mentally ill to community nursing homes. Unfortunately, the era was marked by a lack of plan-ning, little consensus on the meaning of deinstitutionalization for the chronically mentally ill, the failure of community facilities to keep pace with the outflow of patients, and slow-to-develop networks or systems of ancillary services for the men-tally ill and their families upon release. The result has been a failed social experi-ment, with jails becoming the "treatment of last resort." While the effects of deinstitutionalization varied from state to state, the period from 1970 to the present brought other social problems related to deinstitutionalization—homelessness, particularly among returning war veterans, housing shortages, substance abuse, victimization, violence, and, ultimately, criminalization of mental illness, as the mentally ill repopulated jails and prisons.

Similarly, President Richard Nixon's 1971 declaration of the war on drugs has come to represent a more than 40-year history of national and state level legislation aimed at a variety of "illegal" drugs. Jails, designed to accommodate smaller populations and shorter lengths of stay soon began to fill with sentenced and unsentenced offenders. Fueled by drug-oriented law enforcement and mandatory minimum drug sentencing laws, the percentage of those in U.S. jails accused or convicted of a drug offense sharply increased in the 1980s, from 9 percent to 23 percent in 1989. Today, jail populations are again swelling as an "opioid epidemic" is sweeping the nation.

Of critical note are the 72 percent of people in jail with a substance use disorder and a serious mental illness. Of these, female detainees have increasingly populated jails and are more likely to present with victimization histories, trauma, substance use histories, and serious mental illness. A recent survey of experienced jail staff reported far greater numbers of seriously mentally ill inmates in their jails compared to 5–10 years ago, with these populations having higher rates of recidivism and more major behavioral and abuse problems. Notably, the Bureau of Justice Statistics finds suicide the only cause of death occurring at higher rates in local jails than in the U.S. general population.

As the number of individuals with mental illness in U.S. jails has reached a crisis level, with the numbers of seriously mentally ill adults admitted to county jails reaching the 2 million mark, national efforts are emerging as part of an effort to reduce their numbers. The Stepping Up Initiative, funded by the U.S. Bureau of Justice Assistance, is led by the National Association of Counties (NACo), the Council of State Governments Justice Center, and the American Psychiatric Association Foundation (APAF). Their Call to Action encourages county leaders to pass a resolution and work with teams of key jail stakeholders (the sheriff or jail warden, judges, district attorney, treatment providers, state and local policy makers, and people with mental illness and their advocates) to reduce the number of jailed mentally ill. Drawing on innovative and proven practices from across the United States, a participants' tool kit is available that includes webinars, distance-learning exercises and opportunities, and resource and funding identification for developing a six-step action plan. To date, 285 counties in 41 states have passed such initiatives.

To address the ongoing issue of training for jail and law enforcement staff, crisis incident training (CIT) is being adopted across the country to address the serious limitations of criminal justice system staff in dealing with mentally ill inmates and offenders. Leading the effort for 29 years, CIT International hosts an annual national conference that continues to disseminate state-of-the-art training, best practices, and resources, and encourages interagency partnerships at the local level to address the issue.

The call for diversion programs for the mentally ill in jails has led to the creation of more than 300 mental health courts (MHCs) nationwide since the 1990s.

Again, relying on partnerships across criminal justice, mental health, and social service agencies, these courts offer judicially supervised treatment options in lieu of jail incarceration. Although a few studies have found several large urban MHCs highly effective in reduction recidivism, the existing research finds MHCs moderately effective, though a promising way to divert mentally ill offenders from jails.

With more than 3,000 jails in operation in the United States, the solution to turning around the centuries-old practice of placing mentally disordered individuals in local community jails is extremely complex and, as usual, in the case of jails, dependent on ever-shrinking local and state budgets to expand diversion programs and create more treatment opportunities. The best hope for changing the trend is decriminalizing mental illness and creating a system where public health and public safety agents work together to develop a more effective and less costly model for managing the mentally ill in jails and as they reenter their communities.

Rosemary L. Gido

See also: Mentally Ill Prisoners

Further Reading

Aufderheide, D. (2014, April 2). *Mental illness in American jails and prisons: Toward a public safety/public health model.* Retrieved October 1, 2016, from http://healthaffairs.org/blog/2014/01/mental-illness-in-americas-jails-and-prisons-toward-a-public-safety-public-health model/html

Bureau of Justice Statistics. (2010). *Mortality in local jails, 2000–2007.* Washington, DC: Author.

CIT International. Retrieved October 1, 2016, from http://citinterntional.org/html

Cornelius, G. F. (2008). *The American jail: Cornerstone of modern corrections.* Upper Saddle River, NJ: Pearson.

Eldridge, L. D. (1996). "Crazy brained:" Mental illness in colonial America. *Bulletin of the History of Medicine, 70*(3), 361–386.

Gido, R. (2012). Mentally ill women in jails: Asylums for the invisible. In R. Muraskin (Ed.), *It's a crime: Women and justice* (5th ed.). Upper Saddle River, NJ: Pearson.

Gido, R., & Dalley, L. (2009). *Women's mental health issues across the criminal justice system.* Upper Saddle River, NJ: Pearson.

Gollaher, D. L. (1995). *Voice for the mad: The life of Dorothea Dix.* New York: Free Press.

Jails and mental health issues [Special Issue]. (2016). *The Prison Journal, 96*(1), 3–161.

Morrissey, J. P., & Goldman, H. H. (1986, March). Care and treatment of the mentally ill in the United States: Historical developments and reforms. *ANNALS of the American Academy of Political and Social Science, 484*(1), 12–27.

Pfeiffer, M. B. (2007). *Crazy in America: The hidden tragedy of our criminalized mentally ill.* New York: Carroll & Graf.

Public Citizen's Health Research Group and the Treatment Advocacy Center. (2016). *Individuals with serious mental illnesses in county jails: A survey of jail staff's perspectives: A research report.* Washington, DC; Arlington, VA: Author.

Resources toolkit: The Stepping Up Initiative. Retrieved October 2, 2016, from https://stepuptogether.org/toolkit.html

Skidmore, R. A. (1948). Penological pioneering in the Walnut Street jail, 1789–1799. *Journal of Criminal Law and Criminology, 39*(2), 167–180.

The Urban Institute. (2015). *The processing and treatment of mentally ill persons in the criminal justice system: A scan of practice and background analysis.* Washington DC: Author.

Vera Institute of Justice. (2015). *Incarceration's front door: The misuse of jails in America.* New York: Author.

Mentally Ill Prisoners

Dealing with mentally ill inmates is currently one of the most difficult challenges facing criminal justice professionals. The number of mentally ill people sentenced to prison is a direct result of the deinstitutionalization movement of the 1960s, which systematically closed many of the state hospital beds for the mentally ill. This was done, in part, because of reforms in medication and a confidence that many of the previously institutionalized mentally ill patients could live a full and productive life in the community. This closing of hospital beds was supposed to be paired with a significant support structure for communities so that they could provide services to keep these individuals outside of institutions. In some areas of the country, this community support structure was initially available, but as resources faded, these programs were the first to go, and in some areas of the country, the resources and support systems were never implemented.

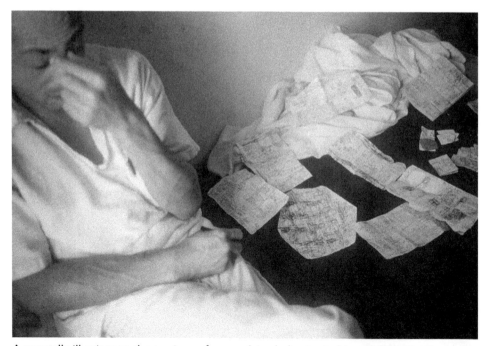

A mentally ill prisoner shows signs of compulsive behavior in his cell, littering the bed with crumpled pieces of paper. Managing mentally ill prisoners often presents an enormous challenge for correctional officers and prison administrators. (Andrew Lichtenstein/Corbis via Getty Images)

The state hospitals released more than 300,000 people between 1955 and 1980. Some of these released patients found support in employment, friends, or family; however, some struggled to figure out how to live on their own. Due to a lack of skills, services, and family support, many of these individuals failed to secure employment and became homeless. Some of them discontinued their medication as needed, or they just could not afford medication.

As the number of unstable mentally ill people increased, this population started having regular contact with law enforcement officers. These officers could find few resources for the many mentally ill people they encountered, and often the local hospitals refused their admission, so the officers began to get creative. It was not unheard of for an officer to buy a mentally ill person a bus ticket to a neighboring jurisdiction. Of course, this was not a long-term solution because officers in neighboring jurisdictions were doing the same thing.

Eventually, the mentally ill individual might do something that justified an arrest, but the arrest was usually just the beginning of another institutionalization. If the individuals were placed in jail for minor crimes, they often quickly began to rack up a variety of more and more serious charges and convictions. This acceleration of offenses was due, in part, to the inability of the individual to understand the rules of the jail or his or her inability to get along with other inmates.

Mentally ill individuals may have been arrested for vandalism, but as a result of their institutionalization, they were charged with additional crimes. Many mentally ill individuals progressed from minor or even borderline criminal actions to serious assaults or threats.

As a natural progression through the system, the mentally ill who accrued additional charges were moved to prisons to serve their time, and these prisons were usually bigger and less equipped to handle this new special population. The prison system was already under stress to manage an ever-increasing and diverse group of inmates. It was at this same time that the sheer number of inmates was on the rise due to the enhanced drug sentencing laws and the increase of gang activity. Prisons were not designed to house mentally ill individuals, and often mentally ill inmates were not able to get treatment for their mental illness or to get psychiatric care for medication compliance and monitoring.

Historians who look at this process often describe the lack of mental health care as a matter of funding, but there was far more to this issue. The corrections systems resisted accepting the treatment of the mentally ill as their problem, so for many years no funding request was even made. The corrections system acted as if they could "will" the problem away or if they did nothing they would get the health care system to take back these people who should be patients and not inmates.

Once it was obvious that the mentally ill inmates were not going to be moved to hospitals, different approaches were taken in prisons across the country. In some systems, medication management became the only mental health treatment offered, but often the budget and staffing of psychiatrists prevented adequate medication therapy. Control, not treatment, of this special population was the primary strategy employed. They were monitored closely, and when their behavior crossed the line they were subjected to controls. These controls would often include full restraints, restraint chairs, placement in a secluded cell, and special meals. The restraints and seclusion also often included use of helmets, diapers, and spit masks.

Once these individuals were placed in these highly controlled environments, policy would usually require a mental health professional to "see" the inmate, but the reality of this policy was that a clinician would "see" the inmate by having a short conversation through a cell door edge or a tray slot. This type of "drive-by" mental health treatment has been the subject of much criticism and litigation. This type of mental health treatment has also led to a very high turnover rate among mental health professionals; after all, this was not the work most mental health professionals went to school to do.

A few systems or facilities were able to develop good mental health treatment approaches such as a therapeutic community or some type of group therapy program. Many jurisdictions also added a new type of prison to their system: the prison for the mentally ill. This was heralded as a great step in the right direction. The ironic part is that many of the mental health prisons were placed in old state hospital buildings (e.g., Kansas). The setting did not change that much, just the name was changed.

The addition of mental health prisons may seem like a great response to the placement of so many mentally ill inmates in the prisons, but the reality of the type of treatment that they received in these special facilities has been the subject of investigation and litigation. In 2015 the Human Rights Watch issued a report: *Callous and Cruel: Use of Force against Inmates with Mental Disabilities in US Jails and Prisons*. This report detailed the use of force that is used against mentally ill inmates as a result of behaviors that stem directly from their mental illness, including detailed case studies. In one such case study, details are presented of a death of an inmate in the Colorado prison for the mentally ill. This inmate died while on a special watch that involved at least one officer who was assigned to constantly watch him. The last six hours of this inmate's life was preserved on video as a part of this special watch status.

The facts that surround this particular case point directly to some of the issues of providing mental health treatment in a prison setting. In this particular case, the staff on duty received additional training for working with the mentally ill—this is not always the case in other facilities. Even with this additional training for the custody staff and the medical training for the clinical staff on duty, the inmate died while under the watchful eyes of employees. Advocates have stated that it is not enough to provide mental health training to custody staff or to increase the number of clinical staff in the facility, but that to properly care for mentally ill prisoners, the culture must also be modified.

Susan Jones

See also: Correctional Counseling; Inmates with Co-Occurring Disorders; Self-Injury in Prison; Suicide in Custody; Treatment in Prisons

Further Reading

American Civil Liberties Union of Colorado. (2013). *Out of sight, out of mind: Colorado's continued warehousing of mentally ill prisoners in solitary confinement.* Denver: American Civil Liberties Union of Colorado.

Curser, D. A., & Diamond, P. M. (2000). Staff opinions of mentally ill offenders in a prison hospital: Implications for training and leadership. *Journal of Correctional Health Care, 7*, 127–147.

Fellner, J. (2006). A corrections quandary: Mental illness and prison rules. *Harvard Civil Rights–Civil Liberties Law Review, 41*(1), 391–412.

Galanek, J. D. (2014, March). Correctional officers and the incarcerated mentally ill: Responses to psychiatric illness in prison. *Medical Anthropology Quarterly, 29*(1), 116–136.

Grassian, S. (1983). Psychopathological effects of solitary confinement. *American Journal of Psychiatry, 140*, 1450–1454.

Human Rights Watch. (2015). *Callous and cruel: Use of force against inmates with mental disabilities in US jails and prison.* New York: Author.

Kitcherner, B. A., Jorm, A. F., & Kelly, C. M. (2009). *Mental health first aid USA.* Annapolis, MD: Maryland Department of Health and Mental Hygiene, Missouri Department of Mental Health and National Council for Community Behavioral Healthcare.

Krelstein, M. S. (2002). The role of mental health in the inmate disciplinary process: A national survey. *The Journal of the American Academy of Psychiatry and the Law, 30*, 488–496.

O'Keefe, M. L. & Schnell, M.J. (2007). Offenders with mental illness in the correctional system. *Mental Health Issues in the Criminal Justice System, 46*, 81–104.

Pustilnik, A. C. (2005). Prisons of the mind: Social value and economic inefficiency in the criminal justice response to mental illness. *The Journal of Criminal Law and Criminology (1973–), 96*(1), 217–266.

Rhodes, L. A. (2004). *Total confinement: Madness and reason in the maximum security prison.* Berkeley: University of California Press.

Slate, R. N., Buffington-Vollum, J. K., & Johnson, W. Wesley. (2013). *The criminalization of mental illness: Crisis and opportunity for the justice system* (2nd ed.). Durham, NC: Carolina Academic Press.

Steinberg, D., Mills, D., & Romano, M. (2015, February 19). *When did prison become acceptable mental healthcare facilities?* (pp. 1–22). SLS Publications; Stanford Law School Three Strikes Project. Retrieved from https://law.stanford.edu/publications/when-did-prisons-become-acceptable-mental-healthcare-facilities-2

Swanson, R. M., Waugh, M., & Lauren Tolle, A. B.-C. (2001). *Colorado state prison administrative segregation for offenders with mental illness: Program review and step-down recommendations.* Aurora, CO: Aurora Research Institute.

Teske, R. H. C., & Williamson, H. E. (1979). Correctional officers' attitudes toward selected treatment programs. *Criminal Justice and Behavior, 6*(1), 59–66.

Torrey, E., Kennard, A., Eslinger, D., Lamb, R., & Pavle, J. (2010). *More mentally ill persons are in jails and prisons than hospitals: A survey of the states.* Paper presented at the National Sheriff's Association.

Methadone Maintenance for Prisoners

Methadone is sold under several brand names, Dolophine being the most common. It is an opioid used to treat pain or a methadone maintenance treatment (MMT) for heroin addiction or to help detoxification in people with opioid dependence. Methadone is usually taken by mouth. It acts on opioid receptors. The drug was developed in Germany in the late 1930s by Gustav Ehrhart and Max Bockmuhl. It was approved for use in the United States in 1947. Research has found that MMT is effective and indeed the best treatment in retaining people in treatment for and in the suppression of heroin use and is approved in the United States. Outpatient MMT must be certified by SAMHSA (Federal Substance Abuse and Mental Health Service Administration) and registered by the DEA (Drug Enforcement Administration). The National Institute of Health concluded that the efficacy and safety of MMT has been undeniably established. MMT remains the most widely used treatment option.

Controversy remains over the use of MMT because it is a narcotic and some people remain in MMT indefinitely. But methadone does not produce the euphoric effect of heroin and the ensuing craving that plagues the addict, making heroin a difficult drug to quit. Heroin has an immediate onset that lasts from 4 to 6 hours and is typically injected but also snorted, several times a day. Methadone has a slow onset and has a 24-hour half-life, resulting in a long-lasting action with no euphoric effect. Methadone also blunts the euphoric effect of heroin, making heroin unattractive for the addict.

Heroin is the most difficult of all drugs to deal with. It is pleasurable and highly addictive, produces a craving like no other, and is extremely difficult to withdraw from because of its physical and psychological effects.

Methadone stops the craving for heroin, the leading cause of relapse, and blocks the painful effects of heroin withdrawal. The widespread use of methadone in the United States began in the late 1960s. It was distributed in liquid form through walk-in clinics. After reaching what is termed a therapeutic dose, heroin addicts are relieved of cravings, the abstinence syndrome is suppressed, and the euphoric effects associated with heroin are blocked. The physical withdrawal effect of methadone is much more difficult than that of heroin. Methadone's effect on the vital organs is more dramatic than heroin. The original recommendation was for MMT to last no longer than three years due to this effect. But in practice, the duration of MMT ranges from a few months to lifetime. The treatment of opiate-dependent persons with methadone will follow one of two routes: (1) MMT is prescribed to individuals who wish to abstain from heroin use but have failed to maintain abstinence for significant periods; and (2) MMT is also suitable for addicted persons who wish to stop using the drug altogether. When used correctly, MMT has been found to be medically safe, nonsedating, and provides a slow recovery from heroin addiction.

It is estimated that about 75 percent of the more than 3 million individuals in prison need some form of drug treatment, but only about 20 percent are receiving any. About 25 percent of inmates have used heroin, and roughly 10 percent have a heroin addiction problem when entering prison. The use of heroin in correctional facilities is very limited.

The use of methadone in prison has stirred debate, but generally the courts have approved its use in prison. Two types of heroin addicts, generally, have tested the courts for MMT in prison: (1) those on MMT before prison and (2) those who need it upon incarceration because of heroin withdrawal. The court, in both types of cases, has used the Eighth Amendment in its argument, finding the denial of methadone in prison cruel and unusual punishment. Some courts, if the prisoner has been enrolled in a methadone program prior to his or her detention, raised a liberty interest, triggering a Fourteenth Amendment due process issue. The federal courts entertained a string of methadone cases in the late 1970s. Generally, courts analyzed the prison medical treatment and found it cruel and unusual punishment. Although the courts originally interpreted the amendment to prohibit torture and other barbaric methods of punishment, modern cases have held that punishments that are incompatible with evolving standards of decency that mark the progress of a maturing society or that involve the unnecessary and wanton infliction of pain are also unconstitutional. The changing notion of the Eighth Amendment in recent decades has settled that the treatment a prisoner receives and the conditions under which he or she is confined are subject to scrutiny. It imposed affirmative duties on prison officials to provide humane conditions. Courts provide a new framework under which to analyze present-day civil rights claims for refusal to provide MMT in prisons.

Abruptly denying MMT causes unnecessary pain and suffering, is not an accepted treatment, and is very likely to cause future harm. The prisoner must prove deliberate indifference on the part of prison officials or medical provider. Somewhere between negligence and intentional conduct is deliberate indifference: an official knows of and disregards an excessive risk to inmate health or safety, an official must be aware of facts from which the inference could be drawn that a substantial risk of harm exists, and an official must also draw the inference.

The courts have held that the patient-prisoner's constant complaints about pain were enough to infer that the prison official knew of a substantial risk of serious harm to the patient. The court has held that the medical staff knowingly took an easier but less efficacious course of treatment and provided grossly inadequate care. The consensus of the scientific community is that MMT is a preferred treatment for heroin/opioid dependence and that if untreated heroin addiction results in withdrawal symptoms, excessive suffering, increased mortality, and a range of illnesses. In addition, ignoring a prior diagnosis and a prescribed course of treatment by a specialist can constitute deliberate indifference.

The story of a substitute for heroin addiction continues—most recently with Suboxone. The expense of the drug at this time makes it unlikely for prison use. The search continues to cure the addiction to the most powerful and pleasurable drug in the world, which was introduced as a cure for morphine addiction.

Craig J. Forsyth and Britain Bailey Forsyth

See also: Drug Use in Prison; Evolving Standards of Decency; Health Care in Prison Populations; Recidivism; Treatment in Prisons

Further Reading

Epstein, E. J. (1974). The Krogh file: The politics of law and order. *The Public Interest*, *39*(Spring), 99–124.

Goode, E. (1996). *Drugs, society and behavior*. Guilford, CT: Dushkin.

Heimer, R., Catania, C., Newman, R. G., Zambrano, J., Brunet, A., & Ortiz, A. M. (2006). Methadone maintenance in prison: Evaluation of a pilot program in Puerto Rico. *Drug & Alcohol Dependence, 83,* 122–129.

Misconduct by Correctional Employees

The need to regulate employee behavior in the workplace has been acknowledged by many professions because the cost associated with workplace misconduct can be high and the consequences can be significant. The most widely researched types of misconduct in correctional environments are those that involve inmate abuse, both physical and sexual, but these types of misconduct are at the extreme end of a continuum of behaviors. Correctional employee misconduct encompasses a wide variety of behaviors that may range from minor infractions to behaviors that are criminal and a threat to public safety.

At the minor end of this continuum are actions where an employee may engage in misconduct that seems unintentional or not very serious. At this end are behaviors such as routinely reporting to work late or helping themselves to office supplies. It could be argued that these actions are common in all types of work settings and may even be accepted or expected practice in some work environments. Some of the employees might even feel entitled to these because of their poor pay. Such feelings of entitlement could be a slippery slope to other inappropriate behaviors. This is especially true if employees see their supervisors or management staff engaging in the same types of acts.

Although these types of minor misconduct violations in correctional settings may seem harmless, they do come with consequences. The first consequence is the cost to the taxpayers who are already shouldering an enormous burden for the corrections system. The second, more troubling issue is that of correctional staff not clearly seeing the difference between right and wrong. It is this issue that has the greatest impact on the corrections environment, especially because corrections employees are supposed to be role models. When the line between doing the right thing or taking advantage of an opportunity becomes fuzzy, the inmates are watching.

This fuzziness has also been explained by some as resulting from working around inmates all day. The idea that the inmates are corrupting staff or encouraging them to bend or extend the rules is not new. Gresham Sykes described this type of reciprocity in his work *The Society of Captives* more than 50 years ago. Sykes described the struggle of correctional employees as they work to maintain power in an environment that depends on working with inmates to get their job completed. The inmates are often needed to assist with specific tasks in housekeeping, maintenance, or the kitchen. They may also be called on to assist officers by helping new inmates adjust to life inside a prison. While the employees navigate this fuzzy boundary, they are also expected to demonstrate appropriate interaction skills and social connections that may help increase an inmate's social adjustment.

At the far end of the continuum of staff misconduct are actions that include boundary violations, such as employees having sex with inmates and/or helping them to escape. The recent high-profile cases involving inmates escaping with the assistance of current or former staff have brought this issue to the forefront for all correctional employees. Many employees struggle trying to understand how this could happen. The simple answer is that these instances are usually the extreme ends of a boundary violation continuum that may have started with minor transgressions.

Misconduct by Correctional Employees   399

Data collected as a result of the Prison Rape Elimination Act (PREA) indicate that the frequency of violations that cross the sexual boundary are far higher than correctional leaders believed. The data indicate that almost one-half of all substantiated incidents of sexual victimization of inmates involve staff.

Researchers have studied other serious criminal misconduct of corrections employees that are directed at the institution, other employees, visitors, and inmates. Corrections employees have committed acts of violence against each of these groups of people, including sexual assault, excessive force, and intrusive search techniques that are assaultive in nature. Although there is no excuse for this type of criminal behavior, the environment may be a contributing factor to these acts. Corrections employees spend a great deal of their waking hours supervising a setting that often includes violence. In addition, corrections officers are given the legitimate power of the state (or other confining authority) to take control of the environment. The exposure to violence combined with this level of power may be the impetus for an employee who no longer sees the difference between right and wrong to take that step toward becoming a perpetrator.

Another key factor of this environment is that people—all people—inside a corrections facility are dehumanized. This dehumanization is a product of the inmate processing and supervision duties, but it is also a part of the process that inmate visitors and even employees may go through. Often dehumanization in corrections is usually only discussed in reference to inmates, but the same types of control tactics can be seen in how the visitors and employees are treated. Inmate visitors are often not valued as human beings, and this type of devaluation easily leads to dehumanization, which may lead to increased opportunity for abuse. Even the corrections employees divide themselves into a hierarchy that has little to do with rank. Terms such as "fish" describe the new employees, "dinosaur" often refers to the older staff, and "split-tail" is a term used to describe female employees. This type of categorization of people allows a dehumanization effect to take over—especially for the employee who may be prone to commit violence in the first place. When an assailant no longer sees the intended targets as human beings, hurting them is much easier.

Command/control strategies and self-regulatory strategies are the two most common approaches to controlling employee actions. The use of self-regulatory strategies is often thought to be more effective because it builds on the employee's values and internal motivation. Bureaucracies, in general, and corrections in particular, often depend on the command/control options. Researchers have studied the issue of rule breaking in the workplace, and they have found that the elements of procedural justice and the effect of a rule violation on the organization or individual influence the decision of an employee to either follow the rules or violate them. Employees may break rules because they feel disengaged, angry, or entitled. Organizational actions to instill a sense of commitment in the correctional employees toward the organization may be a good mechanism to reduce employee misconduct.

Researchers have provided recommendations for correctional leaders that include specific ethics training. Training is often considered the "fix" for many issues in correctional systems, and it is an important component, but training to address issues of ethics and misconduct must be coupled with other organizational support and components. Background checks of employees have been adopted as a policy

400   **Misconduct by Correctional Employees**

in many jurisdictions as a result of the PREA standards, which require background checks to be completed at five-year intervals for current employees and checks for all new employees prior to reporting for duty. Random screenings for employee drug use have been a part of many systems for the last 20 years, but many jurisdictions have also added a system to check for credit status. Although this has been argued by some correctional employees as intrusive and not relevant to their job, the number of jurisdictions that have added this to their processes continues to increase because the connection between money issues and corruption has been well established in many professions. Internal monitoring units, such as Internal Affairs Units (IAUs), are now a customary part of most correctional systems, and they implement many of these monitoring actions. Additionally, some correctional systems have tasked these units with developing an early warning system that mirrors the processes seen in other law enforcement professions.

Although these recommendations may work to "catch" employees who are engaging in a wide range of misconduct, they may also work as a preventative tactic. Employees may alter their behavior if they see that the system has incorporated a variety of approaches to monitor many aspects their behaviors. Internal systems to monitor employee behavior may improve outcomes if they are built on an awareness of the unique characteristics of the corrections environment.

Susan Jones

See also: Correctional Officer Subculture; Correctional Officer Training; Correctional Officers and Discretion; Inmate Subculture; Prison Rape Elimination Act; Sykes, Gresham

Further Reading

Beck, A. J. (2015). Staff sexual misconduct: Implications of PREA for women working in corrections. *Journal of Research and Policy, 16*(1), 8–36.

Calhoun, A. J., & Coleman, H. D. (2002). Female inmates' perspectives on sexual abuse by correctional personnel. *Women & Criminal Justice, 13*(2–3), 101–124.

Hamilton, L. (1995). The boundary seesaw model: Good fences make for good neighbours. In A. Tennant & K. Howells (Eds.), *Using time, not doing time: Practitioner perspectives on personality disorder and risk*. Wiley Online Library.

Haney, C. (2008). A culture of harm: Taming the dynamics of cruelty in supermax prisons. *Criminal Justice and Behavior, 35*(8), 956–984.

Hepburn, J. R., & Knepper, P. E. (1993). Correctional officers as human service workers: The effect on job satisfaction. *Justice Quarterly, 10*(2), 315–335.

Jacobs, J. B., & Retsky, H. G. (1975). Prison guard. *Journal of Contemporary Ethnography, 4*(1), 5–29.

Jensen, J. M., & Patel, P. C. (2011). Predicting counterproductive work behavior from the interaction of personality traits. *Personality and Individual Differences, 51*(4), 466–471.

Jones, S. (2015). Recommendations for correctional leaders to reduce boundary violations: Female correctional employees and male inmates. *Women & Criminal Justice, 25*(5), 1–19.

Morrison, E. W. (2006). Doing the job well: An investigation of pro-social rule breaking. *Journal of Management, 32*(1), 5–28.

Pollock, J. M. (2004). *Prisons and prison life: Costs and consequences*. Los Angeles: Roxbury.

Ross, J. I. (2013). Deconstructing correctional officer deviance: Toward typologies of actions and controls. *Criminal Justice Review, 38*(1), 110–126.

Spinaris, C. G., Denhof, M., & Morton, G. R. (2014). *The corrections profession: Maintaining safety and sanity.* Retrieved from http://nicic.gov/library/027907 and http://nicic.gov/library/027908

Sykes, G. M. (1958). *The society of captives: A study of a maximum security prison.* Princeton, NJ: Princeton University Press.

Vardi, Y., & Wiener, Y. (1996). Misbehavior in organizations: A motivational framework. *Organization Science, 7*(2), 151–165.

Vera Institute of Justice. (2012, February). *The price of prisons: What incarceration costs taxpayers.* New York: Center on Sentencing and Corrections, Vera Institute of Justice. Retrieved from https://www.vera.org/publications/price-of-prisons-what-incarceration-costs-taxpayers

Walker, S., Alpert, G. P., & Kenney, D. J. (2000). Early warning systems for police: Concept, history, and issues. *Police Quarterly, 3*(2), 132–152.

Misconduct by Prisoners

The expansion of the American prison system during the last 50 years has contributed to the increased awareness among scientists of the problem of prison misconduct. The widespread overcrowding across correctional institutions has created numerous challenges, often resulting in a diminished capability to supervise offenders. In addition, the war on drugs has often led to the incarceration of gang members within the same facility, creating opportunities for inside group solidarity, often used to control other inmates and oppose institutional control. From a social control perspective, reducing the incidence of prison misconduct is one of the main goals of prison administrations. Keeping the order within a correctional facility allows for the fulfillment of broader correctional objectives, such as offender rehabilitation. At the individual level, prison misconduct might mirror offenders' inability to follow rules and conform to mainstream social norms, hindering their ability to reintegrate into society upon completion of a prison sentence.

It is understood that prisons are ugly places housing many dangerous individuals. Many inmates might be able to avoid victimization by acting tough, dominating others, or joining violent gangs. However, criminologists have prioritized the analysis of inmates' adaptation to prison using measures that reflect social conformity, so as to anticipate how an inmate would reintegrate into society after a period of confinement. Today, the focus on prison misconduct in a growing body of prison research reflects a widespread concern about the consequences that inmates' lack of adaptation might bring to the criminal justice system and society at large. The contribution of numerous contemporary criminologists has so far allowed for the development of several theories explaining prison misconduct.

IMPORTATION MODEL AND FUNCTIONALIST MODEL

Two dominant theoretical models can be traced across studies on prison misconduct: the importation model and the functionalist model. According to the importation model, inmates' prison experiences are shaped by the personal and background characteristics that they bring with themselves to the correctional facility. Criminologists have focused on the importation model as a way of reconstructing offenders' subcultural values and the influence that those values might have on the inmate's ability to integrate within the prison system.

Although field researchers have insisted for the implementation of the importation model as an expression of the intersectional powers of both inmates' demographics and their personal experiences, many quantitative studies have failed to create statistical models including the intersection of multiple measures. This might suggest that, while the importation model has helped researchers better understand how personal and background characteristics shape an inmate's prison experience, those measures have been mostly studied separately, limiting researchers' ability to fully reconstruct the impact that an inmate's cultural values might have on his or her own prison experiences.

The functionalist model focuses on the inmates' prison experiences as a function of the institution's characteristics. The research on prison adaptation provides criminologists with two separate versions of the functionalist model: the deprivation model and the situational model. The deprivation model—the most commonly employed between the two functionalist models—posits that inmates all respond similarly to the harsh environment of the prison. The idea is that all humans react similarly to the social and physical barriers that they experience during confinement. Conversely, the situational model specifically focuses on the characteristics of each institution and argues that specific features of a correctional facility might affect an inmate's behaviors and ability to adapt. Examples of prison situational characteristics explored in research are overcrowding, hours spent in segregation, number of people in a cell, and exposure to natural light. A more recent application of the functionalist models has allowed for the development of transfer theory. This theory focuses on the impact that inmates' mobility within the U.S. prison system might have on their response to incarceration and their propensity to break rules.

Another traditional theoretical approach to the study of prison misconduct is the management perspective. This approach focuses on the analysis of inmates' misconduct as a reaction to the management style and leadership model employed within the prison system. This approach has proven particularly useful for studies focusing on the macrolevel analysis of prison misconduct, allowing for a comparison across facilities based on their approach to leadership.

Other theoretical perspectives employed in the study of prison misconduct are general strain theory and social control theories. These perspectives were originally developed through the analysis of crime and deviance in general. Considering incarceration as an additional source of strain allows for the opportunity to focus on the continuous effect that strain might have on an individual's life transitions.

Similarly, using social control theories provides us with the opportunity to include elements of inmates' personal characteristics (such as self-control), social ties, and response to correctional control and supervision. All these theoretical approaches have provided us with the opportunity to advance with the analysis of inmates' responses to confinement and their propensity to engage in prison misconduct.

MISCONDUCT AND INDIVIDUAL CHARACTERISTICS

Misconduct is broadly defined in research as an inmate's propensity to break prison rules. There is no consensus in research on how to categorize misconduct. Some studies distinguish between physical and verbal assaultive behaviors. Instead, other studies categorize misconduct based on the severity of the outcome and differentiate between minor and major prison rule violations. It is, however, relevant to the reader that—as research evidence suggests—all types of rule violations share similar correlates.

Existing research indicates that prison misconduct is associated with inmates' characteristics and their past experiences. In addition, prison misconduct is often influenced by features of the institution in which offenders are confined. Institutional characteristics might be either related to the physical and architectural structure of the prison or to the organizational structure and management style of the correctional facility.

Demographic characteristics, such as gender and age, are associated with the incidence of prison rule violations. Younger offenders, especially offenders under the age of 21, are often found responsible for prison rule violations across U.S. facilities. Younger individuals, in general, tend to have less self-control; aggression and anger are not uncommon among young inmates. Youth who are affiliated with gangs or were involved in violent crimes are also more likely to be found guilty of prison rule violations and prison violence.

As for gender, female inmates are less likely to break prison rules or to be found guilty of prison rule violations. Findings from recent empirical studies show that gender differences in patterns of misconduct remain similar even after controlling for a number of risk factors, such as substance abuse, mental health problems, and history of incarceration. Differences between female and male offenders in patterns of misconduct might be also explained by the fact that women in prison are less likely than men to be incarcerated for violent offenses, and violent offenders tend to break prison rules more often than nonviolent offenders. Because women in prison are more likely than men in prison to be parents and to be solely responsible for their children, women might be more likely to comply with prison administrative rules to avoid extended periods of incarceration due to misconduct.

The relationship between race and prison misconduct appears to be less clear than that of gender and misconduct. Some studies show that minorities in prison are more likely to be written up or found guilty of prison rule violations than white Caucasians. Scholars have speculated that the struggle to integrate that many young minorities experience in the outside world might also characterize their carceral experience. However, research has provided us with mixed results in the analysis of the association between race/ethnicity and prison misconduct. Differences across studies might be also associated with the geographic location of the prison itself. It is possible that subcultural values that characterize each region of the United States and the level of racial integration in those areas influence the integration of minorities within the prison system as well. As it is suggested in current studies, this might be especially true for prisons that house inmates from large metropolitan/urban areas of the United States.

Overall, inmates suffering from mental health problems tend to break prison rules more often. Similarly, inmates serving longer sentences are also more likely to engage in prison misconduct, although findings are not always consistent across studies. A few studies consistently found that spatial distance is a relevant factor to take into consideration when analyzing prison misconduct, suggesting that inmates who are housed in facilities farther away from home are, on average, more likely to break prison rules than those confined in facilities located closer to home. This might have something to do with the level of support that offenders receive from family members during incarceration.

It seems intuitive that inmates who are incarcerated in facilities closer to home might receive more visits from family and/or friends. However, the evidence from empirical studies suggests that other factors might contribute to explain the effect of spatial distance on inmates' misconduct. The effect of visitations on prison misconduct is not consistent across studies with some studies showing that the number of visits had no effect on inmates' rule violations. Recent research clarifies that preprison experiences as well as social networks developed prior to confinement all tend to influence the association between spatial distance and prison rule violations. This appears to be especially true for younger inmates.

At the individual level, participation in prison programs tends to reduce one's propensity to break prison rules, but important differences are found across empirical studies. Some studies found that while educational and vocational programs tend to positively influence inmates' behavior and limit their propensity to break prison rules, other studies found that participation in such programs did not reduce prison misconduct. Perhaps, in some cases, inmates who are active within the prison also have more opportunities to move around and interact with other inmates and members of the correctional staff. Such mobility might also increase the opportunity for disagreements and altercations (either verbal or physical). The association between program participation and misconduct might be also explained by the characteristics of the prison itself or the supervision/administrative style of the facility.

INSTITUTIONAL FACTORS CONTRIBUTING TO MISCONDUCT

At the institutional level, prison overcrowding is the single most important factor in the analysis of prison misconduct. This is especially true for facilities that house large numbers of young inmates. The interaction between prison overcrowding and percentage of youth in the facility is the best predictor of prison misconduct among all the institutional-level measures. It is intuitive that the problem of overcrowding must be taken into consideration when assessing the safety of any correctional facility. Similarly, facilities housing higher proportions of violent offenders tend to record higher prison rule violations than those with fewer violent offenders.

Other important institutional-level variables associated to prison misconduct are staff-to-inmate ratio and the presence of rehabilitation programs (educational, employment/vocational, religious, family visitation, and substance abuse). However, contrasting findings can be found in research on prison misconduct with respect to the influence of prison programs. Some studies have consistently found that correctional institutions that promote the use of programs and keep inmates occupied also record lower rates of prison rule violations.

However, other studies found that some programs have limited to no effect on the reduction of prison misconduct. Although facilities that offer educational programs tend to have lower rates of misconduct across studies, the effect of educational programs is consistent only for facilities that offer college-level education programs. These findings are important in that they might suggest that allocating resources to support prison education, especially college-level education, might prove to be beneficial in the long run.

Although criminologists have so far developed relevant theories on what risk factors are most likely to be associated with prison misconduct, the presence of contrasting findings still limits our ability to draw conclusions from current studies. The empirical evidence coming from sophisticated multilevel analyses, focusing on the interaction between individual- level and institutional-level variables has so far produced the most consistent results across studies. Instead, research that has exclusively used individual-level measures has proven to be less reliable across the numerous studies published in the last four decades. As researchers develop new statistical methodologies, it is possible that there will be more consistency across studies that utilize random samples of prisons and inmates.

Because the decision-making process in the field of corrections has to be evidence-based, much research is still needed to inform prison administrators on the implementation of programs and policies that would make prisons safer and more likely to rehabilitate offenders prior to their release back into our communities. Moreover, consistency across studies would better inform policy makers on the needs for prison programs and on the overall effectiveness of resource allocations across correctional facilities.

Monica Solinas-Saunders

See also: Deprivation Model; General Strain Theory and Incarceration; Importation Model; Inmate Subculture; Violence in Prison

Further Reading

Blevins, K. R., Listwan, S. J., Cullen, F. T., & Jonson, C. L. (2010). A general strain theory of prison violence and misconduct: An integrated model of inmate behavior. *Journal of Contemporary Criminal Justice, 26*(2), 148–166.

Cochran, J. C. (2012). The ties that bind or the ties that break: Examining the relationship between visitation and prisoner misconduct. *Journal of Criminal Justice, 40*(5), 433–440.

Flanagan, T. J. (1983). Correlates of institutional misconduct among state prisoners. *Criminology, 21*(1), 29–40.

Lahm, K. F. (2008). Inmate-on-inmate assault: A multilevel examination of prison violence. *Criminal Justice and Behavior, 35*(1), 120–137.

Lahm, K. F. (2009). Educational participation and inmate misconduct. *Journal of Offender Rehabilitation, 48*(1), 37–52.

Lahm, K. F. (2009). Physical and property victimization behind bars: A multilevel examination. *International journal of offender therapy and comparative criminology, 53*(3), 348–365.

Lindsey, A. M., Mears, D. P., Cochran, J. C., Bales, W. D., & Stults, B. J. (2015). In prison and far from home: Spatial distance effects on inmate misconduct. *Crime & Delinquency.* doi:0011128715614017

Morris, R. G., & Worrall, J. L. (2014). Prison architecture and inmate misconduct: A multilevel assessment. *Crime & Delinquency, 60*(7), 1083–1109.

Solinas-Saunders, M., & Stacer, M. J. (2012). Prison resources and physical/verbal assault in prison: A comparison of male and female inmates. *Victims & Offenders, 7*(3), 279–311.

Stacer, M. J., & Solinas-Saunders, M. (2015). Physical and verbal assaults behind bars: Does military experience matter? *The Prison Journal, 95*(2), 199–222.

Steiner, B., & Wooldredge, J. (2008). Inmate versus environmental effects on prison rule violations. *Criminal Justice and Behavior, 35*(4), 438–456.

Wooldredge, J., Griffin, T., & Pratt, T. (2001). Considering hierarchical models for research on inmate behavior: Predicting misconduct with multilevel data. *Justice Quarterly, 18*(1), 203–231.

Mitchell, Joyce (1965–)

Joyce Mitchell was a prison seamstress at the Clinton Correctional Facility in Dannemora, New York, who was convicted in 2015 of helping two inmates escape and sentenced to two and one-third to seven years in the Bedford Hills Correctional Institute. In addition to the prison sentence, she was fined $6,375 and ordered to pay $79,841 in restitution. Mitchell admitted in court to smuggling tools into the prison inside hamburger meat, including a drill bit and hacksaw blades. She claimed she helped inmates David Sweat and Richard Matt escape because they threatened to hurt her family; however, Clinton County Court judge Kevin Ryan said he didn't find Mitchell's explanation to be credible. Both inmates were serving life without parole for murder. Sweat was found guilty of murdering a sheriff's deputy in 2002, and Matt was found guilty of murdering and dismembering his former boss in 1997.

Joyce Mitchell appears in court with her attorney wearing a bulletproof vest. Mitchell aided two inmates in an elaborate escape attempt from the Clinton Correctional Facility in Dannemora, New York. (G.N. Miller/Getty Images)

During the police investigation, Mitchell claimed she wanted to leave her husband Lyle. Mitchell claimed she wanted to have Matt kill her husband so she could be romantically involved with Sweat after the escape. Mitchell agreed to smuggle in the contraband tools so the inmates could dig their way out of their maximum security prison cells at night. The three planned to have Mitchell meet the inmates by a manhole outside the prison after the escape. Because prison correctional officers are continually roving the prison perimeter in vehicles, Mitchell said her idea was to make it look like she was making a phone call when she pulled over to wait for the two inmates to escape. Mitchell said she agreed to be the getaway driver and to meet the two inmates in a jeep, so they would have a vehicle that could withstand driving in the woods. Mitchell said she agreed to bring street clothing with her so the two inmates could change out of their prison uniforms after the escape. She also agreed to bring along a tent, fishing poles, a GPS, money, cell phone, and a shotgun. Their plan was to camp out in the woods while on the run and survive off the land. She said their plan was to hide out in the woods of Dannemora for 6 to 7 hours or until the search quieted down from the escape. Mitchell said their plan was for Matt to go off on his own the day after the escape so she and Sweat could be a couple. Mitchell admitted to having sexual encounters with both inmates while they were incarcerated in maximum security. She also admitted to having romantic feelings for Sweat but not for Matt. Mitchell said she was unhappy in her marriage and got caught up the fantasy of being romantically involved with Sweat after she helped the two escape.

During their incarceration, Mitchell said she got to know both inmates beyond her duties of a prison seamstress. Mitchell gave Matt gifts in exchange for a portrait of her three children. Some of the gifts Mitchell brought to Matt included homemade brownies and cookies, a pair of boxing gloves, and pepper. To aid in the escape, Mitchell said she gave Matt two pairs of glasses that had lights so the inmates could see while they worked at night preparing for their escape. Although she admitted to having romantic feelings for Sweat, Mitchell admitted to having frequent sexual encounters with Matt for approximately two months prior to the escape. Mitchell said her sexual encounters with Matt began when he grabbed her and kissed her. After he kissed her, Matt asked Mitchell to bring him a screwdriver bit, and she agreed. After kissing Matt on several occasions, Mitchell said he asked her to perform oral sex on him, and she agreed. Mitchell said during the two-month time frame before the June 2015 escape, she provided Matt with several sexual photos of herself. Mitchell reported she never had sexual encounters with Sweat but admitted to writing him numerous sexually provocative notes.

Approximately one month prior to the escape, Mitchell said she provided Matt with hacksaw blades by hiding them inside frozen hamburger meat and then placing the frozen meat next to tubes of paint. Mitchell said if the metal detector went off, correctional officers would think nothing of it when they saw the tubes of paint, as they knew Matt was an artist. Mitchell said she also brought Matt multiple chisels and packed them inside of frozen hamburger meat as well.

On June 5, 2015, Mitchell said the inmates told her they planned to escape that night. That evening, she told her husband she was having chest pains after dinner, so he brought her to the emergency room. She was admitted overnight for observation. During the investigation, Mitchell claimed that her husband was the only thing that was keeping her and Sweat from being romantically involved. Because she wanted to be involved with Sweat, the three devised a plan to have Matt kill Mitchell's husband Lyle. Although Mitchell agreed to be their getaway driver, she said the more she thought about their escape plan, the worse she felt. Mitchell said she backed out of the escape because she loved her husband and felt guilty. Mitchell claimed Sweat and Matt took advantage of her weakness because she was suffering from depression, and both threatened to hurt her family if she did not assist them with their escape plan.

On the night of June 5, 2015, Sweat and Matt escaped from the Clinton Correctional Facility in Dennamora, New York, by tunneling out of their maximum security cells and through underground pipes to a manhole just outside of the facility. When Sweat and Matt were discovered missing during the 5:30 a.m. count on June 6, 2015, one of the largest manhunts in New York history was launched, costing approximately $23 million when it concluded about three weeks later. The manhunt involved the Federal Bureau of Investigation (FBI), the Bureau of Alcohol, Tobacco, Firearms and Explosives (ATF), U.S. Customs and Border Protection (CBP), the New York Forest Rangers, the U.S. Marshals Service, the Royal Canadian Mounted Police (RCMP), and the state and local police.

When interviewed by police on June 6, 2015, Mitchell lied and said she had no knowledge of the escape plan. A day later, law enforcement found the external breech, a manhole, where the inmates escaped from the prison. The inmates dug their way out of the south wall of the prison with the hacksaw blades brought into the prison by Mitchell. Although both were incarcerated for murder, they were being housed in the Honor Block, a privileged housing unit, where they had access to televisions, telephones, showers, playing card tables, and cooking stations.

For days following their escape, the inmates slept in the woods and in empty vacation houses. During the manhunt, law enforcement discovered vomit and feces in an empty cabin the two had broken into, which was forensically linked to Matt. The vomit and feces led authorities to believe Matt had consumed bad food or water while on the run.

On June 26, 2015, the Border Patrol shot and killed Matt when they found him in the woods of Elephants Head, approximately 50 miles from the Clinton Correctional Facility. Matt's autopsy revealed a blood alcohol level (BAC) of .18 percent, which is nearly twice the BAC allowed by New York State law for driving under the influence. Two days later, Sweat was shot by a New York State Trooper near Constable, New York, and taken into custody. Constable is approximately 16 miles from where Matt was shot and killed and approximately 1.5 miles south of the U.S. and Canadian border.

When questioned by law enforcement, Sweat claimed he separated from Matt because Matt was sick and intoxicated, and he was slowing down their escape plan. After a thorough investigation was conducted by law enforcement, David Sweat pleaded guilty to two felony counts of first-degree escape and one count of promoting prison contraband. He was sentenced to three and one-half to seven years, to be served consecutively with his current life sentence for murder. Sweat was also ordered to pay $79,841 in restitution, a partial amount incurred by law enforcement during the search.

A year after the escape, the inspector general (IG) of New York released a report that found "longstanding, systemic failures in management and oversight" that "enabled two convicted murderers to meticulously orchestrate their escape from a maximum security facility almost in plain sight." The report further indicated that 20 correctional employees, including both uniformed and nonuniformed personnel, were responsible in some manner for the escape of the inmates. Aside from Mitchell and a prison correctional officer named Gene Palmer, who was also criminally charged with aiding in the escape and smuggling into the prison multiple tools in exchange for paintings by inmate Matt, no other employees were charged criminally, but administrative action was taken, which included one demotion, two suspensions, and several resignations and early retirements. The IG's report indicated a lack of cooperation among correctional employees during the investigative process, which included several employees being purposefully misleading during interviews and outright lying to investigators.

Kim Schnurbush

See also: Maximum Security; Misconduct by Correctional Employees; Misconduct by Prisoners

Further Reading

Ahmed, S. (2015, June 8). Employee questioned in New York prison escape. *CNN.*

Associated Press. (2015, September 14). Joyce Mitchell, woman who helped killers escape in N.Y., says she was depressed. *Washington Times.*

Botelho, G., Almasy, S., & Kaye, R. (2015, June 11). Dogs hit escapees' scent at gas station near prison. *CNN.*

Chuck, E. (2015, November). David Sweat, New York prison escapee, pleads guilty to all charges. *NBC News.*

Esch, M. (2015, June 19). Joyce Mitchell, N.Y. prison worker, discussed having convicts kill husband, prosecutor says. *Washington Times.*

Feyerick, D., Field, A., & Ford, D. (2015, June 28). David Sweat shot and captured alive after New York manhunt. *CNN.*

Genis, D. (2015, June 10). New York State's scariest prison. *Vice.*

Ghosh, B. (2015, June 25). Arrested prison guard denies knowing of inmates' escape plot. *Washington Times.*

Hill, M. (2015, July 28). Joyce Mitchell, prison worker who helped 2 killers escape, gets up to 7 years. *Washington Times.*

Hill, M., & Virtanen, M. (2015, June 12). Joyce Mitchell, prison employee, accused of supplying contraband to escaped convicts: D.A. *Washington Times.*

Katersky, A., Avianne, T., & Chiu, D. (2015, June 20). New York police search Allegany County for possible sighting of 2 escaped convicts. *ABC News.*

Kekis, J. (2015, June 14). Joyce Mitchell, prison worker, charged with aiding escapees appears in court. *Washington Times.*

Margolin, J., Katersky, A., & Shapiro, E. (2015, June 26). Escaped New York inmate Richard Matt shot and killed by police, officials say. *ABC News.*

McKinley, J. (2015, July 28). Prison worker who aided escape tells of sex, saw blades and deception. *New York Times.*

Morganstein, M. (2015, September 28). Joyce Mitchell, who aided prison break, going to prison herself. *CNN.*

Scott, C. L. (2016, June). *Investigation of the June 5, 2015 escape of inmates David Sweat and Richard Matt from Clinton Correctional Facility.* State of New York, Office of the Inspector General. Retrieved from https://ig.ny.gov/sites/default/files/pdfs/DOCCS%20Clinton%20Report%20FINAL_1.pdf

Shapiro, E., & Keneally, M. (2015, June 8). NY prison break and how it compares to *Shawshank Redemption. ABC News.*

Siemaszko, C. (2016, February 3). David Sweat, prison escape mastermind, sentenced for breakout. *NBC News.*

Winter, T., & Connor, T. (2015, July 28). Prison seamstress Joyce Mitchell pleads guilty in escape. *NBC News.*

Muslim Inmates

The population of U.S. residents professing Islam as their faith has been estimated at up to 3.3 million individuals. Muslims, therefore, represent nearly 1 percent of the population (roughly 1 out of 100 people), a proportion that some expect to double by 2050. In 2014, there were more than 2 million individuals incarcerated, more than 1.5 million of those in prison. If the proportion of Muslims was in prison what it is in the general population, Muslim prisoners would number somewhere around 15,000 or more than 22,000 if those in local jails are included. Yet, the proportion of Muslims in the U. S. prison system is not comparable to that in the general population; it is, in fact, much higher. Some estimates suggest a Muslim inmate population as high as 350,000, fueled, in great part, by rates of conversion, between 30,000 and 40,000 converts a year. These estimates may be too high. A recent Pew Research Center survey of prison chaplains found that they estimated the Muslim population in their respective facilities at between 5 and 9 percent of the population—something closer to between 75,000 and 135,000.

Prisons are "total institutions"—establishments where the individuals are under conditions of total control. Erving Goffman wrote that such places are distinct in that "all aspects of life are conducted in the same place and under the same single authority" and that "the various enforced activities are brought together into a single rational plan purportedly designed to fulfill the official aims of the institution" (Goffman, 1961). The official aims of all correctional institutions are a combination of imposing deterrent punishment, incapacitating potential dangers from harming the general public, and rehabilitating prison wards so that they are ready to reenter society, fully restored as law-abiding citizens. In all these aims, religion may play a central role. In Pew's survey of chaplains, 7 in 10 noted that religion was "absolutely critical" to rehabilitative programs, with an additional 23 percent saying that religion was "very important."

Prison institutions are but one type of social system, a network of actors working toward some common end. All systems seek to exert control, to guide or direct individual action through physical means, through manipulating access to resources, through the influence of social relations, but also, frequently, through moral persuasion. If depth of control is measured by how constant, intense, and compelling it is, moral authority is truly a powerful mechanism of control. As morality is often drawn from theology, religion, then, may be among the most useful methods of directing the actions of individuals toward desired behaviors and away from disfavored ones. Viewed this way, the presence of Islam in prison may prove quite desirous. In a study of Muslim inmates in England, Basia Spalek and Salah El-Hassan found that inmates attributed their Islamic practice to reducing their levels of aggression, increasing their sense of structure, and providing an important coping mechanism for dealing with the rigors of prison life. This finding has been supported by a number of other studies. Moreover, the degree to which Islam encourages close relationships between Muslims combines the intensity of an individual's own commitment to its moral message with the behavior-modifying influence of social expectations, applying a strong cultural control over the actions of its faithful. This includes adherence to prosocial scriptural commands, such as the Quran's instruction to "vie, one with another, in good works."

The prosocial influence of Islam may be especially important as it has long been an alternative means of religious belief for disaffected Christians. Spalek and El-Hassan's sample of Muslim converts were mostly black men who had been raised as Christian, maintained a belief in God during a period of disillusionment, and found Allah after a period of what Mark Hamm calls "searching"—that is, "seeking religious meaning to interpret and resolve discontent" (Hamm, 2009). African American inmates have long flocked to varying iterations of Islam, from Americanized forms, such as the Moorish Science Temple, Nation of Islam and, later, the Nation of Gods and Earths (also "Five Percent Nation" or "Five Percenters") to traditional Shia and Sunni variants. In contrast to the population outside of prison,

Muslim prisoners pray in a visiting room at the Ferguson Unit, a prison facility within the Texas Department of Criminal Justice. (Andrew Lichtenstein/Corbis via Getty Images)

blacks constitute the large majority of Muslim prisoners, and most of these were converts during their incarceration. Some have argued that Islam resonates well with populations who see themselves as oppressed or lacking social power due to its emphasis on egalitarianism and brotherhood. Groups like the Nation of Islam were formed explicitly for that purpose, to promote black pride through preaching the black superiority. Still, what the (scant) research in conversion to Islam has revealed is that more orthodox versions of the faith are the fastest growing, and African American prisoners report being drawn to these not out of some search for superior status but merely to gain a sense of one's own equal worth.

Prisons, as institutions concerned with inmates' compliance with measures of control, may therefore be helped by inmates who turn away from Christian denominations toward Islam as opposed to rejecting the positive effects of religion as a whole. Nevertheless, systems of control may have competing goals and values: if Islam acts as a regulatory force, there may be some situations in which its tenets grate against the goals of the prison administration. In this sense, religion may be a negative force—a negative system of control—obliging members to act in opposition to the norms promoted by correctional facilities. This has, in fact, become a predominant concern among prison administrators noticing the increasing number of Islamic practitioners under their charge. National security scholars have also rung the alarm for the potential of terrorist recruitment in U.S. prisons. Hamm has warned about the rise of "Prison Islam," where inmate groups adopt "gang methods of coercion and 'cut-and-paste' versions of the Koran to recruit new members" (Hamm, 2009). In a series of interviews conducted with 30 inmates at Franklin Correctional Institution in Florida and Folsom Prison in California, Hamm found "a fairly consistent pattern of radicalization among young Islamic prisoners in maximum-security custody" (Hamm, 2009). Radicalizers appeared to target those inmates sentenced to long prison terms and disconnected from their loved ones. Pew's survey of chaplains presents discomforting assessments of the prevalence of extremism among Muslims in their facilities: a majority reported that Islamic extremism is either very or somewhat common.

It is important, however, to consider another of Hamm's observations—that only an infinitesimally small proportion of even radicalized Muslim prisoners will ever act on their convictions to engage in actual terror incidents. In a conversation-turned-book, human rights activist Maajid Nawaz explained that Islamic extremism can be conceptualized as a set of concentric circles with increasing threat, but diminishing numbers, as one gets to its core. Near that point, there are "Islamists," those who seek to impose Islam on society regardless of free choice. Although that group itself forms only a small part of the Islamic world, it is only an even smaller subgroup of those that seeks to impose Islamic practice using force. Interestingly, Nawaz himself is a practicing Muslim using Islamic doctrine to argue against extremism, as does the Islamic Studies Program at Folsom Prison, showing that Islam, like other religions, can be a beneficial aspect of prison life.

Kwan-Lamar Blount-Hill

See also: Constitution as a Source for Prisoners' Rights, The; Deliberate Indifference; Evolving Standards of Decency; Folsom State Prison; Inmates and the Freedom of

Religion; Judicial Involvement in Prison Administration; Prison Populations, Trends in; Radicalization of Inmates; Total Institutions

Further Reading

Ammar, N. H., Weaver, R. R., & Saxon, S. (2004). Muslims in prison: A case study from Ohio state prisons. *International Journal of Offender Therapy and Comparative Criminology, 48*(4), 414–428.

Goffman, E. (1961). *Asylums: Essays on the social situation of mental patients and other inmates.* Garden City, NY: Anchor Books.

Hamm, M. S. (2009). Prison Islam in the age of sacred terror. *The British Journal of Criminology, 49*(5), 667–685.

Harris, S., & Nawaz, M. (2015). *Islam and the future of tolerance.* Cambridge, MA: Harvard University Press.

Kaeble, D., Glaze, L., Tsoutis, A., & Minton, T. (2016). *Correctional populations in the United States, 2014* (NCJ 249513). Washington, DC: Bureau of Justice Statistics, Office of Justice Programs, U.S. Department of Justice.

Mohammed, B. (2016). A new estimate of the U. S. Muslim population. *Fact tank: News in the numbers.* Washington, DC: Pew Research Center. Retrieved September 24, 2016, from http://www.pewresearch.org/fact-tank/2016/01/06/a-new-estimate-of -the-u-s-muslim-population

Pew Research Center. (2012). *Religion in prisons: A 50-state survey of prison chaplains.* Washington, DC: Author. Retrieved September 24, 2016, from http://www .pewforum.org/2012/03/22/prison-chaplains-exec/#muslims-protestants-seen-as -growing-due-to-switching

Sowa, J. L. (2012). Gods behind bars: Prison gangs, due process, and the First Amendment. *Brooklyn Law Review, 77*(4), 1593–1631.

Spalek, B., & El-Hassan, S. (2007). Muslim converts in prison. *The Howard Journal, 46*(2), 99–114.